Demon Lovers

DEMON LOVERS

Witchcraft, Sex, and the Crisis of Belief

WALTER STEPHENS

THE UNIVERSITY OF CHICAGO PRESS CHICAGO AND LONDON

WALTER STEPHENS is the Charles S. Singleton Professor of Italian Studies at The Johns Hopkins University. He is the author of *Giants in Those Days: Folklore, Ancient History, and Nationalism* and coeditor of *Discourses of Authority in Medieval and Renaissance Literature*.

The University of Chicago Press, Chicago 60637
The University of Chicago Press, Ltd., London

Printed in the United States of America

11 10 09 08 07 06 05 04 03 02   1 2 3 4 5

ISBN: 0-226-77261-6 (cloth)

Title page illustration: *Devil Seducing Witch,* illustration for Ulrich Müller (Molitoris), *Von den Unholden und Hexen* (Konstanz, [1489?]).

Library of Congress Cataloging-in-Publication Data

Stephens, Walter, 1949–
Demon lovers : witchcraft, sex, and the crisis of belief / Walter Stephens.
p. cm.
Includes bibliographical references and index.
ISBN 0-226-77261-6 (alk. paper)
1. Witchcraft and sex—History. 2. Demonology—History. 3. Trials (Witchcraft) I. Title.

BF1572.S4 S74 2002
133.4′09—dc21

2001043393

∞ The paper used in this publication meets the minimum requirements of the American National Standard for Information Sciences—Permanence of Paper for Printed Library Materials, ANSI Z39.48-1992.

For Janet and Catherine

She said something even stranger,
Which causes me great horror:
That the Devil became a man
And took ardent lustful pleasure
With her. Oh, God, what horror!
Great God, what a strange couple!
O true God, Jesus, what a transgression!
The woman is married to the Devil!

—Martin Lefranc, *Le Champion des dames* (1441)

CONTENTS

ILLUSTRATIONS

Figures

Diagrams

Acknowledgments

My greatest debt is to my wife and daughter, to whom this book is dedicated with my dearest love. My wife, Janet, has been everything that authors say on these occasions and more, at every level from finding a title to simplifying the language of the final draft.

To thank every colleague who contributed an insight, criticism, or reference would be impossible. Several have been indispensable to me, however: Charles T. Wood, Charles Stinson, and Walter Simons at Dartmouth; Salvatore I. Camporeale and Thomas Izbicki at Johns Hopkins. Stephen Greenblatt's course on witchcraft at the School for Criticism and Theory in 1992 was a major inspiration.

Special thanks go to my students at Dartmouth College and at The Johns Hopkins University for their enthusiasm and curiosity and to Arthur Scott.

I am grateful to many librarians, but especially to Patricia Carter and Marianne Hraibi at Dartmouth's Baker Library, Bett Miller and Sue Waterman at Johns Hopkins's Eisenhower Library, and Carolyn Smith at the Peabody Library. My research has benefited from collections at Cornell University, Harvard University, the University of Pisa, the Scuola Normale Superiore di Pisa, the Biblioteca Apostolica Vaticana, the Biblioteca Nazionale Centrale di Firenze, the Kunsthistorisches Institut in Florenz, Villa Spelman of The Johns Hopkins University, and Villa I Tatti of Harvard University.

Grateful acknowledgment goes to Duke University Press, Peter Lang Publishing, and Wayne State University Press, respectively, for permission to revise material that previously appeared in the following publications: "Witches Who Steal Penises: Impotence and Illusion in *Malleus maleficarum*," *Journal of Medieval and Early Modern Studies* 28, no. 3 (fall 1998): 495–529; "Desperately Seeking Satan: Witchcraft and Censorship in *The Name of the Rose*," in *Umberto Eco's Alternative: The Politics of Culture and the Ambiguities of Interpretation*, ed. Norma Bouchard and Veronica Pravadelli, 99–126 (New York: Peter Lang, 1998); and "Incredible Sex: Witches, Demons, and Giants in the Early Modern Imagination," in *Monsters in the Italian Literary Imagination,* ed. Keala Jewell, 153–76 (Detroit: Wayne State University Press, 2001).

Randolph Petilos, my editor at the University of Chicago Press, has made this book possible, not least by finding two of the best readers imaginable for a book on witchcraft. The vast knowledge and meticulous care of Richard Kieckhefer and Brian Levack have corrected many inaccuracies and oversimplifications. The ones that remain are obviously my own. Joseph H. Brown has been a demanding and exacting copyeditor, saving the manuscript from many inaccuracies and non sequiturs.

The Office of the Dean of Faculty of the Krieger School of Arts and Sciences at The Johns Hopkins University has provided generous subsidy support for publication. Both Johns Hopkins and Dartmouth have been generous with research support, in part through professorships established by the generosity of the late Professor Charles S. Singleton and the late Paul D. Paganucci.

NOTE ON TRANSLATIONS

Quotations from works for which no translation is included in the list of works cited are my own translations. Where specialized terms are used in the original language, I have often included them in brackets within the translation. I have done the same in cases where there could be some ambiguity about the closest modern English term. In a few cases, I have left the original term untranslated all or most of the time, both in the text and in translations. This is particularly the case with terms like *maleficium* and *praestigium,* which belong to the specialized vocabulary of witchcraft. Translations of such terms (in this case, "witchcraft" and "illusion," respectively) would either be imprecise or require clumsy phrases.

INTRODUCTION

SEX FIENDS

Now this is certain, that in the sayings and actions of men, whereas we desire a true estimate, we ought to consider, *Cui bono,* that is, for what end or advantage they were said and done.

—John Wagstaffe, *The Question of Witchcraft Debated* (1671)

On 20 September 1587, Walpurga Hausmännin, a licensed midwife practicing at Dillingen in the diocese of Augsburg in southern Germany, was burned at the stake as a witch. Walpurga confessed to a long list of *maleficia,* as deeds of harmful magic were called. Most of these were related to her profession as a midwife; in twelve years, she had supposedly killed forty-one infants and two mothers in labor. But she also confessed to attacking other people: Georg Klinger's small son, the wives of the governor and town scribe, Hans Striegel's cloistered daughter, and Michel Klingler. Of these five people, three were not expected to live, according to the contemporary account of Walpurga's trial. Nor was her maleficence limited to people, it was claimed: she was blamed for the deaths of nine cows (although "she confesses that she destroyed a large number of cattle over and above this"), a horse, and an unspecified number of pigs and geese. And she attacked crops, causing hailstorms "once or twice a year."[1]

For a time, scholars viewed Walpurga's case as "sadly typical" of witchcraft trials. Walpurga's advanced age and her profession were, William Monter said, normal features of the accused witch in this era of very high infant mortality.[2] More recent research has thrown into doubt the notion of a typical witchcraft trial as well as the notion that midwives were the class of women most likely to be accused. But, while Walpurga's supposed confession is not "standard," as Monter thought, he was right in maintaining that it displays "the full gamut of the ordinary witch's *maleficia.*"[3] The record of Walpurga's trial is a kind of encyclopedia of the crimes that were attributed to witches; although it does not describe a commonplace witchcraft *trial,* it is instructive as a collection of the commonplace or stereotyped *ideas* that characterized such trials from about 1400 to 1700. Perhaps this completeness, along with its sensationalism, is what made Walpurga's trial interesting to the correspondent of the multinational Fugger banking firm who transmitted the record of her trial. Walpurga was, in a sense, an unwilling media star of her period.[4]

Walpurga's case has one feature that is both unsettling and prominent: its obsessive attention to sex. Sexuality is of course implicit in most of Walpurga's alleged crimes since many of them have to do with childbirth. But sexual intercourse, particularly fornication with demons, is a major theme of her trial record. Even if we knew that Walpurga genuinely believed that she had committed such acts, the priority that her judges accorded them would still require explanation. Walpurga's whole career as a witch is traced with minute attention to sexual causes: in 1556, thirty-one years before her trial, and nineteen years before her first alleged murder, she supposedly propositioned a fellow worker while the two of them were harvesting grain for Hans Schlumperger. Recently widowed, she lived alone, so the two agreed to meet at her lodgings, "there to indulge in lustful intercourse." On the appointed night, as Walpurga sat waiting and "meditating upon evil and fleshly thoughts,"[5] the coworker whom she was expecting arrived, and they had sex.

Or so she thought. No sooner had they finished than Walpurga saw unmistakable signs that her paramour was not Bis im Pfarrhof, the man she had lusted after, but the Devil himself, disguised as a human. Although he otherwise had the "guise and raiment" of Bis, the Devil betrayed his identity in several ways: one of his feet was actually a cloven hoof, while one of his hands seemed to be neither animal nor human but "as if made of wood."[6] When she realized what she had done, the horror-struck Walpurga spoke the name of Jesus; the being thereupon disappeared, thus confirming that he was the Devil.

Yet Walpurga confessed that, despite her initial terror, she yielded to the Devil on the very next night, when he returned in the same form. She surrendered her soul as well as her body to the Devil, and, since she could not write, she allowed him to guide her hand as she signed a pact in her own blood. After this, Walpurga supposedly embarked on a continuous orgy of sexual excess, all of it performed, as far as the record shows, with this devil, whom the record variously refers to as her "paramour" (*Buhl*), her "demon lover" (*Buhlteufel*), or "Federlin" (little feather). These names reflect some confusion in the account. It appears that Walpurga initially confessed to being Satan's paramour but then changed her mind and demoted her demonic lover to the rank of an ordinary devil. Although her personal devil was called "the Devil" (*der Teufel*) and "the Evil Spirit" (*der böse Geist*) at his first appearance, she also "confessed" that she later met "the Great Devil" (*der große Teufel*) at a Sabbat, or witches' festival.[7] Appearing as "a big man with a gray beard, who sat in a chair like a great prince, and was richly attired," this "Great Devil" required Walpurga to reiterate her dedication of body and soul and to renounce everything having to do with Christianity: "Thereupon the Great Devil baptized her afresh, naming her Höfelin ["Little Court Lady"?] and her paramour-devil Federlin."[8]

Sex is repeatedly identified as the primary motive for Walpurga's initiation into witchcraft and her perseverance in crime. Federlin's sexual hold on her was considerable: he fornicated with her "in many divers places, . . . even in the street by night," and even after her capture and imprisonment. Federlin made Walpurga kill the forty-one children, exhume some of them, create ointments and other paraphernalia of witchcraft from their bodies, and even eat roasted children. He also made her mock the Virgin Mary as an "ugly hussy," trample crosses and consecrated wafers, steal holy water, and destroy its vessels. Even Walpurga's widowing is presented more as an excuse for fornication than as a cause or intensifier of poverty. The record only briefly acknowledges Walpurga's poverty, saying that the Devil "made her many promises to help her in her poverty and need, wherefore she surrendered herself to him body and soul." The only other reference to any of her physical needs besides sex is the statement that she sometimes ate "a good roast or an innocent child"[9] at the Sabbat.

Misogyny

The emphasis on demonic sex in Walpurga's trial is not at all uncommon. But how should we interpret the sexual features of texts written four, five, or six centuries ago? Until the 1970s, scholars construed them as ✓ evidence that witchcraft mythology was related to or even dictated by Christian hostility to sex and that it reflected the psychological conflicts imposed by repressing natural sex drives. In 1959, Rossell Hope Robbins wrote that "a combination of prurient inquisitors and hysterical young women about to be burned produced most of the accounts, which are completely the product of erotic and neurotic imaginations."[10] Since the 1970s, the attention to sexual relations between devils and women in witchcraft writings has seemed suspiciously like an effort to "demonize" women in particular: "Much of the basis for legends of demon lovers stemmed from the belief that women were sexually insatiable and could not be satisfied by mere mortal men."[11]

Statistics compiled by historical research reveal that about 80 percent of the victims of witch-hunts were women.[12] The conclusion that witch-hunting was an exercise in "woman hunting" requires a short step: "To claim that witch hunts were not woman hunting is to deny the most obvious fact about them."[13] Although many writers have reached similar conclusions, the late Christina Larner was a notable exception. She asserted that the witch-hunt criminalized women as a group for the first time in Western history. Yet she also insisted that "witchcraft was not sex-specific but it was sex-related" because "the substantial proportion of male witches in most parts of Europe means that a witch was not defined exclusively in female terms."[14]

Historical scholarship has uncovered a complicated interplay of motivations behind witch-hunting, discrediting the notion that men's misogyny was a conscious, programmatic motivation that somehow eclipsed all other social tensions and pressures.[15] Recent scholars consider such polemical feminist interpretations as products of a particular moment in the late-twentieth-century women's movement. In a chapter sardonically titled "A Holocaust of One's Own: The Myth of the Burning Times," Diane Purkiss traces the persistent, unfounded legend that nine million or more female victims died in witch-hunts inspired and directed by misogynistic men to books like Andrea Dworkin's *Woman-Hating*. The actual figure will never be known, but reliable researchers estimate a total of thirty to sixty thousand victims of both genders over about three hundred years.[16]

From studies of German trials, Lyndal Roper concludes that most witchcraft accusations were made by women against other women:

> Relations between mothers, [other persons] occupying maternal roles, and children formed the stuff of most, though not all, witchcraft accusations in [Augsburg]. To this extent, early feminist works which focused on birth and midwives were making an important observation. But though trials were concerned with the question of motherhood, they were not . . . male attempts to destroy a female science of birth, nor were they concerned with wresting control of reproduction from women. What is striking is that they were typically accusations brought by mothers, soon after giving birth, against women intimately concerned with the care of the child, most often the lying-in maid and not the midwife.

Roper asserts that, "so far from being a simple expression of misogyny," witch-hunting in early-modern societies can be seen as a way of "tak[ing] the fears of the mother seriously, supporting her search for the culprit,"[17] rather than blaming her for infant illness and death or dismissing her fears and accusations as hysterical.

Clearly, misogyny is not the whole story, and there is no easy explanation of the fact that men—and children, some of them reputedly as young as eight—were also tried and executed as witches.[18] In many early trials, men constituted the majority of the accused. As late as 1522–23, the trials at Mirandola in northern Italy inverted the statistics that we have come to expect: of the ten persons executed, seven were men and only three women. The alleged ringleader of the group was not a woman, or even a man with a criminal reputation, but a parish priest, and there were several other priests among the accused.[19] Even in the seventeenth century, clerics could be put to death for witchcraft on evidence provided exclusively or predominantly by women: Louis Gauffridi was accused by nuns of Aix-en-Provence in 1611, Urbain Grandier by nuns of Loudun in 1634, and Thomas Boullé by nuns of Louviers in 1647.[20] Certain stereotypes about witches resembled myths about necromancy or ritual magic, the practitioners of which were almost exclusively learned clerics. Strong thematic and historical links bound witch-hunting to the late-medieval persecution of heretics, the victims of which were equally likely to be men as women.[21] In many early trial transcripts and treatises, it is unclear whether the crime being prosecuted is witchcraft or heresy. The accused, who look like witches to us, are frequently designated by names linking them to major heresies, especially Waldensianism and Catharism.[22] In all these cases, early and late, sexual excess was a prominent accusation whether defendants were men or women.

The case of Johannes Junius, put to death for witchcraft in 1628, offers a useful counterpoint to Walpurga's story. Sexual relations with demons are as prominent among his alleged crimes as they are in her case. A panic, or large-scale witch persecution, was under way in Bamberg; several hundred persons are said to have been burned, and Johannes's wife had already been executed as a witch before his arrest.[23] As former burgomaster or chief magistrate of the town, he was one of its leading citizens, not a pauper like Walpurga; William Monter estimated that only a dozen cases of more prominent victims were recorded.[24] Johannes was rich enough to have lost six hundred florins in a lawsuit; this economic setback supposedly occasioned his initiation into demonic sex.

As he was sitting in his orchard lamenting his loss (the record claims that he was "sorrowful" but "not despondent"), he was accosted and enticed into sex by what appeared to be a woman. As with Walpurga, Johannes's paramour turned out to be a demon; as soon as they had copulated, the "wench" was transformed into a goat, which "bleated" that it would break Johannes's neck unless he renounced God. The "transformed spirit" then made good its threat, grabbing him by the neck. Like Walpurga, Johannes reacted by speaking a holy name, exclaiming, "God help me!" Vanishing only long enough to demonstrate that it was indeed a demon, the spirit "came straightway back," bringing a number of people with it. Collectively, they forced Johannes to deny God and be rebaptized "in the evil spirit's name." He was renamed "Krix" and instructed to call his paramour "Vixen" (*Füchsin*). This demonic mistress or succubus supposedly demanded that Johannes commit *maleficia,* in particular, that he kill his daughters and his youngest son. Instead, he used the powder that the demon had given him to kill his own horse. Unlike Walpurga, Johannes did not have to confess killing forty people—or even one—in order to be put to death. One horse was enough.[25]

Johannes's case differs in another important way. Since he was both literate and wealthy, Johannes was able to write a letter to his daughter—after his hands and arms healed from the devastation of the thumbscrews and the strappado—and to bribe a guard to deliver it to her. In general, his account squares with the minutes of his trial, but it differs on several important points, and he reports a chilling conversation with the executioner in charge of torturing him. Noting that he had borne a day of thumbscrews, leg vises, and the strappado without confessing anything, Johannes tells his daughter: "When at last the executioner led me back into the prison, he said to me: 'Sir, I beg you, for God's sake confess something, whether it be true or not. Invent something, for you cannot endure the torture which you will be put to; and, even if you bear it all, you will not escape, not even if you were an earl, but one torture will follow another until you say you are a witch. Not before that,' he said, 'will they let you go, as you may see by all their trials, for one is just like another.' "[26]

"One [trial] is just like another." Interrogators needed to hear *a certain kind* of answer, but they could not tell defendants precisely what to confess in every detail. Thus, defendants regularly had to guess the answers that their interrogators wanted, and interrogation became a kind of horrific charade, played with inadequate clues. Walpurga's case shows that the guesswork could be extremely tricky: initially, she had to confess that she had had sex with *the* Devil, that is, Satan; but later, in response to a new line of questioning, she had to realize (and pretend to remember) that her paramour was only *a* devil, namely, Federlin. This revision was required by the stereotyped scenario that her interrogators had in mind: witches had to be formally introduced to Satan at the Sabbat, under awe-inspiring circumstances. Walpurga did not know at any given moment exactly what her interrogators wanted to hear her confess. If they had dictated her confession in detail, hearing her repeat it would have done them no good. They required that she convince them that she was telling the truth. Their fascination with demonic copulation is an important clue for understanding why this was so.

Scholars have observed that every witch trial was a complex dialogue between the accused, the prosecutors, and witnesses called by the prosecution. But the dialogue between defendants and prosecutors was governed by an unfair balance of power, particularly when torture was used. So it is crucial to ask the legal question, Cui bono? that is, whose interests were best served by a particular confession, the defendant's or the prosecutor's? We can sometimes hear the trace of an individual defendant's concerns, such as the Oedipal anxieties and sexual frustrations of the Augsburg defendant Regina Bartholome, whose case Lyndal Roper examines.[27] Far more often, we can hear the anxieties of the judges and interrogators if we stop assuming that the confessions that they coerced are significant only as evidence of social control or irrational sadism.

Let us go further and leave aside anything that could be learned about individual persons. Then the question becomes, What kind of *argument* is best served? To ask Cui bono? about accusations and confessions rather than individuals raises the suspicion that demonic copulation became a routine accusation because one could *not* simply assume that humans regularly had sex with demons. What is universally recognized or firmly believed does not need constant reaffirmation through violent coercion. If the confessions are not simply dictated but must be laboriously extracted through a "cat-and-mouse" dialogue, then something truly important is at stake.

So let us entertain the idea that confessions like Walpurga's were necessary *because the concept of sex with demons needed constant reinforcement.* The hypothesis that demonic copulation was at best problematic makes sense for one historical reason: Western Christian theologians were worrying about it and other problems of demonic anatomy and physiology for centuries before the first witch trial. These problems were then exhaustively discussed in the earliest treatises on witchcraft, composed between about 1430 and 1530. If demonic copulation had been an obvious and axiomatic fact of life, it would not have received the minute, voluminous exposition and vehement defense that these treatises devoted to it. Writers reviewed every possible objection, both theological and scientific, to its possibility and then claimed to resolve all the difficulties. But they could not hide their own deep doubts about the plausibility of sex between humans and demons.

Seen in this light, it is even more suspicious that accusations of demonic copulation filled trial records. Whether a trial was dependent on any particular treatise is beside the point: to the extent that trials and treatises shared themes, they implicate concerns common to both those who prosecuted accused witches and those who wrote treatises. Unless we can show that there was *no* contact between prosecutors and writers, widespread accusations of demonic copulation reinforce the evidence of a culturewide problem.

Witchcraft Theory

Realizing that demonic reality must have been in doubt provides a new perspective on many otherwise puzzling aspects of the behavior of interrogators and judges. The motivations and phobias of interrogators are usually assumed to be obvious, or at least close to the surface of trial records. Historians have increasingly focused on accusers and defendants, assuming that their motivations are less easily comprehended. Such research is extremely important for understanding the total phenomenon of witchcraft. But the dominant motivations of the interrogators were far from obvious. The problem of demonic reality was rarely posed explicitly in trials, yet it drove the logic of interrogation in many cases, providing a plausible motivation for seemingly irrational proceedings. Evidence of that logic has been overshadowed by the sheer human interest of the *stories* that defendants were forced to tell about themselves. Narrative is always more gripping than theoretical explanation, and records of witchcraft trials contain stories and anecdotes that provoke in a modern reader strong reactions of pity, righteous anger, and even titillation.

Nor is the problem usually explicit in the anecdotes about trials that systematic witchcraft treatises recounted. Here as well, the sheer human interest of vivid narrative often overshadows the theological logic that that narrative illustrates, making the goals of the writers seem arbitrary, contradictory, or illogical.[28] Treatises reserved explicit discussions of demonic reality for their drier—that is, more technical, theoretical, and *theological*—passages. Without reading these theoretical passages carefully, paying attention to their asides and parenthetical remarks, we cannot appreciate how problematic demonic reality in fact was.

Witchcraft was a complex notion, informed by demonic copulation and by several other distinctive assumptions, meticulously elaborated in specialized handbooks for inquisitors and other technical treatises written after about 1430. Understanding such treatises and the importance of sexual and corporeal thematics within them is crucial to understanding what *witchcraft* meant in the periods when identifying witches was a compelling social problem. Yet scholars have rarely approached these writings as carefully as they have trial records and narratives. And *what* the treatises say has received far more attention than *how* they justified witch-hunting. Unless we read treatises as carefully as we read narratives, we can be misled by unexamined assumptions about what motivated concern with witches. We risk reducing the inquisitors to two-dimensional, "demonized" stereotypes as fantastic as the stereotype of the witch.

In this book, I examine witchcraft treatises almost exclusively. Actual trials, like those of Walpurga and Johannes, will be discussed only occasionally, to illustrate certain real-world resonances of the themes that I treat. I will normally refer to my authors, not as *judges, inquisitors,* or *interrogators,* but rather as *witchcraft theorists.* I will attempt to show, not that witchcraft trials and witchcraft theorists influenced each other directly, but only that the theorists had certain recognizable common concerns. I will specify, however, that I use the word *theorist* in the same sense that it has acquired in the modern concept of the *conspiracy theorist.* Witches were imagined as saboteurs or secret agents, and they were discussed to explain why the ideals of Christianity remained unfulfilled—and explanations varied considerably. I will not refer to these writers as *demonologists.*[29] They were theologians first and foremost. Their interest in demons was inseparable from their theological concerns, not an eccentric sideline.

In 1977, Sydney Anglo somewhat testily described the problem that treatises on witchcraft theory present: "It appears to be tacitly assumed by many scholars that discursive arguments by the learned have little relevance to the reality of witch persecution. It is usual to pass over long, and often elaborate, treatises with a few casual remarks; to summarize their intricacies in a single paragraph, or to cope with their obscurities by ignoring them. Many of these books are well known and frequently cited; yet there has been little analysis of their structure, arguments, language, and interrelation."[30] I think that Anglo was right to assume that there is more than a little relevance of learned arguments to witch persecution, although we may be wary of defining the connection too exactly. I would add that neglect of theory in favor of narrative and "reality" may stem from an unjustified *fear of being bored.* And I would rebut that, on the contrary, a little more scrutiny pays immense dividends in intellectual and human interest. Witchcraft persecution was a complex phenomenon, but the motives of its defenders were comprehensible, familiar, and *rational.*

Since 1977, more attention has been paid to witchcraft theory. But even scholars who distrust sensational anecdotes and concentrate on theory pay insufficient attention to *how* witchcraft treatises argued, to what Anglo called "their structure, arguments, language, and interrelation." Stuart Clark's *Thinking with Demons* (1997) is a case in point. This magnificent book is a landmark in the history of witchcraft studies; its contributions will not be supplanted for decades, if ever. Clark analyzes practically everything that modern scholarship has written about the "scientific" demonology behind witch-hunting; he surveys most of the innumerable treatises on witchcraft theory as well as many pamphlets and trial transcripts. His bibliography alone runs to eighty-six pages. Yet the effort required to synthesize an immense literature kept Clark from achieving everything he would have liked. Given the scope of his project, he regrets "not spending more time on individual authors and individual texts, instead of so often submerging them in general descriptions."[31]

One result is that Clark never questions whether theorists of witchcraft believed their own theories. He explicitly refuses to consider what we presume when we talk about *belief:*

> Naturally, those who *believed* in witchcraft thought that their *beliefs* did correspond with reality. From within the vantage point of a language it is customary to *suppose* that signs describing reality do work in this way; and if it is the only (or even the main) language the users have to think with, they cannot, without absurdity, think that their *belief* is wrong. Neither, indeed, can their historians, for whom some form of relativism is just as much a necessity. Whether witchcraft *beliefs* did in fact correspond with reality becomes, therefore, a question not worth asking—because there is simply no way to arrive at an extra-linguistic answer to it.[32]

Clark correctly decides that it is not worth asking whether witchcraft theories corresponded with reality, but he begs in advance a far more important question: Did those who propounded and defended such theories actually *believe* that they corresponded to reality? Their texts provide strong evidence that they did not, not even usually.

Witchcraft theorists did not suppose that their theories corresponded with reality: they were *testing* to discover *whether* a correspondence existed and dreading that it might not. Just because they *claimed* that they believed something or that they never doubted something else does not oblige us to take their word for it. To do so is to confuse rhetoric with logic and rationalization with reasoning. Clark's brilliant analysis of the overt skepticism that opponents of witch-hunting voiced about the reality of witchcraft is no substitute for testing its defenders' expressions of belief and credulity.

The challenge of testing belief in witchcraft requires reading, cover to cover, what several early defenders of witch-hunting wrote. The texts of witchcraft theory must be considered as complete wholes, driven by motivations that are probably *not* obvious. Insight will come if we read these treatises as carefully as we would novels or autobiographies, paying attention to their themes, their rhetorical strategies, their use of logic, and their strategic silences. By assessing the points of agreement and contention among treatises, the following chapters compile a detailed psychological and intellectual profile of the subculture that created the earliest theoretical justifications for persecuting witches. The way in which these writers argued reveals that they were not smug and credulous, although their language often was. They were intensely worried, for they were striving to resolve contradictions that, for them, threatened the credibility of witchcraft, demonology, and Christianity itself.

1

WITCHCRAFT THEORY: COPULATION WITH DEMONS AS CARNAL KNOWLEDGE

Theory of a grand kind tends to break out when routine social or intellectual practices have come unstuck, run into trouble, and urgently need to rethink themselves.

—Terry Eagleton, *Literary Theory*

Demonic Bodies, Fiendish Sexuality

Modern readers have generally reacted to the representation of women's bodies and sexuality in witchcraft literature without noticing how these topics relate to portrayals of demons' sexuality and corporeality.[1] This bizarre topic is completely foreign to the Western view of the world since at least 1800. Yet it is crucial to understanding the motives that drove literate European men to construct the myth of witchcraft crimes.

Demonic corporeality and sexuality are not even "hidden" topics; they have been staring us in the face all along, in what we know about the peculiarities of European witchcraft between 1400 and 1700. Witchcraft in this period differed from witchcraft in other cultures—including the culture of European intellectuals and churchmen before 1400—in its twofold emphasis on *maleficia* and demonolatry.[2] *Maleficia,* or acts of harmful magic, are the basis for any definition of witchcraft around the world; but demonolatry, the intentional worship of and subservience to demons, is peculiar to early-modern European witchcraft. Summarizing the relevant scholarship, Brian Levack asserts that "many individuals tried for witchcraft were not accused of performing any *maleficia* at all; their crime was simply worshipping the Devil. Whenever large witch-hunts took place, those persons who were implicated by confessing witches were almost always accused simply of attending the sabbath, not of practicing specific acts of magic."[3] And sexual relations with demons were conceptualized as the most common expression of demonolatry or "demonomania," as the jurist Jean Bodin called it in the late sixteenth century.[4] Sexual submission to demons was defined as a ritual act, demonstrating the witch's servitude, in both body and soul, to the demonic familiar and to Satan, the archenemy of God. This sexual slavery was allegedly undertaken eagerly by the novice witch, but she—or he—was often portrayed as enduring it with regret and even loathing after the initial trysts.

Sex with demons was only one aspect of a more general European fixation on *physical interaction with demons.* Demons, appearing in human or animal form, required their human devotees to worship them "in person." They demanded formal contractual agreements or "pacts" with humans; one "sold his soul to the devil" as if selling a horse or a field. Most dramatically, demons required that humans engage in outlandish, orgiastic sex with them. Strangely, while scholars of witchcraft have devoted much time to cataloging the great variety of such corporeal interactions between demons and humans, they have overlooked the significance of corporeal interaction itself. What would it have meant in 1430 or 1680 to assert that humans could interact with demons in the same way in which they interacted with other humans? What was the cultural and philosophical meaning of *commerce, association,* or *fellowship* between human society and the society of hell? Thus far, only the moral dimension of these concepts has interested scholars. But there are compelling reasons to suspect that moral condemnation of human-demon interaction was often a facade, an alibi for preoccupations of another sort entirely.

Why Demons, Why Then, Why There?

Persecution of witches had tremendous positive emotional value for everyone but the "witches." There were at least two kinds of reasons, "neighborly" and "elite," for discovering and persecuting witches. Those who accused their neighbors of witchcraft "were almost always concerned exclusively with *maleficium,*" or harmful magic.[5] To the uneducated mentality, *maleficium* was *somehow* caused by the witch herself, in mysterious ways. Neighbors displayed far more concern about her presumed motives, her desire to harm, than about how she produced harm. Accusations of witchcraft grew out of violent quarrels or long-simmering rancors among neighbors. Enmity could begin with a dispute between propertyholders, or a village outcast could attract hostility from all sides. When misfortune happened, one suspected one's enemy or the outcast of having caused it. In one common pattern, those who refused charity to village paupers suspected them of avenging themselves; feelings of guilt transformed the needy into figures of power and malice.[6]

"Elite" groups were not necessarily rich, but they were educated, able to read. For most of the period of witchcraft, this meant clerics, who could read Latin, the language of law, medicine, philosophy, and theology. Literacy affected people's most basic assumptions about witches and witchcraft: "Witch-beliefs . . . which concern the relationship between witches and the Devil were mainly the property of the literate and ruling classes and not the common people."[7] It is well documented that accusations of interacting with demons (demonolatry and copulation) were introduced into the trial proceeding by literate interrogators. They "usually did not arise in witchcraft trials until that stage of the proceedings when torture was applied," and they were frequently *scripted*.[8] Interrogators had formularies, long lists of stock questions to be asked, in order, of the defendant, concerning presumed interactions with devils as well as *maleficium*. False starts and incongruities occur often enough in defendants' answers to indicate that such confessions were rarely, if ever, imposed verbatim. Defendants were tortured, badgered, and wheedled into providing confessions varying in details and coherence but with stereotypical outlines. They verified demonic copulation, attendance at the Sabbat, and other physical interactions with demons.

For a long time, the demonological concerns of interrogators were probably incomprehensible to ordinary farmers, shopkeepers, and parents: "Illiterate peasants could not fully understand the sophisticated theories of the demonologists, . . . monks and theologians. Their concern with, and fear of witchcraft centered on the witch's ability to cause harm by occult means, not her relationship with the Devil."[9] Of course, many individuals may have had witch-hunting motivations that stemmed from both sources: an inquisitor, for instance, could have been born in a peasant environment where witches were blamed for agricultural and interpersonal disasters. Eventually, the common people adopted the elite concern with demons, being educated into it through sermons, the solemn pageantry of trials and executions, and, eventually, their own literacy.

But education and propaganda could not guarantee absolute uniformity of assumptions about witchcraft. Although Johannes Junius was literate and his trial came late in the history of witch-hunting, his assumptions about witchcraft were markedly different from those of his interrogators. His letter to his daughter reveals important differences between what he remembered confessing and what his interrogators supposedly recorded as he spoke. Most of the differences concern his interactions with demons.[10]

Neither Johannes nor Walpurga could have realized that they were being required to confess undergoing a revelation. That is, their supposed crimes were interpreted as having a "scientific" by-product, granting them valuable *knowledge* about demons and the supernatural world. As usual with indictments for demonic copulation, they had to admit that their paramours initially seemed to be ordinary humans. Not until after sexual consummation did either defendant's sex partner reveal that it was a demon. This stereotyped sequence indicates that, for the interrogators, sexual relations permitted the defendants to discover the true nature of their demonic paramours. If interrogators had wished only to degrade or humiliate Walpurga and Johannes, they could have forced them to confess knowing from the start that their tempters were demons. Instead, they accused them—or, rather, credited them—with *acquiring* the knowledge that they were interacting with demons. So sex was not simply a way of "demonizing" them or demonstrating their radical difference from good Christians.

The phrases *carnal knowledge* and *knowing in the biblical sense,* based on Genesis 4, were once pious euphemisms for having sex. In the more open sexual culture prevailing since the 1960s, they can hardly be used without irony. But sexual relations do imply the acquisition of *knowledge* as well as pleasure. Sex is the most intense and intimate possible form of interpersonal contact.

The possibility of having unmistakable contact with demons through sex was anything but unproblematic between 1400 and 1700. Sex with demons was a highly complex idea. It had evolved very slowly within the literate culture since about 1150, and it had to overcome philosophical, physiological, and theological objections of tremendous weight and variety. In a nutshell, the objections had one source: Western Christian theologians had proclaimed for centuries that angels and demons are "pure spirits" and as such have no bodies at all.[11]

This doctrine raises crucial questions: How is it possible to have sex with a being that has no real body? How can one do so with the firm conviction that one's partner is fully human? Why did defendants recognize their mistake *immediately* after consummation? More important, from the standpoint of witchcraft interrogations, what logic was served by *forcing* someone else to confess such experiences? Once again, the experiences of Walpurga and Johannes provide valuable clues. How could Johannes's evil spirit grab him by the neck if it had already changed into a goat? Goats have hooves, not hands. Within the logic of the interrogation, however, the anatomy of goats' forelegs is not the issue. The "goat's" show of force reveals that *a spirit* was capable of inflicting real *bodily* harm through physical contact rather than simply frightening Johannes from a distance. It had previously demonstrated its true demonic nature by the ease of its metamorphosis from alluring wench into disgusting goat. Walpurga's demon clearly betrayed that it was an evil spirit by displaying a cloven hoof and a wooden hand. Her failure to recognize these defects until after sexual consummation does not imply that she was stupid; rather, her shocked discovery insinuates that the demon's imitation of the human body and its sexual performance was almost perfect. Both confessions depend on the goat as a traditional embodiment of gross materiality and sexuality: the goat represents and confirms the reality of beings that are normally immaterial or even antimaterial.

Most of the interrogators who required such confessions would have known that demons were supposed to be purely spiritual. Thus, they appear to have enforced nonsensical, delusional confessions. Yet they presumed that the defendants were both sane and willful. Similar contradictions have traditionally been addressed, if at all, through speculation about the probable psychology of defendants, judges, or both. But here we would need to explain why defendants consistently made such confessions: Was postcoital depression and guilt so widespread that it made people "demonize" their sex partners? As for the interrogators, surely not every cleric had phobias about sex; not every married judge was a prude or an impotent voyeur.

Neither defendants nor interrogators were demonstrably insane, stupid, or neurotic; rather, their interactions took place within the confines of a great problem that was both complex and delicate. Although we cannot ascertain the preoccupations of individual interrogators in witch trials, we know that theoretical treatises about witchcraft had to create elaborate and often fragile explanations to resolve the contradictions between demonic incorporeality and demonic copulation. As time went on, these explanations depended increasingly on illustrations drawn from trials. Late-sixteenth- and early-seventeenth-century treatises are filled with confessions that are used to explain away the contradictions of demonic copulation.

Theorists and interrogators did not constitute a social class, but they shared fundamental assumptions based on literacy and theology. Their emphasis on demonic sexuality illustrates a profound difference between their mental world and that of defendants and accusers. After about 1200, the literate elite had less and less reason for uncomplicated belief in the reality of devils, angels, and the whole world of spirit; by 1400, the entire notion was demonstrably in crisis. Most, if not all, witchcraft theorists—and probably the majority of witchcraft interrogators—were interested in sexual and other corporeal relations between humans and demons because they were anxious to confirm the reality of the world of spirit. They considered the carnal knowledge of defendants their most valuable proof of that reality.

There are numerous indications that the elite exploited and misinterpreted common people's beliefs about the spirit world in an attempt to repair and rehabilitate their own.[12] People who could not read and write were obviously unable to leave firsthand records of their beliefs about spirits: the descriptions that we have inherited were recorded by the literate and are probably tainted by literate presuppositions and anxieties. Nonetheless, it appears that, throughout the history of European witchcraft, the illiterate accusers and defendants in trials had a firmer, less complicated belief in the reality of spirits than did the literate elite who forced them to discuss spiritual reality. Fairies, elves, and other beings foreign to the biblical and theological tradition were probably mentioned initially by defendants or accusers, not interrogators.[13]

Although we cannot know the realities of popular beliefs or precisely how those beliefs were distorted and exploited in trials, we know that witchcraft theorists assumed that common people believed more readily. Indeed, phrases like *for the witches firmly believe* occur with great frequency when witchcraft theorists discuss the nature of demons. This makes for a startling and shameful irony about European witch mythology. Although witchcraft treatises discuss *maleficium* in detail, their primary concern was the demonstration that demons are real. As a result, in the early treatises, *maleficium* was often invoked explicitly as a demonstration of demonic reality.

Corporeal Interaction

After 1400, Western witchcraft mythology insistently repeats that witchcraft is a combination of *maleficia* and *corporeal interaction with incarnate devils.* In a definition of *witchcraft* from 1505, the individual crimes imputed to witches are all familiar, but there is a strikingly insistent repetition of the words *corpus, res corporales, corporaliter.* This litany underscores at every turn that these crimes were committed through the interaction of human and demonic *bodies.*[14]

The arena par excellence of human interaction with demons was the Sabbat, or "witches' dance," or "witches' game." Accused witches like Walpurga and Johannes allegedly met the Devil (or a devil) for the first time when they were alone and vulnerable to discouragement or lust. But devils and witches had a social life as well. They supposedly gathered at immense meetings, often by the thousands. The most sordidly fascinating aspects of witchcraft mythology concern this mass meeting of witches and devils, where they engaged in a wide variety of shockingly perverse activities. According to Francesco Maria Guazzo, a theorist of the early seventeenth century, witches denied the Christian faith and withdrew their allegiance from God; they repudiated their baptism and their godparents and accepted a new name from the Devil. They gave their clothes, blood, and children to the Devil and begged him to inscribe their names in the "book of death"; they vowed to strangle or suffocate a child in his honor once or twice a month; they allowed themselves to be branded or marked by the Devil; and they repudiated the church's sacraments.[15]

As to the specifically sexual transgressions of the Sabbat, according to Guazzo, after dancing and singing and banqueting in the Devil's honor, "in the foulest manner they copulate with their demon lovers."[16] The witchcraft theorists' obsessive attention to sexual transgression is even more striking because of the joylessness of the sex that they describe. Early theorists often quoted witches on "the intense pleasure of diabolic intercourse," but often witches "confessed" that sexual relations with demons were anything but pleasurable.[17] Later theorists tended to collect anecdotes proving that demonic copulation was "entirely devoid of pleasure" and that witches felt "the most acute pain" during intercourse. In fact, by the late sixteenth century, the Devil "always had a member like a mule's . . . as long and thick as an arm." Sometimes the demonic penis was covered with barbed scales or was composite in nature, even being half flesh and half iron. Devils' penises might have two or three prongs, for simultaneously penetrating more than one orifice. The devil's semen was often ice-cold and painful, sometimes spoiled and rancid.[18]

A cui bono analysis suggests that, if their demon lovers had ever existed, witches might initially have been deceived by them but that, once they experienced such degrading sex, they would have done their utmost to avoid it rather than eagerly seeking it again, as they were usually made to confess. Still, nothing about the mythology of the Sabbat implies that demonic copulation served only to demonize sexuality or women. Literate interest in copulation with demons was hardly driven by prurience, misogyny, or puritanical fervor. Literate men craved demonstrations that even sexual intercourse, the most intimate sort of bodily contact, was possible with demons. Copulation offered valuable perspectives on the life of demons, their corporeality, and the possibility of interacting meaningfully with them.

Like the rest of the activities at the Sabbat, demonic copulation served to *anthropomorphize demons.* Sabbatic evidence demonstrated that real *human* interaction was possible between witches and devils. The idea of bodily contact organizes the whole concept of the Sabbat. There, the sexual orgies and other activities were supervised by Satan himself, to whom witches paid homage through a variety of degrading and disgusting rituals involving bodily contact.[19] At times, Satan appeared in the guise of a relatively normal human being. At other times, he appeared in animal form. And sometimes his body showed a mixture of human, animal, and even inanimate characteristics. Whatever his physical form, Satan always interacted with his devotees in a strictly human and corporeal fashion: he distributed money and food, oversaw a sexual orgy, and beat or berated witches who displeased him. The Devil's rewards and punishments resembled those that a human tyrant might have meted out, not the unmistakably superhuman actions of a god, even a pagan one. He did not change people's nature or annihilate them, as Greco-Roman gods were supposed to do. Because his rewards and punishments were overwhelmingly corporeal and evil, he offered a striking moral contrast to God, the angels, and the saints; but, most important, *he behaved exactly like a human being.*

There was no defeatism or despair behind theorists' enthusiastic descriptions of the hordes attending Satan's meeting. The Sabbat was literally "hell on earth." It amounted to a transferral of Satan's court from the invisible realm of spirit to the sphere of bodily interaction; and it was *visitable.* It provided evidence that intimate contact with demons was available on a large scale, often involving thousands of people at once, for witches had to testify that they had seen each other there. Large-scale witch panics happened when such testimony—rather than evidence of *maleficia*—was systematically demanded by judges.[20]

Early Witchcraft Theory

Not only were fantasies of the Sabbat driven by the satisfaction of discovering human enemies; they also provided the exhilarating confirmation that suprahuman or supernatural enemies were *real.* This shines dramatically through a document from 1460 describing alleged gatherings of a group of heretics. The Latin text describes these people as "Waldensians," but the French equivalent, *Vaudois,* was already a synonym for *witch:*

> Thus by their four senses, one of them interior (i.e., the power of thinking or considering) and three exterior (i.e., sight, hearing, and touch, particularly in sexual embraces and intercourse [*amplexu et copula*]), and sometimes even by the sense of smell [*olfatum seu odoratum*], and through the intellective faculty, and by many signs that would take far too long to describe here, the Waldensians know that incubi [*dyabolos,* male devils] are different from men and succubi [*dyabolas,* female devils] are different from women. And consequently, if such a thing should happen there, they would know the difference between a real woman and one being represented by a succubus [*dyabola*]. And similarly the power of thinking and considering distinguishes between a man and an incubus; because the Waldensians are frightened by the sight of a demon in whichever sex he appears [*in quocumque sexu appareat*], even though they are used to seeing that demon, for he commonly has a terrifying face and violent bodily manners or gestures.[21]

The passage makes clear that, whatever the writer's moralistic pretensions, he is really interested in *knowledge*. And he considers carnal knowledge the most complete form: "An assertion [*accusatio*] is already certain when based on sight; more certain when based on hearing and sight; but it is most certain and vehement and of greatest possible weight when based on touch—particularly that of carnal embraces—along with sight and hearing."[22]

Other early writers, who are more recognizable as witchcraft theorists than as heresiologists, gave a similar significance to demonic sexual encounters. Nicholas Jacquier, a French Dominican inquisitor, wrote his *Flagellum haereticorum fascinariorum* (*Scourge of Heretical Enchanters*) in 1458. He was anxious to demonstrate that the confessions of witches were not based on hallucinations or dreams. He declared categorically that,

> in the first place, experience clearly teaches that sexual intercourse [*operationes Venereae*] and the transports of carnal delight cannot take place or be consummated by people who are asleep, even though such experiences might originate in sleep by means of illusions or filthy fantasies. Thus, almost all the heresies, and the sects of witchcraft [*maleficiorum*], or those who practice enchantment [*fascinariorum cultores*] (many of whom, both men and women, confess this spontaneously and with signs of shame), affirm that in their gatherings, which they undertake in order to worship devils, they sometimes take perverse carnal delights with demons who appear visibly to them [*ipsi cum daemonibus apparentibus, quandoque ad invicem inordinate carnaliter voluptantur*]. And they do this so strenuously (as has been discussed already), that many of them remain ill and weakened for several days thereafter. It is clear that such apparitions take place in reality, and not to people who are dreaming, but to those who are wide awake.[23]

It hardly needs pointing out that everything in this pathetic proof—the spontaneous confessions, the shame over sexual perversity, and the health-sapping athleticism of the sex itself—serves to demonstrate the reality of these "apparitions." Jacquier's use of the term *apparitiones* implies, not insubstantiality or ghostliness, as the English term now does, but rather that only through exuberantly sexual embodiment can something spiritual *manifest itself* so clearly to the senses.

And Jacquier could not let it rest. He needed reassurance that people could be found who were evil enough to encounter demons; then he needed proof that their interactions were real. He claimed to have interviewed the servants of those who fornicated with demons, who testified that they often found their masters and mistresses bedridden and exhausted on Friday. Some even stayed abed several days thereafter. The servants were puzzled at first, for their employers could give no plausible reason for this extreme debilitation. It later became clear, says Jacquier, that the cause was sexual overindulgence at the Sabbat, which is always held on Thursday night. Jacquier's conclusion: "Thus the gatherings of these perverse witches are not an illusion formed by the imagination but a practice that is real, corporeal, and personal."[24]

Jacquier implies that the reality of this interaction is entwined with the reality of Christian faith. Many people refused to believe in the miracles of Christ, he says; likewise nowadays, many people who know all about the *maleficia* perpetrated by witches, and all about their spontaneous confessions, still refuse to believe in the existence of this evil sect. Worse yet, these skeptics disturb and obstruct the inquisitors who are trying to combat witchcraft. Skeptics should know that the Devil is inspiring their interference because he is trying to prevent the annihilation, or at least the repression, of his antireligion (*perfidia*).[25] Demons want their followers to invoke them and conjure them up for two reasons. Primarily, they intend to alienate their followers from the Catholic faith and procure their damnation in the afterlife; but demons also employ witches to help them molest faithful Christians with innumerable *maleficia* and other physical calamities during their earthly life.

Jacquier explicitly argues from the reality of *maleficia* to the reality of human-demon interaction and thence to the reality of demons themselves. "Since these *maleficia* happen *in reality,*" Jacquier claims, "it is clear that these heretical witches have joined themselves to devils with a pact, and adore them worshipfully *in reality,* and not in their imagination, and attend the synagogue where the devils interact with them *perceptibly.*"[26] Jacquier's proof makes several presuppositions. *Maleficia* were physical harms, possible only on the basis of bodily contact, and they could be performed only by demons. Witches were guilty, not of inflicting *maleficia,* but rather of commissioning them. On the basis of "his" pact with a witch—itself based on bodily contact between them—the demon inflicted bodily harm on the witch's chosen victim. Although the afflicting demon was usually invisible and incorporeal while inflicting the *maleficium,* the injury was, from the victim's perspective, a form of direct, involuntary bodily contact with a demon.

Sexual exhaustion, spontaneous confessions, the evil miracles of *maleficia:* these are Jacquier's evidence that demons are real. Such logic is momentous, for it evinces the opportunistic principle at work behind righteous indignation over *maleficia.* Moral crusades against sorcerers and witches make metaphysical investigations possible. Evildoers are necessary and *desirable* to the degree that they provide these metaphysical clues.

Girolamo Visconti, a Milanese Dominican related to the ducal family, wrote two treatises around 1460, the *Opusculum . . . in quo probatur lamias esse hereticas,* or *A Little Work about Witches* (printed in 1490 as *Opusculum de striis, videlicet an strie sint velud heretice iudicande*), and the *Lamiarum sive striarum opusculum,* or *On Lamias or Witches.* Like Jacquier, Visconti imagined that confirmed witches enticed newcomers into their sect by describing the sensual pleasures of the Sabbat: "Furthermore, people are initially invited to the witches' 'game' by someone who is expert in the art of witchcraft. To attract men, he promises that they will enjoy beautiful women, while handsome youths are promised to women. And every kind of pleasure and sensuality that one can enjoy will be found at the 'game.' And if they accept the invitation, they gather there above all to enjoy sexual pleasures." All witches "prefer to deny their faith and baptism rather than be deprived of the pleasures of the 'game.' " But more women than men go to the Sabbat, says Visconti, and, anyway, the most interesting sex acts do not happen between humans. All those in attendance, men and women, noble and common, are assigned a demon, an incubus or succubus "with whom they have sexual intercourse, and who appears to them often, both in the home and outside it, when they are wide awake, as they themselves affirm."[27]

Giordano (Jordanes) da Bergamo, another Dominican, wrote his *Quaestio de strigis* (*Inquiry into Witches*) about 1470. Giordano claimed to know a woman who had an incubus. He was fascinated by incubi, but even more by succubi. In this he appears to be in the minority of witchcraft theorists, who were usually more interested in women and incubi than in men and succubi. His case suggests that a particularly strong interest in succubi betrayed a desire to experience direct corporeal contact with demons rather than relying at secondhand on the confessions of women. At any rate, Giordano claims that an old and trustworthy man who lived at Peschiera on Lake Garda in northern Italy told him that the Devil once took on the appearance of a beautiful girl and seduced a hermit who lived about a mile from town. When the intercourse was over and the hermit stood up, the Devil taunted him: "Look what you've done! I'm not a girl or a woman, in fact, but the Devil!"[28] As usual in such tales, the Devil disappeared immediately, proving that his words were true. But he had extracted so much semen that the poor hermit dried completely out and died within a month of the fateful coitus.

As proof of his veracity, the trustworthy storyteller showed Giordano the very spot where this event happened and "many others." Thus, Giordano anticipated by four centuries Mark Twain's legendary proof that a miracle took place near a tree: "Well, there's the tree."[29]

The French Dominican inquisitor Jean Vineti wrote his *Tractatus contra demonum invocatores,* or *Treatise against Those Who Invoke Devils,* sometime between 1450 and 1470. Vineti declared that "it can be plausibly concluded that the depositions and confessions of some women, who confess that they have coupled with demons, should not be treated as if they were false and impossible."[30] Although Vineti's treatise is far less misogynistic than the infamous *Malleus maleficarum* would be a few years later, it foreshadows the *Malleus*'s condemnation of women in one important way: Vineti's title announces a moral crusade against a group of people, but his moral condemnation of their activities is *logically* necessary so that he can use those activities to argue "scientifically" for the reality of demons. Consequently, only about two of his seventy-seven pages discuss invokers of demons; the rest of the book is consumed by proofs that demons are real. The scientific argument about demonic reality engages Vineti's attention far more deeply than the immorality of demon invokers does. As his title indicates, his interest in these people is determined almost entirely by their supposed ability to make demons *appear.*

Vineti's treatise is organized into four major parts, each containing a number of Scholastic *quaestiones,* or, as Vineti significantly calls them, *doubts* (*dubia*). The first part "inquires about the nature of demons, and their names"; the second is "on the apparitions and operations of demons in assumed bodies." Not until the third part does Vineti discuss magic, while *maleficia* are left until the fourth. Except for the title and a brief preface, invokers of demons are not even mentioned until well into the second part. Vineti makes no effort to hide his consolation at knowing that someone can invoke demons and interact corporeally with them. Here are the first sentences of part 1: "Those who assert that spirits [*substantias separatas*] do not exist in nature fall into the error of the Sadducees, both as regards philosophy and as regards Catholic faith. The philosophical error will be clear if you recall to memory the arguments brought forth by Anaxagoras, Plato, Aristotle, and Avicenna. Anaxagoras was the first philosopher (as Aristotle testifies in the third book of *On the Soul*), and he posited the existence of an incorruptible first principle, that is, an intellect who formed this universe [*mundum*] by separating its elements from primeval chaos [*commixta*]."[31] In three sentences, Vineti moves from the existence of spirits to the existence of God. Vineti's God is not just a "principle" but an animate being capable of creating and *caring* for the world.

As many nervous Christians after him would do, Vineti denounces the Sadducees, a Jewish sect from the time of Christ whose disbelief in the afterlife was interpreted as a materialistic refusal to believe in spirit at all.[32] Quoting Aristotle, Aquinas, and Augustine, Vineti goes on to compare the Sadducees to ancient Greek and Roman materialist philosophers like Democritus, Epicurus, and Lucretius (whom he may have known only by reputation). These philosophers denied the existence of spirit, for they "said that everything that is, must be corporeal," and thus that only matter exists.[33] Vineti provides some of the earliest ✔ evidence that the existence of witches was vehemently defended because it gave indirect proof of the existence of God by proving that other spirits were real.[34]

Vineti then brings forth the frightening idea that undergirds his whole condemnation of interaction with demons:

> This also refutes the presumptuous and heretical-sounding opinion of those who say that demons do not exist, except in the imagination of the common people, so that a man imputes to a demon the terrors that he has impressed on himself by the exercise of his own imagination, and that on account of a vehement imagination, some figures can appear to the senses exactly as a man has thought of them, and then it is believed that he is seeing demons. But these ideas are repudiated by the true faith, through which we believe that angels fell from heaven and are now demons.[35]

Vineti's reasoning must be understood in all its skeptical implications: he supposes that the experiences of demon invokers prove that contact with devils is possible, but how does he know that such experiences are not imaginary? What if corporeal interaction with devils were imaginary *precisely because* devils were imaginary? If frightening thoughts can cause us to perceive things that are not really there, can we be certain that demons, whom Christians are admonished to fear and loathe, are real?

Vineti hastens to assure his readers—and himself—that this dismaying possibility can in no way be true and so initially seems far less worried than the anonymous reviler of "Waldensians," his contemporary. Yet Vineti's reasoning is circular: We need to know whether demons are real. Demon invokers and witches say that they are. But what if we are not satisfied by the testimony of these people? Then we have to fall back on faith: we have to believe that devils exist simply because the Bible and Catholic doctrine assert that they do.

There is a remarkable conceptual unity about demons and their human allies in these early texts. The overt ethical and moralistic slant of these works defined witches and their immediate forerunners as hostile, aggressive assaulters of good Christians. The moralism was reinforced by defining witches as "demon lovers," the paramours of devils. Yet, despite reviling witches as *malefici* and *maleficae,* male and female "evildoers," the earliest witchcraft theorists were not primarily interested in witches' magical assaults on good people. Far more enthusiasm was reserved for witches' physical interactions with demons. Those interactions were imagined as fully corporeal and included sexual intercourse, conceptualized as a form of knowledge gathering.

The philosophical attention that theologians lavished on this stereotype reveals that the real demon lovers, the persons who most ardently desired physical relationships with embodied devils, were the theologians themselves. Their desire for "carnal knowledge" of demons was, not pornographic, but metaphysical. Their fantasy of witches' corporeal ravishment translated their own desire for an overwhelming intellectual conviction, one that would annihilate their involuntary resistance to the idea of demonic reality.

Resistance to Skepticism

To say that witchcraft theorists did not believe their theories is not to say that they thought like modern educated secular people. With two or three centuries of scientific thinking and rationalistic skepticism in his or her mental baggage, the modern educated layperson looks at elements of the mythology of witchcraft and thinks: "Such things cannot happen." Yet, at some point in the distant past, activities attributed to witches, and powers attributed to devils, must have commanded belief among literate Europeans. Before the twelfth century, writings about interactions between demons and humans sometimes betray no doubt. They are told straightforwardly, with a matter-of-fact attitude toward the possibility that such encounters could actually take place. These pre-twelfth-century writings are short on theory and demonstrate no apparent need for complicated explanations.[36] There are no convoluted chains of proof, no attempts to head off the reader's skepticism with elaborate preemptive refutations. The internal logic of these writings seems to express a mental attitude to the effect that "this is how such things must happen, this is the most satisfactory explanation." It seems therefore quite safe to qualify such writings as expressions of belief.

The thirteenth century was a watershed in the history of Christian beliefs about spirits. David Keck has demonstrated that, "as late as 1200, scientific angelology . . . was still in its infancy. By contrast, fifty years later, both Aquinas and Bonaventure had developed thorough, systematic, comprehensive angelologies that addressed all of the major natural and metaphysical issues concerning angels."[37] Because demons were defined as fallen angels, no discussion of angelology could ignore them. But the search for precision and certainty about a world that was invisible to humans generated significant perplexities and doubts. In this respect, witchcraft theory was a direct outgrowth of thirteenth-century angelology and demonology.

As thirteenth-century angelology evolved toward fifteenth-century demonology and witchcraft theory, literate discussions of the spirit world progressively accumulated the telltale signs of bad faith that were missing from the earlier literature. The luxuriant proofs of the 1400s and 1500s display neither belief nor rationalistic skepticism. Instead, they are saturated with an attitude best expressed as "these things cannot *not* be happening in the way in which I propose." The older, late-antique and early-medieval mentality had been "this must be true." The modern rationalist stance is "this cannot be true." The early-modern contention was "this cannot *not* be true." Witchcraft theorists often employed this very phraseology.

The early-modern attitude thus occupies an uncomfortable halfway point between belief and skepticism, an attempt to maintain belief while fighting off skepticism. The attitude of witchcraft theorists toward their theories was not belief but rather *resistance to skepticism,* a desperate attempt to maintain belief, and it betrays an uncommonly desperate *need to believe.* That is why I will continue to speak of witchcraft *theories* and *theorists* rather than *beliefs* and *believers.*[38] The witchcraft theorists' resistance to skepticism preceded, conditioned, and made possible the overt and candid skepticism about witchcraft, demonology, and the spirit world that erupted after the middle of the sixteenth century.

The official skeptical tradition of the sixteenth and later centuries, which has been studied by historians of philosophy and science, grew out of a long process of damage control. The Western Christian "will to believe" in the reality of spirit progressively lost ground for centuries before anyone could decide to abandon it.[39] Overt expressions of disbelief grew directly out of increasingly unconvincing attempts to *construct* belief.[40] Between about 1400 and 1700, witchcraft theory was the most visible and socially disruptive phase of this *resistance to skepticism,* but it was preceded by other phases, beginning as early as 1150. (And, needless to say, resistance to skepticism did not end when witchcraft persecutions did. One need think only of "creation science" and its prehistory in the resistance to Darwinism.)[41]

No sophisticated literary theory is needed to analyze resistance to skepticism, but it may be helpful to review a distinction drawn by Umberto Eco. Eco notes that older literary theories habitually concentrated their attention on the intention of the author but that, since the 1950s, literary theorists have decided that authorial intention is "very difficult to find out and frequently irrelevant for the interpretation of a text." Thus, modern literary theory has concentrated increasingly on "the intention of the interpreter who (to quote Richard Rorty) simply 'beats the text into a shape which will serve for his purpose.' " But, says Eco, "there is a third possibility. There is an *intention of the text.*" This *intentio operis* (to use Eco's medieval-sounding term) may even be unconscious on the part of the author, but it can be discovered. Yet how can the intention of the text be proved to our satisfaction? "The only way is to check it upon the text as a coherent whole."[42]

As Eco observes, this is an old idea, as old as Saint Augustine's fourth-century *De doctrina Christiana,* or *On Christian Doctrine:* "Any interpretation of a certain portion of a text can be accepted if it is confirmed by, and must be rejected if it is challenged by, another portion of the same text. In this sense the internal textual coherence controls the otherwise uncontrollable drives of the reader." But how can we know whether we are exaggerating the evidence of internal cohesion and overinterpreting the text, by reading things into it rather than out of it? Eco several times invokes a principle of *textual economy:* Is it economical to assume that the text functions in this way? Not if it can be shown that our interpretation "could not coexist with other hypotheses that proved to be reliable in order to explain phenomena that [it] did not explain."[43] And not if refuting those other hypotheses requires much effort. This is, in a sense, an updated and expanded version of the logical maxim called *Ockham's razor:* "One should not multiply explanations and causes unless it is strictly necessary"; the most valid interpretation is the one whereby "everything is explained, using a smaller number of causes."[44]

I do not mention the fourteenth-century Scholastic philosopher arbitrarily. Without Ockham's Scholastic predecessors, either there would have been no witchcraft theory, or it would have had a drastically different shape. Ockham's advice is paramount for two purposes: for testing our own hypotheses about witchcraft theory but also for testing the hypotheses of witchcraft theory itself. Often, as chapter 2 below will show, a failure to recognize uneconomical explanations in witchcraft treatises leads scholarship into uneconomical and thus demonstrably wrong interpretations of "the author's obvious motives."

Interpretations of texts about witchcraft err to the degree that they do not stop to ask whether such elaborate theories are necessary in order to achieve the ends that witchcraft treatises ostensibly pursue. Was all this theological reasoning about spirits necessary if the primary goal of witchcraft theory was the social control of humans? Was such reasoning merely a demonstration of its authors' deeply held beliefs? Why was that necessary?

To paraphrase Hamlet's mother, herself something of an Ockhamist in psychological matters, "They did protest too much, methinks." To recall my earlier distinction, we must distinguish the *logic* of the text's organization from the *rhetoric* of its protestations about its author's uncomplicated belief; we must separate its reasoning from its rationalizations. The logic of an uneconomical explanation is inherently shaky; confidence and certainty must therefore be claimed by rhetorical means, through loud disclaimers and protestations.

By discussing texts, I do not wish to imply that we can learn nothing about the men who wrote the treatises that I will be examining. On the contrary, texts betray the human insecurities that made witchcraft theory and prosecution possible. Regardless of whether the *empirical author,* the historical person to whom a book is attributed, ever existed, our interaction with the text accumulates the profile of an *implied author,* the type of individual who would or could have written such a text.[45] What kind of person would have needed or wanted to construct such a text? Whether the empirical author is correctly identified as Vineti, Jacquier, or Visconti, the intentions of the text create our sense of "that kind of person." Thus, it is ultimately irrelevant whether a text's empirical author was an inquisitor, a secular judge, or an ivory-towered scholar, whether he was famous, infamous, or unknown. Irrelevant, that is, to asking *why a society* produced texts about witches for so long and why it did things to people identified as witches.

Witchcraft treatises demonstrate a systematic logic, and they resemble each other. They display their anxieties systematically—not openly, as a rule, but between the lines, through repetition, innuendo, approach/avoidance, and allusion. In a sense, the authors—whoever they were "in fact"—could not have told us more about their motivations had they stretched out on a psychiatrist's couch. But, like the psychiatrist's patient, they did not and could not always "tell the truth" in their overt declarations. What they claimed to worry about is not usually what their reasoning shows them to be worrying about, and what they loudly profess to believe with complete serenity often betrays nagging philosophical and theological doubts.

For this purpose, it is also useful for us to know *what else* has been attributed to a particular author, whoever he may have been. Unless the attribution is recent and conjectural, the combination of texts can be eloquent. Do the other writings mention witches or have other themes in common with the witchcraft treatise? What practices do the other texts condemn or defend? Can these concerns be observed in other fields or disciplines? Were they noticeable in earlier writings by others? Do texts by others—both older and contemporary—show similar anxieties, or do they present the same issues serenely?

Witchcraft theory became quite uniform. Its stereotypes and commonplaces crystallized, not just because theorists read each other, or because they read previous theologians, but also because there was a logic to the "cumulative concept" that appealed to most theorists.[46] That logic is thoroughly implicated by the fundamental doctrines of Christianity concerning the nature of *spirit*. Anyone engaged in the prosecution of witches must have felt its attraction, whether he was familiar with formal witchcraft theory or not.

That logic, I shall argue, implied that the identification and persecution of witches was nothing less than a defense of fundamental Christian principles. Those principles remained central to Christianity from long before Martin Luther until long after the Council of Trent. They were not moral or ethical questions about conduct, as we have been led to believe, but scientific problems of being and knowledge, concerning devils, angels, the human soul, the truthfulness of the Bible, and the evidence of God's existence and presence in the world. Witchcraft theory was far more than a demonology. It was not an anomaly in the history of Western Christianity. It was an expression of Christianity's deepest and truest logic, although in oversimplified and neurotic form. Not that its practitioners were usually treated as fanatics or obscurantist crackpots; they participated in the most vital, wide-ranging, and up-to-date philosophical and scientific debates.

I am not arguing for some eternal, unchanging battle between science and religion of the sort that nineteenth-century liberal historians like Andrew Dickson White hypothesized.[47] The failure of witchcraft as an explanation of the world and God is not directly related to the rise of modern science. Witchcraft theory evolved out of a history of debates in natural philosophy—not our "science," but its predecessor. Natural philosophy, as Roger French and Andrew Cunningham argue, was "before science"; and it "was created by thirteenth-century Christians in order to serve as a weapon against the threats that they perceived [Christianity] was then facing."[48] It was "a new subject" in the thirteenth century, created by writers of the new Dominican and Franciscan orders, philosopher-theologians like Saints Thomas Aquinas and Bonaventure.

Natural philosophy was built up through the application of Aristotelian philosophy to Christian theology, and one of its uses was the polemical refutation of heresy. The most important opponent of orthodox Catholicism in the thirteenth century was the tremendously influential Cathar heresy. Cathars claimed to be able to prove that the world was fundamentally evil. They denied the existence of a single, omnipotent, benevolent God and postulated another god, a thoroughly evil and immensely powerful being who had created the world. There was not one God but two, and their antagonism explained why the world is not uniformly good. One goal of natural philosophy was defeating this heresy and showing that "God is good, His creation is good, the goodness and the causality of the Creation are evidence of the goodness of God. . . . [T]his new concern with nature was thus God-centred, and the point of it was to convey a certain message about God. Nature was to be studied, discussed, disputed about and even observed and investigated, not primarily for itself nor for the sake of disinterested knowledge but for what it said about God its creator."[49]

This did not become any easier with the defeat of the Cathar—or any other—heresy. Rather, every victorious explanation created, hydra-like, new contradictions and the need for further explanations. One of those new explanations was witchcraft, built on the demonology of just those authors who were instrumental in creating natural philosophy.

The concerns of this larger cultural history illuminate the preoccupations shown by the intentions of the text in witchcraft treatises. Although the social viability of witchcraft faded sharply after 1700, resistance to skepticism did not. Both phenomena are more comprehensible when viewed within the history of attempts to defend God and the world of spirit. The skepticism about Christianity that natural philosophers opposed may have been external to them in the thirteenth century, as it was in the heresies of the Cathars. But skepticism was infectious; many later authors fought it because they had internalized it, and it riddles their texts with clashing logic and rhetoric. Witchcraft theory was an impassioned protest that "these things cannot be imaginary!"

2

WHY WOMEN? THE *MALLEUS MALEFICARUM*

> But theologians will tell you that these things *can* be done by the Devil. . . . And you can understand many examples from the book of the Germans Friar Heinrich and Friar Jacob, excellent theologians of the Dominican order, called *The Hammer*. . . . And you can have this hammer, if you want to use it against those who are hardheaded, and don't want to believe the truth; so you can either bend them to believe what they are supposed to, or else smash them into a hundred thousand pieces.
>
> —Gianfrancesco Pico della Mirandola, *Strix* (1523)

Metaphysical Voyeurism

The anxieties of witchcraft theorists were of another order than ours because the hopes and fears of their epoch were not those of our own. Although it often seems like "Scholastic pornography," sex-obsessed demonology was not driven by sexual repression or sexual anxiety in any modern sense.[1] Psychiatrists like Sigmund Freud, Jacques Lacan, or Melanie Klein may yet have something to tell us about the anxieties of witchcraft theorists, but not until we have understood how their treatises cohered *as theory*. Until we know in detail what they were arguing for, it is unhelpful to apply modern psychoanalysis to them.

The arguments of witchcraft theorists demonstrate that they were *metaphysical voyeurs,* not dirty old men or repressed prudes. What they wanted to see was not hidden behind bedroom walls or memories of their mothers. It was closed off by the barriers that separated life from the afterlife, humanity from the demonic and the divine.

The Malleus maleficarum *and Misogyny*

These precautions need repeating with regard to the question of gender. For most of our theorists, "having a female body was the one factor most likely to render one vulnerable to being called a witch."[2] But the literate men who developed the theory of witchcraft were not driven by misogynistic motivations of a sort familiar to feminist criticism.

Caution is particularly necessary when reading the text that has become synonymous with witch-hunting, the *Malleus maleficarum,* or *Hammer of Witches,* published in 1487. (For the sake of convenience, let us refer to the author of the *Malleus* as Heinrich Kramer. But I shall initially discuss the text itself, without reference to an author.)[3] The *Malleus* has been justly condemned for its remorseless misogyny. Its habitual word for witch, *malefica,* is feminine, and it declares that witchcraft "is better called the heresy of witches [*maleficarum*] than of wizards [*maleficorum*], since the name is taken from the more numerous [*potiori*] party."[4] The *Malleus* consolidated the misogynistic impulses scattered in previous witchcraft treatises and hardly ever quoted their evidence of male witches.

But hatred of women was not the sole or even the primary motive for compiling the *Malleus.* The misapprehension that misogyny explains the *Malleus* comes from misunderstanding the medieval theology and philosophy undergirding the book's argumentation. The *Malleus*'s reasoning is no different from what we have seen in its forerunners. However, the *Malleus* is far longer and more meticulous: it is a *summa,* and the works written before it were pamphlets by comparison.

Part of the problem is language. Little interpretation of the *Malleus* in the past three decades has been based on the original Latin text. This prevents understanding the *Malleus* historically, for modern translations are often inaccurate, sensationalized, or made artificially relevant.[5] Reliance on translations distorts the most basic assumptions about the book's history and intended audience. Anne Llewellyn Barstow, a writer who flatly equates witch-hunting with woman hunting, claims that the *Malleus* "was soon translated into German, French, Italian, and English."[6] But, until the twentieth century, no translations *at all* of the *Malleus* were printed.[7] If you didn't read Latin, you didn't read the *Malleus.*

For readers dependent on translations, the single most comprehensible chapter of the *Malleus* is part 1, question 6, an infamous and very complete collection of everything evil or unflattering that its author could find about women in the Bible, classical literature, and Christian theology.[8] This chapter[9] of the *Malleus* has monopolized the attention of twentieth-century readers, distorting their understanding of every aspect of the book, starting with its misogyny. Stuart Clark notes that "overreliance on this one [chapter] has obscured the almost mechanical nature of its arguments, citations, and illustrative tales, as well as the existence of a yet more explicit clerical misogyny in other fourteenth- and fifteenth-century writings." He goes so far as to maintain that "on the whole . . . the literature of witchcraft conspicuously lacks any sustained concern for the gender issue; and the only reason for the view that it was extreme and outspoken in its anti-feminism is the tendency for those interested in this subject to read the relevant sections of the *Malleus maleficarum* and little or nothing else."[10]

In his remarks on part 1, question 6, Henry Charles Lea, the late-nineteenth-century historian of witch-hunting and inquisition, observed that "the demonologists found an easy explanation of the greater propensity of women to become witches in the weakness and depravity of the sex, which was the favorite object of monkish objurgation [rebukes]." Lea was careful to observe, however, that the *Malleus* does not "indulge in the customary monkish abuse of women" until this chapter.[11] He was aware, that is, that something besides misogyny had been at stake up to this point and that misogyny had just made a grand entrance.

The *Malleus*'s denunciations of women *as women* are both perfunctory and localized. To ignore this is to misread the book's fundamental purpose, its *intentio operis*. Relying on Montague Summers's 1928 English translation of the *Malleus,* Anne Barstow asserts that 49 of 275 pages constitute a "tirade against women's sexual powers."[12] If about a fifth of the *Malleus* is dedicated to "women's sexual powers," we should still wonder what the rest of the book is about. But most of the pages to which Barstow refers are not primarily about women or sex. Rather, they examine such varied—yet intimately related—topics as imagination, the sacraments, divine justice, and the activity of incubus devils.

The only pages of the *Malleus* devoted specifically to women and sexuality are those in part 1, question 6. These seven pages constitute only 14 percent of what Barstow calls the *tirade against women's sexual powers*. More important, they represent only 2½ percent of the whole *Malleus maleficarum*. To paraphrase Umberto Eco, is it economical to presume that the ideological purpose of the *Malleus maleficarum* is to justify hatred of women?

The Uses of Misogyny

The misogyny of the chapter is obvious and undeniable; it claims that "women do all things because of carnal lust, which . . . is insatiable in them. Wherefore for the sake of fulfilling their lusts they consort [*se agitant*] even with devils." It identifies several kinds of witches, and says that some are more dangerous than others, but claims that all of them "practice carnal filthiness [*spurcicias carnales*] with devils." It assures us that witches necessarily "indulge in diabolical filthiness through carnal copulation [*spurcitijs diabolicis per carnales actus*] with incubus and succubus demons" and concludes that they "devote themselves body and soul [to devils]."[13]

These assertions express the fundamental idea of the *Malleus,* but they require interpretation. Writers of the sixteenth and seventeenth centuries interpreted the *Malleus* as I have interpreted its forerunners, reading it as a defense of the reality of demons and a theory of physical interactions with them. Gianfrancesco Pico della Mirandola, an early devotee of the *Malleus,* described it in 1523 as a hammer for smashing *skeptics* rather than women.[14]

Careful examination of the *Malleus* supports Pico's interpretation. The book was written to prove that demons are not imaginary and that their copulation with witches proves that they are real. The tirade against women was written to argue that women's nature, both psychological and physical, makes them the ideal sex partners of demons. The many parts of the book that are not focused on women or copulation explore the important *theological* consequences of the demonstration that demons are real.

The *Malleus* is filled with evidence that its author, Heinrich Kramer, was never quite convinced by his own claims. His discussion of demonic copulation openly betrays how hard-won his belief in it really was: "The theory that modern witches [*maleficas*] are tainted with this sort of diabolic filthiness does not depend so much on our own opinion, as on *the expert testimony of the witches* [*maleficarum*] *themselves, which has made all these things credible.*"[15] Kramer defends the credibility of witches' testimony by quoting Aristotle: "That which seems true to many cannot be altogether false, according to Aristotle in the seventh book of his *Ethics,* and at the end of his *On Sleep and Waking.* And now also in modern times, the deeds and sayings of witches, who do such things truly and in reality, *bear witness*" to the reality of demonic copulation.[16]

Modern scholarship on the *Malleus* has not prepared us to notice or evaluate Kramer's reliance on witches and Aristotle for proof of an assertion about demons. What could the most reviled category of women have in common with the philosopher most respected by medieval theologians? Answer: a theory that real proof and certainty come from sensory data and bodily experience. Witches provide the empirical proof—*experta testimonia* means both "expert" and "experienced" testimony—that bodily contact with demons is possible. Like previous witchcraft treatises, the *Malleus* is asserting that witches have carnal *knowledge* of demons. The witch knows demonic reality by experience because she has voluntarily submitted to a demon's sexual assault and allowed her body to be penetrated by his. By treating witches as expert witnesses, the *Malleus* translates metaphysical definitions into legal concepts and categories. The courtroom is now officially a kind of observatory where evidence of demonic reality can be collected. Legal proof has become subservient to metaphysical proof. In fact, legal proof has *become* scientific proof.

Witches' expert testimony does not simply affirm the reality of demonic copulation: it *contradicts* the accusation that Kramer has an overactive imagination, that "the theory depends only on his opinion," to paraphrase him. The importance of this rhetorical strategy cannot be stressed enough. The function of the witch is, as Kramer baldly admits, to *make credible* the notion that devils have regular bodily interaction with human beings.

The Front Page

Kramer did not reel off his arguments without effort. While composing the book, he made drastic changes to its structure, constantly hoping to argue more effectively. Throughout the process of revising, his overriding concern was to remove any doubt that demons prove their reality by copulating with witches.

In the final, printed version of the *Malleus,* the witches' testimony to demonic reality does not get mentioned until nearly halfway through the book. But it was part of Kramer's earliest concept. In an early draft, some time before going to press, witches' expert testimony appeared very near the beginning of what was certainly a shorter treatise. Even now, the first page of the *Malleus maleficarum* reveals that it was written to demonstrate that demons are not imaginary: "Those who say there is no such thing as witchcraft [*maleficium*] except in the imagination [*estimatione*] of men do not believe that demons exist either, except in the imagination of the common people [*vulgi*]; and they think that a man creates terrors for himself from his own imagination and then attributes them to a demon's activity; indeed, they assume that a powerful imagination [*imaginatione*] can cause certain figures to appear to the senses exactly as a man has thought of them, so that we say he only thinks he is seeing demons, or witches [*malefici*]."[17] This passage corresponds almost verbatim to a passage from Jean Vineti's *Tractatus contra demonum invocatores* that we examined in chapter 1 above (see p. 25). Vineti's treatise was first printed four years before the *Malleus,* so this passage could have been copied from it. But in fact both authors were copying from a standard theological source.[18]

Montague Summers garbled the *Malleus*'s first page badly in his English translation.[19] Thus, discussions of the treatise have neglected the core of Kramer's witchcraft theory, ignoring his deep anxieties about the power of the imagination, the reliability of sensory evidence, and the possibility of gaining knowledge about the world of spirits. Kramer admits from the beginning how worrisome he finds these problems and declares his intention of addressing them by investigating witchcraft as *knowledge gained by physical means.*

The *Malleus* implies that a central tenet of faith, the existence of demons, requires an *empirical* demonstration to be convincing. But then, just as Vineti's did, Kramer's treatise falls back on the idea that the existence of demons must be believed because it is an article of faith, as if empirical reasoning is also inadequate: "But in fact, [the theory that demons are imaginary] is repudiated by the true faith, through which we believe that certain angels fell from heaven and are now devils. And indeed we confess that because of the great refinement [*subtilitate*] of their nature, devils can do many things that we humans cannot do; and those who induce them to perform such [wonders] are called witches [*malefici*]."[20] The rhetorical flourishes—"true faith," "we believe," "we confess"—convince neither a modern reader nor Kramer himself. By bringing the process full circle, he reveals that neither dogma nor witches' empirical testimony gives satisfactory proof of demonic reality.

When focusing on the *Malleus*'s presentation of women, scholars often claim that its argumentation is illogical, but this is inaccurate. The logic is there, but it aims to prove something other than what we expect it to prove.[21] The logic of the *Malleus* is abominable, but not solely because it is misogynistic: the *Malleus* exploits misogyny to reinforce a demonology—and, ultimately, a theology—that Kramer found unconvincing. To say that he exploited theology in order to demonize women requires turning his logic inside out.

The issue is not misogyny per se but rather its ideological usefulness, the cui bono question again. Of course the *Malleus* was misogynistic, but what, for Kramer, was the *use* of misogyny? To read his treatment of demonic copulation as a tirade against women's sexual powers is to miss his point entirely. If anything, his tirade is *for* women's sexuality. The issue was not keeping women in their place or controlling their sexuality. Heinrich Kramer did not fear that women were associating with demons: he *hoped* that they were. His whole theology *depended on* women's sexual transgression, and it would have collapsed if he had ever had to admit that women's behavior conformed to the patriarchal ideal of chastity and submissiveness.

The Malleus: *A Work in Progress*

The first two parts of the *Malleus* lay out Kramer's theory of witchcraft, while the third part describes how to prosecute witches effectively. A major task of the first two parts is defining how to identify people who might be evil enough to seek the company of devils and properly equipped to vouch for their reality. The notorious "women's-evil" chapter was written to demonstrate that women were inherently suited for these tasks. Textual evidence shows that this chapter was written quite some time after Kramer decided to focus on demonic copulation as a way of demonstrating that demons were not imaginary.

Kramer's anxiety over the effectiveness of his arguments is betrayed by substantial changes that he made to the *Malleus* before completing the second of its three parts. Textual evidence allows us to track these revisions precisely, and it provides crucial insight into the way in which Kramer thought and reasoned while composing the *Malleus*. His revisions were clearly designed to make the connection between women's evil and demonic copulation more plausible. Considering the importance of Kramer's treatise for the development of witchcraft theory and how thoroughly it has been misunderstood, we are well advised to pursue these insights.

At least once before sending the *Malleus* to press the first time, Kramer edited his treatise by "cutting and pasting," perhaps with literal scissors and paste. He thereby left conclusive textual evidence that the women's-evil chapter replaced a purely technical discussion of copulation between women and demons. The technical discussion was then repositioned much later in the text of the *Malleus*. Kramer had decided that he needed to discuss the theological ramifications of demonic copulation, and above all its moral preconditions, before discussing *how* it took place.

The Latin text of Kramer's women's-evil chapter still shows evidence that this revision was made abruptly and somewhat clumsily. In the Latin *Malleus,* the chapter's title does not mention the general evil of women. Instead, it reads "Here follows what pertains to those witches [*maleficas*] who subject themselves to demons; and it is the sixth question and division of the work." The first paragraph of the chapter also bears no relation to the topic of women's evil. Most of it concerns the anatomical and physiological characteristics of demonic bodies. The paragraph outlines seven topics as if Kramer intended to discuss them in the chapter, but he never does:

> There is also, concerning witches who copulate with devils, much difficulty in considering the methods by which such abominations [*spurcicias*] are consummated. *On the part of the devil, first, of what element the body is made that he assumes;* secondly, whether the act is always accompanied by the injection of semen received from a human male; thirdly, as to time and place, whether the devil commits this act more frequently at one time than at another; fourthly, whether he commits this act [*se agitat*] in a way that is visible to bystanders. *And on the part of the women,* it has to be inquired whether only they who were themselves conceived in this filthy manner [*ex huiusmodi spurcicijs*] are often visited by devils; or secondly, whether it is those who were offered to devils by midwives at the time of their birth; and thirdly, whether the actual venereal delectation of such women is of a weaker sort [i.e., than what they experience in sex with human males].[22]

At this point, Kramer suddenly declares that he will defer discussion of the seven points in order to discuss the evil nature of women: "*But we cannot here reply to all these questions,* both because we are only engaged in a general study, and because in the second part of this work they are all singly explained . . . in the fourth chapter. . . . *Therefore, let us now chiefly consider women;* and first, why this kind of perfidy is found more in so fragile a sex than in men. *And our inquiry will first be general, as to the general conditions of women.*"[23] This announces the topic of the chapter as we now have it, that is, women considered in themselves and defined as agents of evil. But notice that the passage introduces the evil nature of women as a necessary precondition for their sexual relations with demons, not as interesting in itself. The *Malleus* is deferring discussion of the technical aspects of demonic copulation to concentrate on the moral character of women.

The change of topic offers no surprise to modern English readers. Montague Summers's translation prepares them for it by retitling the chapter: "Concerning Witches Who Copulate with Devils; Why It Is That Women Are Chiefly Addicted to Evil Superstitions." Since modern readers are more interested in women than in demonic copulation, they have still less occasion for surprise. However, Kramer's *original* audience might well have been puzzled. Once they got past the first paragraph, Kramer's title looked completely inappropriate.

Although the discrepancy between the content of the women's-evil chapter and the chapter's original title is invisible to the English reader, it is our strongest clue to how the *Malleus* evolved. The stranded title reveals that, originally, the chapter was about *only* the mechanics of demonic copulation. The summary paragraph tells quite clearly what the original contents of the chapter were, describing them in seven headings.

The problem discussed was, not women's evil, but the discoverability ✔ of demons. The first four headings are exclusively about how devils copulate. Only the last three headings concern women, and none of them considers women from a standpoint of moral condemnation. Instead, headings 5–7 discuss technical or "scientific" aspects of women's sexual contact with devils. Headings 5 and 6 pose the problem of defining what sort of women are "*often* visited by devils." Taken together, these two headings raise the question whether *some* women are predisposed to frequent contact with demons, either through genetics (women who were sired by devils) or through ritual (women dedicated to devils at birth or before baptism).

The last of Kramer's three points about women focuses on their "actual venereal delectation" during copulation with demons. As his

treatment of this theme will show, *Kramer wants to know whether sex with* ✓
demons is as satisfying to women as sex with ordinary human men is. The
technical character of these seven points and their lack of hypocritical
moralizing make it clear that Kramer's interest is not prurience but
provability. There is nothing here about women's general behavior and
no discussion of their morality.

After writing the chapter in its original form, Kramer decided that
the reader's acceptance of demonic copulation must be more carefully
prepared. So he wrote a new chapter on the inherent evil of women in
order to make their motivation for demonic copulation as plausible as
possible. He replaced the technical discussion of demonic copulation
with the discussion of women's evil and wrote a transitional paragraph
to show how they were related.

In the transition, Kramer promised that the technical questions about
demonic copulation would be exhaustively treated in the fourth chapter
of part 2, and that is almost precisely what he did. The title of part 2,
question 1, chapter 4, announces a discussion of "the way whereby
[witches] subject themselves to incubus demons," and the whole seven-
point discussion has been moved there.[24] A new first paragraph repeats
the seven points with slight changes in wording.[25] This detail is peculiar. Kramer recopied the paragraph rather than moving it out of the
women's-evil chapter because he wanted the reader to notice the repetition and remember the connection between women's inherently evil
nature and the technical aspects of demonic copulation. If he had wanted
to discuss women's evil for its own sake, why not write a new title and
summary for the chapter?

Other than recopying the summary paragraph, Kramer made no
noticeable changes to the discussion of demonic copulation after moving
it to part 2. In fact, the discussion continues to mention topics that "we
will treat in the second part."[26] But the discussion is *already* in part 2:
Kramer forgot to change its cross-references to reflect its revised position
in the book. This oversight confirms the evidence of the nearly identical
summary paragraphs: the discussion was originally located in part 1, at
just the point where Kramer now discusses women's evil. It has been
moved, not composed specially. What changed was the rest of the
Malleus, starting with a new chapter on women's evil.

✓ ✓✓ To summarize: while composing the *Malleus,* Kramer decided that his
treatment of demonic copulation presupposed characteristics of women
that he had not yet proved. He could not discuss the scientific aspects
until he established that women were morally predisposed to seek sex
with devils. So he split off the technical material on demonic copulation
from its summary paragraph in part 1, question 6. He then filled the

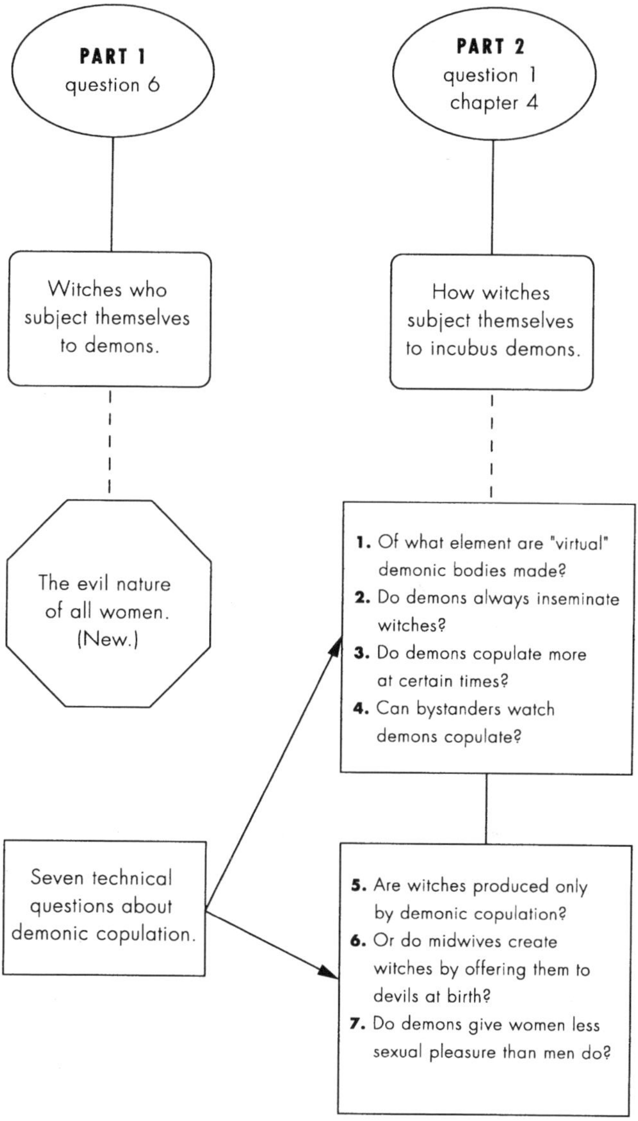

DIAGRAM 1 Author's revisions while composing the *Malleus maleficarum*. Demonic copulation: the mechanics.

empty space with a newly composed demonstration that women are inherently evil. Finally, he reserved the discussion of demonic copulation until he composed part 2 of the *Malleus*. (See diagram 1.)

In part 2, the long-deferred discussion of demonic copulation closely follows the order laid out in its summary paragraphs.[27] Kramer's seventh point, the last of the three concerning women, argues that women demonstrate demonic reality by experiencing demonic virility: "If it be asked: Whether the venereal delectation is greater or less with incubus devils in assumed bodies than it is in like circumstances with men in a true physical body [*in corpore vero*], we may say this: It seems that, although the pleasure should naturally be greater when like disports with like, yet that cunning artificer [*artifex*] can so bring together the active and passive elements, not indeed naturally, but in such qualities of warmth and temperament, that he seems to excite no less degree of concupiscence."[28] Kramer wants to discover just how real demonic copulation is, and he presumes that, the stronger a woman's sexual pleasure is, the more likely it comes from interaction with a real being.

Kramer does not feel that he can claim that women find demonic copulation more intensely pleasurable than intercourse with men. But his wording betrays that, if he dared, he would assert exactly that: he compromises by saying that a demon can satisfy a woman *no less well* than a man can. Here, in the concluding paragraph of his entire discussion, he reveals that the plausibility of demonic copulation, its *verisimilitude,* is a matter of *virisimilitude.* Demons must be real because witches testify that they are every bit as virile as men (*viri*). Indeed, this is the chapter in which Kramer bases that claim on the expert testimony of the witches themselves.

This is a misogynistic assumption because it presumes that, for any woman, ultimate sexual pleasure can come only from being penetrated and ravished by a force that is unambiguously male. But it is not *about* hating women or trying to punish their sexuality. It is about hunting women only to the extent that it focuses on exploiting their sexuality to discover something about demons. *Cherchez la femme* means *cherchez le diable.*

The last sentence of Kramer's relocated discussion preserves a snapshot of his mind at the moment he realized that he would need to write some material on women's evil before he could discuss demonic copulation properly. He promises to discuss demonic copulation "more fully later with reference to the qualities of the feminine sex," but there is no trace of such a discussion anywhere in parts 2 and 3 of the *Malleus.* The only such discussion is the one about women's evil in part 1, question 6.

So Kramer was interested in the mechanics of demonic copulation well before he produced his perfunctory and unoriginal discussion of women's evil. But the important question is not which chapter was written first. Kramer concluded that it was *logically* necessary to prove the evil nature of women before he could assert that women copulated with devils. Despite their drastic separation in the final version of the *Malleus,* everything about the two chapters indicates that they form a thematic unit. The repetition of the summary paragraph in both places was intended to ensure that women's general propensity to evil and the evidence of their sexual encounters with demons would remain firmly connected in his readers' minds, despite the expanding volume of proofs.

Ultimately, the connection did not hold. Part of the fault was Kramer's, for the changes made it too difficult to remember the connections. Accidents of cultural history did the rest. By the twentieth century, readers had very different priorities. The existence of demons had become an obsolete, uninteresting problem, while the nature of women was a topic of passionate cultural and legal debate.

Another Revision

Kramer wanted to demonstrate that he was not credulous to assert that demons can prove their reality. In the discussion relocated to part 2, he introduced the idea that witches are expert witnesses to the reality of demons because they have sex with them. For the sake of thoroughness, he gave other, corroborating testimony and concluded: "Therefore this matter is fully substantiated by eyewitnesses, by hearsay, and the testimony of credible witnesses."[29]

However, the expert-witness arguments were not moved from part 1, question 6. Textual evidence demonstrates that they were originally in part 1, question 5. This means that Kramer originally introduced the idea of witches' expert testimony before he even discussed the mechanics of demonic copulation, much less women's evil. Not only is the idea that witches give the best proof of demonic reality the central idea of the *Malleus;* it is probably the oldest.

The evidence is conclusive. First, the expert-testimony material forms a large, coherent block. Second, it intervenes somewhat clumsily between two questions that Kramer moved from part 1, question 6, concerning the mechanics of demonic copulation. The interpolation was not foreseen in the summary paragraph about mechanics, in either the old location or the new.

Other traces reveal the original position of the expert-testimony material, as we can see from a comparison of the first sentence of part 1, question 5, and a subheading of part 2, question 1, chapter 4:

> Whether it is in any way Catholic to hold that *the origin and multiplication* of the works *of witches* [*maleficorum*] result from the influences of the celestial bodies, or from the superabundant wickedness of men, and not *from the filthiness of incubus and succubus demons . . .* ?

> How in modern times witches [*malefice*] perform carnal acts with incubus demons, and how they are multiplied by this means.[30]

These two passages have telling analogies with each other. One asserts that female witches multiply by means of copulation with demons, the other that *maleficia,* the *works* of both male and female witches, do so. Their overall implication is the same: the increase in witches' activity comes from an increase in demonic copulation.

But the text of part 1, question 5, drops the assertion completely and concentrates on refuting two alternative explanations, one attributing the increase in *maleficia* to astrological influences, the other attributing it to moral degeneration. Proof that the true explanation is increased insemination of witches by demons has been moved to part 2 and mixed in with the relocated material on the mechanics of demonic copulation. It interrupts the transition between two technical questions, "of what element the body is made that [the demon] assumes" and "whether the act is always accompanied by the injection of semen received from a human male."[31] (See diagram 2.) Demonic copulation is still identified as the origin of witchcraft, but astrology and human depravity are no longer even mentioned as alternative explanations. Witches' expert testimony has a new, slightly different function: it now proves that Kramer has correctly described the mechanics of demonic copulation.

Another example of sloppy editing confirms that the material came from part 1. When Kramer defends his practice of accepting witches' expert testimony, he claims that "there was no question of credulity in accepting their stories because they freely [*sponte*] turned to repentance; for they all agreed in this, that they were bound to indulge in these lewd practices [*spurcitijs*] in order that the ranks of their anti-religion [*perfidia*] might be increased. *But we shall treat of these individually in the second part of this work,* where their particular deeds are described."[32] Once again, these words are already in part 2. Like the seven mechanical questions about demonic copulation, the expert-testimony material has been moved from part 1; in the process, two questions or chapters were combined into one. (See diagram 2.)

So Kramer's earliest arrangement of the *Malleus* introduced demonic copulation to explain how witches proliferated and called on witches as expert witnesses to the process, even before attempting to explain how demonic copulation could be physically possible.

The relocated material indicates that the original part 1, question 5, also argued that, before 1400, true witchcraft did not exist. This is extremely important: it shows Kramer trying to explain why anxiety over witchcraft exploded around the year 1400 rather than sooner. Kramer was aware that his concerns were, not age-old, but pretty recent.

Before 1400, Kramer argues, there must surely have been witches, for history attests to their *maleficia;* likewise, incubi and succubi existed

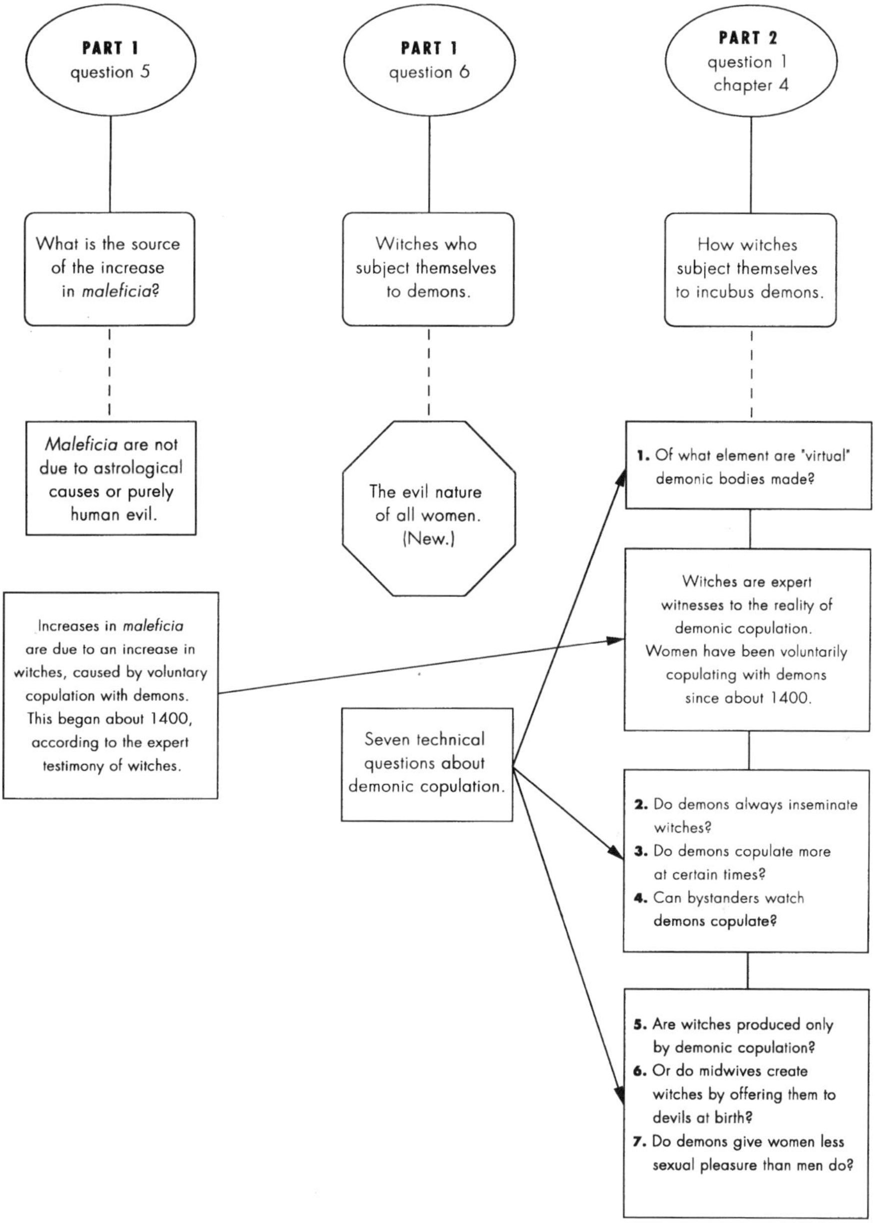

DIAGRAM 2 Author's revisions while composing the *Malleus maleficarum*. Demonic copulation and *maleficia*.

in those olden times, for theologians and canon lawyers record many things about them.[33] However, evidence of interaction between incubi and makers of *maleficia* is elusive: Kramer claims not to know whether *maleficae* of former ages copulated with incubi. Moreover, he has noticed that even authors from the turn of the fifteenth century still referred to incubi as molesting unwilling women. "Let us say," he concludes, "that it is unknown what was done by *maleficae* of former times, before the year of our Lord 1400 or thereabouts; whether, that is, they were addicted to this filthiness [*his spurcitijs inserviebant*], as modern *maleficae* have been since that time. Experience has shown us that nowhere up to now has history spoken of this."[34]

This waffling is a clear sign that Kramer, who preferred to rely on long-standing Catholic tradition, could find no support in it for his contemporaries' definition of witchcraft as a combination of *maleficium* and demonic copulation. To be truly authoritative, a definition would have to be traceable to the fathers and doctors of the church or the canon lawyers, and Kramer knew that this one could not be found there. The elements of witchcraft—incubi, succubi, and women performing *maleficia*—were attested only separately before 1400. But the *oral* expert testimony of the witches themselves guarantees what *written* tradition does not: it proves that the combination of *maleficia* and demonic copulation is a reality. The clincher, Kramer says, is that modern women admit that they "*willingly* subject themselves to this stinking, miserable servitude for sheer pleasure."[35] The witches themselves necessarily vouch for their corporeal experience of demonic reality because more respectable authorities provide no such evidence.

The Original Malleus

This much is certain about the earliest draft of the *Malleus:* Kramer needed proof that demons were real, not imaginary. He decided that witches' confessions to copulating with demons would give that proof. Having argued that, he realized that he needed to explain how such copulation could be physically possible. No sooner had he finished that proof than he wondered whether his readers would believe women to be morally capable of such nefarious behavior. At this point, he sought out his commonplace books and strung together every unfavorable opinion about women that he could find. These changes obliged him to move his whole discussion of demonic copulation from the beginning of the *Malleus* to the middle.

As a result of this scissors-and-paste editing, the *Malleus* now has a different logical progression than it did when Kramer began it. He must have begun to rethink his logic and organization after completing the initial draft of part 1, question 6. He appears to have remained largely satisfied with the first four questions, for they changed little, if any. There is some repetition in them that shows him vacillating over when to discuss aspects of demonic copulation, but they show no evidence of drastic transpositions.

All the first six questions heavily emphasize the physicality of interaction between witches and demons. Question 1 announces that witchcraft proves the existence of devils. Witchcraft is therefore necessary to Catholic faith; disbelief in witchcraft is heresy. Toward its middle, question 1 insists that any witch "has truly and actually bound herself to be the servant of the devil, and this was not done only in fantasy or the imagination [*se tota obtulit et astrinxit diabolo vere et realiter et non fantastice et imaginarie solum*]." It is necessary, Kramer continues, that a witch cooperate with the devil "truly and bodily [*vere et corporaliter*]."[36] This declaration unambiguously foreshadows the explicitly sexual arguments to follow.

Question 2 asserts that demons and witches need each other to perpetrate bodily harm on victims. It extends the definition of corporeal interaction by discussing *maleficium* as bodily harm (*maleficium* relates victims corporeally to demons, just as copulation relates demons and witches). Bodily interaction becomes more explicitly sexual in question 3, "Whether children can be generated by incubi and succubi." The answer is yes. Kramer argues that demons could sire children invisibly but that they *prefer* "to perform this visibly as a succubus and an incubus . . . there being, as it were, actual bodily contact."[37]

In the summary of question 3 written for the *Malleus*'s table of contents, the theme of corporeal contact ties questions 2 and 3 even more closely: "Secondly whether . . . a demon must always cooperate with a witch to produce a malefic effect, or whether one without the support of the other can produce this effect. Thirdly, whether . . . such effects are produced in this way by incubus and succubus demons. Also that real human beings are procreated by such demons for the origination and proliferation of witches [*maleficorum*]."[38] Here, Kramer reveals a concern to show that incubi and succubi *in particular,* of all possible kinds of demons, perform both *maleficia* and demonic sex.

In its current form, question 3 fails to discuss incubi and succubi as particular species of demons. Instead, question 4 inquires whether all demons, or only some, "perform the operations" of incubus and succubus: do these terms describe species or only activities? The hesitation suggests that Kramer was still thinking on his feet. And he still does not declare unequivocally whether copulation is universal among demons.[39]

Instead, he announces, among other ideas, that demons never perform "unnatural" sex acts. Thus, he implies that demonic copulation is always potentially procreative.

In the original part 1, question 5, as we saw, Kramer discussed witches as expert witnesses to the reality of voluntary copulation with demons and, thus, to demonic reality. He argued that such voluntary corporeal interaction had begun around 1400. In question 5, he also repeated some arguments from question 3 regarding how demons inseminate witches.[40]

Having established the reality of demons and demonic copulation on the authority of witches, Kramer then examined the mechanics of demonic copulation in part 1, question 6. He first discussed the four problems about demons' corporeality and sexuality, then three problems about witches. He stopped just short of asserting that demons provide women stronger sexual delectation—better orgasms—than men do. Here again there is overlap since the seven problems revisit ideas discussed in original questions 3 and 5.

It is clear, then, that, in Kramer's original plan, before he began transposing chapters to part 2, he intended for the first six questions of the *Malleus maleficarum* to describe a smooth curve. He began with the question of demonic reality and moved to the possibility of corporeal interaction with demons through both *maleficium* and demonic sex. He then introduced the subject of incubi, succubi, and their ability to copulate with human beings. He went on to assert that witchcraft—the combination of *maleficium* and voluntary corporeal interaction with demons—had begun around 1400, when women stopped resisting the sexual advances of demons. He concluded with a detailed exposition of the mechanics of demonic copulation.

Very early on, at the end of question 2, Kramer revealed his plan for the remaining trajectory of part 1. This plan jibes with what we have seen so far: "And because among all the actions [of witches] two above all contribute to the multiplication of their numbers, that is, [their association with] incubus and succubus demons and their sacrilegious sacrifices of small children, we will therefore treat these topics most particularly, so that in the first place we shall discuss the demons themselves, secondly, the witches, and thirdly, we shall mention the divine permission."[41] As we saw, questions 3 and 4 do treat demonic copulation from the perspective of the demons themselves. All the original six questions concern the demons themselves and discuss witches only to define demons.

The new question 6 somewhat disrupted this original focus on demons. It shows Kramer deciding that he would have to discuss witches as *women,* as people with motivations, not as mere instruments for measuring the reality of demons.[42]

With questions 5 and 6, the need for serious revision made itself known. After question 6, the revisions to part 1 slowed or stopped. Questions 7–11 still correspond to the second division of Kramer's early outline, "the witches." These five questions concentrate on witches' *maleficia,* or crimes against other people, constantly reminding us that witches can do nothing without demons. Question 7 inquires whether witches can cause love and hatred between spouses and concludes that *devils* can, with witches' assistance.[43] Questions 8 and 9 argue that witches can obstruct conception and cause an illusory yet very effective form of castration—but only through the agency of devils. Question 10 explains witches' seeming ability to transform themselves and others into various animals—through illusions produced by devils. Question 11 delivers the long-promised discussion of how witches, particularly those who are midwives, perform "sacrilegious sacrifices of small children" to devils.

Questions 12–18 constitute a theodicy: as Kramer promised in question 2, they discuss why God permits witchcraft to exist. Significantly, the *Malleus*'s table of contents concludes its outline of question 18 by stating that part 1 forms a perfect circle, whose first and last questions both explain how and why God's permission is necessary for witchcraft to happen.[44] Not only does God have good reasons for allowing witchcraft, but he has also provided ways to counteract it.

After revising part 1, Kramer decided to add a second major section to part 2.[45] There he discussed *maleficia* in more detail and described the "remedies" that God provides against them, particularly through the Catholic sacraments and the persecution of witches. Part 3 moves from theory to practice by prescribing how to entrap, try, and destroy witches.

Thus, demonic copulation is not simply a perverse sidelight of the *Malleus maleficarum.* Witches' carnal knowledge of demons is the thematic keystone of the entire book: witches attest to the existence of demons through sexual experiences and *maleficia* that are demonstrably real. Demons are the ultimate cause of all afflictions visited on humanity. But demons need witches because human malice provides the opportunity for demons to cause harm.

As Kramer implies in the first two questions of part 1, witchcraft is a complete Christian theory of reality. Witchcraft explains the relations among the most basic agents and forces of Christian "physics": "For [witchcraft] to take place, three things concur, to wit, the devil, the witch, and the permission of God."[46] This delicate balance of human, demonic, and divine interaction organizes the chapters or "questions" of part 1 of the *Malleus maleficarum*. Thanks largely to Kramer's treatment, the interaction of demons, witches, and the permission of God provided the common core of all witchcraft theory down to the 1690s and Cotton Mather.

The Two States of the Malleus

The discussions of astrology and general human sinfulness that remain in part 1, question 5, probably bore most modern readers as thoroughly as the discussion of women's evil distresses and offends them. But changes to question 5 are important for showing what Kramer was arguing *against*. He had powerful reasons for believing that he could not simply argue *for* demonic reality. In his fifth question, Kramer had originally written a proof that widespread voluntary demonic copulation caused a "population explosion" of witches after 1400 and that witches themselves vouched for the truthfulness of this claim. After completing that argument, he realized that his task was more complex than he had thought. He could not vindicate demonic copulation as an explanation of increased witchcraft until he proved that witchcraft was real.

The other indispensable aspect of witchcraft—*maleficium*—was not universally accepted as a real cause of human affliction. It was all well and good to prove that demons were real, but, if all they did was copulate with women, how worrisome could they be to the world at large? Kramer therefore needed to prove that *maleficium*—cooperation between witches and demons to harm innocent people—was a reality. To do this, he had to demonstrate that other explanations could not account for the afflictions that he attributed to *maleficium*. As we saw, the first sentence of question 5 still asks whether "the origin and growth of works of witchcraft proceed from the influence of the celestial bodies, or from the abundant wickedness of humanity, *and not from the abominations of incubus and succubus demons*."[47] Some potential explanations were based on astrology; they were scientific or, in Kramer's terms, natural. Others were theological and presumed that sheer human depravity was to blame. All the explanations implicitly or explicitly excluded demons; all implied that devils were imaginary or irrelevant.[48]

During the early stages of composing the *Malleus,* Kramer grew increasingly worried by the possibility that such causes could provide better explanations of the misfortunes that he was attributing to *maleficium*. He had been rebutting such arguments piecemeal throughout his first four questions but had spent most of his effort on demonic copulation. Now he decided that a more thorough response was necessary.

Once again, summary paragraphs provide solid evidence for the sequence of revisions. When Kramer sent the *Malleus* to press, he prefaced part 1, question 5, with a long and confusing title and summary:

> This, then, is the question about the influences of celestial bodies, in which three additional errors are condemned; and it is the fifth question in order.
>
> But for a better elucidation of the foregoing, and also to obviate any sort of would-be objections whatever, the works of witches [*maleficorum*] will be examined with respect to five possible causes, four of which will be rejected as having no influence. The fifth, which will be vindicated, in fact, is an intellectual power, from which they [i.e., the works of witches] have to derive. Although this intellectual power [i.e., demons] is good according to its nature, it is nonetheless evil according to its will. Thus four causes are rejected, to rebut those who deny the existence either of witches [*maleficas*] or of their deeds: and that is, the influences of the celestial bodies, the movers who move the celestial bodies and their spheres, the increasing wickedness of human beings, and the efficacy of images, characters, and words.[49]

One could assume, says Kramer, that the heavenly bodies alone influence events on earth or that the influence comes from the mysterious Aristotelian "intelligences" moving the spheres. One might suppose that humans were able to harness these powers through a purely natural form of magic, involving incantations not addressed to devils. One could even argue that people just go from bad to worse. All these arguments are specious and wrong.

This is the order of discussion in the new question 5, except that the fifth, "vindicated" hypothesis, demonic copulation, was moved to part 2.[50] This passage also suggests how Kramer revised question 5. He must have initially just piled all the refutations in front of his discussion of demonic copulation. But he was not long satisfied with this solution. Probably the expanded question 5 was simply too large. Question 5 is still one of the two longest in part 1, even after Kramer transferred the discussion of demonic copulation. Kramer saw that, to reduce the chapter's bulk, he could transfer the witches'-expert-testimony material to part 2 and combine it with the technical discussion of demonic copulation.

After the transfer, part 1, question 5, remained *only* a refutation of the alternatives to *maleficium*. But Kramer did not remember to indicate where the relocated material could be found; he made no further changes to question 5's title or summary paragraph. This oversight doomed the summary paragraph. It is so contorted that it must have been confusing even in the sixteenth century, and its topics did not correspond to part 1, question 5, as printed. It went missing from the *Malleus* sometime between 1519 and 1580, probably deleted deliberately by an editor.[51] The elimination isolated question 5 even more, breaking any visible link between its arguments and the arguments of the questions surrounding it. So, on the basis of question 5's first sentence, someone simply retitled it: "Whence proceeds the increase in witchcrafts." Since Montague Summers translated from a very late edition, the whole summary is missing from his English translation.

Overall, the revisions that Kramer made in the *Malleus* constitute a classic case of self-defeating encyclopedic anxiety. As happened with the birth of Tristram Shandy, an author found a topic so important that he deferred and prefaced it far longer than was useful to the reader. But Laurence Sterne was joking, while Kramer was in earnest. He came to feel that he had to prepare more carefully for his definitive treatment of demonic copulation, but, the more proofs he added, the more he seemed to need. By the time he was ready to analyze demonic copulation, he had pushed his treatment far from its original position: about a hundred modern pages, in fact. He was so obsessed with refuting the objections to his theory of human-demon interactions that the logical connections were all but lost in the complications of the rearranged text.

Despite all his efforts, Kramer failed to rewrite thoroughly enough. By neglecting to create new transitions and cross-references or delete obsolete ones, he left his treatise disorganized. Some editors were already confused in the sixteenth century. But, had Kramer reorganized the *Malleus* more carefully, he would have erased the clues that reveal its original intention. Given the complexity of his arguments, the *Malleus* might appear even more illogical than it now does.

Thanks to the traces of his revision, we can observe two different logics of argument. But the notion of demonic copulation as an index of demonic reality is fundamental to both logics, and its importance drove Kramer's revisions. His lack of attention to crucial textual detail reveals how important demonic copulation was to his outlook from the beginning and how hard he worked to make it seem plausible.

What the Malleus *Means*

Kramer did not fear feminine power; on the contrary, he needed it, and he felt compelled to defend the notion that "so fragile a sex," defined as *powerless* in itself, could truly excel at evil.[52] He was attempting to explain what he and his contemporaries still perceived as an anomaly. He knew that his readers would not automatically assume that women had voluntary access to demonic power. They did not simply assume that, because Eve was tempted by the serpent in Genesis, women could initiate contact with demons whenever they wished.[53] In the lived reality of social and intellectual interaction, the picture was far more complex.

As Norman Cohn wrote in two finely argued chapters, the notion that women could have voluntary access to demonic power was new and strange in the early fifteenth century. Before 1400, before witch-hunts or witchcraft theory, clerics imagined the deliberate invocation of demons as a privilege of people like themselves, literate men. The necromancer or ritual magician of the late Middle Ages called on demons to manifest themselves and perform services for him. But he was "a very different figure from the witch as she was imagined at the time of the great witch hunt," as Cohn explained. The necromancer was "more often male than female, a commander of demons rather than their servant, a specialist skilled in the most elaborate technique." The legend of the magician Theophilus, who contracted his soul to the Devil, entered Latin tradition in the eighth century. By the thirteenth century, it was "one of the most familiar and best-loved" of a number of tales about deliberate interactions with devils.[54]

Necromancers possessed lore that no simple village person, particularly a woman, was thought capable or worthy of having. They exploited their highly specialized knowledge of writing, theology, and philosophy in elaborate attempts to contact and dominate demons. They usually claimed to work in the name of God and appeared confident of avoiding eternal damnation.[55] The early-sixteenth-century story of Doctor Faustus entered Western European tradition after the stereotype of the witch had formed, but it still looked back to the earlier ideal of contacting demons as an activity for learned men. It showed the influence of witchcraft mainly in its unrelenting emphasis on Faustus's evil intentions and his sexual relations with demons.

Questions of sex and gender are central to witchcraft in somewhat unexpected ways. Necromancers were not stereotyped as sex partners of demons. This was not simply because they were men but because, being men, they could read. Because most women were illiterate, their sexuality was the only trait that literate men could imagine bringing them into contact with demons. Since women's sexuality was defined as passive, women were imagined as being dominated by demons rather than as controlling them. Kramer could imagine women as the ideal witnesses, the *testes expertae* to demonic reality, because a woman who confessed to being ravished by a demon was testifying to the existence of a suprahuman presence that left her no choice but to believe in its reality.

Even this was not an easy step: the idea of women voluntarily initiating *any* form of contact with demons was so strange that Kramer had to explain how it came about. As we saw, he asserted that, until about 1400, women were molested by incubus demons against their will. In fact, this was the consensus of ancient and medieval literature on incubi until the rise of witchcraft theory. Kramer had to argue for a momentous historical change just to defend the idea that modern women were voluntarily copulating with demons.

Among early witchcraft theorists, Kramer was the author who most thoroughly argued for a preponderance of female witches. His emphasis on women is closely related to his insistence that "carnal lust" is the root of all witchcraft and that all witches practice "carnal copulation" with demons. Kramer's main reason for casting women as the prime sex partners of demons was his assumption—or his *will to believe*—that women were highly sexed yet passive in their sexuality. Women are "more carnal than men" and thus crave sex more intensely, but their role in copulation is to *receive* the actions of a man or an embodied spirit.

To Kramer, women were necessary for ensuring that, as the "active" and "dominant" partners in copulation, demons *imposed* their reality on humans. He clearly wanted to believe that demons could prove their reality better by penetrating human beings sexually than by allowing humans to penetrate them. If the vagina is the marker of a passive sexual role, then women are necessary sex partners for demons so that demonic reality can be passively *suffered*. If demons were to take the "passive" and "receptive" female roles, they would be subordinated to humans. By that token, there could be no certainty that demons were not imaginary.

So, in Kramer's logic, the witch's reaction of "carnal delectation" demonstrates that she is being acted on, and, the more intensely she enjoys, the more intensely real is the agent who is acting on her. Kramer showed little interest in stories of sex between succubi and men, and he declared, as practically every writer on the *Malleus* observes, that men are less prone to such "filthiness" than are women.[56] Kramer was terrified of sodomy, so he was not about to imagine men being buggered by incubi (although other theorists did). In fact, he declared that all demons abhor sodomy and other "crimes against nature"; his incubi practice only vaginal copulation with women. Although he discussed succubi infrequently, he appears to have imagined that they also practice vaginal copulation exclusively.[57]

These are not gratuitous expressions of misogyny and homophobia; they were based in Kramer's need to prove that demons were not imaginary. Vaginal copulation was necessary so that demons could prove their reality by inseminating women. Since crimes against nature are by definition contraceptive, Kramer's horror of sodomy is consistent with his need to verify demonic reality. His emotional attitudes toward sex between men (which were indeed negative) are not directly relevant to this logic.[58]

The same active/passive reasoning applies to the immaterial realm of the intellect. Kramer says that women's minds are weaker than men's but "more impressionable" and that they are therefore "more ready to receive the influence [*impressio*] of a *disembodied* spirit" than men are.[59] Although invisible, these *impressiones* are as literal as footprints or fingerprints, the marks of an actual pressure or penetration. To a great extent, Kramer regarded women as geologists regard seismometers, as instruments for detecting and measuring the force of phenomena that cannot be observed directly.

Papal Ratification of Kramer's Definition

Kramer's ideas about witchcraft were not spread exclusively by the *Malleus* or even by other treatises. They were approved and given a much wider diffusion through Pope Innocent VIII's bull *Summis desiderantes*. Scholars consider this document a milestone in the legitimation of witchcraft theory and witch persecution. It was "truly fundamental, if only because it was perceived that way by its contemporaries; at the level of their psychological attitudes it was extremely deleterious. . . . [T]o speak *ex cathedra* about the reality of witchcraft meant to support the efforts of those who persecuted it."[60] Kramer and others argued in all seriousness that, if witchcraft were imaginary, there would be no laws against it. The very idea that the church could be in error was impious.[61] They were right in a way: the bull established the reality of witchcraft through legislation.

The *Malleus* and the *Summis desiderantes* were the two most influential documents yet created about witchcraft: one gave the most elaborate theoretical explanations, the other the most detailed papal condemnation of such crimes. There is a fundamental agreement between the *Malleus* and the *Summis,* for the pope's letter implicitly identifies demonic copulation as the origin of witchcraft: "It has recently come to our attention, not without great pain to us, that . . . many persons of both sexes, unmindful of their salvation, and straying from the Catholic faith, *have transgressed with incubus and succubus demons,* and with their incantations, spells, conjurations, and by other abominable superstitions and sortileges, offenses, crimes, and misdeeds, they cause and procure the perishing, suffocation, and extinguishing of the offspring of women, the young of animals, the produce of the earth, the grapes on the vine, the fruits of trees. . . ."[62] And so on for another half page of *maleficia*. The pope issued this bull in 1484, three years before the *Malleus* was printed, explicitly to authorize the inquisitions of Heinrich Kramer and Jacob Sprenger, the individuals whom the *Malleus* claims as its authors. The *Summis* was printed in most early editions of the *Malleus* as a kind of preface, lending papal authority to the book.

The *Malleus* cites the *Summis* as proof that demonic copulation is a reality. An explicit linkage between demonic copulation and infanticidal *maleficia* recalls the proximity of these crimes in the bull:

> Let us likewise consider that, for the propagation of their antireligion [*perfidia*] they are required to perform four actions in particular, to wit: to renounce the Catholic faith, in whole or in part, through the most sacrilegious oaths [*ore*]; to devote themselves body and soul [to the devil]; to offer up unbaptized children to that same Evil One; to indulge constantly in diabolical filthiness through copulation [*per carnales actus*] with incubus and succubus demons—and would that all these things were completely untrue and could be said to be made up [*figmenta*]! If only the Church were immune to the infection of such a great spiritual leprosy!
>
> However—alas!—this is not true, as is shown both by a determination of the truth in a bull of the Apostolic See, and by Experience, the teacher of all truth [*rerum magistra*], who has convinced us, by means of [the witches'] own confessions and the evils [*flagitijs*] they have perpetrated, that we can no longer refrain from investigating them, lest we imperil our own salvation.[63]

A priori, the bull lends the highest credibility to witchcraft as demonic copulation and *maleficium,* so Kramer mentions it even before the inquisitorial *experience* of hearing confessions of witchcraft. Thanks to the *Summis desiderantes,* he need not rely exclusively on the expert testimony of the witches themselves. Although the bull is recent, it provides the written authority that Kramer had vainly sought in Catholic tradition before 1400: proof that demonic copulation and *maleficia* occur together.

The close agreement between the most explicit witchcraft bull and the most explicit treatise raises the suspicion that the pope might have granted the bull because the future author of the *Malleus* convinced him that demonic copulation was fundamental to witchcraft. Kramer might even have provided "boilerplate" or ready-made text to the papal scribes once the pope had approved his ideas. Theoretically, of course, Innocent could have convinced Kramer of this idea; the latter could have written his book to explain the pope's theory. Or the two could have reached their conclusions separately: after all, the *Malleus*'s ideas were not original, only more elaborate than usual. Still, Kramer sought the bull actively; the pope granted it in response to the inquisitor's complaints that other authorities were obstructing his inquisitions.[64]

At any rate, whether either man influenced the other is finally irrelevant. Thanks to this bull, the intimate connection of *maleficia* and demonic copulation received papal approval three years before the *Malleus* went to press. Once his book was printed, Kramer argued in it that the *Summis desiderantes* proved that his witchcraft theory correctly described crimes rampant in the real world. Along with Kramer's restless editing of the *Malleus,* the bull indicates that tremendous energy was expended between 1484 and 1487 to have demonic copulation recognized as the foundation of all witchcraft.

3

SEXY DEVILS: HOW THEY GOT BODIES

> For as the Damascene says in the third chapter of book two, "Angels and demons are incorporeal beings, thus it is a bestial error to say that demons have hands or feet."
>
> —Ambrosius de Vignate, *Tractatus de haereticis* (1468)

> In this whole field Aristotle must be most carefully avoided, not because he committed more errors, but because he has more authority and more followers.
>
> —Petrarch, *On His Own Ignorance and That of Many Others* (1371)

How did the problem of demonic copulation become such an obsession of Western Christian theology? The fundamental problem was whether demons were imaginary. The only way of proving that they were real was to demonstrate that they could interact physically, perceptibly, and undeniably with human beings. Certainty would have to depend on corporeality, for the body and the senses provide us with the information that forms our picture of reality. *Reality,* a word whose Latin root means "thing-ness," was originally a learned idea and seems to have arisen in the twelfth or thirteenth century. Like the concepts *quantity* ("how-much-ness") and *quality* ("which-ness"), it arose in a culture that was coming to grips with ancient philosophy.[1] Medieval Catholic thinkers rarely confronted ancient philosophy directly, however; it was transmitted to them through Arabic and Jewish sources. Needless to say, this dependence could present a problem from the religious perspective, as Islam and Judaism were both regarded as inimical to the truth of Christianity.

The most prestigious of the ancient scientists was Aristotle; he was simply *Philosophus,* "*the* Philosopher," for the late Middle Ages. The stakes were high for reconciling Aristotelian methods with Christian presuppositions about reality. His analyses of human and nonhuman bodies and of sensory information opened exhilarating prospects for exploring the world. But his ideas about the human soul and the possible existence of suprahuman beings were difficult to understand. What could be understood was often distinctly foreign to Christian dogma and thus intensely worrisome. Yet Aristotelian method had undoubted advantages for many types of philosophy and theology. Developments after 1500 would largely discredit the idea that Aristotelian concepts of the soul and suprahuman beings were compatible with Christian doctrine. But, between 1100 and 1500, Christian theologians spared no effort to *make* them compatible. One key arena for this effort was demonic corporeality.

The definitive answers to the problem of corporeal interaction with demons were given by the most authoritative Aristotelian theologian of the Middle Ages, Saint Thomas Aquinas (d. 1274). Aquinas provided rigorously argued, protoscientific explanations of demonic corporeality and physiology in Aristotelian terms, with a view to proving that physical interaction between humans and demons was possible. This is not to imply that Aquinas was responsible for the attempt to verify demonic corporeality through witchcraft theory and witch-hunting.[2] He certainly did not recommend the discovery and prosecution of witches in the way in which these things were practiced after his time. Moreover, his anxieties about the verifiability of spirit were inherited from previous Christian theologians.

Understanding whether—or, ostensibly, how—demons could interact perceptibly with human beings had already become important by the twelfth century, and it became crucial in the thirteenth. The problem was implicit by about 1150 in Peter Lombard's influential *Sententiarum libri quattuor,* or *Four Books of Sentences.* This was the standard university textbook of theology throughout the Middle Ages and into the early-modern period. As David Keck states, "The history of angelology in the thirteenth and fourteenth centuries and beyond is the history of the commentaries on the *Sentences.*" While desultory speculation about angels and demons was traditional, Christianity did not acquire "an organized, systematic, and near-comprehensive treatment of the angels and their nature" until the *Sententiarum* entered the theology curriculum of the University of Paris.[3] Every degree candidate in theology had to demonstrate his grasp of the field by commenting publicly on this text. As a result, the *Sententiarum* virtually founded demonology and its happier twin, angelology, as systematic fields of study.

The style of intellectual inquiry that characterized medieval Scholasticism was highly competitive, especially at the prestigious University of Paris. This predisposed medieval and early-modern theologians to discussions of minutiae:

> That prospective masters of theology had to deliver commentaries on the *Sentences* meant that theologians would have a professional incentive to explore in greater and greater depth the questions raised by the Master's

> text. An ambitious theologian could not simply repeat what Lombard had stated, rather he had to delve deeper, probe more tenaciously, and reason more accurately than not only Lombard but also other commentators if he were to establish himself as a leading theologian. Lombard's text thus provided the Scholastics with a formal occasion for angelology by presenting a coherent structure for discussing the nature of the angels that was open to new categories and concepts.[4]

The institutionalization of angelology between 1150 and 1400 was not as uniformly positive as it might appear from Keck's account. It was not just a story of occasions and opportunities. Angelology was about the fallen angels as well as the good ones, and even speculation about good angels was fraught with perplexity and outright worry. Arguing about good angels may even have led to some of the more extreme hypotheses about bad angels; this seems to be the case with attempts to show how one might interact unmistakably with suprahuman beings.[5] For thinkers who distrusted human sexuality, carnal knowledge of good angels was not an option that attracted discussion.

The entire second book of Peter Lombard's *Sententiarum* is devoted to ontology or manner of being. As its title—"On the creation and formation of corporeal and spiritual things, and about many other things pertaining to the same subject"—intimates, it defines and classifies beings according to whether they have bodies.[6] Here is the first systematic discussion of a number of angelological and demonological questions that would haunt Scholastic theologians and eventually inspire the specialized subculture of witchcraft theorists.

Several distinctions of book 2 were particularly important. Distinction 4, "Whether God created the angels perfect and blessed, or miserable and imperfect," exonerated God from responsibility for the evil committed by devils: they were created as good angels but fell by their own fault. Distinction 7 declared that, once Satan and his legions had fallen, no further change was possible in the nature of angels and demons: "Good angels are confirmed by God's grace so that they cannot sin, and the evil ones are so hardened in their evil that they do not wish to live well." Distinction 11 claimed that God delegates a guardian angel to every human soul and that a devil is assigned to test its use of free will.[7]

But distinction 8 was by far the most influential, making the issue of demonic corporeality a part of the standard curriculum in theology: "Whether angels have bodies, as has seemed to some writers, with whom Augustine seems to agree, saying that, before the fall of Satan, all angels had subtle and spiritual bodies but that, since then, the evil angels' bodies have become grosser so as to enable them to suffer."[8]

Lombard reveals that no consensus had been reached in previous Christian scholarship as to whether angels and demons had a *physical presence* as well as a spiritual one: Did they have bodies, or were they pure spirit? Lombard posed the question by asking whether Augustine, the most authoritative of the church fathers, had really believed that God created bodies for the angels.[9] Neoplatonic writers before Augustine had defined the *daemon* (Greek *daimon*) as a being intermediate between gods and humans and naturally endowed with a body made from some substance like air. Augustine quoted the philosopher Apuleius's definition of daemons as "of an animal nature, passive [i.e., passible, able to suffer] in soul, rational in mind, *aerial in body,* eternal in time."[10] But this demonic body was not problematic for Augustine. He merely noted that humans should not envy daemons "because they have better bodies" than we do, bodies that can suffer but do not die.[11]

Augustine's discussion of suprahuman beings was quite thorough, occupying over half of book 8, all of book 9, and much of book 10 of the *De civitate Dei,* or *City of God.*[12] A momentous contribution was his redefinition of all daemons as *demons,* that is, as fallen, evil angels. In his defense of Christian monotheism, Augustine declared that the gods worshiped by pagan Egypt, Greece, and Rome had all been demons who misrepresented themselves to humans. This meant that idolatry was a form of demon worship. And pagan literature did not represent the gods as pure spirits. Although the gods could change their appearance at will, they had bodies that were as real as any human's, and they interacted constantly with mortals in very physical ways. This was particularly true in the texts that future theologians studied to refine their knowledge of Latin, Virgil's epic *Aeneid* and, especially, Ovid's *Metamorphoses*. The latter is declaredly about the transformations of bodies, and its treatment of sex is often quite explicit. Greco-Roman stories of sexual liaisons between gods and humans would eventually be exploited by witchcraft theorists to imagine demonolaters' physical interactions with demons. The question was, what *kind* of bodies had these "gods" or demons actually had?

The Sex Life of Aerial Bodies

As Peter Lombard's presentation intimated, the notion of demonic bodies was problematic for the Christian notion of angels and demons as spirits. After Lombard, important Scholastic writers took the problem seriously and attempted to resolve it. The most influential was Aquinas. Any modern Christian who hears about demonic copulation for the first time will immediately think of the physiological contradiction that Aquinas purposes to eliminate. He explains that angels and devils are pure spirit: thus they are immortal. But by definition they cannot have bodies since mortality is defined by the destruction of a body. Yet, he says, Scripture speaks of angels and devils as if they do have bodies.[13]

Like witchcraft theorists after him and Christians throughout history, Aquinas cannot accept this kind of contradiction between the text of the Bible and the theology that he wants. Although he does not say so, it is clear that he must find a way to prove that both Scripture and the theological definition of angels are correct; giving up and conceding that one is right and the other wrong is not an option. To paraphrase Umberto Eco, where yes and no are opposed, Aquinas's solution was to combine them and create a "nes."[14]

Without declaring it in so many words, Aquinas argues that angels and devils have bodies that both are and are not real. This in-between state of reality is accomplished by the creation of a *virtual* body: "The angels, then, assume bodies made of air, but condensed by divine power in an appropriate manner."[15] Aquinas's virtual bodies were an innovation with respect to Augustinian tradition. Lombard had asked whether Augustine agreed with the Neoplatonists that bodies were a natural component of demonic being. Aquinas answered negatively and maintained that Augustine was merely citing the Neoplatonic view in order to refute it. This is untrue. In the *De civitate Dei,* Augustine accepted the idea of such aerial bodies and apparently saw no problem with the notion that they were not subject to death and decay. Yet his discussion allowed for Aquinas's innovations by relying heavily on if-then formulations.[16] It would have been difficult to prove that Augustine argued *against* Aquinas's idea.

Aquinas exposes the human need that inspired the idea of angels' optional bodies. He stipulates that "angels do not need bodies for their own sake but for ours." Angelic bodies are a kind of allegory or, to use Aquinas's word, a representation (*repraesentatio*): "When an angel assumes a body the resulting union is . . . of a mover with a body that represents its movements. Such representation is in line with the Scriptures' way of making use of sensible things as images of what is, properly speaking, only discernible by intelligence [i.e., a mode of knowing that does not depend on sensory impressions but instead intuits the truth directly]. The angels, by divine power, formed bodies for themselves which in some degree represented their intelligible attributes. This is what is meant by their 'assuming' bodies."[17] Aquinas explains that angels do not actually eat, or drink, or talk, or have physical sensations, but only appear to. Since they have no true bodily functions, virtual bodies are clearly of no use to the angels and demons themselves.

The only reason for virtual bodies must be to represent the invisible and intangible reality of angels for human benefit. Aquinas finds support for this idea in the apocryphal Book of Tobit, where the archangel

Raphael tells Tobias: "Whilst I was with you I seemed to eat and drink, but my [actual] food and drink is invisible."[18] Thus, says Aquinas, "to the extent that vital functions resemble other activities, they can be performed by angels through the bodies they assume": that is, angels and devils can mimic eating, walking, and other activities by moving their artificial bodies appropriately, even though no real eating or walking is happening. When the Bible describes angels eating, "the food they took was not changed into their assumed bodies, nor were these bodies such as could assimilate food."[19]

But eating and walking are not the activities that most interested Aquinas or the witchcraft theorists who would read him so avidly. All of them were intrigued by incubus and succubus demons, sexual predators that had been mentioned by ancient writers, particularly Saint Augustine. Between Augustine's time and the twelfth century, Catholic writers had not been seriously concerned with incubi, but Saint Bernard of Clairvaux (d. 1153) had supposedly liberated a woman from an incubus that tormented her, and, in the early thirteenth century, Caesarius of Heisterbach had collected a number of tales about demonic copulation in his *Dialogus miraculorum,* or *Dialogue on Miracles.*[20]

Of all the books of the Bible, the Book of Tobit was most interesting in this respect because it seemed to tell of an incubus. In Tobit, the angel Raphael's major task is showing Tobias how to repel a murderous demon. Tobias wishes to marry his kinswoman Sarah, but the demon Asmodeus has killed each of her first seven husbands on the wedding night, and Sarah remains a virgin. Without Raphael's help, Tobias would doubtless be number eight.[21] Yet nowhere does the Book of Tobit state or imply that Asmodeus had sex with Sarah; the demon simply kept her from having relations with men.

Aquinas himself never refers to Asmodeus as an incubus; but it does not seem irrelevant that, immediately after citing the Book of Tobit to define how angels give the appearance of eating, he ends his discussion of angels and devils by treating incubi and succubi and defending their reality. The order of his arguments thus implies that copulation is the ultimate form of bodily activity; later writers could thereby assume that Asmodeus was an incubus.[22] They could assume either that the Bible vouched for the reality of incubi or, conversely, that incubi required investigation because, appearing in the Bible, they must somewhere exist in reality.

Wondrous Births as Proof

Aquinas reminds his readers that Saint Augustine had discussed stories of incubi and succubi in the *De civitate Dei.* Although many of these tales were told by pagans, Augustine declared that it would be rash to reject entirely the evidence that such authoritative witnesses offered. (The doctrine of authority held, in essence, that something implausible told by a respected writer was more plausible than the same thing told by an unknown or minor writer.)[23]

Some Jewish and early-Christian writers had even argued that, in Gen. 6:4, the "sons of God"—whose union with the "daughters of men" produced giants—were obviously angels and, thus, incubi. Although he was unwilling to oppose the authority of those who offered other evidence of incubi and succubi, Augustine rejected this interpretation, on the grounds that it would have involved a second fall of the angels, long after the fall of Adam and Eve. Like nearly all Western Christian writers, Aquinas accepts Augustine's objection and concludes with him that the sons of God must have been purely human. They were probably the good descendants of Adam's third son, Seth, while the daughters of men must have been evil and thus descended from Cain.[24]

Unlike previous commentators on the biblical giants, Aquinas did not reject their angelic parentage and then drop the subject. Instead, he offered a scientific hypothesis explaining precisely *how* angels and women *might* have sex, regardless of who the sons of God were: "But let us suppose that occasionally an offspring *is* born from copulation with a devil. In such a case, the semen would not come from the devil himself, properly speaking, nor from the body he had assumed; it would be taken from a man for that purpose; and the same devil would receive semen from a man and impart it to a woman. . . . And the child so begotten would not have the devil for its father, but the man whose semen had been used."[25]

Witchcraft theorists would later adopt Aquinas's idea enthusiastically: to sire human children, a demon first becomes a succubus by constructing the body of a woman from air and vapors. The demon assumes or inhabits this body, using it to steal semen from a man by having sex with him. Then the demon transgenders itself, giving its virtual body male form and becoming an incubus. Having sex with a woman, the incubus injects the stolen semen into her.

There was a bonus to this theory, as some witchcraft theorists came to understand. If Aquinas's hypothesis could ever be proved, it would mean that Gen. 6:4 neither argues against the reality of incubi nor argues for sexual relations that are impossible. Even if the sons of God were fully human, incubi could still have participated in the generation of giants.[26]

Aquinas's bizarre mechanics of demonic insemination was not the only possible one: Alexander of Hales (d. 1245) had been content to hypothesize that demons simply "gather the natures by which the child is generated from the hidden sources [*occultis sinibus*] of all things, and inject them into women."[27] Even this cleaner explanation had already been adaptable to the idea that, since incubi could sire real children, demons must be essentially as real as human beings. But Aquinas's explanation has the merit of recognizing that "the hidden sources of all things" is not a very precise or realistic-sounding explanation. If demons are going to be truly *virisimilar,* then they will have to copulate and beget as much like real human men as possible. Given that demons have no proper bodies, artificial insemination by a virtual body with switchable gender is the closest approach possible to ideal virility. Aquinas's entire consideration of angelic and demonic corporeality in the *Summa theologiae* ends with this demonstration, thereby giving pride of place to demonic copulation.[28]

Admirers of Aquinas are usually shocked and indignant at the suggestion that his demonology could derive from doubt rather than confidence.[29] But, whatever his motives in defending the idea that demons could sire fully real children, his explanation became central to the theory of witchcraft and the practice of witch-hunting. Without this ✓ explanation, the concept of witchcraft as corporeal interaction with demons could not have evolved as thoroughly, or influenced society as profoundly, as it did. Witchcraft theorists quoted it verbatim, including Aquinas's stricture that the child is actually sired by the man whose semen was stolen rather than by the demon, whose virtual body cannot produce the necessary sperm. This apparent concession allowed theorists to project a detached, objective persona while still protecting the most important idea: that demons have bodies that are *real enough* to have sexual relations that produce offspring. Sex is the ultimate proof of reality, in its results, if not in its preconditions.

To modern eyes, all this looks either pornographic or hopelessly pedantic. How can a body that is not real have real sex? But that quandary is precisely the point. Aquinas is careful to stipulate that, although the bodies of angels and devils are not real, they are truly representational and thus are not untruthful or fictional. Virtual bodies impart genuine knowledge of the invisible and intangible beings that they represent:

> Just as the figurative expressions used in the Bible to convey truths that are beyond the reach of our senses are not lies—because in speaking in this way Scripture does not identify one order of things with another, but merely avails itself of certain analogies in the sensible world [i.e., the world that the senses experience] to give us an idea of purely intelligible properties [i.e., properties that cannot be known through sensory impres-

> sions but must be directly intuited, like geometry]—so it is no slur on the truthfulness of the holy angels that the bodies they assume should seem to be living men when in fact they are not.
>
> For the whole point of these "bodies" is to signify, through human actions and attributes, the spiritual actions and attributes of angels. Indeed it would be less to the purpose if real human bodies were assumed, for then the visible properties would lead the mind to men and not to angels.[30]

Here, Aquinas expounds the deepest reasons why *virisimilitude* is necessary to angels and demons. The whole point of angelic corporeality is to *represent* angelic reality in human terms for a human audience. Otherwise, we would have no way of experiencing them and no proof that they are not imaginary.

By defining the angelic body as a representation, Aquinas turned a liability into an asset. He salvaged the Bible passages that speak of angels' bodies while protecting the notion that angels are incorporeal or bodyless and therefore immortal. However, only a short step separates defining the angelic body as a representation of invisible reality from defining the demonic body as a *proof of the reality* of the invisible. Aquinas himself admits that, if angels and devils had no other way of teaching us about themselves than by possessing live human beings or reanimating cadavers, they could not prove that they exist, "for then the visible properties would lead the mind to men and not to angels."

Aquinas's best-known discussion of angelic reality is in part 1 of the *Summa theologiae,* questions 50–64. As its title implies, the massive *Summa* was his greatest attempt to give definitive order and system to Catholic theology, even though he abandoned it, still unfinished, in 1273. Among other works, Aquinas repeated his systematic demonology in his treatise *De malo,* or *On Evil.* This work was cited by witchcraft theorists about as often as the *Summa theologiae,* and its attraction for them is not hard to see. Its discussion of demons may have been written around the same time as that in the *Summa,* but it seems more likely that it came somewhat later. In any event, the discussion of demonic corporeality in the *De malo* seems to have been added after the rest of that treatise was already in circulation, which suggests that Aquinas could not leave the subject alone. Yet he declares that "the question of whether the demons have or do not have bodies naturally united to them makes little difference in regard to the teaching of Christian faith."[31] This is a curious statement in context since the *De malo* devotes about twice as many pages to the problem of angelic corporeality as the *Summa* does.

Aquinas is known to Catholic tradition as the *Doctor Angelicus* in homage to his interest in angels, but he could also be called the *Doctor*

Diabolicus because he rarely discusses angels in isolation from demons. He was less anxious about the provability of demonic reality than the witchcraft theorists among his followers would be. But his repeated treatments of suprahuman corporeality show that the problem concerned him deeply. He posed with great precision the epistemological question whether humans can be certain that demons exist. Several of his treatises contain lengthy examinations of angels' and devils' manner of being, and he usually begins from the problem of angelic and demonic corporeality.[32]

In Aquinas's systematic discussions of angelology and demonology examined above, the problem of suprahuman reality is not overtly worrisome. Aquinas does admit that some learned men have maintained "that angels never assume bodies, and that all the angelic appearances of which we read in the Scriptures were prophetic visions; that is, they took place in the imagination."[33] He handily dispatches this objection, although he does hint that even the Bible may not prove that interaction with angels takes place in physical reality rather than in the internal arena of the imagination.

Such occasional betrayals of anxiety seem to have magnified the uneasiness of Aquinas's disciples. As Jean Vineti, Heinrich Kramer, and other followers would realize with increasing alarm, there may be no important empirical difference between a prophetic vision and a hallucination. Moreover, Aquinas did examine the reality of angels and demons *explicitly* while discussing other topics. Vineti's and Kramer's references to "those who say that demons exist only in the imagination of the common people" are direct quotations from Aquinas's commentary on a question regarding the sacraments, not the attributes of angels and devils.[34] The fact that Aquinas made the remark parenthetically and then changed the subject made his followers even more nervous.

The other authority on demonic corporeality was Saint Bonaventure. He differed in one profound way from Aquinas over the nature of angels and demons. Bonaventure accepted the Aristotelian doctrine of *hylomorphism* more completely than Aquinas did. This doctrine made fundamental distinctions between form and matter and specified that every living being must be composed of both. Bonaventure therefore concluded that angels and devils could not be pure spirit, altogether lacking bodies. That would mean that they had no matter and thus that, in Aristotelian terms, they could not exist. For Bonaventure, pure spirit, pure *immateriality,* was an attribute of God alone.[35]

David Keck summarizes the differences between Aquinas and Bonaventure on the question of suprahuman corporeality. For Bonaventure, "matter is capable of being either spiritual (if joined to a spiritual form) or corporeal (if joined to a corporeal form), whereas for Aquinas 'matter' is always corporeal" because "Aquinas defines 'matter' as a physicist." That is, "for Aquinas, matter is equivalent to corporeality; he considers matter as it is already in existence in the world. For Bonaventure, matter is a metaphysical construct that is equivalent to indeterminate potency," that is, a category of things that do not yet exist but are "capable of being rendered into existence by being joined to a form."[36] Because Bonaventure did not equate matter with what we now call *atoms*, or *stuff*, or *material*, he could imagine spiritual matter, whereas Aquinas, thinking more as we do, could not. The problem of *spirit* in Aristotelian terms also affected the human soul; this may be why so many demonologists and witchcraft theorists slid from discussing the verifiability of demonic presence into worries over the immortality of the human soul.[37]

Because Aquinas treats angelic and demonic corporeality more starkly as a problem of matter *versus* spirit, his answers to the problem of demonic reality were more attractive to witchcraft theorists.[38] The problem of spiritual matter did not have much impact, for, if such matter existed, human senses could not detect it anyway. Even Bonaventure's angels would have to make themselves perceptible by creating a second body out of something more substantial, like compressed air. Other Scholastic theologians provided answers along one line or the other. So witchcraft theorists often mentioned Bonaventure and other angelologists to support Aquinas's solutions to the problem of demonic reality rather than to oppose them.[39]

Unless questions of demonic corporeality could be answered with precision, the ontological category of angels and devils would remain unverifiable in external reality. So any explanation of demonic bodies was problematic for a long time. Aquinas's solutions were condemned by the University of Paris in 1277, while they were still extremely new. But eventually they won out over Augustine's assumption that there was no problem of demonic corporeality. Then, once Aquinas's doctrines were accepted, Augustine's attitude became worrisome. The *Index librorum prohibitorum*, or *Index of Prohibited Books*, eventually censored references to demons' bodies even in the subject indexes of Augustine's works.[40] Since Augustine's theology was so fundamental to Christianity, the perception that he had been wrong about demonic bodies was damaging.

Aquinas was a Dominican and Bonaventure a Franciscan. This meant that their explanations of demonic corporeality and copulation, viewed as mutually supporting, passed directly into the cultural and intellectual baggage of the two religious orders, which supplied most of the early witchcraft theorists. These pioneers then transmitted their assumptions and methods to later witchcraft theorists and witch-hunters, Catholic and not.

No Solitary Vices

Although all witchcraft theorists shared the basic fear that demons were imaginary, each had characteristic anxieties. Each tried to be as resourceful as possible in locating new evidence that demonic copulation was real or at least possible, so each developed a distinctive manner of arguing the case. The lengths to which fifteenth-century writers pushed Aquinas's speculations about incubi and succubi are sometimes extremely bizarre.

Alonso Tostado (d. 1455) discussed incubi and succubi twice. This Castillian Spaniard received his degree in theology at the age of twenty-two and was said to have been "the wonder of the world, who discussed everything that is knowable."[41] He was a teacher, not an inquisitor, and, instead of burning heretics, he made his reputation by writing an immense commentary on the text of the Bible. (Ironically, in 1443, he had to defend some of his own writings against charges of heresy.) His first reference to incubi appears in his commentary on Genesis 6, where we would expect it in connection with the giants; there he rehearses all the themes that we have seen so far. Tostado accepts Aquinas's incubus theories as proof that Gen. 6:4 does not disprove the existence of incubi and succubi.[42] But this solution was apparently unsatisfactory to him.

It is a measure of Tostado's inventiveness that, to determine whether masturbation is a sin against nature, he returns to the subject of incubi and succubi in his commentary on Matthew's account of the Sermon on the Mount. He decides that it is, even though the Bible, with its encyclopedic lists of sins, says nothing to that effect. As we might expect, he observes that a masturbator sins because he is having sex for pleasure and not as Saint Paul prescribed, with a legitimate wife, for the sole purpose of procreation or paying the debt of marriage. So is the act of masturbation against nature because technically it cannot lead to the creation of progeny? Ah, but things are not so simple.

Tostado concedes that a man who masturbates is "using his own thing [*utitur re sua*]" and does not intend to pollute a woman by adultery or fornication. But masturbation is still an unnatural act, for demons can add another layer of sin by making a man procreate involuntarily:

> It is true that from masturbation itself progeny cannot be had. But once in a while procreation can happen incidentally [*per accidens*] through the agency of incubus and succubus demons, on which see Augustine, book 15 of the *De civitate Dei*. For in the form of a succubus the demon

> can gather the semen thus emitted; thence, having turned himself into an incubus, he can deposit it in the vessel of a woman, and the woman will conceive. And nonetheless that conception will not be caused by the demon, but rather by the man[43] who through masturbation [*molliciem*] emitted the semen; and the man will be called the father of the progeny that is born, even though he has never seen the woman it is born from. And it is thought that this sometimes happens in the case of those whom popular tales [*vulgares historie*] say were children of the Devil. Moreover, it is said in Genesis 6 that giants were born in this way before Noah's Flood. Nonetheless this happens incidentally because that filthy or weak [*mollis*] man did not intend for the conception to take place since he thought it was impossible.

Tostado goes on to discuss, from the demon's point of view, the relative merits of collecting semen from masturbators as opposed to those who "pollute themselves" involuntarily while having erotic dreams in their sleep: the degree to which the demon can "apply his organs," whether or not he has to become visible, and so on.[44]

Who is to say whether Tostado believed that such things could happen? Certainly, masturbation was the last thing on Saint Augustine's mind in the passage that Tostado cites, and Tostado can hardly have misunderstood since the passage was crucial to all discussions of incubi and succubi. True belief would seem more plausible if such speculations were not subordinated to the demonstration that demons are not imaginary. As it is, these beliefs resemble make-believe. They are *made* beliefs, a semideliberate attempt to nurture a sense of demons' reality by fomenting fears that are irrational only if their logical utility escapes our notice.

Like Tostado, Heinrich Kramer adopted and magnified Aquinas's concerns over demonic reality, refusing, as both Aquinas and Tostado did, to abandon the possibility that the Bible described sex between women and incubi. Quoting Aquinas almost verbatim, Kramer declared:

> In conclusion, in spite of the contention of some that devils in assumed bodies can in no way generate children, and that by the "sons of God" [in Gen. 6:4] is meant the sons of Seth and not incubus angels [*sic*] . . . nevertheless *the contrary is clearly affirmed by many*. And that which seems true to many cannot be altogether false, according to Aristotle in the seventh book of his *Ethics* and at the end of *On Sleep and Waking*. And now in modern times the deeds and words of witches who truly and actually perform such things prove this as well.[45]

Kramer expanded Aquinas's speculations on how demonic copulation *might* take place by asserting that witches are expert witnesses to its reality. He even claims that Aristotle provides the criterion that gives witches' testimony its irrefutable authority. The supposed Aristotelian phrase "that which appears true to many cannot be altogether false" became a favorite tag of witchcraft theorists when attacking skepticism about witchcraft or demonic reality.[46]

Kramer pushed Aquinas's arguments about demonic conception. But Kramer's chapter on witches' expert testimony shows that he did not have to push terribly hard:

> Notice also St. Thomas, [in his commentary on] the *Second Book of Sentences,* distinction 4, article 4, in the solution of an argument, where he asks whether those begotten in this way by devils are more powerful [*maioris virtutis*] than other men. He answers that this is the truth, basing his belief not only on the text of Scripture in Genesis 6 ("And the same became the mighty men which were of old"), but also on the following reason. Devils know how to ascertain the virtue in semen: first, by the temperament of him from whom the semen is obtained; secondly by knowing what woman is most fitted for the reception of that semen; thirdly, by knowing what constellation is favorable to that corporeal effect.[47]

This passage makes it clear that Kramer collected everything that he could find in Aquinas about the reality of demonic copulation but also that Aquinas pushed as hard as he could on the text of the Bible. Perhaps the sons of God in Genesis 6 were not incubi. But Aquinas's speculations about demons' genetic expertise, and about the probable size and strength of children who *could* be sired by incubi, created a space for the idea that Genesis 6 does not refute the possibility of demonic copulation.

Kramer accepts Aquinas's three points enthusiastically and contributes one of his own: "We may add, fourthly: *from their own words* we learn that those whom they [i.e., devils] beget have the best sort of disposition for devils' work. When all these causes so concur, it is concluded that men born in this way are powerful and big in body."[48] This suggests that Kramer used torture to corroborate all Aquinas's speculations about demonic copulation by making people confess it (at least that is what he claims). Women provide expert testimony that they can have real sex with demons and can bear children who are genetically endowed with the perfect temperament for becoming witches. For demons, making these children large and strong would be no more difficult.

Kramer repeats that witchcraft originated in demonic sex and can be identified with it:

> Therefore, to return to the question whether witches had their origin in these abominations [*spurcitijs*], we shall say that they originated from

> some sort of pestilent mutual association with demons, as was clear in our first point. But no one can deny that witches multiplied precisely by means of those abominations [*spurcitijs*] mentioned in our second point, even though the demons' purpose is not [their own] pleasure but corruption [of the witches' souls]. And the process must be like this: a succubus demon draws the semen from a wicked man; and if he is the man's own assigned [*deputatus*] devil and does not want to make himself an incubus to a witch, he passes the semen to the assigned demon of that woman or witch [*mulieri seu malefice deputatus*]. And that demon, under a horoscope [*constellatione*] that serves his purpose that the man or woman so born [*genitus vel genita*] should have great powers for the performance of witchcraft, becomes an incubus to the witch.[49]

Kramer tells us not to worry that "those of whom the text speaks" in Genesis 6 "were not witches but only giants and famous and powerful men."[50] After all, he states, there was no witchcraft in those early times; only after witchcraft was invented did demonic copulation produce witches as well as giants. Never mind that one of the principal occupations of witches—in fact, the only one that Kramer attributes to all witches without exception—is voluntary copulation with demons. Never mind that he is even now arguing that, for all practical purposes, witchcraft *is* demonic copulation. For the moment, *maleficium* is the furthest thing from Kramer's mind.

All the dithering, all the circular argumentation, all the misogynistic assumptions and rickety proofs of such passages have one overriding message that shines through every apparent digression, lapse, or contradiction: demons are not imaginary; they are real. Thus, in the present passage, Kramer claims that demons never use semen collected from "nocturnal pollutions" or wet dreams. His ostensible reason is that sperm emitted during coitus is more fertile; but he also needs to keep full-fledged demonic copulation at the forefront of his reader's attention.[51] Dozens of pages later, when he is discussing *Wechselkinder* or changelings, he reverses himself and says that devils may produce such children from semen that is *either* emitted in wet dreams *or* received by a devil "as a succubus," implying that actual copulation is not always necessary.

There was a reason for the contradiction. In the second case, Kramer was defending, not demonic copulation, but rather, as his chapter title indicates, other "dark and horrid harms with which devils may afflict men." One example of these horrid harms is the "strange children" that demons sometimes substitute "for the real children." Here, the reality of the demonic intervention is proved, not by a woman's sexual experience, but rather by the strangeness of the child: "Though they are very heavy, they are always ailing and do not grow, and cannot receive enough milk to satisfy them, and are often reported to have vanished away." The strangeness of the child, especially the tendency to vanish, proves its connection with demons.[52] Since Kramer admits that the child is not the woman's *real* child, he feels no need to argue that it was real enough to be conceived through demonic copulation.

Others quickly followed Kramer's example. Silvestro Mazzolini, known as Prierias (after his birthplace of Priero in Piedmont), was a Dominican who served as inquisitor in and around Milan between 1508 and 1511 before being called to Rome to teach theology. In 1515, he was appointed master of the sacred palace, or personal theologian, to Pope Leo X, a post that he held until his death in 1523.[53] He wrote about witches in two of his works: first in the *Summa sylvestrina,* a theological encyclopedia that he dedicated to the new pope in 1514, and then at more length in his *De strigimagarum demonumque mirandis,* or *On the Wonders of Witch-Sorceresses and Demons,* published in 1521. Mazzolini's two discussions were among the earliest to be heavily influenced by Kramer's *Malleus.*[54]

Building on the *Malleus,* Mazzolini misrepresented Aquinas's conclusions more than Kramer had. The *Malleus* inspired an overt claim that the birth of wondrous children confirms the *reality* of coitus between women and spirits. After discussing witches' *maleficia,* Mazzolini says, "The second effect [of human association with devils] is sexual delight [*voluptas*] taken with incubi and succubi, that is, according to the gender of the witch. And this effect is indeed wonderful [*mirabilis*], so that a person can have either active or passive coitus with a spirit; *and this coitus is so real* [*adeo realiter*] that from it are born no ordinary men, but actual giants, as all theologians are agreed." Kramer, more than Aquinas, inspired Mazzolini to claim that "all theologians are agreed" that giants were sired by demons. Mazzolini seems almost overwhelmed by the implications of demonic copulation. He promises to investigate its causes in the first book of the *De strigimagarum* and warns the reader that "infinite questions" about it will have to await resolution until book 2.[55]

Problems with Aristotle

There were precise philosophical reasons for Aquinas's and his followers' uneasiness about demonic corporeality. From the late eleventh century on, as Aristotle became *the* Philosopher for Scholastic theologians, Catholic angelology and demonology evolved by means of the attempt to reconcile biblical accounts of suprahuman encounters with Aristotle's description of nature and being.[56] But how successful did their attempt seem to the Scholastics themselves?

By far the most important variation between the arguments of Aquinas's *Summa theologiae* and those of his *De malo* is an admission that haunted all witchcraft theorists either consciously or unconsciously. At a crucial point in the *De malo,* Aquinas acknowledged that Aristotelian philosophy was hostile to the concept of demons: "Having seen these things about the corporeal and the incorporeal, it must be noted that in regard to the demons, the peripatetic followers of Aristotle did not affirm the existence of demons, but said that those things attributed to demons come to pass from the power of the heavenly bodies and of other natural things."[57] This admission, in combination with the possibility that demons were a hallucination of common, uneducated, unscientific people, haunted later clerics like Jean Vineti and Heinrich Kramer.

There were rumors of open, unashamed doubt as well. As early as 1340, the existence of angels and demons had been openly questioned by a Christian cleric, Thomas Scoto. In 1520, Gianfrancesco Pico claimed to have seen court records of Pietro d'Abano's indictment for impiety (ca. 1315), containing the allegation that "among other things he denied that demons exist, and said that they can by no means be found in nature."[58]

But, when Kramer referred to those who "do not believe that demons exist except in the imagination of the common people," he was thinking of Aquinas's Aristotelians in this passage in the *De malo,* as questions 1, 2, and 5 in part 1 of the *Malleus* demonstrate. And Kramer returned to the problem with even more concentrated anxiety in part 1, question 8, again referring explicitly to this passage in the *De malo.* These skeptics claim, says Kramer, that, "through ignorance of hidden [*occultarum*] causes which no man understands," we wrongly "ascribe certain natural effects to *maleficia.*" They say that we are mistaken to argue that certain phenomena "were effected by devils working either by themselves or in conjunction with witches [*per se vel maleficos*]" since the real causes, although mysterious, are wholly natural. But Aquinas has defeated this objection, says Kramer,

> in his questions concerning evil [*questionibus de malo*], where he treats of devils, and in his first question, whether devils have bodies that naturally belong to them [*naturaliter sibi unita*], among many other matters he makes mention of those who referred every physical effect to the influence [*virtutes*] of the stars. . . . And he says: "It must be considered that the Peripatetics, the followers [*sectatores*] of Aristotle, held that devils did not really exist, but that those things which are attributed to devils proceeded from the power of the stars and other natural phenomena. . . ." And the error of these [thinkers] is plain, since they referred everything to hidden

> causes in the stars [*causas occultas siderum*], holding that devils were only fabricated by the imagination of men [*tantummodo fabricarentur ex opinione hominum*].[59]

To deny that devils and witches can cooperate or copulate is to deny that devils can demonstrate their reality and to accept that they must in some sense be imaginary, including the possibility that they are totally nonexistent.

This in turn would mean accepting that everything that we experience has a natural cause rather than a *super*natural one, even if the natural cause is "occult" or hidden from us.[60] Aquinas and Kramer found astrology objectionable, not only because it deprives human beings of their free will (the traditional objection, which aims to protect God from the imputation of ultimate responsibility for evil), but also, and equally importantly, because it explains everything in terms of pure matter and thus implicitly denies the existence of spirit. The heavenly bodies may be heavenly, but they are still bodies, not spirits, and, if they can affect our lives directly, then there is no necessity for angels and devils to exist.[61] These anxieties are seen most drastically in Heinrich Kramer's revision of part 1, chapter 5, of the *Malleus,* which, as we saw, evolved from a declaration that the proliferation of witches was due to demonic copulation into a systematic refutation of the idea that the alleged effects of *maleficia* could have natural (astrological or purely human) rather than supernatural or demonic causes.

For Kramer, if we deny demonic copulation and other forms of interaction between demons and humans, we are opposing the doctrinal consensus of Christianity as a whole: "They who maintain that there is no witchcraft in the world go contrary to the opinion of all the Doctors, and of the Holy Scripture." This is why Kramer asserts that to deny the existence of witchcraft is a great heresy, one that amounts to abandoning Christianity.[62] Both Scripture and the consensus of the church doctors "declare that there are devils, and that devils have power over the bodies *and imaginations* of men. . . . Wherefore, those who are the instruments of the devils, at whose instance the devils at times do mischief to a creature, they call witches."[63]

If the imagination as well as the body is not constantly vulnerable to demonic influence, we could suspect that the imagination itself has "imagined" the existence of devils. Kramer declares that Aquinas's passage in the *De malo* distills "the common opinion [*communis ratio*] of all Doctors . . . against all who err in this way by denying that there are any witches." But Kramer is aware that he is reading between the lines and forcing conclusions: this "common opinion," he says, "is very weighty in its meaning [*sententia*], even if it is expressed in few words."[64] The meaning of Aristotle, also expressed in few words, was itself oppressively weighty in the minds of those who defended the existence of demons.

Aquinas and his followers among the witchcraft theorists were not alone in their uneasiness that Aristotelian philosophy did not support the existence of demons and might actually oppose it. Late-medieval and Renaissance writers who wanted nothing to do with witch-hunting or its logic shared this fear of Aristotle.[65] A particularly striking example is Agostino Steuco (d. 1548), a Neoplatonic philosopher from Gubbio in central Italy. Steuco was renowned for his *De perenni philosophia,* or *On Perennial Philosophy,* an exhaustive and learned demonstration that the most important doctrines of Christianity had been espoused by philosophers and theologians of all times and places.

Modern scholars have repeatedly observed that, by making previous religions agree with Christianity about everything, Steuco defeated his purpose and made Christianity superfluous.[66] Likewise, on the subject of demons, Steuco betrayed his fear that Christian doctrines needed supporting evidence from other religions, and he hinted that even such a consensus might not be enough. Unlike Aquinas, and unlike Kramer and almost all the witchcraft theorists, Steuco made no attempt to hide his knowledge that it was not simply Aristotle's followers who had no use for demons but the master himself as well: "Thus all of Chaldean, Egyptian, and Hebrew theology is in agreement about the depraved nature of demons—*and also agrees that demons exist.* And Aristotle cannot deny this consensus of such ancient and venerable theologies, unless he is completely without shame."[67] Although as a philosopher Steuco needed Aristotle's methodological rigor and clear thinking, he could not repress his consternation over Aristotle's refusal to validate the world of demons.

Thus, he presented Aristotle as a renegade, the only philosopher in all of history who failed to understand the obvious:

> From all these doctrines, introduced gradually over time and depending one upon another, there remains *the single conclusion* that *demons are evil,* and this has been recognized and preached not only by Christians, but by all nations, and particularly by the most ancient philosophers; it has been confessed by Empedocles, Plato, Xenocrates, Chrysippus, and also by Hermes Trismegistos, Pherecides, Sirus, in short, by all mortals, and all centuries. So that *two things* have been spoken and proclaimed by everyone, two things that not even Aristotle could completely deny: all ages, all religions agree that *demons exist,* and that *they are evil.*[68]

Confirming the adage about protesting too much, Steuco forgets that he ostensibly has only one point: demons are evil. He cannot resist making explicit the more fundamental point: demons are real. He wants to be sure that we understand that saying that demons are evil is not like saying that blue six-legged cows are lazy. In fact, Steuco's discussions of Aristotle and demonology are peppered with parenthetical phrases like *et daemonas esse* (and that demons exist) and *et quod sint* (and that they exist).

Steuco was anything but a scatterbrain. He was a sophisticated theologian and philosopher who was justly renowned for his erudition and wide reading and rose eventually to become head of the Vatican Library. But he knew that the existence of angels and demons was no longer an unproblematic concept, and he left hints that he doubted that anyone had seen either in a long time: "In those former centuries, when the earth was not yet polluted [*violata*] by idolatrous religions, angels were often seen in many different lands."[69] In fact, the only sightings of angels and devils that he discussed are from the Bible. Like Aquinas and Kramer, his favorite was the story of Raphael and Tobias.[70] Yet, even when referring to this story, Steuco concentrated on good angels. He refrained altogether from collecting stories about incubi and succubi, and he mentioned the idea of demonic copulation only to heap scorn on it.[71]

As a good Neoplatonic Christian, Steuco had no use for Aquinas's virtual bodies. Like Augustine, Bonaventure, Plotinus, and Marsilio Ficino, he allowed himself to imagine that angels and demons had bodies of their own that were real yet composed of some immortal material that was too insubstantial to be perceived by human senses.[72] Nonetheless, he longed to see and experience such bodies—or to believe that someone could. He allowed himself to imagine that, even in his day, some particularly holy people might perceive angelic bodies: "They have no flesh at all; instead their nature [*compositio*] is spiritual, like fire, like air. Their bodies can be perceived only by those who are under the guidance of the spirit of God. No one else can see them."[73] Steuco was the very opposite of a witch-hunter: he wished to believe that saints could see good angels, not that women had sex with bad ones. But his basic desire was the same as that of the witchcraft theorists: to believe that angels and demons really existed and, if possible, to find proof of this "belief."

The anxieties about Aristotle that haunted writers from Aquinas to Steuco were well-founded. This was shown dramatically in 1567, with the posthumous printing of a work written nearly half a century earlier, in 1520. The delay in publishing Pietro Pomponazzi's *De naturalium effectuum causis, sive de incantationibus,* or *On the Causes of Effects in Nature; or, On Magical Charms,* is understandable. Pomponazzi (d. 1525) was an

Aristotelian philosopher who knew his author inside out, and he refused to pretend that Aristotle had been a Christian before Christ. Pomponazzi was already in deep trouble for having published, in 1516, his terrifying *De immortalitate animae,* or *On the Immortality of the Soul,* which demonstrated that Aristotle's philosophy argued against human immortality in any form.[74] This may help explain why the *De naturalium effectuum causis* was not published any sooner. It argued cogently that the Philosopher also opposed the reality of miracles, magic, *maleficium,* and demons.[75]

With surgical precision, Pomponazzi quoted the passage that provoked the deepest anxieties of witchcraft theorists and other Christians: Aquinas's admission that some people say that demons exist only in the imagination of the common people and that natural causes can account for *maleficia* and everything else attributed to demons.[76] Pomponazzi showed just how right Aquinas had been and that Aristotle was the foremost of these skeptics. He used precise passages in Aristotle to argue that natural causes could explain anything Christianity called *supernatural,* including *maleficia:* "Aristotle did not argue for the existence of these spells and *veneficia* [i.e., *maleficia*]; in fact we are told that he said these charms were the fantasies of simple women [*muliercularum figmenta*]. And he does say this, in *De historiis animalium,* book 8, chapter 24. But since the Church argues for *maleficia,* and since Plato and other serious authors defend *maleficia* as well, I will try to respond to [their] arguments by following the way of Nature, without demons. And I will show that if such things can be done *by* demons, they can also be done *without* demons."[77]

Pomponazzi wanted to cut off every avenue of escape, so he attacked the quibble behind which Aquinas and witchcraft theorists habitually took shelter. They admitted that Aristotle does not support the existence of demons but claimed that he nowhere argued against it explicitly. True, said Pomponazzi, and he gave four possible causes for Aristotle's omission.[78] First, death could have simply cut Aristotle down before he got to demons—although he died in old age and so could presumably have found time for them. Second, perhaps Aristotle thought that he had said enough here and there in his works and that intelligent readers did not need to be led by the hand. Pomponazzi favors this explanation; he has collected everything that Aristotle said on the subject, and *De naturalium effectuum causis* shows that the Philosopher had no use for demons and no need to belabor the point in a special treatise.

Of Pomponazzi's two other possible explanations, neither is flattering for Scholastics and other Christians. The third is that Aristotle knew that Athens had put Socrates to death for impiety and that he is supposed to have said that he did not want to make her sin against philosophy a second time. This makes sense, says Pomponazzi, because we know from Plutarch that Anaxagoras was also afraid to explain his ideas about natural causation. Long before Aristotle, this philosopher knew that most people could not understand the concept and that "they suspected that anyone who investigated such things was guilty of the crime of impiety and wanted to diminish the power [*numen*] of God by surrounding it with limits and the concept of necessity."[79] How can God be omnipotent if certain things happen regularly, by necessity? If most of what happens is natural, including what we thought was miraculous, can there be any room for the supernatural?

Pomponazzi's fourth conjecture is even worse. Maybe Aristotle *did* say all these things openly, but his book was destroyed. At the end of his *De licitis libris et illicitis,* or *On Lawful and Unlawful Books,* Albertus Magnus says that Aristotle wrote a book called *De morte animae,* or *On the Death of the Soul,* "in which many things are said against the gods, societal laws, and the priests." So, says Pomponazzi, "perhaps that book was destroyed by the pagan priests, *or perhaps by our own popes.* In his *De vitis pontificum,* or *Lives of the Popes,* Platina says that many books have been destroyed by the popes."[80] How far is the church willing to go to silence what it does not want to hear?

In general, says Pomponazzi, philosophers have always been hated by common people and priests because they explain the world without reference to gods, demons, or miracles. So, if Aristotle did not systematically discuss demons and *maleficia* anywhere in his works, he had good reason. And the church has good reason to be wary of Aristotle: "Aristotle condemned and completely rejected the kind of philosophy that proceeds by riddles, metaphors, and fictions—the kind of philosophy that Plato practiced more than anyone else. So it is no wonder that Plato has been exalted by the ignorant [*vulgaribus*] and by priests, who have rejected and disparaged Aristotle."[81] No one could have made it clearer than Pomponazzi: Aristotle gives no support to demons, *maleficia,* or supernatural, "spiritual" causation. If you need them, you need another philosopher.

It would be naive to assume that Pomponazzi's critiques made it impossible to enlist Aristotle in favor of demons. This was shown forcibly in 1580 by Andrea Cesalpino. Cesalpino was an Aristotelian philosopher of repute, so, when he became interested in demonology, he entitled his treatise *Daemonum investigatio peripatetica,* or *An Aristotelian Investigation of Demons.* First, Cesalpino had to provide an elaborate demonstration that Aristotle believed in the existence of demons, despite all evidence to the contrary. This consumed four of his fifteen chapters. Having done this, Cesalpino devoted his remaining eleven chapters to witchcraft. Not surprisingly, witches prove that demons are not imaginary: "Even now there flourish among us in many places people who use certain magical practices [*superstitionibus*] and observances to perform *maleficia* that sound incredible and are most monstrous [*portentosa*]. Most of these people are women or men from the lowest classes, and many of them who have been apprehended by the authorities have confessed, when tortured and examined by the judges, not only to their shameful crimes, but to the principles on which they are received into this sacrilegious calling. From these confessions a not inconsiderable knowledge can be had concerning those things about which we are seeking certainty."[82] For his time, Cesalpino was a genuine scientist, a physician and botanist who discussed a hypothesis about the circulation of blood before Harvey and was the first to classify plants according to their reproductive organs.[83] Yet, despite his scientific outlook—or because of it—he could not help looking to witches for certainty about demons. His investment in Aristotelian precision did not prevent him from copying most of his witchcraft theory straight out of the *Malleus maleficarum*.[84]

A Tour de Force

The depth of anxiety beneath discussions of demonic reality is flamboyantly displayed in the works of Bartolomeo Spina (ca. 1475–1546). Spina was a Dominican and Mazzolini's star pupil. He was at various times an inquisitor, an important director of the Dominican order, and a professor of theology. As his teacher had done, Spina became master of the sacred palace. Pope Paul III enlisted Spina's theological expertise for initial phases of planning the Council of Trent (1545–63), where Catholicism responded to the challenge of Protestant reformers.

But Spina's career as a defender of the faith began much earlier. In 1519, he wrote an indignant attack on Pomponazzi's proof that Aristotle did not support human immortality. Between 1518 and 1520, he served the inquisitor Antonio da Ferrara as vicar in the city of Modena.[85] Spina's *Quaestio de strigibus*, or *Inquiry into Witches*, was probably finished in 1523, when this experience was still fresh.[86] It shows that he was willing to use almost any kind of evidence to support the reality of witchcraft and demons.

Yet Spina is disorientingly frank about his anxieties; he seems at times to flaunt them. On the subject of demonic copulation, he says that witches claim to perform three kinds of miracles that are often dismissed as impossible. The second of these wonders is "the appearance of demons in human form or even that of beasts, and the consummation of venereal acts with them in divers ways according to the demons' apparent gender [*pro apparente sexus diversitate*]."[87] Such copulating demons are called *incubi* and *succubi*, Spina declares, and he will prove that they exist.

Once he has exposed the basic weakness of the proposition that he is arguing, Spina scrupulously makes the strongest possible case for every objection that can be raised against it. Unlike previous theorists of demonic copulation, he begins by admitting that "there is no example of this, or any other express authority for it, in Holy Writ." Spina flatly concedes that biblical commentators "rebuke the opinion of some who say that the 'sons of God' who sired the giants were incubus demons." Thus, he silently corrects his teacher Mazzolini's misleading claim that all theologians use the sons of God to prove the existence of incubi. He admits that the case is more complex than that: it is true that "all doctors of theology assert that they exist and are found in nature." And it is also correct that "they claim this most commonly when they comment on that place in Genesis 6 where it says that 'The sons of God seeing the daughters of men, etc.'"[88] But, as Spina admitted at the outset, that is not the same as saying that the Bible proves that incubi exist; true to this admission, he invokes neither the sons of God nor Asmodeus.

Spina describes the situation accurately: at least since Aquinas, theologians had circled the text of Genesis 6 and probed it from every angle, but the best that they could do was demonstrate that it could not be used to *disprove* the existence of incubi. Even Aquinas could not dismantle Augustine's objection about a second fall of the angels. All that he could do was point out that Augustine was unwilling to doubt the authority of those who told *other* stories about incubi. Spina frankly concedes that this is the true state of the question and correctly observes that the whole idea of incubi is supported only by hearsay:

> Indeed, the holy doctors are not moved by any reason or revelation to believe these things [about incubi,] . . . and they proclaim other things [about witches] to Christians as truth, on no other basis than their mere faith in those who tell the stories [*non nisi sola fide narrantium*]. This shines forth most especially in Saint Augustine, who in his writings was the first among Catholics to describe these things as not only possible but real [*facta*]. In book 15, chapter 23, of the *De civitate Dei,* he says this: "There is a very widespread rumor, which many claim to have experienced [*se experti*], or to have heard from others who had experienced it and whose trustworthiness [*fide*] is undoubted, that sylvans and fauns, which the common people call incubi, have been shameless with women, lusting after them and performing copulation with them. And it is said that some demons, called duses by the Gauls, tirelessly attempt and carry out this filthiness, so that it would seem impudent to deny it." Thus says Augustine.[89]

Not only Aquinas, says Spina, but other holy doctors, such as Gregory the Great and Isidore of Seville, affirm that incubi and succubi exist, and none of them has any justification other than Augustine's authority "since this [the existence of incubi and succubi] cannot be found in Holy Scripture, nor in any revelations to the ancients, nor in the normal and natural course of things."[90] Spina would seem to have destroyed his case.

However, Spina has already unobtrusively made his move to vanquish our resistance to the idea of incubi. He has misrepresented Augustine by simply omitting his next sentence. Augustine went on to admit that, on the basis of these assertions about *silvani, fauni,* and *dusii,* "I dare not determine whether there be some spirits embodied in an aerial substance (for this element, even when agitated by a fan, is sensibly felt by the body), and who are capable of lust and of mingling sensibly with women."[91] By omitting this sentence, Spina quotes Augustine's hesitation or ambivalence as if it were a dogmatic statement of plausibility: in fact, the most that Augustine would say was that he *could not* say whether incubi existed.

To doubt the testimony of an authoritative witness was more than a simple breach of courtesy; it was tantamount to a personal assault, so Augustine refrained. Moreover, he seemed not to consider the question very important because he abandoned it here.[92] But Spina attempted to place his readers in the same predicament that Augustine felt, by making them unwilling to doubt the positive assertions of an authoritative witness. To achieve this, he obscured the fact that Augustine never asserted anything and, indeed, refused to assert. By truncating the quotation, Spina implied that Augustine found the evidence for demonic copulation overwhelmingly convincing.

Spina concludes that readers should therefore accept the word of theologians that incubi exist, just as the theologians have accepted Augustine's word and as Augustine himself accepted the testimony of authoritative witnesses. Except, of course, that Augustine's acceptance was at best passive and partial. This misrepresentation shows how weak Spina's case was; but many readers could have missed it. Yet they had to notice how Spina seems to undercut his contention by emphasizing that the whole doctrinal tradition about incubi hangs on Augustine's mention of them.

Still, Spina knew what he was doing. He was attempting to condition his readers, to talk them into relinquishing their own experience in favor of authoritative hearsay. The key words *expertus* and *fides,* in the passage quoted above and in others to be found throughout Spina's witchcraft theory, show that he wanted to encourage a passive attitude toward everyday reality as well as toward the Bible: forget what seems logical to you on the basis of your experience. Instead, have faith in what you are told, and have faith that it is based on someone else's experience.

This pretended emphasis on sensory experience allows Spina to invoke Aristotle as if the two of them agreed perfectly about what constitutes empirical evidence:

> A report [*fama*] that everyone spreads [*famant*] does not die out completely; and it is impossible that what everyone reports [*famosum*] should be completely false, as Aristotle says in the book *On Sleep and Waking* and in the seventh book of his *Ethics*. This holds true above all when the story is based on the certainty of the senses. Indeed, the external senses cannot fail with respect to their proper objects of perception, as he says in the second book of *On the Soul*. Now all these people tell about supernatural things that they themselves have seen and done; and eyewitnesses testify that those things are true, on the basis of several kinds of perception. And it is public and universal knowledge that all of them agree that the things they have perceived were done bodily [*corporaliter*].[93]

Clearly, Spina is no longer discussing theologians and church doctors. He has invoked Aristotle to reinforce a very different kind of authority, that of witches and their accusers.

Like Heinrich Kramer, the anonymous anti-Waldensian of 1460, and their fellow witchcraft theorists, Spina is a *pretend Aristotelian,* arguing from alleged sensory experience. In so doing, he provides a decisive clue to the connection between Aristotelian philosophy and the need to argue for demonic copulation. Aristotle stresses sensory experience: if demons provide none, how real can they be? So witches must speak as *testes expertae* about their own experience; their accusers must be eyewitnesses or *testes de visu;* both witches and accusers must formally swear that everything happened bodily, not in a dream or vision.

Spina clearly knew the limits of his argumentation, claiming only that not all witchcraft is imaginary: "Thus these things must not be considered completely false; nor should it be thought that all such persons are deceived or deceivers." A modern reader expecting to find evidence of this inquisitor's credulity may thus be surprised that Spina's barrages of proof have led to such a subdued conclusion. These are not the claims of a man who is either credulous or irrational but rather an exquisitely calibrated exercise in damage control.

Nor is Spina discussing only demonic copulation here; rather, that topic provides the occasion for reconsidering all the activities attributed to witches. And he seems to weaken his case further: having told us that we should believe in witchcraft on the strength of our faith in those who tell us about it, he now concedes that some things are harder to believe than others. For a moment, he sounds as if he is about to tell us that we should believe whatever we like:

> Let us suppose that something is more incredible than whatever is being discussed, or even equally incredible, and nonetheless it is believed by holy doctors and proclaimed as certain, for the sole reason that it is recounted and corroborated by a multitude of both men and women, both those who have experienced it [*experti*] and those who have learned about it and become acquainted with it through those who experienced it. Then there is all the more reason for everyone to believe the thing that is more believable or at least equally believable, and which is equally widely known and affirmed by those who have experienced it, or by those who have learned about it through the truthful report of those who have experienced it.

No other aspect of witchcraft strains credibility as badly as demonic copulation, declares Spina, ending any illusion of his credulity on that score. No cynical skeptic could make a stronger case for laughing demonic copulation out of court than Spina now does:

> Every other thing that witches are said to do in that diabolical Sabbat [*cursu*] is more credible than what they say happens to them, I mean, that demons are incubi and succubi to them—than this same thing, which it is unbelievable that demons could carry out there or anywhere else. . . . That this is more incredible, and is obviously more foreign to all possibility, is evident from the fact that demons are spiritual creatures. Thus they are no more capable of bodily pleasures or delights, and can no more enjoy them with the delight of the senses, than stones can. For just as stones do, the angels lack senses to enjoy those delights, and consequently such delights are clearly foreign to the desires of those spirits.[94]

Once again, Spina seems to have destroyed the credibility of demonic copulation. But he is not about to relinquish anything. The Sabbat is "less incredible" than demonic copulation, but that is no reason for deriding the latter. True, the only reason for believing in demonic copulation is that eminent theologians say that they believe in it. *But that should be enough* because, if anyone is qualified to decide what should be believed, it is the theologians: "For since it is a sign of frivolity to believe immediately without a good reason, as it says in Ecclus. 19:4, 'He who believes quickly is light-minded,' such a fault must be all the more foreign to the most holy and authoritative doctors of holy church than to anyone else whatever, for they are both naturally and supernaturally endowed above all other people with the gifts of understanding [*intellectus*]."[95]

It is not that the doctors are gullible or hasty for believing in demonic copulation, as the quotation from Ecclesiasticus might imply. By definition, it is impossible for them to err; they have the discernment to distinguish reliable and trustworthy testimony from delusion, *even about what seems manifestly impossible*. Therefore, we can believe even what seems completely incredible, simply because these theologians say that they believe it. So, if anyone denies what witches say about the rest of their activities and says that such confessions are the ravings of crazy people, "then he should [logically] believe that those who recount less credible things are even crazier: *yet the holy doctors believe these things*, as we have said, and consider them ascertained by the reports of people who are not crazy."[96]

However incredible demonic copulation may seem, it has been certi- ⌐ fied as real by theologians, who have used careful criteria to establish the truth, relying on the lived experience of witches and the eyewitness testimony of others. Thus, says Spina, we should believe *everything* that we hear about witchcraft. ⌐

There is, of course, a massive contradiction at the heart of Spina's scholarship. He tells his readers that they should believe in demonic copulation because authoritative theologians declare with certainty that others have experienced it. Yet Augustine never claimed to believe in it, while the convoluted arguments of Aquinas, Kramer, Mazzolini, and Spina himself reveal their own inability to believe. That is why the latter three had to enlist the expert testimony of the witches themselves. To his readers, Spina was declaring, "You must believe this because we tell you that we believe it"; yet his attitude toward accused witches implied, "I want to believe this because you tell me that you have experienced it and therefore believe it." Thus, he accords even more authority to ✓ accused witches than to theologians. Although the theologians make the incredible credible to the faithful, it is the witches who make all these things credible to the theologians themselves, just as Kramer had said.

Spina's convoluted arguments show well enough that he was not credulous. He did not even expect credulity from his readers. Spina assumed that belief in witchcraft, most especially belief in demonic copulation, was an arduous enterprise. Far from being automatic, credulity was extremely hard-won. Spina understood that belief—*fides* or faith—was not a gift or an innate talent: it had to be constructed. Rather than carelessly or ineptly presenting his case, he showed the sensitivity of a psychoanalyst, elucidating the conflicts clearly, and then providing the reader a method for reasoning through them.

The entire elaborate exercise was constructed for two reasons, one overt and one covert. The overt reason was to salvage the concept of demonic copulation by showing that the confessions of witches and the beliefs of the church doctors prove each other. In this, Spina did nothing new, but he took unprecedented risks at every moment by refusing (except in the misquotation of Augustine) to minimize the difficulties of believing in witchcraft. And that has to do with the covert reason for defending demonic copulation. What is truly breathtaking is Spina's willingness, despite all his talk about philosophy and method, to reduce witchcraft theory to a matter of faith and faith alone: witchcraft and Catholicism are not simply complementary; they require identical psychic energies. *Fides* is the word that Spina uses both for belief in the mysteries of Christianity and for acceptance of the reality of witchcraft.

The writings examined here demonstrate that witchcraft theorists and other early-modern intellectuals inherited two frightful anxieties from Aquinas: they feared the power of the human imagination, and they dreaded that the concept of nature sufficed to account for the world around us. If natural causes adequately explain our experience, there is no need for the supernatural, and we may have simply imagined it. Assurance that demons could interact bodily with human beings seemed to provide a way of assuaging these fears. Without demonic corporeality, there was no proof that demons were real, and thus the implication was that nature—pure matter, rather than spirit—could adequately explain everything that humans experienced.

Ironically, of course, witchcraft theorists were expecting matter to disprove its own sovereignty by proving the dominance of spirit. Consequently, there was an escalation of anxiety from Aquinas through the early-fifteenth-century inquisitors and theorists to Kramer and Spina as each writer absorbed and reacted to the undeclared nervousness in his predecessors' arguments.

Despite the ever-growing backlog of authoritative pronouncements on demonic copulation, each theorist had to demonstrate its scientific plausibility to himself. Kramer's treatment of the theme was so complete that subsequent theorists could have discussed the matter very briefly as a fact of common knowledge, had they so chosen. Tellingly, few, if any, theorists took this option. Each new treatise reviewed the same basic collection of authorities and sources; each usually added some new detail, a bit of bibliography or a fanciful explanation. And each treatise had its own characteristic touches of doubt, hesitation, and exaggeration.[97]

4

INCREDIBLE SEX: CONFRONTING THE DIFFICULTY OF BELIEF

> If he could induce others to believe what he said, then for him the statement acquired some degree of truth, a reflection of their belief that it was true; and this reflected truth might grow stronger with time and repetition until it became conviction, indistinguishable from ordinary factual truth, or very nearly so.
>
> —Patrick O'Brian, *The Thirteen Gun Salute*

The need to convince oneself that the world of spirit was real increased dramatically from Aquinas's 1270s to the 1520s of Bartolomeo Spina. The more each writer tried to satisfy the need, the more involuntary skepticism he generated in his successors and, usually, in himself. As a result, Spina had to admit quite consciously how difficult belief was. Without a diabolophany, a shattering personal encounter with a demon, the need for belief in demonic reality could never be satisfied. Involuntary skepticism was exacerbated, rather than comforted, by mere logical demonstrations that demons are real. This paradox was vividly illustrated in a work that Spina read while working on his *Quaestio de strigibus,* or *Inquiry into Witches.* In a treatise published with the *Quaestio,* Spina expressed admiration for the work of Gianfrancesco Pico della Mirandola:

> When I had finished my *Quaestio de strigibus,* and during the time its publication was being delayed (contrary to the hope of those who were asking to see it), I happened across and read in some haste a remarkable treatment of the same question by the distinguished count of Mirandola, Giovanni Francesco Pico. And I ascertained that it indeed agrees with my principal conclusion. Yet each of us may take pleasure in his own work: I have neither found anything objectionable in his work nor borrowed anything from it to ornament my own, even though I am confident that he also sets out the truth.[1]

Gianfrancesco Pico della Mirandola (d. 1533) was the nephew of Giovanni Pico, the philosopher who, along with Marsilio Ficino, had the greatest influence on Neoplatonic, magical, and occult thinking in late-fifteenth-century Europe. Gianfrancesco is now much less known than his uncle, but he was no less influential in European intellectual history. He was a tireless defender of the truths of Christianity against the crescendo of skepticism that he felt Aristotelian science fostered by encouraging an empirical attitude toward the world.[2] He brilliantly understood that the way to fight skepticism was with skepticism itself. So, to defend Christianity against Aristotelianism, he co-opted the methods of Sextus Empiricus (d. 220 C.E.), the most thoroughgoing and radical of the ancient Greek skeptics. According to Charles Schmitt, Gianfrancesco's *Examen vanitatis doctrinae gentium et veritatis Christianae disciplinae,* or *Examination of the Vanity of Pagan Doctrine, and of the Truth of Christian Teaching,* published in 1520, was the first work since the end of Greek philosophy to give serious consideration to Sextus.[3]

Albano Biondi characterized Gianfrancesco's skepticism as an antihumanistic "one-way street." Eugenio Garin observes that Gianfrancesco used Sextus's skepticism to build arguments that would strengthen religion by destroying philosophy. Schmitt explains that

> Pico subscribes to the *fides quaerens intellectum* [faith seeking understanding] formula of the Middle Ages and considers the mistake of the pagan philosophers to lie in the fact that they took their starting point in *intellectus* rather than *fides.* For him the sceptic critique of philosophy has shown conclusively that [*intellectus*] cannot be a legitimate starting point, and in writing the *Examen Vanitatis,* he hopes to convince his fellow Christians of this fact. So, in the final analysis, the sceptics furnish a useful method that is applicable to the conditions of his own time, and for that reason he has studied it and given it extended consideration in his work. To go beyond this and to say that Pico attempted to revive scepticism as an end in itself would be incorrect. It is merely an instrument to be used in the demonstration that the unique source of truth is found in Christianity, and beyond this function [skepticism] is of no interest to him.[4]

Precisely because nothing can be known with certainty, Pico argued, Christians should abandon Aristotle and all of ancient philosophy because the philosophers encourage us to rely on our senses, which are fallible. Rather than allowing such empiricism to destroy our faith, we should humbly submit to the truths about the world that are divinely revealed in the Bible and the works of the church fathers and doctors.

Spina, who was at least honest about the difficulty of belief, obviously appreciated this quality in Gianfrancesco's work. The book that Spina praises so highly is not, however, Pico's massive and erudite *Examen vanitatis* but his relatively short and grippingly reportorial *Strix, sive de ludificatione daemonum*, or *The Witch; or, On the Illusions of Demons*. This little book was published in Latin in 1523. The *Strix* displays such invincible credulity that it seems to have been written by someone completely lacking Pico's philosophical sophistication. This impression is wrong, however, because the *Strix* is as learned in its way as the *Examen vanitatis*.[5] It does not *demonstrate* Pico's credulity; instead, it attempts to *construct* it or make it possible.

The following year, with Pico's knowledge and cooperation, the Dominican Leandro Alberti translated the *Strix* into Italian. Together, Pico and Alberti widened the audience for witchcraft theory, making it accessible to people who knew no Latin: the translated *Strix* was the first printed discussion of witches in vernacular Italian.[6] Thanks to Alberti's translation and another made by Abbot Turino Turini in 1555, even illiterate Italians could *hear* a systematic exposition of practically everything that had been discovered about witches by the first quarter of the sixteenth century.

Previous witchcraft theorists assumed that laypeople believed automatically and uncritically in the reality of demons. Translations of Pico's *Strix*, by contrast, assume that even simple people need indoctrination; their credulity about witchcraft must be shaped and reinforced. Alberti tells the reader not to marvel that he has translated Pico's elegant Latin into such a rough-and-ready vernacular Italian. He knows that his translation is inelegant, and he lists the principal theorists and practitioners of literature in Italian to show that he has the knowledge to do better. But he has translated "rather for the rough common people [*rozzo volgo*] than for learned men. . . . [I]f I had wished to observe all the rules and observations written by those estimable men (or, rather, brilliant lights of our century), the work would not have been so easily understood. . . . And so for now we have left aside, in translating this little work, that culture and ornament that it merited."[7]

The Dominican order was known as the Order of Preachers, for its task was to ensure that the common people were exposed to orthodox dogma in their own languages. Alberti assumed, probably from experience, that demonological theories of witchcraft were foreign to common people. In his letter of dedication to Pico's wife, Giovanna Caraffa, he noted that such matters were still "known only to the learned [solamente dalli dotti intesi]."[8]

There is an autobiographical dimension of the *Strix* that goes far beyond Pico's experience as an erudite philosopher. He was the prince of a small domain where a spate of witch trials took place in 1522–23. As a secular ruler, he was the ultimate authority responsible for the execution of least seven men and three women, burned as witches between 1522 and 1525. The victims came, not only from Pico's own Mirandola, but also from Concordia, the ironically named territory of his estranged sister-in-law. Pico's exact role in this affair is not clear, but it is evident, as Albano Biondi remarked, that he "did a lot more than simply lend the power of the arm of the secular law" to the convictions obtained by the Dominican inquisitor and vicar.[9]

Both Pico and Leandro Alberti disclose that Pico was actively involved in the trial: *connivance* and even *instigation* may not be excessive descriptions of his role in this miserable affair. Alberti states that Pico wrote the *Strix* in answer to public outcry over the trials:

> Many began to say with insulting words that it was unjust that these people had been so cruelly killed since they had not done anything deserving of such a consequence [*guiderdone*]. And that what they had said about the Game [*Giuoco,* i.e., the Sabbat] had been said out of folly or brainlessness, or else from fear of the harsh tortures. They claimed that it did not seem plausible that people could have committed so many disgraceful insults and mockeries against the consecrated host, or the crucifix, or against our most holy faith; they said that this could be easily proved because many of the defendants who had first confessed later steadfastly denied their confessions, which they would not have done if they had truly committed such crimes. And beyond that they said many other things to strengthen their blameworthy arguments,[10] so that from day to day such mutterings were increasing among the common people.

If we can believe Alberti, it was not until this point that Pico stepped in. But, even if Alberti's version of the timing is true, his portrayal of Pico's motivations is nonetheless disquieting:

> These things came to the attention of your grace's most loving consort, the illustrious Lord Prince Giovanfrancesco, who is a man certainly no less Christian than learned and erudite. Being somewhat uncertain about this affair, he decided that he wanted to understand it completely and through subtle investigation to acquaint himself with both its causes [*fondamento*] and every least detail deriving from them.
>
> First he attended and was present at the examinations of the defendants before the inquisitor; afterward he interrogated them himself in private [*da sé a sé, a parte per parte*] about that wicked Game and the abominable rites and profane customs and impious [*iscommunicati*] behavior and damnable actions that take place there all the time. And he heard this not from only one of them, but from a great number, and found that they agreed about

> the most important things (although in some very minor things they seem to disagree somewhat, either through lapse of memory or because of the deceptions and frauds of the evil demon). He found that they are immersed in so many filthy vices that the chaste and modest ears of a Christian cannot hear them without great discomfort.
>
> And since he is a true servant of Our Lord Jesus Christ and also a learned and erudite man, he has seized his sharp pen and written a work in three books about this culpable, wicked, and perverse school of the Devil, so as to unmask the ambushes and hidden traps of the Devil and to help spread the shining truth of the faith of Christ in every place, so that everyone will protect himself from the frauds of our crafty enemy and be better able to track him down wherever he is.[11]

From Alberti's account, it appears that Pico actively meddled in the trials and even followed them up with private interrogations, taking advantage of the fact that defendants who had confessed under torture were theoretically required to reiterate their confessions "freely," that is, without active torture.

Strangely, Pico himself claimed a far smaller role in the proceedings: "When you hear the witch speak in this little work, believe [*putes*] that you are hearing unmitigated history, which I gathered partly with my eyes, and partly with my ears, when the transcripts of the interrogations were read to me."[12] Given Pico's characteristic deviousness, I am inclined to believe Alberti's enthusiastic, if somewhat naive, account of Pico's intense involvement.[13]

Spina saw Pico's *Strix,* his own *Quaestio,* and Mazzolini's *De strigimagarum* as a perfect trinity for the creation of belief.[14] After he had finished reading Pico's book, he says,

> I happened across the work that, I remembered, my teacher, the most illustrious master of the sacred palace, had published some time ago [i.e., in 1521], which was even more filled with that same topic and many other things of a similar nature. I had deliberately refrained from using it because it did not consider the topics that I intended to treat in my own work. Filled with joy that I was in every way imitating the perfection of my teacher's doctrine, I never borrowed the least word from his work, even though he and I use authorities, reasons, and specific examples that are consonant or even at times identical.
>
> This I did so that the truth, confirmed by three witnesses [*testibus*], might command the fullest possible trust [*fides*] from everyone. When it is known that none of us borrowed from the others' publications, this will cause everyone to have a firmer faith [*fidem*].[15]

This declaration is disingenuous about a lot of things, but Spina is right to assert that the three works complement each other. Like Spina and Mazzolini, Pico set out to prove that witchcraft was absolutely real, doing so by raising every conceivable objection, then meticulously refuting them all.

Pico could have matched the two Dominicans' analytic thoroughness; he had written other treatises, notably his immense attack on Aristotle. But his greatest contribution to the development of witchcraft theory was abandoning the arid treatise format of professional theologians such as Mazzolini and Spina. Pico turned theory into theater by writing a dramatic dialogue in four voices. He was not the first to structure a witchcraft treatise as a dialogue. Around 1437, the German Dominican Johannes Nider had written a long dialogue, the *Formicarius,* or *Anthill,* that included a section on witchcraft, and, by 1440, Martin Lefranc was writing his *Le Champion des dames,* or *Defender of Women,* a debate in vernacular French verse. In 1489, Ulrich Müller, who signed his works with the Latin translation of his name, Molitoris (Miller), had in the *De lanijs* (or *Von den unholden*) used the dialogue form to defend the prosecution of witches.

Pico understood that witch-hunting and witchcraft theory were essentially *narrative* enterprises: they depended on the multiplication and repetition of stories to make points and create convictions. Like Spina, he understood that the reader's faith in the reality of witchcraft could never depend on logic, which created only greater skepticism. Instead, the reader had to be convinced that the reality of witchcraft was guaranteed by someone's lived experience—the witches' *experta testimonia*—and merely corroborated by the theologian's expertise in supernatural matters. This testimony would be far more convincing if a way could be found to lighten the erudite commentary and prevent it from suffocating the human interest and sensationalism of supposed lived experience.

The dialogue offered the ideal medium. Pico's choice of dialogue form probably convinced Alberti that translating the *Strix* for common people was possible. Alberti claims that the *Strix* is written "with such order and such various doctrine and delightful entertainment [*festa*] that, once he has begun it, the reader cannot avoid following it all the way to the end, always reading things that are curious, rare, and learned . . . always hoping to find others no less to his liking."[16] It is hardly mass entertainment, but the combination of dialogue and vernacular Italian gave it a chance at a wider audience.

Beyond the problem of maintaining readers' interest, Pico understood that even the most methodical Scholastic treatise on witchcraft was ultimately an educated man's dialogue with himself, his attempt to conquer his own skepticism. Thus, Pico structured the *Strix* as a dialogue among four people, taking place over two days. The dialogue stages and *dramatizes* the difficulty of belief with great resourcefulness. In it, three characters attack the almost invincible doubts about the reality of witchcraft expressed by a fourth character, one Apistius.

In his translation, Alberti says that Apistius is a Greek name meaning "infidel."[17] But Pico's Apistius claims to be a faithful Christian and says that he has never for an instant doubted the truthfulness of Catholic doctrine. Rather, he is Pico's mouthpiece for every kind of doubt about the reality of witchcraft: Apistius wants to believe that Christianity can get along without witches. The task of the dialogue is to convince him that he is wrong, and that task is entrusted to the other characters. Apistius's friend Phronimus (meaning "prudent," says Alberti) is a Christian humanist, an expert in classical literature; the inquisitor Dicastes (meaning "judge") repeats all the arguments of theologians and inquisitors.

The remaining character is a radical innovation: Strix (meaning "witch") is the voice of lived experience, an expert witness to the reality of *maleficia* and demonic copulation.[18] The dialogue is thus an archetype: its structure analyzes and summarizes the process of *creating belief* in witchcraft that had been going on for over a century. As theologians ✓ constructed *the witch* to silence *the skeptic* in their own minds, so Pico's Strix presents all the arguments considered most likely to convince skeptics. Moreover, the *Strix* is supposedly a *documentary* investigation of real life. Despite the allegorical names, the reader is admonished to "believe that you are hearing unmitigated history, which I gathered."

Pico's decision to make the witch—an illiterate woman—participate in a discussion with three well-educated men was revolutionary from the standpoint of literary history: the dialogue's form echoed that of others written by the most idealistic Platonists and other humanists of the Renaissance. But the choice was obvious from the standpoint of witchcraft theory. Pico took the conversation of witches and inquisitors out of the torture chamber and restaged it as an earnest but lively philosophical discussion. Heinrich Kramer had maintained that "the expert testimony of the witches themselves has made all these things credible," so Pico simply put Strix on the witness stand—or, rather, in a chair at the seminar table.

Strix's testimony is often conclusive. Of course, her authority is not based on democratic conceptions of gender or class equality or human rights. Far from it. Although she is never tortured during the dialogue, there is no attempt to conceal that she was tortured earlier, until she confessed what Dicastes wanted to hear. During the time she is onstage,

Strix does suffer some verbal abuse. But this vituperation cannot disguise the joy and hope that Pico's other three characters feel whenever she confesses her atrocious deeds.

Alberti acknowledges this, claiming that "whoever is a lover of Christian faith can take pleasant delight and sweet profit" from the dialogue.[19] The three men often behave with surprising, apparently illogical tenderness toward Strix, sometimes addressing her as "my good woman" or even "my good witch" ("But you, my good witch, did you ever kill children?").[20] Such deference is not misplaced because Pico's Strix is the star of his dialogue. Without her expert testimony, Phronimus and Dicastes could never convince Apistius that witchcraft is real.

As the book's subtitle (*On the Illusions of Demons*) might lead us to expect, Pico's real subject is demonic reality and its relation to illusion and untruth. On the second day, Dicastes tells Apistius that witches are persecuted and captured by inquisitors, not for being carried by demons to the Sabbat, but for renouncing their faith, mocking the church's sacraments, despising Christ, and adoring the demon. "What do we care whether they do it in their bodies or only in their minds?" he asks. "And yet," he says, "beware of thinking that most of them are not carried there in their bodies!" He decides that it is time for expert testimony from the witch:

> DICASTES: And now, so that he may have more faith [*fides*] in all this, come here, Strix, and swear on this most holy book, which I place in your hands. And know that, in so swearing, if you break your word, or if you lie in the least thing, you will never be forgiven, either by us, or in the life to come.
>
> STRIX: I swear it.
>
> DICASTES: Were you carried to the Sabbat [*ludum*] in the body or only in your mind [*animo*]?
>
> STRIX: In both body and mind together [*simul*].
>
> DICASTES: How do you know that you were carried through the air in your body?
>
> STRIX: Because with these very hands I touched that demon, who was named Ludovicus.
>
> DICASTES: What exactly did you touch?
>
> STRIX: His body.
>
> DICASTES: Was it the same as the body of anyone of us here?
>
> STRIX: Softer!
>
> DICASTES: Were there others there [at the Sabbat] in the body?
>
> STRIX: A huge throng.
>
> DICASTES [*to Apistius*]: So respond all those I have put to the ques-

tion, even when I have not used torture; so respond all those examined by other inquisitors, who say that they all answered as if with one voice. And they say this even though they understand that they are not being tortured or punished for this reason but rather because they have broken the faith that they promised to God. Thus they speak with one mouth, both male and female, in this town and in other lands. . . .
[*After a digression:*] But let me return to you, Strix. What kind of coitus did you have with the aerial body of the demon?
STRIX: I don't know what kind of body he had, but I do know this: I had greater pleasure from him than from my own husband![21]

Chi si scusa, s'accusa: excusing yourself is another way of accusing yourself. Dicastes' explicit, unsolicited denial that inquisitors tortured accused witches in order to make them talk about the bodies of demons is the most damning evidence that we have yet seen.[22] It is as good as a confession, and the reason that Dicastes himself gives for torture, the broken faith of renegade Christians, comes out sounding like the mystification that it was.[23]

Earlier, Strix told Apistius that her demon, Ludovicus (Luigi or Louis), seemed to be a man in every respect except his feet: they looked like those of a goose and were reversed so that they pointed backward.[24] Dicastes helpfully explains that all the trial records of the inquisition reveal that the Devil can create a nearly perfect facsimile of the human body but never can get the feet to come out right: God makes the feet come out *inversos et praeposteros* so that people will know that they are in the presence of a devil and not be fooled into thinking that he is human.[25] Thus, they have no excuse for sinning. The corollary, which Dicastes does not state, is equally important: imperfect feet are an infallible way of recognizing demons, so *we* should not fear that witches mistake ordinary humans for demons.

Like his translator Alberti, Pico was aware that speculation about the composition of demonic bodies was not a part of oral peasant culture. His Strix usually limits herself to describing the visual and tactile qualities of her demon's body. At one point, she even has to describe her demon's genitals:

APISTIUS: We know that demons have neither bones nor flesh. How then can they eat? How can they copulate?
STRIX: The parts put on by them are similar to flesh and bones, but bigger [*crassiores*] than those of any mortal.[26]
APISTIUS: Can you compare them to anything so as to give us some indication or communicate an analogy that will help us learn about their members?

> STRIX: I don't know, except that they are bigger than human ones, and softer, and very similar to flax or cottonwool that has been bundled and densely packed.[27]

Despite her mention of "parts put on," Strix reveals no obvious knowledge of the Scholastic doctrine that demons fabricate bodies of compressed air; rather, she gives a detailed description of how demonic bodies *feel.* It looks, however, as if Pico wants to have things both ways: Strix has to provide accurate details while remaining ignorant of theoretical concepts.

Apistius is fascinated by demonic copulation, but his interest is not remotely pornographic. At one point, he returns to the subject of goose feet and ends up witnessing a sort of epiphany; his reaction betrays the nature of his interest:

> APISTIUS:[28] Oh, but tell me, witch, did he ever show any sort of feet other than gooselike (so to speak) when he came to you?
> STRIX: Never any other.
> APISTIUS: On what terms did he appear to you?
> STRIX: Sometimes when I called him, and sometimes on his own.
> APISTIUS: And always in human form?
> STRIX: Never any form but human if he intended to copulate with me.
> APISTIUS: Oh, what kind of copulation can there be with a wrinkled old woman?
> STRIX: Oh, woe is me, woe is me!
> DICASTES: What are you afraid of?
> STRIX: Look, all of you, look!
> DICASTES: Where?
> STRIX: At the wall!
> DICASTES: In what shape?
> STRIX: Of a sparrow!

Rather than accuse Strix of inventing her vision in order to change the subject, the three men excitedly discuss it as evidence that she can see what they cannot. In fact, Dicastes' question "In what shape?" suggests that such interruptions have happened before. In a real-life situation, his leading questions during torture would have given Strix the idea for this apparently spontaneous diversion: "Where is your demon now? Can you see him?"

Leandro Alberti's embellished translation of the men's ensuing discussion captures their mood even better than Pico's original:

> DICASTES: Pray look well, both of you, how he has now taken the shape of an extremely lascivious bird, *in complete conformity with the discussions of this evil woman,* who surpasses all the monsters of filthy lust with her insatiable and unbridled cravings!
> APISTIUS: Oh, how I marvel that not one of us has seen this feigned sparrow, except for her!
> DICASTES: However hard I look, I can't see it, and it seems to me that none of us can see it!
> APISTIUS: Oh, this is certainly a wondrous thing![29]

This scene cannot but appear comic to us, but its unmistakable intent is to provide a model for our enraptured wonderment.

The three men's interest in the witch's sexuality may strike modern readers as prurient or pornographic, in view of some of the things that she recounts. She says that she and Ludovicus did not copulate only at the Sabbat. He used to accompany her to the market sometimes, and, one evening when they were returning, they made love three times before arriving at Strix's house, although she lived only a mile from town. The ideological function of the witch's apparent nymphomania is not to disparage her womanhood (although the three men do plenty of that at other times). Rather, as in the works of previous theorists, it demonstrates the demon's reality through the intense pleasure that copulation with him causes her. Apistius understands this implication, yet he still seems genuinely puzzled:

> APISTIUS: But I still cannot understand the meaning of all this copulation. . . . Nor can my understanding grasp the reason for so much sexual pleasure [*voluptas*].
> DICASTES: Witches claim they are so overcome by it that they swear there is no pleasure like it on earth. And I can think of several reasons why that would be true. First, because those rebellious spirits put on a most pleasing face. Next, because their [virile] members are of an uncommon size. With their faces they delight the eyes, and with their members they fill up the most secret parts of the witches. And beyond that, they pretend to be in love with them, which is perhaps the most welcome of their miserable miracles. And probably they can stimulate something very deep inside the witches, by means of which these women have greater pleasure than with men.[30]

√ More pleasure, more reality—for Dicastes as well as Heinrich Kramer since he mentions the demons' sexual potency three times.

Pico's purpose is to demonstrate demonic reality rather than to denigrate women, for he goes right on to discuss the intense sexual pleasure that succubi can provide for male witches. Seven of the ten witches tortured and burned with Pico's connivance were men, and their alleged ringleader was a priest, Don Benedetto Berni.[31] Pico's *Strix* shapes and fictionalizes the atrocities that took place, and it idealizes the witch by stripping her of any recognizable personal identity and making her an archetype. But Don Benedetto is Pico's prize bête noire, and he is several times vilified by name. Pico offers him as proof that men can experience demonic sexual reality just as thoroughly as women can: "Nor do I think it is any different with those who sin with succubus demons," says Dicastes.[32]

In his portrait of the old priest, Pico displays an even stronger *metaphysical* prurience than earlier writers on succubi did, as if Pico himself wished to be ravished by a succubus. Don Benedetto was a connoisseur: he knew good sex when he found it, says Dicastes. Although the priest had his pick of all the women in his "sect" (what moderns would call his *coven*), he swore that "he took more delight with the demon named Armellina than with all those women he had had sex with. And lest you think he had possessed only a few of them, he had known even his sister carnally, and they said he had had a daughter by her." Dicastes assures Apistius that "this is all most certainly recorded in the transcripts of my interrogations."[33]

Like Strix, who took her demon, Ludovicus, to market with her, Benedetto flaunted his relations with Armellina. People other than the inquisitor misinterpreted his conduct, however. "The poor fool was so thoroughly in love," Dicastes reports, "and burned with so much lust for Armellina, that he often walked and talked with her in public, although no one else could see her. *Thus, whoever heard him talking with her, not being able to see her, thought he had gone mad.*"[34] Is there *any* truth in all this? The unfortunate Don Benedetto could have been an outcast: he may have had a lot of enemies, or he may simply have been somewhat eccentric. Was he actually just muttering to himself in public, or was he praying or reading in his breviary as he walked about?

Or was absolutely everything made up? If so, by whom? One element suggests that poor Don Benedetto blamed his inquisitor for inventing or embellishing these slanders. When the old priest was forced to give the name of his demon lover, he replied, "Armellina." This imaginary name is based on the surname of the real-life inquisitor, Gerolamo *Armellini*. Not coincidentally, Dicastes is Pico's fictionalization of Armellini: Pico has Dicastes refer to Benedetto and other of Armellini's real-life victims as his own. On Armellini's recommendation, Benedetto was publicly stripped of his ecclesiastical insignia, hanged, and then burned. It looks as if the old priest knew, consciously or not, that Armellini was twisting and molding his confession and sent a coded accusation to posterity.[35]

Perhaps even worse than Don Benedetto, conjectures Dicastes, was another crazy fool named Il Pivetto.[36] Pivetto loved a demon named Florina, who appeared to him in the form of a stupendously beautiful woman.[37] He enjoyed her carnal delights for forty years and became so insanely enamored that, when Dicastes questioned him, he declared himself ready to endure any torture rather than abandon her. In fact, Pivetto now believes that there is no other God than her (*ut alium esse deum non existimet*). That is how it goes with those who fall under the spell of incubi and succubi: "Some become atheists [*Athei*], others simply despise God and his things, which they were baptized into, and so they desert the faith."[38] Once they have done that, then they easily fall into all sorts of *maleficia,* harming good Christians to stay in the good graces of their demonic paramours.

In all of witchcraft literature there can be few more revealing examples than these two fictionalized defendants for understanding how and why witchcraft theorists projected their metaphysical need for carnal knowledge of demons onto the targets of their supposed moralistic loathing. Dicastes' slanders against Don Benedetto and Il Pivetto reveal that, for Pico (and probably for the inquisitor Armellini), sex was not sex, or at least not sex alone: it was *proof* of metaphysical realities. What Stuart Clark calls *witch hating* expresses the self-styled hater's *envy* of persons whom he imagines experiencing those devastating proofs of spiritual reality that he craves but knows he cannot have.[39]

Witch Hating and Religious Doubt

Protestant Christians did not habitually target Catholics as witches, or vice versa; typically, each religious group preyed on its own numbers in a search for the enemy within, the hypocritical subversive. This search for internal subversion already hints that the need to identify witches was the symptom of an awareness that, in some sense, one's religion was not "working." Pico's *Strix* was published around the time that witch persecutions suddenly went into a decline that lasted for decades (when persecutions eventually resumed, they quickly reattained and even surpassed their previous ferocity). Brian Levack reports the widely known fact that records also indicate that "there was a forty-year lull in the production of witchcraft literature. Very few treatises were written during that period, nor were new editions of the older works forthcoming. . . . After 1570, however, there was a marked upsurge in witchcraft prosecutions, and this development stimulated the printing of the old treatises and the authorship of new ones." Levack observes that this hiatus in publication was contemporaneous with two developments: the decline in actual prosecutions and "a preoccupation of the educated élite with the Protestant Reformation."[40]

Levack and other recent historians are reluctant to see a direct causal relation between witch-hunting and religious strife in early-modern Europe.[41] But there is another way of considering the relation: not as direct, but as inverse. It may be that open religious strife gradually *replaced* witch-hunting in the period between Luther's ninety-five theses and the onset of the French Wars of Religion (1517–62). Certainly, witchcraft theory provided an indirect means of confronting implausibilities and contradictions in Christian theological dogma long before they were discussed in polemical exchanges between Catholics and Protestants. Similarly, I suggest, witch-hunting could have served to sublimate doubt and skepticism about dogma by acting them out, testing and verification taking the place of intellectual discussion.

Such acting out would have been a useful reinforcement of doctrine, not only for the illiterate and unsubtle, but also for individuals capable of sophisticated intellectual wrangling. While simple folk might hope merely to identify the source of their ills, thinkers even moderately versed in theology would be predisposed to look for evidence of real interaction with spirits. There is evidence in trial records that prosecutors occasionally offered to free defendants if they would make their demonic familiars appear in court, either in corporeal form or by empowering the defendants to perform wonders.

Given these conditions, any large-scale religious conflict that brought doubts and anxieties about the validity of Christianity into the open might reduce witch-hunting. The analogy with Freudian psychology is not inappropriate: anxieties, whether sexual or metaphysical, demand attention. If we avoid confronting them directly and repress them, they find expression in bizarre form as symptoms. It is not impossible that the increasingly bitter polemics of the early Reformation served as a kind of Freudian talking cure for the anxieties that Western Christian intellectuals had *acted out* symptomatically over the previous century when they constructed witchcraft through trials, torture, and treatises.

But, if this is in fact what happened, there was a relapse. Once the doctrinal positions of the major disputants had solidified, once attempts at compromise and reunification had failed and organized conflict had begun, each Christian denomination was left alone to cut its losses, consolidate its gains, and repress its own characteristic doubts. Witchcraft theory was already available for repressing doubt, so a relapse into it was almost inevitable on the publishing front. The same could have happened in social life, providing one reason why sixteenth- and seventeenth-century witch-hunters persecuted their own coreligionists as much or more than their declared religious enemies. By defining the insidious enemy within, witchcraft theory objectified, allegorized, and dramatized the internal contradictions of dogma, as Pico's *Strix* so eloquently showed. Because witch-hunting, like witchcraft theory, depended on an absence of open discussion, it could have provided a comfortably camouflaged way of exploring doubts about the validity of one's Christianity.

Whether this hypothesis has any value for social history remains to be seen. But there was a peculiar escalation in sensational writing about demonic copulation after 1570. After that date, the sexual acts that witches were forced to confess committing with devils were far more violent and lurid than those typical of the period ending in the 1520s. In fact, every aspect of demonic copulation underwent terrific exaggeration during the reprise. No longer was intense pleasure or physical exhaustion an adequate sign that demonic copulation was real. The devil had to demonstrate his virility by going beyond the bounds of *virisimilitude* (and of verisimilitude). His penis had to be enormous, his ejaculate incredibly copious; both had to be so cold as to cause intense pain. The Devil could have a three-pronged penis, said Pierre De Lancre in 1612, so that he could simultaneously penetrate his victims vaginally, anally, and orally. If he was uninterested in fellatio, he could reduce his penis to only two prongs. De Lancre's expert witness added that the Devil's "member" could sometimes be half iron and half flesh, at other times completely made of horn. The Devil also increasingly appeared as a hybrid, not simply having inappropriate feet, but materializing largely or even wholly in the shape of an animal to copulate with his devotees. Although such sadistic fantasies had appeared occasionally before the 1570s, they became normal and necessary after that time.

Now not only women and men but children as well were forced to admit copulating with devils. Two German writers at Bonn and Würzburg recorded in 1629 and 1630 that children three and four years old, "to the number of three hundred," were said to have had sex with devils. One claimed that children as young as seven had been put to death for this crime; both said that children between ten and fourteen were routinely being burned for it.[42] Already in 1580, Jean Bodin had claimed that twelve was the age of consent for females and thus that twelve-year-olds *could* be routinely fornicating with demons. De Lancre claimed to have seen "hundreds of confessions" of six- to twelve-year-olds.[43]

These are the claims, not of credulous people, but rather of people who *need* to believe and cannot quite manage. Like some forms of drug use and sexual experimentation, fantasies about witches required their addicts to increase the dosage constantly; otherwise, the fantasies lost their ability to satisfy the underlying compulsion, even temporarily. The less one believed in the verifiable presence of the Devil, the more exaggerated claims one made for his being everywhere, at all times, in all forms.

English Witchcraft

The pattern of forcing accused witches to confess to attending the Sabbat and copulating with devils was largely missing from witch trials in England. (For historically determined reasons, Scotland conformed to the pattern established on the Continent and prosecuted people for having sex with demons.)[44] There was only one period when accusations of demonic copulation were prevalent in England: between 1644 and 1647, the infamous freelance "Witch-Finder General" Matthew Hopkins was able to take advantage of the turmoil of the English Civil War. Hopkins made his services desirable by charging high prices for them, and the number of accusations of demonic copulation rose noticeably.[45]

Except during this interlude, the picture of the typical English witch that emerges from the period "has nothing to do with the Continental one," as Barbara Rosen writes:

Vampire!!

> The [English] Witch almost never sees the Devil, and if she should meet him, it is alone; and his guise is that of a vagrant or an unremarkable animal. Most characteristically, the witch is given or adopts an animal which becomes her familiar, and executes her evil wishes. Her "pact" with it consists in giving it a living thing at intervals and allowing it to suck her [own] blood. "Pact" and "mark" become confused in the concept of an unnatural teat somewhere on the [witch's] body from which the animal is regularly suckled on blood. These ideas of the animal familiar and the supernumerary teat are . . . very nearly unique to England.[46]

"The witch's pact," notes Rosen, "was with the subsidiary, the minor devil who lived with her as cat or dog or toad, a being small enough to be in some degree in her control, yet large enough to demand some services." Rosen explains that "the element of affection in the alliance, which, on the Continent, took the form of surrender and worship, and bestiality [i.e., copulation] with demons was in England expressed by the cosy, slightly perverted relationship of a lonely and poverty-stricken woman to her pet animal."[47]

These characteristics can be related to the fact that torture was illegal in England. On the Continent, an established inquisition and Roman law encouraged the use of torture for obtaining confessions. These structures were never allowed to take precedence over English law. Without torture, confessions of demonic copulation and attendance at the Sabbat could not be obtained.[48] So English judges (and juries—another feature that distinguished England from the Continent) had to make do with whatever evidence of demonic activity could be found or fabricated. As Rosen remarks, "The English *did* see old women with pets."[49]

This meager raw material was transformed into evidence of intimacy with demons: one of the earliest familiars was a cat supposedly named Satan.[50] The witch's teat and the animal familiar thus served well enough to prove the same basic contention as confessions of demonic copulation: that someone was having corporeal interactions with demons. The corporeal contact involved in suckling is about as intimate as sexual intercourse. Although the physical sensations may be more sedate, they are still sensuous, and there is an exchange of bodily fluids (to use the current mechanistic euphemism). In early-modern physiology, milk was supposed to be produced by the transformation of blood in the mother's body, so there was no essential difference between suckling a familiar with blood and giving milk to one's child.

The concept of demonic copulation was familiar to English witchcraft theorists from their readings in demonological treatises written and printed on the Continent, particularly the *Malleus maleficarum.* English writers, whether defenders of witch-hunting or scoffers like Reginald Scot, discussed demonic copulation in their own works.[51] So there is no reason to believe that the absence of this motif from trials reflects some fundamental difference between the actual activities of English defendants and those of their Scottish and Continental counterparts. Nor is it likely that English stereotypes primarily reflect animosity to women's biological role as mothers and nurturers.[52] Even within the mythology of demonic copulation, maternal relations were at issue when abnormal children were discussed as the trace of sexual intimacy with a demon. The differences between England and the rest of Europe cannot obscure the demonic common denominator between characteristic accusations of suckling familiars disguised as small animals and copulating with demons. Both were treated as proof that humans could have intimate physical contact with embodied demons.

Tellingly, in England and the rest of Europe, no one claimed that the actual contact between demons and humans could be directly observed by witchcraft judges or theorists. Rosen observes of English trials that "the indispensable familiars—devils in animal form—are never produced in court as evidence, or even found by those supposedly searching a witch's house for them. Their beds and feeding dishes are solemnly produced, but they [the familiars] are always 'vanished away.'"[53]

Cui bono again: unless the ideological function of the familiar was to demonstrate the reality of interaction with demons, there was no reason why an animal could not have been produced in evidence. Conversely, to have brought the demonic familiar into court would have meant exposing it to skepticism and scorn by revealing how little it could possibly differ from ordinary cats, dogs, or toads. The ability to vanish was a defining characteristic of demons. If an instantaneous disappearance was demonic, any absence could be proposed as proof that a demon had *once* been present.

This reliance on absence was the great flaw in the laboriously constructed mythology of corporeal interaction with demons. Numbers of reasons were brought forth why everyone should believe witches' confessions that they had committed this heinous sin: (1) the confessions were spontaneous (calling confessions *spontaneous* served to disguise the fact that they were made during torture or under the threat of it—or, in England, after prolonged sleep deprivation and enforced walking); (2) the confessions were sacramental as well as juridical, and witches knew that if they lied—did not confess every accusation—they would be punished in the afterlife as well as in this one; (3) witches knew that they were going to die, so they confessed (*a*) to save their eternal souls or (*b*) because they no longer had anything to gain by trying to hide their egregious crime. Still, it must have been frustrating to realize that the defendant's confession to having a demonic familiar was the only available substitute for an actual examination and interview of the demon. Confessions and eyewitness testimony had to take the place of watching a woman and a demon interact.

Some prosecutors clearly fantasized about this possibility. In the Chelmsford trial of 1566, the queen's attorney offered to free Agnes Waterhouse if she could produce her familiar, Satan: "'Well,' said the Queen's attorney, 'well, can you make it come before us now? If ye can, we will despatch you out of prison by and by.'"[54] Speaking of the Swedish "Blockula" trials of 1670, Cotton Mather asserts, "The Judges would fain have seen them show some of their tricks; but they unanimously declared, that since they had confessed all, they found all their witchcraft gone; and the Devil then appeared very terrible unto them, threatning [*sic*] with an iron fork to thrust them into a burning pit, if they persisted in their confession."[55] Matthew Hopkins, the infamous witch-hunter of the English Civil War period, placed defendants "on a stool in the middle of the room, perched with their feet off the ground and watched for up to three days without food or sleep in the hope . . . that their familiars might come to them."[56] To suggest that these were nothing more than attempts to prove guilt is naive, given the history of witchcraft theory.

There seems to be no example of an inquisitor or a judge commanding a witch to produce her demon and copulate with it. Yet it is unlikely that prosecutors in witch trials would have passed up the opportunity to stage such trysts if they had been able to do so in a way that seemed intellectually convincing. It is not a question of their reluctance to collaborate with or connive at sin. The elasticity of inquisitorial morality and principles in other areas makes it unlikely that prosecutors in witch trials refrained from conducting such tests on moral grounds. Given the kinds of reasoning that we have seen, they could have easily explained away their complicity in *any* kind of experiment.

So the problem remained in the back of many minds. Heinrich Kramer was noticeably frustrated that inquisitors were unable to catch women flagrante delicto with their demon lovers. As usual, he expressed his dissatisfaction in a positive-sounding way by developing a complex theory. "Insofar as actual experience has taught us [*quantum experientia nos edocuit*]," Kramer says, "the incubus demon has always operated in a form visible to the witch." The fact that the witch is bound to the devil by an express contract or pact (*federatum pactum et expressum*) means that "there is *no need* for him to approach her *invisibly*."[57] This double negative is a way of admitting that no one but witches *can* see demons: seeing is a privilege conferred by the pact.

For this reason, and because both women and demons are so crafty, Kramer implies, bystanders cannot normally observe their copulation. However, "the witches themselves have often been seen lying on their backs in the fields or the woods, naked up to the very navel, and it has been apparent from the positioning of those limbs and members which pertain to this filthiness [*illius spurcicie*] and from the agitation of their legs and thighs, that, all invisibly to the bystanders, they have been copulating [*cooperantibus*] with incubus demons; yet sometimes, at the end of the act a very black vapour, of about the stature of a man, rises up into the air from the witch. But this only happens very rarely." Devils produce this visible indicator so rarely, confides Kramer, because they do so only when they are sure that "they can in this way seduce or pervert the minds of girls or other men standing by."[58]

The hidden problem triangulated by these theories seems to be that inquisitors have never observed demons copulating with women. Kramer could be arguing that, since inquisitors are incorruptible, there would be no point in the devils allowing them to witness copulation.

But to stop here would be tantamount to admitting that inquisitors will always be prosecuting crimes that remain invisible to everyone but the criminals themselves.[59] Thus, Kramer still needs a reliable eyewitness: "But it is certain that the following has happened. Husbands have actually seen incubus devils doing such things with their wives, although they have thought that they were not devils but men. And when they have taken up a weapon and tried to run them through, the demon has suddenly disappeared, making himself invisible."[60] So much for the argument that copulating devils allow themselves to be seen only by their paramours; and so much for the exception that devils allow bystanders to see them copulate only in order to stimulate their lust. Husbands confirm what no one else but witches can: the *virisimilitude* of demons, who cuckold them as effectively as human lovers.

Maliciously, Kramer claims that the wives—presumably when unhurt by the sword thrusts—throw their arms around their husbands and mock them for believing what they have just witnessed.[61] It goes without saying that Kramer is uninterested in the fate of wives whom demons do not snatch from the sword thrusts of their irate spouses. It would be a mistake to expend too much emotional energy on the travails of these women, as erroneous as asking how extensive the problem of demonically sired children is. Kramer's speculations have nothing to do with actual social problems. He cannot provide a single case study or name to document his claim that disappearing demon lovers or *Wechselkinder* are problems that inquisitors address by persecuting witches. The problems that haunt him are theological, not social, and he has little interest in knowing what living people actually do in society.

Filthy Pictures

All this puts into somewhat different perspective the fairly numerous fifteenth- and sixteenth-century representations of nude women interacting with demons or performing rituals that suggest witchcraft. Depictions and suggestions of relations between women and demons reflected a specific theological tradition of witchcraft theory. They conditioned the spectator, including the illiterate one, to imagine—that is, to *visualize*—corporeal interaction with demons as real. While actual copulation between women and demons was rarely depicted, it was made available to the visual imagination, even to spectators unfamiliar with theological demonology.[62]

Although there were antecedents in the manuscript tradition, one of the earliest printed illustrations of an embodied demon seducing a woman appeared in the German translation (1489) of Ulrich Müller's witchcraft treatise (fig. 1).[63] As Walpurga Hausmännin would confess a century

FIGURE 1 *Devil Seducing Witch*. Illustration for Ulrich Müller (Molitoris), *Von den Unholden und Hexen* (Konstanz, [1489?]).

later, this demonic seducer has inhuman hands and feet; as with the Ludovicus of Pico's *Strix,* these appendages—and an apparent tail—are birdlike. His paramour, who despite the crudity of this woodcut appears to be young and attractive, seems not to notice: she is absorbed in gazing at the demon's face, as Pico's Dicastes described witches doing.

Demons did not have to appear in anthropomorphic shape in order to cavort with women. They could appear in a variety of animal shapes. The most libidinous example is the dragonlike creature that extends its long tongue up toward the abdomen of an attractive nude young woman in one of Hans Baldung Grien's erotic drawings from 1515 (fig. 2). This copulatory suggestion is doubled and reversed by the strange flamelike columns issuing from, or perhaps entering, the vulva-like growth at the end of the dragon's tail. As the woman grasps one of the columns and looks over her shoulder into the dragon's face, she and the dragon complete a kind of sexual closed circuit, each appearing to penetrate the other. They pay no attention to the two weird putti (or are they damned infants of some sort?), whose gaze is locked on the dragon's tongue and the woman's pelvis.[64]

Perhaps not all Baldung's representations of nude women in equivocal postures are correctly identified as being of witches; but, like this one, several suggest that women are sexually available to demons. One of his more frequently analyzed drawings portrays three playful nude women of varying ages, including an obviously elderly woman, suggesting the sexual availability of all women to invisible observers, whether men or demons.[65]

Obvious representations of erotic encounters between demons and women are rare, compared to the wealth of illustrations depicting demonic corporeality from the twelfth through the seventeenth centuries. As Jeffrey Burton Russell and others have documented, the figure of the Devil assumed his modern form, both theologically and pictorially, in this period.[66] Given the massively increased scientific interest in the reality of demons beginning in the late twelfth and early thirteenth centuries, this is hardly accidental. In fact, the pictorial arts were as important as philosophical speculation for reinforcing the sense of demonic reality. It is belaboring the obvious to repeat the scholarly commonplace that religious art could function as books for the unlettered; it is more significant that visual representation reinforced the notion of demonic reality for *literate* observers. A plausibly represented corporeal devil could make the entire construct of Catholic theology seem more real to theologians themselves.

Paintings and engravings document this increasing preoccupation with the corporeality of the Devil. In the twelfth century, Satan began

FIGURE 2 Hans Baldung Grien, *Naked Young Witch with Fiend in Shape of Dragon* (1515).

to acquire animal characteristics. By the thirteenth century, he had acquired wings, which changed from angel wings to bat wings as the century progressed.[67] Fifteenth-century devils are a riot of corporeality, sprouting horns and antlers in inappropriate locations and combinations, faces on their abdomens, knees, and buttocks, strange, luxuriant ears, and reptilian skin tones and textures.

Michael Pacher's *Altarpiece of the Church Fathers* shows a grotesque horned, fanged, antlered, multieared, frog-headed, bat-winged green devil with an anorexic human torso and limbs, eyes in his buttocks, a tail that functions as a long nose, and a dripping, fanged, red-lipped mouth for an anus (fig. 3). One might expect him to be tempting a woman into copulation, but, instead, the demon is holding a missal—a book of Catholic masses—for a mitred ecclesiastic, Saint Wolfgang (fig. 4). This picture neatly allegorizes the utility of demonic corporeality for maintaining Christian faith in the late fifteenth century.[68] The overwhelming materiality and corporeality of Pacher's Devil—so intense that it has no rhyme or reason—serves the same ideological function as confessions of copulation with other demons. It presents him as indisputably corporeal and therefore real.

The riotous corporeality of this single devil was multiplied ad infinitum in representations of Saint Anthony's temptation. As Charles Cuttler showed, two themes underwent a "sudden efflorescence" at the end of the fourteenth century: Anthony being tempted by a demon embodied as a woman and being savagely beaten by multiple grotesque demons. The favorite of these representations was, not the scene of sexual temptation, but the beating. Its depiction as a full-scale physical *assault* became the dominant scene in Anthony's iconography.[69] Between 1470 and 1510—a period that neatly brackets the first wave of printed witchcraft treatises—three famous depictions of the saint's mauling by demons took hold of the European imagination.

The earliest, by Martin Schongauer (fig. 5), was an engraving. It was highly innovative, according to Cuttler, and was widely influential since it was multiplied by printing. It had a profound effect on Michelangelo, among others.[70] Indeed, the engraving must have been successful if Israel van Meckenem chose to copy it and sign it as his own, altering it only by mirror reversing it.[71] One of Schongauer's innovations was to have the assault take place in the air rather than on the ground, as in the standard hagiographic account of Anthony's temptation. Cuttler observes that other examples of such "levitation" are "known . . . chiefly in relation to witchcraft. [Previously] Anthony himself had been subjected to elevation, though by the hand of angels, rather than by devils, the latter having attempted to prevent his passage, as is told in the Athanasian account of

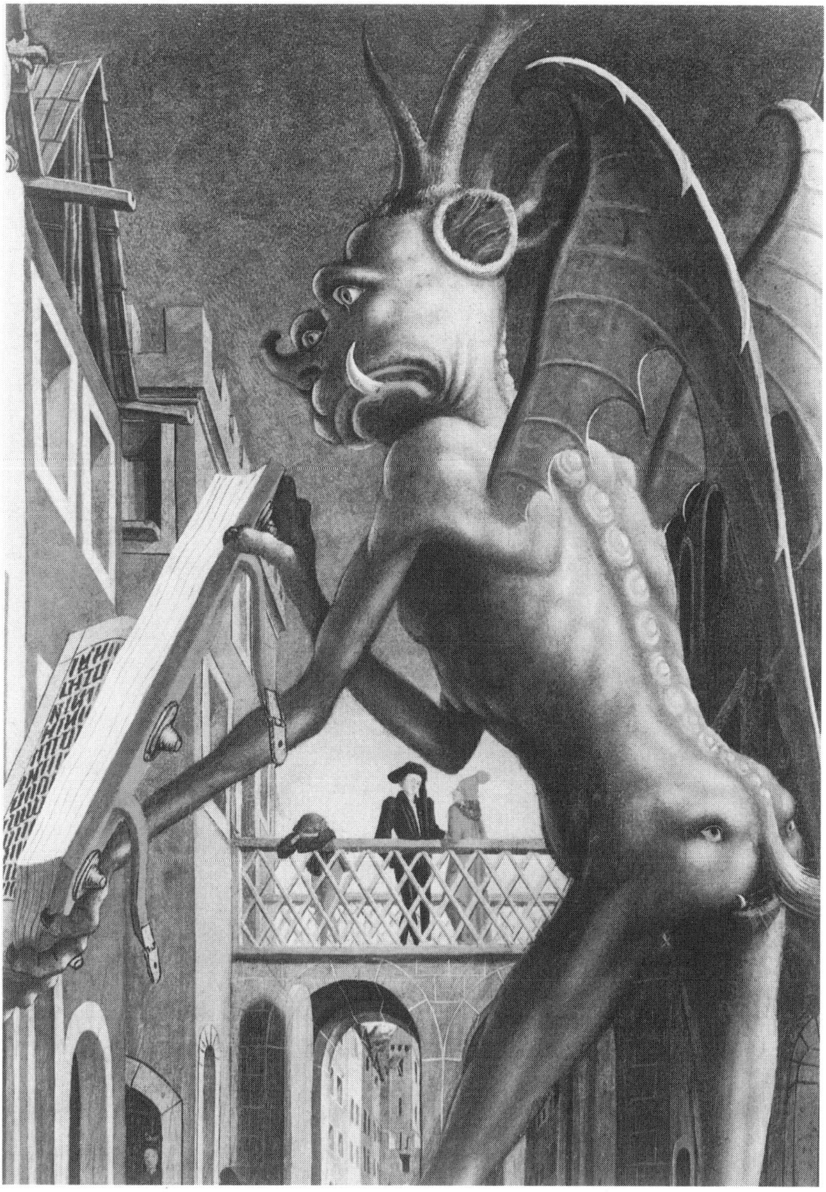

FIGURE 3 Detail of Michael Pacher, *Saint Wolfgang and the Devil,* from the *Altarpiece of the Church Fathers* (ca. 1475–79). Munich, Alte Pinakothek.

FIGURE 4 Michael Pacher, *Saint Wolfgang and the Devil,* from the *Altarpiece of the Church Fathers* (ca. 1475–79). Full image of which figure 3 above is a detail.

his life."[72] Since witchcraft involved physical interaction with demons, this is no surprise.

Demonic transportation was, like copulation, a supposedly definitive proof of real, corporeal interaction. Schongauer's engraving is thus a milestone in the representation of demonic corporeality. His devils illustrate the seemingly contradictory qualities of demonic bodies, both a chaotic materiality and an "airy" lightness, for some of them have no well-defined wings. They exhibit nearly every conceivable form of grotesque corporeality—birdlike, quadrupedal, and fishlike as well as humanoid—

FIGURE 5 Martin Schongauer, *Temptation of Saint Anthony* (ca. 1470).

but their ability to *carry* the saint through the air at the same time as they assault him implies the indisputable physical reality of the encounter.

Lucas Cranach the Elder carried Schongauer's fantasy of demonic corporeality even further in his 1506 engraving of the assault on Saint Anthony (fig. 6). The corporeality of Cranach's demons is so heterogeneous—it now includes insect and crustacean forms as well—and the scene so crowded that the boundaries between one body and another are at times entirely obscured. Levitation is also more emphatically represented. Schongauer's landscape had taken no more than a corner of the picture. Cranach's more extensive landscape, occupying more than half the picture, leaves the spectator in no doubt that the assault takes place high in the air.

Since it happens on the ground, Matthias Grünewald's 1510 portrayal of the saint's mistreatment (fig. 7) might seem to represent a step backward. But the Isenheim altarpiece yields nothing to its predecessors in riotously grotesque corporeality; as a painting, it adds a vivid display of color to the preexisting iconography. Grünewald contextualizes the event by setting it against a larger backdrop of demonic violence. Demons appear to be destroying an edifice of some sort, and they are engaged in combat with angels, under the watchful eye of the deity. Thus, Grünewald draws the imagination of the spectator upward through a kind of chain of being, from the monstrous materiality of the demons, to the ethereal but anthropomorphic corporeality of the angels, and finally to the deity, who must logically be the incarnate Son. As Hieronymous Bosch and many later artists understood, Saint Anthony's travails provided the perfect occasion for exploring the luxuriant paradoxes of demonic corporeality.[73]

Male witches do not seem to appear alone with incarnate succubi, although succubi do appear to Anthony and other male saints in art.[74] However, there is one representation of an incarnate male-gendered demon that implies his sexual threat to a male. Urs Graf's 1512 drawing of a hermit and a grotesque devil (fig. 8) shows a holy man descending from a mountain and heading toward a city. We know that the hermit is male because his beard protrudes from his voluminous hood. Perhaps the notion of the city as a place of temptation thus accounts for the demon's proprietary attitude toward the hermit; but, traditionally, the desert or wilderness was conceptualized as the battleground where hermits faced the temptations and assaults of demons, as in the legend of Saint Anthony.

Nor does tradition account for the demon's menacing sexuality. This hardly looks like a scene of temptation: it is more like the prelude to a rape. The demon's scrotum is clearly in view, and his long gnarled tail, curling upward between his legs, either hides or mimics a large erect

FIGURE 6 Lucas Cranach Sr., *Temptation of Saint Anthony* (1506).

FIGURE 7 Matthias Grünewald, *Temptation of Saint Anthony* (1510). From the Isenheim altarpiece, Unterlinden Museum, Colmar.

FIGURE 8 Urs Graf, *Hermit and Devil* (1512). Pen-and-ink drawing. Öffenliche Kunstsammlung Basel, K.17.

penis. The two figures' physical stances give the overwhelming impression that the demon is about to sodomize the hermit. The drawing leaves open the question whether the crucifix and rosary that the hermit carries will protect him from the demon's sexual assault. Literary tradition would suggest that, although the hermit might welcome an encounter with a demon, he would not succumb without resistance to this incubus's advances, as witches were supposed to do.[75]

Such ugly representations are often given a moral interpretation: devils were hideous because people believed that they were evil.[76] But such pictures also emphasized the scientific point that demons were not *mere* spirits. Their grotesque bodies demonstrated that they could become palpable and real. One might believe (at least momentarily) that they were pure body or pure matter. And a brutal, furious sexual assault would make the point even more dramatically.

The gross materiality of the invisible is one message of Albrecht Dürer's 1513 engraving *Knight, Death, and Devil* (fig. 9). Dürer's famously hideous devil and his companion, pale Death riding a skinny nag, are as perfect in their materiality as the elegantly armored Christian soldier astride his gorgeous charger. And yet, and yet: something is amiss. We can agree that the firm-jawed knight is "steadfast on the road of faith" and "undeterred" by the figure of Death, whom he could be resolutely ignoring.[77] But can we be certain that he even sees the demon since it is completely behind him? Has he, like Christ, said "get thee behind me," or is all this luxuriant corporeality visible only to the spectator? What does it mean that Death is only slightly less corporeal or grotesque than the demon and even needs a horse? Is the horse corporeal and real? If it is not real, are Death and the demon real? How far can corporeal representations of invisible realities be extended before they stop seeming real?

The ugliness of embodied demons was not universal. Witches' bodies could be elegantly erotic or distastefully decrepit; demons too could flaunt their corporeality as physical beauty, even charm. By the early sixteenth century, devils could be almost indistinguishable from elegantly physical human specimens. Luca Signorelli's fresco of the Last Judgment, painted between 1499 and 1504 (fig. 10), is in the cathedral of Orvieto. Signorelli's devils have batlike or birdlike wings and from one to four horns, but they have no tails, talons, or hooves. Their bodies are as graceful and well muscled as any of the men whom they are tormenting. Their faces as well are distinctly human, although distorted into unpleasant leers or fierce concentration. Their worst trait is their skin tone, often deathly white, gray, or green, in whole or in part. Their grotesquerie comes from this odd combination of overall human beauty, desultory nonhuman details, and hints of decomposition.

FIGURE 9 Albrecht Dürer, *Knight, Death, and Devil* (1513).

The message of these demons' largely human corporeality is that interaction with them is no different from physical oppression by extremely powerful human beings. As if to punctuate the violent message with hints of sex, in the center of the composition three of the five most visible devils are torturing attractive young women. One of them (fig. 11) is carrying a nervous woman piggyback. They hover between watchful

FIGURE 10 Luca Signorelli, *The Damned* (ca. 1503). Orvieto Cathedral, Cappella Nuova (Cappella di San Brizio).

FIGURE 11 Detail of figure 10 above.

good angels standing on clouds in their splendid armor and the desperate, writhing mass of anatomically perfect nudes below. (Two other airborne devils have just dropped men whom they were carrying in the same fashion.) Is the woman airborne because she was a witch in her earthly life, or is the devil simply flaunting his physical strength? Why are his fingers interlaced with those of her left hand—is this a meaningless detail or a gratuitous taunt by the devil, or does it imply that the two once had "a relationship" in this life as well? Why is the woman looking apprehensively over her shoulder at a good angel? Shouldn't her misgivings be a reaction to the devil carrying her?

These questions cannot be answered, but Signorelli's ambiguous display of human beauty emphasizes that, as a genre, the Last Judgments of the Middle Ages and the Renaissance served to argue pictorially for the reality of demons and the afterlife. The pain and suffering of the human body left to the mercy of demons, like the sexual experiences of demon-loving witches, were offered to the spectator as proof of such reality. Analogous proofs of good spiritual realities were offered, and not only by pictures. Signorelli's elegant devils adorn the church that houses the relics of the eucharistic miracle of Bolsena, the greatest and most famous manifestation of the Lord's body in medieval times.[78]

Analogous developments can be found in literature. Despite the author's ambiguous claim not to know whether he traveled "in the body," Dante's *Divine Comedy* is an intensely corporeal demonstration of the reality of the afterlife, particularly in hell and purgatory. Moreover, personalities whom Dante encounters make statements implying that his body is indeed present. Dante assures his readers that the torments of hell and the penances of purgatory are real, above all by explaining how such suffering happens. After death, he claims, the human soul feels such nostalgia for its lost body that it confects a temporary body for itself by condensing air and vapors. This provisional, substitute body suffers torments in hell and expiates sin in purgatory, until the Resurrection will make it obsolete. The provisional body that Dante imagined is the human equivalent of the virtual bodies that Aquinas and others hypothesized for angels and demons needing to interact with humans.[79] Without it, Dante intimates, the afterlife does not make sense.

Given the scientific value of corporeality, we should not assume that early-modern pictures of witches are merely whimsical or pornographic in their intent.[80] Depictions of nude women, or women in lascivious poses, as witches presented them as objects of interaction for demons and not only as objects of the lust of human men. Prurience was not irrelevant, of course. If demons were *virisimilar,* a picture that aroused human lust made an implicit argument for demonic lust; Milton would articulate this insight when he portrayed Satan's physical appreciation of Eve.[81] Even speculation about demonic malice could not eliminate prurience. Theologians agreed that the lack of a proper body prevented demons from feeling true lust; what demons lusted after was, not sexual intercourse for its own sake, but the perdition of the human soul.[82] Yet some witchcraft theorists interpreted Saint Paul's demand that women cover their heads in church "for the angels" as a measure intended to prevent arousing the lust of incubi.[83]

Whether demons were interested in sex or spiritual sabotage, the female body was conceptualized as a lure or bait for them. It could be pictorially represented in a variety of poses and expressions; it could be young and erotic or old and decrepit, inviting expressions of distaste as well as expressions of lust. (One thinks of Pico's Apistius and his disgusted puzzlement over the idea that an old woman was having sex at all, much less with a demon.) It could express both vulnerability and depravity, qualities essential for demonstrating demonic reality. Even highly aestheticized representations of nude witches, like those of Hans Baldung Grien, reflected theoretical, theological traditions of speculation about corporeal interaction. For learned spectators, eroticized visual depictions of witches and demons probably had the same effect as Pico's vivid dialogues, using art to counteract the difficulty of belief.

Sincere moral condemnation of sexuality seems to be about the only element missing from pictorial representations of witches and demons, as from written ones. From the standpoint of learned culture, the whole problem of witches was that, like Pico's Dicastes, the inquisitor or theorist himself *could not see* the reality of the demon that he was pursuing. For this reason, pictorial representations must have been something of a consolation to learned men. Pictures were better than nothing; they were far better than the thousands of words required for logical or narrative proof.

Aside from these surrogates of visibility, the elusiveness of demons—the only alternative to their nonexistence—must have been intensely frustrating. To obtain the proof that intimate contact with demons was really possible, inquisitors and other prosecutors of witchcraft had to extort confessions *about the past* from accused witches. Although confessions came from real people, they were secondhand, vicarious experience, as Bartolomeo Spina revealed in his use of the term. His and others' witchcraft treatises, as well as some early trial records, suggest that a fundamental rationale for persecuting witches was to compensate for this lack of direct perception. So, if a prosecutor was truly inquisitive about demonic reality, his net progress in satisfying his metaphysical voyeurism was always and ever zero. If he was not a prosecutor, a witchcraft theorist was even less likely to find satisfaction. Compiling expert testimony gathered by others was thirdhand contact, yet it was the closest thing to firsthand experience with demons that witchcraft theorists could expect.

Belief was hard to come by. Contrary to the fundamental assumption of modern scholars and historians, witchcraft theorists were not credulous, nor, in all likelihood, were most active hunters of witches. They were not trying to convince others of something in which they truly believed. They were anxious to convince *themselves.*

5

FROM DREAMS TO REALITY: WHY WITCHES FLY

"I recognize you, Witch."
—newspaper advertisement for Strega liqueur, showing an attractive nude young woman holding a broom

The notion that witchcraft was a real and heinous crime is not a medieval or Dark Age idea. Witchcraft theory and the persecution of witches are Renaissance phenomena, and they lasted into the Age of Reason. Throughout much of the Middle Ages, churchmen condemned the belief in witchcraft as a delusion of the uneducated based on their ignorance of true theology. Clergy were expected to combat belief in witchcraft among the laypeople, teaching that it was incompatible with Christian belief, administering penance to and even excommunicating those who persisted. Yet, around 1400, a sizable number of clerics began defending the reality of witchcraft. Harsh penalties were carried out to punish crimes that churchmen had previously dismissed as imaginary.

No satisfactory explanation has been provided for this ironic reversal, perhaps because *witchcraft* is too vague a term, susceptible to many variations in meaning. If, instead, we examine what happened to the concept of corporeal interaction with demons during the late 1300s and early 1400s, we can observe the process that led to the characteristically Western concept of the witch. Theologians' need to verify the possibility of corporeal contact with demons provided the nucleus around which many other ideas, including the reality of *maleficium,* were pulled into orbit.

Witchcraft theorists' maturity or thoroughness in defining witchcraft is often measured by the relative complexity of their concepts of the Sabbat, but this is an unreliable index. Kramer's *Malleus* was the most thorough treatise for a century, yet it does not have a developed concept of the Sabbat as a formalized mass meeting of witches.[1] The two things that Kramer and other key writers did argue for unanimously were *maleficium* and corporeal contact between witches and demons. For writers of the sixteenth century and later, the appeal of elaborate Sabbats was not sheer complexity but multifaceted corporeal interaction with devils. The reality of this interaction was still guaranteed by witches' confessions and mutual accusations—the expert testimony of the witches themselves.

Transvection, the concept that witches were carried bodily by demons, was central to witchcraft theory far longer than descriptions of the Sabbat. Contrary to modern cliché, witches could not actually fly because they were defined as powerless in themselves. Like *maleficium,* a witch's flying could only be performed for her by a demon. In exchange for the witch's submission ("body and soul," by means of the pact), the demon struck her victim with disease or misfortune, and it was the demon who carried aloft the witch's broomstick or other aircraft, enabling her to fly. Demonic transvection exerted the same fascination over witchcraft theorists as demonic copulation, for both involved intimate physical contact between humans and demons. This is why transvection became an indispensable part of the Sabbat, once such meetings became a regular feature of the witchcraft myth. Many theorists imagined that witches might occasionally walk to the Sabbat or take some other conventional means of transport; after 1500, few authors imagined Sabbats without regular demonic transvection.

Transvection and the Sabbat are linked by an extremely curious historical origin, however. To read the document that spawned them both is initially an exercise in puzzlement. Unless the concept of corporeal interaction is borne firmly in mind, this text seems far removed from witchcraft. Sooner or later, all fifteenth-century witchcraft theorists quoted a text that described how "some wicked women, perverted by the Devil, seduced by illusions and phantasms of demons, believe and profess themselves, in the hours of night, to ride upon certain beasts with Diana, the goddess of pagans, and an innumerable multitude of women, and in the silence of the dead of night to traverse great spaces of earth, and to obey her commands as [if she were] their mistress."[2]

This passage was widely read throughout the later Middle Ages because it had been included about 1140 in the standard reference work on canon law, that is, the laws that were enforced by Catholic confessors and ecclesiastical courts. It is part of a law known as the Canon *Episcopi,* which, as its title suggests, is a directive to bishops enjoining them to stamp out certain unorthodox beliefs in their dioceses. Throughout the Middle Ages, it was thought that the Canon *Episcopi* had been passed by the Council of Ancira (modern Ankara) in 314 C.E. It is more likely that it dates from the mid-ninth century, and it seems to reflect the difficulties of evangelizing the laypeople of Carolingian Europe, when pre-Christian religions and folkloric practices still survived alongside Catholicism, competing for the allegiance of simple people.

The Canon *Episcopi* is the oldest and most important source for the Western Christian mythology of the witch's "flying" and for the notion that she attended nocturnal mass meetings of witches. Its centrality has long been evident to everyone interested in witchcraft, beginning with the earliest witchcraft theorists. The latter discussed it more passionately than they did any other text.

They did so for good reason. The Canon *Episcopi* offers *no* support for the concept of the witch that developed around 1400. On the contrary, it concludes that the nocturnal traveling of women is nothing but an illusion or a dream. The same goes for nocturnal gatherings: the Canon *Episcopi* declares that, when these women think that they experience "things joyful or mournful, and persons known or unknown," they are plunged into unreality because, "while the spirit alone endures this, the faithless mind thinks these things happen not in the spirit but in the body." Belaboring what seems obvious to him, the Canonist asks, "Who is there that is not led out of himself in dreams and nocturnal visions, and sees much when sleeping which he had never seen waking? Who is so stupid and foolish as to think that all these things, which are only done in spirit, happen in the body . . . ?"[3]

The worldview expressed by this text seems eminently sensible and almost modern: on one side stands what is physically possible, corresponding to a condition of full wakefulness; on the other side stands the impossible. Yet the latter is often experienced in dreams as if it were possible. A closer look shows that the crucial distinction drawn by the Canon *Episcopi* is not between truth and falsehood, or between waking and dreaming, but rather between *body* and *spirit*.

Herein lay its fascination for early witchcraft theorists. The Canon *Episcopi* does not equate truth with waking and falsehood with dreaming; rather, it asserts that, under some circumstances, the spirit can have real experiences in which the body does not participate. Holy men like Paul and Ezekiel received true revelations, yet they never believed that their wondrous experiences happened to their bodies: "The prophet Ezekiel saw visions of the Lord in spirit and not in the body, and the Apostle John saw and heard the mysteries of the Apocalypse in the spirit and not in the body, as he himself says 'I was in the spirit.' And Paul does not dare to say that he was rapt in the body."[4]

So the Canon *Episcopi*'s first level of reasoning is that the women are mistaken: if prophets and holy men can have good and true visions only in the spirit, then simple laywomen are deluded to believe that their visionary experiences happen in the body. This belief is not simply mistaken: it deserves condemnation, for it implies that the believer "loses the [Christian] faith, and he who has not the right faith in God is not of God, but of him in whom he believes, that is, of the Devil."[5] Anyone who believes that such travel is real "belongs to the Devil" simply because it is impossible.

In complete contradiction to early-modern witchcraft theorists, the Canon *Episcopi* declares it heretical to believe that women travel supernaturally at night. Centuries later, Heinrich Kramer and others would condemn as heretical the *failure* to believe in the reality of such travel. And they used the same terms as the Canon *Episcopi* does: *body* versus *spirit.*

The Canonist—the author or authors of the Canon *Episcopi*—differed from the witchcraft theorists in his crucial presuppositions about the nature of this travel. The idea that a person could "traverse great spaces of earth" at nighttime, on the backs of "certain beasts," and do so *in the body* is contrary to the experience of ninth- or twelfth-century people because it implies travel at great speed. The same holds for the fifteenth century, except that witchcraft theorists interpreted this travel as transvection or flight. However, nothing in the Canon *Episcopi* implies that women or their confessors were thinking of aerial flight. In fact, the Canonist's touchstone is probably travel on horseback. At issue is a distance—great spaces of *earth*—so excessive that to travel it on the backs of beasts would require an improbable or inconceivable speed. Flight, altitude, birds, wings, or broomsticks are never mentioned: this is *riding,* not flying.

For the Canonist, the issues are simple. His concept of reality is empirical and experiential, based on what we perceive when we are certain of being awake. But reality is also based on dogma. Not only does night travel contradict everyday experience of travel; it goes against what the Bible says about people and animals. It assumes that "Diana, the goddess of pagans," could change both animals' nature, to give them the power for unnaturally rapid travel, and people's nature, to endure it. The Canon *Episcopi* equates this assumption with idolatry. To believe "that anything can be made, or that any creature can be changed to better or to worse, or be transformed into another species or similitude," by anyone other than God is implicitly to worship that being as one's god because the Bible tells us that such powers are God's alone. As proof, the Canonist quotes John 1:3: "All things were made by him."[6]

This text should have prevented witchcraft theorists' elaborate fantasies about witches and the Sabbat. It was the most authoritative obstacle to belief in the reality of transvection, secret nocturnal mass meetings, and shape-shifting (the metamorphosis of witches into cats or wolves).

Instead of giving up, witchcraft theorists approached the Canon *Episcopi* as a fearsome challenge. They had to attack cautiously; since they believed that it had been issued by a council of the church, they could not declare categorically that it was wrong. A favorite tactic was to claim that the Canon *Episcopi* condemned, not the women's belief in their night travels, but only their belief that Diana empowered them to perform these rapid peregrinations; such belief implied polytheism and idolatry. Other writers attempted to prove that the women described were different from real witches; since witchcraft was a new heresy, the long-ago writers of the Canon *Episcopi* could have known nothing about it, so the document was irrelevant. Still other writers proclaimed that, whatever the truth about the ancient women of the Canon *Episcopi*, modern witches could experience the Sabbat both ways: "in the spirit" during dreams and "in the body" in waking reality.

The question remains why such a persistent effort of revision was felt to be necessary. There are two related reasons. First, the Canon *Episcopi* disturbed early witchcraft theorists because it did not support their need to believe in the empirically demonstrable reality of the visionary experiences on which crucial biblical doctrines are based. That is to say, the Canon *Episcopi* does not make corporeal interaction the criterion for judging the reality of supernatural experiences. Even prophets like Ezekiel and saints like John and Paul, it declares, never believed that their bodies had been involved or present when they received important revelations, yet those revelations were truthful. The Canon *Episcopi* calmly accepts that truth and falsehood are not perfectly aligned along the axes of illusion and reality, or of wakefulness and dreaming, or, most important, of body and mind (or spirit).

The Canon *Episcopi* envisions, not two possibilities, but three. The Devil can cause dreams that are both counterfactual and untrue, while God can inspire visions that are true yet contrary to everyday experience. Such visions, the Canon *Episcopi* implies, may be "ecstatic": the soul may actually be "standing outside" (ex-stasis) the body. There is a third possibility, for illusory dreams can also happen without any intervention by either Satan or God.[7] This the Canonist calmly implies when he assumes that everyone is often "led out of himself in dreams and nocturnal visions, and sees much when sleeping which he had never seen waking." By the early fifteenth century, this third assumption was profoundly disturbing. Not that the phenomenon of dreaming had been neglected in the meantime: Thomas Aquinas had suggested a typology of dreams that began from related premises.[8] By the fifteenth century, it was difficult to know how one might distinguish a natural dream from a supernatural one, and some writers, at least, craved empirical confirmation of the distinctions.

This desire relates to the second way in which the Canon *Episcopi* disturbed early-modern clerics—through its concept of Satan. The Canon *Episcopi* repeatedly declares that the Devil is the source of idolatrous illusions, but it gives no guidance for detecting Satan's presence, other than the everyday behavior of certain people and the nonconformity of their beliefs with Christian dogma. Yet the whole point of the Canon *Episcopi* seems to be that truth and illusion, possible and impossible, body and spirit, can be easily distinguished. For the reader of about 1400, the Canon *Episcopi* suggested questions that it could not answer: If certain things happen only in the spirit, how can one be certain whether Satan—or God, for that matter—causes them? Worse yet, what is the difference between a divinely or demonically inspired dream and a neutral, natural dream of the sort that everyone has? On what basis could we distinguish them?

Worst of all, the Canon *Episcopi* is tantalizingly confident about the mechanism that Satan uses to delude his women victims: "Thus Satan himself, who transfigures himself into an angel of light, when he has captured the mind of a miserable woman and has subjugated her to himself by infidelity and incredulity, immediately transforms himself into the species and similitudes of different personages, and deluding the mind which he holds captive and exhibiting things, joyful or mournful, and persons, known or unknown, leads [the victim's mind] through devious ways."[9]

The appearance of precision here is deceptive, for the Canonist has no theory as to how Satan does this and feels no need of one. In some unspecified way, on some unspecified stage (but one that must correspond at some level to the human mind), the Devil impersonates people, replicating the bodily appearance of persons whom his victim may or may not know. On this basis, he is able to construct whole scenarios that appear to be real experiences.

The Canonist feels no need of theory because he has no difficulty accepting the Bible literally. He casually quotes Saint Paul's dictum that Satan "transforms himself into an angel of light" (2 Cor. 11:14) to deceive unwary Christians. He shows every sign of interpreting this verse literally, yet he does not explain *how* it is true and feels no need to justify his omission. In this, he differed radically from his fifteenth- and sixteenth-century readers. Most of those readers feared that the problem of reality runs much deeper than the Canonist suspected. If experience is divided into events that happen to the spirit only and events that happen to both body and spirit, they reasoned, how is it possible to describe Satan's activities precisely unless they affect the body of his victims? How do we know that he is present? How could he ever be observed in operation? How do we know that such illusions are not produced by worry, frustration, hunger, drunkenness, drugs, or disease? Where is the line between natural and supernatural causality?

Fear of Nature, Fear of the Imagination

The Canonist could never have imagined these problems. He lacked two important fears that developed between about 1140 and 1400. First, he did not fear the power of the human imagination; he feared no contradiction in the assertion that Paul, John, and Ezekiel had experiences that were true but contrary to normal experience. Second, he did not fear the power of nature, either in itself as a limitation on human activity and knowledge or as a basis for explaining human experience. It is not even likely that he had an idea of *nature* rather than of *normality* or that he articulated an opposition between *natural* and *supernatural*.[10] As a result, he had no need of empirical or bodily proof about the reality of interactions with Satan. Thanks to his third category, *noncorporeal but nonetheless true,* his reality was a continuum, not a dichotomy.

During the centuries following the Canonist's time, theologians became aware of needing to confront Aristotelian philosophy. Aristotle stressed concepts like cause and effect, the importance of observation and sensory perception. By 1200, what the Canonist had accepted as truth revealed in the Bible now coexisted uneasily with notions of truth *acquired* by purely human means. The biblical "Creation" was defined by philosophers as nature, and nature seemed at times to be autonomous. It threatened to encroach on the sovereignty of God, making him almost unnecessary to describing the world. Already in the twelfth century it was possible to suspect Christian philosophers of following ancient pagans "who say that nothing exists beyond bodies and the corporeal; that there is no God in the world besides a concourse of elements and a natural temperament."[11] Aquinas would state this frightening idea with deceptive nonchalance before refuting it in his famous five proofs of the existence of God: "If a few causes fully account for some effect, one does not seek more. Now it seems that everything we observe in this world can be fully accounted for by other causes, without assuming a God. Thus natural effects are explained by natural causes, and contrived effects by human reasoning and will. *There is therefore no need to suppose that a God exists.*"[12] The new philosophical outlook suggested that, to be real, interactions must be verifiable by sensory evidence. Where did this leave the women of the Canon *Episcopi*?

The implication that these women were not interacting physically and perceptibly with Satan stimulated resistance to the Canon *Episcopi.* This resistance created the nocturnal mythology of corporeal interaction at the Sabbat. The myths developed slowly, over the course of something like a century.

About 1354, the Dominican preacher Jacopo Passavanti was writing in Italian (in *Lo specchio della vera penitenza,* or *The Mirror of True Repentence*) that "some people say they see dead people and talk to them, and that they go by night with witches [*colle streghe*] to their *tregenda.*"[13] Many such people are simple impostors, he says: they take advantage of others' bereavement for financial gain or out of sheer malice. Nonetheless, some people do sincerely think that they see dead people. This is impossible, says Passavanti (presumably because these souls are in hell or purgatory and are not allowed out). But people are seeing *something* that is real. The Devil can take on the semblance of dead people and falsely impersonate them, as he did when the Witch of Endor claimed to show the ghost of Samuel to Saul:[14] "And we find that demons sometimes take the form of living men and women, and of horses and asses, and go about in a horde at night in certain regions. And when people see them, they think the devils really are those people whose shape they display. And this in some countries is called the *tregenda.* And the demons do this in order to spread an error and to create a scandal, and to slander those persons whose shape they take on, by seeming to do illicit [*dishoneste*] things during the *tregenda.*"

In fact, the *tregenda* that Passavanti describes is not what we now call the Sabbat; it is probably a reminiscence of what folklorists call the *wild host* or *wild hunt.* It may also reflect the legend of Saint Germanus, who is supposed to have exposed and shamed a band of demons who took on the shape of certain people and went about trespassing and carousing at night to ruin their reputations.[15]

Passavanti makes assumptions that were crucial to defending corporeal interaction with demons: (1) that the people whom he is discussing are awake, not asleep; (2) that demons—in the plural—are performing some sort of masquerade; (3) and that the demonic theatrical presentation seems absolutely lifelike ("they think the devils really are those people"). Moreover, if devils can impersonate horses and asses, Passavanti could be implying that the Canon *Episcopi* wrongly dismissed night travel by women. In fact, Passavanti is already combining ideas of the wild hunt with the women of the Canon *Episcopi,* as the next part of the passage shows: "Yet certain persons can be found, especially women, who claim that they themselves go by night in a group to this *tregenda;* and they list great numbers of their company by name. And they say that the women of this throng [*torma*] who lead the others are Herodias, who had John the Baptist killed, and Diana, the ancient goddess of the Greeks. We should give some thought to the manner of this, and how it can be possible." Passavanti has clearly read the Canon *Episcopi* or quotations from it, as the references to Diana and Herodias indicate. He is evidently reconciling those references with his notion of *tregenda*—people's nocturnal but *waking* interactions with demons who have taken on the shape of humans or animals.

Passavanti shows by his last sentence that, unlike the Canon *Episcopi,* he does not consider any of this lore obvious or self-evident, in itself or in its implications. The lore is not profoundly disturbing to him, but *how* such things happen requires some explanation to fit into his view of the world. Moreover, before treating dreams and visions, Passavanti carefully introduces the idea so conspicuously missing from the Canon *Episcopi:* the Devil can transport people bodily: "There is no doubt whatever that, by his natural powers, the Devil can lead and carry men and women, whether few or many at a time, from one place to another, however he wishes, if he is not held back by divine power." Yet Passavanti concedes immediately that bodily experiences are rare; normally, the Devil produces exactly the kind of imaginational or spiritual experiences that the Canon *Episcopi* described:

> *But it is rarely found that he does this.* The other way, which is more likely [*verisimile*], is the one discussed above: that he can make it *seem* to a person that she or another person is something that she is not, or is doing something that she is not doing. And he does this whether the person is awake or asleep, by changing the imagination and the phantasy, and impressing on it the images and semblances of those things that he wants the person to think she is, or is doing or saying. So that, while the person is in her own bed, it will seem to her that she is traveling, and doing marvelous things; and later she will recount these things in the belief that she has really done them. And this commonly happens to witches of both sexes [*malefici*], or to bewitched persons [*persone maleficiate*], that is, those to whom or by whom some act of maleficent magic [*alcuno malificio d'arte magica*] has been performed; or to people who have faith [*fede*] in such things. (emphasis added)

Passavanti's categories for analyzing demonic interaction with humans are more precise than the Canonist's distinction of body from spirit. First, he adopts principles of Scholastic Aristotelian psychology, with its definition of the imagination or phantasy as a discrete faculty of the total human being. This is far more nuanced than a simple distinction between body and spirit. In addition, he discusses what the Canonist called happenings *in the spirit* by reference to demons' ability to cause movement from place to place, even within the human imagination. This psychological explanation draws on a range of ideas in Scholastic physics, most of them Aristotelian in origin, particularly the concept that every motion in matter must have a spiritual cause.[16]

Passavanti is not particularly disturbed by the implication that most experiences of the Devil happen only in the imagination and do not involve actually transporting a human body from place to place. But notice that his theory of how the Devil deceives is considerably more detailed and mechanistic than that of the Canon *Episcopi,* which had been content to accept the authority of a verse from Saint Paul. Over the course of the next 150 years, Passavanti's relatively tranquil admission that bodily experience of the Devil is rare would disappear, as theorists tried ever harder to prove that it was commonplace and verifiable, striving to explain it with minute precision.

I do not intend to claim that Passavanti's text was crucial in the development of the stereotype of the witch; it may have been, but that is beside the point. He exemplifies *a stage* in the development of the assumption that, for the reality of the spiritual world to be convincing, there had to be proof that someone had experienced it corporeally.[17] Many of the texts that I discuss could be replaced by others of the same period that make the same assumptions. What remains true is that the encounter between Christian theology and ideas of experiential reality evolved according to something like the chronology that I am describing.

"Exploding" the Canon Episcopi

After Passavanti, theorists became far more anxious to show that the Canon *Episcopi* could not disprove the idea of bodily interaction with demons. According to Nicholas Jacquier's *Flagellum haereticorum fascinariorum,* or *Scourge of Heretical Enchanters* (1458), witches are different from the dreaming women of the Canon *Episcopi;* demons can and do appear bodily to modern witches when they are awake and do carry them bodily from place to place.[18] Jacquier adds many details of such interaction and develops a theory of the Sabbat, collecting most of the soon-to-be classic myths about copulation, ceremonial demon worship, child sacrifice, devil's marks, and *maleficia.* Like other early theorists and inquisitors, he refers to the witches' *synagogue,* rather than to their *Sabbat,* creating an alternate link to anti-Semitic stereotypes.[19]

Jacquier repeats with mechanical regularity that everything happens in reality and in the body, not in dreams or hallucinations. He includes testimony from his own inquisitorial practice. At one point, he claims that the reality of witchcraft is proved by the testimony of upright persons worthy of credence. These good people swear under oath that, while traveling at night, they have accidentally run across the synagogue and recognized certain of the witches present. What is more, some of those very witches have confessed under oath that they saw the wayfarers as well! The wayfarers say that they were struck with terror and disease, and the witches confess that they were beaten by their devils for being discovered.

Despite the emphasis on mutual recognition and concordant testimony, only these alleged beatings guarantee that demons, as well as the human defendants and witnesses, were present: "Thus we should not marvel if *the abovementioned trustworthy witnesses did not see the devils along with the witches,* because a devil that has assumed a body can appear to one person and not to another, even when they are present at the same time. . . . Therefore the actions of this abominable sect are not illusions of people who are asleep, but true and concrete actions, performed by people who are awake."[20] Clearly, Jacquier is reaching for any explanation that will guarantee demonic reality.

Jean Vineti, the inquisitor of Carcassonne, stated baldly in his *Tractatus contra demonum invocatores,* or *Treatise against Those Who Invoke Devils* (ca. 1470), that "devils can actually take on the semblance of bodies. To affirm, therefore, that devils appear materially and visibly to humans and really talk [*loquantur*] with them does not involve contradicting the Canon *Episcopi.*" Vineti declared that a careful reading of the Canon *Episcopi*'s wording showed that it was discussing people who were different from witches, that is, from "modern heretics, who invoke and adore devils while awake, wait on and follow their advice, pay them honor, and—something that exceeds the ferocity of wild beasts—sacrifice their own children or, often, the children of others to devils and have recourse to their [sexual] filthiness."[21]

To demonstrate that these interactions were real, Vineti examined the idea that demons transport witches bodily to the Sabbat. He maintains that "an angel, good or evil, if God permits, can through its natural powers transport a man bodily from one place to another and even carry him a long distance," for the simple reason that spirit is superior to matter.[22] Vineti attempts to domesticate the concept of nature by insisting that the powers of angels and demons are natural, not supernatural. Far from being a concession, this amounts to demolishing the distinction between natural and supernatural in order to assure the reality of the latter.

Vineti's crucial arguments against generalizing from the Canon *Episcopi* are biblical rather than empirical: he cites the example of Habakkuk (Dan. 14:33–39), whom an angel carried by the hair from Judea to Babylon and back.[23] He adds that, if anyone claims that only a good angel and not a devil can perform such actions, "he goes against the truth of the Gospels" because Matthew says that Satan carried Jesus to the pinnacle of the temple of Jerusalem. These Bible incidents make it clear, he concludes, "that angels, and even devils, can transport people physically from one place to another." Thus, it is clear that we have to take seriously "the depositions and confessions of those who confess that they were transported bodily from one place to another by demons, not only at night, but also in the daytime."[24]

Giordano da Bergamo (ca. 1470) also wished to make room in the Canon *Episcopi* for devils to interact bodily with witches. His *Quaestio de strigis,* or *Inquiry into Witches,* has been described as defining "the moderate position of a theologian careful to establish the truth with respect to hearsay" because, unlike most of the works already seen, it does not maintain that practically everything that witches confess happens corporeally.[25] He may be more careful than other early theorists, but Giordano's fears are the same as theirs. To get around the Canon *Episcopi,* he specifies that demons can deceive witches in three ways: with illusions perpetrated while they are awake, with disturbances of their imagination when they are asleep, and by bodily transporting them from one place to another.[26]

The first method explains how witches can believe that they are having sex with demons but also how they can believe that they have been transformed into cats for the purpose of sneaking into houses and killing children. Witches are deluded to think that they are truly turned into animals; devils simply make them believe this, even though they are wide awake. This mistaken belief in literal metamorphosis is disproved by the Canon *Episcopi,* says Giordano, which reminds us that only God can change the true form of his creatures. The second manner of deceit is also a concession to the Canon *Episcopi,* repeating its explanation of things seen in sleep and dreaming. In both cases, however, the Canon *Episcopi*'s explanations are carefully modified by constant recourse to Aristotelian explanations.

The third manner of deceit is where Giordano salvages what the Canon *Episcopi* most threatened, that is, the reality of demonic transport. Demons deceive witches about transvection in two ways, he says. First, they let them think that mere unguents have power to make sticks and brooms transport them, whereas devils do the carrying. Second, devils open and close doors and gates so quickly that witches think that they have flown right through solid obstacles.

Thus, it is clear, Giordano declares, what the faithful must believe about witches. In the first place, we must remember that truth is the whole purpose of our faith. There is no way that falsehood can be the basis for faith.[27] So, regarding witches, we must believe only what corresponds to the truth, and it is as wrong to believe that witches are not carried bodily by demons as to believe that they are truly turned into cats. To believe "that witches cannot intervene in the reality of things through the power of the Devil, but only act on appearances, and in their fantasy or when asleep," is wrong. Such skepticism is as ignorant as believing everything about witches, for the skeptics "do not know how great is the power of the Devil to effect such things when divine justice allows it." The faithful, Giordano concludes, "must completely banish certain beliefs about witches from their hearts, while they must firmly believe others."[28] From the beginning, witchcraft theorists had been hinting that a belief in witchcraft was necessary to proper Christian faith: about 1470, Giordano may have been the first to say it out loud.

Resisting the Explanatory Power of Mental Illness

Late-sixteenth-century opponents of witch-hunting claimed that the myths of demonic witchcraft could be explained by natural causes. Critics like Johann Weyer and Reginald Scot claimed that most witches were plainly affected by melancholy.[29] This was not mere sadness but a complex physical and psychological disease. It was brought on by an excess of black bile, one of the four "humors" that were supposed to circulate in the body and determine its "complexion," or characteristic physical makeup and psychological moods. Witches could be out of touch with reality for a variety of reasons, said these critics: poor diet, old age, and even the mere fact of being a woman could predispose one to melancholia.[30]

But witchcraft theorists had foreseen this argument a century before Weyer and Scot. In his *Opusculum* (ca. 1460), Girolamo Visconti penned a systematic demonstration that witches were *not* melancholics and did not imagine their experiences but had them in reality. Visconti declared that, "since all those who say that such women are deceived take their arguments from the chapter of *Episcopi* mentioned above, I want to prove by that same chapter that this sect is not afflicted [*non laborare*] by a melancholic humor that would impede its members' use of reason and their freedom of the will." Visconti went on to discuss the signs of melancholia as defined by medical authorities and then argued that real witches exhibit no such symptoms. If we say that witches are sick and only imagine their doings, Visconti argued, many people will maintain that they are not heretics and should be pitied rather than persecuted: "For as Aristotle writes in the *Ethics,* we do not censure those who suffer from an ailment that does not originate in their will; instead, we have compassion for them, and take pity on them, as we do the deaf, the blind, and fools."[31]

This possibility enraged Visconti: "Truly, this opinion is extremely dangerous, and, as I will show, it is contrary to the faith and to the honor of Almighty God. Therefore it must be refuted with all our powers and banished far from the borders of Christendom."[32] Visconti clearly understood that, if we cease punishing witches, we necessarily imply that their interactions with devils, and possibly the devils themselves, are imaginary. Visconti's ultimate insinuation is that witches must die in order to preserve the credibility of devils and, hence, the credibility of the entire world of spirit.

This is particularly clear in his next few sentences: "In his commentary on chapter 4 of Matthew, while explaining that saying of the Savior's, 'Begone, Satan! Scripture says "You shall do homage to the Lord your God and worship him alone,"' John Chrysostom relates that we must never countenance outrages against God." Jesus teaches us, says Visconti (still quoting Chrysostom), to put up nobly with insults directed against ourselves. But we must not even listen (*nec usque ad auditum sufferre*) to insults directed at God: to disregard them is impious and wicked.[33] If we admit that the Sabbat is imaginary, we weaken our faith in God and offend him.

Despite his wish to write a *medical* proof that witchcraft is not imaginary, Visconti ends up falling back on biblical proofs, particularly Matt. 4:5–11, which we saw Vineti worrying about: the point where Satan takes Christ bodily to the pinnacle of the temple and then to the top of a high mountain. The argument about "outrages against God" comes from Chrysostom's commentary on just those verses. In his *Lamiarum,* Visconti returns to the same Bible passage while discussing witches' bodily interaction with demons. He informs us that, according to the *Glossa ordinaria,* the oldest compilation of Latin commentaries on the Bible, Satan's temptation of Christ was "done in the body [*corporaliter*], and [so] it is not strange [*mirum*] if he who permitted himself to be crucified also permitted himself to be carried about."[34]

"Thus," concludes Visconti, "we should not scoff [*deridere*] at those who say that they have sometimes seen the Devil in human form, or in the form of a wolf, a goat, or other such animals, since this both can and often does happen."[35] But the physicality of Christ's encounter with the Devil does not just support the testimony of witches. If both Christ and the witches offer proof that real contact with devils is possible, then witches confirm that the Bible account of Christ's transvection is true.

Tellingly, Visconti calls on demonic copulation to corroborate the proofs offered by demonic transvection: "If, therefore, it is possible that demons can transport people from place to place and have sex with them [*commisceri*] as well, . . . then it is evident that this Sabbat [*ludum*] is real [*verum*] and not an imaginary illusion or a dream."[36]

Ulrich Müller or Molitoris published a treatise on witchcraft theory in 1489, hoping to prove that witches were guilty of real crimes. But, after twice quoting the Canon *Episcopi* verbatim, Müller had to conclude that witches do not travel at night and do not gather at the Sabbat in reality. These experiences happen "only in their dreams, or, as we have said, because of an excess of imagination." Witches see only "the representation of the similitudes of the appearance of things [*per representationem specierum similitudinarium*]," which are impressed on them by the Devil: "Thus deceived [*illuse*], they think after awakening that everything happened to them in reality [*vere*]."[37]

Müller says that he wrote the dialogue in response to a request by Archduke Sigismund of Austria that he help resolve the witchcraft controversy. Accordingly, Müller cast himself, the archduke, and a university professor of civil and canon law as the speakers. The most striking feature of this dialogue is that he assigned the role of skeptic to the archduke. Müller and Schatz, the lawyer, have the difficult task of convincing Sigismund that witchcraft is a real crime even though many of its effects are based on illusions produced by demons. As Maria Rosario Lazzati observes, this position involves "an apparent contradiction."[38]

Even if his logic is faulty, Müller's rhetorical strategy is quite astute: by overcoming the doubts of the supreme political and legal authority, he implies that no one else has any reason or right to doubt the criminality of witchcraft. One side effect of this strategy, however, is that the archduke's doubts brutally unveil the theological agenda of witch-hunting:

> SIGISMUND: Furthermore, I ask whether these wicked [*maledicte*] women[39] can straddle a stick covered with a certain unguent, or a wolf or another animal, and be carried by the Devil from one place to another, where they drink and banquet and fornicate with [*cognoscant*] each other and give themselves over to pleasure.
>
> ULRICH: First, however, we must hear your opinion, Honored Prince.
>
> SIGISMUND: We know that the Devil is an incorporeal spirit; he has neither hands, feet, nor wings, and he has no spatial dimensions; how then can he carry a man, who is corporeal?[40]

Hard question. Having searched strenuously for nonbiblical evidence of demonic reality, Müller ultimately must fall back on the Bible. To vindicate the idea that devils can interact bodily with humans and even carry them about, he mentions Habakkuk and other examples already brought forward by witchcraft theorists. Not at all surprisingly, he adds, "And also about Our Savior it is said in the Gospel of Matthew, chapter 4, that the Devil took [*assumpsit*] him and carried him to the pinnacle of a temple, and so forth. Thus I am convinced that the Devil can appear in human form [*specie*] and to human beings and interact [*conversari*] with them."[41]

Müller's title, *De lanijs et phitonicis mulieribus,* or *On Witches and Prophetic Women,* is one clue to his familiarity with arguments in the *Malleus maleficarum.* Kramer attempted to create a formal Scholastic definition that would differentiate between the deluded women of the Canon *Episcopi* and the evil witches of his day:

> The category under which the women [of the Canon *Episcopi*] are contained is called the category of pythons [*species phitonum*], through whom a demon either speaks or produces wonders [*mira*]. . . . But the category under which witches [*malefici*] are contained is called the category of witches [*malefici*]. And because they differ greatly from each other, it is not fitting that anyone who performs something under one category should be included under other categories. Thus, since the Canon speaks of those former women, and not of witches [*maleficis*], those who want to see this kind of imaginary bodily transport [*imaginarias deductiones corporum*] behind each and every category of heresy [*superstitionis*], so that all witches [*malefice*] would be carried in their imagination only, like the women [of the Canon *Episcopi*], are interpreting the Canon falsely.[42]

The people who use the Canon *Episcopi* to argue that transvection cannot be real, Kramer says, generalize quite inappropriately from one passage

> where it is said that witches are only transported in imagination [*tantum fantastice et imaginarie*]; but who is so foolish as to conclude from this that they cannot also be bodily [*corporaliter*] transported? Similarly, at the end of that chapter it is set down that whoever believes that a man can be changed for the better or the worse, or can be transformed into another shape [*speciem*], is to be thought worse than an infidel or a pagan; but who would conclude from this that men cannot be transformed into beasts by illusory tricks [*prestigiosa illusione*], or that they cannot be changed from health to sickness—that is, from better to worse?[43]

Persons who argue in this manner, says Kramer, are merely "scratching at the surface of the words [*in cortice verborum*]" of the Canon *Episcopi.*

Instead, we must "study the inner meaning" of those words (*ad nucleum verborum attendere*), as Kramer himself has done in the first hundred pages of his treatise. Then we will see that a literal reading of the Canon *Episcopi* is "contrary to the opinion of all the Holy Doctors, and, indeed, against the teaching of Holy Scripture."[44]

Here, Kramer implicitly compares the activity of reading to eating walnuts. Ironically, this comparison was a topos, a scholarly cliché employed to describe the technique of interpreting pagan poems allegorically. Break the shell (*cortex, integumentum*) of the text, and discard it; extract the true, useful, nutritive kernel (*nux, nucleus*) of meaning. Medieval interpreters had recourse to allegory whenever the literal meaning of the classics contradicted the theology that they wished to propound. The comparison of the text to a nut symbolized a necessary violence and a degree of arbitrariness.[45] Kramer's adoption of the nut topos is doubly ironic: in order to argue for a literal interpretation of demons in the Bible, he must throw away the literal text of the Canon *Episcopi,* which depends on biblical literalism for its demonology.

Kramer feared the legal consequences of dismissing witches as ill or deluded. By confusing witches with the women of the Canon *Episcopi,* someone could argue "that a witch [*maleficam*] only cooperates in the infliction of debilitation or sickness through witchcraft [*effectum maleficiale*]" by means of her imagination.[46] He fears that someone may argue that, *since* witches only imagine being transported by demons, they also only imagine that the rituals of witchcraft cause the infliction of real harm. This fear of the Canon *Episcopi*'s authority is fundamental to the *Malleus:* much later in the treatise, after a long chapter on how witches are transported from place to place, Kramer declares that,

> since the public report of this sort of transvection is continually flying about [*volat*] even among the common people, it is unnecessary to add further proof of it here. But we hope that this will suffice to refute those who either deny altogether that there are such corporeal transvections, or try to maintain that they are only imaginary and phantastical. And indeed, it would be a matter of small importance if such men were left in their error, were it not that this error tends to the injury [*contumeliam*] of the faith. For notice that, not content with that error, they do not fear to introduce and publish other errors also, to the increase of witches [*maleficarum*] and the detriment of the faith. For they assert that all witchcraft—of which witches are justly, truly and realistically [*realiter*] accused as instruments of the devil—can only be ascribed to imagination and illusion, as if witches were really harmless, just as their transvection is only imaginary [*fantastica*].[47]

If witches are not carried by demons, there is no proof that witches are the instruments by which devils inflict *maleficia* on humanity. *Maleficia* must have some other source, and demons must be either imaginary or irrelevant. This, says Kramer, is "a cause of great reproach [*contumeliam*] to the Creator."[48] We know from Kramer's first chapter that disbelief in witchcraft implies disbelief in demons: if demons are not responsible for *maleficia,* who is? Is anyone responsible? Is God? For demons to be real, witches must be guilty because only humans can be apprehended and tried.

Kramer's whole system depended on the reality of demonic transvection. So he could not content himself with mere textual interpretation: he needed expert, empirical testimony from the witches themselves. But could he prove that witches were *always* carried bodily, that they *never* imagined their flights? No, the best that he could do was claim that the confessions of witches, both "those who have been burned" and "those who have returned to penitence and the faith," confirm that "they are transported *both* bodily and phantastically," both in reality and in their imagination.[49]

Kramer says that preachers must teach this truth to their congregations, and he takes personal credit for obtaining proof of it from witches' confessions:

> Among such there was the woman in the town of Breisach whom we asked whether they could be transported only in imagination, or actually in the body [*an ne fantastice et illusorie aut corporaliter*]; and she answered that it was possible in both ways. For if they do not wish to be bodily transferred, but want to know all that is being done in a meeting [*contione*] of their companions [*consodalibus*], then they observe the following procedure, as she did herself. In the name of all the devils, she would lie down on her left side, and then a sort of bluish [*glaucus*] vapour came from her mouth, through which she could see clearly what was happening. But if she wished to be bodily transported, then it was necessary to follow the method which has been told [i.e., to anoint a chair with an unguent made from unbaptized babies and be carried by a demon].[50]

Kramer's presentation of his method is chilling. To refute the Canon *Episcopi,* he interviewed this witch as one might interview any expert about some specialized activity or technique; but he clearly did so using torture. His inspiration for this gruesome interview—if it took place—almost certainly came from his readings in earlier theorists. Hardly any of their arguments failed to find an echo in his exposition.

Witch mythology was shaped by a process of damage control. Witchcraft theorists' objective was to preserve as much of the spirit world as possible from the encroaching, corrosive evidence that it was either imaginary, unprovable, or inaccessible. As Bartolomeo Spina announced, "I will prove that it must be believed by everyone, and *in no way doubted,* that these things happen in just the way inquisitors claim they do."[51] Nowhere is this attempt to neutralize skepticism better shown than by theorists' attempts to circumvent the authority of the Canon *Episcopi.* The issue is not whether they were fundamentally dishonest or specious when they claimed that more than one interpretation of the Canon *Episcopi* was possible or even when they argued that it could not be used to prove that all witches were dreaming. Of course, multiple interpretations of any document are always possible, within certain limits. But, at bottom, these writers were always arguing one thing: that the Canon *Episcopi* could not disprove the reality of demons.

Anything needing such elaborate defense is already in doubt, regardless of how strongly the proof constructor claims to believe. Defenses of demonic reality have another characteristic that betrays how little they were motivated by belief or credulity. Whether written early or late, treatises on witchcraft theory were not structured as a simple confirmation that demons are real. Rather, each treatise was organized by the necessity of refuting doubts and objections that had been or could have been *already* raised about the plausibility of physical interaction with demons. The Canon *Episcopi* was merely the most famous and authoritative sourcebook for such skepticism.

Even when precise sources of doubt cannot be identified, it is clear that, logically and grammatically, "They really do exist" is the appropriate rebuttal to a prior assertion that "Such phenomena do not exist." The fundamental proposition of any witchcraft treatise is that demons are not imaginary because the witches who interact bodily with them are not asleep, deluded, or ill. From the standpoint of logic, this proposition is a double negative. It proposes, not that "Demons exist," but rather that "Demons *do not not* exist." Every major assertion of a witchcraft theorist amounts to "This is not incredible," and tag phrases like *Incredibile non est* or *Nec inverisimile est* are common in the phraseology of witchcraft theory. Even when they do not occur explicitly, such phrases are tacitly presupposed by convoluted argumentation and elaborate accumulations of evidence: "Are you still not convinced? Here are some more proofs."

Handbooks of rhetoric define a phrase like "It is not incredible" as litotes or understatement. Grammatically, litotes is a double negative. In the rhetoric of witchcraft theory, however, double negatives are not understatements but rebuttals of actual objections. Witchcraft theory depends on a rhetoric of overstatement and "protesting too much," not on understatement.

Scholars have devoted a lot of attention to the apparent illogic in the mythology of witchcraft. But the argumentation of witchcraft theory follows *another* logic, an implicit logic, rather than no logic or faulty logic. That logic is double negation, the negation of negation. Curiously, historians and other scholars have largely passed over the double-negative logic of witchcraft theory as if it were perfectly normal and unworthy of attention. Perhaps as a result of this neglect, no sustained attention has been paid to instances where, in their attempts to prove that witches interacted verifiably with demons, inquisitors and other judges engaged in actual experimentation.

In the Western tradition, one vindicates a theory through either philosophy or science, that is, by offering proofs that are either logically sound or verifiable and repeatable through experimentation. If an experiment fails to confirm a hypothesis, the experimenter is expected to explain. Treatises on witchcraft theory are fundamentally structured as logical demonstrations, but they also contain accounts that supposedly record the results of experiments with witches. All the experiments failed to verify human-demon interaction, so the failures had to be explained away. This damage control was entrusted to the logic of double negation. The number of experiments recorded is sufficient to provide a crucial perspective on the motives that impelled individual theorists to defend or engage in the hunting of witches.

6

EXPERIMENTS WITH WITCHES

> One of the most amazing failures of historic theology has been the failure to employ, in the substantiation of religious belief, the same kind of empirical evidence which has long been used in support of scientific belief.
>
> —D. E. Trueblood, *The Logic of Belief*

> In a world dominated by the demon of science and technology, in which science seems to devour the space of the sacred, see what a paradox emerges: science confirms the sacred, recognizing with fairness and dignity that scientific truth is not the whole truth.
>
> —Nicola Nasuti, *L'Italia dei prodigi eucaristici*

If the Canon *Episcopi* did not provoke the earliest experiments with witches, it furnished the frame of reference for interpreting them. The most recognizable experiments investigated whether women flew or attended the Sabbat.[1] Interpretations of the "data" provided by these experiments underwent a complete reversal during the fifteenth century. Initially, experiments were interpreted as proof that witches did not and could not attend the Sabbat. When they continued to fail, experiments were interpreted double negatively as evidence that transvection and the Sabbat were *not unreal,* despite an appearance of unreality. A few later experiments, performed when the persecution of witches was waning, led to the same negative conclusions as the earliest fifteenth-century experiment.[2] Despite controversy and reinterpretation, the format of the experiments did not change appreciably over the centuries. Ultimately, they revealed far more about human motivations than about demonic transportation.

In the early seventeenth century, Cervantes alluded to these experiments in his short story *The Dogs' Colloquy.* In this philosophical tale, one dog tells another about his conversations with a witch, who told him that

> "some people think we go to these gatherings only in our imagination, and that through it the devil presents to us images of all those things

which we say afterwards have happened to us. Others deny this, and say that we really go, body and soul. I myself hold that both these views are true, for we don't know whether we go in imagination, or in reality, because everything that happens to us in our imagination happens in such an intense way that it can't be distinguished from the times when we go really and truly. *The inquisitors have made some experiments on some of us whom they have apprehended, and I think that they have found that what I say is true.*"[3]

Experiments with witches are startling for what they reveal about the connection between witchcraft theory and scientific inquiry during the early-modern period. It is no accident that *inquiry* and *inquisition* come from the same root or that Sir Francis Bacon referred to science as "the inquisition of nature."[4]

If we can believe the accounts left by witchcraft theorists, literate men began experimenting with live women only gradually. If surviving accounts are trustworthy (a big if), women resembling those mentioned in the Canon *Episcopi* probably began the experimentation themselves. I base this conjecture on one of the earliest known references to an experiment, in the Bible commentaries of Alonso Tostado.[5] When discussing the Book of Genesis, Tostado related:

> There are some women, whom we call witches [*maleficae*], who claim to travel whenever they wish, by means of certain unguents and the observance of certain words, and they claim that men and women gather in certain places where they enjoy every sort of pleasures, both in food and in sexual intercourse [*in complexibus*]. One simple woman [*muliercula*] of this sect was not believed when she told of this, and so she promised to undertake it in the presence of many people. After the ritual of words and annointing with unguent, she lay down as if dead in the presence of bystanders. When she returned to her senses after several hours, she declared with conviction that she had been in such-and-such places and claimed that she had enjoyed various pleasures with a great number of people belonging to that same sect, and she named people who were known in that region. Those who were present realized that she was deceived about this business because she had lain there unconscious in front of them and had never left the place.[6]

Wishing to put the whole matter to a test (*ut magis eam rem experirentur*), the bystanders had burned and beaten the witch while she slept, but neither the burns, which Tostado says were quite cruel, nor the equally serious beatings woke her. When she did awake at long last, the bystanders argued that she had never left their presence, much less done the things she claimed.

At first, she contradicted them steadfastly, for she had felt nothing of all this mistreatment. But, gradually, she began to notice the painful burns and bruises on her body. Eventually, she agreed with the bystanders that she had dreamed everything. Tostado concludes that it is certain that the woman was alive throughout the experience (a fact that would not have been as easy for the fifteenth-century bystanders to ascertain as it might be for us). Yet, he says, the woman was so thoroughly deprived of her senses (*tam forti alienatione a se distractam*) that, if the bystanders had killed her, she would never have felt a thing.[7]

This anecdote raises several possibilities, assuming that it relates something that actually happened. First, the unguent that the woman rubbed on herself evidently contained a psychotropic or mind-altering drug. It had anesthetic effects that lasted even longer than the hallucinations that it caused. People like this woman may have known certain plant extracts or animal secretions (possibly from poisonous toads) that caused these profound stupors and vivid dreams. The woman's experience seems to have had one phase in which she underwent intensely realistic dreams about traveling, feasting, and sexual intercourse. Her dreams may have had an element of wish fulfillment, which would account for the feasting and possibly for her recognizing people known to the community at the celebration.

More important, the woman accepted her audience's conclusion that burns and bruises proved that her body had remained in their presence and could not have traveled anywhere. She assessed her physical pain on awakening as proof that her pleasures and travel had been illusory. The mental or spiritual experience was actually disproved by her physical, bodily experience. Perhaps, if her body had not been burned and bruised while she thought that it was experiencing pleasure, if, say, she had merely been tied down before beginning the experiment, she might have argued that her mental experience was real, despite her body's exclusion from it. The seventeenth-century Benandanti studied by Carlo Ginzburg appear to have believed something similar, to wit, that the soul can travel and have real experiences while the body remains inert and seemingly lifeless.[8]

It is not evident what the woman assumed her audience would see—whether she expected them to report that she had flown away, or ridden off on a horse or another beast, or somehow simply disappeared. It is certain, however, that the anecdote does not mention devils or other supernatural beings. Nor does Tostado refer to the gathering as a Sabbat or a witches' game or dance. There is no mention of anyone presiding over the celebration that the woman dreamed of attending. Even in Tostado's unsympathetic narrative, the celebration has an air of community and equality about it; Satan does not tyrannize it, as in a stereotypical Sabbat. Most remarkably, neither the woman, her audience, nor Tostado mentions issues of sin or heresy, much less the transgressions of the Sabbat. Husbands later became important in this kind of anecdote: their role was to reveal the witchcraft secrets of their wives by finding their ointments or surprising them during their ceremonies and denouncing them to inquisitors.[9] But Tostado mentions neither secrecy, husband, crime, nor punishment. Perhaps this is not accidental since he also does not mention a clergyman or judge being present.

The answer to the question, Cui bono? therefore seems to be that this dream was in the woman's own interest and no one else's. She undertook the experiment on her own initiative, to convince her acquaintances (one can hardly call them friends, considering their treatment of her) that she was experiencing something real. She was deeply disappointed that her experience was a dream and not a reality. Rather than an experiment *on* a witch, this was an experiment *by* a woman. We have no guarantee that Tostado's anecdote reflects genuine peasant practices, but it does feature the kind of wishful fantasy that a poor person, possibly living alone, might plausibly dream.

One would expect a scholar who told this story to consider witchcraft a delusion, based on mental simplicity or the harsh conditions of peasant life. We might think that he would agree wholeheartedly with the Canon *Episcopi,* despite not mentioning it here. Tostado did discuss the Canon *Episcopi* in another of his commentaries on the Bible; indeed, he quoted and paraphrased it extensively, in a largely positive vein. But he staunchly defended the reality of witches' transvection; despite recounting this woman's failed experiment, he never claimed that her experience was typical. In fact, Tostado may have been the first scholar to claim that transvection was a real and regular occurrence.[10]

In his second discussion of transvection, Tostado begins by using the Canon *Episcopi* to pose the question "whether men can sometimes be carried by the Devil to different places." He admits that "some people say this is not possible since the church, at the Council of Ancira, rejected this belief, as is clear from the Canon *Episcopi.*" After faithfully expounding the position of the Canon *Episcopi,* he sets out to prove that it cannot apply in all cases: "Nonetheless, it must be said that, in spite of [what the Canon *Episcopi* affirms,] devils can transport men both with and without their consent, to different places, both by day and by night, *and that sometimes this transvection happens in reality* [*et etiam aliquando hoc fit*]."[11] In fact, says Tostado, it was not the Canon *Episcopi*'s intention to affirm that women can never be carried by devils; it merely states that they are wrong to believe that they are following Herodias or Diana and shows that they fall into heresy by believing that Diana is a goddess.

Tostado declares that *these* women are not dreaming. Their experiences are happening in reality, but Diana, Herodias, and the beasts that the women ride are actually devils who have taken on false semblances. The reality of night flying is proved by the apprehension and punishment of many women for doing it. Tostado hints that nonwitches (his grammar suggests that they are men) have performed experiments to duplicate the women's experience of transvection: "And some persons [*aliqui*], wishing to imitate their unspeakable ceremonies, have experienced great misfortune. Nor can this be said to happen only in dreams since, not only those [*ipsi*] who suffered them, but also many others were witnesses to this fact. There is no reason to doubt this." It is true, says Tostado, that such things can happen in a dream and be mistaken for reality "since even prophetic revelations often happen like this, by means of imaginary visions. Nonetheless, it is not denied that these things can truly happen in external reality [*realiter exterius*]." He argues that there are "dreams in which a man does not suffer any of the things he thinks he suffers; but this does not exclude the possibility that such things can really [*realiter*] happen outside of dreams."[12] Thus, concludes Tostado, we should not interpret the Canon *Episcopi* to mean that it is heresy to believe in demonic transvection.

The work of damage control has advanced considerably since Passavanti. Passavanti had been willing to admit that demons rarely carried people about. Now Tostado will go only so far as to admit that "demons rarely carry anyone against their will." Even this concession nearly gets retracted on the same page, for Tostado claims to have witnesses that it *has* happened and declares that it would happen much more often if God did not prohibit it.[13]

Biblical Literalism and the Need for Witches

The implied contradiction between Tostado's anecdote and his overall position on witches' transvection was caused by his uncoordinated attempt to prove that the Bible is literally true. The Canon *Episcopi* had simply accepted the Bible as the yardstick of truth, but Tostado felt pressured to defend the scientific accuracy of two widely separated passages in the Bible. Each passage implicated a different kind of science.

Tostado recounted his skeptical anecdote about the dreaming witch in his commentary on the Book of Genesis, where he was at pains to demonstrate that there was nothing implausible about God creating Eve from Adam's rib. Could God make Adam sleep so soundly that he would not feel this extreme mutilation of his body? How could such pain be ignored? Tostado is not content with the argument that God can do whatever he likes, although he does repeat it favorably. This answer does not explain normal reality, in which pain is one of the strongest forces known. However, Tostado knows something about anesthesia. Thus, he introduces a scientific explanation:

> But furthermore there are some substances that by their very nature take away the sense of pain. If parts of the body that have to be cauterized [*urende*] or cut are anointed with these mixtures, there will be no sense of pain. And we know that there is one kind of ointment that causes so much loss of consciousness [*mentis alienatio*], and such an abstraction of the person from himself, that for a certain period of time no sensation can be found in anyone who has been anointed with it. And nowadays here in Spain this often happens. There are women whom we call witches. . . .

At precisely this point, Tostado recounts the story of the woman who failed to wake when burned and beaten by her neighbors. He concludes by asking, "How much more easily could it have happened through God's own handiwork that the rib was taken away and yet Adam felt nothing?"[14]

Tostado's story, then, is not skeptical at all. It is a defensive reaction to skepticism caused by the concept of nature: if witches are undergoing a perfectly natural form of total anesthesia, then God could have administered it to Adam before "operating." The Bible is not a naive fiction; it does not contradict the physiological principles of nature.

In Tostado's commentaries, the figure of the witch coalesces from various arguments that have no other necessary logical relation. Their only common denominator is the implication that the Bible is literally true, or at least not implausible as a record of historical and physical fact. In his commentary on Adam's rib, Tostado's mention of witches is something of a red herring. Despite his use of the term *maleficae,* there is no mention of *maleficia,* women do not actually fly, and their whole experience is an illusion. Although Tostado examines demonic copulation in detail elsewhere in the Genesis commentary, he makes no mention of anyone voluntarily experiencing it and asserts that incubi molest unwilling women.[15]

However, in his commentary on the first five chapters of the Gospel of Matthew, his *maleficae* look considerably more like the witches of the full-blown myth or cumulative concept: they do fly, and they are guilty of *something* that involves collaboration with devils. Tostado discusses demonic transvection while commenting on the story in Matthew and Luke where Satan tempted Christ by carrying him to the pinnacle of the temple and thence to a high mountain, where he showed him the entire world.

Other writers mentioned this story in passing, but Tostado considers its verisimilitude so important that he devotes ten immense double-column pages to it. He considers every possible objection to the literal truth of the story, suggests a dizzying array of possible answers, and concludes that all are wrong or irrelevant. His worry reduces to this: if devils cannot carry modern people literally and bodily, this Bible story conflicts with reality. Such a contradiction is not unthinkable—otherwise Tostado could have written far less—but it is inadmissible because it threatens the very foundation of Christian doctrine.

Tostado's defense of transvection is tortuous and circular. His final proof that witches are truly carried by demons is the biblical account of Satan carrying Christ:

> To maintain therefore that a man can be transported through the air by the Devil is not the same as having faith in the Devil, nor thereby to fall away from the true faith, since Holy Scripture affirms such things, for example, when Christ was carried by the Devil. Thus we must not deny that maleficent women, and men as well, when they have completed some abominable superstitious rites and anointings, are taken by devils and transported to various places and that many of this kind of people gather in one place, and offer tribute to the devils, and abandon themselves to libidinous and filthy acts [*turpitudini*].[16]

But Tostado is writing a Bible commentary: he introduced the subject of witches solely to defend the scientific plausibility of Satan's carrying Christ. By reversing his argument, Tostado intimates that witches and their activities lend more credibility to the Bible than they gain from it.

The basic premise of Tostado's commentary is that events narrated in the Bible are always literally true and must *therefore* have definite analogues in modern experience. Tostado's clinching proof that modern analogues exist appealed strongly to subsequent theorists: "Besides, everyday experience [*experientia*] itself demonstrates this—and I only wish that such experience were not so well known! For we know of many who, as if in a single instant, have been carried from one place to another very distant place through the ministration of demons, who are the masters of witchcraft [*principes maleficiorum*]. And the truth of this is so manifest that it would be imprudent to deny it since a thousand witnesses [*testes*], who are aware of having experienced this themselves, vouch for it."[17]

Heinrich Kramer reasoned the same way, using many of the same arguments.[18] Decades before the *Malleus maleficarum,* Tostado anticipated its argument that expert witnesses could be found who would certify the reality of corporeal interaction between humans and demons by citing their own lived experience. The transparently insincere rhetorical flourish of wishing that corporeal interaction were not undeniable also appealed to Kramer and later theorists as a means to disguise their need for witchcraft to be true.

As if his point were not already clear, Tostado devotes two interminable pages to demonstrating that Satan could not have shown Christ the whole world in a vision or through some trick of optics.[19] His overt—and theologically valid—reason is that, given Christ's divinity, it would have been scandalous for him to allow Satan to tamper with his mind. But, since Christ and the witches are locked in mutual dependence and neither can be defended as plausible without the other, Tostado cannot tolerate the idea that Satan interfered with Christ's perception of reality. This would imply that the Canon *Episcopi* could be right when it asserts that witches are only dreaming. The converse is also true, for the Canon *Episcopi* could impugn the reality of Christ's experience of Satanic transvection. Any hint of illusion in either text will destroy the precarious reality of witchcraft *and with it the credibility of the Bible.*

Tostado lived in the middle of five or six centuries when clerics were driven by what Don Cameron Allen called a "pious obsession," their desire "to prove that the Bible did not disagree with recent historical and scientific findings." Tostado's gigantic commentary was a crucial development in that obsession. Confronted with stories such as Noah's Flood, Christian Bible commentators labored interminably, devising "scientific" explanations of *how* the whole earth must have been flooded. They speculated endlessly as to what God did with the excess waters before and after. They estimated the precise measurements of the Ark and calculated how it stayed afloat, how much space was needed for the animals and their feed, how Noah solved his titanic sanitation problems, and every other conceivable scientific problem. This process culminated in Athanasius Kircher's elephantine *Arca Noë* of 1675, an immense volume that made Noah's Ark the crucial episode of a huge historical novel that Kircher presented as scientific Bible commentary.[20]

Allen noted that Tostado and company were, not silencing heretics, but arguing against themselves. Ancient and early-medieval Christian theologians dismissively "branded . . . as pagan impertinence or heretical observation" many questions about the literal truth of the Bible. After the twelfth century, increased interest in natural philosophy exposed the inefficacy of such rhetorical tantrums. Late-medieval Bible commentators, particularly Tostado and his predecessor Nicholas of Lyra (d. ca. 1349), had to confront these questions and so, according to Allen, they "offer their remarks as resolutions of the *normal* objections to the story." As Allen showed, Tostado "began the process of fictionalizing the account" of the Flood, "imagining what Noah thought and did" to make the assertions of the Bible more congruent with everyday reality.[21]

The process that produced (and still produces!) scientific justifications of the historicity of Noah's Flood created the construct of witchcraft as corporeal interaction with demons—during the same historical period and by identical means. Scholastic theologians adopted Aristotelian scientific principles because the verisimilitude of the Bible, its agreement with the data of everyday experience, could no longer be dismissed as irrelevant to faith. Science as we know it did not exist in 1440, but Tostado exemplifies the problem of biblical verisimilitude in an age of empirical reasoning. The problem was alive and well four centuries before Darwin, half a millennium before the Scopes Monkey Trial (1925) or the Kansas school board's ban on teaching evolution (1999). Then, as now, a lot of imagination and fantasy, what Allen called *fictionalizing,* were necessary to combat the evidence that Bible stories are unscientific, mythical, fantastic, or fictional. By Tostado's day, one no longer just rebutted the carping of pagans or heretics; one first had to resist *one's own* suspicion. To doubt the literal truth of any passage in the Bible threatened one's confidence in Christian dogma.

Tostado's logic implies unambiguously that to deny demonic transvection to witches means denying it to Christ, thus negating the Bible's claim to truthfulness. Yet Tostado never quite said this out loud. Eighty years later, Bartolomeo Spina was to have no such scruples, and he still saw the Canon *Episcopi* as the crux of the problem:

> It is false . . . and in fact extremely dangerous to say that that text [the Canon *Episcopi*] indiscriminately teaches that these things must not be believed and that they are not done in the body, as if they could *never* be done in the body, and yet to state in the same breath that those [church] fathers asserted in their commentaries that Christ was carried in the body onto the mountain by the Devil, and so on. This way of speaking implies either that the Gospel is not to be believed [*credendum*] or else that the church council [Ancira, where the Canon *Episcopi* was thought to have been passed], whose precepts we are supposed to obey in everything, teaches something false and contrary to the Gospel. Neither assertion expresses healthy [*sanam*] faith on the part of anyone who makes it. . . . And to say that we should not be concerned about the example of Christ is to say that we should not be concerned about the Gospel. And we can

> see how much faith this reveals in anyone who says it, whoever he may be. For the proof of the possibility of this demonic transvection is founded on and inferred from the truth of the example of Christ. *Whence to deny that [demons carry witches] is to deny the Gospels.*[22]

Spina's final two sentences execute a bizarre logical about-face. This maneuver summarizes the importance of transvection in witchcraft theory. The Bible proved that witches were telling the truth, but, far more important, *witches' confessions guaranteed the truthfulness of the Bible.*

A Second Experiment

Apparent contradictions are also found in the work of Johannes Nider, a German Dominican whose writings about witches may be slightly older than Tostado's. Nider's *Formicarius,* or *Anthill,* was not printed until 1475, but he probably completed it in 1437 or early 1438, dying the latter year.[23] Subsequent editions of the *Formicarius* subtitled it "A dialogue using the example and nature of ants to exhort readers to lead a Christian life," but the book also contains a lot of information on the supposed activities of witches. Much as Tostado did, Nider defends the idea that witches exist yet recounts an experiment on a woman that should have discredited the idea of corporeal interaction with demons.

Nider claims that his own teacher knew a Dominican friar who once met an old woman in a country village. The woman was so crazy (*dementata*), says Nider, that she believed that she was carried about through the air (*transferri per aera*) at night in the company of other women and Diana, the pagan goddess. Nider gives no indication as to when the encounter took place—assuming that it actually happened—but, if the Dominican was a generation older than Nider, it could have happened by about 1380, the year Nider was born. When the friar "attempted to cast out this perfidious notion with salubrious words," says Nider, "the stubborn woman declared that she believed more in experience [*se plus credere experiencie*]" than in his words.[24] So the Dominican asked her to let him be present the next time she left on one of her night travels. The woman agreed, assuring him that he would observe her departure with his own eyes.[25] She even invited him to bring along suitable witnesses (*testibus ydoneis*). On the appointed date, the Dominican arrived at her dwelling with his trustworthy (*fidedignis*) witnesses.[26]

In Nider's anecdote, by contrast with Tostado's, there is no crowd of unruly and abusive neighbors but a skeptical representative of the church. This detail colors several aspects of the story. Although Nider's witch is also injured during her experiment, the injury is accidental and self-inflicted. Nider claims that the old woman placed a kneading tub on top of a stool, climbed into it, and sat down. Then, as Tostado's witch did, she rubbed an unguent on herself, spoke some words, and fell into a deep sleep. Because she jostled around from the excitement of her dream, calling out in a soft voice and clapping her hands, she accidentally rocked the tub off the stool, falling onto the floor. The fall injured her head so much that she woke up. We cannot know whether the story happened or happened as Nider tells it, but the woman's rickety perch means that no one had to beat or burn her to wake her up. She, not the Dominican, was responsible for her injury. Her stupor seems to have been considerably less deep than that of Tostado's witch. There was no uncertainty whether she was alive: she was far from immobile during her dream, even clapping her hands and "exulting," as Nider says, and woke up after less extensive injury than Tostado's witch suffered.

The presence of the Dominican friar and the transmission of the tale through Dominican channels account for resemblances between this experiment and actual witchcraft investigations, resemblances that were missing from Tostado's anecdote. Nider's protocols of witnessing have become more formal, and he insists on the appropriateness and trustworthiness of the witnesses chosen by the friar, presumably for their objectivity. Moreover, Nider leaves no doubt that the woman's activity was evil. His witch spoke, not "ritual" words as Tostado's did, but actual "words of witchcraft," *verba malefica.* This is particularly significant because the original meaning of *maleficium* is "evildoing" rather than "magic," so these words of witchcraft are not simply "magic words." He relates that the woman immediately fell asleep *thanks to the demon* (*opere demonis*) as soon as she had spoken the words.

Despite these danger signals in the story, we need not fear for the old woman's safety. Resemblances aside, this was not a witchcraft trial, and Nider's Dominican did not deal harshly with her. Although her activity is construed as evil, she is portrayed as deluded, not evil. The friar contented himself with taunting her, "rubbing in" his victory and making her acknowledge it. As she lay immobile on the floor, Nider tells us, the friar leaned over her and asked, "Where, pray tell, are you? Do you think you were with Diana? Everyone here is a witness that you never moved from your tub!" On the basis of this experience (*ex his gestis*), the Dominican convinced the woman to abandon her errors and return to being a proper Christian. It would have been customary for the Dominican to prescribe some form of penance, but Nider mentions no trial or punishment.

Nider was searching hesitantly for a demonic explanation of the same procedure that Tostado presented as natural. The resemblances between Nider's anecdote and a witchcraft investigation depend on two short references, one to *verba malefica* and one to a demon's influence. These references clash with the internal logic of the story and appear to be an editorial insertion by one of the clerics who transmitted the story (Nider, his teacher, or the original Dominican). The woman's words to the Dominican did not mention a demon; although her offer to demonstrate her practices to him looks dangerously naive, she would surely have tried to conceal her activities had she believed that she was conjuring demons. Given the Dominican's relatively gentle treatment of her, he also must not have attributed her experience to the willful invocation of a demon. It seems more probable that Nider or his teacher added the demonic details, particularly the *verba malefica.* The story would have been more coherent without them, and someone was nudging it in the direction of demonic interaction.

Given the story's benign ending, the stipulation "thanks to the demon" does not seem intended solely to condemn the woman. It also excludes the idea that her dream was caused solely by the natural properties of her ointment. Yet natural properties would seem to be precisely the point of the original story. Without the editorial insertions, Nider's story would carry the same message as Tostado's: natural substances can cause deep sleep and powerfully realistic dreams. That message has been blunted, if not eliminated. As a result, while Tostado describes the erroneous belief in transvection as a mistaken conclusion about unguents, Nider treats it as potentially heretical. Like the Canon *Episcopi,* and probably under its influence, Nider also links the dreaming woman to pre-Christian polytheism through references to Diana and Venus, whereas Tostado does not. Because Nider states that a demon is somehow responsible for the woman's hallucination, her beliefs become the battleground on which a representative of the church implicitly *does battle* with the devil, defeating his delusions by convincing the witch.

Nider does not seem to have known what he thought of this anecdote. He told it three times over a period of several years, changing his interpretation each time. Catherine Chène observes that, in his *Preceptorium divinae legis,* or *Handbook of Divine Law,* a manual for confessors probably written before the *Formicarius,* Nider cites the old woman as an *exemplum* to illustrate the Mosaic commandment against worshiping other gods. He tells the story in extremely compressed form, in two long sentences. He does not mention Diana, and there is no reference to a demon, to words of witchcraft, or to witnesses other than the friar. Nider related the tale once more in an undated collection of sermons, again in reference to the First Commandment. Here, Nider nudges the story in the direction of *maleficium* and something that looks like transvection. He refers to the old woman as one of "the *unholda,* who cause a lot of misfortune (*vil unglucks*)." *Unholda,* like *Hexe,* was a term used to designate "witches" in Nider's time; he says *unholda* "make the ointment [*salb*], and go on trips [*enweg farent*]," and he says that the woman fell from her perch "in the Devil's name." Although he refers to witches' travels and their ointment in the same breath, Nider still maintains that *this* old woman went nowhere. Similarly, Nider claims that *unholda* break the first commandment with their idolatry, an extremely serious accusation. Yet he says that their errors are laughable.[27]

Despite changeable details in three tellings, the basic plot of Nider's anecdote retains strong resemblances to that of Tostado's anecdote. Given the anecdotes' outlines, it is truly strange that neither author told his story expressly to support the skepticism that the Canon *Episcopi* advocated. In isolation, the anecdotes could hardly make any other point, for, in both cases, the observers' initial skepticism is vindicated. Contrary to the logic of his tale, each author refers to "witches" or "witchcraft" (*maleficae* or *maleficia*), and each elsewhere defends the reality and physicality of human interactions with demons.[28]

In the *Formicarius,* as distinct from the other two works, Nider discusses ✓ the dreaming witch while attempting to articulate a comprehensive theory of dreams. The entire second book of the work is dedicated to "truthful seeming good revelations [*de verisimilibus bonis revelacionibus*]," while the third book is about "false and illusory visions [*de falsis et illusorijs illusionibus*]."[29] In the chapter on the dreaming witch, Nider bases his analysis of dreams on the dialogues of Gregory the Great and the *Summa theologiae* of Aquinas.

Nider arrives at five potential causes of dreams: internal and corporeal; external and corporeal (conditions of the sleeper's immediate environment); external and astrological (influences of the heavenly bodies on the sleeper's body); external, spiritual, and evil ("such as when a demon moves the phantasy of someone to knowledge of something mysterious or to come [*alicuius occulti vel futuri*]"); and external and good ("coming forth in the phantasy and mind of man from God, but through the ministry of good angels"). In addition, says Nider, we learn from Aquinas that the cause can be internal and psychological (*animalis,* or relating to the soul) "in that those things on which a man's thinking and feeling dwelt while awake recur to his phantasy while sleeping." These causes, according to Nider, require different ways of interpreting dreams. Dreams should be interpreted only by either theologians or philosophers—*philosopher* being a term that includes physicians (*medici*) and astrologers (*astronomi*) as well as natural philosophers.[30]

Nider implies that interpreting dreams is a tricky business, and the sleeping witch's story appears aimed at discouraging laypeople from interpreting or trusting their dreams.[31] In this, he follows a long Christian tradition of distrust concerning dreams. Jacques Le Goff has observed that Christian dream interpretation differed from pagan practice, on which it was partly based, by placing more value on the source of a dream—God, Satan, or the human body—than on its structure and content. According to Le Goff, early Christianity "showed first an interest in dreams, then anxiety about them, and finally, uncertainty." This uncertainty and distrust lasted into the early Middle Ages, as Le Goff shows. But it did not end or significantly attenuate in the twelfth century, as the historian implies.[32]

Instead, attention began to focus on the notion of corporeality as a potential index or guarantee of distinctions between dreams and reality. The body, angels, and demons were now investigated both as *causes* of dreams and as entities that might conceivably interact with one another *outside* dreams. This involved a shift or expansion of attention: the question was no longer only, as in antiquity and the early Middle Ages, whether one should take dreams as omens. What Le Goff calls *the Christian distrust of dreams* had expanded to include the very state of dreaming and, by implication, that of wakefulness. It may be that, before interacting with observers, Nider's or Tostado's witches believed that their experiences took place in some alternate reality. For clerical observers, the women posed the problem whether it was at least possible to distinguish *someone else's* dreaming from wakefulness.[33] While the affirmative answer seems to have satisfied the original observers, Nider and others found it worrisome.

One cannot help but wonder whether such experiments were common. In the light of concern over the implications of the Canon *Episcopi,* we might suspect that they were. However, given their resemblances, it is possible (although unlikely) that both our anecdotes could derive from a single event. Nider and Tostado were both present at the Council of Basel, which met in that city (1431–37) before transferring to other locales. Several early witchcraft theorists were present at this council, which has been called "an important site for the exchange of ideas" about witchcraft.[34] Many early witch trials took place in the dioceses in and around this area of Switzerland.[35] Perhaps a story with this basic structure was told by one of the learned clerics who met in Basel for the council. Repetition and embellishment of the story would have created two variants over several years, particularly if one or both of our authors heard the story at second- or thirdhand. In that case, their variations would derive less from actual fact than from the differing attitudes of successive storytellers. Certainly, other aspects of witchcraft theory

Mountains
Isolation

developed through the repetition and variation of stories as well as doctrines.

Clearly, we must be wary about advancing such possibilities: interpretation of these stories cannot serve as reliable evidence of how witchcraft theories actually evolved. I have implied that Tostado's anecdote antedated Nider's only because it does not mention clerical witnesses or demons. The history of stories is not bound to follow my logic, but these early stories of dreaming witches at least reveal that the Canon *Episcopi* had become intensely problematic. Skepticism about the bodily reality of certain experiences no longer expressed an easy confidence that Christianity was superior to paganism. Skepticism had broken its bounds and menaced Christian doctrines of the spirit world. Witchcraft theory and its tales of experimentation with witches evolved to address this uneasiness.

About-Face?

There are later stories of experiments with witches. By far the most suggestive was recounted almost a century after Nider by Bartolomeo Spina, in the *Quaestio de strigibus,* or *Inquiry into Witches* (1523). Like Nider and Tostado, Spina asserted that witchcraft was real yet recounted an experiment performed on a witch that seemed to disprove his contentions. Spina's anecdote is far more disturbing than the earlier ones, however. He unambiguously rejected the possibility that witchcraft was *ever* reducible to delusions or empty dreams. Whereas Tostado and Nider had defended witchcraft intermittently and almost in parentheses, as it were, Spina composed a formal treatise solely about the reality of witchcraft. He was an inquisitor as well as a Scholastic philosopher and theologian, so he collected all the arguments of real or imagined skeptical opponents and then refuted them systematically.

As his predecessors had done, Spina recounted an experiment that appears to demonstrate that transvection is a mere illusion. Anyone reading only this segment of Spina's treatise would mistake him for a staunch opponent of witchcraft theory:

> In the fifth place, certain experiments [*experientiis*] have demonstrated the falsity of the idea that witches are carried by the Devil to the Sabbat [*ludum*] or to other distant places, as a result of having used some unguent. . . . And let us begin by recalling what happened to the illustrious Prince N., in times recent enough to be remembered by many. This prince heard that a certain witch, who confessed that she had been carried many times to the Sabbat [*cursum*], was being held in the prison of a

> certain friar inquisitor. The prince conceived a desire to find out through experience [*experiri*] whether such things were true, or simply dreams, and, summoning the reverend inquisitor, he finally convinced him to permit the woman to be brought before the two of them and a large number of noble witnesses. They agreed to make her anoint herself with the unguent that she normally used so that they might see whether she would truly be carried through the air to the Sabbat [*cursum*] by a devil and whether the devil would present himself visibly or invisibly [*a diabolo visibiliter vel invisibiliter apparente*].

Spina recounts that, after the accused witch anointed herself, nothing at all happened: "She remained immobile; nor was anything unusual able to happen to her at any time."[36]

This is a systematic experiment worthy of the name, and it has many odious features. The woman herself appears to have had no part in organizing the demonstration. Instead, the initiative supposedly came from an inquisitive petty despot, and the woman was forced into a performance before a large audience. The ideological positions on transvection had shifted. Not the woman but the inquisitor maintained that witches are carried by demons. The skeptical role of Nider's ecclesiastic passed to Spina's worldly Prince N. As Spina portrays him, the prince did not begin by categorically denying the reality of the Sabbat. Instead, he reserved judgment, intending to rely on empirical evidence. According to Spina, Prince N. and the inquisitor arranged the experiment to test two propositions: (1) either witches are carried to Sabbats by devils, or they are not; (2) if witches are carried by devils, then the devils act either visibly or invisibly.

We cannot know whether the woman had ever used an unguent or thought that she traveled before confessing under torture to demonic transvection. But did she even exist? She is a mere cipher in Spina's calculations, "a certain witch." For that matter, the prince and the inquisitor are also ciphers. The initial *N* is probably not a clue to the "illustrious prince's" actual name: it looks like the standard abbreviation for *nomen* (name), used for confession templates, such as those in part 3 of the *Malleus maleficarum*. Its normal meaning is "insert name here." We do not even hear where this experiment supposedly happened or when: just how old does one have to be to remember it? Except for the story's inconclusive outcome, this featurelessness could make us suspect that Spina simply invented the story.

If Spina did invent this story, he certainly chose a roundabout way of proving the reality of transvection. He relates that "nothing unusual" happened during the experiment and that the witch simply had a sound nap. So he is initially forced to conclude that "it is clearly false that witches are carried to the Sabbat when they so desire [*pro voto*]."[37] He then continues arguing as if he were an opponent of witch-hunting. He observes that physicians have used purely natural ingredients to create unguents that, applied to the skin, can cause chronic insomniacs to fall into a profound slumber. Thus, he argues, there is no need to search for supernatural, unnatural, or demonic causes for the transvection or flying of witches. Dreams induced by hallucinogens seem to be the simplest explanation of transvection and the Sabbat.

It might seem that Spina has painted himself into a corner by taking his opponents' arguments so seriously. But it would be a mistake to presume that he will admit defeat. Once he has assessed the experiment, he devotes the next eighty pages to rebutting all arguments against the reality of witchcraft. Spina's long rebuttal displays every kind of reasoning and proof available to witchcraft theorists.

One argument seems particularly lame to modern eyes. Spina says that Prince N.'s experiment may have failed because of demonic malice. The devil may have sabotaged it, hoping that Prince N. would decide that witchcraft was imaginary, ignore the warnings of inquisitors, and cease cooperating in the persecution of witches. Here, Spina seems to hint that Prince N. commissioned the experiment because he needed an excuse to stop cooperating with the inquisitor rather than from a more objective curiosity. As a secular ruler, Prince N. was expected to execute witches remanded to him by the inquisition since the church maintained the pious fiction that execution was a decision to be made by the secular authorities. Perhaps Prince N. had no enthusiasm for making his judicial machinery punish crimes that seemed imaginary to him. Such a possibility is not far from Spina's mind. "In fact," he declares, "by not believing in such things, nobles and other laymen never cease to detract from the honor due to inquisitors, accusing them of directing their investigations at little old ladies and fools [*anicularum vel fatuorum*]."[38]

Contrary to what we might expect, Spina asserts that God also had reason to sabotage the experiment:

> On the part of divine justice, whose ministers inquisitors are, God justly prevented the woman from being carried off, for the purpose of glorifying justice itself. Thanks to divine justice, witches who fall under the jurisdiction of inquisitors no longer enjoy the assistance of the Devil. Nor indeed during the whole time that they remain under the jurisdiction [*actuali iudicio*] of the inquisitor are they able to harm anyone, or escape from prison, or be freed in any other way with the Devil's help, or be carried off anywhere else. Indeed, God caused good to result indirectly from this evil.[39]

Thus, although God's purposes are completely opposed to those of the Devil, they complement them exactly: neither had a good reason for allowing the witch to be carried off by her demon. God even agreed with the Devil that the unnamed inquisitor should be humiliated for cooperating with the prince's experiment. The inquisitor was ridiculed by the curious prince and his noble witnesses for abusing the powers of his office and persecuting foolish, harmless women (*fatuas mulieres*).[40] Although Spina condemns this conclusion, he implies that God allowed it to prevail in order to punish the inquisitor. Spina explains that right-thinking people, who did not share the prince's and the nobles' curiosity or their desire for empirical proof, condemned the inquisitor for putting his fear of human opinion before the fear of God.

God had another, more positive reason for causing the experiment to fail, according to Spina. Because the witch was not carried off by her demon on that occasion, the curious nobles, wrongly concluding that such things never happen, were prevented from testing the ointment on themselves. Its failure left them no hope of experiencing with their own bodies what harmful curiosity had made them investigate through the bodies of others (*ut haec experirentur in corpore suo, quae noxia curiositate cognoscere quaerebant in alieno*).[41]

This sentence has fascinating implications. Transvection would seem to be irresistible: Spina implies that, if the witch had flown off, everyone would have rushed to test her ointment on themselves. Spina's own curiosity and his own desire to believe that transportation by demons is a reality seem to shine through here. Spina's interest in the psychology of Prince N.'s witnesses reveals that issues of corporeality, sensory experience, and experimentation engage his attention more than questions of morality and *maleficium*. His comment about the courtiers' curiosity implicitly defines the witch as a proxy, someone who attempts (or can be made to attempt) experiments that one both desires and fears to perform. This idea of proxies was powerfully attractive to Spina.

Some lucky people did not need witches as proxies. There is a whole genre of stories about curiosity and experimentation with ointments featuring ordinary and innocent people. These nonwitches chanced to observe the rituals of witches, impulsively imitated them, and were instantaneously transvected. The earliest of these stories comes from Apuleius's *Metamorphoses,* or *Golden Ass,* which theorists usually present as if it were scientific testimony rather than a kind of novel.[42] Spina also tells of a girl in his own time who was supposedly transvected from Bergamo to Venice. Waking in the middle of the night, and observing her mother fly out the window, she tried her mother's witch ointment without pausing for a second thought.[43]

According to witchcraft theorists, these reckless experimenters provide independent corroboration that transvection is real. They are emphatically not witches and have no desire to perform harmful magic, but their curiosity is powerful. As "curious innocents," they rub the ointment on themselves without realizing the danger of harming or even damning themselves. They show no awareness of being carried by demons and assume that they fly thanks to some power hidden in the ointment. The theorists who tell these tales always warn the reader not to make the same mistake: only demons can cause humans to fly.

Curiosity is not the only motive that inquisitors attribute to transvected nonwitches. Spina's teacher Mazzolini tells of a man whom sexual obsession led to experience transvection and the Sabbat. Paradoxically, the experience redeemed him, making him come to his senses and abandon all his sins:

> Add to this a surprising incident that a certain man of Piacenza often told about *his own experience.* This man, if perchance he has not died recently, is now a Benedictine monk named Gerolamo, in the Congregation of Saint Justine. Before becoming a monk, he fell in love with a girl and possessed her, thanks to the help of a witch-sorceress [*strigimaga*]. And he promised the witch that he would attend the Sabbat. The witch took the young man and the young woman to the Sabbat, *with the Devil's help,* by following this ritual: uncovering his wrist, Gerolamo anointed it by using the witch unguent to trace certain characters, according to the instructions of the witch, who did the same. And the young woman, who was present and had just been possessed sexually by Gerolamo, did the same as well. And suddenly all three of them *were taken up into the air,* passing out through the chimney. All three *were carried* to the great walnut tree of Benevento, *on the back, as it seemed, of a neighing horse, and at such great speed that the air gave off a sharp whistle as they cut through it.* At the walnut tree were many thousands of men and women who were dancing in the uncertain light.[44]

When the Sabbat was over, Gerolamo was taken back home by way of Venice. He observed many rivers and towns on both parts of his journey, places that he had never seen before, but he recognized all of them as soon as he saw them, particularly Venice.

According to Mazzolini, Gerolamo "returned home and satisfied his passion on the girl once more. But then, thanks to God's mercy and his own natural honesty of mind, he was overcome with disgust at so much impiety. So he went to the bishop, or to his vicar, confessed all that he had done, and was solemnly whipped in the church, behind closed doors. Thanks to divine mercy, he became a monk and lived righteously afterward, and he may still be alive."[45]

Obsession with crime cannot be the reason for telling this remarkable story because there is no mention of the witch being pursued, much less caught and tried. And Gerolamo, who is both a fornicator and a near witch, gets off comparatively easy, for he is never even publicly humiliated. As the italicized passages reveal, the only significant motivation for recording this story is its demonstration that demonic transvection is possible and can be experienced by anyone willing to take the risks. The Sabbat itself is dismissed in a single sentence; it functions simply as a proof that Gerolamo was carried through the air by a demon. More strangely still, Gerolamo recognizes Venice and other places and landmarks immediately, even though he has never seen them before. To modern ways of thinking, this feature is a sure sign that Gerolamo was dreaming, but Mazzolini takes it as confirmation that the transvection was both wondrous and real. He tantalizes his readers (or intends to) with the possibility that Gerolamo may still be alive and able to confirm the truthfulness of this narrative. He further insists: "Anyone who wants to be absolutely certain about this matter must question [*interroget*] Friar Andrea of Genoa, a man eminent both for his religious life and for his learning, who is now enrolled in our order of Blessed Dominic. The witnesses I bring forth are alive [*Testes vivos exhibeo*]."[46]

At other times, stories of curious experimentation recount failure on a small or grand scale. Spina admits that "it has been proved by other experiences [or experiments: *experientiis*] that, in fact, many people who had thoroughly anointed themselves" with unguents taken from true witches "neither were transported by the demon nor fell asleep." He tells of two men who saw two old women (*vetulae*) anoint themselves and take flight out the window. Like the Bergamask girl, the men decided to try the unguent on themselves. But, even though they applied it several times (*pluries*), nothing ever happened: "They neither left that place nor yet fell asleep."[47]

A far greater disaster befell a curious magistrate. According to Bernardo Rategno da Como's *De strigiis,* or *On Witches,* written about 1505 or 1510,

> At Mendrisio, a city in the territory of Como, a wondrous incident happened almost fifty years ago [i.e., about 1460], which is still well-known both at Como and at Mendrisio; at Mendrisio a number of people are still living who remember what happened. An inquisitor, Bartolomeo da Omate, the *podestà* Lorenzo da Concorezzo, and the notary Giovanni da Fossato were prosecuting the witches [*strigias*]. One day, the *podestà,*

> overcome by curiosity and wanting to know *by experience* whether witches journeyed to the Sabbat truly and in the body [*quadam curiositate ductus, volens experiri an vere et corporaliter illae strigiae irent ad ludum*], came to an agreement with a witch that she would take [*conduceret*] him to see such a Sabbat. He left late one Thursday night with his notary and another citizen and came to a certain place outside the city, just as that witch had described it [*praedixerat*]. And when the three men approached closer, they saw a large number of people gathered around an individual (who was the Devil in human form) sitting there in the manner of a great lord. But suddenly, on orders from the Devil, all the people gathered there began beating that *podestà* and his two companions with sticks, so badly that all three of them, *podestà,* notary, and the other one, died of their injuries within fifteen days. And God permitted it in order to punish them for their curiosity. Who then will say that this happened in the imagination or in dreams [*in phantasia aut in somniis*]?[48]

We should not be misled by the implication that the curious officials walked or rode ordinary horses to this Sabbat or that the witch did not accompany them after all. We are told that their purpose was to test *by experience* the idea that witches attended the Sabbat bodily. Presumably, seeing the demons "in person" would have been enough to convince these men that others had reached the Sabbat via demonic transvection. The tale of the battered officials reveals the witchcraft theorists' metaphysical voyeurism in action, completely without proxies, flagrante delicto. Despite its ostensibly unhappy ending, it recounts a theorist's dream come true.

Mazzolini's version differs from this one somewhat: he specifies that the witch who directed the men to the Sabbat was their prisoner; and he adds a colorful, realistic detail: the men had just enough strength left to drag themselves home after their beating. But he agrees that they died within fifteen days and that the beating took place on orders from the Devil, although with God's permission. Both Rategno and Mazzolini tell the anecdote self-consciously and with some defensiveness. Mazzolini prefaces his account by wishing that all skeptics about the reality of the Sabbat could have the same experience as these curious experimenters.[49] In context, it is hard to know which of Mazzolini's impulses was stronger: the desire that such people should be punished for acting on their curiosity or the wish that all such curiosity could be satisfied.

These stories have not hitherto been discussed as the supposed record of experiments. Yet that was their purpose. In line with the principle enunciated by Kramer, they are *experta testimonia,* testimonies of lived experience. Someone has duplicated witches' experience of physically interacting with demons, but without concluding a demonic pact, performing *maleficia,* or incurring damnation. We need not depend on the confessions of heretical criminals—who by definition are untrustworthy—or the application of torture to know that demons are real. Rategno's story of the curious magistrate even has the structure of a primitive laboratory report: do as I say, says the witch, and your results will duplicate mine, and so they do. Like modern lab reports, such stories did not serve solely to convince anonymous or hypothetical readers; whoever repeated the expert testimony had to construct or organize his convictions as well.

Convictions were often hard to acquire, particularly if one did not dare attempt the experiment. Mazzolini vividly betrays his need to be convinced when he describes how inquisitors (himself included?) interview children to learn details of the Sabbat. Strangely, the interviews produce no information about transvection. Dancing must "stand in" for transvection, and most of the dancing seems to be taking place among humans: devils are merely the dance masters:

> On this matter, so that these same diabolical games and spectacles will not be taken for mere dreams, I will tell you something else. Often, thanks to the teaching and exhortation of inquisitors, children of twelve or ten or eight years see the error of their ways. *And the inquisitors command them, as a miraculous proof of such an important event, to dance as they do at the Sabbat.* These children dance in such a way that no expert could deny that they have been taught according to some art that is supernatural and transcends the human. In fact, these dances are completely unlike human dances: the woman is held behind the back of the man, and they dance not by stepping forward but by moving backward. At the end of the dance, when they have to reverence the devil who presides over the Sabbat, they turn their backs to him and bow their heads not forward but backward; and they do not bend their legs backward but rather forward, raising themselves into the air. These children perform all this with such grace and elegance [*venustate*] that it seems impossible that they should have learned it so quickly and at such a young age. . . . I do so wish that one of our reverend cardinals would take it on himself to ship ten of these boys and girls to Rome (which would be quite easy) so as to offer a great spectacle to the city and remove the veil of blindness, which is somewhat widespread, from the eyes of the incredulous.[50]

The dance is so ridiculous that it can misdirect our attention since every move is an obvious reversal of conventional dancing. Yet Mazzolini does not interpret the dance's features as irreverence to Christianity or societal norms. His tone expresses self-hypnotic wonder, not polemical anger or righteous outrage. He reads every element as proof that the children can have been taught only by devils. Because children are young and inexperienced, any child who can perform such feats must be under supernatural influence. Mazzolini's reliance on *children's* dances betrays his desperation, for he really needs proof of *adults'* physical interaction with demons. In short, as the French say, Mazzolini is tickling himself to make himself laugh, with no more success than usually crowns that exercise. One cannot help wondering whether he tried to elicit stories of flying from these children: if so, his attempts must have failed.

No modern reader needs to be reminded of the parallels between these texts from the 1520s and the hysteria over satanic ritual child abuse during the 1980s and 1990s. Mazzolini's pupil Bartolomeo Spina makes a startlingly twentieth-century claim about the value of children to interrogators. Many boys and girls, "and that sort of innocent and simple people," corroborate the testimony of convicted witches, "and in their case it would easily be noticeable if they were lying or pretending [*si fingerent mendacium*]; for this reason the testimony of children is considered absolutely reliable [*certissimum dicitur*]."[51]

Mazzolini's dancing children are the closest thing in all of witchcraft literature to an experiment that works. Although the proof is pathetic, there is at least an element of continuity between what the children do under the inquisitor's gaze and what they supposedly did at the Sabbat. Mazzolini was arguing that the devils have left a *trace*. But, in order to discover that trace, Mazzolini had to look elsewhere than to actual witches. Experiments with witches, like that of Prince N., never worked outside daydreams. They left no discernible trace of demonic presence. Not until witch's teats and witch's marks or devil's marks (*stigma Diaboli*) were regularly sought on defendants' bodies could experiments on witches claim to work. These corporeal symptoms had to be interpreted as *unnatural* because they were insensitive to pain, colder than the surrounding flesh, or in suspicious locations. As with the children's dances, *unnaturalness* had to be construed as something *supernatural* and hence *demonic*. And, like the children's dances, the *stigma* was only conjectural proof of *past* corporeal contact with demons.[52] True voyeurism—real firsthand watching—was impossible.

It Ain't Necessarily Not So

Perhaps Tostado and Nider were not systematic enough to realize that the experiments that they described undercut the reality of witchcraft, but Spina was a consummately systematic writer. Why, then, did he describe the experiment of Prince N., which seems to refute everything that he wants to prove? If, as it seems, he invented the story, could he not have done better? Why not invent something more like the curious magistrate of Mendrisio? The probable answer is not obvious. Spina wanted to prevent other curious people, whether inquisitors or laymen, from performing such experiments because he knew that they were doomed to failure.[53]

Spina has a variety of stratagems for contesting the validity of experiments with witches. We have seen his grandiose claim that God and Satan cooperate to thwart such harmful curiosity. At the other extreme, he can claim that experiments failed because witches or their curious observers were using the wrong ointment. Spina declares that the best medical authorities agree that *true* witches' ointment contains nothing that could cause sleep through natural means. He does not deny that physicians can use natural substances to induce sleep, but he stipulates that such ointments always or nearly always work. Identical causes produce identical effects on comparable subjects, he says, arguing as the good Aristotelian that he is not. By contrast, the hallmark of the true witches' ointment is its unpredictability: it works only if the Devil wants it to work. Spina was neither joking nor, in terms of his own logic, stumbling when he declared that "it has been proved by other experiences [*experientiis*] that, in fact, many people who had thoroughly anointed themselves" with unguents taken from true witches "neither were transported by the demon nor fell asleep."[54]

However, it is simply not true that nothing diabolical is happening to witches: in fact, the Devil's apparent absence is the strongest possible clue to his presence:

> From all these things it is clear that, even if some people fall asleep after using the genuine, abominable [*execrabilem*] ointment, this happens for no other reason than the Devil's ill will [*malitia*], so that he can sometimes deceive those who watch or hear about such things. Thereby [because they have seen nothing happen] the observers will believe that no one is ever taken to the Sabbat [*ludum*], even when they anoint themselves correctly, and they will think that everyone who claims to go there is deluded. Because, just as the Devil can transport such people through the air, so, thanks to the freedom of his will, he can cause them to fall into a very deep slumber, either immediately or within a short time.[55]

The proof that demonic forces are at work is precisely the unreliability of the experiment, which is construed as *unnaturalness*. Because the true witches' ointment has no natural, inherent powers, the Devil can protect his interests by choosing freely whether to make it work. Spina's logic is not irrational, therefore; it simply can never be allowed to demonstrate the absence or nonexistence of demons. Spina knows that, if life were as simple and straightforward as experiments with witches seem to indicate, it would have no room for demons.

What, then, are we to do? It would seem that we have a simple choice between believing our eyes and believing Spina's logical but rickety explanations. Spina knows that this choice would be intolerable: it would cause either perplexity or skepticism, and his whole effort would therefore be fruitless. There is a solution, however. We can accept the testimony of witches themselves. We can choose to believe their version of what happened—as presented by the witchcraft theorist—and thus to disbelieve our own senses: "If, therefore, certain persons affirm that they were carried off, even though they appear to lie there immobile or seem to sleep a true bodily sleep [*corpore dormientes*], we must not conclude that they themselves were truly sleeping there or that their bodies were even there. Rather, if they swear that they were bodily carried off, we must believe [*putandum est*] that the Devil has taken on their likeness and lain there in their stead."[56] Clearly, Spina is opposing the whole prior tradition of experiments with witches. He is willfully confusing voluntary drug users, like the witches of Nider and Tostado, with the poor souls who make ventriloquized confessions under torture.

If seeing is believing for most people, it often appears that believing is seeing for the very religious. But, in Spina's case, as with all witchcraft theorists, the problem is more complicated. Although he asserts it, Spina does not believe the Devil has disguised himself as the witch and sent her off to the Sabbat. He *refuses* to believe that such a thing is *not* happening or cannot happen. In a word, he is exercising resistance to skepticism: he is claiming that "you cannot prove that the Devil does not do this." Even he would never put his case quite that baldly, for to do so would be to admit just how implausible it is. But he implies the admission by the premises of Prince N.'s experiment: (1*a*) either witches are carried to Sabbats by devils, (1*b*) or they are not; (2) if witches are carried by devils, then the devils act either (*a*) *visibly* or (*b*) *invisibly*. Alternative 2*b* ensures that alternative 1*b* can never be proved, and, in this, Spina's logic is paradigmatic. The whole mythology of witchcraft can be reduced to the proposition that invisibility or imperceptibility is never the same as unreality.

Spina's program for resisting skepticism thus has two parts. On the one hand, we must disregard the evidence of our senses. Equally important, we must decide in advance to believe all those who swear in court that they have been carried away by demons. Above all, we must avoid experiments like the one conducted by Prince N. As far as proving the interaction of humans and demons is concerned, judicial evidence is more reliable than empirical testing or evidence gathering.

This substitution of judicial evidence for experimentation is what permitted the persecution of witches to take place. And it was a substitution: in the evolution of experiment stories from Tostado and Nider to Spina, we can observe that substitution taking place. Nor was the switch made ingenuously: we cannot claim that Kramer or Spina did not know the difference or that the concept of empirical evidence was foreign to them. Both of them elevated the witch to a position of supreme authority, as an expert witness reporting on lived experience. We are required to take her word—as recorded by Kramer or Spina—for what demons did to her body.

There were other, supplementary guarantees. Spina claims that witches have confessed, "not only judicially, but also sacramentally [*sacramentaliter*], under the care of the lord inquisitors, who desire their conversion and salvation."[57] Forget for a moment the cruel hypocrisy of that last clause. Because an inquisitor was entrusted with purifying the faith, a witch's confession was never, at least in Catholic courts, merely legal. It was sacramental because the witch had to receive absolution or spiritual cleansing from the church's representatives—the inquisitors—or else be condemned to hell. The stakes were not simply civil; they were eternal. The church always disclaimed responsibility for putting convicted witches to death: that was up to the civil authorities. But, while death affected the body only, damnation was final, and witchcraft theorists construed the threat of damnation as the ultimate guarantee that the expert testimony of witches was reliable.

Along with other theorists early and late, Spina invokes this terrible solemnity, and the psychic desolation that it produced in witchcraft defendants, as proof that they had no reason to invent their confessions: "Nor can those who have lost all hope of saving their own lives, as happens in the case of relapsed heretics, be suspected of divulging such things out of a fear of incurring the pain of death if they do not confess. . . . [I]ndeed, often when such persons know they are going to lose their lives, they show that they know it, so that anyone can judge that it is not out of a fear of imminent punishment that they confess."[58]

To see the significance of this move, lay aside for the moment the overwhelming evidence—including what Spina says here—that most of what witches confessed about their interactions with demons was suggested by the leading questions of their interrogators and shaped through the strategic use of torture. Instead, look at the ways in which Spina enhances the value of witches' testimony about their supposed lived experience. In one passage, he compares it favorably with the experiences of saints. While celebrating mass in Milan, says Spina, Saint Ambrose (d. 397) fell asleep with his head on the altar. The congregation spent three hours waiting impatiently for him to come to his senses and deliver the benediction so that they could leave. When Ambrose awoke, he claimed that he had spent those hours hundreds of miles away, in Tours, France, conducting the funeral of Saint Martin:[59] "And it is said that, as testimony of such a wondrous thing, he left in Tours the glove [*chirothecam*] that, as a bishop, he wore when officiating. Both Ambrose's own affirmation and that concrete sign [*signo*] show that he was most truly there among the people of Tours, in his own real body [*verissime corporaliterque*], and that during that time an angel took his place at the altar in Milan, after putting on a body similar to Ambrose's."[60]

The same thing happened to Saint Clement (d. 101). While celebrating mass in Rome, he also seemed to fall asleep for three hours. When he returned, he told the congregation that Saint Peter had appeared and commanded him to go straight to Pisa and consecrate a church being dedicated to Peter: "And to demonstrate this beyond a doubt, he left three drops of his own blood on a marble stone in that church, which to this very day are held in the highest veneration in the cathedral of that town. From which it is clear that an angel in the shape of Saint Clement was in Rome during the time that the saint himself was in Pisa, having been carried there and back by another angel."[61] The glove and the drops of blood are proof positive that miraculous transvection took place. As Mark Twain said, "Well, there's the tree."

But, for transvection to occur, each traveling saint's body had to be replaced in church by an illusory double, formed by yet another angel. If a miracle is necessary to make another miracle possible, so be it: two miracles are better than none. Otherwise, we would have to conclude that the two saints dozed off while celebrating Christianity's holiest ritual. Since this cannot be, Spina argues, transvection and impersonation by demons obviously happen in an identical way when experiments with witches appear to fail: "It would have been wrong, therefore, to believe either of these men if he had said that he was asleep during that time. By the same token, therefore, witches must be believed when they say that they have been to the Sabbat in the body [*corporaliter*]. And, if in the meantime we see them sleeping somewhere else, we should believe that it was actually the devil in their shape or figure that we saw."[62] Suddenly, after all his emphasis on the value of expert testimony about lived experience, Spina changes his mind. Discount all testimony if—and only if—it denies the corporeal intervention of demons. Even saints must not be believed unless they say what we want to hear.

Spina is shockingly explicit about the value that he sees in witches' confessions. More openly than we could have imagined, he admits that Christian faith is not a strong-enough guarantee that the spirit world exists: "[Through witchcraft,] we come to know three things by familiar experience, three things that we formerly knew only by faith [*tria cognoscimus familiari experientia, quae sola fide prius cognoscebamus*]—although these things are still questioned by those who wish to measure everything according to their own intellect. First, we learn that in our own regions certain intellectual creatures can be observed, whom we call demons, and who are incomparably superior to all humans in power and knowledge."[63] Unlike Luther, whom his teacher Mazzolini was once delegated to refute, Spina's motto is not *sola fide* or "faith alone."[64] In Spina's mouth, *sola fide* is an admission that true conviction is lacking.

Only experience—and remember that *experience* and *experiment* are derived from the same Latin word—is an adequate guarantee that demons exist. This admission is so baldly stated that one wonders how Spina could bear to make it. Yet the logic of his argumentation bears out the centrality of such thinking to his witchcraft theory. In fact, although his arguments look unscientific and even antiscientific to modern eyes, Spina presents himself as an empiricist, someone whose motto is "experience above all!"

> All these truths are proved believable in exactly the way inquisitors preach them, and the reason for this is experience herself, who is called the teacher of all things [*rerum magistra*]. And we argue thus: that which is proved by a multiplicity of experience cannot be denied. Indeed, nothing is more certain than what is known through the senses, that is, the kind of knowledge that comes from experience. And those things that are told by witches are also proved in many other places by the experiences of persons who are not witches, as far as the substance of the deeds is concerned. Regarding bodily transportation, . . . let me now simply bring forth those things that have been recounted in our time by persons who had certain knowledge of them.[65]

Before taking Spina's word that he is merely using the experience of nonwitches to corroborate that witches are transported by demons, remember that he is already using witches' confessions about transvection to prove that demons are real. The common denominator is, as Spina indicates explicitly, that *experience proves that demons are real, so we need not believe in spiritual realities on faith alone.*

Clearly, the experience that Spina champions is not direct experience. For Spina, *experience* is another word for faith, not for empirical thinking. He doubts that he or his readers will ever see or interact with demons, so he proclaims that one's own experience is never to be trusted. The curious should beware of experimenting with witches because he has demonstrated why God and demons doom experiments to fail. Experience must be left to the experts, to people whom one can trust: saints, doctors of the church, and witches.

Spina can justify referring to an act of faith as empirical thinking because his goal is to convince readers that their own experience is always anomalous, always the exception that proves the rule: "Whatever is asserted by a numberless multitude of persons of both sexes, and whatever is uniformly spoken of, as if with one mouth [*quasi uno ore*], by all people in every place and in various times, is always upheld and must be believed beyond any doubt."[66] Witches are only one category of *testes fide digni* or trustworthy witnesses to the fact that demons and humans interact physically. The same testimony is offered by the neighbors who accuse them, by children (who are too young and innocent to dissemble), by a few successful experimenters, by the best philosophers, and by theologians, popes, and inquisitors (who by definition cannot err in this matter). If your own experiences contradict this consensus, dear reader, you are deluded.

Spina admits that witchcraft reinforces the credibility of Christianity by demonstrating that demons are real. But it does so in a second way as well, by explaining the origins of everyday evil: "Second, because the work of witchcraft is evil, we know demons to be evil. We can almost feel with our hands [*sensim veluti palpamus*] how demons seduce men and women into innumerable crimes, deceptions, and frauds."[67] It is noteworthy that Spina implies that the evil deeds of witches constitute palpable proof, not of their own evil character, but of demons' power over them.

Elsewhere, Spina states that witches' *maleficia* corroborate the proofs of demonic contact furnished by transvection and the Sabbat. Most of witches' crimes are committed during the Sabbat, he says: "Thus, since it must be concluded from the preceding that these people do not commit their crimes through illusion but in reality [*non illusorie, sed vere*], it must be true that they do not travel or get transported to the Sabbat in their dreams, but truly and in reality, and consequently that eyewitness testimony against them must be believed."[68] If the crimes are real, then the Sabbat, and the physical contact with demons that it requires, must be real.

The alternative to considering accusations of *maleficia* as proof, says Spina, is simply unthinkable:

> It should also be understood that, if we do not believe witnesses against other people because we think that they are deluded, there would be no

> reason for believing those who accuse themselves or make a proper juridical confession that such things happened to them because it would be equally proper to think that they were also deluded and that we should take pity on them and not carry out sentences against them if they should say that they never did such and such a thing except at the Sabbat, or that they never committed such things willingly [*ex corde*], or that they never held a wrong opinion about the faith. Which is something that no sane person would permit, and it runs counter to the practice of all inquisitors.[69]

Caution and skepticism must stop somewhere, Spina says. If we could not accept testimony as proof of reality, human society would be impossible.

At one point, Spina drops all pretense and admits that he is recommending faith rather than empirical thinking:

> If, then, faith [*fides*] were not bestowed on such a large multitude of witnesses to such things, and if such things were treated as if they had not been seen, there would be no point in believing anyone who described things that the listener did not know about *from his own experience.* And thus the benefit of human interaction would cease, nor would there ever be an end to disagreement. That there is such a great multitude of people confessing that such things take place in the body [*corporaliter*] is already ascertained *for the benefit of the whole world* by the multitude of people who fall under the jurisdiction of inquisitors in every region of Christendom. For, in the diocese of Como alone, often in the course of a single year, over a thousand such people are subjected to inquisition and trial by the current inquisitor and his deputies (who always number eight or ten or more), and almost every year more than a hundred of these people are burned.[70]

Faith is not the evidence of things not seen. No, faith is *earned* by the evidence that certain things *have* been seen—and touched. That's what evidence *is.* Witnesses prove guilt, and confessions of guilt prove that things happen really and truly, not in someone's imagination.

The final proof of reality is that people die for their guilt. That a hundred people a year, or even one, might have been burned at Como is a terrible thought, but whether these deaths actually happened is irrelevant for discovering how Spina thought. He asserts that death is, not only the consequence of guilt, but also its proof or confirmation. This circular argument appealed to every defender of witch-hunting.

There can be no doubt that Spina was more concerned with vindicating the reality of interactions between people and demons than with demonstrating that witches deserve to die because they are evil. His rage at witches helped make possible his belief that they had real, nonimaginary experiences with demons. Only by constantly stimulating his own moral indignation with proofs that witches were guilty of *maleficia* did he maintain his faith in the reality of the demons who did the real work of *maleficia*. Put another way, Spina did not fear that witches have real contact with demons; he *hoped* that they did. He did not wish to eliminate such activity; he wanted to find as much of it as possible. He was not interested in social control as much as in *thought* control, and that meant *self*-control.

The hoary question why, about 1400, significant numbers of learned Christians suddenly began looking for witches depends on a more fundamental question that has not been asked until now. Why did large numbers of educated men like Tostado and Nider suddenly begin fearing that the reality of human interaction with demons was not self-evident? Bartolomeo Spina's work of the 1520s is crucial to answering this question, for he was not an unusual witchcraft theorist; he was simply more systematic than many and more explicit than most. The question whether human interaction with demons truly happened was quite simply the only compelling reason for experimenting with witches or writing about such experiments, as Spina did so extensively.

There are good and explicit historical reasons why the problem arose. We will never know what the women were doing who attracted the attention of the first clerical experimenters. They may have been folk healers experimenting with drugs for medicinal purposes or using them as an escape from misery and want. Other women and men may have belonged to non-Christian fertility cults like the Benandanti or nighttime dream travelers studied by Carlo Ginzburg, or they may have been shamans of some other sort.[71] Certainly, many early witches died because they were suspected of heresy, which is mentioned almost interchangeably with witchcraft in the early texts.[72] Many witches, particularly in later times, died, not because they had done something wrong, but simply because someone being tortured spoke their names. What does remain clear is that the early stories of experimentation appealed to many ecclesiastics because of their potential for demonstrating demonic reality.

Most of the early witchcraft theorists were more intrigued and worried by a single short *text*—the Canon *Episcopi*—than by real people and their activities. It is striking how much time and energy they invested in coming to terms with the Canon *Episcopi*. Details drawn from it infiltrated their interpretation of anything they heard about women, demons, dreaming, or supernatural traveling. When Nider mentioned that the crazy old village woman in her kneading tub thought that she was traveling with Diana, he may have been describing what an actual late-fourteenth- or early-fifteenth-century woman thought she was doing. But this detail could also have crept in from the Canon *Episcopi,* for Nider and his Dominican elders had certainly read it.

The Legacy of Damage Control

Witchcraft theory was not irrational or unscientific. It expressed both prescientific and antiscientific impulses. It grew out of and depended on the tradition of Scholastic natural philosophy, the ultimate aim of which was to vindicate the goodness of God and the truth of the Bible.

The insecurities that produced experiments with witches are not a thing of the past. Both witchcraft theory and Scholastic natural philosophy resemble the creation science of late-twentieth-century Christian fundamentalists. All three attempt to make knowledge of the physical world conform to the most literal possible interpretation of the Bible. This is always an exercise in damage control: how much of the Good Book can be salvaged when experience collides with tradition and authority?

The articles "Theology of Demon"[73] and "Demonology"[74] in the *New Catholic Encyclopedia* (1967) provide a particularly disquieting example of damage control. They are dominated by a discussion of experimentation with spirits. "Theology of Demon" notes that "the present, more detailed knowledge of the universe has forever destroyed the crude concept of a three-storied world in which angels and demons materialize with ingenuous frequency." *Ingenuous frequency* is a curious phrase because it implies that demons obviously materialize, but less frequently than unscientific ages naively thought. The writer cannot prove this, however, for "demonology has not been the object of very much serious study in the twentieth century. Yet the need for such study is apparent."

Why is study necessary? "The Church is committed to a belief in angels and demons, but the meaning of this belief in terms that are both comprehensible and relevant to modern man has not been adequately presented." That is, angels and demons *have to* exist, even though "more detailed knowledge of the universe" given by modern science has not *yet* confirmed that they do. Since the church cannot abandon belief in spirits, they must be made relevant. So science needs to answer the question, *How* do spirits *really* exist? Asking science to address this question reveals a purely psychological problem: how to go on believing in spirits.

When science is mentioned, experimentation cannot be far behind. "A question can be raised," "Demonology" declares, "about the permissibility of performing an experiment in which there is a possibility of diabolical intervention. *Must such experiments be avoided?*" (emphasis added). The whole thrust of the article has prepared this dilemma. There is a serious moral danger here, according to the writer: experiments might be arranged so that one would seem to be expecting devils to manifest themselves.

To confront the danger, the writer dusts off the thirteenth-century theory, perfected by Aquinas, of formal versus implicit pacts with devils. If one "expressly calls upon" a devil, this reveals intent to make a formal contractual agreement. However, a pact may be merely implicit "when a person does not expressly ask the devil for a favor, but from the nature of the thing sought or the way in which it is to be obtained, it can only be concluded that the devil is tacitly invited to grant the request. In such a case, a kind of knowledge, or the performance of a kind of deed, is sought that could not be performed by human powers alone."[75] (We observed this latter phrase in Mazzolini's description of experiments with dancing children.)

How can we avoid making these tacit invitations to devils? The best that the writer can do is quibble. He says that the consensus of tradition holds that, "if there is only a *possibility* of diabolical intervention, it is permissible, *for a just cause,* to conduct such experiments" (emphasis added). Nevertheless, he adds, "prudence would seem to require the experimenter to disavow any intention of seeking diabolical aid, and to state that he positively does not want it." Extreme caution is required, for, whenever, "instead of a *possibility,* there is a notable *probability* of diabolical intervention, it is evident that there is no moral justification for such experimentation." History could have taught this writer that the possibility of diabolical intervention, much less its "notable probability," was a long-ago daydream that did not survive experimentation.

Without wishing to impugn the writer's sincerity or ethics, I suggest that he has precisely described the psychology that led witchcraft theorists and hunters to daydream of experiments with witches. As they did, he wants to preserve the possibility of contacting demons, and the point of his writing, as of theirs, is that contact *must* be possible. Yet he wants the contact to happen without his approval. This places him in a double bind: to create a situation where his desire for demonic contact might be fulfilled, he would need to repudiate the desire explicitly. Thus, he would have to depend on the demon to respond to the logic of his actions rather than to the rhetoric of his words.

The question raised by the encyclopedia article is not whether its author or the Catholic church consciously intends to explore deeds "that could not be performed by human powers alone" in order to find demons. Catholics have been no more inclined to experiment with demons than Protestants have, although Catholicism has a longer and more systematic tradition of demonology. The point is that experimentation *necessarily* becomes a temptation as soon as dogma about the existence of demons is confronted by a tendency to test hypotheses empirically. Experimentation with witches did not wait for the development of the scientific method: it was sufficient that investigators recognize a distinction between theory and experience.

When Francis Bacon referred to the *inquisition* of nature and compared "her" to a witch, he was not expressing some radical new insight. Experimental attitudes toward demons permeated the logic of witchcraft theory, if not its rhetoric. Moreover, explicit experiments with demons had already been undertaken: before the rise of witchcraft theory, learned exorcists and necromancers attempted to interview devils at firsthand. The dissatisfaction caused by these inconclusive interviews eventually led, by a process that was only partially conscious or intentional, to the hope of secondhand interviews. Perhaps one could forcibly interview other *persons* to find out about demons. People whose activities were suspicious or unorthodox might have demonic contacts. Finding someone else who had demonic contact—or would confess to it—was a tantalizing solution to the scarcity of firsthand encounters among the men most interested in demons.

So inquisitors and theorists vigorously searched their surroundings for evidence of superhuman encounters. Sometimes they revealed this intention through the logic of their arguments; sometimes they confessed it with shocking explicitness, as did Kramer, Mazzolini, and Spina. Anticipating the ideal, morally acceptable, and cautious experimenter that the *New Catholic Encyclopedia* describes, witchcraft investigators were calling on spirits to prove their existence, but being careful not to admit it. They could "disavow any intention of seeking diabolical aid"; they could "state positively" that they did not want it and declare loudly that they were working to stamp it out.

The longing to discover deeds "that could not be performed by human powers alone" has driven a number of fads and hysterias among the American public, from the "spectral evidence" that ran amok at Salem, Massachusetts, in 1692, to the satanic ritual child abuse and alien abduction crazes of the 1990s. Promoters of the most outlandish incidents have followed Mazzolini's lead by emphasizing the value of children's testimony, declaring or presuming that children are too innocent to lie and impervious to suggestion or ventriloquism. This is not a sentimental idealization of children: it reflects a desperate need for children's testimony to be taken seriously in an *adult* context. It betrays the unspoken hope that children's pure belief will stimulate the adult participants' more laborious credence. Children's fantasy life and suggestibility are dragooned into service of the anxiety-ridden, doubt-riddled fantasy life of adults.

The writings of fifteenth- and sixteenth-century witchcraft theorists should caution us against dismissing present-day accusations of commerce with demons or suprahuman aliens as irrational or credulous or attributing them to entrenched systems of belief. It is clear that actual belief did not provoke the speculations of witchcraft theorists: belief is what they were *seeking*. Their natural philosophy was driven by the desire to defend God and the Bible. Science, which has evolved from natural philosophy, has no such bias. This makes the problem of spiritual reality even more acute for the modern would-be believer. Today, it is clearer than ever that the loud declaration that "these things definitely happen" is often a coded way of protesting that "these things *cannot not* be happening." Because the Bible says they do . . .

7

THE THEORY OF WITCHCRAFT POWER

Fair is foul and foul is fair.
—*Macbeth*

Where did the power of witchcraft come from? In general, the answer was "from demons." Transvection by demons explained how witches seemed to fly. Demonic power was also behind the harms inflicted by *maleficia*. The sources and mechanics of demonic power have not been fully explored by scholarship, however.

Historians of European witchcraft have written extensively about "countermagic," the "good magic" that Christian clerics and layfolk employed to counteract the "bad magic" of witchcraft.[1] Countermagic is sometimes described as an accommodation, a way of making Christian theology fit the folkloric, preliterate, essentially non-Christian worldview of the medieval laity. Perhaps. But the countermagic of early witchcraft treatises would have been incomprehensible to common people. It was intensely learned, logical, and rational. It was also profoundly interwoven with notions about demons and the power of witchcraft.

To understand how countermagic related to witchcraft, we must first understand it in isolation. The rituals identified today as countermagic were defined by formal Catholic theology against a broader theory of the sacraments, that is, of the rituals necessary for practicing Catholicism.[2] The complete theory of the sacraments evolved between about 1150 and the closure of the Council of Trent in 1563, that is, during the centuries when theologians were preoccupied by the problem of corporeal interaction with demons. After discussing and arguing over which rituals were essential, theologians between about 1150 and the Council of Florence (1439) agreed that there were seven sacraments: baptism, confirmation, eucharist (communion), penitence or confession, matrimony, extreme unction, and ordination. This definition was formally accepted and placed beyond discussion by the Council of Trent.[3]

Sacraments were momentous: most were experienced only once by an average layperson, and the exceptions, eucharist and penance, were repeatable because they were crucial to individual salvation and communal harmony. To take communion, one had first to confess one's sins, do penance before God, and often make amends to other people. To be denied communion (excommunicated) was to be cut off from both eternal salvation and normal human interaction until formally readmitted. Layfolk ordinarily could not celebrate sacraments; only priests could because the capacity to celebrate sacraments could be gained only through another sacrament, ordination into the priesthood. The great exception was baptism, which layfolk could perform in an emergency. Since baptism was essential to salvation, an infant or a person wishing to convert could be legitimately baptized by a layperson if in danger of dying before a priest could arrive.[4]

According to the *New Catholic Encyclopedia,* "the sacraments are not magic."[5] There are historic reasons behind the need for this disclaimer.[6] The misperception that sacraments are magical derives in large part from the oversimplifications of sacramental theory introduced by witchcraft theorists. Rather than referring to *magic,* it is more accurate to discuss sacraments in terms of their alleged effects. The most mainstream theologians, along with the most extreme witchcraft theorists, declared that sacraments had effects that were real. Their disagreements lay in details—very important details.

Catholic sacramental theology, as it evolved from the twelfth century to the sixteenth, is a theory of signs and signification that is based on concepts reaching back to Saint Augustine in the fourth century. But, in orthodox Catholic dogma, sacraments are not *mere* signs. They are "signs given by God, and not invented by men, which have the *power* to *effect* the same holy thing that they signify."[7] That is to say, sacraments *perform* exactly what they signify. Sacraments do not merely "re-present"; they simultaneously "present." They do not stand for something located elsewhere in space or time; they bring it *here* and *now,* at the same time as they stand for it. The signifier *creates* the signified.

This is more foreign to modern thought than it may initially seem. Modern secular theories of signification do not make room for considerations of power, not in any literal sense. Modern theories assume that a word represents a thing by eliciting a thought in a human mind; in addition, a written word represents a spoken word. In both cases, the thing signified can as easily be absent as present, for there is no necessary link between the sign (or signifier) and the signified. This is because signifiers have conventional meanings established by human custom. They have an arbitrary link to their signifieds and differ from culture to culture: *bread, Brot, hleb, pane, pain.* My interlocutors will understand me as long as they share my linguistic and cultural conventions.

Just as an ordinary sign does, a sacrament makes something present in human minds; it *signifies* that thing. But the sacrament also makes the thing present *in reality,* during the very time in which it signifies it. That is, in the Aristotelian definitions given by Scholastic theologians, a sacrament *causes* an *effect* at the same time as it signifies the process of causing the effect. This happens because God has created a necessary link between the ritual signs and their referents.

For example, baptism is a sacrament that cleanses the soul of original sin. The grace that cleanses the soul is invisible, as are the cleansing and the soul. But the process is represented, while it is happening, by the baptismal water, the priest's words, and his gestures.[8] Moreover, the water as physical thing is a necessary part of the sacrament; without it, the words do not make a sacrament. So sacraments are not mere signs; they *do* at the same time as they tell. In terms of twentieth-century sign theories, they *resemble* what we now call *magic words*. But sacraments are not identical with magic.

One crucial difference between sacraments and magic should already be apparent. Assuming that it works, magic causes things to happen in such a way that bystanders can agree whether anything happened. The effects of magic ceremonies are perceptible when they work.[9] The same cannot be said of sacramental signification.

This is dramatically evident in the most important and controversial example of sacramental signification, the consecration of the eucharist during the mass. When the priest *says* "This is my body," the sacramental elements cease to be bread and wine. The bread and wine *become* the body of Christ, his true, literal flesh and blood. But the eucharistic wafer continues to look like a wafer of bread. This lack of a perceptible effect caused centuries of discussion and, from the twelfth century on, much turmoil in Western European society. Many sincere Christians doubted or denied that any real effect happened, even when they wanted to believe that it did. Even formal sacramental theory conceded that the eucharistic "transubstantiation" was invisible and unverifiable by the senses. It had to be believed on faith.

The difference between sacraments and magic was vivid for the thirteenth-century Scholastic theologians, particularly Aquinas, who contributed the most to defining the sacraments. The Scholastics did not assert that the sacramental words or rituals in themselves caused the sacramental effect. The effect could come only from God, through an act of grace. The phrase *ex opere operato* was coined by Scholastics attempting to define how the sacraments caused their real, physical effects.[10] This concept was not intended as an assertion that "the mere outward ceremony, apart from God's action," caused the sacramental effect. Sacraments could not cause their effects infallibly or automatically. Rather, the sacramental causes and effects were governed by complex conditions and precise interactions between God, the priest celebrating the sacrament, and the congregation or recipients. Sacraments had to be celebrated with the explicit "intention of doing what the Church does," and they had to be received in the proper way. Efficacy *ex opere operato* was theorized to avoid imputing the sacramental efficacy to human action or attitudes and to protect the complexity of the process.[11] The church defended these ideas in 1439 and 1547 at the Councils of Florence and Trent.[12]

Those defenses were necessary. Ironically, Protestant reformers came to interpret the concept as if the actions of the priest or the ceremony itself produced the effect, an idea that they found redolent of magic or even witchcraft.[13] But the misinterpretation did not spring up fully formed, all at once. Sixteenth-century Protestants thought of efficacy *ex opere operato* as magical because fifteenth-century witchcraft theorists had already defined witchcraft in magical terms and sacraments in opposition to witchcraft. An essential trait of fifteenth-century (and later) witchcraft theorists was their inability to believe that the imperceptible effects and energies of the sacraments were real, not imaginary. After all, those effects had been described since the thirteenth century in the Aristotelian terms of *cause* and *effect, matter* and *form, substance* and *accidents.* There must be *some* way of verifying them. The problematic verification of sacramental effects was a crucial stimulus to theories of witchcraft.

Here, an important distinction must be made. Witchcraft theorists wished to view the sacraments from what we could call a scientific viewpoint; they presumed that any sacramental effect must be perceptible in some way to be real. Accordingly, they interpreted the Aristotelian terms of sacramental theory with absolute literality, as if discussing physics or chemistry. In this, they differed from the clerics who defined sacramental theory in the decrees of church councils. These decrees used words like *substance* approximatively, without philosophical rigor, when defining sacraments. For instance, the Fourth Lateran Council (1215) mentioned *transubstantiation,* not as a scientific term with a precise definition, but rather as an approximate description of something that necessarily had to remain a mystery.

Similarly, when Aquinas used the vocabulary of Aristotelian philosophy, he did not assert that the realities of faith could be adequately described in these scientific terms. On the contrary, he consistently argued according to a "principle of analogy." That is, he approached the supernatural mysteries revealed in the Bible "as if" they could "in a certain fashion" be described with terminology appropriate for understanding the world of nature and humans. His argumentation used an exquisitely self-conscious and careful version of the linguistic imprecision that characterized definitions given by church councils. And this had to be so: as clerics, both Aquinas and the conciliarists had to assume that, like God, his sacraments passed human understanding. They would have been aware that the Latin term *sacramentum* was a translation of the Greek *musterion*—mystery—not just a tag for a particular group of standardized rituals.[14]

These subtleties were lost on the clerics who became witchcraft theorists; in fact, that is *why* they became witchcraft theorists. By demanding that sacramental causes and effects conform literally to Aristotelian terminology, they turned the sacraments from supernatural mysteries into natural processes. They carried out a process well described by Salvatore Camporeale. Understanding sacramental causes and effects in a literal way required conceptualizing them with reason, thus subtracting them from the sacred mysteries of faith and "desacramentalizing" them. By regarding sacramental effects as part of the natural order, witchcraft theorists mechanized them, made them automatic, and turned them into perpetually identical objects, or reified them. To view transubstantiation, for instance, as if it were adequately defined by Aristotelian categories had serious consequences. To quote Camporeale, "The celebration of the mass, gradually reduced almost to a single significance . . . was stripped of the rich spiritual and sacramentary semantics proper to the eucharistic liturgy." This led to "an unavoidable *desacramentalization* of the eucharistic celebration . . . and a kind of cultic *reification*." That is, "it seems as if the priest no longer has any other function than to be the performer [*operatore*] . . . and administrator of the sacred," a kind of manufacturer, as it were.[15]

The analogy with witchcraft theorists' insistence on demonic corporeality is striking. Like demons, sacramental effects must be made perceptible by human senses in order to allay the suspicion that they are imaginary. Faith is not enough, or, rather, it is impossible.

Witchcraft theorists hoped to restore their faith in the reality of sacramental processes by demonstrating two things: first, that the effects of *maleficium* and other witchcraft activities were perceptible; second, that witchcraft energies were of the same kind as sacramental energies but produced opposite effects. They defined witchcraft and sacraments as releasing energies that were contrary in orientation but not different in kind, somewhat as we represent positive and negative electrical charges.[16] That is, witchcraft was a *countersacrament*.

Witchcraft theorists saw that important theologians, including Aquinas and Bonaventure, had discussed *maleficium* and sacraments together.

But, unlike Bonaventure and Aquinas, they were consumed and obsessed by the relation between *maleficium* and sacraments. Witchcraft theory was seductive to these clerics because it offered a way of mapping the literality and reality of sacramental energies.

Witchcraft theory and Protestantism emerged between 1400 and 1600 as manifestations of the same crisis of confidence in the efficacy of the sacraments, that is, in the reality of their energies and effects. The effects of the sacraments had come to seem imaginary because they were imperceptible. Where Protestantism openly contested sacramental efficacy, witchcraft theory attempted to defend it, but it did so covertly, indirectly, and in bad faith. Protestants exhibited, and witchcraft theorists resisted, their skepticism and doubt.

Because witchcraft theory was so strongly motivated by resistance to skepticism, the theory that witchcraft was a countersacrament rarely underwent in-depth discussion. However, countermagic received more considerable attention. Because countermagic was defined within the theory of sacraments, witchcraft theorists' discussions of countermagic help us understand their presuppositions governing witchcraft as countersacrament.

Most of the rituals now defined as countermagic were called *sacramentals* rather than *sacraments*. Theologians had perceived that some rituals, while important, were less central to Catholicism than the sacraments. These *sacramentals* (*sacramentalia*) were ultimately not defined as full-fledged sacraments (*sacramenta*), but they seemed nonetheless to have something sacred about them.[17] The sacramentals—holy water, blessed salt or bread, blessed candles and wax, making the sign of the cross, and so on—were less momentous than sacraments. They could be as freely and effectively used by layfolk as by clerics, and they were subject to unlimited reiteration.

For theologians of the Middle Ages and the early-modern period, sacramentals were not countermagical but counterdemonic. One of their principal functions in daily life was to drive away demons. Anyone could make the sign of the cross or speak a holy name, and at certain times holy water and other blessed articles would be distributed to layfolk for their protection from demonic menaces.[18] Sacramentals counteracted the *opera Diaboli,* or works of the Devil, one of which was *maleficium.* By contrast, the sacraments were defined as *opera Dei,* works of God.[19] Sacraments and sacramentals were therefore complementary: sacraments were a work *by* God, while the sacramentals were a work *against* the Devil, his works, and his collaborators.

This antidemonic function caused modern scholars to define sacramentals as countermagical. Indeed, witchcraft theorists' treatments of the sacramentals look very much like discussions of magic. The most familiar sacramental that they discussed is the use of holy water to repel demons and counteract their harm. Every witchcraft treatise features examples of demons who were routed by this remedy. Kramer even recommended making accused witches drink holy water to break the "*maleficium* of taciturnity" through which their demonic familiars prevented them from confessing.[20]

Nider's discussion of the relation between sacramentals and *maleficium* is crucial to the theory of witchcraft, and it does indeed look magical: "Moreover, it is well-known that witches [*malefici,* the masculine plural] confess that their *maleficia* are obstructed [*prepediri*] by the rites of the church when these are properly observed and venerated: for example, by the aspersion of holy water, by the taking of consecrated salt, or of candles on the day of the Purification of the Virgin [Candlemas], by the rightful use of consecrated palm fronds on Palm Sunday, and by other such things. This is because the church exorcizes these objects so that they will weaken the powers of demons."[21]

Nider's theory is not based on popular misconceptions. It is precise, explicit, and theological. It depends on the learned concept of efficacy *ex opere operato,* or sacramental efficacy. But it simplifies the complex theological idea, turning it into something mechanical and automatic. It *reifies* the idea, emphasizing the mechanical manipulation of objects rather than the process of signification.

Heinrich Kramer similarly oversimplified the theology affecting the words pronounced during the performance of sacramentals. Moreover, he allowed the oversimplification to affect his thinking about the sacraments, an even more serious lapse: "It cannot be objected that God conferred a power [*vim*] on words, as he did on plants and stones; because if some forces [*virtutes*] belong to words or sacramentals or other benedictions or lawful charms [*carminibus,* incantations], they have these not on account of being words, but from the divine institution and ordination, and from a covenant [*ex pacto*] of God. It is as if God had said, 'Whoever does this, I will do that grace [*gratiam*] for him,' and thus the words in sacraments perform [*efficiunt*] what they signify."[22]

There was a dangerous ambiguity in Kramer's presentation. By so strongly emphasizing that sacramental *words* are performative, Kramer contradicted his assertion that God conferred no power on words. The long-standing definition of sacraments as *signa efficaces* or performative signs was complicated, and Kramer simplified it drastically, implying that the words were powerful in themselves. By this failure, he slid precipitously from faith into magic. Hence his reference to "lawful charms," a distinctly unsacramental idea.

Witchcraft theorists ignored or even explicitly denied the importance of the performer's intentions. They presumed that sacramentals worked automatically, regardless of the faith that one placed in them. Their extreme assertions of the sacramentals' automatic power contrast vividly with definitions provided by mainstream theorists, who declared that no sacrament or sacramental could be performed without the proper *intention.*[23] Faith was essential to the sacramentals' supposed efficacy, and intention was actually more important to the sacramentals than to the sacraments. Sacramentals worked, not *ex opere operato,* but *ex opere operantis:* it was the work of the performer (*operans* or "operator") that gave them efficacy, and the most important work was the faith that the performer invested in the sacramental.

The sign of the cross provides dramatic examples of this *reification* of the sacramentals. Crossing was one of the sacramentals most frequently cited in the testimony of witchcraft defendants and witnesses. Witchcraft theorists asserted that the sign of the cross functioned as a demonifuge regardless of the conscious intentions of those who performed it. Their works are filled with anecdotes of devils who disappeared when innocent people blundered into Sabbats, took fright, and crossed themselves. More dramatically, theorists tell of terrified witches who imprudently crossed themselves while being transvected by demons, only to be dropped and injured when the demons disappeared.[24]

Sacramentals are best understood in their specific relation to *maleficia;* continuing to speak of *witchcraft* is not useful and sometimes counterproductive. It is clear from discussions of crossing and holy water that sacramentals and *maleficium* were stereotyped as polar opposites in witchcraft theory. That polarity led to conceptualizing the sacramentals' effects as magical: unless their effects were reliable or even infallible, sacramentals could seem imaginary. After all, their effects could not be seen or otherwise perceived directly. However, the effects of *maleficium* could. So it was sufficient to believe in the reality of *maleficium.* If one accepted the idea that *maleficium* was real, any sacramental that seemed to neutralize a *maleficium* could be defended as having a perceptible effect; thus, it had to be real.

There was a bonus. For witchcraft theorists, *maleficium* was caused by demons, not nature, mere words, rituals, or some mysterious force of human malice. So, if a sacramental eliminated a *maleficium,* it implicitly defended the reality of demons along with its own. If it chased away an embodied, perceptible demon, all the better.

Good layfolk who employed the sacramentals for healing could be presented as "antiwitches," at least in the early days of witchcraft theory.[25] Nider's *Formicarius* tells of several remarkable women, near saints in fact, who were devoted to the sacramentals. One, called Seriosa ("serious," an interesting name in itself), was what we could call a faith healer. Nider discusses her together with witches yet makes clear that, far from being a witch, Seriosa was a model believer who took Christian ceremonies "seriously":

> I knew a spinster named Seriosa, who lived in the diocese of Konstanz. She was a mother and a mirror [good example] to all the girls of that neighborhood, and she had the highest faith in the life-giving [*vivifice*] sign of the cross and in Christ's Passion. She lived in a hovel and was voluntarily poor in that village, which was a place where witchcraft [*maleficia*] was known to be rather common. One of her friends was struck in the foot by a serious witchcraft [*maleficio*] and could not be healed by any art. After many remedies [*remedia*] had been tried without success, she visited her friend, who asked her to perform a benediction. She agreed and silently recited the Lord's Prayer and the Apostles' Creed and repeated signs of the life-giving cross. The sick man, instantly feeling himself healed [*curatus*], wanted to know, for future remedies, what sort of charm [*carminacionis*] she had used. And she answered: "Because you have bad or weak faith [*mala fide vel debili*], you do not observe the divine and approved practices of the church and often treat your illnesses with forbidden charms [*carmina*] and remedies. And this is why you are struck, rarely in the body, it is true, but often in your soul, by such things. But if you had faith [*speraretis*] in the efficacy [*efficaciam*] of prayers and lawful signs, you would easily be cured. In fact, I applied nothing to you but the Lord's Prayer and the Apostles' Creed, and you are already healed [*sanatus*].[26]

"Moreover," continues Nider in a passage that we have already seen, "it is well-known that witches [*malefici*] confess that their *maleficia* are obstructed by the rites of the church when these are properly observed and venerated." This antagonism confirms that the sacramentals are real.

Seriosa's healing ritual looks like magic to modern eyes, but Nider clearly presented it as the *contrary* of certain "forbidden charms." To avoid misunderstanding, consider Seriosa's ritual in terms of its effects. Nider says that she was healing an injury caused by *maleficium,* so in this sense we can speak of counterdemonism. Yet the "forbidden charms" that Seriosa denounced are not the *maleficia* that caused the injury; instead, she criticized "good" charms that had proved inefficacious for healing. If healing by means of words is magic, then Seriosa's use of the sacramentals was better magic. But, just as injuries from *maleficium* were caused by demons, so Seriosa's healing came from God. In either case, the human rituals did nothing: by recalling a pact with God or a demon, the words constituted a request or a prayer.

The real problem of countermagic is not magic—a question of labels—but rather the notion that a ritual like making the sign of the cross could have effects on physical health. A modern reader will find this idea "primitive," "un-Christian," or "unspiritual," according to his or her religious inclinations. Most Christian sects no longer officially encourage their adherents to think that prayer or ritual gestures will have real effects on their physical health and safety. That the effects of a Christian ritual were equal and opposite to the effects of a demonic ritual makes the idea even more unsavory to a modern mentality. But Nider, like other witchcraft theorists, wanted to convince his readers of all this.

Seriosa provokes the reflection that Nider and other witchcraft theorists might have preferred to argue overtly for the sacramentals' beneficial physical effects. However, figures like Seriosa are rare in witchcraft theory. The counterdemonic effect most often ascribed to sacramentals is not healing but the disappearance of a devil. Even pronouncing holy names was supposed to repel demons, and the examples of this practice that witchcraft theorists give can look deceptively like examples of magic words. Both Walpurga Hausmännin and Johannes Junius were forced to confess this power of words: when Walpurga spoke Jesus' name, and when Johannes pronounced that of God, their demonic seducers disappeared, at least temporarily. In general, stories of disappearing devils illustrated the contention that witchcraft was not the only means of interacting physically with demons. Good people could also interact with them by driving them away or neutralizing the physical afflictions that they caused.

The idea that evil spirits vanished when confronted with sacramentals is so commonplace that scholars customarily assume that anyone who alluded to such demonic pest control believed implicitly in its efficacy. By the early 1400s, belief was clearly not universal or easy, and stories of demonic disappearance rarely seem to satisfy witchcraft theorists. Their difficulty believing is understandable since the stakes were so high. Just as proof of demonic reality was necessary to a belief in the world of spirit, so verification that sacramentals chase demons away was needed to show that God takes care of his own. The two concerns were linked in disquieting ways: for one thing, they were reversible. Stories of demonic disappearances and reappearances were supposed to illustrate the efficacy of sacramentals; but that efficacy depended on proving the reality of the demons that were driven away. And, to say the least, proof of demonic reality was not easily obtained.

The accounts of Johannes Junius's and Walpurga Hausmännin's trials reflect this dilemma. The disappearance of their demon lovers at the sound of holy names should have demonstrated that they were spirits since normal flesh and blood cannot vanish before our eyes. But the disappearance per se failed to guarantee the demon's reality. Supplementary proofs, including copulation, had to be added. Still, like disappearance, copulation was only an implicit proof, and logic required more explicit ones.

When the demon supposedly commanded Johannes to renounce God, he refused and invoked God's name instead: "Thereupon the spirit vanished *through the power of these words.*"[27] The explicit reference to the power of God's name shows that the disappearance of the spirit was intended precisely to demonstrate that power. Yet this anxiety raises a curious paradox: If the point of the disappearance was to demonstrate the power of God's name, why did the spirit return almost immediately? The story's overall logic intimates that the spirit could not demonstrate the power of God's name until it had demonstrated its own reality. The spirit would have proved nothing if it had simply disappeared and stayed away; easy success might even have caused the suspicion that the spirit was a hallucination. So the demon not only came back but brought a crowd of real people with it. The human entourage demonstrated in the most emphatic way that the spirit itself was not an illusion.

Walpurga's demonic paramour also disappeared when she spoke the name of Jesus, although it took longer—until the next night—to return.[28] In both cases, the spirit had proved its reality through copulation and other physical interactions before disappearing. The temporary effects of the divine name reflected, not that its power was limited, but rather that the spirit that it routed was real. The spirit's reappearance, even more than its disappearance, confirmed its reality. Proof of the spirit's reality also proved, by extension, that the power of divine names was not an illusion. Here as elsewhere in the illustrative anecdotes of witchcraft theory, the redundancy of implicit proofs can obscure their common logic. Without the explicit reference to the power of God's name, the redundant, tangled proofs in the story of Johannes's spirit would not reveal their common logic.

Personal Experience and Experimentation

Stories that witchcraft theorists told about the sign of the cross and *maleficium* consistently betray anxiety over the reality of Catholic sacramentals. In the *Formicarius,* Johannes Nider quotes the experiences of Judge Peter of Bern, a Swiss lay magistrate. Nider finished his book in 1437 or 1438, while Peter ceased prosecuting "the sect of witches" sometime between 1406 and 1417.[29] Thus, the *Formicarius* reflects the earliest phases of literate concern over witchcraft, when heretics and male sorcerers abounded, female *maleficae* had no prominence, and the polarity between *maleficium* and the sacramentals was starkly evident. Nider's quotations from Peter show that this prototypical witch-hunter was obsessed with verifying the counterdemonic efficacy of the sign of the cross. Anguished by a series of disastrous hailstorms that had caused famine in his territory, Peter managed to find a culprit. Nider says that Peter told him this revealing story about his experiences:

> "When," he said, "I had captured Scadelem, who had gravely damaged our territory with hailstorms and a famine and had destroyed many things with lightning, I interrogated this guilty man about the truth of the matter. After suffering four yanks of the strappado, he initially gave me this answer: 'I can easily procure hailstorms, but I am not able to cause damage whenever I want [*ad libitum*]. I can harm only those who are deprived of God's protection [*auxilio*]. Those who protect themselves with the sign of the cross will not perish by my lightning bolts.' " And the judge [Peter] asked: "How exactly do you go about causing thunderstorms and hail?" The guilty man replied: "In the first place we use certain words to invoke the prince of all the demons, begging him to send one [of his demons] to strike whatever we have indicated. When the demon arrives, we sacrifice a young black rooster to him by throwing it up into the air at a crossroads. When the demon has accepted the offering, he immediately calls up the winds. But he does not always send lightning and hail to the places we designate, for he must act in accordance with the permission of the living God."[30]

In Peter's theory, *maleficium* and the sacramental gesture are antithetical, for witchcraft can work only in the absence of sacramental energy. When confronted with verifiable disasters, Peter wished to believe that such harm could happen only because the holy sign was missing.

Whether Judge Peter's desire to believe was at all popular or folkloric, Nider certainly interprets it as theologically valid, so for our purposes it is an elite theory. Peter's theory was more complicated than it may appear, for it had to accommodate the possibilities of failure. Another sorcerer supposedly told Peter that, once when he attempted to convince a demon to attack a man with lightning, the demon replied that he could not, for the man had strong faith and protected himself conscientiously with the sign of the cross. However, the demon continued, if the sorcerer wished, he could spoil the eleventh part of the man's crops.[31] Despite acknowledging the possibility of such partial counterdemonic failures,

Peter went to great lengths to convince himself that the sign of the cross guaranteed God's protection against the assaults of demons and that physical harm could happen only when crossing was neglected.

Peter's most important proofs were supposedly based on personal experiences. They were made possible by convincing himself of living under constant attack by witches and demons. Peter told Nider that "for a long time witches tried to avenge themselves on him, but he kept a good faith and always protected himself with the sign of the cross. So, being alerted to their presence on several occasions, he avoided encountering them in those situations where they are wont to perform *maleficium*." Thus, says Nider, "Peter always came away unharmed, thanks to the adroitness [*astucia*] of such precautions."[32]

But something is wrong with this logic. Rather than deflecting or counteracting a specific *maleficium,* as in the testimony that Peter elicited from his tortured defendants, the protective energy of the cross helped Peter avoid all contact with witches. This notion of total prophylaxis suggests that he needed to account for his own lack of danger rather than a superabundance of it. Ironically, the passage suggests that Peter's constant crossing himself helped him understand why he *rarely* encountered witches. Subsequent theorists would repeat that witchcraft should be treated as a *crimen exceptum,* subject to otherwise illegal forms of evidence gathering, precisely because it was so difficult for investigators to have direct experience of it.[33] Yet, like Peter, they seem to have had no trouble discovering other people's experience.

There is already something suspicious about the monotony of Peter's praise for the power of crossing. But there is more to his obsession than simply protesting too much. Peter was a witch-*hunter:* he needed and desired contact with his quarry. To maintain faith in the sacramentals, it must have been essential that he account for the absence of witches when he expected to encounter them. Even the idea of total prophylaxis seems not to have been particularly comforting.

One of Nider's stories reveals that, despite, or perhaps because of, the frequency with which Peter crossed himself, he needed to discover an exception to confirm his rule of obsessive crossing and total prophylaxis. He needed to connect *lack of safety* with *lack of sacramental protection.* Otherwise, how was he to convince himself that the people he persecuted were truly harmful or that crossing himself counteracted some real power? So Peter's experience made room for this vital logical link—but without the satisfaction of direct encounters with witches.

Nider says that there was one occasion when, "because of his own crime [*ex delicto proprio*], Peter merited not being completely protected by God, as he told me." One evening, Peter went up to bed and as usual crossed himself in preparation for sleep. But he was planning to get up during the night and write some urgent letters since he needed to travel the next day. Waking during the night, he was deceived by an unexpected, "artificial [*ficticia*]" light into thinking that day had already come. Nider says that Peter was "filled with rage," but not for the reason that we might expect. He was angry, not because he overslept, but rather "because, as he thought, he had neglected the night, not protecting himself as he should in his usual way." That is, Peter thought that he had forgotten to cross himself.[34] So he dressed and stormed downstairs to his study. Finding it closed, "which ignited an even greater rage in him," Peter turned and stalked rapidly upstairs to his bedroom again, grumbling all the way. "And, out of indignation, he emitted a single curse [*malediccionem*] with a rather brief saying, as if to say 'In the Devil's name!'[35] And behold, immediately, in those deep shadows, Peter was thrown headlong down the stairs so violently that his servant, who was sleeping comfortably under the staircase, woke up and came out to see what had happened." The servant found Peter at the bottom of the stairs, his candle still lit, but Peter himself "deprived of the use of reason, injured in all the parts of his body, and bleeding copiously." The whole household was awakened, but "no one could discover the cause of the fall."

Apparently, no one, least of all Peter, suspected that running up and down dark staircases in a towering rage was sufficient cause for a fall. Or, rather, Peter *preferred* to believe that, by invoking the Devil in a moment of thoughtlessness, he had canceled the protection acquired by crossing himself. Consciously or unconsciously, he staged his own experience of a supposedly commonplace occurrence. Demonological literature is filled with admonitions against uttering the Devil's name lightly or joking about him with phrases like *Devil take it* or *Devil take you*. There was a long tradition of these stories: in the thirteenth century, Caesarius of Heisterbach told two in the *Dialogus miraculorum*.[36] This precaution is the converse of the idea that merely pronouncing a holy name, even through surprise or accident, was sufficient to drive demons away automatically, regardless of the speaker's intent.

The polarity is significant. We could say that Peter thought of himself as inadvertently performing *countermagic on countermagic*. This is betrayed by his claim that his rage was motivated by an *erroneous* belief that he had forgotten to cross himself during the night. In fact, he later reasoned, he had crossed himself normally, but the imprecation "in the Devil's name" had canceled the protection. Peter gave no explanation why he thought that he had forgotten to cross himself. Given the otherwise circumstantial detail, this omission points to the unasked question whether crossing oneself has any real effects. Peter needed proof that protection had been canceled despite his intent; he needed to avoid suspecting that the fall was *accidental,* despite his routinely crossing himself. Proof that he had truly forgotten would not have addressed his anxieties at all. So Peter chose to believe that his curse canceled his crossing and that witches had therefore been able to attack him, sending demons to cause his fall.[37]

This is not the end of the story. Because Peter had *seen* no witches, he needed further proof of the causal link, and only the confessions of witches could provide that. Nider relates that, "finally, thanks to the grace of God, Peter recovered the use of his reason, but he did not regain his bodily health for over three weeks. And although he suspected witches, whom with all his might he desired to cancel from the face of the earth, nonetheless he remained ignorant as to who was guilty of the crime committed against him." Yet, says Nider, the mystery did not remain unsolved for long because, "truly, nothing is covered up that will not be revealed."[38]

Now that Peter had found personal motivation for discovering witches, Nider reports, he soon got his wish. One day, a stranger drinking in a tavern looked into his glass and claimed that in the wine he could see a person he knew who was at that moment stealing the baited fishhook that he had set out in waters near his house. But this was taking place "six long Teutonic miles" from where he was sitting, so the drinking companions realized that he was watching the theft with help from a demon (*opere demonis*). They denounced him to Peter. He underwent severe torture for two days without revealing anything, but, when Peter had him tortured again on the third day, he confessed his crime and incidentally solved the mystery of Peter's fall.

Peter had previously decided that his injury was caused by five witches in particular, a woman and four men. His defendant's confession now confirmed the judge's suspicion that, even before his fall, they had "met in a certain place" and perfected techniques "to harm him gravely or to kill him, he being as yet unaware of these fraudulent practices."[39] By this confession, the defendant became an informer, confirming that Peter had been magically injured in order to obstruct his pursuit of witches. Thus, a man trying to impress his drinking companions, or perhaps even joking with them, was burned at the stake. This was his reward for assuring Peter that the sacramentals can keep demons and their human collaborators from harming us unless, by our own negligence or sinfulness, we neglect our protection and perform *counter-countermagic.*[40]

In fact, Peter squeezed the maximum confirmation out of this poor fellow. The confession took place on a Saturday, and the accused "added that on the previous two days, being held back by the machinations of demons, he had not been able to answer under torture. But, because, *as he said,* Saturday was holy to the Blessed Virgin, as soon as services had been celebrated in her honor, he suddenly became able to tell the truth." Despite the italicized words, it seems unlikely that the defendant made this counterdemonic conclusion without prompting. The mass enacted the supreme sacrament, the transubstantiation of the eucharistic host, but Peter was more interested in proving that Saturday masses provoked the Virgin to intercede and expose the truth. Like the sign of the cross, the mass had deprived demons of the ability to harm or deceive the pious witch-hunter.

Despite his constant harping on the power of the sacramentals, Peter faced an acute problem when he captured an accused witch. If witches were so powerful, and if the sign of the cross prevented encounters with them, why did he never seem to need sacramental protection when he met them face-to-face in the daytime? Evidently, he needed supporting explanations:

> As far as public [i.e., secular] justice goes, all the witches [*malefici*] whom we mentioned above gave testimony, both by their words and through experience [*verbo et experientia testimonium dederunt*], that, as soon as witches are captured by the officials of secular [*reipublice*] justice, all their power is instantly destroyed. Thus, when Judge Peter, whom we have often mentioned, wanted his agents [*famulos*] to capture the above-mentioned Scadelem, such a trembling took hold of their hands and bodies, and such a disgusting stink assailed their nostrils, that they almost lost hope of daring to capture the witch. But the judge told them: "Seize this miserable man confidently because, as soon as he is touched by public justice, his evildoing will lose all its powers." And, indeed, the outcome or effect [*effectus*] of this incident proved his words true.[41]

Clearly, Judge Peter forced his witches to provide testimonials that they lost all their powers when apprehended. Here, there is no sacramental counterdemonism; the sorcerer's power is neutralized by secular agents and brute force (although Peter may have considered it as having a divine origin).[42] But, if that was true, why so much emphasis on crossing oneself to avoid encounters with demons? The confident tone of this passage is an anomaly; it contrasts starkly with Peter's obsession with crossing himself.

Heinrich Kramer, an avid reader of the *Formicarius,* would provide lengthy explanations of witches' instantaneous loss of power when captured. In Kramer's case, the problem was more urgent: unlike Nider, he had decided that nearly all witches were women. How was one supposed to be afraid of a terrified woman, who was often old and decrepit to boot?[43] Despite adopting Nider's theory of constabular counterdemonism, Kramer still needed to reinforce his belief in an ongoing titanic struggle. Kramer could not risk an emotional anticlimax in these situations, so he recommended that inquisitors remain on their guard with paranoiac determination even after the arrest. They must avoid touching witches and should carry sacramentals—blessed herbs and salt or an Agnus Dei of blessed wax—to avoid being bewitched. Moreover, any witch must be brought before her prosecutors backward so as to be seen before seeing.

The bewitching that Kramer most feared in these circumstances was evidently not the physical harm that sacramental precautions usually counteracted. He claimed that, if the witch looked at the inquisitor before he could look at her, she might make him "lose his anger" and set her free. Kramer said that he offered this advice as "true testimony" of his own experience, implying that he "lost his anger" and let someone go because he took pity on her.[44] This fiasco made him aware of needing time to activate his hatred of witches before meeting the gaze of a defendant. As with Peter of Bern, Kramer's obsessive counterdemonic practices maintained his fear and witch hatred in a constant state of alarm. Belief in the need for counterdemonism was essential to preserving belief in the reality of witches' power.

The mechanics of attitude maintenance could be even more elaborate. Kramer required that the witch be carried bodily into court, to prevent her feet touching the ground, for "many who have been about to be burned have asked to be permitted at least to touch the ground with one foot; and when this was denied them and they were asked why they wanted only to touch the ground, they answered that if they *had* touched it, they *would have* freed themselves, striking many others dead with lightning."[45] Kramer's wording betrays the key point: if these defendants were not completely imaginary, invented to prove Kramer's point, they *were not* allowed to touch the ground. Their testimony to their own perilousness was comforting; experimental exploration of it was undesirable.

These make-believe beliefs reveal that the trial was an ordeal for the inquisitor as well as for the accused witch. Having to release a defendant or even feel pity menaced the sense that one was prosecuting a real crime. Unless the witch's aura of menace could be maintained, the theological superstructure with its delicate balance of supernatural forces would collapse. Therefore, even more explicitly than Nider, Kramer theorized the struggle between the inquisitor and the accused witch as the visible evidence of a largely invisible battle. The witch will not confess unless a good angel overpowers her demon and forces him to stop helping her maintain the "witchcraft of silence" (*maleficium taciturnitatis*). The fact that her immense powers have vanished so quickly must be proof, not that they were imaginary, but that the power of God wielded by the inquisitor was greater than the power of the Devil.[46]

Witchcraft as Countersacrament

The binary and symbiotic relation that bound *maleficium* to the counter-demonism of the sacramentals was repeated in the conflict between witchcraft and the sacraments. We have seen that Judge Peter thought of sacramentals as counterdemonism, but he could also envision a counter-counterdemonism capable of annulling their protection, regardless of his conscious intentions. By the same logic, witchcraft was theorized as a *countersacrament*. Witchcraft was defined as a real force, identical in type, but opposite in orientation, to the power of the sacraments. The relation between these forces was even more intimate, for witchcraft power could be traced ultimately to the power of the sacraments and sacramentals. For some authors, witchcraft energy was not simply identical in type to sacramental energy; it was the *very same* energy, but with its "polarities" reversed.

Overall, the practice of witchcraft was imagined as a *countersacramental* interaction with demons. This idea was perhaps suggested by the idea that the sacramentals counteracted the power of demons. By that logic, any voluntary interaction with demons was countersacramental. This appears abundantly in the *Formicarius*. Nider asserted that Judge Peter discovered exactly how witches "learned the art" of witchcraft: "The witches came to a certain meeting and by their own efforts visibly saw [*visibiliter viderunt*] the demon in the assumed image of a man. To him the disciple had to promise [*fidem dare*] to abandon Christianity, never to adore the eucharist, and to trample the crucifix, whenever he could do so in secret [*latenter*]."[47] Here, Nider implies that witchcraft becomes possible as a result of two countersacramental transgressions, avoiding the eucharist and stamping on the crucifix. In the first century of witchcraft theory, these two activities are practically universal elements in the initiation ceremonies of witches.

The logic behind both actions is precise. By never adoring the eucharist, the witch withdraws faith from it, either as belief in its powers or as allegiance (faithfulness) to it. Indeed, the promise to abandon Christianity is presented as a kind of counterfaith (*fidem dare*). Thus, the witch forfeits the Christianizing effects that periodic communion maintains. Witches could avoid the eucharistic energies in a more graphic fashion, by accepting the eucharistic host but removing it from their mouths rather than swallowing it. This gesture is all but ubiquitous in the first century of witchcraft theory. By trampling the crucifix or some other sign of the cross, the initiate witch counteracts its benefits as counterdemonism and demonifuge. The crucifix did not have to be a stolen work of religious art; some texts speak of witches trampling crosses made of sticks or even drawn in the dirt. The implication is that the sign itself is magical. Nider or his informant barely avoids claiming that these two countersacramental actions make possible the initial encounter with the demon; other theorists made the cause and effect explicit.

The concept of countering or avoiding sacramental protections is implicit linguistically in the most widespread term for witchcraft, *maleficium*. This word means nothing more than "evildoing"; the nouns related to it, *maleficus* and *malefica,* simply mean "evildoer." Nider and, after him, Kramer attempted to draw a link between *maleficium* and witches' apostasy or renunciation of *fides*. Yet they were aware that the word revealed its origin in the verb for doing (*facio, fare*), not the noun for believing.[48] *Maleficus / malefica* implies nothing as precise as what is implied by the words *witch, wizard, sorcier / sorcière, strega, strix, Hexe,* or other early-modern words for those who practice witchcraft.

Instead, the word *maleficium* had sacramental resonances. Given the causal link between avoiding sacramental protections and learning witchcraft, it cannot be accidental that the term *beneficium* was used to designate the concrete benefits of receiving the sacraments. Saint Bonaventure made the connection between *maleficia* and sacramental *beneficia* explicit when discussing the form of sorcery that most intrigued him (as it did Aquinas and the canon lawyers). Referring to male sexual impotence (*impotentia coeundi*), Bonaventure declared: "This kind of sorcery [*sortilegium*] is a diabolical *maleficium,* but matrimony is a remedy and a divine *beneficium;* but a divine *beneficium* is stronger than a diabolical *maleficium;* therefore matrimony will sooner dissolve a *maleficium* than a *maleficium* will block matrimony."[49]

Bonaventure called matrimony a divine *beneficium* because it was a sacrament. That he made the opposition explicit over a century before the first systematic witchcraft theories confirms that the peculiarly Western European construct of witchcraft as *maleficium* evolved by a logic that was sacramental. *Maleficium* is a countersacrament, just as the sacraments and sacramentals are counterdemonism.

As we might suspect, Heinrich Kramer made the link between the *beneficia* of sacraments and the *maleficia* of witchcraft more systematic than he found it. In the second part of the *Malleus maleficarum,* he defined the basis of *maleficium* as the perversion or misuse of sacramental materials and ceremonies. He declared that "in all their methods of working injury [*maleficiandi*] devils nearly always instruct witches to make their instruments of witchcraft [*sue malicie*] by means of the sacraments or sacramentals of the church, or of anything divine or consecrated to God: as when they sometimes place a waxen image under the altar-cloth, or draw a thread through the holy chrism, or use some other consecrated thing in such a way." Kramer went on to claim that witches work their *maleficia* "first by means of the sacraments and secondly by means of the sacramentals."[50] He thus defined the sacraments and sacramentals as essential to *maleficium;* it is created from them.

To explain how sacraments can be forced to produce *maleficium,* Kramer told of a witch whom he convicted of burying a consecrated eucharistic host in a jar with a toad. Once the two had decayed and mixed together, the witch confessed, they would have become raw material for working *maleficium.*[51] It was certainly possible to interpret sacramental energies as moral or spiritual rather than physical and mechanistic. But Kramer's story, the only example that he gives, implies that witches redirect or invert the sacraments' energies and harness perverted energy to work physical *maleficia.*

Although Kramer contends that *maleficium* depends on desecration, desecration is by nature secondary. As the word indicates, *de*secration depends on a prior *con*secration, the dedication of an object or action to God. Consecration sets something aside for God, making it his (this setting aside is the primary meaning of the Latin term *sacer*). Desecration attacks and reverses this process. Early witchcraft theorists' discussions of *maleficium* and desecration depend on the idea that consecration was more than symbolism or ceremony. It was a real physical *process* that made available certain *literal* energies that were physically beneficial to Christians. Those energies could be perverted and turned into negative versions of themselves. In this way, desecration produced *maleficium* from *beneficium.*

Not Parody: Countersacrament

Scholars of witchcraft assume that initiation rituals and other atrocities described as taking place at the Sabbat were parodies or travesties of Catholic rites. The term *parody,* drawn from literary criticism, describes actions that take place at the level of ideas and opinion. But the activities of the Sabbat were defined as producing effects on external reality; they created literal physical energies that were equal and opposite to effects of the sacrament. Once again, we must be careful to distinguish the rhetoric of witchcraft theory from its logic. It is true that early witchcraft theorists portray witches and demons as *expressing* contempt for Catholicism; they describe witchcraft ceremonies as *intended* to mock or dishonor Christ and the sacraments. But theorists maintained that, as *actions,* witchcraft ceremonies produced physical energies and perceptible effects. These assertions betray a logic of respect. Yet, in these stories, witches and demons explicitly deny respecting the sacraments.

A need to feel respect for the sacraments and a desire to receive real benefits from them can be traced only to the theorists who told the tales. The concept of witchcraft *maleficium*—physical harm—takes for granted that sacramental *beneficium* was a physical effect, not just a comforting idea. To define this process as parodic is thus to miss its significance in witchcraft theory.[52]

The countersacramental process of desecration or perversion is starkly portrayed in Nider's descriptions of witches' initiation into their "sect." Nider's informant Judge Peter evidently tortured a woman into this confession: one of witches' main activities was killing small children, either in their cradles or right in their parents' beds. This was performed so stealthily that the children seemed to have died a natural death. The woman continued: "Then we secretly steal them from their graves and cook them in a cauldron [*caldari*] until the whole flesh comes away from the bones and becomes a soup that may easily be drunk. . . . [A]nd with the liquid we fill a flask or skin. Whoever drinks from this, with the addition of a few other rituals [*ceremoniis*], immediately acquires much knowledge and becomes a leader [*magister*] in our sect."[53] Drinking the broth of murdered babies is the centerpiece of an initiation ritual. It provides an arresting illustration of antisacramental activity.

More precisely, the broth and its effects are represented as the antithesis of the eucharist. The broth is not a parody of the eucharist; it is a countereucharist. Through its effects, it is portrayed as *a better eucharist.* The superiority is implied through references to ingesting infant bodies. For their broth, the witches used a baby that was both literal and publicly perceptible. Medieval mystics who adored the eucharistic host often imagined it as an infant and sometimes had ecstatic visions of infants during communion. But no one else could see these visions. The public sphere had an equivalent. Stories about Jews who stole and tortured the eucharistic host often connected the desecration with miraculous apparitions of the Christ child. These eucharistic children could be visible to more than one person, sometimes even including bystanders. These horrible slanders could have been indirectly reinforced by another factor, the myth of ritual murder. This was a durable stereotype that accused Jews of abducting young Christian boys and killing them in ways that were reminiscent, not only of the crucifixion, but also of the celebration of the eucharist. Often, the murdered children produced miracles that reflected eucharistic doctrines.[54]

The witches' initiation inverts late-medieval eucharistic mythology by proposing equal and opposite antieucharistic effects for the ingestion of *unsacralized* children. The witch confessed that unbaptized babies were the most highly prized for confecting the initiatory broth.

The effects of this ritual are physical and perceptible, not spiritual or mystical. The issues of perceptibility and reality organize the contrasts between the witches' ceremony and the eucharist. By contrast with the Catholic host, which imparted both body and blood in the form of a wafer, the witches' broth of babies was a liquid, derived from a solid. It was a sensorially verifiable way of ingesting body and blood simultaneously.

This detail reflects problems in eucharistic theology. After a long debate, Catholic theologians had decided by the 1400s that it was unnecessary for laypeople to partake of communion in both species, that is, to consume both bread and wine. The consecrated wafer was declared sufficient for laypeople because, in the moment the priest spoke the words "This is my body," every particle of both bread and wine was transformed into both the body and the blood of Christ. Not all Christians accepted this innovation; in Nider's time, Hussite dissidents in Bohemia insisted on receiving wine as well as bread, as would many of their Protestant successors.

Anxiety about eucharistic reality could evolve rapidly, as we see from the two known versions of the *Errores gazariorum,* or *Errors of the Heretics,* a short treatise from the 1430s.[55] Both versions of the story are found in manuscript collections of documents connected with the Council of Basel, which historians now consider an important venue for early speculation about witchcraft. In what is certainly the older version, it is claimed that, at their "synagogue," the heretics "urinate and defecate in the wine cask, and they do this to insult the eucharist." In the second, amplified version, we read that "they urinate in the wine cask and also put solid excrement in it. When questioned why they do this, they say they do it in contempt and mockery of the sacrament of eucharist because [*quod*] it is made from the said wine."[56] The second writer turned a purely imaginative slander into a confession by specific (although probably imaginary) people. He also implied that the same wine that the heretics sabotage will be used in celebrating the eucharist. If he thought like Nider and Kramer, this writer assumed that contamination would render the eucharist inefficacious. If so, we should wonder why he was so concerned with inefficacious eucharists that he needed to explain their production or punish their producers.

Anxieties about the eucharistic wine could have inspired the half-hopeful fantasy that the same people *might* be both sabotaging the Catholic sacrament and performing their own more efficacious countersacrament. Judge Peter extracted detailed confirmation of the powerful effects of the witches' antieucharistic broth from another of his victims. This young man also described the overall initiation ritual centered on consumption of the broth:

> "This is the kind of order [*ordo*] by which I have been seduced," he said. "It is necessary initially for the future disciple and his teachers [*magistri*] to go into a church early on a Sunday morning, before the holy water has been consecrated. There, in front of them, he has to deny Christ, his faith, his baptism, and everything about the church. Then he must do homage to the *Magisterulus,* that is, the Little Master, for thus, and in no other way, do they name the demon. Finally, he drinks from the above-mentioned[57] wineskin. As soon as he has done this, immediately, in the deepest part of himself, he feels himself conceiving and retaining the images [*ymagines*] of our art and the principal rites of this sect."[58]

This man confirmed and amplified the first witch's testimony: the enemies of Christ had a better eucharist, one whose effects were easier to experience perceptibly. Contrary to the eucharist, the witches' broth *worked* instantaneously and unequivocally, the moment it was ingested. It canceled whatever vestiges of faith remained in the initiate after he formally renounced Christianity and at once gave him everything he needed to know to adhere faithfully to Satan's antireligion.

The initiation mimicked the effects of two other sacraments, baptism and confirmation, as well as the eucharist. It conferred favor or grace, strengthened resolution, and gave knowledge of a sort that Christians had to acquire through catechism and preaching.[59] The experience was wonderfully intense: the initiate felt himself conceiving *and retaining* his new religion in the most vivid way, through images. And he instantly knew, without being taught, how to perform the rituals that expressed his complete fulfillment of his antireligious obligations.

In isolation from the medieval and early-modern Catholic theory of sacramental efficacy, this ritual looks like a hodgepodge of irrational horrors. But, in terms of that theory, the broth ceremony was both coherent and highly expressive. Its effects were more satisfactory to the metaphysical imagination of Judge Peter and Johannes Nider than anything claimed for the eucharist. Heinrich Kramer found Nider's description so reassuring that he quoted it verbatim, thus bequeathing it to generations of witchcraft theorists and enthusiasts.

The Witches' Countermass

This young man's pathetic fictional confession obeys a precise logic of reversal, whereby the effects of the Catholic sacraments are transformed into equally strong but opposite effects under the Devil's control. Ceremonies must be reperformed, but in reverse; objects and forces must be inverted, transferred, or neutralized. Because Sunday is the Lord's Day (*dies dominica*), and because any church is his house, the witches' initiation must take place there. The inductee must repudiate everything pertaining to the church from within the church building itself, for that is where baptism and confirmation, the rituals of initiation into the church, take place. All this undoing has to be completed before the holy water is consecrated. Satan and his minions would obviously be unable to enter the church after this ceremony because holy water is consecrated through exorcism and hence functions as a demonifuge. However, until the holy water has been consecrated, the church is simply another building, and demons can enter it as easily as anyone else can. After all, they are everywhere, always awaiting their chance.

Like Christ, Satan is a military leader as well as a *magister*—teacher and master—so his disciples, *discipuli,* are also soldiers. The initiate had to do homage (*homagium,* the technical term of feudal allegiance) to the Devil in person. Judge Peter probably imagined the convert to witchcraft placing his hands inside the clasped hands of the Devil, as in the ceremony of homage, in order to demonstrate how the Devil held him completely in his power. The initiate was literally becoming "the Devil's man" or vassal, as if deserting one feudal army and joining another.

This *maleficus* admitted that, by becoming a witch, he had joined a new *ordo,* a term used to designate religious orders. *Ordo* implies, not just a new organization, but one that was completely *orderly*. The convert belonged to a new *ordo rerum,* a new order of things, almost a new universe; it was more emotionally satisfactory and less intellectually puzzling than the *ordo* of orthodox Catholicism. This clerical fantasy about the witches' ceremonies, sacraments, and community may initially look like a dystopia based on fear, but its logic reveals it as a kind of envious, inverted utopia.

The Need to Know

The human suffering through which Judge Peter obtained confessions indicates how badly he wanted to know what he wished to believe. This passage of Nider's *Formicarius* is one of the most horrifying in all of witch-hunting literature. The young man who confessed these things had, along with his wife, already escaped Peter's persecution on another occasion. This time, however, Peter managed to trap the couple, along with the woman who first spoke of the broth, and convict them of mass infanticide. Although the wife refused to confess, the husband confessed and "repented." According to Nider, the young man then "offered himself up joyfully [*laete*] to death" because "he had heard from literate men [*litteratos*] that he would obtain complete pardon [*veniam omnimodam*]."[60] One would dearly love to know who these literate men were and just what they promised. Were they clerics? As a lay judge, Peter had no authority to discuss such pardons with a defendant.

It sounds as if, in exchange for providing the information that Peter craved about witchcraft, the young man made the best of a very bad bargain. He was promised a complete absolution of all the sins that he had ever committed. Given the way this complete pardon was expressed, the man may have been allowed to hope that he could also cancel sin preemptively. Certainly, he was preparing to sin under duress. By falsely confessing to being a witch, constructing fables about the initiation ceremonies of witchcraft in concert with Judge Peter, he was about to sin against the sacrament of confession. Since he knew that he would be executed, he would also have known that a false confession would cause his eternal damnation unless he could annul it before death. Other defendants often realized this, and many retracted their confessions, only to be tortured again until they reconfirmed them. Forcing defendants into damnation through torture scandalized sixteenth-century opponents of witch-hunting as much or more than the torture itself, more even than their suspicion that defendants had committed no crime. So the young man may have hoped to obtain absolution by exploiting the ambiguity of that "omnimodal" pardon.[61]

The young man probably had a more personal sin on his conscience as well: betraying his wife to Judge Peter. Nider says that, although the wife had been "convicted by witnesses to the truth, [she] refused to confess either during torture or in the face of death. After her pyre had been prepared by a guard, the woman cursed him with evil words and was burned." It is reasonable to imagine that the young man and his wife had agreed to deny the charges and rely on their innocence and their resistance to torture. Nider specifies that they were kept in separate prisons, so they probably could not have changed their strategy or otherwise communicated freely. If there was an agreement, the young man reneged on it, for Nider says that he told Peter, "I believe my wife is so obstinate that she will rather endure the fire than confess the least part of the truth." Peter seems to have made her an offer like the one her husband accepted: Nider refers to her, not as impenitent (*impenitens*), but as unpersuadable (*impersuasibilis*). Nider concludes sanctimoniously that the wife's conduct shows "just how harmful is the icy antireligion [*perfidia*] that kills children and newborns" and that her husband died "in great contrition."[62] The last clause, at least, is believable.

Sacramental *beneficia* and the *maleficia* of witchcraft were separated by nothing but the opposing polarities of their powers. Although locating the origin of *maleficia* in sacramental energy may look blasphemous today, it had a considerable ideological advantage. Had witchcraft theorists postulated a simple opposition between good and evil powers, without explicitly tracing evil power to the perversion of good power, they would have risked two grave dangers. To imply that sacramental energies merely counteracted demonic ones might create the impression that evil had an autonomous origin and essence rather than being a mere privation of good, as Catholic tradition since Augustine maintained. Given the focus on demonic power in witchcraft theory, this could have implied belief in a Manichaean or dualistic theology and cosmology, a world in which Satan's power was equal and opposite to God's own. The church had spent decades in the twelfth and thirteenth centuries combating this heresy among the Albigensian Cathars of southern France.[63] So, although the Devil of witchcraft theory often seems nearly as powerful as God, a formal equation of their powers was unacceptable.

One of the main tasks of witchcraft theory was to demonstrate that God's control over the physical and moral cosmos was perfect, despite all appearances to the contrary. Locating a single source of supernatural energies was a necessary corollary to the idea that the ultimate reality was single and good, not double and self-contradictory. If moral evil was a perversion of moral good, then evil energy clearly needed a comparable definition. Otherwise, there was no proof that God was not somehow responsible for evil or incapable of stopping it.

Danger was present on another very different front. Unless sacramental *beneficia* and maleficial energies were somehow causally related, witchcraft could provide no definite proof of sacramental reality. As Peter's canceled act of crossing himself showed, complete absence of a sacrament could mean that the sacrament was irrelevant to the production of physical effects. Likewise, Nider's descriptions of the witches' initiation ceremony never imply that ritual power came only from the unconsecrated flesh of the stewed babies. Readers might decide that the act of cannibalism was horrific and unnatural enough to confer an evil power all by itself, whether sacraments had any reality or not.[64] Therefore, Peter or his learned commentator had to make explicit that real power was inherent in the sacraments by framing the cannibalism in a ritual context that mimicked and reversed Catholic rituals within the sacred space of a church.

To show that *maleficium* depended on *beneficium* was to create a theory that allowed both to be verified—or at least to hold out the hope. These syllogisms, however, were anything but complacent. Like their preoccupation with demonic corporeality, witchcraft theorists' treatment of the causes and effects of *maleficium* demonstrated, not firm belief, but rather a network of hypotheses. Only an overheated rhetoric of fear and hatred allowed the hypotheses to look like unquestioned belief. The hyperbolically inflated fear of witchcraft's ill effects *sounds* authentic when accompanied by expressions of hatred, bigotry, credulity, and superstitiousness. But the rhetoric of hatred and fear masks a relentless logic of desire. Expressions of superstitious credulity disguise a proto-scientific drive to verify the ill effects of witchcraft. Only thus could one locate and contemplate the good, sacramental energies that witches and demons had neutralized.

The paranoid fantasies of Judge Peter throw into question whether he, Nider, or other "upright" Christians who repeated these abject theories or killed other people for confessing their truth were truly contemptuous of witchcraft or horrified by it. Contempt and condescension were exactly the emotions that theorists of witchcraft *never* genuinely evinced when they wrote about the antireligion that they had invented. Witchcraft was necessary to explain the potential shortcomings of Catholicism. If witchcraft energy was imaginary, then so were the energies of the sacraments. As Nider intimates, witchcraft was *enviable,* and it evolved into an ideal construct that could fulfill any number of wishes.

Witchcraft theorists' fascination with topics that we find disgusting or cruel does not convict them of inconsistent religious motives. Their deepest concerns about religion were metaphysical, not moral. Witchcraft made perfect *logical* sense as part of a Christian system, and it was emotionally attractive because it presupposed physical interaction with beings that, by definition, good Christians could not seek to encounter. For someone to associate physically with those beings was indispensable. Without such people, there was no convincing case that the world of spirit was anything more than make-believe and wish fulfillment.

8

"THIS IS MY BODY": WITCHES AND DESECRATION

> The tabooed object is always an indication of the deepest interest of the society that forbids. All the forces that combined to intensify the prohibitions against sexual activity outside marriage, tended in practice to increase the importance of sex in the total picture of human life.
>
> —Ian Watt, *The Rise of the Novel*

The notion that witchcraft *maleficia* were produced by perverting the energies of sacramental *beneficia* was useful for maintaining credence in sacramental energies and effects. The most important sacrament of all was the eucharist or holy communion. The claims made for it by orthodox theologians surpassed everything claimed for the other sacraments: every day, in thousands of places, Christ became flesh and blood once more in the hands of his priests, and his body was eaten by believers. Each time mass was celebrated, the sacrifice of the son of God was repeated, and it was a real sacrifice, not a symbol or a ritual reminder of a long-ago incident. When the priest pronounced the words "This is my body," a miraculous transformation took place: bread and wine became true flesh and true blood.

But none of this was visible: what had been bread and wine still looked like bread and wine. One had to believe that the change had taken place, but without any kind of sensory confirmation. A lucky few people claimed to have experienced it; but their experience was private and mystical, even visionary.

Was there any way of knowing that the miraculous transformation happened in external reality? To know that it did, one would have to see the blood at least. For complete certainty, one would need confirmation that one was not alone, that others had had the same experience. By the thirteenth century, a number of stories about miraculous public transformations were circulating. In a few cases, holy people had caused the sacrament to reveal its nature by becoming perceptible flesh or blood. But the majority of the transformations were caused by violent mishandling or desecration. Desecration made the eucharist declare its nature: the effects of its consecration by a holy man were imperceptible, but they became perceptible through the violence of an unholy person. These stories offered expert testimony; one might never experience eucharistic verification, but there were witnesses that it had happened and that it had happened publicly.

Ironically, the need for sensory verification was stimulated by increased precision in defining how the bread and wine became Christ's flesh and blood. The central eucharistic dogma is the *presence* of Christ in the consecrated elements of bread and wine, yet that presence cannot be perceived by the human senses. Traditionally, it had sufficed to believe that the words of Scripture meant that there was a *real presence* of Christ in the elements of holy communion: Christ himself was *somehow* present in the bread and wine once the priest had spoken the words of consecration. In the ninth century, literate Christians had begun to worry whether Christ's statement "This is my body" became literally true when repeated by the priest at mass or was only a reminder of Christ's sacrifice on the cross.[1] By the eleventh century, it was becoming clear that the doctrine of real presence was no longer adequate.

Something more precise and scientific was needed. In 1059, and again in 1079, Berengar of Tours, who had opposed the literalist interpretation, was forced to swear that, after consecration, the eucharistic elements became "the true and proper and vivifying flesh and blood of Jesus Christ, . . . the true body of Christ, which was born of the Virgin."[2] In 1215, the Fourth Lateran Council, under Innocent III, included the word *transubstantiated* in its decrees concerning the eucharist; literalism, already traditional, was now official for all Christendom.[3] All Western Christians were to be taught that the wafer or host was literally, absolutely, and completely transformed into the body of Christ.

Transubstantiation was a logical outgrowth of the earlier orthodoxy. Scholastic theologians explained more precisely, in terminology shared with the physical sciences of the time, *how* Christ became present in the wafer. Only the appearances (or species or accidents) of bread and wine remained, completely unsupported by the reality (or substance) of bread and wine, which had been invisibly supplanted by the reality of Christ's body and blood.[4] For ecclesiastical authorities, transubstantiation also justified the withholding of the chalice of eucharistic wine from the laity, a practice that had begun with the intention of avoiding the scandal of spilling Christ's blood. Since every particle of the consecrated host became both body and blood, there was no need for layfolk to partake of the chalice.[5] These doctrines would be reiterated by the Council of Florence (1439) and the Council of Trent (1551).[6] Such reinforcement was necessary: transubstantiation and even real presence were resisted by several important groups of heretics in the late Middle Ages, even before the rise of Protestantism.

The mythology of desecration offered an indirect way of defending eucharistic reality against doubt. Only an unbeliever had reason to mishandle the sacrament deliberately, and, in tales of desecration, the eucharist reacted to disbelief by making its sacramental reality suddenly obvious to the senses, overpowering them with fear or revulsion. This transformation from pure sacrament to filthy desecration was intimately related to the beneficent powers supposedly produced by the sacrament. That is, *per*version of the sacrament resulted in an *in*version of its characteristics. Spiritual energies became materialized; the undetectable became detectable.

A fundamental characteristic of early witchcraft theorists was their craving for empirical confirmation of eucharistic reality, made evident by their frequent and vivid descriptions of witches mishandling the sacrament. Eucharistic desecration was necessary to the logic of witchcraft: it too was *corporeal interaction* with the supernatural. The eucharist was commonly defined by theologians as *corpus verum,* the true body of Christ. Just as the virtual body of demons had to make imperceptible demonic reality evident, so the Lord's body was required to demonstrate its hidden nature to human perception.[7] The *corpus demonis* and the *corpus domini* were subject to the same doubts, and only a real body would calm those doubts.

Heinrich Kramer provides a fascinating example of eucharistic desecration that he claims to take from his own witch-hunting casebook:

> And now, as to just how they perform such [*maleficia*], first by means of the sacraments, and secondly by means of the sacramentals, we will refer to some recent happenings, discovered by us through an investigation [*per inquisitionem*].
>
> In a town which charity and reason prevent me from naming, when a certain witch received the body of our Lord, she suddenly lowered her head, as is the detestable habit of women, placed her garment near her mouth, and taking the body of our Lord out of her mouth, she wrapped it in a small cloth. Afterwards, at the suggestion of the Devil, she placed it in a jar in which there was a toad, and hid it underground in a stable near the storehouse of her house, together with several other things, by means of which she was going to work her *maleficia.* But with the help of God's mercy this great crime was detected and brought to light.
>
> For on the following day a workman was going on his business near that stable, and heard a sound like a child crying; and the closer he came to the paving-stone under which the jar had been hidden, the more

> clearly he heard it. And thinking that some child had been buried there by the woman, he went to the Mayor or chief magistrate, and told him what had been done, as he thought, by the infanticide [*parricida*]. And the Mayor quickly sent his servants and found it to be as he had said. But they were unwilling to exhume the child, wisely deciding [*sano usi consilio*] to stand watch and wait to see if any woman came near the place; for they did not know that it was the Lord's body that was hidden there.
>
> And so it happened that the same witch came to the place, and hid the jar under her garment while the others watched from their hiding-place. And when she was taken and questioned, she laid bare her crime, saying that the Lord's body had been hidden in the jar with the toad, so that by making her powders from them, she might be able to cause injuries to men and other creatures whenever she wished.[8]

Notice that Kramer never openly asserts that this incident proves the sacramental reality of the eucharist. Anyone familiar with basic eucharistic dogma can understand the point of the story by paying attention to its circumstances.

Kramer made his point with a minimal expenditure of rhetorical energy, so he may look like a believer. Yet the logical weaknesses of the story expose it as a response to the need for verification. The workman and the authorities demonstrated neither common sense nor compassion: suspecting that a child was buried under the paving stone, they set an ambush for a witch rather than attempting to rescue the child. And they did this precisely because "they did *not* know" that it was the eucharist rather than a real child that was in terrible distress. Kramer allows himself one momentary outburst of pious indignation ("this great crime"). But his indignation is not directed against the abuse of children. In fact, he is not indignant about the abuse of the sacrament, either. The logic of the story is about sacramental reality and the unconfessable hope that desecration will verify it; that logic makes any indignation about the witch's actions look insincere.

Whatever Kramer says, his real purpose for torturing the woman into this confession (assuming that he did not invent the entire story) was to reassure himself that the eucharist could *do something* other than just lie there like any other lump of bread. This he proved both by having the witch confess how the desecrated sacrament would have caused *maleficia* and by finding witnesses to its vocal protest against the misdirection of its miraculous energies. While the vocal protest established Christ's real presence in the consecrated host, the *maleficia* that its desecration would have produced were supposed to derive from the perversion of that presence and its energies.

Tales like this exude as strong an aura of repressed skepticism as tales of demonic copulation. Just as the taboo against demonic copulation was not primarily about sex, so tales of desecration were not ultimately concerned with respectful comportment. Although Kramer does not do so in the anecdote just examined, theorists regularly asserted that desecrating witches intended to insult and humiliate Christ. This implies that witches already believed that Christ was present in or around the sacrament. Otherwise, there would have been no reason to portray their motive as mockery. (What good is a public insult if its target is not thought capable of perceiving it?) Yet witches' malice allegedly made them incapable of properly interpreting the outcome of their desecrations. In these highly convention-bound stories, witches never foresee that their desecrations will produce actual, empirically verifiable results. But no desecration story fails to provide this nasty surprise. A desecration that did not produce flesh or blood would have served the witches' purpose but not those of the tales' tellers.

Worse yet, witches habitually drew the wrong conclusions—*obviously* wrong conclusions—when their desecrations produced tangible results, as if they had never heard of real presence or transubstantiation. But witches were by definition renegade Christians, so they could not have avoided such knowledge. Eucharistic desecrations were not discussed only among theologians: they were also the subject of sermons and pictures aimed at the unlettered.[9] Thus, there were fundamental contradictions in the supposed behavior of witches toward the sacrament. Strangely, witchcraft theorists never comment on the contradictions, despite vilifying witches as stupid wretches. However, like Kramer, other theorists were scrupulously careful to provide the correct interpretation of the empirical results through the logic and circumstances of their tales.

Attention to these sorts of cues confirms that witchcraft theorists told stories of desecration to demonstrate that the eucharist was neither an empty ceremony nor a mere symbol of some intangible benefit. Just as stories of demonic copulation demonstrated that demons were not imaginary, so stories about eucharistic desecration proved that the sacraments worked tangible effects on external reality, not just in the spirit or the imagination. This defensiveness can be seen more clearly in stories of eucharistic desecration that circulated before the construct of the witch was fully evolved. In these stories the need for verification is not yet sufficiently camouflaged; logic and circumstance are not allowed to do all the work.

Alonso de Espina's *Fortalitium fidei,* or *Fortress of the Faith* (ca. 1460), can be considered a witchcraft treatise because it has a section denouncing the allies of demons. However, de Espina's tale of eucharistic desecration does not come from his alleged personal experience. It is a much-repeated traditional story that had circulated for at least two centuries before de Espina. And it concerns, not a witch, but rather a Jew.

Alonso claimed that a Jewish usurer had once obtained a eucharistic host from a Christian woman. Having recently pawned her best dress with the Jew, the woman wished to borrow it back so as to be properly dressed on Easter Sunday. The usurer would not consent to this act of kindness; rather, he eventually convinced the woman, against her conscience and better judgment, to accept an impious bargain. She could have her dress back for good, rather than for a day, but in exchange she had to remove the eucharistic host from her mouth at Easter mass and bring it to him. As soon as the usurer was alone with the object, he threw it into a kettle of boiling oil and water. But first he spoke to it, daring it to prove its reality:

> "Are you that god of the Christians? Are you that Jesus Christ whom the crazy credulity of the Christians considers and believes absolutely to be God? If you are that man, whom my fathers gave up to be beaten, then I hereby commit you to the boiling waves! If they tortured you with the cross, I give you up to cooking! They gave you to death when you were alive, but, now that you are dead, I will give you death again! If you want to talk, *if you are God, show whatever power you have,* and defend yourself from the fire!"
>
> Spewing these and similar wickednesses from his mouth, he threw the body of Our Lord Jesus Christ into the boiling waters. Instantly, the Jew and his children saw the beautiful form of a little boy walking about on the boiling water. Seeing this great sign and miracle, the Jew was *not* converted to God; rather, just as holy Moses tells us Jewish people always do, he behaved like a Jew and remained stiff-necked and hardened in his mind [*animo*].
>
> Several times he tried to use the iron poker in his hand to plunge the little boy, who was shining like the sun, under the boiling waters of the urn. But he could not even touch the boy; divine wisdom so guided the Christ child [*puer Iesus*] that, just as the Jew thought he saw him in the middle of the urn, he would appear on the right side of it. And, when he tried to injure him there, he would appear on the left side. The Jew wrestled with the little child there but could never overcome him in this trial [*causa*].[10]

As the last word indicates, this is a trial or an ordeal, and Christ wins, vindicating his real presence in the sacrament and the reality of transubstantiation. Like the witches who would come after him, the Jew is too cruel and stubborn to give in and believe the empirical evidence; his wife and children, however, convert to Christianity and abandon him to his fate.

The bishop of Paris arrives too late to see the Christ child. He finds only a perfectly preserved eucharistic host. This he accepts as proof, not that nothing has happened, but that a miracle has happened. Everyone says that the wafer was boiled, became a child, and so on, yet here it sits, fresh as the moment it was consecrated. So the bishop has the Jew put to death for desecration. The Jew's last request is to be burned with the Talmud, which he says will preserve him from death because it makes its believers immortal. The book naturally fails the test and is burned to ashes with the Jew.[11]

This tale was one of the most famous stories of eucharistic desecration in all the Middle Ages.[12] It had been told dozens of times since the thirteenth century, and there were dozens of similar stories. In the transition from de Espina to Kramer, we can watch the process whereby, in the 1400s, witches inherited a role that formerly had been largely reserved for Jews: the "enemy of Christ." This personage demonstrates hatred for Christ by abusing the eucharist, in order to assault him *literally*. Stories of Jews and witches were ideologically useful as narratives of lived experience, for they told how Christ responded *personally* to doubt about Christianity's claim to be the one true religion and to skepticism about the reality of its miraculous claims.

From the standpoint of sacramental theory, these narratives of experience look very much like accounts of *experiments*. They are the most vivid illustration of a pattern that the historian of science Lynn White observed in late-medieval discussions of the eucharist: "It was as though Europe had become populated with doubting Thomases eager to thrust their fingers into the very wounds of Christ. To an extraordinary degree the new eucharistic cult was empirical in temper, permitting the constant seeing and handling of God."[13] Many dogmas of Christianity were immune to experimentation, but the theology of sacraments tantalized Christian theologians with the possibility of empirical verification because sacraments combined ritual gestures and linguistic performances in ways that were supposed to produce real effects. The obligatory references to eyewitness testimony and confessions in stories about desecration show how ardently verification was desired.

Stories of witches' and Jews' eucharistic desecrations were important confirmation of sacramental reality, but not all confirmed the same doctrines. Each story emphasizes one of the two related dogmas about the eucharist. A bleeding eucharist suggests or confirms that the host is transubstantiated, literally the body *and the blood* of Christ; a vocal wafer that wails and weeps, or becomes an actual child, demonstrates real presence, the idea that Christ is somehow present whenever the eucharist is celebrated. In all cases, the miracle happens because *Christ himself* has been subjected to a humiliating and disgusting outrage, his body having been impiously broken or contaminated.

There is another difference: stories of desecrating Jews often begin with a Jew's quasi-scientific curiosity about the claims that Christians make for an object that he considers a mere bit of bread. The stories then describe his single-minded determination to test the reality of those claims. The Jews' experiments are invariably successful—usually the eucharist bleeds, although other forms of literalization, like de Espina's visible Christ child and Kramer's audible voice, are possible.

Clearly, the logic of these tales betrays the interests of their tellers, far more than of skeptical Jews. In the first place, the Jewish desecrator almost never converts, although Jewish bystanders sometimes do. Some desecrators, while not converting, become frightened and attempt to get rid of the wounded host, but miraculous obstacles always frustrate their efforts, making discovery of the desecration, and its resultant miracle, inevitable.

The stereotypical Jew was valuable and desirable to the teller of such tales precisely because of his reputation as "Christ killer." His paradoxical refusal to believe what he sees is rhetorically condemned as hard-heartedness, stupidity, or sheer unmotivated malice. But, from the Christian viewpoint, the Jew's malice is the crucial element that makes the experiment succeed. The experiment was intensely *desired* by the Christian tellers of these tales, but the experiment required a "researcher" raised since childhood to disbelieve in the divinity of Christ. The Jew's disbelief was not adequate: he must be desirous of certainty and devoid of inhibitions yet too prejudiced to accept the overwhelming obvious.

The Jew in the story is an inverted self-portrait of the Christian who told his story. Although the narrator opposed the attitude of the Jew in his tale by desiring a vindication of eucharistic literality, he exploited his protagonist as a surrogate, a "lab assistant" who could perform the forbidden experiment. The Jew carried out the experiment for all the worst reasons and proved, against his own intention, that the claims made for transubstantiation of the sacrament *were not untrue after all*. Thus, he provided a scapegoat onto whom the Christian narrator projected his own doubts or anxieties. By vilifying the Jew, the narrator condemned and atoned for his own doubts, camouflaging the projection with time-honored and theologically sanctioned stereotypes and hatreds of Jews.[14]

The witch's paradoxical failure to convert was a theme that the early witchcraft theorists probably inherited from stories of Jewish desecrators. Neither repents when confronted with the evidence of a miracle, much less expresses belief in eucharistic reality. At most, witches might express horror at the bloody mess that they created or repent and confess belief once they were caught and prosecuted. Cui bono? Unlike the stereotypical Jew of desecration narratives, a witch's whole religious education had presumably focused on making her believe the claims of eucharistic literality. Since witches were supposed to be deliberate renegades from Christianity, any witch who saw a miraculous host would have been a simpleton not to return to the church since this was a miracle that confirmed Christ's words at the Last Supper, "This is my body, given for you" (Luke 22:19).

Jews, and the witches who partially replaced them, were not to remain surrogate desecrators forever. In the early Reformation, within seventy years of de Spina, Swiss Protestant iconoclasts would publicly issue challenges and taunts to eucharistic hosts before desecrating them. In 1528, iconoclasts from Bern built a fire in a Franciscan chapel, "into which they threw the consecrated hosts." In Neuchâtel in 1530, "the mob destroyed every cultic object in the church, ransacked the sanctuary, and consumed the consecrated hosts as if they were common bread." Later, in Geneva, they rampaged "even to the extent of feeding the sacred host to a goat and saying 'Now he can die if he wants; he has received the sacrament.'" Following a fiery sermon by Guillaume Farel in 1535, Protestants invaded the cathedral of Geneva. The mob took about fifty consecrated hosts and fed them to a dog, whose owner quipped, "If they really are gods, then they won't let themselves be eaten by a dog." The defenseless wafers—"dieux blancs," as they were called—were quickly consumed by the dog.[15]

This behavior of real-world Christians, on the same territory that produced witches, increases the likelihood that desecrating Jews and witches in earlier narratives were vicariously acting out the repressed desires of medieval Christians for confirmation of eucharistic reality. Surely not all desecrators of the 1500s were completely convinced that the hosts could not respond to their provocation. Even if they were, their desecrations must have had a powerful effect on bystanders. After so many centuries of stories about hosts that responded instantly to desecration, what could it mean if nothing happened?

Great care is needed in interpreting narratives of eucharistic desecration, precisely because of their polemical attitude toward groups of people who were violently persecuted. The social realities of prejudice against Jews and the persecution and mass murder of them on the pretext of eucharistic desecration are all too tragically evident. Many, if not most, desecration narratives about Jews had been repeated in order to justify bloody assaults—pogroms—against them. My analysis is not intended to explain how such tales about Jews *originated.* Such tales, whether about Jews or about witches, had many ideological uses. They could be used to justify violence against people who had already been singled out as worthy of destruction, but that was not their only utility.[16]

When the storyteller portrays his motivation as unquestioning credulity about truths that the enemies of Christ deny, something besides human hatred is at stake. Whatever their attitudes toward groups of real people, some late-medieval theologians were eager for demonstrations of doctrinal validity. Stories about Jews and witches served that theological purpose, which could be "compartmentalized" and distinguished from the social function of defending and rationalizing atrocities. Indeed, there is evidence that, although they often recounted such anti-Semitic tales as these, Christian ecclesiastics often condemned violence against Jews in their writings and sometimes attempted to prevent or halt massacres of them.[17]

Rather than unmotivated hatred of Jews or bad conscience about atrocities, de Espina's tale exemplifies *motivated* hatred. The context in which he tells it is the construction of a symbolic, textual "fortress" of Christianity (*Fortalitium fidei*), to defend the faith against all who doubt or scorn it. De Spina's tale was centuries old, but Heinrich Kramer told a completely new story, claiming to have tortured a live woman into the "Toad Witch's" confession. As far as ideological utility goes, it is not relevant whether Kramer actually did this despicable thing or fabricated the entire story without physically harming anyone. The ideological burden of both tales, despite their differences, is the same: something really happens when the priest speaks the words of consecration ("This is my body") over the bread of communion. If one were evil enough, as evil as a Jew or a witch, one might personally experience the reality of that transformation. By mobilizing Christian hatred of outcasts, stories of desecration betrayed a hope that Christians were not condemned to remain eternally in doubt about the reality of the sacraments.

Witchcraft theorists depicted witches and Jews engaging in eucharistic experiments. Unlike Jews, however, witches were usually not portrayed as prototypical scientists: they show no awareness of experimenting. The Jew acts because he is skeptical, the witch because she at least believes enough eucharistic doctrine to think that she will insult Christ by mishandling the host. This is clear even when there is no mention of her belief in transubstantiation. This, in its way, is revealing. Given the rich history of supposed experimental desecrations by Jews, it looks as if the theme of experimentation was being repressed in stories about witches. As with demonic copulation and demonic transvection, the logic of these narratives betrays powerful urges, while the rhetoric of pious credulity and bigoted hatred disowns them.

The inhibitions against such experimentation were powerful. Witchcraft theorists could never have performed it themselves, for it was impious. There was another reason too. As with experiments about witches' transvection, there was always the danger that the experiment would fail, yielding no advance in knowledge. Failure would imperil the experimenter's soul by further weakening his faith. It was more satisfying to imagine someone else taking the risks and discovering the desired result. Even more satisfying would be a successful experiment performed without the awareness of experimenting. Thus, theorists constructed the witch as a de facto experimenter, unaware of the "scientific" implications of her actions.

The Positive Version

Such behavior illustrates the paradoxes of proof. The more late-medieval theologians insisted that the wafer was the *corpus verum,* or real body of Christ, the more desire they created for empirical proof, both among themselves and, apparently, among pious laity. Even liturgical practices cried out for dramatization of proof: part of the Easter celebrations in some medieval churches involved placing a consecrated host in a make-believe tomb in the church sanctuary on Good Friday, from whence it would be "resurrected" during the service on Easter morning.[18]

Moreover, narratives about eucharistic verification were not told only about evildoers. Miri Rubin tells of a Jewish woman who unconsciously demonstrated the reality of both eucharist and baptism:

> A Jewess moved to another region where she was unknown, and pretended to be a Christian. When she lay on her death-bed and was visited by a priest, she confessed to him that she had never been baptised. The priest tried to persuade her to convert but failed, until he remembered that in the early church ("primitiva ecclesia"), people were often healed following baptism, as [the Emperor] Constantine's case amply illustrated. On hearing this, the Jewess decided to be baptised, and she was healed. On a subsequent visit to her [the confessor] learned from the woman of her regret. Whereas in the past she had always received a vision of a pretty little boy in the priest's hand at church, this vision disappeared once she had been baptised. The priest patiently explained that faith is not proven by seeing but by belief. Before she was converted the vision was sent to persuade her; as a Christian she no longer needed such proof.

Rubin interprets this as a "complex tale about the instability of conversion and the ease with which Jews might invade Christian spaces." Equating rhetoric with logic, she asserts that "the affirming visions are inserted in passing, as a common occurrence, just as natural as eucharistic truth."[19]

But "eucharistic truth" was not "natural"; it only gets represented that way through rhetoric. This story presents dogma through a priest's patient explanations instead of an inquisitor's accusations. Here, the *innocently disbelieving* Jew stands in for her Christian counterparts in a less-threatening manner than witches or Jewish men, but the same polemical points are made as in tales of deliberate eucharistic desecration—along with a bonus vindication of the corporeal benefits of baptism. The polemical points are scored more effectively through understatement and circumstance than they could have been through explicitness and overstatement. But the ideal audience is still Christians, not Jews.

Even devout Christians were supposed to experience the reality of transubstantiation and real presence on occasion. Carolyn Bynum and other historians have discussed late-medieval eucharistic legends about innocent believers who experienced visions of miniature children, bleeding hosts, and hosts containing bits of flesh or even tiny arms and legs. Down through the fourteenth century, such grisly experiences were regularly attributed to female mystics, as Bynum exhaustively documents.

According to Bynum, popular piety truly believed in transubstantiation: "The proliferating eucharistic miracles of the twelfth and thirteenth centuries—in which the host, lying on the paten, shut away in the tabernacle, or raised high in the priest's hands, turned visibly into Christ—were not (as some have argued) the result of the doctrine of transubstantiation. Rather, they were an expression of the sort of piety that made such doctrinal definition seem obviously true." Bynum's contention may be true for many people in the period before the birth of the term *transubstantiation*. But after 1215, at least, popular miracles were prized by some clergy because they offered proof that dogmatic definitions of Christ's real presence in the host were obviously true. Clerics (always men) habitually controlled the process of recording women's experience of eucharistic miracles. Thus, given the increasing interest in proof, it is difficult to know just how accurately they portrayed the women's experiences and beliefs.[20]

Christian laity were not allowed to handle the consecrated host except to consume it, so their miracles were purely subjective and left no empirical evidence. But, like Jewish men, Christian clerics, including priests officiating at mass, had eucharistic experiences of doubt, disbelief, and empirical confirmation. Like the experiments of Jewish men, priestly miracles often produced tangible evidence by leaving behind pieces of flesh or staining the accoutrements of the mass with enough blood to create relics. Like the hosts desecrated by Jews, these priestly relics could then be displayed to the faithful as empirical proof of transubstantiation.

In fact, the most famous of all eucharistic miracles, the "Miracle of Bolsena" (which, strangely, Bynum never mentions),[21] supposedly happened to a skeptical priest officiating at mass in 1263. A German or Bohemian priest, unable to believe the literality of transubstantiation, supposedly prayed to God for a sign that would convince him. As if on cue, the instant that he uttered the words of consecration, "This is my body," the host sprayed him and the vestments of the mass with droplets of blood shaped like tiny human figures. Owing in part to the publicity surrounding this miracle, the feast of Corpus Christi, which celebrated every aspect of the corporeality of the sacrament, was increasingly revered.[22] This miracle provided empirical proof of transubstantiation, publicly literalizing the term enshrined by Lateran IV. To this day, the relics are conserved and venerated in the cathedral of Orvieto, in central Italy. Afterward, the Miracle of Bolsena inspired other eucharistic miracles, as it had presumably been inspired by previous ones.[23]

Thomas Aquinas was crucial in the process of pursuing belief: he explained the theory of transubstantiation, promoted the new feast of Corpus Christi, and may have composed hymns in honor of the sacrament.[24] Aquinas apparently knew the stakes for belief. In his commentary on Peter Lombard's *Sentences,* he entertained the idea that "if what is done occasionally for the strengthening of faith were done always, that would not be a mockery of faith, but an even greater confirmation. And sometimes, *in order to strengthen the faith of someone who is doubtful about this sacrament,* the body of Christ shows itself under the *species* [appearance or form] of flesh, as we read in the life of Saint Gregory and in the lives of other fathers. Thus it would not be a mockery if the eucharist always showed itself in its own *species* [i.e., as flesh or blood]."[25]

Nonetheless, Aquinas concluded, it is better that such miracles be occasional because humans abhor cannibalism. If the body of Christ were not presented under the *species* of bread and wine, the faithful would suffer horror "because man does not only flee from touching unclean things out of abomination, but also from touching holy things, out of devotion."[26] But the cat was out of the bag, as it were: far from remaining occasional, eucharistic miracles proliferated after Aquinas's time in a way that seems excessive and even obsessive, particularly since so many miracle stories featured enemies of the faith.

We could imagine, as scholars often have, that some people truly thought of themselves as witches and were actively hostile to the sacred objects and signs connected to Catholic ritual. But, within the context of witchcraft theory, the question whether real people intentionally desecrated the eucharist, and, if so, for what end, is largely irrelevant. However, while witches were imaginary, stories about them addressed preoccupations about the behavior of real people. From the eleventh century on, there were several waves of opposition to dogma about the sacraments, particularly the eucharist. Many Christians contested the doctrine of real presence before transubstantiation was formally championed in the thirteenth century by Innocent III, Aquinas, and other influential churchmen.

The protests were growing by the late fourteenth century and the early fifteenth. John Wyclif and Jan Hus both inspired movements of heretics, in part by opposing eucharistic orthodoxy. Sacramental theory was central to Catholic theology and ritual practice, so opposition to definitions of the sacraments was not a peripheral feature of heresy: it was crucial, from the eleventh century to the consolidation of Protestantism half a millennium later.[27] Official endorsement simply could not guarantee the doctrine's universal acceptance, miracle stories or no.

However, stories of eucharistic miracles did grow dramatically in popularity among the laity throughout the late Middle Ages. Between 1263 and about 1400, popular veneration of the eucharist and pilgrimages to the sites of eucharistic miracles greatly increased. In late-medieval Germany, there were over a hundred such sites, according to historians. Such popular enthusiasm caused a clerical backlash: while some churchmen affected and encouraged credulity about eucharistic miracles, others took a cautious approach.

By the turn of the fifteenth century, some influential churchmen were distrustful of eucharistic miracles and the spectacle that they excited at places where they had occurred. Jan Hus opposed pilgrimages to the extremely popular site of Wilsnack in 1405; a year later, he criticized the veneration of bleeding hosts in general. Hus would be burned as a heretic in 1415 and become a martyr of "Hussite" resistance to Rome, but criticism of eucharistic enthusiasm was not lacking within the Roman hierarchy. Cardinal Nicholas of Cusa was a pious philosopher and a negotiator with Hussites. He forbade the veneration of bleeding hosts throughout Germany in 1451, only to be overruled by papal decree two years later. And, Heinrich Kramer aside, Dominicans were in general wary of stories of eucharistic miracles, at least where bleeding hosts were concerned.[28]

To consider eucharistic miracle narratives in isolation from this ongoing polemical context would be naive. It is clear what interests were served by making people confess under torture—or, in the case of mystics and priests, by encouraging, recording, and broadcasting their willing testimony—that the eucharistic host distilled real blood or otherwise reacted like a sentient being when subjected to extremes of belief or disbelief.

Witches and the Eucharist

Rather than accurately describing the external realities of heresy, transformations in the stereotype of the desecrating unbeliever betrayed the deepening uncertainty of believers about the provability of sacramental doctrines. Witches were a new kind of desecrating heretic, imagined as more threatening than the stereotypical Jew. They were more numerous, and they had easy access to the sacred object. Witches were more dreadful than traditional heretics, for their alliance with Satan was willful and hateful, not the result of ignorant misunderstandings over doctrine. But the sense of threat and dread was not entirely unpleasant; it had its emotional utility, and it was actively sought out through the repetition of stories.[29] Rather than being authentically frightened or outraged, some clerics were obviously comforted.

Desecration of the host became a regular feature of witchcraft mythology at an early stage. From the beginning, witchcraft theorists were as interested in evidence of desecration as in crimes of *maleficium* against living persons. Before 1440, trials in Swiss dioceses were already forcing testimony of ritual desecration during gatherings of heretic-witches.[30] In her examination of some of these earliest trials, Martine Ostorero documents that inquisitors were finding evidence of crimes against the eucharist simply because that is what they were looking for.[31]

In 1460, Girolamo Visconti was describing enemies of the faith who look more like witches than heretics to modern eyes. He related that "such people confess that they have sometimes taken the true body of Christ," that is, the *corpus verum,* or consecrated eucharistic wafer, "to the witches' game. In fact, when they receive the host in church, they pretend to wipe their mouths and thus remove it secretly. Later, at the witches' game, they either stamp on it or offer it to the Devil."[32]

Visconti did not, however, mention any eucharistic miracles. This became a subject of worry for his editor, who tried to correct the omission. Visconti wrote around 1460, but his treatises were not printed until 1490, by Alvisio Della Croce, a monk and canon lawyer. As Visconti's editor, Della Croce declares that he made one modification to the text: "I added an explanation why the body of Christ allows itself to be trampled on by this kind of criminal."[33] Della Croce must have been profoundly disturbed by Visconti's assertions, for he gives two contradictory reasons why Christ allows the desecration to happen. In so doing, he revealed how deeply problems in eucharistic doctrine could affect confidence in Christianity.

Visconti had simply said that it was no wonder that Christ allowed the eucharist to be trampled since he had voluntarily submitted to crucifixion. Visconti's uncomplicated identification of the consecrated host with the body that died on the cross obscures a long history of contention. Doctrine held that there were not two bodies of Christ, only one, yet commentators struggled for centuries to understand how Christ's body could be expanded ad infinitum through the eucharist and still remain in heaven at the right hand of God, in exactly the same form as on the first Easter morning.[34]

Della Croce's editorial intrusion shows that he was dissatisfied with Visconti's identification of the body of Christ crucified (the *corpus historicum*), the body of Christ resurrected (the *corpus gloriosum*), and the body eaten in the eucharist (the *corpus verum,* or "true" body). Perhaps he was outraged at the idea that Christ could be in heaven even as he was being desecrated.[35] Or he may simply have found the identification of the various bodies paradoxical, as many heretics had and would. So Della Croce introduced another reason for Christ to allow desecration: "Or, like me, add this to the author's response, and say that it is not strange or contrary to his divine goodness that he allows his most reverend body to be trampled underfoot since through his ineffable mercy he daily permits it to be taken at the altar by evil persons as well as good, even by fornicators, profaners of holy things [*sacrilegis*], robbers, murderers, and numberless other criminals."[36] Della Croce simply eliminates the *corpus historicum* and the *corpus gloriosum* so as to limit his attention to the *corpus verum.* He has not denied their sameness, but the heavenly *corpus* is out of the limelight.

After all, says Della Croce, Saint Paul tells us that anyone who receives communion unworthily, while he is still polluted by unconfessed sin, is not really receiving a sacrament, not receiving the body of Christ in the full sense. Instead, he is eating his own damnation, for he behaves as if he does not believe that the eucharist is the body of Christ. By the same token, those who trample the consecrated wafer are not really mistreating the body of Christ, at least as regards its divine powers and efficacy; they do not injure God's glory or majesty, but only themselves.[37]

Yet Della Croce is no happier with this explanation; now he is distressed by the idea that the consecrated wafer might sometimes be the body of Christ and sometimes not. So he adds another explanation and begins to address his deepest concern: "Nor is it strange [*mirum*] that no miracles happen because of this crime, because in other places many miracles have been shown, and since our evil actions provoke God every day, the showing of miracles would have to go on infinitely, which is against Aristotle."[38] Miracles that happened every day would not be miracles; they would be natural and ordinary. So we should not be concerned if witches do not add to the stock of eucharistic miracles.

Della Croce chooses not to consider transubstantiation itself a daily miracle. Indeed, he tries to wrest his discussion away from miracles, but with no success:

> Nor does our faith derive its power [*virtutem*] from miracles. For faith has no merit where human experience and human reason concur. And indeed God even strikes those who merely treat the sacrament thoughtlessly, as we read of Oza, whom God struck and killed for his thoughtlessness because he put out his hand to steady the Ark of the Covenant when the oxen drawing it stumbled. And he strikes those who insult or obstruct [*improperantes*] his own servants the prophets. For the earth swallowed Dathan and Abiron alive because of the insolence and irreverence they showed to God's servant Moses. If God so punishes insolence to his servant, how much more will he avenge it if it is directed at himself? Let no one therefore believe that he is escaping divine judgment when he dares to treat the sacrament so abusively.[39]

Della Croce seems to be proving his perfect indifference to miracles by citing a long string of them. His last sentence, moreover, returns to his anxiety over not hearing that miracles take place when witches desecrate the eucharist. The weakest, least-sincere statement of all is his assertion that faith does not depend on miracles: as far as the abstract definition of faith goes, that is perfectly true, but not in Della Croce's discussion.

A Career in Defense of the Eucharist

Concerns about the efficacy of the sacraments defined the career of Heinrich Kramer. His fascination with witchcraft was entwined with these complex anxieties, as revealed by the Toad Witch story and the theory that *maleficium* depended on sacramental energies. Kramer's career after publishing the *Malleus maleficarum* bears out dramatically the link between his anguished theological skepticism about the eucharist and his desire for witches. The need to defend eucharistic reality stimulated most of his writings.

Nine years after the publication of the *Malleus,* Kramer brought out a collection entitled *Tractatus varii cum sermonibus contra errores adversus eucharistiam exortos*, or *Various Treatises and Sermons against Errors about the Eucharist*.[40] As its title indicates, this is a collection of treatises and sermons defending eucharistic reality as defined by orthodox Catholic theology. In addition to thirty-six sermons about the eucharist, the collection contained "a little treatise concerning the miraculous host preserved under the species of blood for 300 years at Augsburg, or a confutation of the error that asserts that, whenever the miraculous sacrament of the eucharist appears in the host in the form of blood or human flesh or a [human] figure, it is not a true sacrament; with the promulgation of excommunication against those who hold this opinion."[41] According to Kramer's Dominican biographers, "Our Heinrich had a serious dispute on account of the daring sermon of a preacher who at Augsburg dared to assert that the Catholic church had not laid down anything definitive about the appearance of blood or human remains in the sacrament of the eucharist, concerning whether Christ is truly present and truly to be worshiped there [in such miraculous hosts] by the people. And [the Augsburg preacher] said that this matter should be left to the judgment of God because regarding it nothing certain has been defined by the church or the holy fathers or doctors."[42]

In the context of fifteenth-century theological quarrels, it is clear that Kramer's opponent was merely urging circumspection in a matter that, since the thirteenth century, had brought ever-increasing sensationalism to the cult of the eucharist. Yet Kramer's biographers conclude that "in this matter Heinrich proved both the zeal of his faith and the authority of his office, condemning the assertions of the aforesaid [Augsburg] preacher, and forbidding, under pain of excommunication, that they be taught by anyone."[43]

Kramer's eucharistic treatises of 1496 also appear to have been motivated by a controversy of the previous year, concerning other issues of real presence and transubstantiation. This time there appears to have been an actual clash between popular piety and the caution of some clerics. According to Kramer's biographers, he was invited to Venice in 1495 to intervene in a controversy over eucharistic devotion. There, before the patriarch of Venice, he disputed publicly and preached several sermons. From a modern perspective, this is already somewhat curious, in that he was by then known as the author (or, officially, the coauthor) of the *Malleus*. Thus, if he was indeed "summoned . . . by the master-general of the order, Father Joaquin de Torres,"[44] his competence as theorist of both witchcraft and eucharist had to be known.

At any rate, his mission came about because of a fairly spectacular eucharistic incident, one in which, moreover, no miracle had occurred. Near Padua, a man collecting firewood discovered two pyxes, or holy vessels containing consecrated hosts. They had been stolen three years previously from a nearby village church. One pyx was the sort used to carry the sacrament to invalids; the other, known as a *monstrance,* was more ornate and was used to display the host for adoration during Corpus Christi festivities. The church's priest, summoned by the wood gatherer, found some eucharistic hosts (*species eucharisticas*) in the pyxes. He therefore fetched a portable altar stone (which was normally used with pyxes for taking the sacrament to the sick and dying). The priest constructed a little shrine (*aedificiolum*) around the hosts and set a guard to watch it "so that nothing unlawful [*illiciti*] might be done," say Kramer's biographers. Meanwhile,

> news [*fama*] of the incident had spread, and people were flocking to the wooded spot; candles were lighted; people cried that Christ was present [*ibidem adesse*] and adored him. As news of the event spread, it was reported to the bishop of Padua, who sent his clerics and inquired into everything. Since in the other container [*in altero vase*] they found only some decayed remainders of sacramental hosts [*corruptasque . . . nonnullas sacramenti species atque reliquias*], in the sight of the people the clerics who had been sent by the bishop destroyed the shrine . . . and carried [the vessels and their contents] away with them. It was forbidden, under pain of ecclesiastical censure and excommunication, for anyone to visit that spot again or worship there. On this occasion, in fact, certain priests preached that the people had committed idolatry by what they had done and asserted that they had worshiped mildew, trees, brambles, and the Devil.[45]

Assuming that this incident is recounted factually, we might wonder why it provoked a clerical faction to accuse simple folk of worshiping the Devil when they obviously thought that they were worshiping the body of God.

The answer probably concerns the declaration that the hosts were *corruptas;* they had decayed after exposure to the elements. Unlike the host of Bolsena and other miraculous wafers, indeed, unlike the host of Kramer's Toad Witch, these gave no sign that they were flesh and blood rather than decomposed bread. They had not even remained miraculously intact, as some hosts were said to do, expelling themselves unchanged from the bodies of sinners or from heaps of dung after several days or even seven years. The common folk who flocked to the site were apparently unconcerned by the actual state of the rediscovered hosts. It was the clergy who reacted, and overreacted, to the decay: "And so grave contentions arose between the clergy and the layfolk [*populo*] over whether the people had sinned there by worshiping Christ's body, which they believed was there, but which nevertheless was not truly [*vere*] there."[46]

This is an exceedingly curious thing for clerics to claim. No one contested the authenticity of the pyxes or the hosts. Since the hosts were found in pyxes of a sort used *only* for carrying consecrated hosts outside the church, and since the hosts are referred to as *species,* it is apparent that no cleric doubted that they had been duly consecrated.[47] Nor did the actions of the thief permit such a doubt. This sacrilegious theft would have been motivated either by the material worth of the pyxes or by the value of the hosts as potential raw material for magic. Yet everything lay where it had fallen. Laypeople probably did occasionally remove consecrated hosts from their mouths and use them for some magical purpose, as Kramer claims in the *Malleus*—although not with intent to desecrate them.[48] But none of this is mentioned either. The one certainty is that anyone who stole the pyxes with a view to appropriating their contents would have had no reason, either in reality or in the clerical imagination, to fill them with unconsecrated or questionable hosts. To steal unconsecrated hosts, place them in vessels intended for consecrated elements, and then abandon them in the wilderness served no purpose that can be documented among early-modern Europeans.

Thus, it appears that what disconcerted one clerical faction was that *no eucharistic miracle had occurred.* Two features betray this: first, that such a sharp polemic arose from the discovery of hosts abandoned in circumstances implying that they had been consecrated and, second, that during three long years the hosts had never shown any empirical sign of their divinity. If the hosts had been properly consecrated, why had nothing vaguely resembling a miracle occurred? Why had they decayed exactly as if they were ordinary bread?

But something more general was at stake too. The passage continues, amazingly, by wondering whether real consecration *ever* takes place: "And indeed the question was raised whether the host should at most be worshiped conditionally, even when it is shown and elevated during the sacrifice of the mass or is carried to the sick, since no one receives any illumination from God or is granted inner [*interius*] certainty as to whether a host has been truly [*vere*] consecrated."[49] This is the question that Kramer's superior called him in to resolve: Should one only *ever* adore the eucharistic host with a mental reservation? That is, whenever one adored the host, did one need to think the conscious thought that, for one's adoration to be valid, the host must have been properly consecrated?[50]

If the account is accurate, what exercised the clerics most of all was not even the lack of a eucharistic miracle. That lack raised the much more worrisome question whether one could *ever* know that the host was truly the body of Christ, even seeing it in a priest's hand. Ostensibly, the question regarded only an uncertainty (either Donatistic or orthodox) whether any particular host had been duly consecrated by a priest. But the controversy quickly took on a universal significance, as the passage quoted above shows.

It appears from Kramer's biography that he was summoned to Venice because the Venetian Dominicans knew of his interest in such eucharistic problems. He may even have been called to Augsburg a year later because of the sermons that he preached in Venice. Certainly, his Dominican biographers connect the two incidents thematically, turning from one directly to the other. If we compare the two incidents, however, Kramer seems to have argued against two almost contrary ideas. In Venice, he opposed the radical idea that, even if one watched a priest consecrating a host, there could be no proof that the consecration was valid. In Augsburg, he argued against an equally radical contention: if blood or flesh appeared physically in a eucharistic wafer, it could *not* be proved that Christ was truly present in the host. This idea menaced a centuries-long tradition of alleged eucharistic miracles.

Together the two cases implied that under *no* circumstances could anyone know whether transubstantiation had taken place, whether Christ was really present in the host. Neither a host that looked like bread nor one that looked like flesh and blood could be proved a valid sacrament. What could have been more threatening to a man of Kramer's anxious temperament?

Kramer's last charge on behalf of eucharistic orthodoxy took place in 1502 when he published his *Sancte Romane Ecclesie fidei defensionis clippeum adversus Waldensium seu Pickardorum heresim,* or *Shield to Defend the Holy Roman Church against the Pikarts and Waldenses.* The Pikarts (or Bohemian "Beghards"), were a radical subsect of Hussites.[51] Kramer wrote the piece while serving as Pope Alexander VI's censor of the faith in Bohemia and Moldavia. From Kramer's standpoint, the Pikarts' most disturbing tenet was their leader Martin Húska's negation of both transubstantiation and real presence in the eucharist. According to Húska, the consecrated host did not become the literal body and blood of Christ, nor was Christ present, *in any sense,* within the eucharistic elements. Húska had been burnt in 1421, but his radical ideas were still current in Bohemia—or at least Kramer feared that they were.[52]

The history of theological dissent in Bohemia throughout the fifteenth century provides a valuable clue to the connection between Kramer's sacramental anxieties and his need for witches to exist. Fifteenth-century Bohemia was the homeland of the most troubling heresies, many of which centered on the reality of the sacraments and particularly on the eucharist. The reformer Jan Hus was burned at the stake in 1415 by the Council of Constance because he had espoused some doctrines of the English cleric John Wyclif (d. 1384). Wyclif's bones and books were burned on the orders of the same council, in part because his attempts to understand the mystery of the eucharist had led him to contradict the doctrine of transubstantiation by proposing *con*substantiation as a better explanation. It seemed clear to Wyclif that, since the bread could still be seen after the words of consecration ("This is my body"), its *substance* had not been abolished. Consequently, it could not be true that the mere appearance or *species* of bread remained, "unsupported by the substance" of bread, as orthodox doctrine had taught since Aquinas. A better explanation, thought Wyclif, was that the substance of God's body had been added to the substance of the bread.[53]

Hus did not espouse this doctrine, and, despite lending his name to the Bohemian movement through martyrdom, he was not a radical exponent of "Hussitism." But Hus did criticize the cult of bleeding eucharistic hosts, both as a member of an archiepiscopal commission and in the treatise *De sanguine Christi,* or *On the Blood of Christ.*[54] Other Bohemians raised objections more similar to Wyclif's, and some had stronger disagreements with eucharistic orthodoxy. As with other late-medieval heresies, one inspiration of Hussitism was a form of biblical literalism and a resultant demand that church practice conform to scriptural precedent.[55] Catholic practice no longer allowed laypeople to take communion "in both species," that is, with both bread and wine; but, from 1414 on, a moderate Hussite sect, the Utraquists (from the Latin *utraque* for "both"), demanded that the chalice also be given to the laity.

After Utraquism emerged, Hussitism began fragmenting over numerous issues, including the existence of purgatory, the veneration of images, the selling of indulgences, and more. A radical wing of "Taborites" was militant in every sense. Adherents expected the end of the world and the second coming of Christ to happen in 1420. Taborites differed from moderate Utraquists in proclaiming that Christ's body and blood were in the bread and wine in a sense that was sacramental and thus real, but not transubstantiative.[56]

Martin Húska's subsect of Taborites, known as Pikarts, carried such thinking to its logical conclusion. Húska defined the eucharist as a mere love feast or commemorative meal and denied both transubstantiation and real presence, thus denying that Christ was present *in any sense* in the eucharist. Húska "deployed the rationalist argument that the physical body of Christ was in heaven, and could not be in the eucharist," an argument that we encountered among the worries of Visconti and Della

Croce. Húska's followers "in the passionate fashion characteristic of Tabor proceeded to empty monstrances and trample on hosts" to demonstrate their disbelief that eucharistic bread was "really" the body of Christ.[57]

As Malcolm Lambert observes, "The eucharist was a highly sensitive issue among all Hussites." Although the Taborites had abandoned transubstantiation, "none the less they were believers in a real presence, and the belief was of great emotional importance."[58] Húska's Pikarts were thus persecuted by a rare coalition between the more moderate Taborites and the Utraquists, who could still agree that the doctrine of real presence was valid. In 1421, Utraquists and Taborites burned Húska to confirm their agreement. When Kramer wrote against "the Pikarts" eight decades later, he was writing against an idea of total opposition to eucharistic orthodoxy. Nothing more radical could be imagined.

The overall fame, the very idea of Hussitism, was synonymous with questioning the validity of the sacraments. To some extent, what Hus or any of his followers actually believed is irrelevant for understanding Kramer and witchcraft theorists. The important consideration is that orthodox clerics accused them of sacramental critiques and that quarreling sects of Hussites multiplied the accusations against one another.[59] Hus himself was unjustly accused of Donatism, the belief that sacraments lost their efficacy when administered by worldly and corrupt priests.[60] Like Hussitism, many heresies between the twelfth and the seventeenth centuries can be called Donatist in a loose sense if they impugned the validity of the sacraments for any reason. Accusations of sacramental invalidity were frequent, made overtly and dogmatically on occasion, more often implicitly and even reluctantly, through calls for reforming clerical corruption and institutional excess.

Late-medieval Donatism has generally been understood as a concern with human imperfection, but it was at times a response to the apparent imperfection or inefficacy of the sacraments.[61] Questions about the sacraments were interlocked with questions about the nature of God and of his relation to humanity. Human unworthiness could be a relatively comforting explanation of the perception that sacraments did not always or reliably appear to connect humanity to God. A far more frightening alternative, one so dreadful that it could be expressed only obliquely, was that sacraments failed because God was indifferent, absent, or imaginary.

Such a fear is already enshrined in Isa. 59:1–2: "Behold, the Lord's hand is not shortened that it *cannot* save; neither is his ear heavy that it *cannot* hear: But your iniquities have separated between you and God, and your sins have hid his face from you, that he *will not* hear." God's unresponsiveness *must be* a result of our sin, not of his impotence or indifference. Paradoxically, the necessity for a perfect society and clergy was a goal whose very unattainability could comfort Christians (especially theologians), for it indefinitely postponed God's responsibility to answer humanity's call. As the anthropologist Mary Douglas remarks: "[One] way of protecting the belief that religion can deliver prosperity here and now is to make ritual efficacy depend on difficult conditions."[62]

The existence of Hussitism and other broad movements suggested that some teachings about God—either those of the established church or those of Hussitism itself—must be in error. The specter of arbitrariness haunted some of the principal exponents of Hussitism, and they showed an instability of conviction that must have been disturbing to onlookers of any persuasion. Stephen Páleč and Stanislav of Znojmo were denying transubstantiation and teaching the Wyclifite doctrine of remanentism or consubstantiation in the earliest days of Hussitism; but, after 1408, they became reactionary supporters of orthodoxy.[63]

By its existence, heresy always implies that belief is based on choice, rather than on unarguable fact—indeed, the Latin *heresia* is derived from the Greek word for "choice."[64] There is nothing more troubling to the dogmatic mentality than the thought that the ultimate realities are subject to human choice or interpretation, for, if that is so, how can they be ultimate, and what guarantee do we have that we have not imagined them? A lack of consensus implies a lack of reality, and this is why an ecumenical yearning has coexisted so easily with its apparent opposite, a self-righteous authoritarianism, among both Christian dissidents and Christian establishmentarians. Beneath the demand for doctrinal consensus lies an uneasy and nearly conscious recognition that the nature of reality always depends on an interpretive consensus. As Kramer repeated, "That which appears true to many cannot be entirely false." But is it *true*?

The chronology of Hussitism, with its problematic attitudes toward sacramental reality, coincides to an uncanny degree with the chronology of witchcraft theory and witch-hunting. Hussitism traumatized Western Christianity from 1411, when Hus was excommunicated, to the end of the anti-Hussite military crusades in 1436. Nider published his *Formicarius* about 1438, while his informant Judge Peter, on whose witch-hunting experiences Nider relied, had ceased the activity sometime between 1406 and 1417. The Council of Basel was held in that town from 1431 to 1437, before continuing in Ferrara, Florence, and Rome until 1445. Several of the earliest theorists, including Nider and Tostado, were present at the council and could have exchanged ideas about the new heresy of witchcraft. Hussitism was a major concern of this council, carried over from its predecessor, the Council of Constance, which lasted from 1414 to 1418 and burned Hus in 1415. The dioceses of Basel and Constance abut the dioceses where the earliest witch-hunts of any size and continuity took place, in the 1430s and 1440s.[65]

Nider and several other early witchcraft theorists frequently mentioned Hussitism, always with alarm and loathing. Nor had Bohemia ceased to trouble Catholic orthodoxy in Kramer's time: Pope Pius II had debated theology with Taborites in 1451, and, in 1462, he denied a request for permanent recognition of the lay chalice; he had also written a history of Bohemia that described it as a homeland of heresy.[66] Kramer's theory of witchcraft was probably affected by contact with Bohemians in Rome during Pius's reign and thus perhaps as early as 1458. In 1485, only two years before the *Malleus* was published, Bohemian Catholics and Utraquists formally agreed to a thirty-one-year stalemate in which each group would keep the parishes that it held, thus institutionalizing two contrary views of the eucharist, one with and one without the chalice.

This is not to claim that Hussitism caused witchcraft theory. Rather, to the extent that early witchcraft theorists worried about both Hussitism and sacramental reality, the ambiguous distinction between witchcraft and long-standing heresies like Catharism and Waldensianism in the earliest witchcraft treatises is more comprehensible. Something was in the air, a generalized malaise about sacraments, their reliability, and what they implied about God. Hussitism was a real expression of that malaise; witchcraft theory was mostly imaginary, but it expressed the same disturbance.

Much of Hussite history occurred before the invention of printing. But, by Luther's time, Hussite views, particularly on the ideal nature of the church, could be efficiently disseminated by this new medium. In 1520, Luther had Hus's *De ecclesia,* or *On the Church,* printed, and the next year was referring to Hus as a saint, claiming, "We are all Hussites without knowing it."[67] Printing also empowered the Catholic counterattack, and one element of that offensive was the evidence that sacraments were after all valid, offered by the printing of works of witchcraft theory, starting with Nider's *Formicarius* in 1475. The doctrinal and social viability of Hussitism nearly outlasted the half-century lull in witch-hunting and the publication of witchcraft theory (ca. 1520–70). As late as 1564, Pius IV, the pope who ratified the final decrees of the Council of Trent, granted limited lay access to the chalice in the archbishopric of Prague.[68] But such measures were no longer of any use. Protestantism had spread to the point that, in France, the Wars of Religion (1562–98) were already becoming a reality; so was the second, more extreme phase of witchcraft theory and witch-hunting. The violent fifteenth-century Catholic war on Hus's ideas about church reform backfired, galvanizing

Bohemian national identity and loosing theological shock waves that reverberated a century later in Luther's revolt and later still in the Thirty Years' War.

Pico's Witch: Hate the Sinner, Love the Sin

Having read the *Malleus* carefully, Gianfrancesco Pico was heir to all Kramer's anxieties, not least the sacramental ones. Pico understood perfectly who benefited from witches' confessions, and, in his dialogue *Strix* (1523), he dramatized the role of the desecrating witch as the reinforcer of her prosecutors' faith. He showed precisely—and consciously, as far as we can tell—how the witch's failure to realize that she had confirmed eucharistic reality strengthened her persecutors' belief in it.

The skeptical Apistius initially resists all arguments used to prove the reality of witchcraft, but a kind of turning point comes in the second day. The witch recounts that her demon, Ludovicus, instructed her to desecrate two consecrated hosts by sewing them into the hem of her skirt. This was supposed to prevent her from confessing. However, once she was captured and the inquisitor Dicastes began threatening her with severe torture if she did not confess, Ludovicus commanded her to throw the hosts into her chamberpot, implicitly contradicting his promise that they would prevent her confession. As she was breaking them up with a stick ("there in the dung," adds the translator Alberti), she saw them begin to bleed. Predictably, she says that she was filled with horror and fear at the sight.[69]

The reactions of the witch's male interlocutors demonstrate the utility of her bizarre, contradictory confession to their faith. Curiously, Dicastes has been absent during this confession, so only the two laymen hear it. The inquisitor has been away overseeing preparations for a meal; he has decided to maximize his friends' time with the witch by saving them the trip home for lunch and back. (Pico probably assumed that the inquisitor's absence would make the witch's confession seem completely unforced, in contrast to her Bible oath that demons are virile lovers, which Dicastes extracted by threats.) Dicastes' absence on a catering errand allows a dramatization of disgust: when Dicastes returns and cheerfully asks if the laymen are satisfied with the witch's answers, Phronimus replies that they are so nauseated (*stomachati*) that lunch may no longer be necessary.[70] Their disgust is ironically the key to their reassurance about the sacraments.

Dicastes cannot have overheard the witch's confession, yet he does *not* ask why his friends are so suddenly off their feed. The stage business of his absence and return, the luncheon arrangements, and the laymen's vehement expressions of disgust cover up all four characters' silence about the witch's miraculous confirmation of eucharistic dogma. In fact, not one of them *ever* mentions this. Because food, blood, and excrement are all under discussion during Dicastes' brief absence, the two laymen's protestations of disgust can easily distract the reader from asking cui bono questions about the witch's confession, such as why the Devil gave such contradictory orders, why he was willing to risk reviving the witch's faith in Christianity, or whether she ever told Dicastes about the miracle. Yet food, blood, and excrement allow for the silent proof of the sacrament's corporeality.

Despite all the stage business, Pico cannot or will not disguise how important Strix's confession is to Apistius. When Dicastes innocently suggests that they take a turn in the garden to regain their appetite for lunch, Apistius blurts out:

> I would never have been able to believe that such crimes [*scelera*] could be thought up! Up to now, I would have easily forgiven such people since I thought that their flightiness [*levitatem*] was the cause of everything; I believed that witches were led into this error because they had been deluded by the trickery [*praestigiis*] of demons. Nor would I swear even now that they are not deluded. But just as I have never not believed in the truth of the Christian religion, so I would never want such ungodly desecrators [*impiis temeratoribus*] of that religion to be spared punishment.[71]

Why should Apistius choose this moment to protest that he has always been a Christian—or, rather, that he has *never not believed* what Christians are supposed to believe (*nunquam non assensus sum*)? Only when he hears about desecrating the eucharist does he declare himself ready to approve hunting down and killing witches.

Moral outrage seems an unlikely motive for this decision: earlier, when Strix confessed to killing many small children, Apistius expressed no outrage at all. Instead, he asked her a number of technical questions: how the children were killed, why they did not cry out and wake their parents, why not all of them died. And he concluded laconically that Strix's explanations sounded improbable.[72] Yet, when he hears that eucharists bleed, Apistius never expresses any doubt—or, indeed, any opinion at all—about the miracle, except to declare that witch-hunting is a good idea. Did Pico think that eucharistic miracles were too commonplace and too evidently real to merit discussion?

Probably not. Dicastes intuits that Apistius is still not ready to believe everything about witches, despite being ready to condone killing them: "If I demonstrate that showing no mercy to witches rightly pertains to the Christian religion, and if I bring before you so many witnesses that you will no longer seek not to believe absolutely that many things in the aforementioned Sabbat are done truly, and, as we are accustomed to saying, in reality (let me be allowed to use this word), I think that you will no longer put up such obstinate resistance." Remarkably, Dicastes' speech continues the double-negative phrasing of Apistius's declaration (*no longer* seek *not* to believe). The inquisitor still stops short of requiring that Apistius believe everything he hears about witches. Indeed, Apistius answers that he is still not completely convinced: "As yet my mind does not incline more in one direction than the other."[73] Yet he is still willing to have witches killed.

The inquisitor's next move seems like a non sequitur. Suddenly, he is no longer discussing witchcraft or desecration: "Tell me, did you ever see a dead man come back to life?" Of course Apistius has not seen such a thing. Ever the well-read humanist, Phronimus interjects that poets and philosophers, including Plato, tell of such things. "But regarding such a crucial and serious thing, I don't believe poets and philosophers," replies Apistius; "I believe the Gospels." He does well, says Dicastes, who adds that modern reality is actually far stranger than the Gospels.[74]

And that is the point: despite Apistius's claim to believe the Gospels, Dicastes knows that he is struggling. Sacraments, witchcraft, and the Gospels are all part of the same problem:

DICASTES: Let me propose another example, which is something that is not contained in the Holy Scriptures. Do you believe that ships leave from the Straits of Gibraltar, and from Lisbon in Portugal, and that, sailing into the west wind, they are carried for about twenty thousand furlongs to a vast land whose real size is still unknown, or, that, sailing with the west wind, they cross the Atlantic to the Gulf of India?
APISTIUS: Why wouldn't I believe it?
DICASTES: *Whom* do you believe?
APISTIUS: Those many merchants who say that they have made such a voyage.
DICASTES: Have you ever spoken to any of them?
APISTIUS: I've never spoken to them myself; but I have spoken with people who had heard it with their own ears from men who declared that they had personally made the trip.
DICASTES: But couldn't those people have deceived you?
APISTIUS: But who would suspect such serious men of taking pleasure in lies?
DICASTES: If, therefore, I produce here among us an equal number of witnesses, of no less gravity [than your witnesses to the existence of

America], who have sworn under oath that witches are carried to the Sabbat [by demons], and that demons in the form of women take amorous pleasure with men, and in the form of men with women, and that they have had this from the mouths of the witches and wizards themselves, who were constrained by the sacrament [to confess all this], will you not be satisfied?

PHRONIMUS: That would make a man seem either foolish or stubborn. Don't refuse, Apistius.

APISTIUS: Why do you say that?

PHRONIMUS: Because when many people are of the same opinion about something, and agree about it as if speaking with one voice, it cannot seem credible [*verisimile*] that someone goes on claiming the right to deny it. Not, that is, unless he is led by a good reason, one so strong as to demolish that commonly affirmed opinion. And I don't believe you have such a good reason.[75]

This exchange shows how far-reaching the myth of witchcraft was in its consequences for Christian faith. Several familiar arguments are recognizable, particularly from Bartolomeo Spina: that witchcraft is less incredible sounding than some other proposition that is clearly true; that it is upheld "as if with one voice" by many people; that something cannot be false if it seems true to many people; that one must believe the testimony of reliable witnesses. Above all, this passage reveals what is actually at stake in Pico's discussion of the reality of witchcraft: the truth value of the Gospels, the sacraments, and Christianity as a whole.

Dicastes did not overhear the witch confess desecrating the host, nor can he know that that confession caused Apistius's outburst against witches' desecrations. Nevertheless, he brings discussion of eucharistic theology out into the open by reminding Apistius that witches' confessions are *sacramental* confessions. Witches are tortured to make them confess, but Dicastes chooses to believe that they are being forced into confession *by the sacrament* (*adacti sacramento*). Penitence or confession was a sacrament, and it was a mandatory preparation for receiving the sacrament of eucharist. Dicastes implies that interrogating a witch is the same as hearing sacramental confession. Strangely, this was the normal view. Therefore, Discastes assumes, the sacraments exert a kind of psychic coercion that no one can resist.[76]

Eucharistic desecration provided indirect confirmation of sacramental efficacy, while direct confirmation took several forms, all supporting the idea that demons and evil effects disappeared when confronted with sacred objects, names, or gestures—the sacramentals. Pico provides a striking combination of the two ideas that involves the eucharist routing demons. This time, it is not Dicastes but Phronimus who tells Apistius of a miracle ("Note this wondrous thing!" exclaims the marginal caption in the Latin first edition). The learned humanist says that he heard the story some time ago, from "a great man, who was outstanding in rank, power, and riches." This is not "something made up by the poets," he assures Apistius, but rather something guaranteed by trustworthy (*locupletissimo*) testimony.[77]

About twelve years previously (i.e., around 1510), there was a good priest who lived in the German Alps. This priest needed to carry the sacrament to a man who was mortally ill and lived far away. Knowing that it was too far to travel on foot, the priest mounted his horse and hung the consecrated host, in its special traveling container, around his neck for safekeeping.[78] After he had traveled for quite a while, he ran across someone who invited him to dismount from the horse and accompany him to see a marvelous spectacle (*rem mirabilem*). No sooner had the imprudent priest got down from his horse than he felt himself swept away through the air with his new companion. A short time later, they were both put down atop a high mountain, in a spacious field surrounded by trees and enclosed by cliffs. In the field were multitudes of people, engaged in every sort of dance, feast, game, and song, along with "whatever else can delight the minds of mortals."[79]

While the poor priest was still reeling from the flight and his new surroundings, his traveling companion asked if he would like to pay his respects to the Lady (*domina; Madonna*) and make her some present, as the others were doing. The priest decided that this lady must be the Blessed Virgin Mary, for she was indeed queenly and beautiful, sitting on a golden throne, being adored by groups who came in orderly fashion and offered her presents. Misled by her title and her appearance, "for he did not know that this was a demonic illusion [*praestigium*]," the priest did what "he would never otherwise have done if he had known that this was a superstition." Deciding that nothing would give the Madonna more pleasure than a gift of the "consecrated body of her only son," he approached the throne reverently, fell on his knees, and laid the pyx containing the sacrament in her lap.[80]

Immediately, the throne and the Lady, who was only an empty illusion (*imago* or image), disappeared, along with the crowd and everything else, including even the demonic companion who had brought the priest there. Realizing too late that he had fallen for a demonic illusion, the priest prayed to God not to abandon him in that savage place. At long last, after wandering among those cliffs without seeing any sign of another human, the priest ran across a shepherd, who told him where he was. He discovered that he was almost a hundred miles (a stereotypical distance in these stories) from the place for which he had set out. Since everything disappeared, we might be tempted to regard the whole experience as a dream; but the "fact" that the priest was so far from home prevents this interpretation.

We might now expect to hear something about the poor invalid whom the priest had set out to visit. Since the priest was taking him the *viaticum,* we know that he was gravely ill, in danger of death, and urgently needed last rites. Yet all we hear is that, when the priest returned home, he notified the imperial magistrate of what had happened. Phronimus is even careful to mention Emperor Maximilian I by name, implying that the story must have been forwarded to him "in exactly the way I have told it to you."[81]

The ideological priorities of the story are clear: the "poor sick man" is nothing more than the excuse for telling the story. The emperor is brought in to imply that no one would have dared tell lies or fantasies to his officials. Another point of the story is made explicitly: Phronimus says that he is telling the story as proof that people can be carried about by demons, as readers will see if they consult the *Malleus* written by the German theologians Henricus and Jacobus.[82] This theme of transvection is familiar but something of a red herring here. Once more, the unspoken eucharistic theme is supremely important.

Pico devotes no attention to explaining why everything disappeared when the consecrated eucharistic host touched the demon, just as he offered no explanations when the witch confessed her horror at seeing the desecrated hosts bleed. The correct interpretations must be inferred logically by the reader, not because they are unimportant, but precisely because they are so overwhelmingly important. To make these points overtly and explicitly would mean admitting that they are at issue. To examine them openly would mean subjecting them to the same scrutiny and involuntary skepticism that makes telling the story necessary.

Witchcraft narratives became necessary because theories of sacramental efficacy were increasingly difficult to believe when stated in the scientific terms of Scholastic theology. Witchcraft theorists intuited that Christian dogma was more convincing when presented as literature. The translation from theory to narrative makes readers' "willing suspension of disbelief" easier by engaging their emotions as well as their intellect. Narrative allows them to confront the theory indirectly rather than head-on. Readers' energy can be concentrated on emotional stimuli: disgust at the witch, anxiety over the fate of the buried child or the dying man in need of last rites, awe at the spectacle of magnificent ceremonies or sublimely terrible scenery.

The theoretical points cannot be made completely explicit for fear of implausibility, so the believability of these tales depends on a high degree of allusiveness. Readers must, if possible, draw the ideological conclusion for themselves, and this is most effective when it happens by reflex ("Oh, yes, for we are taught that . . ."). Alternatively, a serendipity will do, as when the Jewish woman's confessor just happened to remember that, in the early church, baptism sometimes healed physical diseases. Yet we should notice how often phrases like "for he (or they) did not know that . . ." are used to ensure that readers understand the ideological point of witchcraft miracles. Authors clearly felt that readers must be guided toward the desired ideological point and prompted to think of it at the proper moment in the story.

In his *Strix,* Pico showed that he understood or intuited this dynamic as well as or better than other witchcraft theorists. The debating among his characters, which lasts the better part of two days, ends only a couple of pages after Phronimus finishes this eucharistic anecdote. At this point, Apistius declares that he now firmly believes in the existence of witchcraft. After clearing up a few other points that he defines as minor, Apistius asks to be renamed, and the inquisitor Dicastes rebaptizes him, almost literally, as Pisticus, "the Believer."[83]

Leandro Alberti saw the significance of this conversion and made a small addition when he translated the dialogue's finale. Instead of having Pisticus and Phronimus simply take their leave of Dicastes, Alberti gave the inquisitor the last word, having him tell the departing laymen "Ite in pace" ("Go in peace").[84] This phrase recalls the words by which an officiating priest ends the celebration of mass: "Ite, missa est." Indeed, the dialogue has more than a little in common with the mass since the witch and her interpreters have demonstrated that the eucharist is a real sacrifice, a complete but normally invisible reenactment of Christ's crucifixion.[85]

Real Presence, Real Blood

In addition to appearing early in the evolution of witchcraft theory, accusations of eucharistic desecration were one of its most durable features. Confessions to desecration were still being extorted around 1600, as attested by the trials of Walpurga Hausmännin and Johannes Junius. Each of them confessed to destroying or spoiling sacramental materials, and, in both cases, their judges were particularly interested in eucharistic desecrations. Walpurga "confessed" that "at their nightly gatherings she had oft with her other playfellows [*Gespielen*] trodden underfoot the Holy and Blessed Sacrament and the image of the Holy Cross. The said Walpurga states that during such-like frightful and loathsome blasphemies she at times truly did espy drops of blood upon the said Holy Sacrament, whereat she herself was greatly horrified."[86]

Why did Walpurga not repent and reconvert? Stereotypical witches and Jews had been making the same egregious mistake for centuries, in stories that she could have heard. Even if Walpurga had truly expressed rebelliousness by mistreating the host, it is difficult to imagine that the experience of seeing it bleed would not have driven her straight back into the church. Since she supposedly did not convert, the adjectives and adverbs describing her desecrations (*holy, blessed, frightful, loathsome, truly, greatly*) reflect the interests of her interrogators, not Walpurga's own.

In Johannes Junius's case, there is further reason for suspicion. When he wrote to his daughter about his interrogation, he recalled: "I had to tell what crimes I had committed. I said nothing. . . . 'Hoist the knave up!' So I said that I was to kill my children, but I had killed a horse instead. It did not help. I had also taken a sacred wafer, and had buried it. *When I said this, they left me in peace.*"[87] Content with the revelation that Johannes had desecrated the host, his interrogators did not force him to confess that he had committed any *maleficia* at all against human beings. The torture stopped definitively as soon as he admitted desecrating the host. The sum total of his *maleficia* (as opposed to the thought crime of apostasy or abandoning Christianity) was thus killing a horse and burying a wafer.

Johannes was not forced to confess witnessing a eucharistic miracle. But the transcript of his interrogation shows that his interrogators had a more complex idea of his crime against the eucharist than he understood: "Once, at the suggestion of his succubus, he had taken the holy wafer out of his mouth and had given it to her. Was obliged occasionally to have intercourse with his succubus."[88] While Johannes remembered confessing only to burying the host, his interrogators connected the desecration to sex crimes committed with his demon lover. What connection could they have presumed between sexuality and sacramentality? It can only have been corporeal interaction as an indicator of reality: the *corpus domini* and the *corpus demonis* pass or fail the reality test together. Such anxieties cannot be attributed to Johannes since he saw no connections between desecration and demonic sex. The corporeal connection that his interrogators sought between the demon, the witch, and the eucharistic host reveals the same anxieties about provability that produced stories of eucharistic miracles.

The visions and other experiences of eucharistic mystics were intensely private and became public only by becoming stories. Relics of eucharistic miracles were displayed publicly, but, to see them, most people had to undertake a pilgrimage. Even then, without stories to explain them, relics would have remained unidentifiable, desiccated lumps.[89] Thus, for most people, including clerics, proof of real presence and transubstantiation was available only through narratives about eucharistic desecrations and miracles.

Moreover, the protagonists of these narratives were not to be imitated since they were much better or worse than the average run of Christians; they were either saintly mystics and ordained priests or heretics, witches, and Jews. The dread and loathing that these narratives worked so hard to incite probably helped assure that actual experimentation remained outside the ordinary cleric's and layperson's direct experience. And, as they were meant to do, the stories probably quelled even the desire for confirmation in most of their audience. But the tellers of these stories show no sign of conquering their own desire.

9

WITCHES, INFANTICIDE, AND POWER

> They ordinarily begin thus: "How does this happen?" What they should say is: "But does it happen?"
>
> —Montaigne, "Of Cripples" (1585–88)

Witches kill children. Witches are cannibals, and their favorite food is children, as Hansel and Gretel found out. Witches are cooks, and their favorite utensil is the cauldron, in which they prepare foods and potions that are both horrible and disgusting. These are such commonplace ideas, so thoroughly overworked in fairy tales, Halloween lore, and cliché that their origin may seem untraceable. Yet all of them received something like their present form at the hands of the early witchcraft theorists. Witchcraft theorists did not invent the infanticidal witch; they adopted her from the folk culture of their illiterate contemporaries. As elsewhere in witchcraft theory, however, there is more to the infanticidal witch than meets the eye. On her shoulders fell the task of defending the sacramental efficacy of baptism and, by extension, the goodness and providence of God. Her crimes were essential to understanding why the innocent suffer and die, despite the protective powers of the sacraments, in a world ruled by a loving God.

The earliest unambiguous example of the witches' cauldron is in Nider's *Formicarius*.[1] Nider maintains that Peter of Bern forced a witch to confess:

> "We set our snares chiefly for unbaptized children and even for those who have been baptized, especially when they have not been protected by the sign of the cross and prayers, and with our rituals [*ceremoniis*] we kill them in their cradles or even when they are sleeping by their parents' side, in such a way that they afterward are thought to have been overlain or to have died some other [natural] death. Then we secretly steal them from their graves and cook them in a cauldron [*caldari*] until the whole flesh comes away from the bones and becomes a soup that may easily be

> drunk. Of the more solid matter we make an unguent that is useful for working our will and our arts and our transformations [*transmutacionibus*]; and with the liquid we fill a flask or skin. Whoever drinks from this, with the addition of a few other rituals [*ceremoniis*], immediately acquires much knowledge and becomes a leader [*magister*] in our sect."[2]

To a modern sensibility, this passage seems calculated to evoke "horror": an ethical recoiling from gross mistreatment of the human person, coupled with a metaphysical terror before the idea that a human body can be treated as nothing more than matter, simple food. Today, these acts are a far more shocking desecration than mishandling the eucharist or other sacraments.

The notion of stewed babies is so unsettling that it distracts scholars from the overall logic governing this passage. Judge Peter's anxieties were sacramental and clearly betrayed by the confessions that he extorted from this alleged witch. She confirmed that little children died because of human and diabolical violence, not by accident. They were not smothered by sleeping parents; nor did they succumb to disease or the natural order of things. The witch implied—doubtless with plenty of help from Peter—that baptism is sometimes able to protect little ones from physical danger and even death. Yet Peter envisioned the sign of the cross reinforcing the protections of baptism; this qualification betrays his realization that he could not claim absolute efficacy for baptism. Even after reinforcing it with crossing, Peter was still unable to believe that baptism was efficacious against crib death. As the tale of his fall down the stairs demonstrated, he also had no firm faith in the efficacy of crossing. So he imagined that a beverage made from infant bodies, especially bodies lacking these sacramental protections, had countersacramental properties.

God's Providential Plan for Infanticide

Infant mortality was one of the most powerful catalysts for anxiety about witches. Trial records and treatises document the anxiety that parents and kinfolk suffered over the fragility of infants' and toddlers' hold on life.[3] When a child sickened or died, this anxiety erupted into accusations of witchcraft: "Repeatedly, witnesses stress the physical character of the victim's agony, which cannot be alleviated by the onlookers or by the mother, and which excites hatred, revenge, and guilt feelings in part because of the sufferer's innocence."[4] For the parents of a dead infant, there was a burden of grief that we can readily understand (for there is no evidence that medieval and early-modern parents loved their children any less than modern parents do). In many cases, the parents may have felt responsible for or guilt over the child's death.

But inquisitors and witchcraft theorists were not distressed by infant mortality for the same reasons as parents were. Clerics' most prevalent anxiety was theological. We cannot know whether parents were comforted by claims that the sacraments protected little children from death. But Judge Peter had plenty of company: many early witchcraft theorists desired to believe that baptism afforded protection from physical harm as well as preparing the soul for the spiritual benefits of Christianity.

This desire was rarely stated explicitly by the earliest theorists, but Bartolomeo Spina provided detailed explanations of the logic behind it. Like his predecessors, Spina declared that Satan required witches to kill small children and, whenever possible, to do so before they were baptized. Then he explained why and how: "[Satan] persecutes the name of Christ with the most intense hatred; and, because the effects of that name shine forth most notably in baptized children, therefore he persecutes them as if he were persecuting Christ himself. Insofar as he can, the Devil prevents the baptism of children, on account of the envy that drives him to plot against human well-being."[5]

Here, Spina attempts to play both sides against the middle: like Judge Peter, he wants to believe that the Devil prefers to have witches kill unbaptized children to prevent their ever enjoying the benefits of Christianity. However, he has to admit that the Devil also attacks baptized children and occasionally succeeds in killing them. To avoid conceding that baptism confers *no* protection, he argues that its very efficacy makes it ineffective. Because baptism makes infants identical to Christ in sinlessness, the Devil is forced to attack them, driven by his envious hatred of Christ.

Spina insinuated that baptism protects the body as well as the spirit by using the term *salus*. To convey that idea, we have to translate *salus* as meaning "well-being," but the word's original meaning is "health." A few lines later, Spina clarifies his understanding of *salus,* asserting that "by the ministry of [witches] the Devil everywhere continues to grow stronger in his assaults on the bodily and spiritual health of Christians [*salutem tam corporalem quam spiritualem*]."[6] The idea that devils and baptism affected bodily health was not a concession to the ignorance of the unlettered. In addition to Spina, remember the converted Jewish woman's confessor, who explained how baptism cured the emperor Constantine of leprosy.

There was a *logical* reason why clerics chose to believe this seemingly irrational idea. Educated churchmen's concern with the physical effects of baptism betrayed excruciating anxieties about the death of small children. Those deaths threatened their confidence in the benevolence of God, for children were *innocent*. Parents could have reasoned the same way, however simplistic their theology. But, for churchmen, the core of the problem lay in the concept of original sin. Saint Augustine had taught that, when Adam and Eve disobeyed God's commandment in Eden, human nature was irremediably corrupted. A tendency to rebellion and sinfulness was coded genetically, as it were, and passed on through the sex act by which humans reproduced. From before their birth, human beings were literally guilty until proved innocent.

The New Testament implied that no one could be saved except through baptism.[7] In Western Christianity, this came to mean that baptism saved the human soul by cleansing it of the stain of original sin. Spiritual purification was not merely symbolic: it was something real, and the soul was quite literally washed clean. By the fifteenth century, Catholic theologians had theorized that baptism actually left a *character,* that is, a letter or an identifying mark, on the human soul, by which God recognized and claimed it as his own. Without that mark there was no salvation. Baptism was a literal act of writing; the Catholic prohibition of repeated baptism was conceptualized as a way of avoiding "overwriting"—garbling the soul's mark by a second or subsequent inscription. The Council of Trent would recommend that, when baptizing adults, one begin: "If you are already baptized, I *do not* baptize you, but, if you are not baptized, I baptize you in the name of the Father, the Son, and the Holy Spirit." This was not a preamble to baptism but the words through which it took place.[8]

Baptism alone could not save, of course. Once a person became capable of understanding sin, he had to manage his own salvation by regularly confessing his sins and doing penance for them. But, until they reached the age of reason and could distinguish right from wrong, children were not capable of committing sin.[9]

Baptism was nonetheless crucial for newborns and small children.[10] By merely being born, children were stained with the filth of original sin, even though they could not *commit* sin. This meant that stillborn infants and other children who died before they could be baptized were automatically excluded from heaven.[11] They were denied salvation on the basis of sins committed by others long before their own conception. Consequently, Aquinas and other theologians recommended that Caesarian section be used to extract and baptize the unborn children of dead mothers, before the fetuses could die. In order to console despondent parents, some clerics as late as the sixteenth century were pretending to revive dead infants for a few moments so that they could be baptized.[12] By contrast, a baptized child was saved and admitted to heaven through no effort of its own. Children with no possibility of committing sin were admitted to heaven or excluded from it without reference to their own actions or even the ability to act.

Even without reference to eternal salvation, the death of any infant seemed a potential indictment of God's justice. The dilemma over which fate was worse is made evident by witchcraft theorists' lack of consensus: they could not agree whether witches and devils preferred to kill baptized or unbaptized babies.[13] From the standpoint of earthly life, the injustice was equal for baptized and unbaptized infants: both were deprived of life through no fault of their own. There was nonetheless a special poignancy to the death of a baptized infant. Baptism had canceled its hereditary or original sin, and, being dependent on others for everything, it was unable to commit sins of its own. So why would God allow this perfectly innocent child to die?

Historically, the fate of unbaptized children was more worrisome to Christian theologians; it had anguished them for centuries. In the fourth century, Saint Augustine initially believed that the souls of unbaptized children would be banished from blessedness without actually being punished. Later theologians would refer to this place of banishment as the limbo of children. However, they had to bear in mind that Augustine had later changed his opinion, deciding that unbaptized children *would* receive punishment, although it would be the mildest of all damnations. Beginning with Peter Abelard (d. 1142), theologians rebelled against the cruelty of punishing unbaptized infants in limbo. Pope Innocent III took the view that unbaptized children would suffer only psychologically, feeling "the pain of being deprived of the vision of God."[14]

Aquinas went further still, teaching that unbaptized children would not suffer even psychological pain. They would feel a natural happiness, but they would not receive the beatific vision of God since this supernatural benefit was available only through baptism.[15] The depth of feeling on the issue can be judged from the fact that, in the mid-fourteenth century, "the very few theologians who, with Gregory of Rimini, stood out for the severe Augustinian view, were commonly designated by the opprobrious name *tortores infantium,*" or child abusers.[16]

Girolamo Visconti was troubled (ca. 1460) by all aspects of God's treatment of infants. That an infant should die was troubling regardless of its eternal fate. He reminds his reader that, writing to a woman on the death of her daughter, Saint Jerome (d. 419) had wondered, "How comes it that often two- and three-year-olds, and even those still taking milk at their mothers' breast, are snatched away by the Devil?" Visconti also recalls that Augustine had meditated gloomily on Ecclus. 40:1, which declares that "an heavy yoke is upon the sons of Adam, from the day they go out of their mother's womb till the day that they return to the mother of all things." Augustine used this summary of human hardships to gain perspective on the death of baptized children: "Even little ones, who by the laver of regeneration [baptism] have been freed from the bond of original sin, in which alone they were held, nonetheless suffer many ills, and in some instances are even exposed to the assaults of evil spirits."[17]

Augustine and Jerome left these questions unanswered and unwittingly raised others that disturbed Visconti. Both implied that devils killed children even after baptism. This was unacceptable to Visconti's way of thinking, for it implied that God was either impotent against the devils or negligent toward innocent children.[18] Worse, the numerous cases of children dying *before* they could be baptized implied that God either could not or would not protect them long enough for the salvific rite to take place. Worst of all, neither author had mentioned witches: both implied that devils killed infants without human assistance.[19] This omission intensified the impression that God was unable or unwilling to protect little children from demons.

Visconti found the problem difficult but not insoluble. Witches made direct conflict between God and demons unnecessary: demons took advantage of witches' sinfulness and used human agency to harm children with *maleficia,* rather than by making frontal attacks on them. Thus, there was no need to wonder whether God could not or would not defend children from demons. Witchcraft eliminated God's responsibility for the attacks by blaming them on human sin.

To prove this, Visconti reminds us that, in Aquinas's *Summa contra gentiles,* "among other effects of the magical arts, we read of these things [injury and death] sometimes happening to innocent children." Therefore, Visconti concludes, "We can clearly see why these children *really* die because they have been taken to the witches' game [or Sabbat], for that game is not fantastical but real." Visconti explains further that witches "sometimes kill their own children, grandchildren, or other infants either just after offering them to the demon [at the Sabbat] or within a certain period of time dictated by [him]." As with other theological dilemmas, so with this problem interviewing witches became a way to verify empirically Aquinas's solutions. Visconti assures us that his description of witches' infanticide "is found in many texts, and I myself have heard it from witches."[20]

Despite the authority of Aquinas and the testimony of witches, Visconti was still not satisfied with God's treatment of little children. The scandal of all infant deaths leaked through his syntax and rhetoric:

> *But who would ever be able* to speak in the following manner and say, "It is clear that God is unjust (*if it is lawful even to say so*) since he permits these things to happen to infants, who are pure and innocent"? We respond that *it is in no way apparent from this that God is unjust.*[21] For, if they are baptized, such infants fly straight to heaven, where they lead a blessed life without end. But even in cases when such dead children have not been baptized—*although witches themselves do admit that they prefer to take baptized infants*—there is still no injustice on God's part because, if these children had survived, they would *perhaps* have been damned. But, if they die unbaptized and before the age of reason, they descend to the limbo of children, where there is no punishment. Indeed, they take great delight from the knowledge of those things that they can know through nature alone unaided by grace, as Saint Thomas asserts in his questions on the punishment of original sin.[22]

It does not take much imagination to perceive Visconti struggling against the thought that, yes, God may be unjust after all, no matter what Aquinas said.

Yet, by Visconti's time, Aquinas's description of limbo was looking a bit too optimistic to some theologians. The Council of Florence (1439) seemed to argue for the actual punishment of souls dying "in original sin alone." And both Reformation and certain key Counter Reformation theologians would return to Augustinian severity about the punishment of unbaptized children. Even Cardinal Bellarmine (d. 1621), the great defender of Catholic dogma against Protestant criticism, "found the situation embarrassing, being unwilling, as he was, to admit that St. Thomas [Aquinas] and the Schoolmen generally were in conflict with what St. Augustine and other Fathers considered to be *de fide* [articles of faith], and what the council of Florence seemed to have taught definitively."[23]

Although he wrote a century and a half before Visconti, Dante (d. 1321) provides an instructive comparison to the witchcraft theorists. Dante declined to discuss the unbaptized infants at all, confining himself to a glancing reference: "The crowds, which were many and large, of *infants* and women and men."[24] Perhaps he glossed over the unbaptized infants because they were etymologically incapable of speech (*in-fantes*) and could not be interviewed. But a lack of curiosity about children on Dante's part seems unlikely. In fact, he took sophisticated liberties with the theology of limbo and changed the subject of it, quite literally, from children to adults.

Tradition held that there were two kinds of souls in limbo: the souls of righteous pre-Christian Jews, mostly adults, were imprisoned in the *limbus patrum;* the souls of unbaptized children were held in the *limbus infantium* or *puerorum.* Christ freed the Jewish patriarchs from limbo, delivering them to heaven, since they had believed the prophecies of the Hebrew Bible about the Messiah. After Christ's crucifixion and resurrection, only the souls of unbaptized children remained in limbo, and they would stay there forever.[25]

Yet, according to Dante's *Inferno,* in the year 1300 limbo still teemed with adult souls. These adults were not Jews, of course: eligible Jews had already been delivered. The adults in limbo were righteous Greek and Roman pagans like the poet Virgil; there were even Muslims. This was curious, for Dante agreed with tradition that the pagans had no notion of the true God or of the Messiah, and he elsewhere classified Muslims as schismatics and damned.[26] Dante's love of learning could plausibly explain his anomalous adults since all were either intellectuals or celebrated in literature.[27] But it does seem remarkable that, after making such large exceptions to tradition, Dante neglected the theology of infant baptism so obviously. He returned to the subject near the end of the *Paradiso,* but there he concentrated on the salvation of baptized infants and their different degrees of blessedness, not even mentioning limbo by name.[28]

Significantly, Dante's early illustrators refused to follow his example: several of them depicted the souls of children in limbo quite prominently, either among the adults whom Dante mentions or even in a group by themselves.[29] They were right to do so: theologians before and after Dante insinuate that, if the children in limbo could have communicated, they would have complained about their fate. Certainly, Dante's adult citizens of limbo complained: although they were not damned, they lived in a state of constant unfulfilled desire, unrelieved even by hope.[30] And they had at least lived. Tradition suggests that the souls of children might have lamented more bitterly and justly than Dante's adults.

On either side of Dante, Aquinas and Visconti grappled openly with the problem of children's eternal separation from blessedness. But, when Bartolomeo Spina took his turn, he left limbo alone. He was more concerned to justify God's ways to children in *this* world. And he found a solution, by blaming their parents as well as witches. Yet he was no more convinced of God's justice than Visconti had been:

> He who considers the most serious crimes [of parents] will understand that it is *not unjust* of the Almighty to permit the death of these little innocents, for the parents most gravely provoke his wrath and vengeance against their children. Not that such children are being punished for any

> crimes of their own. Rather, they *not unjustly* suffer punishment for the sins of their parents, whether their own immediate parents and ancestors or our common parents Adam and Eve. Indeed, we should consider that *God has permitted the most egregious evils and the most severe spiritual injuries,* beginning with the falls of the angels and the first man, just so that no one's free will should be seen to suffer violence. Thus, we will not marvel that *God permits the death of children who are in themselves innocent since he does not wish to obstruct the malice of witches and demons as if by violence.* And there are other reasons why this is required by his own justice, for he is God who is blessed for ever and ever. Amen.[31]

Spina ends his whole treatise on witchcraft right here. His conclusion suggests that the phenomenon of infant death was the principal stimulus behind his need to believe in the reality of witchcraft. And, if we want to wonder why Spina trails off into a prayer rather than analyzing God's "other reasons," we might ask ourselves how emotionally satisfying Spina's God can possibly be.[32] A God who finds the free will of witches and demons more important than the earthly suffering or eternal exile of innocent children is not very different from a devil. Yet there was no better solution to the death of children, so long as sacraments were interpreted as Spina and his contemporaries wanted.

Witchcraft Power

Infanticidal witches were invaluable in one further way for defending the reality of the sacraments. Their delight in the flesh of unbaptized infants was more than cruelty or perversity; they supposedly found it useful. Nider's informant Judge Peter learned that witches produced two magical substances from the children they boiled in their cauldrons, a broth and an unguent. Each product had a different function. As we saw, the broth was reserved for the witches themselves. Whoever drank it, admitted Peter's witch, "with the addition of a few other ceremonies, immediately acquires much knowledge and becomes a leader in our sect." This effect was mental or spiritual and thus intangible. But the unguent made from the undissolved residue left in the cauldron had tangible *physical* effects.

The unguent was crucial to theories of transvection and *maleficium,* especially after Nider's time. Nider himself was still vague about the unguent's effects, saying only that it was useful to witches in their pleasures, their arts, and their "transmutations."[33] If interpreted loosely, the word *transmutacio* could perhaps refer to transvection. But it more likely designates the process whereby witches supposedly changed themselves into cats to kill children without being detected.[34]

In witchcraft theory after Nider, the unguent had two distinct and complementary sets of effects. Witches were supposed to consider some of its effects beneficial to them, particularly transvection and the metamorphosis into animals. In addition to these devilish or inverted *beneficia* toward witches, the unguent caused *maleficia*—illness and misfortune—when rubbed or sprinkled on faithful Christians. When it was used for this latter function, it was sometimes described as a powder.[35]

Heinrich Kramer was fascinated by Nider's description of the cauldron and the initiation ceremony. In the *Malleus,* he quoted most of Nider's chapter on these things. Moreover, Kramer tortured the "Witch of Breisach" until she confirmed his interpretation of Nider's passage (or so, at least, he claims). He concluded triumphally that "her account of the method of professing the Devil's faith [i.e., the initiation] undoubtedly agrees with what has been written by that most eminent doctor, Johannes Nider."[36] But Kramer differed from Nider by clearly interpreting one effect of the unguent as "transportation": he quoted Nider's witch as mentioning *transvectionibus* or "transvections" instead of *transmutacionibus* or "transformations."[37] Kramer was quite explicit about how the unguent derived from children enabled transvection to take place:

> Now the following is their method of being transported. As was explained in the foregoing, they have to make an unguent from the limbs of children, particularly of those whom they have killed before baptism, and, following the demon's instructions, anoint with it a chair or a broomstick; whereupon they are immediately carried up into the air, either by day or by night, either visibly or, if they wish, invisibly. . . . Although the demon for the most part performs this by means of this unguent, to the end that children should be deprived of the grace of baptism and of salvation, yet he often seems to effect the same transvection without its use. For at times he transports the witches on animals, which are not true animals but devils in that form; and sometimes even without any exterior help witches are visibly carried solely by the operation of the Devil's power.[38]

Overall, Kramer could not decide whether witches preferred to kill infants before or after baptism.[39] In this passage, he went further and implied that the unguent might be altogether unnecessary for transvection. But this concession simply reflected his desire to believe *everything* theorized about how demons transported witches. He still needed to believe that devils prefer to have witches kill unbaptized children and that most of the time the unguent must contain their remains in order for witches to be transported, so he accepted Nider's theory.[40]

The idea of a necessary link between transvection and lack of baptism was endlessly appealing, and Kramer could not allow it to be supplanted by alternative solutions. He passed the connection on to Mazzolini, who claimed that the Devil commands witches to make "a certain unguent from the bones and limbs of children, and especially [*praecipue*] those who have not been reborn at the baptismal font." Mazzolini quoted Judge Peter of Bern via Nider and Kramer, repeating that witches attack "especially [*maxime*] those not baptized, and those not protected by the sign of the cross, so that they cannot be baptized and saved."[41] By Mazzolini's time, the idea that the unguent "of babies" was necessary for transvection had become institutionalized.

The bodily detritus of unbaptized children presumably caused its demonic effects because the crucial sacramental energies of baptism were absent. By enabling demonic transvection and *maleficia,* the unguent proved the reality of the *energeia,* the energy or effect of baptism and signs of the cross—not directly, but by default and inversion. Demons were attracted by the absence of baptism and crossing, just as they were repelled by their presence.

The absence of sacramental effects did not mean that the bodies of unbaptized children were neutral. Witchcraft theorists reasoned as if the little bodies were filled with something evil, a kind of maleficent mana or power that demons recognized and responded to. Doctrinally, that mana corresponds to the stain of original sin, which no baptism had canceled. The concept of mana is an anachronism here, and assertions that unbaptized flesh contained such power are nowhere explicit in witchcraft theory. Kramer denies it explicitly.[42] But, logically, devils' affinity for original sin can be inferred from their predilection for the flesh of unbaptized babies.

This attraction demonstrated by default that baptism and signs of the cross removed the negative mana. The rites could have protected the dead children from demonic attentions, but, because they were missing, the children's bodies were still able to attract demons, even after being cooked and made into unguent. The very matter of unbaptized children's bodies was thus conceptualized as a kind of bait, transmitting a signal for demons in somewhat the way carrion attracts scavengers. Original sin apparently tainted the body as well as the soul, just as baptism protected the "health" or "salvation" (*salus*) of both.

The concept of negative mana was implicit in the general defense of sacramentals that Johannes Nider worked out from Judge Peter's "data." Nider implied that negative mana was omnipresent in matter and that demons are everywhere: "Moreover, it is well-known that witches [*malefici,* the masculine plural] confess that their *maleficia* are obstructed [*prepediri*] by the rites of the church when these are properly observed and venerated: for example, by the aspersion of holy water, by the taking of consecrated salt, or of candles on the day of the Purification of the Virgin [Candlemas], by the rightful use of consecrated palm fronds on Palm Sunday, and by other such things. This is because the church exorcizes these objects so that they will weaken the powers of demons."[43] Like unbaptized infants, all matter, including the physical elements of holy rituals, is infested with demons. The exorcism of holy water and other objects makes them off-limits to demons, ending the infestation. Demons thus precede the sacramentals, both logically and in time. Not coincidentally, exorcism was an integral part of the baptism ceremony: before original sin could be washed away, demons had to be chased away.[44]

Once exorcism has taken place, holy objects acquire an automatic power to drive demons away and keep them from helping witches or harming good Christians. Salt could be consecrated and was used in the preparation of holy water, so some witchcraft theorists claimed that Satan avoided serving it at the Sabbat. This fiction harmonized with the supposed automatic efficacy of salt as a demonifuge; the connection was so obvious that there was no need to make it explicit. Someone was bound to complain about the lack of salt at Satan's banquets because they were unpalatable even when they featured no disgusting or horrifying foods. So several theorists told of a husband who followed his wife to the Sabbat out of curiosity. He naively but forcefully insisted on being served salt with the banquet and suddenly found himself alone, either because the salt was brought or because he exclaimed, "Praise God! Here's the salt!"[45]

Real Presences

The diverse functions of the unguent were linked at the deepest level by the assumption that the negative mana of unbaptized children called up a demon, making him present himself "in person," either visibly or invisibly. Only witches could normally see devils, but others could see their effects or energy (*energeia* means effect) because the witch appeared to be flying on a broomstick or the good Christian was afflicted with *maleficium*.

In fact, although the unguent of babies was regularly discussed in connection with baptism, its effects presupposed the categories of eucharistic theology. The necessary *presence* of the demon for transvection and *maleficium* was the polar opposite of the real presence of Christ in the consecrated host. Kramer's Toad Witch confessed that her powders for working *maleficium* contained a desecrated eucharist and the body of a toad, but she did not mention unbaptized babies. Since toads were considered innately evil and poisonous, their bodies had a negative quality comparable to the mana of unbaptized children. Kramer's substitution clarifies the notion that demonic presence could be called up by unconsecrated baby flesh. As the concept of sacramental countermagic presupposed, Christ and the demons were antithetical presences: one would always dominate or exclude the other.

The same eucharistic logic about presence applied throughout witchcraft mythology. At the Sabbat, witches allegedly had to trample a eucharistic host, a crucifix, or some other object intimately connected with Christ's body. The first occasion was their initiation, when they renounced Christian faith and transferred their allegiance to Satan. Pico's Strix recounts that her devil, Ludovicus, commanded her always to remove the consecrated wafer from her mouth, as soon as the priest had placed it there, by pretending to wipe her mouth. She was then to wrap the host in a linen handkerchief and bring it to the Sabbat, where it would be trampled, mocked, and even urinated on.[46] We must assume that the rationale for abusing the host was to insult and offend Christ "in person," thanks to his real presence in the host.

Pico's witch asserts in another passage that abusing the eucharist produced demonic presence as effectively as using the unguent of unbaptized babies. The demon seemed to *replace* Christ's presence:

> APISTIUS: Did you prepare for the arrival of the devil, or did you simply wait for him to carry you?
> STRIX: I made a circle and anointed myself, and straddled a bench, and was immediately carried to the Sabbat [*ludum/giuoco*]. At other times I trampled the consecrated host inside this circle, *with many insults,* and then Ludovicus appeared instantly, and I coupled with him as much as I liked.
> APISTIUS: What is your *damnable* unguent made from?
> STRIX: For the most part it is made from the blood of little children [*infantium/fanciullini*].[47]

The opposition between sacraments and demons was diametrical. If one was missing, the other was bound to be present. So, for witchcraft theory, any action involving a sacrament had to result in *some sort of presence.* Heinrich Kramer summarized this logic when he stated that all *maleficia* were based on the perversion of sacraments or sacramentals.[48]

Logically, if a sacrament was perverted, it would make present something perverse because sacraments were *signa efficaces,* producing the effects that they signified. When a witch desecrated sacramental material, the energy released from it became perverted (literally rerouted) and available for evil purposes. The invisible *beneficia* of the sacrament were reversed in other ways as well; they were also made visible or otherwise perceptible, as *maleficia* or a demon. As perverse presences, demons became unambiguously evident to human senses through a physical process of reversal, concretization, and perceptibility.

The logic of mirror reversal and symmetry could concretize presence in several ways. Desecration could make Christ's presence visible through bleeding or other protests, but Pico assumed that it could also make Christ's *absence* visible by summoning a devil. The demonic presence represented Christ's absence to the senses, the implication being that desecration offended Christ and drove him away. This process represents perversion of energies as inversion of presences: visible for invisible, evil for good, horrible for comforting, *maleficium* for *beneficium*. The presence of Christ in the consecrated host was invisible, but his absence became visible antithetically because a devil became *verifiably present* when the host was desecrated. Thus, Christ must previously have been *really present* in the host. In modern terms, the idea that perverted sacraments produced present absences can be conceptualized on the analogy of nuclear fission. The energies holding the atom together are imperceptible until we do violence to the atom: then the energies are displayed with incalculable violence. Clearly, it will not do to push the analogy of nuclear fission too far, but *energeia* as a literal and physical *effect* was clearly presupposed in all stories of perverted sacraments confessed by witches.

No Spiritual Vacuum

Pico's Strix "admitted" that demons could be attracted or summoned by both desecrated hosts and the unguent of babies. Bartolomeo Spina carried the equivalence further, modifying the recipe for unguent. He declared that *true* witches' unguent contained desecrated sacramental materials in addition to the remains of unbaptized children: "From those same children . . . they make that aforementioned unspeakable unguent, which demons find perfectly delightful [*valde delectantur*], mixing into it sacramental materials in contempt of the faith."[49] In this way, he implied, the unguent's attractive power was doubled: it exploited both the absence of sacramental energies and their perversion: "This is why it happens that, when women anoint themselves with a certain execrable ointment, the demon appears in answer to their prayer and carries them to various places. For, in confecting the ointment, they have thrown together many abominations, mixing them abusively with sacramental elements, while taunting the faith and the name of Christ, and doing it all in the name of the Devil." Spina went on to claim that people with no person-to-person relation to demons could be transvected by using the ointment, even when they were ignorant of its true nature: "And, indeed, sometimes persons can be carried about by demons in this way even though they themselves did not create that baleful ointment or even establish any sort of explicit pact with the Devil to the end of being carried."[50]

Spina's unguent reifies the sacramental principle of efficacy *ex opere operato:* it can work automatically, on anyone, as long as it was made under a demonic pact. The user's intentions toward the Devil are irrelevant. Yet Spina seems to be trying to have it both ways. He does not claim that the unguent *always* works automatically: if heaven intervenes, or if the demon fears that some good might come of the transvection, the unguent will fail to have an effect. Spina also says that, at least sometimes, the demon must answer an explicit prayer, not just respond reflexively to a stimulus.

Still, Spina's vacillation respects his sacramental theory of signs. The unguent is a sign with efficacy *ex opere operato,* so a devil always notices it. But devils have free will, so they can refuse to make it work. "Because of the explicit or implicit pact undertaken by these people with evil spirits or by others who did so before them," he says, as soon as anyone is anointed with the ointment it acts "as a sign, and the devil appears immediately of his own volition."[51]

We saw earlier that the devil's free will handily explained the failure of experiments under controlled conditions, such as happened to Prince N. Spina declared that the power of the unguent was not at all natural; it had nothing to do with the materials used or the human actions undertaken, but only the devil's caprice. Therefore, it would not work infallibly, but only when the devil wished. Here, as well, he claims that "it must in no way be thought that there is any natural power [*virtutem*] inherent in this unguent." There is no way the ointment could constrain the devil, he says, "nor is the Devil in thrall to the natural powers of corporeal things," for the simple reason that "he is nobler than them and unfettered [*absolutus*] by anything material."[52]

Spina attempted to avoid making the process of desecration crudely mechanical, too much like what we would call physics or chemistry. But here he adds that the unguent works because, "just as an animal is drawn by food, so a spirit is by signs, as Augustine says."[53] His last sentence weakens Spina's attempt to avoid a mechanistic concept of desecration, for it intimates that he wanted to believe that devils could not ignore the true witches' ointment any more than animals can ignore food. This magic quality appeared elsewhere: Spina maintained that magic words are necessary to the ointment since witches have to confect it "while taunting the faith and the name of Christ and doing it all in the name of the Devil."[54] The force of these insults to Christ is necessary for the ointment to become a lure for demons, even though the words were spoken long before the ointment is used.

By imagining the unguent as an automatic but ignorable homing signal, Spina makes it conform to the dogma that sacraments are signs that effect what they signify. As in a sacrament, the unguent's efficacy is not a natural power; it does not come from the physical materials. Instead, the efficacy is supernatural, deriving from the proper combination of words, things, and gestures at the moment of its creation. Just as Christ can respond to misuse of the consecrated host, so the devil can respond to misuse of his antisacrament, its use by people with whom he has no pact.

In fact, Spina's description of how the unguent was made corresponds neatly to the Scholastic definition of a sacrament, which was repeated by the Councils of Florence and Trent in the fifteenth and sixteenth centuries. A sacrament must have two elements, matter and form. The matter (*materia*) is material things (*res*): water for baptism, bread and wine for the eucharist, and so forth. The form (*forma*) is provided by the words (*verba*). Power to create the physical effects of a sacrament comes from God; power to create the effects of the unguent comes from a demon. Together, form and matter constitute the ceremony of the sacrament.

Form and matter are of course the Aristotelian categories that go to make up the hylomorphic theory of bodies. Sacraments and bodies implicate each other in many ways, the most dramatic of which are the definitions of the eucharist and matrimony as sacraments that *incorporate,* or form a body, from two or more "members."[55] The similarity of the unguent-making ritual to a sacrament seals its polar opposition to sacramental effects—although such a seal was hardly necessary for recognizing the opposition, it shows an urgent need for system and correspondence. No clearer proof could be desired that the unguent was a countersacrament.

Witchcraft as Theodicy

The ramifications of involuntary skepticism about the sacraments went far beyond purely sentimental concerns about infant mortality. Skepticism affected the ultimate questions of theodicy, that is, the branch of theology concerned to explain why an omnipotent and benevolent God allows evil to exist. The classic statement of the problem was in Aquinas's *Summa theologiae,* which reduced the dilemma to its harshest terms: "*It seems that there is no God.* For if, of two mutually exclusive things, one were to exist without limit, the other would cease to exist. But by the word 'God' is implied some limitless good. If then God existed, nobody would ever encounter evil. But evil is encountered in the world. *God therefore does not exist.*" Aquinas went on to resolve the problem through five proofs of God's existence.[56] But, by the fifteenth century, his purely logical proofs were considerably less convincing, at least to witchcraft theorists.

Johannes Nider was very clear about the comfort that he found in witches' reassurances that witchcraft was real:

> From these things it is therefore clear that the mercy and wisdom of omnipotent God, which reaches mightily from end to end of all things, uses the *maleficia* of these most evil men and devils most delightfully [*suaviter*]. Thus, while they attempt through their antireligion [*perfidia*] to diminish and weaken the kingdom of Christ and his faith, they actually strengthen that faith in the hearts of many and make it take root more hardily. Thus, many advantages [*utilitates*] can accrue to the faithful from the evils that we have been discussing because thereby faith is strengthened, the Devil's malice can be examined, God's wonderful power is manifested to men, they are exhorted to the care of themselves, and they are inflamed to reverence for the Passion of Christ and for the ceremonies of the church.[57]

Historians of witchcraft consider Nider's *Formicarius* as a formative text for the ideas that prevailed in later witchcraft theory. Most scholarly attention has been focused on book 5 of the work, where Nider discusses witches overtly.[58] This is probably because sixteenth- and seventeenth-century compilations of witchcraft treatises included only book 5. But there are four other books in the *Formicarius,* and they fit a carefully designed plan that Nider announces in the very first sentence of the book. "As I have traveled about," Nider writes, "I have often heard, particularly in some parts of Germany, the complaints of some who are lazy in their faith, asking why God no longer strengthens the church with miracles, as he formerly did, and does not illuminate it with holy revelations for the protection of the faith and the inculcation of virtues necessary for living well."[59] Nider put the problem bluntly: if miracles are possible, why are they no longer happening?

Needing to demonstrate that God has not abandoned Christians, Nider set out to prove that miracles were still commonplace if one knew where to look. He describes this plan for his treatise on its first page: "The first book will principally address the rare examples of good men and their works; the second will be about truthful-seeming [*verisimilibus*] good revelations; the third about false and illusory visions; the fourth about the powerful works of the saintly [*perfectorum*]; the fifth about witches [*maleficis*] and the illusions that they create."[60] Beginning from a perceived absence of God's miracles, Nider progressed methodically to a demonstration that these absences are illusory and that the illusion of absence is sometimes produced by Satan and his minions.

Although Nider does not mention sacraments here, he construed them as daily miracles that bind humanity to God, important signs that God was present and at work in the world. Anything that damaged sacramental credibility raised the specter of God's absence. Faith healers like Seriosa, who believed in the power of sacraments and sacramentals, gave Nider one proof that positive miracles were still possible. But, when sacraments seemed inefficacious, there had to be a reason. Nider's informant Judge Peter provided the evidence that witches regularly attacked the sacraments.

Bartolomeo Spina made the connection between witchcraft and theodicy even more emphatically than Nider, in a passage that we have already examined in part:

> [Through witchcraft,] we come to know three things by familiar experience, three things we formerly knew only by faith (although they are still questioned by those who wish to measure everything by their own intellect). First, that in our own regions intellectual creatures can be observed, whom we call demons, who have infinitely more power and knowledge than humans. Second, because the work of witchcraft is evil, we know demons to be evil. We can almost feel with our hands how demons seduce men and women into innumerable crimes, deceptions, and frauds. Third, we come to know with what ferocious hatred demons persecute Our Lord Jesus Christ and those devoted to him; how they inflict various injuries, above all on the innocent; how they persecute the faith of Christ and *by every possible means expose the sacraments of the church to contempt, mockery, and disgrace so that they are dishonored.*[61]

As Spina's third point makes explicit, witchcraft had something to do with exposing the sacraments to mockery and contempt.

Spina was not referring to witches' supposed desecrations, such as stamping on crucifixes or torturing the consecrated host. Rather, he needed to explain why sacraments appeared not to protect Christians from "various injuries," inflicted "above all on the innocent." He claimed that the defeat of witchcraft vindicates the truth of Christianity even when the sacraments appear not to work: "Because of witchcraft, what was already clear in itself becomes obvious to everyone: namely, that the Catholic faith is blessed with every kind of truth and perfection, and that it leads the faithful to blessedness despite the efforts of those evil spirits. Indeed, demons can achieve only those results that will frustrate their malice and iniquity. Thus, we find reason to bless and praise Almighty God, both for the good things that he disposes and for the evil things that he permits."[62]

Gianfrancesco Pico thought along similar lines. Just before his witch told Apistius about killing children and desecrating eucharists, Pico overtly instructed his reader about the doctrinal usefulness of witchcraft, explaining how it reinforced the faith of wavering Christians. Pico implied that theology could use some help, by putting the explanation in the mouth of the philosopher, Phronimus, rather than that of the cleric, Dicastes:[63]

> PHRONIMUS: *I want to add two more words here.* I think that God himself has with great providence decided to confirm and establish the faith in the minds of the faithful in several ways, so as to spread the Christian religion far and wide in this *unhappy* time, when it seems that everything is going from bad to worse.
>
> APISTIUS: In what ways, exactly?
>
> PHRONIMUS: In three ways, principally. First, through the coming to pass of things that had been prophesied; second, through miracles divinely performed; and, third, by allowing us to discover the crimes committed in these wicked rites [of witchcraft]. We have seen come to pass the *bloody* wars, the *cruel* famine *and want,* and the *horrendous* plague, exactly as they had been divinely announced so many years ago.[64] Anyone who was without faith[65] would be prostrated by the magnitude of such calamities, and people might easily suspect that they happened either randomly [*casu*] or because of some kind of fate [*fato*], were it not that faith had been reawakened and made to thrive on account of so many miracles performed by the Virgin Mother of God in this very town [*in hoc oppido*]. All by themselves these things confirm the truth of Christian faith, but the confessions of witches also corroborate it incidentally [*ex accidenti*]. By means of these confessions, taken from a numerous multitude of witnesses [*testium*] of both sexes, we have learned that demons are the malignant enemies of the truth of Christianity. But the harder they try to defeat and denigrate Christianity, the more it is exalted and shines brightly everywhere.
>
> APISTIUS: You have reasoned well. But tell me, my good witch [*bona strix*], did you ever kill any children?[66]

Miracles, the crimes of witches, and the coming true of prophecies are all ways of strengthening faith. Each reinforces the others.

Biblical prophecies of doom and the well-attested reality of witchcraft assure us that evil does not exist randomly or by necessity. Without this evidence, we would have to conclude that fortune or fate rules the world, rather than divine providence. This would mean that God cannot prevent evil, does not care to prevent it, or is responsible for it. So God has given us prophecy, miracles, and witches so that we will not doubt his existence or his good intentions toward us.

Witches are as necessary to Pico's theology as miracles or prophecy are because they are witnesses that demons are responsible for evil and the apparent inadequacies of Christian teaching. Apistius's asking the witch whether she has killed children is not a digression, for the death of innocent little ones seems arbitrary and unnecessary. It is the strongest argument against God's benevolence.

The "Primitivism" of Witchcraft Theorists

These are hardly the arguments of "credulous" or "irrational" people, unable to think deeply without contradicting themselves. Witchcraft myths about infanticide and sacraments were theological damage control, invented to address exquisitely logical dilemmas. A major advantage of witchcraft was to let God off the hook of seeming injustice. God's defenders "framed" the Devil and witches, making them the scapegoats for the unfairness of life and the afterlife. This formulation is not extreme: witchcraft theorists showed little confidence in their convoluted explanations of God's justice.

By theorizing witchcraft to protect God's benevolence and the reality of the sacraments, early-modern literate elites acted out a thought process that the anthropologist Mary Douglas associates with unsophisticated layfolk and so-called primitive peoples:

> By and large primitive religions and the ordinary layman's acceptance of more elaborate religious philosophies coincide: they are less concerned with philosophy and more interested in the material benefits which ritual and moral conformity can bring. But *it follows that those religions which have most emphasised the instrumental effects of their ritual are most vulnerable to disbelief.* If the faithful have come to think of rites as means to health and prosperity . . . there comes a day when the whole ritual apparatus must seem an empty mockery. Somewhere the beliefs must be safeguarded against disappointment or they may not hold assent.
>
> One way of protecting ritual from skepticism is to suppose that an enemy, within or without the community, is continually undoing its good effect. On these lines responsibility may be given to amoral demons or to witches and sorcerers. But this is only a feeble protection, for it

> affirms that the faithful are right in treating ritual as an instrument of their desires, [yet it] confesses the weakness of the ritual for achieving its purpose.[67]

Douglas's analysis is doubly damning, for it was not the backward, illiterate, and "primitive" layfolk of early-modern society who invented demonic witchcraft to salvage a degree of belief in the efficacy of the sacraments.

Witchcraft was constructed by just those persons who had the strongest interest and the most expertise in sophisticated theology and philosophy. Long before these intellectuals sanctioned and theorized the hunting of witches, parents had found comfort in asserting that witches had killed their children, as parents still do in many cultures. But the intellectual elite "discovered" the link between witches and devils to explain how God could decline to protect some children from death and others from eternal exile.

Witchcraft and the Sacraments in Practice and Theory

Three examples illustrate how thoroughly witchcraft remained entwined with issues of sacramental reality and infant welfare throughout the period of witch-hunting. Bartolomeo Spina says that, about 1522, he heard a strange story that had happened some years earlier. One night, a girl who lived at Bergamo with her mother suddenly found herself in Venice, an immense distance from home. The girl wound up in the bed of her cousin—the very man who told the tale to Spina's informant. The girl was discovered the next morning; because she was both their cousin and stark naked, the rest of the family demanded an explanation. Weeping, she allowed herself to be dressed and then told this story:

> "Last night I was awake in bed, and I saw my mother get out of bed. Thinking I was asleep, she took off her nightshirt and began smearing herself with an unguent that she took from a little jar hidden beneath the bricks of the floor. And, picking up a stick that she had there for the purpose, she mounted it as if it were a horse: she then suddenly took flight out the window and disappeared from my sight. I also got out of bed and greased my body as I had seen my mother do. Feeling myself being carried out the window, I also took flight, and, in an instant, I was transported into this house, where I discovered my mother attempting to harm a sleeping little child. My mother was upset by my arrival and began threatening me. Terrified by all this, I called on the names of Jesus and the Blessed Virgin, and, from that moment, I no longer saw my mother. But I remained here alone and naked."[68]

Once he had heard all this, the girl's kinsman wrote to the inquisitor of Bergamo and informed him of the whole affair. The inquisitor had the girl's mother arrested, tortured her, and obtained a full confession to the daughter's accusations. The mother added that the Devil had transported her more than fifty times into that house to kill her kinsman's child. But she had never succeeded in killing him because he was always protected by the sign of the cross and the pious prayers of his parents.[69]

Assuming, as always, that Spina did not invent this story, it presents some discontinuities that are both a little confusing and extremely suspicious. The young woman was having an illicit sexual affair with an uncle or a cousin. Her willingness to incriminate her mother for witchcraft and attempted infanticide suggests that strife between the two was the daughter's primary motivation. Since the girl's kinfolk were surprised to see her, she was probably a runaway and perhaps betrayed her mother to avoid being returned to her in disgrace. The naked girl knew enough—either on her own or in concert with her kinsman lover—to understand that accusing her mother of attempted infanticide was the way to get rid of her. She ably exploited the sensibilities of her kinfolk, shifting their anxiety from her own sexual invasion to their hopes for the survival of this little male heir (*puer, filius*). She brilliantly turned the child's mother from sexual competitor to ally against her own mother. Perhaps the most plausible element in the story is the ferocity that a child's kinfolk would have shown toward anyone accused of threatening it.

The interests of the girl and her kin were shaped and exploited by the inquisitor. In Spina's telling, it was clearly the inquisitor who introduced the idea that the witch had tried more than fifty times to kill the child. No previous attempts on the child's life were mentioned until the witch was in custody. The daughter would have jeopardized her pretense of innocence by showing any previous knowledge of her mother's infanticidal bent. It is therefore highly significant that the Bergamask inquisitor and Spina both insist that the reason for the old witch's repeated failures was bedtime prayers and signs of the cross. By exaggerating the original charge of attempted infanticide, the Bergamask inquisitor was trying above all to convince himself that these were efficient ways of ensuring children's physical safety. Spina's treatise demonstrates the same anxiety.

Neither cleric was an isolated anomaly in his wish to demonstrate that the sacramentals had real effects on the physical safety of children. Spina's story remained seductive to Catholic readers for centuries. In 1854, Gaetano Moroni was still citing it in his *Dizionario di erudizione storico-ecclesiastica,* being careful to end by saying that "the father inquisitor of Bergamo had the witch imprisoned and with torture obtained from her the confirmation of what her daughter had reported, and he found out moreover that the demon had many times taken her into that room so she could kill the child, but she had not been able to do it because she found it armed [*munito*] with the sign of the holy cross and because of the prayers its parents had made for its safety."[70]

The 1587 account of Walpurga Hausmännin's trial is filled with references to the countermagical power of sacramentals for defeating demons. She had supposedly rubbed the wife of the governor with a demonic salve, "but as [the wife] wore a neck-ornament with blessed medals on it the salve did not work." The men who condemned Walpurga to death were even more interested in confirming that baptism preserved children from physical harm. She had to confess that her demon lover "compelled her to do away with and to kill young infants at birth, even before they had been taken to holy baptism," and that she did so "whenever possible." Walpurga's interrogators attempted to defend the efficacy of baptism without fortifying it with sacramentals or prayers, but they could not get around their knowledge that infants often died despite being baptized. So, to salvage their belief that baptism *somehow* protected little children, these men had to imagine it as something subtler than a vaccination against crib death:

> Walpurga confesses further that every year since she sold herself to the Devil, she has on St. Leonard's Day exhumed at least one or two innocent children. With her Devil-Paramour and other playfellows she has eaten these and used their hair and their little bones for witchcraft.
>
> She was unable to exhume the other children she had slain at birth, although she attempted it, *because they had been baptized before God.*
>
> She had used the said little bones to manufacture hail. . . .[71]

Walpurga's interrogators could not convince themselves that baptism prevents death in infancy, so they forced her to confirm that it prevents the little cadavers from being desecrated. This betrays a process of theological negotiation or damage control.

Even this defense was not adequate; Walpurga had to confess that she often polluted the holy water used in baptism: "She could work the children no harm if they were protected by holy water. But if she herself gave the child holy water, she was able to do it damage, as she had previously passed water [*harnte,* "urinated"] into it."[72] Although this fiction implies difficulty policing the distribution of holy water, there is nothing unusual or unorthodox in the implication that Walpurga baptized some infants herself.[73] But Walpurga's interrogators learned that, if holy water did not have the effects that they had imagined it would, she and her devil had spoiled it. This fiction served the same purpose as the notion that baptism should be reinforced by prayers and signing the cross but admitted no inadequacy in baptism itself. In this, her interrogators espoused a "primitive" religion: "[One] way of protecting the belief that religion can deliver prosperity here and now is to make ritual efficacy depend on difficult conditions. . . . This is a narrowly instrumental approach, magical in the most pejorative sense."[74]

Walpurga's interrogators further buttressed their confidence in the powers of baptism by making her confirm that the bodies of dead unbaptized children contained a maleficent mana that baptism could have neutralized. She revealed that the bones of unbaptized children could be turned against good Christians as destructive hailstones. Their blood was one of the principal ingredients in the salves and ointments that her devil gave her for spreading other kinds of *maleficia*.[75]

The ideological point behind having Walpurga confess all these things is clarified by the final blanket confession that she was forced to make: "She admits that she would have caused still more and greater evils and damage if the Almighty had not graciously prevented and turned them away."[76] Because she took responsibility for forty-three human deaths, the eternal loss of heaven by several unbaptized infants, the destruction of much livestock, and devastating hailstorms that happened "once or twice a year," Walpurga reassured her tormentors that they lived in the best of all possible worlds. It was her fault if baptism and the sacramentals did not bring the material benefits that these men expected. Think of what she and her demonic coterie could have done had God not stayed their hands!

We can never be sure exactly whose voice we are hearing in a witch anecdote. But it is clear from the stories of Walpurga and the "Witch of Bergamo," over the period of a century and a half (from ca. 1522 to 1587) that the desire to believe that baptism and sacramentals counteracted physical harm was felt by the interrogators, not by the defendants. Nor is it likely that such countermagic originated from clerical condescension to popular simplicity. Educated men had exquisitely *theological* reasons for ventriloquizing or imagining witches' confessions of sabotaging sacramental efficacy.

A third example of sacramental defenses in witchcraft theory shows clerical anxieties even more clearly than the previous two. Strangely, it is not later but far earlier than the others, from the early fourteenth century. I refer to a single, anomalous trial in Ireland that, in its insistent themes of corporeality, sacraments, and *maleficium,* strongly resembled witch trials of a century and more later. In 1324, Dame Alice Kyteler was convicted of *maleficium* and demonic copulation by the tribunal of the bishop of Ossory, Richard Ledrede. Alice fled Ireland for England, but her servant, Petronilla of Meath, was captured and tortured until she admitted arranging sexual trysts between her mistress and a demon named "Robert, the son of Art" (*Robertum filium Artis*), "from the depths of the underworld." According to trial records, Petronilla admitted consenting "to a pact whereby she would be the go-between [*mediatrix*] for Alice and the said Robert." Petronilla also confessed watching while Alice and the demon Robert had sexual intercourse in broad daylight: "After this disgraceful act, with her own hand [Petronilla] wiped clean the disgusting place with sheets (*kanevacio*) from her own bed."[77]

The original accusations against Alice Kyteler were only for *maleficium*. She was accused by children of her husbands. By 1324, three of her husbands were dead, while a fourth was near death, supposedly from Alice's witchcraft. The stepchildren had economic motives: they were contesting Alice's inheritance of what they considered their property.[78] But, in the hands of the bishop, the trial turned into a vindication of sacramental efficacy. Ledrede had been appointed to his bishopric by Pope John XXII, who was obsessed by *maleficium* and heresy. He prosecuted members of his court for these crimes in 1318; he was also the author of the decretal *Super illius specula,* which accused "many who are Christians in name only" of "binding themselves to demons."[79]

Bishop Ledrede shared these obsessions: he accused Petronilla, Alice, and other members of the "sect" of using unbaptized children's clothes to prepare potions, powders, and unguents. They supposedly used these things to "kill as well as to afflict (*affligendum*) the bodies of faithful Christians." A hundred years before Nider and Judge Peter, this accusation suggests a need to explain how physical harm can afflict those who should enjoy God's protection. Another clue is provided by the description of how Alice and her "sect" obtained demonic cooperation for their magic (*sortilegia*): "The sorceresses would deny faith in Christ and the church for a whole month or for a year, according to the extent of what they wished to obtain from the sorcery. During that time, they would believe in nothing that the church believed, they would not worship the body of Christ in any way, they would not go into a church, they would not hear mass, they would not eat the holy bread or drink [*sic*] the holy water."[80] Avoiding sacraments and sacramentals removed Christ's protection and permitted the interaction of demons and humans to take place.

Contrary to later theorists, Ledrede imagined that Alice and her group repeatedly renounced faith and the sacraments and then returned to them with no lasting ill effects. He had no notion of a binding relation comparable to Nider's and Kramer's. This fiction has the same implications as repeated appearances and disappearances of demons: it reinforces the sense that the sacramental energies are real by repeatedly switching them on and off. Moreover, belief itself—rather than mere allegiance to dogma—could be switched on and off at will.

As later theorists would do, Ledrede imagined that dead unbaptized children transmitted a malefic mana to faithful Christians, momentarily erasing their sacramental protection. In fact, he expanded his theory while interrogating Petronilla. At first, he indicted her for using the clothes of unbaptized children, but later she confessed during torture that she had also used their brains.[81] Ledrede stopped short of imagining antieucharistic soups and cannibalistic feasting on infants. He thought of sacramental energies as being "on" or "off"; the idea that their polarity was reversible seems not to have occurred to him.

Ledrede even tried to harness the power of the eucharist in his quarrels with secular officials who would not surrender accused persons to him. Once, he entered the seneschal's court with a consecrated host "in its decorated gilt vessel" and, "reverently lifting up the host, he requested from the seneschal, the justice, the sheriff and the bailiffs, that in respect and love for Christ, whom he was holding in his hands, he should be granted a hearing in the cause of faith." The seneschal, unimpressed, "ejected the bishop, with the body of Christ, from his presence and chased him from the court": "'Woe, woe, woe,' cried the bishop loudly in front of them all when he observed this, 'That the Christian faith should be reduced to this, that Christ should be sent to stand at the bar in his own cause before a mortal judge in the presence of Christians, a thing unheard of since he stood trial before Pontius Pilate!'"[82] Here is a case of reification indeed. The consecrated wafer *is* Christ, and Ledrede waves it like a magic wand.

Ledrede succeeded in burning the unfortunate Petronilla, who was left unprotected when her mistress fled to England. But Alice had escaped him; so, in prefiguration of Heinrich Kramer and other witchcraft theorists, he wrote a book. Ledrede's account of prosecuting Alice was not printed until the nineteenth century, so it cannot have influenced the thinking of Nider, Kramer, and other fifteenth-century theorists. Rather, both Ledrede and later theorists were following the logic inherent in orthodox sacramental theory. Ledrede did have some influence on subsequent witchcraft legend in the British Isles, thanks to the repetition and expansion of his fantasies by a few chroniclers. By the sixteenth century, they had imagined all sorts of eucharistic crimes for Alice and her circle.[83]

The Prehistory of Sacramental Maleficium

The trial of Alice Kyteler is the first instance of a trial for crimes that can be defined as witchcraft, rather than *maleficium* alone. It is the first recorded moment when accusations of bodily interaction with demons, particularly copulation, appeared in a trial for *maleficium*.[84] Given its early date, Bishop Ledrede's prosecution of Alice and her friends also shows a singularly vivid and complete set of sacramental anxieties. We have established that theories of *maleficium* and demonic copulation were thoroughly intertwined with anxieties about the reality of the sacraments and of spiritual beings throughout the fifteenth century. It is therefore tempting to look for a catalyst of sacramental and spiritual anxiety in the upheavals of the fourteenth century. This was one of the most calamitous periods of European history, afflicted by, among other tribulations, the Great Famine of 1315–22, the Black Death of 1347–52, that plague's several recurrences, and, on the purely human level, the Hundred Years' War (1337–1453).[85]

To understand what literate Europeans thought of these disasters and how their religious thinking was affected by them, we could turn to Boccaccio's introduction to the *Decameron*. Boccaccio was an eyewitness to the fearsome outbreak of plague in Florence during 1348, and he paints an almost unimaginably shocking picture of destruction.[86] All distinctions between humans and animals were erased, says Boccaccio: people died like cattle, and pigs died like people. What could cause such widespread death? Boccaccio is uncertain whether to attribute it to God's righteous anger at human sin or to an astrological "dis-aster," a strange and deadly alignment of the planets. In other words, Boccaccio hesitates over just that choice of causes that Aquinas and the witchcraft theorists dreaded making: God or astrology, spirits or bodies.

This is not to claim that natural and human disasters caused witchcraft theory to emerge; but the vast disasters of the fourteenth century came after Scholastic theologians had been wrestling for more than a century with the problems of evil and its origins, the existence of God, whether he was both all-powerful and perfectly just, whether the existence of angels and demons could be proved, and problems of sacramental efficacy. Increased interest in the Book of Job reflected these concerns; during the twelfth and thirteenth centuries, Job became a favorite proof of demons' power and malignancy for theologians wrestling with the conundra of theodicy.[87] Moreover, the thirteenth and fourteenth centuries were marked by institutional crises in the church. Popes competed with the emperor for political power. At times, there were two and even three men claiming to be pope (the Great Schism, 1378–1417).

Opposition to the structure and teachings of the church and calls for the reform of the clergy created large movements among the laity that were condemned as heretical and frequently put down by force.

Salvatore Camporeale speaks of a "travail of Christendom" in the fourteenth through the sixteenth centuries, a painful upheaval with many social and intellectual causes: the Black Death, the Great Schism, but also broader ferment and change at all levels of Christian activity: teaching, preaching, methods of theological research, the liturgy, mysticism, and many other areas. For Camporeale, the "travail of Christendom" was a "real and definite theological crisis."[88] The rise of Protestantism and the polemical response of the Roman church in the Counter Reformation are only the latest and most easily categorized aspects of this two-century-long upheaval. Protestantism and Roman Catholicism emerged at the end of this period having undergone many positive changes, but doubt, anxiety, and mental torment about the identity and validity of Christianity continued. Whatever triumphs the Western churches can show were bought dearly.

But Christendom's travail did not suddenly begin around 1300 or even with the Scholastic theology of the previous century. Symptoms of anxiety can be seen much earlier. Accusations of interaction with embodied demons and trials for crimes that implied the reality of the sacraments had been evolving since the early eleventh century. Self-styled orthodox writers had exploited these accusations to soothe theological anxieties that foreshadowed those of witchcraft theorists.

Already in 1022, Adémar de Chabannes was accusing heretics of adoring the Devil, "who appeared to them first as an Ethiopian and then as an angel of light, and who daily brought them much money." One of the heretics supposedly "carried about with him the ashes of dead children, by which he soon made a Manichaean of anyone to whom he could give them."[89] Writing a half century later, another writer, discussing the same group in more detail and with more imagination, declared that the heretics met at night in a certain house, where "they chanted the names of demons until they saw descend among them a demon in the likeness of some sort of little beast." Apparently having no precise notion of demonic corporeality and no idea that demons could prove their reality by copulating with humans, this writer claimed that, "as soon as the apparition was visible to everyone," all the lights were put out, and each man "seized the woman who first came to hand, to abuse her, without thought of sin." He saw sexual transgression by humans as heinous enough, claiming that the heretics willingly copulated with their mothers and sisters and with nuns. When the women gave birth "from this filthy union, on the eighth day thereafter a great fire was lighted and the child was purified by fire in the manner of the old pagans, and so was cremated."[90]

The combination of purely human sex crimes, infanticide, deprivation of baptism, and pagan ritual supposedly brought out an evil mana from the flesh of the dead child: "Its ashes were collected and preserved *with as great veneration as Christian reverence is wont to guard the body of Christ,* being given to the sick as a viaticum at the moment of their departing this world. Indeed, such *power of devilish fraud* was in these ashes that whoever had been imbued with the aforesaid heresy and had partaken of no matter how small a portion of them was scarcely ever afterward able to direct the course of his thought from this heresy to the path of truth."[91]

Centuries before Judge Peter or Johannes Nider, these writers arrived at their concept of a magical antieucharist by forcing the logical connections among various sacraments. The same stories were repeated a century later, in 1114, to vilify another group of heretics, and they kept on evolving.[92] Although these tales were a stock in trade of the Latin church, practically identical accusations were collected by the Byzantine writer Michael Psellus (d. 1078) in his *De operatione daemonum,* or *On the Works of the Demons.* Despite its title, Psellus's book was mostly concerned with the *corporeality* of demons and their abominable interactions with Near Eastern heretics.[93]

These stories imply that clerics were already having doubts about the efficacy of the sacraments in the eleventh and twelfth centuries, as much as two hundred years before sacramental dogmas had been thoroughly elaborated or made formally explicit by Scholastic theologians. There was a real-world basis for such doubts: many of the groups slandered by these early stories actually had denied that one or more sacraments had any real efficacy. A group in 1025 denied the efficacy of baptism, particularly baptism of infants. This group also claimed that "the sacrament of the Lord's body and blood [was] nothing more than that which the eyes of the flesh behold" and further denied the efficacy of penance and "despised" matrimony in favor of rigid chastity.[94] Often, critics declared that sacraments were invalid when they were administered by priests who lived in luxury or kept concubines. Scholars trace this Donatism to the moralistic concern with human imperfection that critics openly voiced, but questions about the sacraments formed a logical closed circuit with questions about the nature of God and of his relation to humanity. Human unworthiness was a comforting explanation of the perception that sacraments did not reliably appear to work; it was far more frightening to suspect that their effects were imaginary.

A number of strategies had evolved for testing or experimenting with sacramental efficacy, both surreptitiously, as Judge Peter did about 1400, and openly, as Bishop Ledrede did in 1324. There was also a doctrinal or at least customary criterion that ecclesiastics could employ to test sacramental efficacy, the ordeal or *ordalium*. In modern English, the word no longer has any precise meaning other than "pain" or "tedium," but in medieval law and custom it was a test: "any procedure of whatever type, through which people believe they can induce supernatural beings to manifest a decision that will have juridical effects."[95] A question of guilt or innocence was taken as the occasion for consulting the will of God, who was invited to pronounce a sentence by causing a person to pass or fail a physical test or by favoring one of two combatants; trial by fire and trial by combat are the two best-known variants of the ordeal, but there were others.

One ordeal sounds ridiculous on the surface (so ridiculous, in fact, that Boccaccio used it as the occasion for a story about low tricksters), yet it could be terrifying. This was the *offa* or *pabulum probationis*. The task was simply to swallow a chunk of food, usually bread and cheese, without choking. First, however, the person on trial had to sit through hours of litanies, anathemas, and invocations calling for entire legions of angels (one ritual refers to twelve thousand spirits), plus the evangelists, the prophets, and so on, to dry up the saliva and seal the throat of the accused if he were guilty.[96]

It should come as no surprise that there was an analogous ordeal of the eucharist or that it was openly based on Saint Paul's saying in 1 Cor. 11:29 that "he that eateth and drinketh [the eucharist] unworthily, eateth and drinketh damnation unto himself, not discerning the Lord's body." Paul's words may be the root of the idea that the energies of the sacraments could be transformed into a force for harm rather than benefit. This verse already implied that eucharist was a test; only the faithful could discern the Lord's body within it.[97]

Whereas the *offa* was used for layfolk, the eucharistic ordeal was usually reserved for ecclesiastics. Tellingly, whereas one was required to confess his sins before normal communion, confession was *prohibited* before trial by eucharist. This stipulation, in combination with the ambiguity of the Bible verse, meant that a trial of human guilt could easily become a trial of divine efficacy, for the point of denying confession to the defendant was the assumption that, if guilty, "he would be struck by more or less immediate punishment, most likely physical, such as a sudden malady."[98]

Combinations of ordeals were possible in practice. Guibert of Nogent reports that, in an incident from 1114, the defendants were made to take communion before being subjected to the trial by water. As the bishop handed them the eucharistic elements, he said, "Let the body and blood of the Lord try you today." Then they were taken to the water: "With many tears, the bishop chanted the litany, then performed the exorcism. Then the men took the oath that they had never believed or taught anything contrary to our faith. Clement [the leader], when cast into the vat, floated on top like a stick, at which sight the whole church was carried away with boundless joy." The man floated because he was being rejected by the water and was therefore guilty. Aside from being the element of baptism, the water had been exorcized and was therefore free of demonic influences. If the defendant sank, the water had accepted him and proved his innocence—at the risk of drowning him. One wonders if the crowd lynched these heretics as joyfully, or as independently of clerical instigation and connivance, as Guibert declares.[99] Or did Guibert feel joy because the ordeal confirmed the guilt that everyone already knew and thus confirmed itself as well?

Anyone familiar with the literature of witchcraft theory and witch-hunting will recall that variants of this ordeal, called *swimming* or *floating* the witch, lasted deep into the seventeenth century, even among Protestants. James Sharpe records cases of swimming in England as late as 1795, although these were usually lynchings.[100]

What is truly curious is that, in 1215, the Fourth Lateran Council had outlawed all clerical participation in ordeals; in theory, this should have put an end to them. Lateran IV was arguably the most important council of the later Middle Ages, and it was overseen by Innocent III, perhaps the most powerful and important of late-medieval popes. R. I. Moore has traced what he called "the formation of a persecuting society" to Lateran IV because it made possible many of the excesses of repression in subsequent centuries.[101] Lateran IV set in motion the doctrinal and legal machinery that enabled the increased surveillance, control, and persecution, not only of the faithful, but also of Jews, heretics, and all the other outcasts who would appear or be imagined after them. For instance, Jews were required to distinguish themselves by their clothing, lest they be mistaken for Christians or even intermarry with them. Moreover, Jews were prohibited from returning to Judaism once they had been converted and baptized.

Lateran IV promulgated the Fifth Crusade against Islam—perhaps to make up for the disastrous Children's Crusade of three years previously or the shameful Fourth Crusade, also promoted by Innocent III, which had seen Constantinople sacked by Catholic forces (in 1203 and again in 1204). In 1208, moreover, Innocent proclaimed a crusade in southern *France,* against the Albigensian or Cathar heretics there. This ferocious, devastating war lasted over twenty years. Pope Innocent encouraged the Franciscans and Dominicans in the early stage of their formation as preaching orders: the preaching friars were necessary for combating the spread of heresy, particularly the Albigensian variant. Finally, Innocent laid important foundations for the inquisitional pursuit of heresy since he "for the first time identified heresy with the doctrine of treason as found in Roman law" and "linked the legal duties of ecclesiastical and lay authorities."[102]

It may thus appear paradoxical that a council and a pope so intent on uniformity of doctrine and repression of religious dissent or diversity should have outlawed the ordeal or, rather, outlawed clerical participation in ordeals. But ordeals were *unreliable.* By 1487, distrust of ordeals was so deep that Heinrich Kramer warned witchcraft inquisitors *never* to allow accused witches to undergo ordeals to prove their innocence. His ostensible reason was that ordeals "tempted God," which is already interesting since *temptare* means both "to tempt" and "to test" or "try."[103] But specifically, Kramer said, when "notorious witch[es] . . . the subject of much public complaint" passed ordeals and were set free, there was "grave scandal to the faith."[104]

Therefore, defendants who requested an ordeal should be ipso facto judged witches: the request proved that they *knew* that devils would help them pass even the fearsome ordeal of carrying red-hot iron for three paces. Devils would either exploit the natural healing properties of herbs or "invisibly interpos[e] some other substance" between the iron and the defendant's hand.[105] The extent to which the mentality of the ordeal nevertheless influenced the trials of heretics and witches is striking. Kramer claims that, in the diocese of Ravensburg, "certain heretics" (he does not say *witches*) were condemned to death but "remained unharmed in the fire." Finally, he says, "their sentence was altered to death by drowning, but this was no more effective. All were astonished, and *some even began to say that their faith was vindicated.*" So the bishop ordered a three-day fast. As a result of the fast, Kramer implies, it was found out that the heretics had "a magic charm sewed between the skin and the flesh under one arm." (A cynic might suggest that, if anything like this story actually happened, the three-day suspension created time for the planting of this evidence.) Once the charms were removed, the heretics were burned with no further ado. According to Kramer, some people say that the happy ending to this near debacle was owed to a necromancer. Informed of the heretics' trick by a devil, he betrayed it to the authorities: Kramer speculates that "the Devil, who is always scheming for the subversion of the faith, was compelled by divine power to reveal the matter."[106]

This look forward to Kramer clarifies some of the potentialities of the Lateran decree. Kramer feared ordeals because, if they failed to prove the guilt that everyone suspected, they undermined people's faith, rather than strengthening it. From a psychological perspective, ordeals were unreliable experiments. The same diffidence, in less conscious form, could underlie the prohibition of ordeals in 1215.

A look at the statutes passed by Lateran IV shows that it legislated several sacramental and demonological definitions that would later be important to witchcraft theorists. A declaration of Catholic faith was placed at the beginning of the statutes, aimed at counteracting the heresies of the Cathars. It declares God omnipotent and says that he created everything, including matter, from nothing (*ex nihilo*). The authors of evil, "the Devil and the other demons," were created by God and were originally good but fell by their own perversity. These definitions oppose the dualistic tenets of the Cathars, who defined matter and the cosmos as evil; they postulated two divinities of equivalent power, one good and one evil, who eternally struggle for domination of the cosmos. Finally, the credo states that "man sinned because of the Devil's instigation."[107] The relation between sinners and demons was thus stated categorically: although there is no god of evil, evil is not purely human.

The anti-Cathar credo goes on to declare that the body and blood of Christ are contained "really" in the eucharist, under the species or appearance of bread and wine, and that this happens through transubstantiation.[108] Statements about other sacraments were added. Discussions of matrimony and baptism, both repudiated by Cathars, imply that the doctrine of transubstantiation is also made explicit for defensive reasons, to address doubt, by Cathars or Christians, regarding whether or how Christ was "really present" in the eucharistic elements.[109]

Crusades against the Albigensian Cathars had been under way since 1208. The council stressed that Catholics who "take up the cross and arm themselves to exterminate heretics" in France would enjoy the same indulgences and privileges as crusaders who "go to the aid of the Holy Land."[110] The historians Roger French and Andrew Cunningham suspect that the crusade was undertaken in frustration over lack of Catholic success in very public debates with the Cathars between 1203 and 1208.[111] The combination of decrees and crusade supports this idea.

The council not only outlawed intellectual opposition to the eucharist but also addressed the possibility of eucharistic desecration for the purpose of committing "abominations." It decreed that all churches keep the chrism oil and the eucharistic elements "under lock and key so that no reckless hand can take hold of them and profane them with unmentionable uses." If the keeper of these things neglected them, he was to be suspended from his duties for three months; if "something abominable" happened to them, he was to receive more severe punishment.[112] These measures may have addressed real abuses; but they also suggested the magical implications that witchcraft theorists imagined in later centuries. At the same time, these measures made actual desecration (or even well-intentioned experimentation) much less likely. Terrible possibilities were suggested at the very moment that steps were taken to make them far less *possible in fact.*

Everyone would now be required to go to confession and take communion at least once a year, at Easter, unless their parish priests decided that they should abstain for a while. Those who refused were to be denied entry into churches during their lifetimes and refused Christian burial at their death. Most interestingly, confession is referred to as medicine (*remedium*) and as healing, while the confessing layman is a "sick man" and the father confessor an "expert physician." Lest anyone interpret this as a mere metaphor, the next chapter is explicitly about physical illness:

> Infirmity of the body sometimes derives from sin, as Our Lord said to the sick man he had healed, "Go and sin no more, that worse not happen to you" [John 5:14]. Thus with the present decree we establish and severely command the physicians of the body that, when they are called by the sick, they should first of all admonish and induce them to call the physicians of the soul, so that, after the spiritual health [*salus*] of the sick has been attended to, recourse can be had to the remedies of corporeal medicine with greater efficacy; for, in fact, when the cause is taken away, the effect ceases as well [*cum causa cessante cesset effectus*].[113]

This is an extraordinary passage, for it ostentatiously employs the Scholastic, Aristotelian language of cause and effect to argue that sin can be *literally* responsible for disease.[114]

Given the frequency of mortal illness in this period, it is significant that the council calls for postponing the physical cures of people who are in mortal danger until the eucharistic viaticum or last communion can be given. Considering the often deadly inefficacy of premodern medicine, this measure was prudent from the practical standpoint. But, by legislating that "bodily cures" could take place only after "spiritual cures" had been effected, the council eliminated the possibility that unexpected healing could be attributed to natural causes alone.[115] It eliminated the possibility of deliberate or accidental experimentation. Enforcement was written into the decree: local prelates were to publish this prohibition in church, and physicians who disregarded it were to be excluded from church (i.e., excommunicated) until they had done penance.

What all this means is that, in the moment that Lateran IV formalized eucharistic dogma for the coming centuries, it also moved to place the sacrament's efficacy beyond doubt or experimentation. Ironically, ordeals and sacramental experimentation continued and even increased. But they became more inventive, less formal, less immediately recognizable. Much of what was done to accused witches—or at least theorized about doing to them—can be classified only as an ordeal. Kramer's recommendation that inquisitors force witches to touch saints' relics, drink holy water or even water in which disks of blessed wax had been immersed, or make them attempt to weep was based on the mechanics of an ordeal.[116]

In some cases, Kramer sought evidence of the *Devil's* intervention rather than God's: "And as for the witch's inability to weep, it can be said that the grace of tears is one of the chief gifts allowed to the penitent. . . . [Tears] are displeasing to the Devil, and . . . he uses all his endeavor to restrain them to prevent a witch from finally attaining to penitence." God's intervention was harder to prove: "Witches should be questioned on the more holy days and during the solemnization of the Mass, and . . . the people should be exhorted to pray for divine help, *not in any specific manner,* but . . . they should invoke the prayers of the saints against all the plagues of the Devil."[117]

Kramer's ideal inquisitor looks for "devilish charms" on the bodies of his witches, but he looks like a witch: he should "wear around his neck consecrated salt and other matters, with the seven words that Christ uttered on the cross." If possible, "he should wear these made into the length of Christ's stature against his naked body, and bind other holy things about him."[118] Kramer seems to have understood that he was conducting a kind of ordeal; in the same chapter, he specifies that the inquisitor should exploit the ordeal of hot iron. The inquisitor should not allow the ordeal actually to take place, but only offer it as an option; he should withdraw the offer as soon as the defendant accepts it.[119] The defendant's acceptance of the offer proves her guilt, and, therefore, the ordeal itself is superfluous. For Kramer, the mere *idea* of the ordeal has become an ordeal and an infallible one: the defendant is guilty whether she accepts or declines. A long chapter follows, dedicated entirely to discussing Kramer's theological and practical objections to formal judicial ordeals; only then can he let the matter drop.

The crises that led to witchcraft theory in the early fifteenth century emerged from a long, uneasy debate between lived experience and doctrinal theory about God, the efficacy of his sacraments, and the demons. These problems emerged with particular force in the Aristotelian discussions of thirteenth-century Scholasticism and were probably worsened by the unremittingly disastrous social and ecclesiastical conditions of the fourteenth century. Traces of Western Christians' negotiation with their doubts about the reality of sacramental energies became far more obvious in the early literature on witchcraft. These works betray important anxieties about the relation of God to humanity: not simply about human sinfulness, but also about God's presence, justice, and providence. The extent of that discomfort was evident in discussions of the eucharist, baptism, and the sacramentals. But there is also strong evidence of it in two areas of witchcraft theory that have hitherto seemed more down-to-earth: the lore of witch-cats and werewolves and the sexual magic of witches.

10

ILLUSION AND REALITY, PART ONE: CRIB DEATH AND STEALTHY CATS

Il ne faut pas faire passer tous les chats pour des sorciers. (We should not make all cats out to be witches.)

—French proverb

Le chat-huant, "screech-cat," i.e., "screech owl"

For witchcraft theorists, and probably for layfolk, witches provided a comforting explanation of misfortunes that had no obvious human perpetrator but could not comfortably be ascribed to God or to chance. The most heartbreaking and scandalous of these misfortunes was infant death. The modern term *crib death* and the more technical *sudden infant death syndrome* both acknowledge that, even today, there is often no obvious explanation for the death of infants. The mystery was even more dramatic in former times, which had more rudimentary ideas of causality. If a dead child had not been accidentally smothered by an adult sleeping in the same bed, if it had not fallen or contracted an obvious throat or stomach ailment, parents were left with an intolerable perplexity. The case was even worse if the child had not been feverish or had seemed normal until just before it died or if, even more problematically, it slowly wasted away without responding to any remedies or showing any obvious symptoms.

As anthropologists have shown, many preliterate or highly traditional cultures profess to believe that no death is ever accidental or natural. In such a view, death always happens because of aggression by an enemy, and the less obvious the attack, the more crafty and stealthy the enemy can be presumed to be.[1] If children are dying for no apparent reason, then witchcraft must be at work, and witches must be extraordinarily stealthy.

Theologians, motivated by theological anxieties rather than the searing personal grief of parents, constructed elaborate theories to explain why God allowed little children to die. But, once theologians resolved the *why* of infant death, they were faced with the problem of explaining *how* infanticide occurred. For these explanations, they relied on and exploited the traditional witch lore of grieving parents.

Gianfrancesco Pico noted several times that witches killed children by sucking their blood. His Strix explained how she avoided arousing parents' suspicions or leaving tangible evidence of her vampirism:

> APISTIUS: But come now, tell me, my good witch: did you ever kill any children?
> STRIX: Not just one, but many of them.
> APISTIUS: With a knife, or with a club?
> STRIX: With a needle and my lips.
> APISTIUS: In what way?
> STRIX: We entered the houses of our enemies at night, by doors and entranceways that were opened for us [by demons], and, while their fathers and mothers were sleeping, we picked up the tiny children and took them over by the fire. There we pierced them under their nails with the needle, and then, putting our lips to the wounds, we sucked out as much blood as our mouths would hold. And I always swallowed part of it—sent it right into my stomach—and part of it I put aside in a little bottle or jar. From it I later made that unguent that we use for anointing our shameful parts when we want to be carried to the Sabbat.[2]

This could well be the layfolk's traditional explanation of crib death. Only the last two sentences show interference by inquisitors or witchcraft theorists.

Pico's inquisitor, Dicastes, does not attempt to disguise how intensely he wants to believe in Strix's explanation:

> DICASTES: So you will not think that this going through the houses of anyone whatever and killing their children is simply fables, or dreams, or imaginations, or illusions, and doesn't happen really and in truth, I can tell you that some truly unfortunate little children have been found. They were still taking milk at the breast, and their fingers had been pierced, with the wounds and holes being found under their little nails.
> APISTIUS: Answer me, Strix: I wonder greatly that these little children didn't weep or cry out loud when you witches pricked them and treated them so badly.
> STRIX: While we are doing it, they are so sound asleep that they don't feel it. But afterward, when they are awakened, they cry out loud, and weep, and wail, and get sick, and sometimes even die.
> APISTIUS: How come they don't all die?

STRIX: Because we heal them. We give them some effective remedies and free them from the illness. And we make a great profit from this healing.
APISTIUS: Who taught you these remedies?
STRIX: The demons.
APISTIUS: This doesn't seem plausible [*verisimile*] to me.
PHRONIMUS: And why not? Don't you know that the Devil knows the powers of all the herbs and that men have learned them too?[3]

Apistius's skepticism about these complicated explanations is as revealing as Dicastes' defense of them.

Screech Owls, Witch-Cats, and Werewolves

How did witches get into people's houses in the first place? Dicastes had a simple but very theological answer: demonic transvection. By this means, he claimed, Don Benedetto Berni, the head of the witch sect, penetrated an otherwise impregnable fortress, sucked the blood of a child, and killed him.[4] Theologians created more elaborate explanations by accepting and modifying folkloric explanations of the causes of infant mortality. This process created many of the early-modern stereotypes of witches, some of which are still part of popular culture.

Silvestro Mazzolini explained how valuable he considered folklore about witches' stealthiness. He related that, in Italy, common people called witches "masks or ghosts or persons who are disguised" (*maschare, id est larvae, aut larvatae personae*).[5] His use of the word *larva* implies that masquerade or disguise is not just hypocritical or stealthy. Disguise makes a person ghostlike, and ghosts can enter where living people cannot. This is clearly no everyday masquerade; it is *powerful.* Mazzolini was aware of connections between masquerading and magic, and he made them fully explicit. These associations characterize the rituals of many primitive cultures, so Mazzolini could be describing ideas that are genuinely folkloric and extremely ancient.

For the elusiveness of witches to have theological value as an explanation, some sort of evidence of their contact with suprahuman or supernatural beings had to be found. Mazzolini thus applied theology to folklore: *maschara* is an appropriate name, he wrote, because witches "commonly go about in the manner of masked or bewitched persons [*larvatorum instar*], made unrecognizable and invisible through the power of demons [*daemonum virtute incognitae et invisae*], and this is how they work their harm."[6]

To explain the peasant concept of *maschare,* Mazzolini depended, not just on theology, but also on Roman and biblical literature. He looked for information about witches and infanticide in the meanings of the words used for witches. According to Mazzolini, all the names demonstrate by their etymology that witches kill children at night by sneaking in and sucking their blood or tearing them apart. Despite his ulterior motives, Mazzolini produced convincing evidence that a desire to attribute infant death to magical enemies has been a constant in Western culture.

As Mazzolini claimed, the Latin and Italian names (*strix, strega, lamia*) used in his day all referred to folklore dating to the ancient Romans about owl-like and woman-like creatures who sucked the blood of babies in their cribs or killed and ate them:

> Sometimes, however, witches are called *strigae* by means of a metaphor, which is used because they are especially prone to work their *maleficia* at night. The *strix* [screech owl] is a nocturnal bird so named because of its screeching [*a stridendo*], because when it calls out it screeches. And the poet Lucan says of it in his *De bello civile* [*Civil War*], "Quod trepidus bubo, quod strix nocturna quaeruntur" [6.689], and it drinks the blood from the little bodies of children. More normally, these people are called *lamiae,* not because of the delightful sex life [*voluptuosa vita*] they enjoy with incubus and succubus demons, but because of the cruelty of their *maleficia.* For in the commentaries to Isaiah 54 the *lamia* is described as a monstrous beast that has the feet of a horse but whose other bodily members mimic [*effingunt*] the human form and aspect. Thus according to Gregory in the thirty-fourth part of his *Moralia in Job* [*Moral Reflections on the Book of Job*], it has a human aspect but the body of a beast. And it is so cruel that it tears apart [*dilaniet*] its own children. Therefore it is called *lamia* as if from *lania* [feminine of *lanius,* a butcher, "one who tears apart"].[7]

Modern scholars agree with Mazzolini that these words for witches reflect ancient Roman fears of screech owls and other nocturnal birds and Roman anxieties about little children's precarious hold on life.[8]

Mazzolini did not pronounce on the reality of Roman monsters, for he was uninterested in Roman times. Unlike the ancient Romans, he assumed that these names did not describe literal monsters or the literal metamorphosis of witches into animals. Yet, since language reflects reality, witches must be called *screech owls* and *lamias* because they behave like these monsters. Mazzolini was interested in the histories of words; he relied on etymologies because he assumed that "names are the consequences of things" (*nomina sunt consequentia rerum*). Witches' most essential activity must therefore be the destruction of children. *Strix* and *lamia* allude to this action; they are metaphors rather than identities.

Gianfrancesco Pico exploited this ancient link between witches, nocturnal birds, and crib death by entitling his dialogue *Strix*. At its beginning, Phronimus first tells Apistius that they should follow the gathering crowd to see whether the inquisitor has caught another witch. The skeptic quips that he would indeed like to see such a rare bird, "sought by me with such desire, but never found anywhere." In this, he anticipates Mozart's joke about another rara avis, the phoenix: "Everyone says it exists, but no one knows where it is."[9] Phronimus, however, is serious, and he buries the skeptic's joke in an avalanche of quotations from Roman writers. When Romans wrote about *striges,* he says, they were speaking figuratively of malicious old women, who "injure newborn children in their cradles, making them cry, and then quickly heal them" so that there is no evidence of their crime.[10] Although the name is metaphoric, it points to a reality.

Although Pico and Mazzolini compared witches to owls and monsters, they and others discussed at greater length the idea that witches changed themselves into cats to kill children. This idea had both literate and folkloric pedigrees. Among literate Christians, the mental habit of associating cats with enemies of the faith predated the period of witch-hunting by a good two centuries. Heretical sects of the twelfth and thirteenth centuries were imagined as having physical interactions with the Devil at secret meetings. Unlike witches, these groups existed, and their enmity toward mainstream Catholicism was real as well.

One heresy in particular terrified the medieval church because of its extent, popularity, philosophical sophistication, and efficient organization. The Cathars, or Pure Ones (from the Greek *Katharoi*), professed a dualistic religion, a religion, that is, that was even more absolute than Christianity in the way it divided good from evil. The Cathars attributed even more power to the forces of evil than Catholics did, for they posited an eternal struggle between a god of good and a god of evil.[11] Thus, Cathars were left vulnerable to the accusation that they actually worshiped Satan. Catholic theologians imagined that, during the secret meetings of Cathars, the Devil would incarnate himself in the form of a large black cat. His devotees would demonstrate their submission to him by an obscene kiss (*osculum infame*) on his anus. Thus, said Alanus de Insulis in the twelfth century, in a libel that became commonplace, *Cathari* are so called from their worship of the *cattus,* or cat.[12]

Kissing the anus of a disgusting demonic animal became a commonplace in the mythology of the Sabbat. In later times, the Devil often incarnated himself as a goat or a goat-like hybrid. Francesco Maria Guazzo's *Compendium maleficarum,* or *Encyclopedia of Witches,* published in the early seventeenth century, contains a woodcut showing well-dressed and presumably noble witches of both sexes lining up to kiss the hindquarters of such a creature and gaily conversing as they wait their turn (fig. 12).

FIGURE 12 *Witch Giving Ritual Kiss to Devil*. From Francesco Maria Guazzo, *Compendium maleficarum*, 2d ed. (Milan, 1626).

The companionship of witches and cats was also a commonplace of English witchcraft theory. The English witch's "familiar," the domesticated demon who carried out her *maleficia,* could be incarnated as a small animal. One of the earliest recorded familiars was a cat supposedly named Satan.[13] It was illegal to torture English defendants into confessing that they had copulated with demons, so the commonplace companionship between a marginal person and her pet was interpreted as a relation between human and demonic enemies of God. The witch demonstrated allegiance to her demonic familiar by allowing it to suckle her blood from the "witch's teat" hidden in some anomalous place on her (or his) body.

Even today, the Halloween witch has one inseparable companion, her black cat. For North American children conditioned by relentless commercial culture, a hissing black cat with arched back is a primary symbol of Halloween.

Misinterpreted pets and misinterpreted Greek adjectives both contributed to the cumulative concept of the witch that was prevalent by the seventeenth century. But fifteenth- and sixteenth-century theorists of witchcraft did not rely on these sources when they imagined relations between witches and cats. Peasant mythology of the time evidently imagined that witches transformed themselves into cats to kill babies in their cradles.

Pico's *Strix* provides evidence that the notion was truly folkloric. In Pico's Latin original, the judge, Dicastes, distinguishes among peasant beliefs: "I actually think some of them are true, that is, founded in reality itself, but some are empty, with no basis in reality, especially what is said by some people about their transformations." When Leandro Alberti translated this sentence for the common lay audience, he added the stipulation "such as that the men and women . . . change themselves into cats."[14]

This metamorphosis is the evident meaning of a well-known woodcut in Guazzo's *Compendium* (1626) showing a cat and a wolflike or canine creature, which apparently represents a werewolf, lurking outside the closed door of a house (fig. 13). As the picture suggests, the mythology of werewolves was consolidated in the same period and by some of the same writers who created early witchcraft theory.[15] Nider explains the thematic importance of lycanthropy or werewolfism to witchcraft theory of the whole period. He describes "certain witches of both sexes who, going against the inclinations of human nature, or, rather, against the nature of all beasts except wolves, are wont to devour and eat infants of their own species."[16] To be a werewolf was not merely "to be a wolf to other men," as the Latin proverb had it, but to kill and eat the infants of one's own species.

FIGURE 13 *Werewolf and Witch-Cat*. From Francesco Maria Guazzo, *Compendium maleficarum*, 2d ed. (Milan, 1626).

A common denominator of witches' associations with owls, cats, and wolves was stealth, invisibility, and unseizability. But folklore about cats offered the most explanatory possibilities for witchcraft theory about infant death. Cats were more useful than wolves for the early mythology of infanticidal *maleficium* because of their domesticity. Finding a wolf in one's bedroom cannot have been a common occurrence—nor one that was easily overlooked. The myths of infanticidal witch-cats must have been inspired by cats' real and proverbial stealthiness and silence. They are a subtle presence, small, and almost uncannily able to evade human detection. Even fog, than which nothing is more silent, "comes on little cat feet."[17]

Cats are consummate stalkers with keen night vision and nocturnal habits, so they shared stereotypical habits with witches. Moreover, cats can be attracted to babies and small children in cradles, for they are curious, attracted by movement, and fond of "nesting" in warm, confined places. It is perhaps for these reasons that, in Europe and North America, folk wisdom has often maintained that cats can accidentally or deliberately suffocate infants. My late father still remembered old wives' tales that he had heard as a child in Alabama in the 1920s to the effect that cats must be kept away from infants or they will "suck their breath away" and kill them.

Even outside witchcraft treatises there is evidence of late-medieval folklore about witches transforming themselves into cats to kill infants. About 1440, the physician Antonio Guaineri recorded that "our common people call [witches] *strigae* or *zobianae,* and say that they often assume the shape of cats."[18] In a sermon of 1427, Saint Bernardino of Siena claimed that he had recently had a witch arrested for killing thirty infants, including her own son; an herbal unguent gave her the impression of being changed into a cat.[19]

Why Pico did not have his witch claim that she became a cat to kill children is anyone's guess. He seems to have known of the myth, or at least Alberti thought so, as we saw above. Perhaps he wished to keep his demons firmly planted center stage; their aid to the witches serves the same role as the peasant myth of witches' transformation into cats, by explaining the stealthiness of their operations.

Bartolomeo Spina, however, recorded very detailed accusations by common people who believed that witches literally transformed themselves into cats. He quotes a Ferrarese couple, Antonio Leone and his wife, as reliable witnesses (*testes fidelissimi*) to the fact that witches become cats to kill babies. Spina's interest in their testimony initially seems foolhardy given that church doctrine since the Canon *Episcopi* had opposed the idea that living beings could undergo actual metamorphosis.

But, thanks to an adroit use of theology, Spina was able to appropriate and exploit the Leones' testimony.

Under oath, this couple told Spina that, around 1520, two big cats entered their bedroom during the night and attacked one of their children. Antonio hit one cat with an iron shovel and caught the other one in a net, but both soon escaped out the window. (Curiously, Spina implies that the window was open during the entire episode, although he previously stated that the Leone family was *securely* locked in the bedroom: *in thalamo suo seris optime clauso*). The same kind of attack happened to the Leones two years later: two big cats, one ash gray (*beretini coloris*), the other black and white, went after a little girl child of theirs. Again, the cats escaped out the window. Both children died completely dried up (*exsiccati*) within a few days of these attacks.

The evidence linking witches and cats is conclusive. "No one can deny," Spina says, that witch-cats often suck so much blood from children that they kill them "because this is affirmed by trustworthy testimony, and it is proved above all by drops of blood found near wailing children after these apparent cats have left them. Nor is it necessary to search curiously for wounds and scars, for they are quite small, and demons can make them heal over instantly."[20] We just saw Pico's Strix and Dicastes claiming the same instant healing. It is clearly irrelevant to Spina whether anyone *sees* cats actually scratching or biting babies. If blood was ever found near babies, their death was *obviously* caused by demonic witch-cats even if no bite or scratch marks can be found.

Spina's informants the Leones lost at least three children, and they made many of the same assumptions that Spina and Pico did about the witch as night-creeping vampire. They differed from Spina and Pico, however, in two crucial ways; they neither assumed that demons were involved nor desired to know exactly *how* witches became cats:

> At night they very often heard the yowling of many cats who were attacking other children of theirs; the cats also attacked the place where they kept the ointment that a certain witch [*strige*] had given them for medicating their children because the children were already bewitched [*strigati*], although not fatally. And yet, as they said, they themselves kept only one small cat in their house. But, when they asked the witch who was burned in recent days about this incident, she told them that what they had seen in their bedroom before was two witches in the form of cats, who had killed their other two children [*alios filios*], and in the way previously mentioned. And she declared that she knew those witches, and she showed them who they were, although only by signs, and not by name.[21]

Spina's reference to a witch who was recently burned implies that these accusations were brought during a case that he was trying. References to the informant witch's ointment for medicating the children imply that the Leones did not suspect or accuse her of killing them. They apparently trusted her but were wary of other local healers. Success and failure of cures probably conditioned their perception of herbalists as helpful healers or harmful witches.[22]

Witch theorists like Spina usually reasoned differently, claiming that anyone who could heal could also harm and therefore that all witches had to be destroyed.[23] Thus, despite the fact that she had tried to aid the Leones, Spina had this helpful witch burned. Since he does not mention the two "culprit" witches again, it appears that he never identified them. Nor does he connect the burned witch with the deaths of the Leone children; rather, he seems to accept and value her expert testimony that other, perhaps unlocatable, witches were the culprits. Individual cases of guilt and innocence did not interest him much: he was more concerned with verifying that witch-cats were responsible for crib death.

Finding the Culprits

Although he did not accept every detail, Spina was highly receptive to his informants' assertion that witches became cats to kill children. He also alluded to apparent folkloric methods for discovering the human witch behind the elusive cat:

> Regarding this apparent transformation of witches into cats, there is another witness in this same town of Ferrara, an artisan named Filippo. And under oath he declared to me this year [1523] that three months previously a certain witch had undertaken to medicate his little boy (whom she herself had perhaps bewitched). But she had told Filippo that, if he should see cats playing about the child or caressing him, he should not interfere. And that same day she had scarcely left when, after an hour, he and his wife saw a large cat that they had never seen before, which walked rapidly right up to the child. The parents became afraid and chased it away repeatedly. Finally they became exasperated by this harassment; Filippo closed the door and began beating the cat severely with a stick, as it fled up and down the room. He eventually forced it to launch itself out the window, which was high off the ground, so that the cat's body seemed to be all broken [*collisa*]. And from that very time the old witch took to her bed for several days with her body all broken [*confracta*]. Because of this, their slight suspicion that she was a witch [*striga*], and that she had bewitched [*strigasset*] their child, who was suffering greatly from the malady that had bewitched [*strigatus*] him, changed into a vehement, indeed a violent, suspicion.[24]

> This is because the blows and wounds that had been inflicted on the cat were all found on the corresponding members of the old woman's body. Innumerable other examples could be brought forward to corroborate this one, but for now let this crystal-clear evidence [*manifestissima testimonia*] suffice. It is contained in public and notarized documents, and anyone who wishes can confirm it by consulting these same witnesses, who are all still alive.[25]

The supposed exact correspondence between the injuries inflicted on the cat and those found on the old woman's body was the only "crystal-clear" evidence that nonintellectuals like Filippo apparently needed to support the idea that witches can change themselves into cats to kill children.[26]

Similar tales were told of witches who became wolves to attack older children and adults outdoors. The same matching strategy was used for discovering the alleged human culprit.[27] A generation before Spina, Kramer told a surreal-sounding story about witch-cats in the *Malleus maleficarum*. Although Kramer's story does not concern killing children, it illustrates how witchcraft theorists, and perhaps even ordinary judges, reacted to the folkloric myth of witch-cats and its implicit method of discovering witches.[28]

In a town near Strasbourg, says Kramer, a man was cutting firewood when three large and fierce cats suddenly attacked him, swarming all over him and "leaping at his face and throat." After crossing himself, the man succeeded in driving away the cats, although with great difficulty, "by beating one on the head, another on the legs, and another on the back." An hour later, he was arrested by town officials and thrown into a dungeon, with no formal accusation or even an explanation for his arrest. Whenever his guards tried to procure him a hearing before the magistrate, the latter flew into a passion, "expressing in the strongest terms his indignation that so great a malefactor had not acknowledged his crime, but dared to proclaim his innocence when the evidence of the facts proved his horrible crime."[29]

Finally, other magistrates convinced the indignant one to grant the woodcutter a hearing. The judge declared: "At such a time on such a day you beat three respected matrons of this town, so that they lie in their beds unable to rise or to move." The defendant protested that he could prove his innocence because he had been at home cutting wood at that hour. The magistrate need only question the arresting officers:

> Then the judge again exclaimed in a fury: "See how he tries to conceal his crime! The women are bewailing their blows, they exhibit the marks,

> and publicly testify that he struck them." Then the poor man considered more closely on that event, and said: "I remember that I struck some creatures at that time, but they were not women." The magistrates in astonishment asked him to relate what sort of creatures he had struck; and he told, to their great amazement, all that had happened. . . . So, understanding that it was the work of the Devil, they released the poor man and let him go away unharmed, telling him not to speak of this matter to anyone. But it could not be hidden from those devout persons present who were zealous for the faith.[30]

Kramer's story clarifies the evolution of witch-cats in the dialogue between common people and the learned. Most evidently, the demonic element appears to have been introduced by one or more of the judges: the woodcutter refers only to women, cats, and "creatures" (*creaturas*).

Kramer himself could have interpolated the demonic explanation, of course—assuming that he did not invent the entire story. Or he may have been one of those "devout persons zealous for the faith" who eagerly added the incident to their proofs of demonic reality. His stipulation that "it is charitable and honorable to withhold" the name of the town where this took place and his enthusiastic remarks about why the story could not be kept secret would allow any of these possibilities.[31] Even if the incident never happened, Kramer's long, detailed narration of it and his careful rationing of suspense, suspicion, and dawning "realizations" show how eagerly he accepted even the weirdest accusations as proof of demonic interference in human affairs.

Kramer and Spina demonstrate that peasant culture posited the transformation of witches into cats and that witchcraft theory needed the idea. Spina's witnesses all appear to be town dwellers, showing that country folk were not the only ones who kept and depended on cats. Yet everyone must have been profoundly distrustful of cats, if only from concern for small children. Kramer showed that inquisitors accepted and approved this distrust; but, typically, he needed to justify the attitude by reference to theology. He remarked that the cat is "an animal which is, in the Scriptures, an appropriate symbol of the perfidious . . . for cats are always setting snares for each other."[32]

The Canon Episcopi *and Metamorphosis*

Despite welcoming peasant theories, neither Kramer nor Spina claimed that witches could *actually* change into cats. Spina carefully stipulated that the metamorphosis was "apparent." Witchcraft theorists agreed with the Canon *Episcopi* that only God can produce such fundamental changes. Because the folk tradition contradicted theological definitions of possibility, witchcraft theorists had to exploit the folklore cautiously. They cautioned their learned readers that common folk often held erroneous beliefs about witches. In fact, theologians claimed, even witches were deluded about *how* they produced their *maleficia;* only their belief in their own guilt was well-founded. Properly trained theologians were necessary for winnowing the truth from the many delusions the Devil produced.

Using witch-cats as an example, Pico's inquisitor, Dicastes, claimed that not every feat attributed to witches could be entirely believed:

> I think that those things are in part true, that is, founded on reality [*ipsa re consistentes; fondate in quella cosa che è*], and in part mendacious and faked [*inanes; fallaci e finte*] and not anchored to any real foundation [*nulla rerum basi fundatas; non firmate in verun vero fondamento*]. This particularly concerns some of those things that some people tell, such as that the men and women of this damnable Sabbat [*maledetto giuoco*] change themselves into the form of cats and other animal figures or that when they have eaten an ox they resuscitate it by placing its bones back inside its skin and having the lady or lord of the game [*giuoco*] tap it with a wand. You can be sure that all these things are imaginations, illusions, and things that the wicked and wily Devil makes seem as if they were real [*in verità*], although in truth they are not, nor can he actually do them. But it cannot be denied, nor reputed false or contrary to truth, that sometimes witches are carried through the air or that they often eat, drink, and take libidinous pleasure with demons in the form of both men and women.[33]

Likewise, although it seems strange, "in the midst of Italy, in a region that is heavily inhabited and frequented by mortals, and otherwise alien to all wildness and bestiality, we have discovered a great company of people both men and women that, at the Devil's instigation, have fed themselves on human blood."[34]

In their theories of witch-cats, Kramer, Spina, Pico, and their fellow theorists had to maneuver very cautiously around the problems of reality raised by the Canon *Episcopi*. The key was to specify carefully what the Canon *Episcopi* was referring to when it spoke of demonic delusion. Having proved to their satisfaction that the Canon *Episcopi* could not be arguing against the reality of demonic transvection, theorists had no problem agreeing with its declaration that only God could change the essential form of his creatures. But to stop here would have prevented them from exploiting the lore about people changing into animals that still flourished among peasants and other laypeople.

Still, the Canon *Episcopi* was not just an obstacle for witchcraft theorists: it offered them positive inducements as well. Because it could be interpreted as condemning only folklore about metamorphosis, it tantalized the clerical imagination. Perhaps someone *was* having contact with demons and experiencing just those idolatrous illusions of metamorphosis that the Canon *Episcopi* described.[35] But how were such illusions produced?

Inner and Outer Illusions

Jean Vineti explained the mechanisms of demonic illusion in general terms: "The demon's illusion can happen in two ways. One way is from within, for the demon can change a man's imagination [*fantasia*] and also his bodily senses so that something will be seen as other than it is. . . . The other way is from without since he can form and configure a body so that, by assuming it, he will appear visibly within it. By the same means he can place any sort of corporeal form around the body of anything whatever so that the one will appear as the other."[36] Vineti was wrestling with the Canon *Episcopi,* resisting the idea that demonic illusion is always produced within the mind. To be *verifiably* demonic, an illusion would occasionally need to be external and corporeal.

A half century later, Bartolomeo Spina explained more clearly and in greater detail, referring specifically to condemned witches' confessions of being turned into cats. Spina declared that the Devil could form "an aerial body in the semblance [*similitudinem*] of a cat" so that, "by interposing an obstacle between the [observer's] eyes and the real human bodies, he permits only the phantasmatic [*phantasticum*] body to be seen." That is, in the same way that a demon can form an aerial body around himself, he can form one that looks like a cat. In the same moment, he can create other obstacles (also from air, apparently) so that, instead of seeing the real body of a witch, we or even the witch herself will see only the illusory form of a cat.[37] Vineti's and Spina's explanations provided a way to account for folkloric evidence that blows inflicted on a witch-cat will leave bruises or wounds on the corresponding members of the witch's own body. Yet they avoid violating the Canon *Episcopi*'s stricture that no one but God can change the actual bodily form of a creature.

The second method of creating illusion is "from within," and it seems even more bizarre to modern eyes. It gives a peculiarly materialistic explanation of how hallucinations are produced inside the mind: "It must be known that the imagination [*phantasia*] is a certain power of the soul connected to the bodily organs in which sensations [*phantasmata*] are received. Thus, the Devil can move the imagination whenever he wishes, just as he can move other bodily things [*corporalia*] from place to place [*localiter*]. And this is particularly true of the bodily humors and of the spirits [*spiritus*] subservient to them, in which the sensations [*phantasmata*] are directly [*immediate*] resident."[38]

Theories of transvection established that demons can move the human body through space. Using the same principles of local motion, the theory of the imagination tried to explain how demons could manipulate thoughts from within the human person. Sensations enter through the senses and are conducted by a system of vaporous spirits and more tangible humors to the imagination, which then presents ("images" or "imaginates") the sensations to the higher or less matter-bound powers of the soul.

Vineti's and Spina's explanations derive from Aquinas. In the *De malo,* Aquinas discussed three related questions: "whether demons can transform bodies by changing their form"; "whether the demons can move bodies locally [i.e., from place to place]"; and "whether the demons can change the cognitive part of the soul by changing the internal and external sense powers."[39] Aquinas's solutions to these questions derive from the same principles as his explanations of demonic corporeality, copulation, and transvection.

Aquinas concluded that demons have no power that is wholly outside the realm of nature; they can employ "naturally active causes" to produce real change, but they are limited to the sorts of change that can be performed by the "power of natural agents."[40] Even so, demons can appear to perform the impossible: "The body of a man cannot be transformed into the body of a beast by the power of natural agents; yet the demons can do this [after a fashion]; for Augustine relates that by the art of magic Circe changed the companions of Ulysses into beasts; and that the Arcadians, when they were swimming across a pond, were changed into wolves, and that women innkeepers changed men into beasts of burden."[41] These stories, related by Augustine in book 18 of his *De civitate Dei,* are a commonplace in witchcraft theory.

But even Augustine's weighty authority would not have made these stories useful had Aquinas not ingeniously reformulated them in terms of scientific demonology. Aquinas agreed that demons "cannot change the distinctive features of the human body into those of a beast according to the truth of the matter [*secundum rei veritatem*] because this is contrary to the order of nature implanted by God." He also agreed that "in fact all the aforesaid transformations were made according to imaginary appearance rather than in reality [*secundum veritatem*], as Augustine makes clear."[42] But Aquinas differed radically on how this was possible. His task would be to bring Augustine up to date, refining and even rejecting aspects of his theory.

As he did when discussing demonic copulation, Augustine began with a fund of legends and fictions from Roman writers and added contemporary hearsay about metamorphosis:

> For if we should say these things are not to be credited, there are not wanting even now some who would affirm that they had either heard on the best authority, or even themselves experienced, something of that kind. Indeed, we ourselves, when in Italy, heard such things about a certain region there, where the landladies of inns, imbued with these wicked arts, were said to be in the habit of giving to such travelers as they chose, or could manage, something in a piece of cheese by which they were changed on the spot into beasts of burden, and carried whatever was necessary, and were restored to their own form when the work was done. Yet their mind did not become bestial, but remained rational and human, just as Apuleius, in the books he wrote with the title of *The Golden Ass,* has told, or feigned, that it happened to his own self that, on taking poison, he became an ass, while retaining his human mind.

Augustine would not accept that demons could change "even the body, much less the soul," of a person, so he needed an explanation.[43]

As with incubi and succubi, Augustine was not particularly worried about scientific precision, not considering it necessary for what he wanted to believe. Admitting that metamorphoses "are either false, or so extraordinary as to be with good reason disbelieved," Augustine chose nonetheless to believe that "God can do whatever he pleases" so that, in his "often hidden, but never unrighteous judgment," he might permit something that resembled metamorphosis. His explanation of how this might happen is both complex and bizarre:

> And indeed the demons, *if they really do such things as these* on which this discussion turns, do not create real substances, but only change the appearance of things created by the true God and make them seem to be what they are not. . . . [T]he phantasm of a man, which even in thought or dreams goes through innumerable changes, may, when the man's senses are laid asleep or overpowered, be presented to the senses of others in a corporeal form *in some indescribable way unknown to me,* so that men's bodies themselves may lie somewhere, alive indeed, yet with their senses locked up much more heavily and firmly than by sleep, while that phantasm, as it were embodied in the shape of some animal, may appear to the senses of others, and may even seem to the man himself to be changed, just as he may seem to himself in sleep to be so changed, and to bear burdens; and these burdens, if they are real substances, are borne by the demons, that men may be deceived by beholding at the same time

the real substance of the burdens and the simulated bodies of the beasts of burden.[44]

Aquinas objected to this explanation for the same reason that we do: Augustine presumed that an individual's imagination or its contents could be physically detached from him, given a body, and presented to another individual: "That statement of Augustine is not to be taken to mean that a demon invests the very imaginative power of a man or even the species [i.e., images or sensory impressions] preserved in it with some sort of body so that he may thus present it to the senses of others, but that the demon himself, who fashions a species in the imagination of some man, either presents another like species externally, after the manner of a body, to the senses of others, or brings about a similar species internally in their senses." Aquinas's objection had another basis. He found Augustine's solution unsatisfactory because it implies that "a demon cannot present anything to man's senses except by way of embodiment."[45]

At first glance, this would not seem to be a very great problem: Aquinas claimed that demons' ability to fashion bodies made possible demonic copulation, which, he implied, was the ultimate test of demonic reality. However, if embodiment were the only way a demon could affect the imagination, his influence on it would be severely limited: a demon could make me aware of his presence, or he could fool me by making me think that Adam was present when Adam was somewhere else entirely, or he could cause me to see a donkey instead of Adam. But embodiment could not make Adam believe *himself* a donkey because that belief comes in part from inside Adam. Therefore, if the demon were limited to what he could do by embodiment, "he could not interiorly enter the organ of imagination, since two bodies cannot be at the same time in the same place."[46]

This was an important moment for the prehistory of witchcraft theory: Aquinas realized that corporeality was not a principle that could invariably demonstrate the reality of demonic interactions with humans. There are times when corporeality can be an impediment, endangering our sense of demonic reality rather than reinforcing it.

Thus, Aquinas concluded that, in some cases, demons must be able to enter the mind. They would affect either the "sentient" power of waking perception (my perception of Adam as a donkey) or the "imaginative" power (Adam's perception of himself as a donkey). They would move perceptions as if they were concrete objects: "In some manner they can transfer the forms [or perceptions] stored in the sensory organs, so that [by means of] these [stored forms] certain apparitions occur." A demon effects this "by transferring [*transituando*] or locally moving . . . the spirits and humors" within the organs of perception.[47] This is the explanation that Bartolomeo Spina and other witchcraft theorists would adopt.

Clearly, the demon could not affect the imagination "by dividing the substance of the organ[, for] a sensation of pain would result." But the demon does not have a body of his own; nor is he attempting to move a fabricated or "assumed" body through the matter of my sensory organs. Thus, there is no wound and no pain.[48] The demon cannot, of course, introduce a completely new sensory perception into my imagination: he can only manipulate the spirits and humors of my body. So he must either call up sensory impressions already stored in my imagination or distort perceptions that are entering my waking consciousness for the first time.

This allows the demon considerable power: although he "cannot make a man born blind imagine colors or a man born deaf imagine sounds," he can convince anyone that the impossible is happening. Mountains of pure gold are impossible, "yet because he has seen both gold and a mountain, a man can by a natural movement form an image of a gold mountain. And in this way also a demon can present something new to the imagination."[49]

This theory was immensely seductive to clerics eager to appropriate the folkloric connection between witch-cats and infant mortality. Aquinas's rigorously scientific explanation of how both Adam and I could believe that Adam was a donkey needed no adjustment to explain how both Joan and I could believe that she was a cat. Thus, although Joan or any other witch was wrong to confess or boast that she could be literally transformed into a cat to suck the blood of children and kill them, the substance of her "claim" (i.e., the accusation against her) was still acceptable.

The *illusory* witch-cat was invaluable for theology: it enabled the identification and removal of persons who disrupted God's plan for the physical and spiritual well-being of little children while constituting one more proof of the reality of demons. Aquinas does not say so in the passages just quoted, and not all his followers made the point explicit, but both he and the witchcraft theorists knew that there was only one alternative to demonic infiltration of the imagination. If demons cannot enter the human body and distort its perception and imagination, then witch-cats and other instances of human metamorphosis, such as donkey-men or werewolves, must be *natural* dreams and hallucinations.

In that case, as with other evidence against the reality of witchcraft, we would have to admit that demons do not exist "except in the imagination of the common people" and that "a powerful imagination can cause certain figures to appear to the senses exactly as a man has thought of them, so that he only thinks he is seeing demons or witches." There could be no *real* witch-cats; so, unless they were an illusion caused by demonic interference in the imagination, demons would be imaginary.

The Evil Empire of Illusion

To my knowledge, there are no fifteenth- or sixteenth-century illustrations of the precise mechanisms that produced the illusion of witch-cats. This is not surprising: an illustration would need to represent both the feline illusion and the human reality underneath. One sixteenth-century illustration shows a witch transforming a man into a donkey, probably as an illustration of the tales mentioned by Saint Augustine. The technique is "stop time": only the man's breast, belly, right arm, and hair remain human; the rest of his body has become fully asinine.[50] This picture could be interpreted to mean that a *real* transformation is taking place, contrary to doctrinal correctness.

Visual representations of werewolves from the early sixteenth century illustrate the metamorphosis as an illusion, but this precludes depicting both the human reality and the lupine illusion. Geiler von Kaisersberg's 1517 *Die Emeis,* or *The Ants,* was a collection of sermons on witchcraft based on Nider's *Formicarius.* When *Die Emeis* discusses lycanthropy or werewolfism as an illusion, a woodcut shows an ordinary-looking wolf attacking an adult wayfarer (fig. 14). This seems to represent the werewolf as he appeared to his victims: frighteningly realistic.[51]

A woodcut of about 1510 by Lucas Cranach the Elder shows the reality underneath attacks by illusory wolves: a raggedly dressed man crawls on all fours in the yard of a country or village house. The ground around him is littered with dismembered human bodies; a dying baby dangles from his mouth as he fixes his gaze on the spectator (fig. 15).[52] Together, the two illustrations form a dyptich representing the real and the illusory phenomena supposedly underlying both werewolves and witch-cats.

There is no representation of a witch-cat comparable to Cranach's picture. Such an illustration would have to show a person sucking the blood of an infant beside a cradle while parents slept in a bed nearby. Showing the illusory cat would add further difficulty. However, witch-cats seem to be depicted in three very similar pictures, two by Hans Baldung Grien and another by Urs Graf, from the period 1510–14.[53] (One of these images is reproduced as fig. 16 in chap. 11 below.) All show a group of nude women performing various acts of witchcraft, especially transvection, cannibalism (apparently of infants), and unction. There are no visible demons. In each picture, a cat appears in the lower-right-hand corner.

FIGURE 14 *Werewolf Attacking Traveler.* Illustration for Johann Geiler von Kaisersberg, *Die Emeis* (Strassburg, 1517).

FIGURE 15 Lucas Cranach Sr., *Werewolf* (ca. 1510).

It could be argued that there is nothing particularly significant about the presence of the cat. How do we know that it is not an ordinary cat or a demon embodied as a cat? One critic refers to the cats as "familiars," implying the latter interpretation.[54]

But, in a fourth picture by Baldung that is related to this group, a cat, still in the lower-right-hand location, is crouched over a book displaying runic-looking symbols. The cat gazes at the book as if reading it.[55]

Clearly, neither ordinary cats nor demons needed to consult texts of any sort. So the reading cat is almost certainly intended to represent a recently transformed woman, rather than a literal housecat or a demonic familiar. We do not see the cat's human reality any more than the reality of the demon transvecting the pitchfork on which an old woman appears to fly through the air overhead. In the center of the picture another cat is held by a standing witch. Most of the cat's body is hidden behind another, kneeling witch. The cat could thus represent either the standing witch's metamorphosis while it happens or the just-completed metamorphosis of another witch.

A decade after these pictures were produced, Gianfrancesco Pico and his translator Leandro Alberti would claim that common people believed that witches were transformed into cats at the Sabbat. Pictures such as Baldung's and Graf's were worth thousands of words by witchcraft theorists like Pico; pictures gave instant substance and plausibility to their learned modifications of laypeople's ideas about witches. By combining the folkloric idea of witch-cats with the learned stereotypes of the demon-loving witch and the Sabbat, these illustrations "retransmitted" folkloric ideas in a disguise that intellectuals found acceptable and comforting. Whoever observed such pictures, even if he were illiterate, would recognize enough of the folkloric concept to prepare his acceptance of the demonological explanation of it.

11

ILLUSION AND REALITY, PART TWO: WITCHES WHO STEAL PENISES

> O imagination, you so steal us from ourselves that we may not notice a thousand trumpets blaring around us. Who is it that moves you, if the senses offer you nothing?
>
> —Dante, *Purgatorio* (1315)

> It is probable that the principal credit of miracles, visions, enchantments, and such extraordinary occurrences comes from the power of imagination, acting principally on the minds of the common people, which are softer. Their belief has been so strongly seized that they think they see what they do not see.
>
> —Montaigne, "Of the Power of the Imagination" (1572–74)

Strange as witch-cats may seem, they were not the weirdest demonic delusion imagined by witchcraft theorists. If we examine one of the pictures discussed at the end of the previous chapter, we note the overtly phallic character of the pitchforks in Urs Graf's drawing (fig. 16). An art historian contends that one of the witches appears to be using the pitchfork she straddles to stimulate herself sexually.[1] Moreover, the stick passes between the legs of another witch who is standing. To make the sexual innuendo even more graphic, a number of limp, tubular objects, identified by the art historian as "sausages," are draped over the stick. The same "sausages" appear, draped over a pitchfork in just the same way, in all three pictures of the group. The art historian further interprets these "sausages" as "phalli," meaning, apparently, that they are either symbols or dildos.[2]

In fact, it is possible that these are neither figurative "phalli" nor sexual appliances but literal human penises, the foreskins of which, facing the viewer in every case, cause the resemblance to sausages. Even if the "sausages" are sausages, they cannot help suggesting penises in the total context of the pictures. If this interpretation is correct, the artists were associating the witch-cat with another peculiar form of illusion discussed

FIGURE 16 Urs Graf, *Four Witches and Cat* (1514).

by witchcraft theorists of their time: the stolen penis. The three pictures suggest an allusion or parallel to the most-famous and least-understood anecdote of the *Malleus maleficarum,* the story of "witches who steal penises."

Whatever these objects were intended to represent, they look as real as anything else in the pictures. However, the stolen penises that the *Malleus* described were illusions of the same type as witch-cats. Like witch-cats, stolen penises were important for demonstrating how thoroughly demons can deceive humans about the nature of reality.

In 1580 the philosopher Andrea Cesalpino summarized and explained Kramer's ideas about illusory stolen penises. Before doing so, he had to define the relation between illusion and witchcraft:

> Now I find that all these people [i.e., witches] engage in four kinds of superstition above all, that is, *praestigium, maleficium,* fortune-telling [*divinationem*], and healing. Of these four, fortune-telling and healing seem to have some appearance [*speciem*] of good in them; nonetheless, the art by which they are performed is shameful and execrable. *Praestigium* is an illusion by which the senses are deceived. Witches [*maleficae mulieres*] use *praestigium* in their nighttime attacks [*incursibus*] when they take on the semblance [*specie*] of a brute beast, such as a wolf or a cat, in order to steal little babies or to poison them with their *maleficia* [*veneficijs contaminent*].[3]

Praestigium was the technical term for the demonic illusion that Aquinas had described and defined as taking place either inside the imagination or in external reality. Witch-cats are one example of *praestigium,* but Cesalpino has an even more intriguing one. "There are men who, through this illusory [*praestigiosa*] art of the witches, seem to have their male organs so thoroughly amputated that absolutely no trace of them remains. It is said that some young men in Germany lost their genitals quite suddenly; when they communicated this to other men, they were warned that this had come about through witchcraft [*maleficio*]. Thus, when they had discovered the witch (who had perpetrated this in revenge for injuries received from the men), she dissolved her *maleficium,* and the young men got back the genitals they thought they had lost."[4] Baldung Grien and Urs Graf had not unambiguously depicted either stolen penises or witch-cats or defined them as an illusion, but Cesalpino does. The men only "thought" that they had been castrated; they "seemed" to have lost their genitals, but in reality no castration took place.

Cesalpino never mentions Kramer or the *Malleus* by name, as if he were deliberately hiding his source. This is not surprising since he claimed to be writing a strictly Aristotelian, "scientific" defense of demonic reality. But he copied the concept of illusory castration, along with most of his treatise, from Kramer's *Malleus.*[5] Cesalpino's mention of witch-cats and stolen penises in the same paragraph shows that he had read Kramer's *Malleus* thoroughly and meditated deeply on its logic, for Kramer did not discuss these illusions in the same part of the *Malleus.*

Cesalpino knew that Kramer discussed illusory castration as an example of *praestigium,* or the type of illusions specific to demons.[6] Both authors valued *praestigium* as proof that, to paraphrase a later demonologist, demons were made by God in nature, not by the intellect or imagination of humans.[7] Cesalpino's use of Kramer shows that, like his source, he needed to believe that demons had nearly absolute control over the human imagination, to avoid admitting that demons were imaginary.

Kramer's discussion of stolen penises was even more bizarre than Cesalpino's brief synopsis would lead us to believe. During his discussion of *praestigium,* Kramer complicates the idea of illusory castration with a weird anecdote:

> And what, then, is to be thought of those witches [*maleficas*] who . . . sometimes collect male organs in great numbers, as many as twenty or thirty members together, and put them in a bird's nest, or shut them up in a box, where they move themselves like living members, and eat oats and corn, as has been seen by many and is a matter of common report [*fama*]? . . .
>
> For a certain man tells that, when he had lost his member, he approached a certain witch [*maleficam*] to ask her to restore his health [*sanitatis*]. She told the afflicted [*infirmo*] man to climb a certain tree, and that he might take whichever member he liked out of a nest in which there were several members. And when he tried to take a big one, the witch said, "you must not take that one," adding, "because it belonged to a parish priest."[8]

Properly understood, this is one of the most important passages in all witchcraft theory. It has profound implications for the treatment of demons, sacraments, and the imagination in Kramer's witchcraft theory and in all other defenses of demonic and sacramental reality.

The strangest aspect of this anecdote is the clear internal evidence that it was originally an anticlerical joke. The joke probably originated in Italy, where double entendres had associated birds and penises since at least the time of Boccaccio.[9] An interest in jokes was not unusual for a preaching friar: sermons were a form of entertainment as well as instruction. Dante was already complaining in the early 1300s that preachers filled their sermons with "gossip." Franciscans in particular were noted for their scabrous sense of humor, and Saint Bernardino of Siena combined humor with withering sarcasm.[10] But this joke would have been less at home in a sermon than among the bawdier tales of Boccaccio, Chaucer, or Rabelais. The sexual endowments and appetites of priests and friars were the subject of scathing jokes and cruel pranks in such literature, reflecting a long tradition of anticlericalism that could be either bitter or lighthearted.

Kramer shows no awareness that the story was a joke, although he lived a while in Rome and claimed to speak Italian well enough to understand sexual innuendo.[11] There are other instances of Kramer's using jokes as if they were transcripts of court proceedings; the impression of insanity radiated by the *Malleus* comes from Kramer's willingness to accept *anything* as evidence that witchcraft and demons were real.[12] Cesalpino, who was Italian, accepted Kramer's authority that the anecdote was a matter of public record and "common report." Like Kramer, he treated it as summarizing a relentless accumulation of legal evidence, attested by sobersided witnesses.

Despite using this anecdote, Kramer does not express a fear of castration. On the contrary, he asserts that castration can be a positive good since it removes the temptation to sexual activity. Kramer was heir to a long tradition of Catholic monasticism and exaltation of celibacy, so he asserted that devils are reluctant to castrate men. Devils know that sexually capable men are most easily led into sin; therefore, they castrate men only when forced to do so by good angels. Even good angels, who recognize the moral utility of castration, are usually reluctant to perform it: they prefer to create the illusion of castration. Kramer tells, without a trace of irony or fear, stories of monks who desired to be castrated: angels obliged them, but without actually removing anything. They simply made their genitals seem to disappear. These stories he offered as examples of angelic blessings.[13]

Nor does Kramer fear that witches castrate in reality, even with the aid of demons. No *maleficium* can cause physical castration, he says: witches can castrate only through illusion or *praestigium*. In the middle of his anecdote about penis stealing, Kramer carefully stipulates that witches can neither remove penises nor cause them to behave like birds. Answering his own question "What is to be thought of those witches . . . ," he declares in the next sentence: "It must be said that it is all done by devil's work and illusion, for the senses of those who see [penises behaving like birds] are deluded in the way we have indicated."[14]

Witches who steal penises are offered only as an example of how demonic illusions or *praestigia* are performed. Kramer is so uninterested in the actual, physical removal of the male genitalia that he categorically refuses to discuss it. He is interested *only* in illusory castration. This is why Cesalpino linked castration to witch-cats rather than to sexual mutilation, fear of women, or other topics that occur to modern readers.[15]

Kramer's penis-stealing witches were essential to his notion of human and demonic interaction. Discussions of them occupy two large passages of the *Malleus* (questions 8–11 of pt. 1 and chaps. 5–9 of pt. 2, question 1). Repetitions between the passages suggest that Kramer divided and reorganized a discussion that he originally intended as a single unit, as he did with the treatment of demonic copulation.

The nest-of-penises anecdote occurs in an explanation of how, with the aid of devils, witches "can take away the male organ, not indeed by actually despoiling the human body of it, but by concealing it with some illusion [*prestigiosa arte*], in the manner which we have already described." This connects to a discussion nearly sixty pages earlier (in Summers's translation) in which Kramer declared that "there is no difficulty in his [i.e., the Devil's] concealing the virile member by some illusion [*prestigiosa arte*]. And a manifest proof or experience [*experimentum*] of this, which was revealed to us in our inquisitorial capacity, will be set forth later, where more is recounted of these and other matters in the Second Part of this treatise."[16] The cross-reference indicates that Kramer claims illusory castration as his own discovery and that he considered it the most convincing example of *praestigium*.

Kramer expounded the mechanics of *praestigium* in terms derived almost verbatim from Aquinas and, perhaps, from Jean Vineti. To give a more general definition of *praestigium,* he quoted the Franciscan theologian Alexander of Hales (d. 1245): "*Praestigium,* properly understood, is an illusion of the Devil, which is not caused by any change in matter, but only exists in the mind of him who is deluded, as to either his inner or outer perceptions."[17] Kramer added that Isidore of Seville (d. 636) defined *praestigium* as "nothing but a certain delusion of the senses, and especially of the eyes. And it is so called from the verb *praestringo* [I fasten or bind], since the sight of the eyes is so fettered that things seem to be other than they are."[18]

Kramer summarizes the Scholastic doctrines of *praestigium* in great detail. He states that "the Devil has five ways to delude anyone so he will think a thing to be other than it is." First, the Devil can use an "artificial trick," of the same sort that human prestidigitators, conjurers, and ventriloquists use, "for that which a man can do by art, the Devil can do even better." The second deception Kramer calls a "natural method": the Devil either interposes "some substance so as to hide the true body" or confuses it "in man's fancy [*fantasijs*]."[19] (Bartolomeo

Spina offered this twofold mode of illusion, internal and external to the mind, as the explanation of witch-cats.)[20]

The Devil's third method, according to Kramer, is that "when in an assumed body he presents himself as something he is not." This is not a reference to demonic copulation, where the Devil presents himself in a fictive body. Kramer is thinking of cases in which the Devil presented himself as a lettuce to a hungry nun, or as a lump of gold to Saint Anthony, in order to tempt them. The same principle can explain witch-cats, for the Devil can "make a man appear like a brute animal"; here, Kramer is thinking of Augustine's story about the donkey-man and attempts to explain it by Aquinas and others, as he shows elsewhere.[21] As this third point shows, there is considerable overlap among Kramer's five methods.

The Devil's fourth manner of deception "confuses the organ of sight, so that a clear thing seems hazy, or the converse, or when an old woman appears to be a young girl. For even after weeping the light appears different from what it was before."[22]

The fifth manner of deception interests Kramer the most, as it had Aquinas. That is when the Devil produces *praestigium* "by working in the imaginative power, and, by a disturbance of the humours, effecting a transmutation in the forms perceived by the senses . . . so that the senses perceive as it were fresh and new images." Given this power, says Kramer, "there is no difficulty in his concealing the virile member by some *praestigium* [*prestigiosa arte*]."[23]

Kramer carefully applies these distinctions to men who thought that they were castrated. In this illusion, says Kramer, "two of the exterior senses, those of sight and touch, are deluded, and not the interior senses, namely, common-sense, fancy, imagination, thought, and memory [*sensus communis, fantasia, ymaginativa, extimativa et memoria*]."[24]

To show how the tree-climbing man was deluded into believing that he saw a nestful of penises, Kramer states that the *interior* senses are deluded "when it is not a case of *hiding* something, but of causing something to *appear* to a man either when he is awake or asleep." This was a case of "a man who is awake [and] sees things other than as they are." He has other examples of deluding the interior senses to show things that are not present, "such as seeing someone devour a horse with its rider, or thinking he sees a man transformed into a beast, or thinking that he is himself a beast."[25] This last example suggests that Kramer's illusory castration was inspired by Aquinas's treatment of Augustine's story about the donkey-man. It also explains witch-cats and werewolves.

When someone sees things that are not there, "the exterior senses are deluded and taken over [*occupantur*] by the interior senses." Kramer describes the process with scientific precision:

> Sensory images [*species sensibiles*] are long retained in the treasury of images of things the senses have perceived, which is the memory—not the intellectual [*intellectiva*] memory, where images of things understandable by intellection or intuition [*species intelligibiles*] are stored, but the memory that conserves purely sensory images—which is in the posterior part of the head. These images are drawn out by the power of demons, as God occasionally permits, and are presented to the common sense of the imagination [*sensum communem imaginativam*]. And these images are so strongly impressed on that sense that a man must necessarily perceive the image [*imaginare*] of a horse or a beast because of the forcefulness with which the demon draws the image of a horse or a beast from the memory; thus the man must necessarily believe that he is actually seeing that beast with his external eyes [*oculos exteriores*] alone. But in fact [*in re*] that beast is not there in the external world: it only seems to be there because of the forceful intervention of the demon, working by means of those images.[26]

Kramer's best example of this process is the nest of penises: "All these things are caused by devils through an illusion or *praestigium* [*prestigiosa illusione*], by confusing the organ of vision through transmuting the sensory images [*specierum sensibilium*] in the imaginative faculty."[27]

Other than the joke and his readings in Aquinas and other theologians, Kramer's documentation of illusory castration and illusory penises is limited to two examples of "expert witnessing." In Ravensburg, he says, a young man wanted to abandon the woman with whom he had had a sexual liaison, but he soon discovered that he had "lost his member by means of an illusion that was cast over it [*prestigiosa utique arte*] so that he could see or touch nothing but his smooth body." Worried about his condition, he confided in a woman, "explaining everything, and demonstrating in his body that it was so." Hearing that he suspected his former lover, the woman advised him to persuade the ex-lover to "restore his health"; if persuasion failed, he should use violence.[28]

The man did as instructed; when his ex-lover protested her innocence, he began strangling her with a towel, whereupon she promised to heal him: "The young man then relaxed the pressure of the towel, and the witch touched him between the thighs with her hand, saying: 'Now you have what you desire.' And the young man, as he afterward said, plainly sensed, before he had verified it by looking or touching, that his member had been restored to him by the mere touch of the witch [*ex tactu dumtaxat malefice*]."[29]

Here is more evidence of Kramer misconstruing common people's notions of witchcraft. The man apparently believed that his genitals had been removed and restored in physical reality, not through illusion. The last phrase suggests that the man believed that the witch alone caused his condition; neither he, his ex-lover, nor the woman in the tavern mentioned demons.

Kramer adds a similar anecdote, claiming to have heard it from "a certain venerable Father from the Dominican House of Speyer." A young man confessing to this priest "woefully said that he had lost his member." Kramer says that the priest related that, "'being astonished at this, and not being willing to give it credence, since in the opinion of the wise it is a mark of lightmindedness to believe too easily, I obtained proof of it [*experientia didici per visum*] when I saw nothing on the young man's removing his clothes and showing the place.'"[30]

This story closely resembles the other. The priest asked if the victim suspected anyone in particular; the young man named a woman living in Worms. Cesalpino assumed, probably correctly, that this suspected witch was also a jilted lover. Although Kramer does not say so here, he elsewhere claimed that most witches are jilted mistresses.[31] The priest of Speyer also suggested that the witch be mollified with "gentle words and promises," although he obviously could not counsel violence if this failed. The young man returned a few days later, "saying that he was whole and had recovered everything. And I believed his words," the priest told Kramer, "but again proved them by the evidence of my eyes [*experientia tamen visus certificatus denuo*]."[32]

In neither story do characters mention demons or seem to suspect that the castration was anything other than real. Moreover, the priest of Speyer seems to make much of his own skepticism about the man's confession, and his claim that he was initially astonished suggests that he had not previously heard of castrating witches.[33] So, assuming that Kramer did not invent the stories, he differed from his informants by assuming three things: that castration by witches was an illusion, that it was a *demonic* illusion, and that witches induced demons to produce it.

The Evil Empire of Illusion Continued

Illusory castration and the nest of penises allow Kramer to redefine the nature of all reality. They prove that devils can distort our perception of reality, turning it upside-down and inside-out. Kramer considers illusory castration an example of how the Devil "deceives men in their natural functions, causing that which is visible to be invisible to them, and that which is tangible to be intangible, and the audible inaudible, and so with the other senses."[34] Conversely, in the nest of penises, what seems perceptible is not there. Together, these two forms of *praestigium* imply that the Devil can exert absolute control over human perception. Given the right conditions (human sinfulness and the permission of God), Satan can make anything seem to be anything else, seem to be absent when it is present, or vice versa.

While leading up to this conclusion, Kramer reveals why he prefers illusory castration as an illustration of demonic omnipotence. Recalling Augustine's story of the man who seemed to be turned into a donkey, Kramer agrees with his assertion that demons could not actually change a man into a beast. "Therefore," Kramer concludes, "it is equally impossible that they should remove *that which is essential to the truth of the human body* (*Hoc quod ad veritatem corporis humani deservit*)."[35] The penis defines the truth about the human body by distinguishing male from female. Kramer implies that, if the Devil can make genitalia *seem to* disappear, he has absolute control over truth because he controls our perception of bodies. Satan can perform an even greater marvel: he can make genitals appear where they should never be and do things that are completely contrary to their nature.[36] Bodies are the measure of reality, and we can know anything only by means of the body; disrupt that knowledge, and we can know nothing.

Kramer's ideas about castration have nothing to do with what we would now call *psychopathology*. Demonic illusory castration, as Kramer defines it, is not psychopathic because *no one* who examines these men can find a trace of genitalia, even though they are still physically intact.

Kramer is so anxious to protect the category of illusory castration that he refuses to discuss the alternatives to *praestigium*. He knows from writers on *praestigium* that other explanations of castration would have to rely on nature or on the power of the human imagination. He concedes that humans can produce illusions by sleight of hand, and he knows that surgical castration is possible; he also knows that melancholia can induce very convincing illusions. But, if he acknowledges that demons might not cause illusions and hallucinations, he will accept the possibility that demons may *be* illusions and hallucinations.

The same fear was raised by the prospect that witches might be dreaming rather than being transvected by demons. In one discussion of *praestigium*, Kramer returns to the Canon *Episcopi* and quotes it extensively to demonstrate that the imagination is "naturally subject to devils, so that they can transmute it, by causing various phantasies." Then, pulling himself up short just in time, he repeats that the Canon *Episcopi* cannot be invoked to prove that demons cause witches to hallucinate transvection rather than transporting them in reality.[37]

Fear of the Imagination, Fear of Nature

The specter of an all-powerful human imagination hangs over the history of witchcraft theory. Only if imagination was infinitely vulnerable to manipulation by devils, or, as Kramer said, "naturally subject" to them, could witchcraft theorists contemplate it with serenity. It was a case of all or nothing: any freedom of imagination menaced the entire demonological construct and, with it, much of Christian theology. It is no accident that Kramer defines the imagination's vulnerability with analogies to demonic possession. Few people are actually possessed, but anyone can suffer from *praestigium:*

> Devils can, with God's permission, enter our bodies; and they can then make impressions on the inner faculties connected [*potentias affixas*] to the bodily organs. . . . [T]he devils can draw out [*educere possunt*] images retained in a faculty connected to one of the organs. For example, he [*sic*] draws [*educit*] from the memory, which is in the back part of the head, an image [*speciem*] of a horse, and transports [*localiter movendo*] that phantasm to the middle part of the head, where is the cell of imaginative power [*cellula virtutis imaginative*]; and finally to the common sense [*sensum communem*], which is in the front of the head. And devils can cause such a sudden change and confusion, that such impressions [*forme*] are necessarily thought to be external things seen with the eyes.[38]

To avoid conceding that the imagination might be autonomous or subject only to purely natural influences, nature and imagination must be tyrannized by the supernatural. Otherwise, nature and imagination will explain away the supernatural.

Kramer's fear of the human imagination is vividly portrayed when he cautions his readers how *not* to interpret the nestful of penises. If we do not apply his principles carefully, they will self-destruct. So readers must not use the principles of demonic corporeality to explain the genitalia strutting about and eating like birds. The illusion was not performed by devils in virtual bodies: "It must not be said that these members which are shown are devils in assumed members, in the way that devils sometimes appear to witches and other people in assumed aerial bodies, and interact [*conversari*] with them."[39]

Kramer exhibits no fear that the nesting penises might have been "virtual members" enclosing real devils. But he needs to exclude the contrary possibility that, when witches believe that they are interacting corporeally with demons, the demons could be simply shunting images inside the human brain rather than constructing virtual bodies in external reality. This would mean that "when demons are said to interact [*conversari*] with witches and other men in assumed bodies . . . they could cause such apparitions by moving [*transmutationem*] the sensory images in the imaginative faculty, *so that when men thought the devils were present in assumed bodies, they were really nothing but* [an illusion caused by] *such transfers of sensory images in the inner faculties.*"[40] If devils lack the truth status conferred by bodies, we have no guarantee that, when we see them, they are not mere images in our brains. Kramer avoids drawing the further conclusion: unless demons sometimes have bodies in external reality, they cannot even prove that at other times they are shunting their own images inside the human brain.

His warnings show that Kramer understood, either consciously or intuitively, that the concept of demonic corporeality is a monstrously efficient double bind. If the Devil has a proper, inherent body, he cannot cause *praestigium* by shunting images in the brain, and human imagination may therefore be autonomous.[41] But, if he does not have a body at all, we can never have proof that he is there in external reality, and, once again, human imagination may be autonomous. The Devil must always be present just when he seems to be absent, like the genitalia hidden under a *praestigium* of illusory castration. Yet Satan must not be absent when he appears to be present, like the illusory genitalia in the bird's nest. He must be present constantly, both when he appears to be present and when he seems to be absent. Satan therefore needs a body that he can wear (the verbs *induo* and *assumo* are often used in just this sense) when proof of his reality is required. But he must be able to avoid corporeality whenever it would hinder his operations. Virtual corporeality defends the demon's reality from objections based on nature, while his intrinsic incorporeality protects it from the threat of an omnipotent human imagination.

Kramer is no more willing to discuss his motivations here than in his discussion of women's evil. He needs to discover and prove an objective reason why the Devil's body can never be a purely mental illusion. Yet he must not reveal his own subjective need for demonic reality. The ideal reason is, as usual, human evil and sinfulness:

> It is to be said that, if the Devil had no higher purpose [*nil altius*] than merely to show himself in human form, then there would be no need for him to appear in an assumed body, since he could effect his purpose well enough by the aforesaid transfer [of images within the head]. But

> this is not so; for he has a higher [*altiora*] purpose, namely to speak and eat with them, and to commit other abominations [*spurcicijs*]. Therefore it is necessary [*oportet*] that he should himself be present, placing himself actually [*realiter*] in sight in an external, assumed body. For, as the Doctors of the Church maintain, Where the angel's power is, there he operates.[42]

Those "other abominations" are sex acts, of course: *spurcitia* is Kramer's favored term for demonic copulation.[43] Although the present passage is quite far from discussions of demonic copulation, Kramer has never stopped thinking about it. By returning to demonic copulation at this point, he once again exploits Christian morality to prove Christian ontology and cosmology: the moral transgression is essential to proving the nature of being and the structure of the world.

The reference to Satan's "higher purpose" reveals Kramer's own. Despite his precautions, he confirms that the ideological purpose of the demon's body is to *convince someone* that he is real, not imaginary. If, as Kramer wants to believe, the penis is "essential to the truth of the human body," then devils must be able to copulate in order to prove their reality. Kramer admits that bodily contact between witch and devil is indispensable because "there can be no proportion between a purely spiritual substance and a corporeal one." Unless the demon has a body, he will differ from a human as zero differs from one, not as one differs from two. Kramer knows that "not even the devils have any power to cause an effect, except through some other active principle" or body. So, if devils cannot fabricate bodies and copulate, then "it does not seem possible that there can be any contact between the demon and human bodies, since he has no actual *point* of contact with them."[44] It is no joke that, for Kramer, the "point of contact" with the human body is the point of the demonic penis.

For Kramer, demons were what modern psychoanalysts would call *the phallus,* a principle of reality. By causing a man to lose contact with his own penis, they overrode all principles of reality based on physicality and sensation. Thus, they guaranteed the reality of what is neither physical nor perceptible: the sacraments, the divine presence, and the entire dimension of spirit.

Defending Sacramental Matrimony

If the psychotic hallucination of a disappearing penis occurred in Kramer's time, it would have symbolized and explained the inability to have or maintain an erection. The shrunken organ would not literally disappear, but extreme shame and mortification might have made it seem to.

There is plenty of evidence that impotence was a major concern of laymen in Kramer's time. Aside from its frequency in imaginative literature, there are famous sixteenth-century cases of impotence, like that of Martin Guerre and Montaigne's anecdote of helping an anxious friend overcome his fear of impotence on his wedding night.[45] Moreover, a frequent type of *maleficium* discussed in canon law was impotence caused by sorcery; many of Kramer's discussions of impotence cite the chapter of Gratian's *Decretum* (*Si per sortiarias*) that discusses magically induced impotence. Of all canon law, only the Canon *Episcopi* receives more citations in the *Malleus*.[46]

Sexual dysfunction was one of the most distressing anxieties of early-modern people, but their reasons for fearing it were not the same as ours. It was most threatening within marriage. Marriage was an economic arrangement far more than a romantic ideal. Childless marriages could have profound effects on inheritance and alliances among families or even countries. Witchcraft could be a convenient explanation of male impotence for both spouses: it preserved the male's self-esteem by identifying an external cause for his inability to fulfill his personal and economic duty. For the wife, as well, self-esteem was at stake: even if an impotent husband did not blame his wife, she could feel that his impotence impugned her sexual desirability.

But these are speculations in modern terms. Kramer never discusses self-esteem, and we have no guarantee that the cases that he mentions were not invented to illustrate a point. As with other social problems, Kramer has no interest in human suffering or practical solutions to it.

Neither Kramer nor the canon law chapter that he cites cares much about impotence unless it occurs within marriage. Obviously, a religion that discourages sex outside marriage can hardly express regret if impotence impedes adultery and fornication. Ecclesiastics were as interested in sex within marriage as married couples were. They shared laypeople's concerns about impotence, but they had their own reasons as well. Like baptism and the eucharist, matrimony was defined as a sacrament. In the case of matrimony, the differences between lay and ecclesiastic sacramental anxieties were even greater than with baptism, the eucharist, or the sign of the cross.

One case shows that even highly privileged and powerful layfolk with some education could disagree radically with theologians over the relation between impotence and sacramental matrimony. It illustrates how ecclesiastics tried to exploit laypeople's fears of sexual dysfunction to reinforce belief in the opposition between demons and sacraments.

Around 1505, Queen Isabella of Castille was told by one of her ladies "that the lady's niece, married to a nobleman, was being troubled [*impedita*] by the art of illusion or of demons, a condition known as being 'ligata' [bound], on account of the witchcraft [*maleficio*] of a certain brother of her husband." The woman asked the queen for help in obtaining a cure for the niece. Initially, Isabella maintained that such sexual witchcraft "should not be asserted or believed among Catholics. It is a wrongheaded opinion of the common people [*vulgi*]."[47]

Nonetheless, Isabella agreed to help. She summoned the Dominican Diego de Deza, who was archbishop of Seville and inquisitor-general, and explained the case to him. Isabella expressed her skepticism about witchcraft, saying that the sacrament of matrimony "is a spiritual thing [*quoddam spirituale*]" and that "in such a holy thing illusions of the Devil or the operations of a demon can achieve no effect." The Dominican disagreed entirely with the queen:

> "Most excellent highness, it does nonetheless happen. The thing itself is certain, and it is accepted by the holy doctors that such an operation of the Devil can take place and has happened many times," as authority for which he mentioned Saint Thomas [Aquinas] and other doctors of the church. Having heard his answer, the most Christian queen said: "I hear what you are saying, sir; but I still question whether *not* believing such a thing is actually contrary to the Catholic faith." He then responded that it was not an article of the faith but that the doctors believe it and insist on it. At length the Catholic queen said: "I agree with the holy church. So, if it is not against the faith [to doubt this], even though the doctors affirm its truth, I will certainly not believe that a demon can exert any power over those conjoined in matrimony and 'bind' them, as it is said. For these things are more due to discord among humans than to interference by powerful demons."[48]

Isabella's interpretation was intelligent, well informed, and straightforward. She reasoned that, if a sacrament is "spiritual" and "holy" because of its association with God, the Devil should be unable to sabotage it.

Her decision to credit human emotions rather than demonic interference looks surprisingly modern and "psychological." Notice, however, that, in discussing this sacrament, Isabella introduced (at least according to the chronicler) the notions of operation, effect (*effectus*), and power (*potestas*). She disagreed with the Dominican very precisely, denying that the effects of the sacrament are physical as well as "something spiritual." In other words, she was invoking the same issues that were at stake in discussions of the eucharist and baptism. The Dominican had to admit that he could not *require* her to believe in a physical struggle between demonic and sacramental energies. He had only the "scientific" authority of Aquinas and other Scholastics to defend the sacrament's effects on physical reality.

Kramer's Defense of Matrimony

Diego de Deza did not mention the *Malleus* in his defense of sacramental literality. But he argued as if he were familiar with his Dominican confrère's discussion of matrimonial dogma, published two decades previously. Like other witchcraft theorists, Kramer worried about infant mortality and the efficacy of baptism, but he was more disturbed by his fear that the sacramental efficacy of matrimony was problematic or imaginary. Hindering the consummation of matrimony is the first witchcraft crime that the *Malleus maleficarum* mentions specifically, and Kramer analyzes it obsessively. Isabella's objection to de Deza actually echoes Kramer's first discussion in the *Malleus:* whether it is heretical not to believe in witchcraft. The first example of witchcraft that Kramer cited in that discussion was "hindering the end of matrimony," that is, preventing procreation within marriage.[49]

Isabella's discussion shows that Kramer's focus was less strange than it seems. As previously mentioned, a common meaning of *maleficium* in Kramer's time was, not witchcraft in general, but specifically impotence brought on by witchcraft, and it was discussed in canon law.[50] A closer look at Kramer's discussions of matrimony shows how little he was concerned by the Freudian anxieties that modern scholars attribute to him. He does not define castration as a primal terror, the way Freud does; it is merely one of several expedients for "hindering the object of matrimony." Real or illusory castration makes men "unable to copulate, and so the contract of matrimony is rendered void, and matrimony in their cases has become impossible."[51]

Kramer never implies that witches make war on the male sex or the hierarchy of gender. He states clearly that they attack sacramental matrimony: "Such hatred is aroused by *maleficia* between those joined in the sacrament of matrimony, and such freezing up of the generative forces, that people can neither demand nor render the debt of matrimony for begetting offspring." He is careful to specify that "impotence of the male to perform the act is not the only *maleficium;* sometimes the woman is caused to be unable to conceive, or else she miscarries."[52]

In some contexts, Kramer does not mention men at all, for his major concern is with the production of children within matrimony. As a Dominican, his deepest concerns emerge when he painstakingly instructs his clerical readers how to preach about witchcraft to the common people. In that passage, he addresses the problems of women, not men. He says that, working through a witch, the Devil "can obstruct the generative forces so that a woman cannot conceive, or so that if she does conceive, he can cause a miscarriage; or if there is no miscarriage, he can cause the children to be killed after birth."[53] The concerns of Queen

Isabella's retainers were thus shared by Kramer: the "bewitched" woman defined *herself,* not her husband, as *impedita* or obstructed.

Kramer displays his desire to believe in the sacramental efficacy of matrimony even more openly than Diego de Deza did. He attempts to demonstrate that Christian sacramental matrimony confers privileges and protections missing from Jewish and Muslim marriages. But to do so he needs witchcraft, for he has to explain why sacramental protections sometimes fail to safeguard Christian marriages. For the sacrament to be real, witchcraft must be real.

To make this defense, Kramer turns from witches' general assault on matrimony to the question of male impotence. In the first question of part 1, he reminds his reader that the authorities of canon law "do not doubt that [impotence] can be brought about by the power of witchcraft." They "do not wonder whether such an effect can be considered imaginary and unreal [*imaginarius et non realis*]." Having established that witchcraft is not imaginary, he turns to the sacrament; it is, he says, "a fact beyond dispute that such impotence can be brought about through the power of the Devil by means of a contract made with him, or even by the Devil himself without the assistance of any witch [*malefica*], *although this most rarely happens in the Church, since matrimony is a most excellent* [*meritorium*] *sacrament.* But amongst pagans this actually does happen, and this is because the Devil sees they belong to him by right [*iusto titulo illos possidere se cernit*]. . . . *But nevertheless in the Church the Devil strives to produce this effect through the medium of witches.*"[54] Kramer wants to draw an absolute distinction between Christian and non-Christian marriage, but he knows that he cannot.

Witches explain why, even though Christian matrimony is "a most excellent sacrament" (according to Paul in Eph. 5:32), impotence can still occur within it, just as it does in non-Christian marriages. Among non-Christians, demons have absolutely free rein over male potency; but, since Christian (i.e., Catholic) matrimony is a sacrament, such absolute power is denied to demons. Only by enlisting human cooperation can demons subvert the sacramental privilege. Even so, Kramer cannot quite bring himself to assert that demons *never* subvert the sacrament without human aid.[55]

Kramer's reasoning is identical with other theorists' defenses of baptismal efficacy against loss of children. A combination of human sinfulness and demonic malice is his only alternative to admitting that the efficacy of sacramental matrimony for procreation is imaginary. Aquinas and the Canonists agree, Kramer says, that male impotence "cannot in any way be said to be illusory and the effect of imagination"; it is "an actual and proven fact," not something "imaginary and unreal." It cannot be true that, "when a man says that he has been bewitched" yet "he is still capable as regards other women, though not with her with whom he is unable to copulate," the reason is always simply a lack of desire—"that he does not wish to [*non vult*], and therefore cannot effect anything in the matter. On the contrary, the truth is upheld by the chapter *Si per sortiarias* and by all theologians and canon lawyers discussing the impediment to matrimony."[56] Unless devils and witches are actively preventing the consummation of sacramental matrimony and the procreation of children according to God's command to be fruitful and multiply, then the sacrament is imaginary. Therefore, witchcraft cannot be imaginary.

Kramer's concept of matrimony is explicitly magical. It is a reification, a mechanical debasement of the dogma that sacraments are "signs *given by God, and not invented by men,* which have the power to effect the same holy thing they signify."[57] But Kramer's exaggeration is not groundless. Catholic matrimonial theory already reflects a literalizing interpretation of the first two chapters of Genesis, the nineteenth chapter of Matthew, and the fifth chapter of Ephesians.[58] And the scriptural passages themselves describe matrimony as a kind of eternal sex act that literally conjoins husband and wife, making them "two in one flesh."

Like the authors of the Bible themselves, Western theologians tended to interpret the body discourse of these passages literally. Formal definitions of the sacraments solidified between the *Sentences* of Peter Lombard about 1150 and the Council of Florence in 1439.[59] Not until the Council of Trent, in 1547 and again in 1563, did the church definitively explicate its doctrine on matrimony and the other sacraments.[60] This long doctrinal consolidation was punctuated by challenges, both real and imagined. Kramer and clerics like Diego de Deza were disturbed by opinions claiming or implying that there was no discernible sacramental efficacy about the eternal conjunction of male and female in Catholic matrimony.

Since infertility can be verified empirically and sacramental efficacy cannot, infertility threatened to belie the Bible passages that grounded the sacramental theory of matrimony. If, as the Book of Genesis claims, God instituted matrimony in Eden, if Adam really meant that all married couples would *literally* become "two in one flesh" like Eve and himself, if Christ correctly interpreted Adam's words to mean that divorce is unlawful, and if Paul correctly interpreted Christ's interpretation, then matrimony should always somehow work. Canon law states that "the consummation of a matrimony consists in its carnal office," and children obviously prove the reality of marital consummation.[61] So consummation and procreation should not be a problem; yet they often are. Worst of all, some men are impotent with their lawful wives, yet they successfully commit adultery and even sire bastards.[62]

Because tradition from Saint Paul onward glorified celibacy and virginity, matrimony was usually defined and discussed as the seventh and last Catholic sacrament. But it is the only sacrament that has indisputable scriptural authority. By this I mean that only one verse in the Vulgate Latin Bible uses the term *sacramentum* in a way that can be interpreted to mean what Western Christians wanted it to mean after 1100. In Eph. 5:32, Saint Paul calls matrimony a *sacramentum magnum*. Kramer's contemporaries interpreted Paul to mean that human matrimony *represents* the indissoluble matrimony of Christ and the church. Catholic matrimony imitates the literal, carnal bond between Christ the head or bridegroom and the "mystical" body of his bride the church. The term *mystical* body excluded all possibility of metaphor, and Christ's relation to the church was not a "metaphoric" marriage.[63] It was the original.

Each individual soul becomes a bride of Christ at baptism, but the incorporation of the church as body or bride of Christ takes place preeminently through the celebration of the eucharist, the supreme sacrament. Like its miniature imitation in human matrimony, the "one flesh" of the church is created literally, not metaphorically. In the case of the eucharist, this marital consummation is even more explicitly literal because it takes place through an act of sacred cannibalism.[64] If matrimony does not always work, the reality of all these intertwined and mutually dependent sacraments, which depend on four or five verses of the Latin Bible, could be threatened.

Kramer and Aquinas on Matrimony, Demons, and the Imagination

Kramer's concern over matrimonial efficacy was inherited from Aquinas and was entwined with his anxiety about demonic reality. At one point, Kramer remarks that the Devil causes so much damage to women's fertility that we should beware the temptation to believe "that the Devil's works were stronger than God's, that is, than the sacrament of matrimony, which is a work of God [*quod opera diaboli essent fortiora operibus Dei, scilicet sacramento matrimonij quod est opus Dei*]."[65] The idea of Satan challenging God by disrupting human fertility comes directly from Aquinas.

Both authors' discussions of matrimony stress the fundamental antagonism between demons and sacraments. Aquinas inquires whether *maleficium* can be "an impediment to matrimony," and he initially seems to prefer an answer in the negative: "It would seem not. For the works of God are stronger than those of the Devil. Matrimony is a work of God and *maleficium* a work of the Devil. Therefore matrimony is stronger than *maleficium*, and cannot be impeded by it."[66] Bonaventure, commenting on the same problem, gives the same initial answer even more plainly: "This kind of sorcery [*sortilegium*] is a diabolical *maleficium*, but matrimony is a remedy and a divine *beneficium*; but a divine *beneficium* is stronger than a diabolical *maleficium*; therefore matrimony will sooner dissolve a *maleficium* than a *maleficium* will block matrimony."[67] As we have seen, the opposition is polar.

But even mere humans can impede matrimony, Aquinas concedes, so the Devil must be able to as well. Finally he concludes that "the Devil himself, as well as matrimony, is the work of God. And among the works of God some are stronger than others. One of them may be impeded by another which is stronger. Whence, *since* [*Unde, cum*] the Devil is stronger than matrimony, nothing prevents that through his agency matrimony may be impeded."[68]

Aquinas begged his own question *whether* the Devil can impede matrimony. He reasoned in a circle, taking his desired conclusion as the major premise of the syllogism that should produce the conclusion. This bit of illogic was not due to ineptitude or inattention. Aquinas was forced into it because he was trying to reason his way around the more disturbing implication that all impediments to matrimony can be explained in natural or human terms, without recourse to demonic agency. Rather than gloss over this problem, he stopped to defend the existence of devils. This could look like a logical error or a digression, but it goes to the heart of the problems that created witchcraft theory: "Concerning *maleficium*, it should be known that some have said that *maleficium* has no existence, and that belief in it comes from a lack of proper faith in God [*ex infidelitate*]. For they would have it that demons are nothing more than the creatures of man's imagination, in that men imagined them and then were terrified and harmed by this process of imagination. But in fact, the Catholic faith insists [*vult*] that demons are something [real], and that they may harm us by their works and impede sexual intercourse."[69] Those words again: Aquinas's meditation on the sacramental efficacy of matrimony and what must be happening when it fails run like a red thread through the early history of witchcraft theory.

In another discussion of the same problem, Aquinas's wording is even more precise and categorical:

> Solution: I respond by saying that some have said that there is no such thing as *maleficium* in the world, except in the imagination [*aestimatione*] of men, who have attributed natural effects to *maleficium* when

> their causes were hidden from understanding [*occultae*]. But this goes against the authority of the saints, who say that demons have power over both the bodies and the imagination [*imaginationem*] of men, when God permits it; thus by means of demons sorcerers [*malefici*] can perform certain wonders [*signa aliqua*]. Now the former opinion proceeds from the root of a lack of faith [*infidelitatis*] or a lack of belief [*incredulitatis*], because they do not believe that demons exist, except in the imagination [*aestimatione*] of the common people [*vulgi*], so that the terrors that a man creates for himself out of his imagination are attributed to a demon. And they think this happens because certain figures can appear to the senses in exactly the same form as a man has thought of them, so that men think they are seeing demons. But the true faith repudiates this interpretation: through faith we believe that angels fell from heaven and became demons, and that owing to the subtlety of their nature they can do many things that we humans cannot. And thus those men who induce demons to do such things are called sorcerers [*malefici*].[70]

As we know from Kramer and other followers, Aquinas's defense of demonic reality is not a digression from his discussion of matrimony: it is a descent to a more basic level of logic. If demons are creatures of the human imagination, impotence can be caused by the imagination or, as we would now say, by psychological factors. In that case, the sacramental efficacy of matrimony is imaginary.

Aquinas's passages on matrimonial impediments are Kramer's precise inspiration for his declaration on the first page of the *Malleus* that he is writing to defend the reality of both witchcraft and demons. Kramer declares that his first chapter is a paraphrase and commentary on the longer of Aquinas's two discussions:

> RESPONSE: Here there are three heretical errors which must be attacked, and when they have been disproved, the truth will be plain. For, according to what Saint Thomas teaches in his commentary to Book IV, distinction 34 [of Peter Lombard's *Sentences*], where he speaks to the impediment [to matrimony] brought about by *maleficium* [*impedimento maleficiali*], certain writers have tried to maintain that there is not such a thing as *maleficium* in the world except in the imagination [*opinione*] of men, who ascribed to witchcraft those natural effects whose causes are hidden [*occulte*].[71]

Aquinas's passage inspired the concern over connections between sexual dysfunction in Christian matrimony and the reality of demons that can be found throughout the *Malleus*.

Like Aquinas, Kramer and other early Catholic witchcraft theorists were disturbed by the suspicion that devils are imaginary, for it menaced their confidence in the reality of the sacraments as well. Unlike Aquinas, however, the witchcraft theorists had an imperious need for empirical confirmation. That devils depended on human coconspirators had to be proved in order to confirm that devils were blocking the sacraments. These human *malefici,* or witches, had to be found.

12

INTERVIEW WITH THE DEMON: FROM EXORCISM TO WITCHCRAFT

> If magicians and witches and the possessed exist, demons exist; but it cannot be doubted that in every age specimens of the former three have been found: thus it is unreasonable to doubt that demons are found in nature.
>
> —Torquato Tasso, *Il messaggiero* (1582)

Redefining Western witchcraft as corporeal interaction with demons discloses that it had a long prehistory. The question whether demons could interact verifiably with humans took on a new urgency around 1400. Theologians in search of proof began speculating that certain people were having sex with incubi and succubi, making pacts with demons to perform *maleficium,* and attending meetings of demons and humans.

The witch was a hybrid figure. Before 1400, each of her activities had been attributed to a different group of outcast or marginal persons. Heretics held secret meetings, both in reality and in the imagination of theologians. The imaginary meetings had far fewer participants than would be imagined for the witches' Sabbat, but the Devil often appeared to heretics in the form of a man or an animal. *Maleficia* were attributed to sorceresses (*sortiariae*) and necromancers.[1] The women discussed by the Canon *Episcopi* stimulated a mental association between sorceresses and heretics. Necromancers were learned men who sought contact with spirits, practicing an art (*necromantia* or *nigromantia*) recorded in books. Their activity gained them an unsavory reputation and occasional execution, but necromancers claimed to pursue worthy and even pious ends. Sorceresses and necromancers resemble the witches of later myth, with one exception: those who seem to have really existed were usually solitary individuals.

Not all contact with demons was defined as evil. The church permitted and encouraged the activity of exorcists, men in priestly orders delegated to tame and expel demons that caused physical and mental illnesses by "possessing" the faithful.

Learned men's interest in varieties of interaction with demons underwent a seamless evolution: there was no distinct "age of heretics" or "epoch of sorceresses." Exorcists claimed biblical precedents for their activity; they were active throughout the Middle Ages and are still a controversial presence in the Catholic church. Necromancers became culturally important in the thirteenth century and remained so into the eighteenth. Fortune-tellers, healers, and other village "wise women" interested theologians for centuries, as the Canon *Episcopi* and the *Si per sortiarias* show.

Witchcraft theory was an advance in that it provided a way of organizing preexisting ideas about relations between humans and demons. It provided a *systematic* description of human-demon interaction. In addition, witchcraft theory defined a way of verifying this interaction, by postulating that it had a physical, even sexual, dimension. Witches' confessions proved that the systematic theory correctly described reality.

However, the concept of witchcraft presented drawbacks as well as advantages. Exorcists and necromancers had no physical contact with demons, but they supposedly interviewed demons directly. The witchcraft investigator had to settle for interviewing the demons' human accomplices. The witchcraft theorist was even further from the source: unless he was a judge or an inquisitor, he had to rely on the interview "data" gathered by someone else. At its freshest, witchcraft information was always *secondhand* information.

Thus, while assembling their theories of witchcraft, writers often paused to reconsider the longer-established, more direct forms of demonic interaction, based on direct interviews. They nourished a stubborn hope that demonic possession, exorcism, and necromancy would yield proofs of spiritual reality furnished by demons at firsthand. Few dared or were permitted to perform "fieldwork," however. Most had to rely on reading the authorities.

Aquinas's writings were particularly esteemed for this sort of research. In the *De malo,* Aquinas discussed firsthand experiences with demons. He declared that Aristotelians' objections against the existence of demons were "manifestly false" because "some operations of the demons are found which in no way can proceed from any natural cause." These operations are of two kinds. In the first, "a person possessed by a demon speaks an unknown tongue." Anyone speaking a language that he himself cannot understand is obviously possessed by a demon. The second operation is necromancy, or the conjuring of demons: "Many other works of the demons are found both in cases of possession and in the necromantic arts, which cannot in any way come about except as proceeding from some intellect." Therefore, says Aquinas, "even philosophers" have been forced to admit the existence of demons.[2]

All this was duly copied out by theorists like Heinrich Kramer. But how much help was it? It was still a defensive move, directed against the awareness that Aristotle did not support the existence of demons. Witchcraft theorists called on Aquinas's authority, but they also forced his implicit skepticism into the open. They investigated *whether* witchcraft, necromancy, and possession offered proof of demonic reality. Their own answers gave them no more satisfaction than his did.[3]

The cross-fertilization of ideas about witchcraft, necromancy, and possession was continuous after 1400, but the proportions of give and take varied. By Kramer's time (1487), it was increasingly writers who had formed definite theories of witchcraft who theorized about possession and necromancy. But, in an earlier stage, dissatisfaction with possession and necromancy had stimulated the formation of witchcraft theory. Jean Vineti's *Tractatus contra demonum invocatores,* or *Treatise against Invokers of Demons* (ca. 1450–70), is only a few years older than the *Malleus,* but it clearly shows the mental progression that created witchcraft from exorcism and necromancy.

Gathering practically everything that Aquinas had ever said about demons, and adding choice passages from a few other, mostly Dominican, writers, Vineti constructed a proof that demons are real and can be contacted. The most direct method is through exorcism. The theoretical bases of exorcism imply two other ways of contacting demons. The first is necromancy; the second involves *maleficium* (specifically, killing children with the evil eye and causing impotence). Vineti's objective was to establish that effects attributed to demons cannot be reduced to natural causes (especially astrology) or to an overactive imagination. He defined necromancy as exorcism gone wrong, using Solomon as the great example: if Solomon was not always a virtuous and proper exorcist, he was sometimes a sinful but redeemable necromancer.[4] Vineti's brief mentions of *maleficium* were parenthetical asides in long revindications of demonic power over nature and the imagination.

According to its title, Vineti's treatise should be a thorough condemnation of necromancy. Instead, necromancers receive little attention and no condemnation that I can find. That Vineti spent so little energy attacking his ostensible enemies does not indicate a lack of interest or logic, however. He was fascinated, and a little envious, as he shows in the third part of his treatise. There, following Aquinas, he distinguishes between positive and negative interactions with demons.

> We can command [*adiurare*] demons by the power of the name of God and repel them like enemies, to prevent their harming us spiritually or corporeally, using the power given by Christ, according to Luke, chapter 10: "Behold I have given you the power to tread on serpents,

> and on all the powers of the Enemy, and nothing will harm you." However, it is not permissible to command demons for the purpose of learning something from them or likewise to obtain anything through their agency, for these things imply that one has some alliance [*societatem*] with them. *Except, perhaps, if this happens through some spiritual suggestion or divine inspiration. For there are some who use the work of demons to produce certain effects, as we read of the blessed James, who forced a demon to lead Hermogenes to him.*[5]

Vineti quotes Aquinas's requirement that anything beyond human powers be requested of God alone. To request favors of demons is as idolatrous as worshiping them. Although they may deny it, magicians obviously expect demons to do things that humans cannot: "In all these things there is apostasy from the faith, on account of a pact entered into with the demon." The magician accepts the pact "either by means of words, if there has been an invocation, or by means of some action." A magician can make a pact implicitly, through his actions, even without saying a word or offering a sacrifice to the demon.[6]

Despite these restrictions, Vineti has trouble maintaining the moral distinction between exorcism and necromancy. His reference to Saint James creates a space for "licit" adjuration that looks very much like necromancy, but the resemblances were already deep. Both D. P. Walker and Richard Kieckhefer observe that the vocabularies of exorcism and necromancy are identical. According to Walker, "The terms *coniuro, adiuro,* and *exorcizo* . . . are essentially interchangeable with each other and with other words meaning 'I command.'"[7] Kieckhefer defines a single "key difference: the exorcist's intent was to dispel the demons, while the conjurer's [or necromancer's] was to summon them."[8] Vineti shows that these diametrically opposed intentions could not be kept separate. There were many shades of grey between the most virtuous exorcist and the worst necromancer.

From Exorcism to Necromancy

Vineti built his *Tractatus* on a framework of quotations from Aquinas. He argued methodically, working carefully toward defining spirit possession and exorcism as the proof of demonic reality. This is a simple strategy, for Vineti's concept of witchcraft was still elementary. Although *maleficium* and its derivative verbs and adjectives occur several times in the *Tractatus,* Vineti mentioned *malefici* only once, in the male form and in passing.[9] Nor had he achieved a systematic concept of bodily interactions with demons. His arguments depend heavily on the idea that exorcists and necromancers have *relatively direct* contact with demons, but physical contact is limited to "certain women."[10]

The structure of Vineti's *Tractatus* reveals how intensely Vineti craved proof that demonic contacts were real. In part 1, he begins from the question *whether* demons exist and attempts to define their being. Part 2 is organized around "whether demons can assume a true body"[11] and discusses *dubia* or "doubts"—a designation that Vineti preferred to the alternative Scholastic term *distinctions*—about demonic copulation and transvection. Part 2 was copied almost entirely from Aquinas, and its overriding topic is still whether demons exist. Part 3 also shows Aquinas's influence. It concerns the overall relations between demons and magic (*artes magicae*). Three chapters inquire whether the heavenly bodies might produce the effects attributed to demons; another chapter discusses whether the effects of *maleficium* happen only in the imagination. Otherwise, *maleficium* is mentioned infrequently, without detailed analysis.

Part 4 is organized by the question whether demons can inflict bodily torment on humans and animals. This allows Vineti to define spirit possession as the model for all forms of *maleficium*. Possession is the simplest form of torment by demons and the oldest attested by Christian tradition.

This progression seems to be defining *maleficium* as proof positive of demonic reality. Yet nowhere does Vineti assume that possession requires *maleficium* or assert that it is caused by *maleficium*. The last four *dubia* of his treatise show just how nebulous the connection still is. They inquire "Whether it can be known with any probability whether a man is being possessed [*vexetur*] by a demon; whether the church has correctly established exorcism for expelling demons from the bodies of the possessed [*obsessorum*]; whether the exorcisms of Solomon derived their effectiveness from God or from other demons; whether possession by demons affects a person's free will in such a way as to constrain it."[12]

Vineti's brief introduction to part 4 shows how clearly he associated doubts about possession with doubts about demonic reality: "Since, as we said above in the eighth proposition of part 3, some people who lack faith [*infideles*] do not believe that demons exist, except only in the beliefs of common people [*estimatione vulgi*], so that the terrors that a man inflicts on himself from his imagination [*ymaginatione*] he attributes to a demon, in this part it will be seen that, as long as God permits it, not only men but brute beasts can occasionally be harassed [*vexantur*] by demons. Whence this part will be organized into seven doubts."[13] Those words again: demons may be a vulgar superstition. Occurring this late in the treatise, they show that Vineti considered possession the crucial proof of demonic reality.

The first sentence of part 4 reveals why possession is so crucial: Vineti declares that "those who claim that demons cannot harass men corporeally manifestly disparage [*detrahunt*] the miracles of Christ." He argues as Tostado did in his defense of demonic transvection: demons, possession, and exorcism must be real because Gospel passages (esp. Luke 6) say that Jesus freed people from demonic possession. Furthermore, says Vineti, Aquinas reminds us that the Jews were wrong to accuse Jesus of casting out demons by the power of other demons. This demonstrates that Jesus was the son of God: "The miracles that Christ performed were sufficient to manifest his divinity for three reasons, as Aquinas says in the same question."[14]

As this last quotation reveals, Aquinas was not discussing possession specifically but rather Jesus' miracles in general. His purpose in that passage was to defend, not demonic reality, but Jesus' divinity. Together, Aquinas and Vineti alert us to the New Testament's use of miracles to prove that Jesus was who he claimed to be. Quoting Aquinas, Vineti contends (1) that these miracles could not have been performed except by divine power; (2) that Jesus performed them through his own power, not by praying to someone else; and (3) that Jesus himself said that he was God, "and if it were not true it would not have been confirmed by those miracles, performed by divine power."[15]

Vineti cannot seem to decide whether his point is proving the reality of demons or the divinity of Jesus. He cites the Gospel story of the Gadarene swine in an apparent effort to prove both. But first he "hypothesizes" that, if demons can torment people, they must be able to molest domestic animals (a common form of *maleficium*). Lo and behold, the Gospels state that Jesus met a man possessed by a legion of devils, made them leave the man, and sent them into a herd of pigs; the devils so maddened the pigs that they leaped into the sea and were drowned.[16] Among the points that he takes from Aquinas, Vineti is most interested in the assertion that Jesus did not allow the demons to persuade him to this act. Rather, his purpose was to teach us (1) how much harm demons can do to humans, (2) that demons could not have harmed the pigs unless Jesus permitted it, and (3) how much more harm demons can do to humans than to pigs, unless divine providence protects us.[17] Weirdly, the confused objectives of this passage make Jesus resemble a witch. Performed by an ordinary human, his miracle would be a *maleficium*. Vineti does not say this, but he does caution against raising "pointless" moral questions about the incident; after all, who created those pigs?[18]

Using the Gospels to assert that demonic possession is real apparently fails to satisfy Vineti. He admits that the body can be tormented by astrological influences acting on its humors; in turn, humors can affect the mind, as happens in melancholia. But demons employ natural causes to inflict their harms on us, so nature *cannot disprove* demonic existence.[19]

Like other witchcraft theorists, Vineti inherited Aquinas's desire to show that astrological influences are not a better explanation of the misfortunes that he attributes to demonic *maleficium*. To concede the plausibility of natural causes would open the possibility that Jesus did not cast out demons but performed medical and psychological cures. Depersonalizing the cause of affliction would endanger the proof of Jesus' divinity.

Vineti has established that demonic possession must be possible if what the Bible says is true, and he is ready to discuss how we can tell when someone is actually possessed. There is a recent empirical case, he says. Some women being tormented by demons "were interrogated about the secrets of Holy Scripture by a group of educated [*litteratos*] men, and they responded as if they had been steeped in sacred literature for their entire lives."[20] So far, so good: following Aquinas's lead, Vineti reasons that, whereas women rarely have theological training, devils have firsthand experience of the realities that theology discusses. Thus, the devils must have suggested or spoken these wonderful answers.

Since Vineti is engaged in demonstrating the truth of Scripture, it is suspiciously appropriate that he chooses an example of demonic possession where exorcists quizzed demons about the Bible. Were the demons simply confirming their presence by giving correct interpretations, the illiterate women being unable to discuss the Bible correctly without their aid? Even if this is true, something is amiss. As we saw, Vineti himself admitted that "it is not permissible to command demons for the purpose of learning something from them or likewise to obtain anything through their agency, for these things imply that one has some alliance [*societatem*] with them."

So why were these educated men comparing notes with demons about the Bible rather than ejecting them and relieving the tormented women? It looks as if their urgent concern was verifying the presence of demons, not exercising Christian compassion. Or was something else at stake? Were the demons also confirming the "educated men's" interpretation of the Bible? Did the "secrets of Holy Scripture" discussed include anything about demonology? Were the "educated men" even exorcists? Did exorcists give nonexorcists access to the women? Finally, whatever the intentions of the "educated men," Vineti had no interest in the anecdote beyond its alleged proof of demonic reality.

The proofs furnished by the possessed women, like so many aspects of witchcraft theory, confirm assertions that Aquinas made to counter the Aristotelian menace to spiritual reality:

> The other part of this proposition is based on Saint Thomas Aquinas, who says . . . "It is known from experience [*ex experimento*] that demons

> can do many things that the power of the celestial bodies would never be able to do, such as when possessed people [*arrepticij*] speak a language they do not know and recite verses and authorities that they have never learned." And indeed, in this matter, as Thomas says in the treatise on spirits [*substantijs separatis*] . . . "the position of Aristotle appears inadequate because many things appear to the senses that cannot be accounted for by the principles that Aristotle teaches. These things appear in people who are tormented by demons and in some works of magicians [*magorum*] that clearly cannot be performed except by some being that has a mind [*intellectualem substantiam*]. *Some of Aristotle's followers have tried to attribute the causes of all these things to the power of the heavenly bodies,* as is clear in Porphyry's letter to Tremefons [*sic*] the Egyptian, *as if some of the wonderful and extraordinary effects of the works of magicians took place only under the influence of certain constellations. They say that it is owing to the workings of the stars that possessed people sometimes predict the future* and that these things come true because the heavenly bodies have an influence on all of nature.
>
> "But clearly some of these things can in no way be attributed to a corporeal cause, such as when possessed people sometimes speak [correctly] about holy things they actually know nothing about. Nay, they speak like this although they are simple and unlearned [*ydiote*] and have hardly ever left the village where they were born: yet now they speak elegantly, in a way foreign to common people." Thus says Thomas.[21]

This passage does not reveal that Vineti had *already* devoted the entire previous book of his treatise to disproving the astrological explanation, beginning from the same texts of Aquinas.

The now familiar words of Aquinas organized the proofs of several chapters, wherein Vineti tried to demonstrate that the works or effects of demons cannot all be attributed to astrology and thus that demons are not simply creatures of the human imagination: "Since, as Thomas says in his treatise on the angels, it is found that Aristotle never once mentioned demons in all his philosophy, some have decided that the effects of the magical arts derive from the heavenly bodies and that there are no demons in all of nature, as Thomas says in the *Summa theologiae*. But, since the true faith repudiates this proposition because we believe that angels fell from heaven and became demons, therefore in the third part of this little work the truth of the faith will be the basis for discussing fourteen doubts."[22] By returning to astrology and Aristotle in connection with possession, Vineti confirmed how deeply he was disturbed by the suspicion that any effect attributed to demonic causes might just as easily be caused by the stars.

Images (including voodoo dolls stuck with pins), jewels, and crystals draw their power, not *naturally* from the influence of heavenly *bodies,* but rather *supernaturally,* by functioning as signs or signals to evil *spirits.* Demons have a pact with necromancers (not witches), so they know which wonders or crimes to perform when presented with certain signals.[23]

In part 3, Vineti could not begin discussing demonic magic until he wrote six chapters demonstrating that neither nature nor the imagination could account for *all* the effects attributed to demons. Part 4 reverses the same logic: it implies that *maleficium* must be real because spirit possession is real, but then Vineti has to prove the reality of spirit possession, which part 3 had already taken for granted. The new proof consists of only one proposition: if illiterate people seem to know or do something beyond their normal powers, then, not they, but a demon is responsible.

The following chapter discusses whether the church rightfully practices exorcism. Vineti declares that "it is fitting that demons are expelled by exorcism *before baptism,* so that they may not obstruct a person's welfare."[24] This proposition is partly familiar, revealing the fear that, unless demons are obstructing the sacraments, the efficacy of sacraments may be imaginary. But Vineti is also implying that exorcism was actually a part of the baptismal ceremony. In fact, Henry Ansgar Kelly observes that "the demonological substance of the baptismal order . . . remained intact in the Roman Catholic ritual . . . [until] 1969, [when] all of the explicitly exorcistic elements were removed, and only a trace of other antidemonic elements was included."[25] Exorcism and baptism were linked, not only in Vineti's time, but for at least twelve centuries previously.

We can now see why witchcraft was related to exorcism in the minds of the earliest theorists. Even if exorcism were not an integral part of the baptismal ceremony, logic would *necessarily* have stimulated witchcraft theorists to ask themselves the disturbing question why demons return afterward to attack small children had it been a preliminary.

When Vineti describes the sacramental process of baptism, he is concerned to demonstrate the literal and physical effects of the rite itself. Because all the priest's actions have a *sacramental* significance, they cannot be merely symbolic. They must have real effects: they must both signify and perform.[26] The same is true of exorcism in general, even though it is not a sacrament:

> Now we must avoid taking the position of some people who maintain that the things that are done in exorcisms have no real effect but are purely symbolic [*nihil efficiant, sed solum significant*]. According to Thomas, in article 3 of the same question, it is obvious that this idea is false because,

> when the church performs exorcisms, it uses verbs in the imperative mood [*imperativis verbis*] to drive out the power of the demon, for example, when we say: "Therefore come out of him, thou damned devil," and such things. And therefore it must be said that exorcisms have some real effect, which is, however, different from the effect of baptism itself.[27]

Vineti has just based the entire reality of the spirit world on the notion that the church would not issue imperatives to imaginary beings.

Demons must be real because *maleficium* and possession are real; but the reality of possession depends on the reality of exorcism. Our ultimate guarantee that exorcism really does anything is our faith that, if an imperative is issued, the being to whom it is addressed must exist, that the church has not wasted its energy these many centuries, defining and issuing orders to imaginary beings. The logic is familiar: we have seen other theorists declare that the church would never punish imaginary crimes and that canon lawyers would never waste their time discussing impotence if it had imaginary or natural causes. Once again, a long string of "empirical" or "experimental" proofs has revealed its real basis in the faith that it was supposed to reinforce.

Necromancy, Exorcism, Witchcraft, Experimentation

Richard Kieckhefer rightly observes that, "in so far as necromancers contributed to the plausibility of claims about witches, they bear indirect responsibility for the rise of the European witch trials in the fifteenth and sixteenth centuries."[28] As we see from Vineti, moreover, clerics who prided themselves on their orthodoxy were as important as actual necromancers in forming the stereotype of the witch. Clerical condemnations of necromancy and defenses of exorcism laid the crucial groundwork for vindicating the possibility of real interaction with demons. The only remaining step was to posit physical, bodily interaction, and, for this, women were most interesting because of stereotypes about their "passive" sexuality.

Necromancers regularly referred to their operations as *experiments*.[29] The term is amply justified, whether the point of the experiment was the acquisition of power over demons (the traditional explanation) or the mere demonstration that *demons are there*. Similarly, the element of experimentation can rarely be discounted from exorcism itself, even in the earliest period of the formation of witchcraft theory.

The temptations that exorcism offered to early theorists of witchcraft are vividly illustrated by Heinrich Kramer. The *Malleus* goes beyond Jean Vineti by claiming that witches can induce demons to possess other people and explaining how. As sole support of these allegations, Kramer once again claims to have personal experience, gathered in Rome during the papacy of Pius II (1458–64), that is, around the time Vineti composed his *Tractatus*.

Kramer says that he made the acquaintance in Rome of a young Bohemian priest who believed himself possessed by a devil. Kramer took an intense personal interest in the Bohemian's case: his descriptions of attempted exorcisms imply that he was in charge of them. This encounter with spirit possession and exorcism influenced his obsession with hunting down and interviewing the "willing accomplices" of devils.

Although Kramer does not quote Aquinas's contention that inappropriate knowledge demonstrates the presence of a devil, he dramatizes it:

> And at last the demon said, "I will not go forth." And when he was asked why, he answered, "Because of the Lombards." And being asked why he would not go forth because of the Lombards, he answered in the Italian tongue (although the afflicted priest did not understand that language), "They all practice such and such things" [*faciunt sic et sic*], naming the worst vice of lustfulness. And afterwards the priest asked me, saying, "Father, what did those Italian words mean which he brought forth from my mouth?" And when I told him, he answered, "I heard the words, but I could not understand them."[30]

Kramer need not mention Aquinas's proof since he can claim the same knowledge through direct experience rather than reasoning or authority.

Kramer's test case reverses the traditional proof: it features a literate cleric ignorant of a vernacular language, not illiterate women or peasants declaiming in Latin or discussing theology. The subject of the devil's declamations is also a departure, for it is not obviously theological. Yet theology is never terribly far from a mind like Kramer's. The "Lombards" in question are almost certainly not an ethnic group in the modern sense but a profession: Italian usurers, about as hated as Jewish moneylenders in many countries and vulnerable to similar kinds of defamation. Kramer's euphemistic wording implies that the Bohemian's devil accused Italian moneylenders of sodomy. This charge was common enough that Boccaccio alluded to it in the first story of the *Decameron*, while Dante's hell placed usurers and sodomites alongside each other under a rain of fire that recalled the destruction of Sodom and Gomorrah.[31]

Sodomy was occasionally connected to witchcraft in theory and trials as a comparably abominable crime. Kramer disagreed with this notion; he declared that devils abhorred sodomy and would have nothing to do with it: "It must be carefully noted that, though the Scripture speaks of incubi and succubi lusting after women, yet nowhere do we read that incubi and succubi fell into vices of any sort against nature, meaning not only sodomy, but also any other sin whereby the act is wrongfully performed outside the proper channel [*extra vas debitum*]. And the very great enormity of those who sin in this way is shown by the fact that all demons equally, of whatsoever order, abominate and think shame to commit such actions."[32] Kramer gave impeccable theological reasons for this opinion, but his own logic required it. Since demons had to mimic male reality even to the point of impregnating women, sex outside the "proper channels" was detrimental or at least not useful for demonstrating demonic reality.

Like demonic copulation, sodomy is more important to Kramer as a demonological sign than as a moral abomination. He can interpret the horror of sodomy as prima facie evidence of demonic presence because he has already defined this attitude as common to all demons. Thus, Kramer expects his reader to notice two unstated proofs of demonic reality: the Bohemian's ignorance of the Italian words issuing from his mouth and the horror of sodomy that the words expressed.

However, the Roman demon did not limit himself to demonstrating his own reality. Like the demons possessing the women mentioned by Vineti, he obligingly furnished proofs about the entire Christian metaphysical system. For two weeks, Kramer escorted the Bohemian to various Roman shrines and holy places, including the supposed pillar at which Christ was flagellated and the site of Saint Peter's crucifixion: "And in all these places [the demon] uttered horrible cries [*eiulatus*] while he was being exorcised, now saying that he wished to come forth, and after a little maintaining the contrary."[33] Finally, Kramer took him to the holiest of holy places in Rome:

> And there was in the Church of Saint Peter a column brought from Solomon's temple, surrounded by an iron fence [*circumferrata*], by virtue of which many who are obsessed by devils are liberated, because Christ had stood near it when He preached in the temple; but even here [the Bohemian] could not be delivered, owing to the hidden purpose [*iudicio*] of God which reserved another method for his liberation. For though [the Bohemian] remained shut in by the column for a whole day and night, yet on the following day, after various exorcisms had been performed on him, with a great gathering [*concursus*] of people standing around, *he was asked by which part of the column Christ had stood,* and he bit the column with his teeth, and, crying out, showed the place, saying, "Here He stood! Here He stood."[34]

One wonders whether the combination of Solomon and Christ gave rise to the idea that the column facilitated exorcism.

At any rate, it is doubtful that Kramer's sole purpose was ejecting the Bohemian's devil. Knowing precisely where Christ had stood in relation to the column could have had little to do with the success of the exorcism. Kramer wanted to make the devil either prove his authenticity by identifying the correct spot or confirm that Christ had stood at the column. In either case, Kramer's discussion reveals that the issue at stake was, not the relief of suffering, but the reality of the spiritual world. His exorcism of the Bohemian did not presume that reality; rather, it set out to prove it. Notice that Kramer waits until this point to mention the numerous witnesses to the exorcism, his signal that he has just said something of major importance.

Kramer used the demoniac to construct a palindromic proof; that is, the proof can be read in two contrasting but complementary directions, like the sentences "Madam, I'm Adam," "Able was I ere I saw Elba," or "Dog as a devil deified lived as a god."[35] Initially, Kramer asserts that people were exorcised near this column because Christ had preached near it. This implies that, if the Bohemian is cured here, we will know that he was possessed. Yet, before the Bohemian can be cured, Kramer invokes the actions of "his devil" as proof that Christ actually stood next to the column. Kramer needed to prove two complementary things: that people were exorcised next to the column because Christ stood there and that Christ must have stood there because people were exorcised there. In other words, the demon is a demon because he knows where Christ stood, but we know that Christ stood there because a demon tells us so. This proof can be made only by a leap in logic: since the Bohemian has not yet been cured, there is no proof (except his claim not to know Italian) that a devil, rather than the man himself, is discussing Christ.

The most remarkable aspect of this exorcism is its failure. The Bohemian remained possessed because, instead of coming out, the demon began to rave about sodomites. Oddly, Kramer expresses no disappointment at this defeat. Instead, he finds a Bible verse that allows him to claim a victory: "Eventually it proved that this demoniac was of that sort of which the Saviour spoke in the Gospel, saying: 'This sort goeth not out save by prayer and fasting.' For a venerable bishop, who was said to have been driven from his see by the Turks, piously took compassion on him, and by fasting on bread and water for forty days [or, for the whole period of Lent], and by daily prayers and exorcisms, at last through the grace of God delivered him and sent him back to his home rejoicing."[36] The Gospel text turns Kramer's failure into success: by surrendering to a longer and more difficult exorcism, the devil proves that he is real. But, because the demon was real, he demonstrated that the Gospel description of obstinate devils is accurate.

To furnish the proofs that were Kramer's objective, the exorcism in Saint Peter's *had* to fail initially. An effortless exorcism would have eliminated Kramer's demonic informant before it could provide the information that he craved. As Vineti intimated, this must be how necromancy of the late-medieval Christian type arose.

Richard Kieckhefer cites recent studies that provide a broader fifteenth-century context for experiments like Kramer's. There seems to have arisen "a heightened consciousness of the possibility that exorcism may be ineffective." Theologians faced a choice. They could argue "that exorcism was indeed effective on the spiritual plane even if residual bodily effects remained." The alternative explanation was "the time-honoured notion that if exorcism did not succeed then *prima facie* the condition was not truly one of demonic possession." The more frequently the latter explanation imposed itself, the more worrisome it became. An apparently contrary fifteenth-century trend, says Kieckhefer, was "*increasing* interest in exorcism as a quasi-liturgical ritual."[37] More manuals were produced, the manuals increased in length, and they suggested increasingly formalized rituals.

These trends were not contradictory or paradoxical. The less satisfactory encounters with demons were perceived to be, the more elaborate the means deployed to improve them. This is the overall trend in witchcraft theory. Conversely, Kramer shows that failure could have its rewards if sufficiently prolonged. Kieckhefer is clearly right to conclude that these trends in exorcism, together with developments in necromancy, indicate "a more general interest in the elaboration and assembly of materials for the commanding of malign spirits" during the fifteenth century.[38]

A Split Personality

Kramer and the Bohemian priest depended on the devil to alleviate their involuntary doubts about the reality of Christianity. But the devil seems to serve a slightly different purpose for each of them. Kramer exploited the devil to verify the reality of sacred relics and the divine person connected to them. The Bohemian's doubts were even more severe than Kramer's, his need for the demon more compelling. Unlike many victims of demonic possession from biblical times on, the Bohemian was apparently not an epileptic. His attacks—it is that clear Kramer is not describing convulsions—did not overtake him without warning. He did not lose self-awareness during the attacks and afterward remembered everything that he had done and said. Kramer states that, "although he was deprived of the power of the sane use of words, *yet he was always conscious of his words,* though not of their meaning." Kramer emphasized that this was an unusual form of possession, differing dramatically from the ones recorded in the Gospels.[39]

Exorcism seemed to call up and *activate* the demon rather than quieting or expelling him, contrary to the symptomology that exorcism presupposed. This anomalous symptom served the same investigative needs as necromancy. The Bohemian slipped easily in and out of possession, at the convenience of his exorcist.[40] Kramer says that, during the time that they were together,

> in all his behavior he remained a sober priest without any eccentricity, *except when the exorcisms began;* and when these were finished, and the stole was taken from his neck, he showed no sign of madness [*irrationalem*] or any immodest [*inhonestum*] action. But when he passed through any church, and genuflected in honor of the Glorious Virgin, the devil would thrust his tongue far out of his mouth; and when asked whether he could not restrain himself from doing this, the priest answered: "I cannot help myself at all, for so he uses all my limbs and organs, my neck, my tongue, and my lungs, whenever he pleases, causing me to speak or to cry out; and I hear the words which he thus speaks through me and with my body [*per me et ex membris meis*], but I am altogether unable to resist; and when I try to engage in prayer, he attacks me more violently, thrusting out my tongue."[41]

The Bohemian's intricate descriptions of the demon's control show that he needed a demon to explain away his own outrageous and sacrilegious behavior in the presence of holy things. He himself was not mocking holy things; rather, the demon was obstructing his attempts to honor them by occupying his body and making it disobey his intentions. His behavior during exorcism was a means of reenacting and modifying his sacrilegious mockeries. Exorcism provided a less ambiguous way to identify the demonic origin of actions that, outside the context of exorcism, would look like his own behaviors.

The Bohemian's detailed reports of what, on other occasions, the demon had told him "in his own words uttered through my mouth" imply that, at times, the possessed man thought of *himself* as interviewing the devil within his body.[42] The origin of his "split personality" could be explained in several ways. Modern readers could interpret the reference to sodomy as a psychosexual symptom. Perhaps the Bohemian had discovered homoerotic tendencies in himself and could not accept them. Or perhaps the conflict was familial. Kramer says that the priest's father accompanied him all the way from Bohemia to Rome and implies that the elder man mediated all his son's contacts with other people there, including other ecclesiastics. Perhaps the priest was overcome by feelings of guilt or hostility toward his controlling father. Perhaps the father had forced him into the priesthood. Translating his generational, Oedipal conflicts with his father into symbolic form, the Bohemian could have acted them out as the ultimate father-son conflict, the primordial enmity between God and the devils. Or could his hostility to the Virgin represent some repressed animosity toward his absent mother, whom Kramer never mentions?

Kramer's narrative suggests a simpler model of repression: the priest had lost faith in the reality of the divine beings described by late-medieval Catholicism. The Christian description of reality had simply lost its power to convince him. He had undergone a kind of reverse conversion, and it filled him with a conviction that he could not face.[43] He was no longer able to observe his religious duties because the whole spiritual dimension described by Christianity simply seemed unreal. He would have been exposed to doubt, for "Hussite" Bohemia in the fifteenth century was the scene of violent conflict over the nature and meaning of the sacraments. Given the dimensions of the conflict, it is unthinkable that a priest working in Bohemia could have remained ignorant of or unmoved by the questions raised.

The Bohemian's psychology fits a pattern that often prevailed in later periods of religious turmoil. Keith Thomas has observed that "obsession by the Devil was a well-known stage preceding the conversion of many Puritan saints" and, more tellingly, that "Devil-worship was one of the temptations experienced by those undergoing the depressive state which usually preceded a Puritan religious conversion."[44] Doubt and vacillation about religious truth had to be experienced as a struggle between the self and someone else. The Devil was the most logical "devil's advocate" for personal convictions that one could not bear to recognize. One outlet for distress was clearly to become possessed. Historians have seen that developing a second and alien personality gained "personal" freedoms of the everyday sort for the Salem girls and the Loudun nuns.[45] But, more important, possession allowed them to express doubts and hostilities about and even ridicule the sacred truths.

Unlike skeptics in later centuries, Kramer's Bohemian could not serenely accept his abrupt loss of belief in the spiritual dimension, much less welcome it as a gain in knowledge, a recognition, a discovery, or an insight. Yet he was apparently convinced that the invisible beings that he had formerly discerned in the cosmos had vanished, leaving a void. His sacrilegious gestures were triggered at moments when he was expected to preach, pray, or converse with supernatural personages, particularly the Virgin. Because these beings no longer seemed real, the outrages that he directed at them them initially were a wordless challenge, daring them to prove their existence, somewhat as Alonso de Espina's Jew dared the consecrated host to prove its divinity. Punishment would have comforted the young priest, as long as it implied the outraged presence of a divine personage.

But there was no response. This anxiety-ridden lack of resolution eventually translated itself symbolically into a stalemate between a pious priest anxious to worship and a devil refusing to let him. Ironically, the devil was extremely accommodating to everyone *but* the Bohemian—allowing exorcists to interview him at any time, putting up with crowds of witnesses. The extreme sociability of "his devil" suggests that the Bohemian felt an overwhelming need, not just for exoneration, but for other people's acknowledgment of his devil's reality. His possession was a cry for help, for forgiveness, for the return of his normality, but also for help recovering his belief.

A few years after the Bohemian, Gianfrancesco Pico della Mirandola performed a similar kind of symbolic representation to recover belief. But Pico pursued belief at a highly conscious level, in a book. Around 1500, he wrote a little treatise called *De imaginatione,* or *On the Imagination,* asking a number of disturbing questions about Christianity. For instance, if Christ was divine, why was he afraid to die? If Christian martyrs went happily to their deaths, why not the son of God? The best answer that Pico found was that Christ felt pity for the Jews because he knew that they would be persecuted for his death.[46] Like Kramer's Bohemian, Pico interpreted the psychology of doubt in demonic terms. Any time we doubt the validity of Christianity, he reasoned, devils must be corrupting our imagination, the weakest part of our mind, making us question the unquestionable certainties of faith.

In other words, doubt *is* the Devil. If we doubt, our minds are controlled by the Devil, who creates a *praestigium* to hide the truth from us. Over the next twenty years, Pico's doubts prompted an ongoing resistance to skepticism. First, he argued in his massive *Examen vanitatis* that we should be skeptical of skepticism and believe what the Bible says. Yet his doubt was so tenacious that, within three years of publishing this anti-Aristotelian masterpiece, he was interviewing witches, quizzing them about the spirit world, and writing the *Strix.*

Kramer's Bohemian priest lacked Pico's resources. Unlike Pico, he did not *reason* that doubt was the Devil; he *imagined* it and enacted it as theater, following the cues of his exorcists. Unable either to believe or to take responsibility for his doubt, the priest felt cut off from the certainties that formerly comforted him. He was nostalgic for his former believing self. Despite his profound doubts, the priest must have been terrified by the challenges that he had issued to the Christian pantheon: *if* these beings were real, he had committed crimes for which explicit and impressive punishments were prescribed, both in this life and in the hereafter. Moreover, purely aside from his inability to believe and his fear of punishment, his actions left him utterly alone: they placed him outside the only community that mattered—the church as community of *belief*—and destroyed his identity.

By attributing his sacrilegious gestures to the "devil," the Bohemian projected his overwhelming doubts about Christianity onto an external agent. When he reinternalized the doubt, allowing it to possess him as a demon, it relieved him of responsibility for doing and thinking the unthinkable. He experienced his alienation from church and profession as self-alienation; he had been invaded, literally *entered,* by the archetypal enemy of faith, the Devil-who-is-doubt. This demonic alter ego was an extra, alien personality that explained and symbolized the evolution of a forbidden, sacrilegious "I," an I-who-is-not-I.[47] It controlled him, not vice versa.

It is significant that Kramer never mentions the Bohemian's mother since most of the "demon's" animosity was apparently directed at the Virgin Mary. The Bohemian's antisacral "id" erupted as a despondent reaction to the silence of putative spiritual beings who were supposed to maintain a constant, comforting contact with humanity. Mary was the most compassionate of these figures. God the Father was more just than merciful, and God the Son could be about as forbidding as his wrathful father: think of representations of the Last Judgment. But Mary was the Mother of Mercy and the Advocate of Sinners: however distant and unresponsive the Father and Son, she was always available. Women could identify with Mary through the experiences of motherhood and grief. Among men, Mary was the object of devotion that was both filial and eroticized. As Alonso de Espina remarked, artists always depicted Mary in the most beautiful and charming terms possible, reserving ugliness and vituperation for devils.[48] No age has willingly depicted Mary as plain or physically ill favored, so it is hardly surprising that her male devotees normally transferred to her all the emotions that they had ever felt for real mothers and beloveds.

This was particularly true of clerics, whose ideal of celibacy forbade the experience of sexual love, and who were often separated from their mothers at an early age to be educated. The tender feelings subtracted from living women were redirected toward Mary; after 1400, her presence was made more concrete through increasingly realistic paintings and statues. To feel Mary becoming distant and unreal must have occasioned a traumatic sense of abandonment in the Bohemian priest. To experience paintings and statues of Mary as inanimate *things* rather than as signs of presence must have further intensified his sense of abandonment. Protestant opposition to images may originally have derived less from abstract theology than from the kind of despondency felt by Kramer's Bohemian priest. This painful psychology of the image as an unintentional mockery must have contributed to the revulsion that many early Protestants felt toward Catholic "idolatry."

Not only could he not acknowledge his doubts, but the Bohemian was also unable to ignore the spiritual void that yawned before him. The more others proclaimed the reality of Christianity, and the more his vocation required him to proclaim that reality through preaching, the less he was convinced.

But the experience of possession had a deeper psychological utility. In Christian myth, Satan and the other devils rebelled against another *presence,* not against an abstract idea of God. By personifying his unwilling resistance to Christian theology as invasion by a rebellious demon, the Bohemian translated his skepticism into the mythological terms of Christianity itself. Once he had personified his doubt as a devil, the persons against whom the devil rebelled were automatically construed as presences. The more the Bohemian's devil mocked Christianity, the more he affirmed it. He addressed Mary as a real presence and spoke to her in the second person, creating an I/thou relationship. (Recall that Vineti based the proof of exorcistic efficacy on the fact that verbs are used in the imperative.)

Even so, the devil's mockeries only partially recovered the presence of Mary. The Bohemian regained her as a presence that was perpetually *about to be lost,* rather than *already* lost. Continuing to repeat the mockery obsessively prolonged the moment just before Mary would abandon the Bohemian, and left him in suspense, halfway between union and alienation, belief and despair. The legend of the rebellious angels thus served as a crucible, alchemically transforming a dread of absence into a hatred of presence. Like demonic copulation, spirit possession called presence into being, gave it a human vessel. Thus, possession recovered the foundation of all Christian theology.

Spiritual Algebra

The priest's private mythology foreshadowed Christian polemicists of more than a century later, who compared disbelief in God to the Greco-Roman myth of the giants' revolt against Jove. The Bohemian transformed his frightening intimations of nothingness into a conflict between two almost equally matched forces, casting himself as passive spectator. This was a personal form of gnosticism, but it was not totally at odds with Christianity. Through the elaborate choreography of possession and exorcism, he staged his psychic conflict in concrete terms. Possession allowed him to imagine that the spiritual void before his eyes was not absolute. The sacred realities were undeniably there, but his inability to venerate them came about because they were being opposed by almost equally powerful forces.

This algebra of positive and negative forces is so starkly schematized that it almost resembles calculations of electrodynamics. This concept of "neutralization" also undergirds *praestigium* as well as the general concept of witchcraft: phalluses, sacraments, and divine personages are all there in reality, but their presence is being systematically hidden by another presence. Zero is not "absolute zero": $0 \neq 0$. Instead, zero is the sum of one and minus one: $0 = [1] + [-1]$. The sacred reality is not "really" absent; it has been *momentarily* overcome or eclipsed by its demonic opposite. When faith is impossible, doubt is incarnated as the Devil. But, precisely because doubt is the Devil, God is possible. Thanks to the Devil, God's presence can be inferred even when his works are imperceptible. Very late defenders of witch-hunting phrased this idea with terrifying lucidity: *Nullus Deus sine diabolo.* Without proof of a devil, there can be no proof of God.[49]

The Bohemian's case comforted Kramer: it implied that, like the man who wrongly believes that he is castrated, we are fooled by demons whenever we become unable to recognize the efficacy of God's sacraments or the world of spirit. Dysfunction, whether sexual or religious, must never be traceable to mental or physical conditions peculiar to the individual or to the natural course of things. A powerful demonic interference *must be* causing our inability to perceive that our fondest hopes and dreams are already realized.

Witchcraft theorists wanted to awake and discover that "it's all true": that what the imagination desires has already come to pass. Not surprisingly, some theorists were fascinated by sleepwalking because it offered a setting in which reality could be identical with dreams, fantasies, or imaginations. One could dream of walking and wake to find oneself actually walking.[50] More often than not, however, reality was a nightmare rather than a golden dream. Witches and devils were essential for explaining why this should be so and why it was not God's fault.

Explicit Theorization

Witchcraft seems a very different concept from necromancy and exorcism, but all three shared the daydream of interacting with demons. Like the witch, the possessed person experienced *corporeal* interaction with a demon—hence the strong emphasis on bodily signs and symptoms in possession and exorcism. The interdependence of witchcraft and exorcism became thoroughly explicit in the literature of exorcism after Kramer's time. He had discussed exorcism to prove the reality of witchcraft; thanks to him, witchcraft was invoked to show that possession and exorcism were not imaginary.

One example can suffice: the *Compendio dell'arte essorcistica, et possibilità delle mirabili, et stupende operationi delli demoni et de i malefici,* or *Encyclopedia of the Exorcist's Art, and of the Possibility of the Wondrous and Stupendous Operations of Demons and Witches,* published by the Franciscan Girolamo Menghi in 1576. It was not a manual for exorcists, although Menghi wrote at least two of those.[51] Rather, as its title implies, it was a refutation of the charge that spirit possession was *impossible.* Menghi aimed to combat the views of

> certain men who are too arrogant in their opinions, and wise only in their own estimation, who have been seduced and persuaded by the father of all errors and lies, so that they not only don't believe, but don't *want* to believe, in the truth of all that is treated in this present work, and moreover go about spreading and persuading this caprice of theirs in the minds of the simple people [*pusilli*]. And this persuasion of theirs has grown so in the mind of the common folk [*volgo*] that many, firmly embracing their error, have tried to defend the idea that the things discussed in this present encyclopedia are fictions and human inventions.[52]

Menghi's *Compendio* rehearses all the arguments that witchcraft theory had found for the reality of demons. It reveals the same fear of nature and imagination, cites the same authorities, and shies away from the same bugbears. As Vineti and Kramer had done, Menghi discussed incidents of possession almost exclusively as proof of demonic reality; most of his examples have the same experimental flavor as Kramer's account of the Bohemian priest.

Not until page 387 of 614 did Menghi begin to discuss spirit possession, and he linked it firmly to the crime of witchcraft. This is not surprising since Menghi's principal source was the *Malleus maleficarum.* Menghi made such extensive use of Kramer's book that he decided to warn his readers. The phrase "the abovementioned authors," he said, should *always* be interpreted as a reference to the *Malleus.*[53]

Menghi still felt that he must reply to objections that modern devils *rarely* gave the signs of their presence that Aquinas had listed, such as speaking languages unknown by the possessed persons. To prove that such objections were groundless, he told the story of Kramer's Bohemian.[54]

13

WITCHCRAFT, BODY, AND SOUL

But surely such apparitions ought to be be feared, not desired.

—Johann von Frankfurt, *Quaestio, utrum potestas cohercendi demones fieri possit per caracteres, figuras atque verborum prolationes* (1412)

By the seventeenth century, epidemics of demonic possession commanded about as much attention as epidemics of witchcraft. The phenomena were often linked causally in descriptions by contemporaries. Several scholars have interpreted this as a "discovery" of the sixteenth century, but Aquinas prepared the discovery more than three centuries earlier. Aquinas connected possession and *maleficia* as demonstrations of the power—and thus the existence—of "some intellect" beyond the human sphere.

Around 1460, when Kramer was exorcising the Bohemian, theorists like Vineti, Visconti, Alonso de Espina, and other frightened Christians were also assembling evidence that spirits were real. Although it is difficult to see a uniform concept of witchcraft in their writings, they all agreed that demonic reality can be proved if corporeal interaction is a fact. Like the other theorists, Kramer intuited a connection between learned theories of possession and exorcism, which were based ultimately on the New Testament and folk concepts such as the night followers of Diana and infanticidal, castrating witches. However, Kramer explained the connections in greater detail than his theorist colleagues, perhaps in part owing to the time that he spent on research. Over two decades elapsed between meeting the Bohemian and publishing the *Malleus*.

Inventing Witchcraft

Kramer was unusually prone to claim firsthand experience as the basis for his explanations. For exorcism and possession, he drew on his own direct experience of the Bohemian's devil. But he also relied on the Bohemian's experience, taking advantage of privileged information that the Bohemian claimed to have received from the devil. Long before

Kramer defined witches as expert witnesses to demonic reality, the Bohemian described minutely how demons operated. This encounter probably stimulated Kramer's interest in witches. At any rate, it is the earliest personal experience that Kramer mentions in the *Malleus*.

Kramer reveals that the Bohemian initially intrigued him because he offered *no* evident support for the reality of spirits and possession. The young man's symptoms suggested a naturally occurring malady:

> It happened that I . . . went into an inn to eat, and that priest and his father came and sat down at the same table with me. We talked together while we ate, as is customary; and the father kept sighing and hoping to Almighty God that his journey might prove to be successful. I felt great pity for him, and began to ask what was the reason of his journey and of his sorrow. Then he, in the hearing of his son, who was sitting next to me at the table, answered: "Alas! I have a son possessed by a devil, and with great trouble and expense I have brought him here to be delivered." And when I asked where the son was, he showed me him sitting by my side. I was a little frightened [*atterritus*], and looked at him closely; *and because he took his food with such modesty, and answered respectfully* [*pie*] *to all questions, I began to wonder* [*hesitare animo cepi*] *whether he was actually possessed, and to suspect that something had happened to him because of a physical infirmity.*[1]

Kramer's "initial fright" is conventional, obligatory, and far less interesting than the doubt that immediately replaced it: whatever was wrong with the young man, Kramer thought, could well have natural causes.

But the Bohemian had a different explanation: "Then the son himself told what had happened, showing how and for how long he had been possessed, and saying: 'A certain witch brought this evil upon me. For I was rebuking her on some matter concerned with the discipline of the Church, upbraiding her rather strongly since she was of an obstinate disposition, when she said that after a few days that would happen to me which has happened.' "[2] Since both priest and witch were Bohemians, it is tempting to speculate that "matters of Church discipline" might have involved Hussitism. Did she demand communion under both species, or did disagreement over other dogma and practice set off the priest's crisis?

Such speculations are less useful than the firm evidence that Kramer provides. His Bohemian's explanation of his malady is a hybrid. It shows the standard formulas of witchcraft accusations made by neighbors: "I quarreled with her; she threatened me; her threat came true; thus she is a witch." By saying that the witch caused his *possession,* however, the priest introduced a devil into the peasant model. Kramer's Bohemian did not invent the connection between spirit possession and witchcraft. Rather, he easily produced the learned theory of witchcraft from raw materials that he found in his two cultures: peasant accusations of *maleficium* and learned theories about spirit possession.

Kramer's and the priest's reactions to the witch show why the hybrid model of demonic witchcraft was so attractive to fifteenth-century clerics. They also show what did *not* interest them. Folk wisdom would have counseled the Bohemian to find the witch and convince or force her to undo the charm, but he apparently never made the attempt. Nor did he show any interest in denouncing her to the inquisition, as witchcraft theorists were beginning to demand in those years. Kramer mentions neither of these solutions here: a highly suspicious omission since he discusses both courses of action at length elsewhere in the *Malleus*. If the two men ever discussed having the witch apprehended and brought to trial, Kramer neglected to tell us. Had she been found and prosecuted, Kramer would not have failed to exult over her downfall and claim personal credit for it, as he did in other cases. Significantly, she is never mentioned again.

Kramer was apparently uninterested even in the expert testimony of this witch. Perhaps at the time, nearly a quarter century before the *Malleus,* Kramer did not yet consider witches expert witnesses. Instead, he and the Bohemian were fascinated by the testimony of the demon. According to the priest, "The devil which possesses me has told me that a charm was placed by the witch under a certain tree, and that until it was removed I could not be delivered; but he would not tell me which was the tree."[3] From the beginning, it appears, the Bohemian was interested only in interviewing his internal devil.

Kramer was fascinated by learning that the Bohemian had been interviewing his devil; but something that the devil told the Bohemian was even more intriguing: "He seemed to have more use of his reason than is usual in the case of persons possessed, and when I asked him about the length of his lucid intervals, he answered: 'I am only deprived of the use of my reason when I wish to contemplate holy things or to visit sacred places. For the devil specifically told me in his own words uttered through my mouth that, because he had up to that time been much offended by my sermons to the people, he would in no way allow me to preach.'" This testimony finally unleashed Kramer's curiosity: he claims that this is why "I, the inquisitor, *wishing for proofs of all these things,* had him taken for a fortnight and more to various holy places."[4]

De singulis certificari volebam: Heinrich Kramer *wanted to be made certain* that the devil was real, and not in the banal sense that exorcists and demonologists routinely claimed. It was not a matter of standard checks for disease or other natural symptoms, nor was the fundamental issue the existence of a particular demon. Rather, if the Bohemian's devil turned out to be real, it offered a possible proof that the entire spiritual dimension was real. There was no more suggestive case of possession than a devil who surfaced *only* to obstruct reverence to God.

Kramer's Bohemian was a prophetic figure. His type of possession took on epidemic proportions a century later, when witchcraft theory and witch-hunting rekindled after the long lull of the early Reformation. It has been observed that only in this second witch-hunting period was possession widely attributed to witchcraft; only then did possession manifest itself in such widespread hysteria. The seventeenth-century cases of Loudun, Louviers, and Salem are three of the latest and best documented.[5] But there were also serious outbreaks before 1600.

In 1580, Andrea Cesalpino, who had read the *Malleus* carefully, cited a number of examples of possession among Pisan nuns. One of these incidents inspired his book as well as another demonological treatise, Francesco de' Vieri's *Intorno a' dimonij volgarmente chiamati spiriti,* or *Discourse about Demons Commonly Known as "Spirits."*[6] In 1574–75, the archbishop of Pisa had consulted a number of theologians, physicians, and philosophers, including Cesalpino and Vieri, about an outbreak of possession in the convent of St. Anne.[7] In conformity with the symptoms defined by Aquinas, nuns in this convent had suddenly begun speaking languages that they were supposed not to know; but they also showed a violent aversion to attending religious services. One Pisan nun, says Cesalpino, ceased being possessed the moment she left the church building.[8]

In what could almost be a retelling of Kramer's story about the Bohemian, Cesalpino adds that the same symptoms afflicted a priest of Speyer, who was brought to Rome to be freed from his demon. This man was perfectly well except when he was in church, where he suddenly became possessed. Cesalpino does not recount the outcome of this case, but the priest's symptoms, like those of the nuns, are identical to the ones exhibited by Kramer's priest: "The possessed testify [*testantur*] that when they are in their right mind they wish to carry out the rites of the church and crave the assistance of the sacraments but that something dwelling [*insitum*] in the members of their bodies opposes this."[9]

Cesalpino was trying to reduce evidence of demons to a science. He admitted that there were ambiguous cases when, "in addition to physical illness, which can appear to have natural causes, no supernatural effects stand out [*ostenduntur*], so that it is uncertain whether someone is suffering because of witchcraft [*maleficio*]." Nonetheless, he claimed that the effects of demons were absolutely clear (*manifestissimi*) in some possessed persons. And "the most certain and inseparable sign of a demonic inhabitant" is when someone is prevented from worshiping, when they can neither speak nor bear to hear holy words, and particularly if they suffer when forced to be present for mass or to carry out ceremonies of the church. Not surprisingly, Cesalpino goes on to generalize from this opposition: the difference between religion and magic is that "the latter uses superstitious means and the invocation of demons, while the former employs divine and sacred names to dissolve every power of the Devil."[10]

The famous outbreaks of mass possession in the 1600s involved women in highly religious communities: particularly Catholic nuns, but also the Puritan girls of Salem. These women were confined and subjected to endless rounds of rigid piety. When they rebelled in the only socially acceptable way, they were often exploited in public spectacles, not only at trials, but in full-fledged theatrical performances, where exorcists and theologians encouraged them to let their "demons" run wild. Nineteenth-century physicians discussed mass possession to illustrate their highly misogynistic ideas about female physiology and psychology, notably "hysteria"—ailments caused by the womb. Responding to their own contemporary cultural givens, modern scholars have suspected pornography and voyeurism in the mania for possession and exorcism. Hollywood filmmakers have obligingly endowed the idea with images and bodies.[11]

But sexuality was not the only or the ultimate reason for these outbreaks, nor was the problem entirely a matter of gender. Although later epidemics of possession occurred largely among groups of women, it is extremely significant that Kramer's very early case involved a solitary male, a cleric. Both Kramer and Cesalpino give other examples of clerics showing these symptoms.[12]

Possession brought repressed sexuality to the surface and displayed it publicly. Men exploited and often provoked these crises, but their motives were not uniquely or primarily pornographic. The sexual agency being ogled by the ecclesiastical managers of such spectacles was demonic, not human. Even more than theorists like Kramer and Cesalpino, these impresarios were *metaphysical* voyeurs. They scrutinized bodies hoping to glimpse "spirit." The problem is complex, but women were culturally determined as the primary sufferers of mass possession for the same reason that they were stereotyped as more likely than men to copulate with demons. Because women were viewed as passive, more material, and less "spiritual" than men, demons would *have* to manifest themselves by acting on women.

The Growth of Experimentation

Kramer's exorcism was an experiment: he needed to convince himself that his initial suspicion of natural causes was invalid. Hearing the priest's tale, Kramer gave in to his experimental inclinations: "But I would have placed no faith at all in his words, if experience [or experiment: *experientia*] had not enlightened me further." Since the Bohemian priest claimed that the devil made his presence known only under certain circumstances, Kramer spent the next two weeks testing every possible variant of those circumstances, "in various holy places," aiming to observe and interview the devil.[13]

Kramer's experiment illustrates Richard Kieckhefer's contention that the "clerical underground" of exorcists gave birth to necromancy. Necromancy was an art, a practice of learned men. Only after several centuries did the idea arise that unlearned people were engaging in a new kind of corporeal interaction with spirits.[14] It is crucial to recall with Kieckhefer that this clerical underground was involved in *experiments*. Many experiments were clearly oriented toward interviewing demons for the purpose of verifying their reality. Obtaining the illicit power stereotypically associated with necromancy was often a minor concern.

Menghi tells of an exorcistic experiment from 1323. A Dominican exorcist, called in by a frightened widow to exorcise the ghost of her late husband, quizzed it on the sacraments, purgatory, and other matters of faith. One of the cleric's companions forced the ghost to guess (successfully, of course) items that he was carrying on his person.[15]

Such experiments help explain why necromancers often made dramatic and apparently sincere claims to be motivated by good and holy purposes, even though church policy officially disapproved of necromancy. Moreover, ecclesiastical disapproval did not necessarily imply a desire to see demonological investigations cease. It was tempting to look for a way of contacting spirits without personally invoking them or making sinful bargains with them. Locating willing or unwilling proxies—the possessed, necromancers, and, finally, witches—ultimately became the favored solution.

In their personal lives, intellectuals like Kramer may never have acknowledged or even noticed the skepticism that drove their researches from exorcism into necromancy and, finally, into witchcraft. But, in their writings, doubts shine brightly through the language that they used and the experimental situations that they described. Doubt was present from the beginning of necromancy and grew throughout the time during which witch-hunting was becoming established. Fuller knowledge of Aristotle's works after 1100 did more than anything to make doubt about spirits possible. We have seen that Aquinas and his followers were profoundly disturbed by the implication that natural causes, including astrology, might be responsible for the magical effects that they wished to attribute to demons. Contact with Muslim scholarship brought other influences as well, among them "new conceptions of the occult sciences, including astrology, alchemy, and related areas of natural magic."[16]

As Richard Kieckhefer observes, this revolution in knowledge created several conflicting conceptions of magic. "The tendency of the uneducated seems to have been to see magic as natural, while intellectuals were torn between three conceptions. Following early Christian writers, they might see all magic (even that of the common tradition) as relying at least implicitly on demons; with the transmission of Islamic scholarship in the twelfth century, intellectuals increasingly acknowledged (whether enthusiastically or grudgingly) that a great deal of magic was natural; yet the real and express invocations of demons by necromancers renewed old apprehensions and made educated people all the more suspicious that magic was really demonic, even if it appeared natural."[17] This admirable synthesis of several hundred years of theology and natural philosophy needs one modification. Acknowledgment that some wondrous effects had nondemonic causes was more grudging than historians have suspected. The "apprehensions" and "suspicions" may have been phrased in condemnatory rhetoric, but more often than not they were motivated by an ambivalent logic that derived from hope as well as from fear. Fear was sometimes largely absent.

The thirteenth century was a crucial period in the development of necromancy as both idea and practice.[18] This was the age of Aquinas, and there is clear evidence that necromancy was already under consideration as a way of investigating whether spirits really existed or were capable of interaction with humans. Around the time Aquinas was born, the German Cistercian monk Caesarius of Heisterbach wrote his *Dialogus miraculorum*, or *Dialogue on Miracles* (1225), which was very influential in the later Middle Ages. Prefiguring Nider and other witchcraft theorists, Caesarius couched his ideas in a kind of catechism, a dialogue between a learned monk and a curious, somewhat skeptical novice. In the fifth *distinctio* (or book) of the dialogue, the novice professes to have "no doubt in my mind" about angels since they are mentioned in the Bible but says that he wants to hear the biblical evidence for demons. When the older monk provides a complete list, the novice then admits: "I do not confess myself satisfied, unless you make these things clear by *living* [or lively: *vivacibus*] examples."[19]

Despite his opening gambit, the novice admits that biblical authority is not enough. Hearing of contemporary experiences with demons would make them seem more real. This attitude is presumably less culpable in a novice than in an older monk, so the latter obliges, using arguments that are by now familiar to us: "That there are demons, that they are many, and that they are wicked, I shall be able to show you by many examples." Then, speaking in the persona of someone other than Caesarius, the monk attributes a story to him about a clerical necromancer and a curious layman:

> There was a knight, whose name was Henry . . . [who] was butler of our fellow monk, Caesarius, when he was Abbot of Prüm. Now, as I have heard from Caesarius himself, this knight did not believe in the existence of demons, but looked upon anything that he . . . ever had heard about them as mere frivolous nonsense; and therefore he sent for a certain cleric named Philip, who was most famous for his skill in necromancy, and besought him earnestly to show him some demons. His reply was that demons were both horrible and dangerous to look upon, and that it was not good for all men to see them. But when the knight continued eagerly to urge his request, he went on, "If you will guarantee that I shall receive no harm from your friends or relations, if by chance you shall be deceived or terrified or injured by the demons, I will consent." And he gave him the guarantee.[20]

On the appointed day, at the fateful hour of noon, Philip placed Henry inside a magic circle and warned him not to step outside it or give or promise the demons anything, lest they kill him. He also commanded Henry not to make the sign of the cross, and, unusually for this kind of story, Henry obeyed, and the efficacy of the sacramental gesture was therefore never tested. While both Henry and Philip had spoken of demons in the plural, only one came to the appointment. Henry interviewed the demon at length, learning firsthand about his power, speed, and knowledge. The demon even knew some of Henry's own sins, including where he lost his virginity.[21]

Predictably, the demon eventually frightened Henry almost mortally: "From that time forward the knight was deathly pale, and never regained his former healthy color; he lived more correctly [*emendatius*], and had no doubts henceforth concerning the existence of demons. He died a little while ago." Paradoxically, Caesarius allows the demon to defend himself against the charge that he is evil: "When the devil asked what he had heard about him, the knight replied 'Very little good and much evil.' To which the devil said: 'Men often judge and condemn me without good cause; I have harmed no one, I never attack anyone unless provoked. Your Master Philip is a good friend of mine, and I of his; ask him if I have ever offended him. I do his pleasure and he obliges me in all things; it was by his summons that I have come to you now.' "[22]

Morality is beside the point in this story. If Caesarius considered necromancy so abhorrent, why did he allow this devil to defend himself? Why is there no condemnation of Philip, a cleric, for experimenting with devils? Furthermore, the devil's self-justification was not entirely specious: he made no attempt to harm Henry until the man denied a number of very civil requests. Of course, Satan is the Father of Lies. Another friend of Philip's, a stupid priest, was killed by a devil when he stepped outside the magic circle, and it is believed (*creditur*) that Philip himself was finally killed by his devil.[23]

Caesarius's story very adroitly refrains from asserting that Henry actually *saw* the devil, although that was his main objective. When the devil arrived, Henry said, "You have done well to come, because I wanted to see [*videre*] you. . . . Because I have heard [*audivi*] so much about you." Yet the devil's arrival is depicted through Henry's *lack* of vision. Initially, Henry heard loud and horrible noises that frightened him, but he did not look away: "Last of all, he saw in a neighboring wood a figure *like a horrible* [*tetram*] *human shadow* higher than the tops of the trees, hastening towards him, and *he understood* [*intellexit*] at once that this was the devil, as indeed it was." The vision did not become much clearer when the devil arrived: "He was in appearance like a gigantic man, very huge and *very black,* clothed in a *dark* robe, and so hideous [*tantae deformitatis*] that *the knight could not look upon him.*"[24] From the beginning, the point of the story was to make the skeptical Henry *see* a devil, but the reader is never certain that the skeptic had more than a glimpse.

What we do know is that Henry *heard* the devil and interviewed him, just as an exorcist would have done. The necromancer, Philip, was suspiciously absent throughout the demonic interview and reappeared only in response to Henry's terrified screams. Yet Caesarius does not present this as a trick. It is proof by lived experience that demons are real, furnished by a witness who, owing to his harrowing experience, is no longer available for confirmation. Since the witness is dead, we have to rely on Caesarius, of course, as the authority guaranteeing that all this happened.

But, in a final paradox, the storytelling monk invokes Caesarius's authority for the veracity of the incident—yet the monk is clearly presented as a fiction created by Caesarius. Where is the truth in this closed circuit? One thing is certain: the entire purpose of Caesarius's fifth *distinctio* is to prove that demons are real. In answer to the novice's doubts, fifty-six chapters narrate numerous other encounters with demons. These demons are not only seen and heard; they interact corporeally: some cause physical harm; others render services to people. At the end of these tales, the novice declares himself convinced "by both teaching and examples, that demons exist, that they are many, that they are evil, and that they are harmful to people."[25]

Nearly four centuries later, Christopher Marlowe's *Doctor Faustus* presents the same uneasy skepticism, with a difference: now, necromancer and skeptic are the same man. In the meantime, the illiterate witch had been invented; she became the primary seeker of demonic experiences, overshadowing the exorcist and the necromancer. So much lore had accumulated about witchcraft that Marlowe's play makes Faustus a hybrid witch-necromancer.

Doctor Faustus also exhibits the striking discrepancy between the rhetoric and the logic of witchcraft theory, for Faustus's avowed goals of wealth and power do not correspond with his behavior. First-year university students are often puzzled by the discrepancy. A typical question in the first hour of discussion is: "Faustus claims he wants money and power; so why does he spend so much time on these stupid practical jokes?"[26] The simplest answer is that Faustus really *isn't* interested in wealth and power. He wants knowledge—in particular, reliable knowledge about the suprahuman and supernatural.

To take the most obvious example, he wastes his time and Mephastophilis's patience with questions that any catechized Christian child should be able to answer: "Tell me, what is that Lucifer thy lord? . . . Was not Lucifer an angel once? . . . How comes it then that he is prince of devils? . . . And what are you that live with Lucifer? . . . And where are you damned? . . . How comes it then that thou art out of hell?"[27] But Faustus is not wasting time: he is interviewing an informant.

Hell is a major problem for Faustus, and he returns to it again and again. Once he signs away his soul, Mephastophilis prepares to fulfill his wishes, but Faustus is suddenly uninterested in power and wealth:

MEPHASTOPHILIS: Now Faustus, ask what thou wilt.
FAUSTUS: First will I question with thee about hell.
Tell me, where is the place that men call hell?

Hearing the demon's eloquent and theologically correct reply, Faustus reveals his real agenda; this provokes a rejoinder that, although apparently banal, is the key to the play's apparent contradictions:

FAUSTUS: Come, I think hell's a fable.
MEPHASTOPHILIS: Aye, think so still, till experience change thy mind.
FAUSTUS: Why? think'st thou then that Faustus shall be damned?
MEPHASTOPHILIS: Aye, of necessity, for here's the scroll
Wherein thou hast given thy soul to Lucifer.
FAUSTUS: Aye, and body too; but what of that?

> Thinkest thou that Faustus is so fond to imagine
> That after this life there is any pain?
> Tush, these are trifles and mere old wives' tales.
> MEPHASTOPHILIS: But Faustus, *I am an instance to prove the contrary;*
> for I am damned, and am now in hell.[28]

Faustus is, not merely a skeptic, but a Sadducee and an Epicurean. The real object of his quest is confirming the existence of spirits, including his own soul. His occasional jauntiness and greed barely disguise this more serious purpose.

Faustus's ideal is a round-trip ticket to hell, an experience that would be firsthand but not terminal: "O might I see hell, and return again, how happy were I then." The Latin word for happy is *faustus,* so Marlowe apparently considered the desire to see hell an essential part of his necromancer's character. Other plays on words reinforce this idea. When Faustus conjures up the specter of Helen of Troy, one of the scholars who requested this favor is so dazzled by Helen's beauty that he exclaims: "For this glorious deed *Happy* and *blest* be *Faustus* evermore." Once Faustus has seen "the face that launched a thousand ships," he cannot be happy without possessing Helen and begs Mephastophilis to make her his paramour. His wish granted, he is in ecstasy: "Sweet Helen, make me immortal with a kiss: Her lips sucks forth my soul, see where it flies!"[29]

Of course, "Helen" is a *succubus,* so the pun is doubly ironic. An assumed body makes the devil disguised as Helen seem as if it were "no spirit, but a true substantial body."[30] In exchange, the succubus seems to make Faustus's soul visible: "See where it flies." In the light of the play's insistence on embodied spirits, we are probably supposed to imagine that Faustus actually sees, or thinks he sees, his soul flittering away. He has wanted all along to see his soul and know that it is real, but now he loses it in the instant he sees it: "Come, Helen, come, give me my soul again."[31]

This demonic kiss is Faustus's last onstage act before the devils destroy his body and carry his soul to hell. Bodies, particularly the ones assumed by Mephastophilis and Helen, have been the medium of proof throughout the play. When Faustus conjured a demon who impersonated Alexander the Great, he did so to satisfy the emperor's curiosity about the bodily characteristics and appearance of Alexander. The emperor commanded Faustus to "let me see some proof of thy skill, that mine eyes may be witnesses to confirm what mine ears have heard reported."[32] This was precisely the skeptical Henry's request to the necromancer Philip four centuries earlier.

Proof has been Faustus's obsession all his life. One of his former university colleagues asks, "I wonder what's become of Faustus, that was wont to make our schools ring with *sic probo.*" Faustus's refrain was "Thus I prove": like the history of necromancy itself, his quest was inspired by the principles of Scholastic philosophy. He was ready to "live and die in Aristotle's works" until he suspected that Scholastic proofs prove nothing: "Is to dispute well logic's chiefest end? Affords this art no greater miracle?"[33] Did he, like Aquinas's other heirs, discover that Aristotle nowhere supports the reality of demons? Only physical contact with an embodied demon can prove that hell and the soul exist, that the soul is a *substance* that can be bought and sold, contracted away like any other *thing*.

That contract shows Faustus's Sadduceeism was never insouciant; it was serious, even despondent. The soul poses a dilemma: the only way to prove that one has a soul is to lose it. So Faustus evolves from reluctant skeptic to despondent believer: "Why wert thou not a creature wanting soul? Or why is this immortal that thou hast? . . . All beasts are happy, for when they die, Their souls are soon dissolved in elements; But mine must live still to be plagued in hell." Where is the solution? Perhaps this: "Let Faustus live in hell a thousand years, A hundred thousand, and at last be saved."[34] But there is no happy ending for Faustus: a round-trip ticket to hell is impossible.

A better question is what the reader or theatergoer should do. Marlowe gives the same answer that Bartolomeo Spina and other witchcraft theorists gave when they discussed experiments with witches: take my word for it, be very afraid, and don't try the experiments at home. "Faustus is gone! Regard his hellish fall, Whose fiendful fortune may exhort the wise Only to wonder at unlawful things."[35] For Marlowe's audience, Faustus's final despair over having a soul was as comforting as his initial skeptical denial was frightening. They might have agreed with a later anguished skeptic who pleaded, "Let heaven exist, though my place be in hell."[36] That hell exists means, at least, that personal annihilation does not.

Faustus systematically tries to verify the supposed truths of Christianity but never discovers a proof that satisfies him. This despondent quest goes a long way toward explaining why real-life necromancers, who, like Faustus, "should have known better," engaged in an activity that they knew was punishable by harsh penalties. Perhaps, after all, their pretensions to virtue and piety were neither hypocritical nor in conflict with their activities.[37] If any of them read Aquinas or witchcraft theorists, they must have intuited that blistering condemnations of necromancy and witchcraft were often a rhetorical feint. For their part, witchcraft theorists, especially professional witch-hunters like Bartolomeo Spina, intuited that necromancy could never provide the ironclad, first-person experience with demons that they craved. They could repress this wish but not eliminate it; it returned to consciousness transformed into the notion that other people must be having the contact with demons that learned and pious men like themselves could never experience.

Like Faustus, witchcraft theorists longed to see hell and return, but they were willing to settle for tales of the Sabbat, which they theorized as a temporary observable hell-on-earth. That they sought testimony of experiences with demons suggests that they had failed in their own attempts at direct contact or were afraid of failure. By collecting these narratives, they became necromancers by proxy, so to speak. Kramer's definition of expert witnesses and the questions that he asked his own expert witnesses suggest that the witch was an unpaid, involuntary laboratory assistant. She served a would-be necromancer who was either incapable of performing the experiments on his own or unwilling to risk their failure. Most of all, he was unable to acknowledge the logic of his activity.

The witch's fictitious confession of firsthand physical experience was extorted or ventriloquized under the cruelest of conditions and was prized as expert testimony to the same demonic marvels that obsessed Doctor Faustus. Her terrible example offered the same admonition as his, to abandon skepticism and embrace fear. The narrative of her crimes and the spectacle of her punishment constituted a warning to "regard her hellish fall" and *only wonder* at unlawful activities, rather than trying them.

The ostensible moral to be learned from Faustus and witches was to avoid damnation; the covert lesson, the one betrayed by their "contradictions" and "illogic," was to avoid disappointment. The deep fear was not that one might be harmed by demons or even by one's coinquisitors. The secret fear was not even that one might repeat Faustus's "hellish fall" and discover having a soul to lose. Rather, one might come to believe that Faustus had been right at the beginning of the play, when he was still a skeptic.

The danger was loss of faith, not loss of salvation, and the deep fear was that we have nothing to fear but nothing to fear itself. Bartolomeo Spina understood this better than almost anyone else: the object of the experiment was to find a demon, but failure to disprove demonic presence would have to suffice. "Here's the demon" was an unattainable goal, so "The demon *isn't not* here" would have to do. Still, there was a hidden bonus: since nothing could disprove the devil's presence, he became ipso facto omnipresent. Witchcraft theorists could blithely argue that his apparent absence was the strongest possible proof of his presence. Like God, he was present both when he appeared to be absent and when everyone agreed that he was present.[38]

The Bohemian's delusion and Kramer's exploitation of it provide a strikingly compact instance of the fundamental syndrome that characterized witchcraft theory, witch-hunting, and mass possession: every suspected absence must be experienced and theorized as a surplus of presence: $0 \neq 0$; $0 = [1] + [-1]$. Kramer and the Bohemian needed to believe that their inability to perceive divine presence was an illusion, a *praestigium diabolicum* caused by a perfect equilibrium of positive and negative suprahuman forces. The alternative to this stalemate was admitting that imperceptible presences were unverifiable by experience and thus potentially imaginary. If spirit was imaginary, was matter the only reality?

Is the Human Soul Immortal?

This is not a modern or "postmodern" idea. It was pre-Christian, and Christianity never entirely stamped it out.[39] One name for it was Epicureanism. Dante inveighed against Epicureans in the early 1300s, condemning them to hell for refusing to believe in the immortality of the soul.[40] A few decades later, Boccaccio said of Dante's contemporary Guido Cavalcanti that "he leaned somewhat toward the opinions of the Epicureans" and that "it was said among the common folk that these philosophical speculations of [Guido's] were solely directed toward the possibility of discovering that God did not exist."[41] (As usually happened in such accusations, Boccaccio presents atheism as an impious, conscious hope rather than an unwilling, dreadful conviction.)

Epicurean ideas reemerged in terrifying detail in 1417, when Poggio Bracciolini rediscovered the long poem *De rerum natura,* or *On Nature,* by the Roman poet Lucretius (d. ca. 55 B.C.E.). Following Epicurus, Lucretius declared that "death is nothing to us, since the nature of the mind is mortal . . . so, when the parting shall have come about between body and spirit . . . then nothing at all will be able to happen to us, [for we] will then no longer be."[42] Here is the original declaration that we have nothing to fear but nothing to fear itself. It is the ancestor of Faustus's skepticism, but with a cheerful face.

No philosophy was as threatening to an insecure Christian as the materialism of the Greek and Roman atomists. These ancient philosophers attempted to overcome the fear of death directly, rather than positing an equal and opposite force of antideath or "eternal life." To a person who has grown up hearing that he must be good because death is not final, nothing is more threatening than the idea that "death is nothing to us." Christians remained terrified by the implication that one's death is both final and cosmically trivial.

As Nietzsche understood from comparing Lucretius to Christianity, it is simplistic to think that the Christian preoccupation with guilt and eternal punishment derives uniquely from a belief in immortality. As witchcraft and spirit possession intimate, Christian belief in immortality has a logical structure that is palindromic. The concept of immortality makes it possible to fear eternal punishment; but fear of damnation makes possible belief in immortality. The palindrome is conditioned psychosomatically, embedded through repetition and ritual.[43]

Because Christian morality and assertions about life after death are interdependent, Christianity can avoid discussing the issue of what Nietzsche called its *selfishness* by concentrating on questions of morality. Christians have denounced Epicureans since ancient times for reducing life to amoral pleasure: "Eat, drink, and be merry, for tomorrow you die." Epicureans were still being reviled from the pulpit in the same terms during my Southern Methodist boyhood. But John Wesley himself feared that he was a closet Epicurean: he wrote to his brother Charles in 1766, "If I have any fear, it is not of falling into hell, but of falling into nothing."[44]

By the time Kramer published the *Malleus,* there had been two printed editions of Lucretius, preceded by a substantial manuscript tradition dating from Poggio's discovery.[45] We will never know whether the Bohemian priest had read Lucretius, but, in unguarded moments, Heinrich Kramer worried about the nature of the world in language that was explicitly philosophical. He eagerly accepted any evidence that he could find that Democritus, Epicurus, and Lucretius had been wrong. In particular, he objected to the doctrine that "altogether denies that the providence of God oversees the things of the world, and maintains instead that the world was made by chance, as did Democritus and the Epicureans." Kramer rejoined that, "since all things *must be* of God, so all things *are* cared for by him, that is, *are* ordained to some end."[46]

He could not allow ideas of randomness or necessity, chance or determinism, fortune or fate, to replace the idea that God personally supervises the world. No, "even defects in nature, even if they arise out of the natural course of things, are subject to divine providence. And therefore Democritus and the other natural philosophers were in error when they ascribed whatever happens in this lower world to the mere necessity of matter."[47] Resisting the idea that nature, matter, and necessity provided ultimate explanations of the world was to proclaim that

God, angels and devils, and spirit in general exist. But not even the expert testimony of witches or interviews with possessing devils could provide final proof.

Kramer was not alone. Three decades before him, Jean Vineti worried that the Sadducees and the ancient materialists could not be right and that spirit *had* to exist. Quoting Aquinas on angelology, he claimed: "The early philosophers went wrong here because they did not grasp the power of intelligence and so failed to distinguish between sensation and understanding. They thought that nothing existed except what could be sensed or imagined; and, as nothing is imaginable except bodies, they thought that nothing but bodies existed, as Aristotle says. The same confusion underlay the error of the Sadducees, who denied the existence of spirit. The truth is that the mere fact that intellect transcends the senses is itself a reason for thinking that there exist spiritual beings [*res incorporeas*] to which only intellect can attain."[48]

In the same period as Vineti, Alonso de Espina listed the Sadducees as his first example of heretics "because they denied [the reality of] resurrection and the angels, not only in opposition to the faith of the Old [*sic*] Testament, but even against the synagogue of the Pharisees, who believed in both." He listed the Peripatetic, Academic, Epicurean, and Stoic philosophers as heretics because, "thinking up a perverse dogma of their own choosing, they fell away from the church."[49]

Espina's namesake Bartolomeo Spina's bête noire was the Aristotelian philosopher Pietro Pomponazzi. Pomponazzi's famous treatise on the immortality of the human soul, published in 1516, scandalized the religious and philosophical intelligentsia, causing some of them to burn it in Venice and to denounce its author as a heretic.[50] Pomponazzi demonstrated that, properly understood, Aristotle's texts offered no proof of the immortality of the human soul and could not be used to construct such proofs without doing violence to Aristotle's principles. This dismayed Spina, who correctly observed that Pomponazzi's *De immortalitate animae* would be better titled *De mortalitate animae,* or *On the Mortality of the Soul.* Pomponazzi opposed more than three centuries of Scholastic scholars, whose primary effort had been to reassure the Christian intelligentsia that Aristotle could indeed be used to demonstrate such crucial Christian doctrines. Three years before Pomponazzi's book was published, probably in response to "leaks" of its contents, a church council condemned it, declaring the immortality of the soul an article of faith.[51]

Pomponazzi's offense was to approach the matter as a scholar: "The question of the immortality of the soul is a neutral problem. . . . For it seems to me that no natural reasons can be brought forth proving that the soul is immortal, and still less any proving that the soul is mortal, as very many scholars who hold it immortal declare." He concluded that since the immortality of the soul "is an article of faith, as appears from the Apostles' Creed and the Athanasian Creed . . . it ought to be proved by what is proper to faith . . . [that is,] revelation and canonical Scripture."[52] While Pomponazzi formally submitted to the authority of Christian faith, he appeared to be saying that philosophical skepticism—properly speaking, the refusal to decide without proof—and religious belief or faith were equally valid in their separate spheres. In more modern times, he would have argued that science was science and faith was faith. Although his books were burned, Pomponazzi escaped further punishment, going on to even greater academic honors rather than to the stake.

Not that Spina didn't try. Outraged by Pomponazzi's treatise, he fired off a blistering and loud refutation of it in 1519, along with a refutation of the *Apologia* that Pomponazzi had written in the meantime to defend his ideas.[53] As John Herman Randall writes, the *Apologia* was "a more detailed and a better book" than the one it defended, and, in it, Pomponazzi declared outright that

> Immortality is no longer a neutral problem; it is wholly contrary to natural principles. [Pomponazzi] is prepared to die for its truth as an article of faith, but he will not teach that it can be demonstrated by reason. "A philosopher cannot do this, especially if he be a teacher, for in so teaching he would be teaching falsehood, he would be an unfaithful master, his deception could be easily detected, and he would be acting contrary to the profession of philosophy." Natural theology [the doctrine that the wonders of nature prove the existence of God] is indeed so weak and ridiculous that it brings Christianity itself into disrepute.[54]

Still, the controversy did not die down, for the immortality of human souls was not the only issue.

As we saw in chapter 3 above, Pomponazzi proved what witchcraft theorists knew: Aristotle offered no support for the existence of angels and demons. Pomponazzi made this clear in *De immortalitate* even before he attacked angels directly in his treatise on wonders. Those who draw an analogy between the human soul and the intelligences or movers of the heavenly spheres on the basis of immateriality and immortality are mistaken, said Pomponazzi: "This clearly contradicts the words of Aristotle, since there is no immaterial substance which does not move a [heavenly] sphere; for in *Metaphysica* xii he holds that the number of Intelligences corresponds to the number of spheres."[55] Further, "since Aristotle did not posit any Intelligence without a body, as in *Metaphysica* xii . . . much less, therefore, can he posit the human intellect without a body, since it is far less abstracted [distinct from its body] than an Intelligence."[56] The analogy between the soul and the Aristotelian intelligences thus serves, not to uphold, but to disprove the immortality of the soul. Similarly, to compare or identify Judeo-Christian angels and demons with Aristotle's intelligences limits their numbers to the total of planetary motions, for it chains those spiritual beings to the task of moving *bodies*.[57]

Pomponazzi takes this discussion to the heart of Scholastic anxieties by stating that astrology can explain certain phenomena better than demonology can. Citing arguments that we have already seen, he attacks and refutes Aquinas's three major contentions: first, that spiritual phenomena occur irregularly, whereas astrological influences are natural and hence regular; second, "that there are some effects in apparitions of this sort that cannot be traced back to the heavenly bodies, like sayings and especially predictions about the future, since such things cannot be done except by one who possesses intellect [i.e., by a demon]"; third, that occurrences like the transformation of rods into serpents (as happened in the contest between Moses, Aaron, and Pharaoh's magicians) "cannot be done by the power of the heavenly bodies."[58]

Aquinas's dependence on possession as proof of demonic presence is invalid: "for all such men are suffering either from black bile [melancholia] or insanity or from a trance or are near to death"; hence they are susceptible to astrological influences, which can cause them to prophesy. These influences can explain the auguries that the ancients took from birds and other animals; thus, they can explain the prophecies given out by certain humans, who are often children or fools and thus not far from sheer animality.[59]

Pomponazzi thus jabbed the raw nerve of the Scholastic fear of nature. He likewise thoroughly irritated the Scholastic fear of imagination. Those who defend the soul's immortality, says Pomponazzi, cite "many experiences" from which they claim immortality can be "conclusively grasped." Foremost among these are encounters with ghosts, both by waking persons in graveyards and by sleepers in their dreams. But "many things are counted among histories which nevertheless are mere fables."[60]

Pomponazzi had worse in store for the idea of ghosts: "Imagination and universal repute also help. Wherefore, as Aristotle tells in *De somno et vigilia* [*On Dreams*], chapter 2, many things are thought to be seen by those living in fear or other passions [strong emotions], even though they be awake, which yet do not exist; just as happens to those ill."[61] This was another application of the argument that worried witchcraft theorists even more than the recourse to astrological explanations: "that a powerful imagination can cause certain figures to appear to the senses exactly as a man has thought of them, so that we say he only thinks he is seeing" what he fears.

Pomponazzi's treatise exacerbated Scholastic fears of the imagination by declaring imagination's supreme power. Two texts that should destroy the idea of the human soul's immortality, says Pomponazzi, are found in Aristotle's treatise on the soul: "Aristotle says at the end of . . . text 12 of *De anima* [*On the Soul*], Book i: 'Knowing is either imagination or not without imagination.' And, although he there speaks conditionally, in *De anima,* Book iii, text 39, he nevertheless says most clearly that there is no knowing without some phantasm—which experience also proves. In no way, therefore, according to Aristotle, does the human intellect have any operation entirely independent of the body."[62]

A phantasm is a sensory impression that is present to the mind, noticed by it. Indeed, in the former passage, Aristotle says that "there seems to be no case in which the soul can act or be acted upon without involving the body; e.g., anger, courage, appetite and sensation generally. Thinking seems the most probable exception; but *if this too proves to be a form of imagination or impossible without imagination,* it too requires a body as a condition of its existence. If there is any way of acting or being acted upon proper to soul, soul will be capable of separate existence [i.e., in isolation from the body]; if there is none, its separate existence is impossible."[63]

To make a long story short, the soul is dependent on the body: it cannot survive without it. And, when the body is alive, the soul depends on imagination to think: "[To] the thinking soul images serve as if they were the contents of perception. That is why *the soul never thinks without an image.*"[64] Pomponazzi repeats these quotations from Aristotle several times throughout his treatise.[65]

To say that all thinking depends on images is to make the imagination the supreme power of the soul. This destroys the Christian view of the soul and, with it, the entire Christian theory of knowledge. According to Scholastic Aristotelianism, the human soul is tripartite, "three souls, so to speak—the vegetative, the sensitive, and the intellective." The vegetative soul is shared with plants and animals, the sensitive with animals; but the highest, or intellective, is peculiarly human. Christianity asserts that the intellective soul survives the death of the body; even during life it supposedly can contemplate truths unverifiable through sense experience. "But," says Pomponazzi, "it is proved that the intellect is inseparable from matter, since it is imagination, or is not without imagination, as is clear in *De anima* i."[66]

Lumping Aquinas and the Muslim commentator Averroës together as misreaders of Aristotle, Pomponazzi declares them wrong to assert Aristotle's belief in any form of human immortality. They wrongly advance a corollary, that the intellect can know without the body, phantasms, and the imagination: "It is strange that Aristotle should have maintained," as they claim, "that at times the intellect knows without any phantasm" since he says "in every passage that there is no knowing without some phantasm."[67]

No, there is nothing for it: what theologians call the *intellective soul* is the same as the *sensitive soul,* for, "according to Aristotle, any knowing thing is the act of a physical and organic body," and "this way of knowing by phantasms is essential to man." Thus, "to say, as they do who assert that the human intellect is absolutely immortal, that the intellect possesses two ways of knowing, one without phantasms at all and the other with phantasms, is to change human nature into divine."[68]

If there is no knowing in isolation from the body, independent of the imagination, and if, as Aquinas's heirs feared, "a powerful imagination can cause certain figures to appear to the senses exactly as a man has thought of them, so that we say he only thinks he is seeing," then what becomes of the beings—angels, demons, ghosts, the immortal soul—of which Christianity speaks? How can we ever be sure that they are present as realities and not as empty images or imaginings? The imagination sometimes has as negative a connotation for Pomponazzi as it does for a modern reader. Dismissing an opinion of Averroës, Pomponazzi sneers that "certainly for me whoever imagines that opinion has a very powerful imagination, and I believe painters have never contrived a finer monster than this monster, besides, it is contrary to Aristotle."[69]

Witchcraft theorists' resistance to skepticism was so ancient and anxiety ridden that, when they found a man who embraced skepticism openly, their hatred became downright gleeful. By attacking him, they could punish every wicked doubt that had ever entered their own minds. Mazzolini and Spina were the pioneers in this exercise. Both discussed immortality at length in their works on witchcraft theory, and Spina also discussed it in his treatise against Pomponazzi. Both heaped condemnation on Pomponazzi and laid claim to a serene belief in Christian dogmas of the spirit. Such belief was manifestly beyond their capacity.

And Pomponazzi would not shut up. In 1520, he wrote *De naturalium effectuum causis,* or *On the Causes of Natural Effects.* There, as we saw earlier, he said explicitly what witchcraft theorists had been dreading. The book was nothing less than a refutation of everything said about demons in the three centuries since Aquinas:

> He [Pomponazzi] saw in nature an orderly uniformity of law that admitted no miracles, no demons or angels, not even any direct divine intervention. . . . [H]e sought to explain all miraculous cures and events through purely natural causes, through natural powers not ordinarily experienced, and through the constant and regular influence of the heavens. . . . The recorded miracles of religion are not events contrary to the natural order [i.e., they are not supernatural]; they are merely unaccustomed and rare. The very conception of an immaterial spirit precludes [its having] any particular operation. "In vain do we assume demons, for it is ridiculous and foolish to forsake what is observable, and what can be proved by natural reason, to seek what is unobservable, and cannot be proved with any verisimilitude."[70]

The doctrines that Aquinas and his disciples had tried to refute were now devastatingly vindicated: (1) natural causes—heavenly *bodies*—account for anything that can be attributed to spirits; and (2) anything that nature cannot explain is ipso facto imaginary.

The way was open for the modern conception of the imaginary as having no necessary basis in reality; but the concept had been implicit in the Scholastic doctrine of the imagination as a power that is potentially infinite and also infinitely deceptive. Scholastic theologians had suspected as much by the thirteenth century; witchcraft theorists had known and feared it, had hinted and alluded to it, had made the sign of the cross at it and thrown holy water at it for over a century. As Aquinas said, mountains of gold may not exist, but we can imagine them, for we have seen both gold and mountains.

That someone had finally spelled out in detail everyone's worst fears about the core of wishful thinking in Christian theology did not bring witch-hunting or the printing of witchcraft theory to an end. Between about 1520 and 1570 there was a decline, but this may have been caused by the expenditure of mental energy that was required to repel open expressions of dissent. Protestants were attacking Catholic practices and sacraments at the same time that Pomponazzi was knocking away the Aristotelian foundations of Christian dogma on spirits. Once each religious group had salvaged whatever "realities" it could from the corrosion of its enemies' skepticism, it was time to face one's own skepticism. An easier solution was to recommence looking for the precise demonic impediments to a perfect world. Each group was free to define *witchcraft* as it chose. But, while the other fellow's Christianity seemed ever more fanciful and blasphemous, showing that one's own variety was not imaginary required a greater effort of imagination.

Skepticism about the world of spirit did not arise suddenly in the late seventeenth century or the early eighteenth to destroy belief in witchcraft. The battle between the skeptic and the believer was inside the thoughts of every writer who defended the existence of demons, witchcraft, or both. Witchcraft theory and witch-hunting *were caused* by skepticism, not by belief or credulity. Every defense of witchcraft and demonic reality was expressed through the negation of negation: "Witches and demons do not not exist; their magic and miracles are not not happening." Witchcraft declined when skepticism overcame the resistance erected against it.

Coming to terms with the imperceptibility, unprovability, and possible nonexistence of the spirit world happened gradually, in step with a reluctant acceptance of the extraordinary power of the human imagination. The subsequent movements that most knowingly exalted the human imagination, either in theory, such as baroque and Romantic aesthetics, or in practice, such as fascination with folk- and fairy tales ("the imagination of the common people"), took place in an atmosphere of emotional exaltation. That exaltation could not have been completely positive: it was in part a manic reaction to dejection and depression. Perhaps the mood was best summarized by a letter that John Keats wrote in 1817: "What the imagination seizes as beauty *must be* truth. . . . The imagination may be compared to Adam's dream—he awoke and found it truth. . . . O for a life of sensations rather than thoughts!"[71] But the only way to avoid thinking was to dream; the search for *those* sensations, promised by the demonic body, proved too elusive. The search for them outside the imagination failed repeatedly.

CONCLUSION

TALKING AROUND THE UNSPEAKABLE

At night after we were in bed, Veronica spoke out from her little bed and said, "I do not believe there is a God." "Preserve me," said I, "my dear what do you mean?" She answered, "I have *thinket* it many a time, but did not like to speak of it." I was confounded and uneasy and tried her with the simple arguments that without God there would not be all the things we see. It is He who makes the sun shine. Said she, "It shines only on good days." Said I: "God made you." Said she: "My Mother bore me." It was a strange and alarming thing to her Mother and me to hear our little angel talk thus.

—James Boswell, *Journal* (1779)

"In a riddle whose answer is chess, what is the only prohibited word?" I thought a moment and replied, "The word *chess*."

—Borges, "The Garden of Forking Paths" (1941)

The French historian Lucien Febvre argued that "the mental equipment available in the sixteenth century made it as good as impossible for anyone to be an atheist, and, perhaps more important, that an atheist could only have been a solitary figure to whom nobody would have paid any significant attention."[1] But not everyone found belief easy or unbelief difficult. Another of Febvre's assessments was more accurate: he referred to the sixteenth century and the three or four preceding as "centuries that wanted to believe."[2]

Stephen Greenblatt argues "not that atheism was literally unthinkable in the late sixteenth century but rather that it was almost always thinkable only as the thought of another." Greenblatt remarks, "People lie readily about their most intimate beliefs. How much more must they have lied in an atmosphere of unembarrassed repression."[3] Repression was not always unembarrassed, either: it was not only the external persecution of societal "others." It was also and fundamentally an internal, psychological repression much like that described by Freud. Like six-year-old Veronica Boswell, educated adults had "thinked" long and hard about those problems but "did not like to speak" of them, except to deny them elaborately or condemn them as the impious and criminal thoughts of others. In *Religion and the Decline of Magic,* Keith Thomas asserts that, in the early-modern period, "the evidence of widespread religious skepticism is not to be underrated, for it may be reasonably surmised that many thought what they dared not say aloud." He suggests that "not enough justice has been done to the volume of apathy, heterodoxy, and agnosticism which existed long before the onslaught of industrialism."[4]

Not that everyone who advocated the pursuit and punishment of witches was an atheist. But the thought was lurking in the logic of their arguments and actions. It was often, to quote Borges, "the only prohibited word." At times, in its disguise as the thought of another, it was painfully explicit. For several centuries, "the thought" was, not atheism proper, but what nervous Christians called *Sadducism* or *Sadduceeism,* a disbelief in the reality of spirit, what we would now call *materialism.* A desire to be convinced of the reality of spirit was the psychic glue that held the witch myth together, from Johannes Nider to sometime in the eighteenth century. This conceptual adhesive accounts for otherwise puzzling resemblances between myths about witches, Jews, necromancers, and heretics.

Without our recognition of this desire to believe, *witchcraft* appears to be a bundle of unrelated, even contradictory beliefs, held together by illogical, even irrational hatreds. *Resistance to skepticism,* the other name for the need to believe, was inherently logical, if only by opposing the logic of skepticism and doubt. The witch supposedly experienced the fondest daydreams of her persecutors, but in an inverted and ostensibly frightening form. She rebutted point for point the objections of the skeptic, that frightening *other self* who haunted the thoughts of witchcraft theorists. Ironically, both the skeptic and the witch existed in the mind of the theologian long before they were found in external reality. In fact, the theologian's witch never existed externally, but the skeptic became an increasingly real presence—during the sixteenth century by opposing witchcraft persecutions and in the seventeenth as the dreaded atheist.

For the writers whose work I have examined, and for many others, witchcraft theory was theological damage control. Their deepest concerns far outlasted the period of witchcraft persecutions. Examples are legion, but four, one from the eighteenth century and three from the twentieth, will suffice.

John Wesley complained to his diary in 1768 that "the giving up of witchcraft is, in effect, the giving up of the Bible." Wesley admitted that, by his time, "most of the learned men of Europe have given up all accounts of witches and apparitions as mere old wives' fables." "I am sorry for it," he thundered, "and I willingly take this opportunity of entering my solemn protest against this violent compliment which so many that believe the Bible pay to those who do not believe it." If only one account of ghosts or witchcraft could be proved true, Wesley fantasized, "all *their* Deism, Atheism, and Materialism" would be refuted and "fall to the ground." Even in the absence of such proof, he concluded, "neither reason nor religion require" that Christians allow themselves to be "hooted out" of invoking the existence of witches as a "weapon" against atheists.[5] Not that Wesley gave up: deprived of witches, he eagerly ✓ investigated whatever encounters with ghosts came to his attention.

In the centuries since Wesley, Christian damage control has evolved to meet new threats, notably Darwinism and Marxism. But the bugbears most favored for reinforcing belief are direct descendants of the witch. Modern fundamentalist Christians profess shock and horror at demonic influences in Halloween celebrations or the Harry Potter novels for children, arousing the suspicion that they are looking a bit too hard for evidence of Satanic subversion. "Satanic ritual child abuse" is an even more noticeable case of forlorn hope masquerading as morbid fear. Love the sin, hate the sinner.[6]

On the other side of the dogmatic fence, Wicca and other self-styled forms of "good" witchcraft, however innocuous their rituals and credos, seem to delight in being considered "satanic" rather than innocuously eccentric or deluded. The legacy of witchcraft theory keeps fundamentalists and modern witches locked in a psychologically ambivalent embrace. Both credos find society's indifference or derision more troubling than the abominations of their favorite adversaries. With enemies like these, who needs friends?

The strangest offspring of witchcraft theory in contemporary society is simultaneously the least obvious and the most thoroughly similar. Large numbers of people—so we are told—believe that they have been abducted, usually from their beds late at night, and taken aboard interplanetary spaceships, often traveling bodily through solid walls to board them. Inside the spacecrafts' futuristic laboratories, alien surgeons and zoological researchers perform bizarre experiments on the abductees' bodies. The aliens force some of these abductees to breed with them, occasionally by forcing them into painful, humiliating sex acts, but more often by stealing eggs and sperm from them. Strange devices, often described as "computer chips," are implanted in the abductees' bodies.

In alien abduction, as in witchcraft, the corporeality of the alleged encounters is prized as conclusive proof of *reality*, provoking strong emotions and allegedly unshakable beliefs in the humans who "confess"

UFOs [marginal note]

to interviewers. Corporeality has evolved with the times, however. The aliens' bodies can now be real instead of virtual, making hybrid human-alien beings easier to conceive. The suprahumans' artificial insemination can also be performed surgically, rather than by old-fashioned copulation. Some abductees suspect that they themselves are hybrids.

The voluntary, solitary witches who call themselves alien abductees perform no *maleficia* and have their own peculiar breed of kindly inquisitors among specialized psychiatrists. Some of these psychiatric researchers, professedly for the most humane, altruistic, and scientific of motives, solicit and record the abductees' "expert testimony" about corporeal interaction with aliens. The most eminent theorist of this movement is the psychiatrist John Mack of Harvard Medical School. Among enthusiasts of alien abduction, Mack has parlayed his impressive credentials and seductive prose into the kind of moral and scientific authority that Heinrich Kramer would have envied.

Unbeknownst to Mack, I am sure, his broadest contentions about the suprahuman world are modernized versions of Kramer's:

> The alien beings that appear to come to us from the sky in strange spacecraft present a particularly confusing *challenge to . . . naturalistic or objectivist ideology*. For they seem to partake of properties belonging to both the spirit and the material worlds, bridging, as if effortlessly, the division between these realms which has become increasingly sacred and unbreachable since science and religion went their separate ways in the seventeenth century. On the one hand, *these beings seem able to be seen by the abductees, who feel their bodies moved and find small lesions inflicted upon them. On the other hand, the beings seem to come, like intermediaries from God or the Devil, from a nonembodied source,* and they are able to open the consciousness of abductees to realms of being that do not exist in the physical world as we know it. Before concluding I will speculate about why *the barrier between the spirit and material worlds* has become so entrenched in the West. For it is *this false dichotomy* that makes our confrontations with beings who do not respect this gulf so shocking.[7]

If this paragraph seems to imply that science is nothing more than an ideology or a sacred cow—like religion—that is what Mack's book attempts to prove.

Mack announces that Western religion and Western science are equally obsolete: he is post-Christian as well as postmodern. Yet, with the exception of *maleficia,* every theme of fifteenth-century Christian witchcraft has analogues in the strange narratives that Mack constructs from interviews with his patients. The psychological atmosphere is the same: fear of the imagination, fear of naturalistic explanations (including traditional psychotherapies), hope masquerading as fear, double-negative formulations, and palindromic reasoning.

As in 1487, a disillusioned literate quester seeks to confirm his metaphysical daydreams by the expert testimony of intellectually, emotionally, and socially underprivileged persons, hoping to discover proof of a reality from which he feels cut off. Mack rebels against the cold impersonality of what he tellingly calls *consensus reality:* "I am often asked," he says, "why, if UFOs and abductions are real, the spaceships do not show up in more obvious form." The answer, predictably, is that these "encounters" are being directed by "an intelligence that provides enough evidence that something profoundly important is at work"; yet this intelligence "does not offer the kinds of proof that would satisfy an exclusively empirical, rationalistic way of knowing." The solution is "for us to embrace the reality of the phenomenon and to take a step toward appreciating that we live in a universe different from the one in which we have been taught to believe."[8]

The difference between John Mack and Heinrich Kramer, aside from their methods of interviewing expert witnesses, amounts to this: the psychiatrist is attempting to recover what the inquisitor was attempting not to lose. The worldview that Kramer vaguely feared has since triumphed and evolved: it is a social reality rather than an indistinct threat, and it often appears overwhelming. Kramer and Mack share the same anxieties, and each could say with the pop singer Bob Seeger, "Wish I didn't know now what I didn't know then."[9]

In his slashing condemnation of Christianity, Nietzsche claimed that "faith means *wanting not to know* what is true."[10] Thomas Aquinas, whose fascination with demonic corporeality foreshadowed the mythology of witchcraft, explored willed ignorance from another angle. According to Garry Wills, "It can be objected that the deceivers in question have first deceived themselves, that they are sincere in their adherence to falsehoods, so they cannot be faulted for acting on genuinely held views. Yet the Roman hierarchy's own most favored theologian, Thomas Aquinas, held that there is such a thing as 'cultivated ignorance,' *ignorantia affectata,* an ignorance so useful that one protects it, keeps it from the light, in order to continue using it. . . . He called this kind of ignorance not exculpatory but inculpatory. It is a willed ignorance, though an unconfessed one."[11] Christians have no monopoly on this kind of thinking. The Christian ideology of spirit continues to exert its appeal even over "post-Christians."

The philosopher Antony Flew tells a parable that purports to expose the fallacy of theistic discourse, or God talk, by self-styled believers.

Flew's parable fits the discourse of witchcraft theory as well as or better than it does discourse about God:

> Once upon a time two explorers came upon a clearing in the jungle. In the clearing were growing many flowers and many weeds. One explorer says, "Some gardener must tend this plot." The other disagrees, "There is no gardener." So they pitch their tents and set a watch. No gardener is ever seen. "But perhaps he is an invisible gardener." So they set up a barbed-wire fence. They electrify it. They patrol with bloodhounds. (For they remember how H. G. Wells's "invisible man" could be both smelt and touched though he could not be seen.) But no shrieks ever suggest that some intruder has received a shock. No movements of the wire ever betray an invisible climber. The bloodhounds never give cry. Yet still the Believer is not convinced. "But there is a gardener, invisible, intangible, insensible to electric shocks, a gardener who has no scent and makes no sound, a gardener who comes secretly to look after the garden which he loves." At last the Skeptic despairs, "But what remains of your original assertion? Just how does what you call an invisible, intangible, eternally elusive gardener differ from an imaginary gardener or even from no gardener at all?"[12]

The answer is that the "Believer's" god, demon, or gardener *feels better.* Flew's Believer is expressing, not belief, but resistance to skepticism, a refusal to believe the empirical evidence that certain things are not happening.

Flew asserts that such discourse is meaningless because it is unfalsifiable—since it cannot be proved wrong under any circumstances, it can never be proved right. Granted, "It does not not exist" is not the same proposition as "Look, there it is." But whether it is intellectually respectable or not, the dialogue between the skeptic and the believer runs on in the minds of many people, educated and not, scientists and not. The emotional stakes are too high to silence it.

In the *Symposium,* Plato's Socrates claimed that the gods never have direct contact with humans. Instead, they employ the *daimons,* beings halfway between gods and humans, as their intermediaries or messengers.[13] Plato's term *daimonion* gave the West its word for demons, his word for *messenger, aggelos,* the word for angels. When God begins to seem impossibly distant, Western Christians rediscover angels and demons. If these messengers begin to seem distant or unreal as well, someone begins daydreaming that somewhere—somewhere *close*—other people *must be* experiencing suprahuman reality, physically, empirically, unmistakably.

Witchcraft treatises were anything but illogical or irrational, and we are still living with their legacy. Their theories were perhaps insane, but insanely *logical.* They were not produced by the sleep or dreaming of reason, as Francisco Goya maintained; they were reason's daydream, produced by its insomnia and hyperactivity.[14] Witchcraft theorists superficially resembled modern proponents of social intolerance and incivility. But a far more important question is how far we—the "good people"—resemble witchcraft theorists. To what degree does Christian morality continue to be invoked, even in post-Christian, secularized form, to reinforce belief in spirits and human immortality?

NOTES

While my system of citation in the notes is in most cases straightforward, it is complicated by the fact that I make use of multiple editions of certain works. It therefore seems useful to outline my basic system first before explaining more complex instances.

If only one work by an author is listed in the list of works cited, just the author's last name is used (e.g., "Spina"). If two or more works by an author are listed, the author's last name and a short title are used (e.g., "Müller, *De lanijs*"; and "Müller, *Von den unholden oder Hexen*"). (Note that, if a note functions simply to give a general reference and not to document a quotation, the title of the work in question is always included [e.g., "see Augustine, *De civitate Dei,* 1.3"].) If two or more translations of a work are listed, both the author's name and the translator's name are used (e.g., "Guazzo/Ashwin"). If two or more editions of a work are listed, the date of the edition being cited is specified (e.g., "Guazzo [1608]").

Citations of theological treatises have been standardized using exclusively Arabic numeration, moving from the largest division of the text to the smallest (e.g., "Aquinas, *Summa theologiae,* 1.51.2").

For Pico's *Dialogus in tres libros divisus: Titulus est Strix, sive de ludificatione daemonum,* I will use my own translations of the Latin original (cited as "Pico, *Strix*") and Alberti's translation ("Pico/Alberti"), with occasional reference to Turini's translation ("Pico/Turini").

For Nider's *Formicarius,* I use Biedermann's photographic reprint of the 1480 Cologne edition collated with Chène's critical edition (Ostorero, Bagliani, and Utz Tremp, eds., 122–99) of manuscripts of *Formicarius*'s "witchcraft" chapters. For the 1480 incunabulum, I will cite both the signature or gathering numbers of the original and the page numbers of Biedermann's reprint (e.g., "Nider/Biedermann, 71 [sig. e4r] [Nider/Chène, 134–36]").

For Kramer's *Malleus maleficarum,* quotations in English are based on Summers's translation, but, where Summers's translation is erroneous or misleading, it has been silently emended on the basis of Jerouschek's facsimile edition. In all such instances, the edition used is not specified (e.g., "Kramer, *Malleus,* fol. 108r [p. 230]," where the page numbers given in parentheses refer to Summers's edition).

For Visconti's *Opusculum,* I quote from the Cornell University manuscript, collated with the only printed text (sigs. c2r–c8v of the 1490 Milan edition). Quotations of the *Lamiarum* are taken from sigs. a1r–c2r of the 1490 Milan edition.

Given the number of editions of Denzinger and Schönmetzer's *Enchiridion symbolorum definitionum et declarationum de rebus fidei et morum* that have appeared over the last 150 years, I cite excerpts by Schönmetzer's paragraph numbers, which remain constant, rather than by page numbers, which do not. I give page numbers (from the 36th ed., 1976) only when citing the Index Systematicus.

Introduction

1. "Urteil . . . ," 105–9. Translated in "Judgment on the Witch Walpurga Hausmännin." Reprinted in Monter, ed., 75–81 (used here). On the context of the trial, see Behringer, 122–29.
2. Monter, ed., 75.
3. Ibid.
4. For the Fuggers' deep interest in witchcraft and demonology, see Roper, 125–44, 171–98, esp. 174–84.
5. "Urteil . . . ," 103; Monter, ed., 75–76.
6. "Urteil . . . ," 103–4; Monter, ed., 76.
7. Ibid. (Matthews ["Judgment on the Witch Walpurga Hausmännin"] translates differently.) Throughout, I will use the term *Sabbat* rather than *Sabbath* to avoid confusion with Jewish and Christian holy days.
8. "Urteil . . . ," 104; Monter, ed., 76–77. The name *Federlin* may have been suggested to Walpurga or her tormenters by the pen (*Feder* ["Urteil . . . ," 104]) with which the demon forced her to sign the pact. There is also a sexual innuendo.
9. "Urteil . . . ," 104–5; Monter, ed., 77.
10. Robbins, 461.
11. Barstow, 137.
12. Levack, 133–37; Briggs, 8.
13. Barstow, 214 n. 13. More judicious is Quaife, 97–112.
14. Larner, *Enemies of God,* 92.
15. Clark, "The 'Gendering' of Witchcraft," and *Thinking with Demons,* 106–33.
16. See Levack, 24–25; Briggs, 8; Purkiss, 7–29.
17. Roper, 201, 211.
18. On child defendants, see chap. 4 below.
19. Pico/Alberti, 15. See chap. 4 below.
20. The essential study is Certeau.
21. Throughout this book, I use the terms *heretic* and *orthodox, Catholic* and *Protestant,* as labels of convenience while attempting to respect the complexity of historical situations and theological nuance. For instance, it is inaccurate to refer to *Catholics* (in the sense of "Roman Catholic") before the closure of the Council of Trent in 1563. I will often refer to *Western* or *Latin* Christianity to distinguish pre-Trent "Catholicism" from Eastern Orthodox Christianity.
22. On the transition from heretic stereotypes to witch stereotypes, see Cohn, *Europe's Inner Demons,* 16–59. Despite believing that witches were real subversives, Russell, *Witchcraft,* 101–32, describes the transition well.
23. Robbins, 35–37, 289; Levack, 21n, citing Larner, *Enemies of God,* 63.
24. Monter, ed., 82.
25. The letter and trial transcript are in Monter, ed., 81–88, and, more completely, in Robbins, 289–93. I follow Robbins here.

26. Robbins, 292–93.
27. On Regina Bartholome (executed in 1670), see Roper, 226–48.
28. Lea referred to "the whole structure of witchcraft" as "an even more extraordinary intellectual aberration than it appears on the surface and an even greater opprobrium to human reason" (1:265). Quaife's assessment is moderate: "To attribute logical argument and impartiality to the *Malleus* is totally rejected by many scholars. There were weaknesses in logic—untested assumptions and assertions, circular arguments and *non sequiturs.* Yet to judge the *Malleus* on modern standards is irrelevant to its standing among its contemporaries. To expect objectivity, the sustained use of inductive reasoning, the evaluation of evidence, a critical cynicism towards authorities and empirical testing of a hypothesis takes us beyond the worldview of the late fifteenth century" (24). I will argue that only objectivity was missing.
29. On the inadequacy of the term, see Clark, *Thinking with Demons,* viii-ix.
30. Anglo, "Evident Authority," 2.
31. Clark, *Thinking with Demons,* x.
32. Ibid., 7, emphasis added.

Chapter One

1. Elliott, 127–56, is the exception and discusses some of the essential primary texts.
2. Compare Evans-Pritchard on African witchcraft.
3. Levack, 9, referring to Midelfort, 52–53.
4. Bodin, *Démonomanie.*
5. Levack, 15, referring to Kieckhefer, *European Witch Trials,* chaps. 3 and 5. *Maleficium* is the singular, *maleficia* the plural.
6. Macfarlane; Briggs; Sharpe.
7. Levack, 28.
8. Ibid., 28 (quotation), 15 (on scripting, referring to Kieckhefer, *European Witch Trials,* chaps. 3 and 5).
9. Levack, 28.
10. See chap. 8 below.
11. There are a few exceptions: see chap. 3 below.
12. Ginzburg, esp. *The Night Battles.* Ginzburg, however, seems not to notice elite anxieties about spirits' reality.
13. On fairies and other beings, see Gui, 444; Bonomo, 7–108; and Ginzburg's work, particularly *The Night Battles.*
14. Plantsch, 260–61. There are approximately fifteen instances of *corpus* and its derivatives on the two pages plus other body vocabulary.
15. Guazzo (1626), 33–44. Guazzo/Ashwin translates the 1608 (1st) edition, omitting crucial material added in the 1626 (2d) edition. Crucially, Guazzo added a chapter on "What forms the devil has usually adopted to deceive men," treating demonic corporeality explicitly. The 1608 chap. 6 (Guazzo/Ashwin, 13–19) thus became the 1626 chap. 7.
16. Guazzo/Ashwin, 38.
17. Examples in Hansen, ed., *Quellen,* 162, 163, 198.
18. Guazzo/Ashwin, 31; De Lancre, 134, 213–33, esp. 224–25; quotations here from Robbins, 464–68. (Scholars often deprecate Robbins's *Encyclope-*

dia, but, despite his reductive theories about witch-hunts, his summaries of primary sources are usually reliable.)

19. See the illustrations for Guazzo's *Compendium,* often reproduced—e.g., in Guazzo/Ashwin; Lehner and Lehner, comps.; and fig. 12 below, p. 282.
20. Midelfort, 85–163.
21. *Recollectio casus,* 174–75 (and see Duvergier). The difference between "male devils" and "female devils" is a matter of demonic art, not nature (*Recollectio casus,* 175). For artificial bodies, see chap. 3 below.
22. *Recollectio casus,* 175–76.
23. Jacquier, 136. See also Lea, 1:276. Pierre De Lancre writes in 1612 that, "whoever does such things, even if the beginning was done in a dream, must wake up during the actual [*formelle*] action because 'rerum natura non capit quemquam coire nescientem' [the nature of things does not allow anyone to have sex without knowing it]" (540).
24. Jacquier, 136.
25. *Perfidia* was often juxtaposed to *fides* as its opposite, in such a way as to exploit the etymology. See Bernard Gui's (439) discussion of Jewish *perfidia.*
26. Jacquier, 138–39, emphasis added.
27. Visconti, *Opusculum,* fols. 2r, 6v, 4r.
28. Giordano da Bergamo (Hansen, ed.), 198.
29. Wills, "The Rescuer," 30.
30. Vineti, sig. b6v.
31. Ibid., sigs. a3r–v.
32. The classic of this later literature is Glanvill's *Saducismus triumphatus.*
33. Vineti, sig. a4r.
34. Henry More would spell this out in 1681, in a letter to Glanvill in the latter's *Saducismus triumphatus:* "The confession of Witches against their own lives being so palpable an Evidence, besides the miraculous feats they play, that there are bad Spirits, which will necessarily open a door to the belief that there are good ones, and lastly that there is a God" (quoted from Kors and Peters, eds., 299).
35. Vineti, sig. a4v.
36. See my analysis of the Canon *Episcopi* in chap. 5 below.
37. Keck, 113.
38. The term *witchcraft theory* is commonly used by, e.g., Monter, ed., 17; and Clark, *Thinking with Demons,* vii.
39. James, *The Will to Believe;* Popkin; Allen, *Doubt's Boundless Sea.*
40. "The irony is that the very attempt to prove that the church has never changed leads to innovating arguments, to *modern adjustments or additions, that just show how ill they accord with the monument they are trying to shore up*—as when the gender of the apostles is adduced to support a male monopoly on the priesthood, after the ancient and real reason for that monopoly, a belief in female inferiority, has become unusable" (Wills, *Papal Sin,* 7–8, emphasis added).
41. See the conclusion below.
42. Eco, *Interpretation and Overinterpretation,* 25, 25, 65. For Rorty's response, see ibid., 89–108.
43. Ibid., 65, 52.
44. Eco, *The Name of the Rose,* 91.

45. Eco, *The Role of the Reader;* Stephens, "Mimesis, Mediation, and Counterfeit."
46. Levack adapts the concept from Hansen, *Zauberwahn.*
47. French and Cunningham, 274.
48. Ibid., 6, 274.
49. Ibid., 202.

Chapter Two

1. Anglo, "Evident Authority," 17.
2. Barstow, 16.
3. My reading of the *Malleus* tends to confirm Hansen's (see Hansen, *Zauberwahn,* 473–79; and Hansen, ed., *Quellen,* 404–7) and Jerouschek's ("500 Years of the *Malleus maleficarum,*" xl–xlvii) assertions that Jacob Sprenger's role in composing the work was probably minimal. On Kramer, see Hansen, ed., *Quellen,* 360–407; Behringer, 71–78; Segl.
4. Kramer, *Malleus,* fol. 23r (p. 47).
5. The Italian translation of the *Malleus* (Kramer/Buia et al.) illustrates this, with its title's pretensions to Freudian precision.
6. Barstow, 171.
7. Before 1900, there is only a German translation, by Kramer himself, of pt. 3 of the *Malleus,* which deals only with judicial procedures. Kramer/Jerouschek, *Nürnberger Hexenhammer 1491,* reproduces the manuscript.
8. Schnyder, 128, observes that much of this material comes from Saint Antoninus of Florence's *Summa theologica.* Antoninus's treatise has a vicious alliterative litany *De diversis vitiis mulierum per alphabetum* ("On the vices of women, in alphabetical order," 3.1.25 [3:116–23]), wherein under *F* we find the definition "Falsa fides": "foemina *femeno* id est minus fide" (False faith: female from *femeno,* that is, lacking faith [3:119]), which Kramer adopted.
9. I will sometimes refer to *chapters;* Kramer refers to these divisions as *questions* (i.e., the *quaestiones* of Scholastic theological debate).
10. Clark, *Thinking with Demons,* 115–16.
11. Lea, 1:308, 307.
12. Barstow, 222 n. 11. I have interpreted Barstow's calculation of page numbers generously, as if it involved only whole pages. In fact, pp. 48–66 are mostly about imagination and illusion; 109–14 are mostly about the characteristics of *incubi* rather than women; 114–17 are about the sacraments; 140–44 are about midwives (and are primarily about theodicy rather than women's sexuality); and 227–30 are about "devils' tokens" and "devils' marks," the signs by which demons signal inquisitors that they have had bodily contact with someone.
13. Kramer, *Malleus,* fols. 23r, 48v, 10v (pp. 47, 99, 21).
14. Pico cites the book's title only as "the Hammer" (Pico, *Strix,* sig. H4r). The wording quoted here is from the 1524 Italian translation of the passage (Pico/Alberti, 188).
15. Kramer, *Malleus,* fol. 54v (p. 111), emphasis added. Mandrou, 131, quotes Bodin as saying that, since women do not habitually boast of their sexual exploits, their confessions to demonic copulation are all the more plausible.
16. Kramer, *Malleus,* fol. 13v (p. 27), emphasis added.

17. Ibid., fols. 4r–v, emphasis added.
18. See chap. 11 below, pp. 318–21.
19. Summers was an anti-Communist English Catholic whose personal theology was thoroughly superstitious. His need to believe in the reality of demons was as desperate as any fifteenth-century author's, as his "credulous" notes to the *Malleus* reveal.
20. Kramer, *Malleus,* fols. 4r–v (p. 2).
21. Anglo ("Evident Authority," 29) asks the ironic rhetorical question, "Were [Kramer's] authorities not evident and his evidence authoritative?" Jerouschek ("500 Years of the *Malleus maleficarum,*" xxxv) thunders, "It would be a mistake to believe that such absurdities, such obvious contradictions and inane syllogisms were the exception in [Kramer's] argumentative apparatus. Quite the opposite: the unconcealed fanatic zeal that drives this call for genocide of women prevents all adherence to the rules of logic, with the result that the *Malleus* can lay no claim to rigor in its drawing of conclusions from false premises."
22. Kramer, *Malleus,* fols. 20r–v (p. 41), emphasis added.
23. Ibid., emphasis added.
24. The discrepancy in numbering suggests that pt. 2 of the *Malleus* became more complex after Kramer moved the discussion of demonic copulation. In fact, unlike pts. 1 and 3, pt. 2 has two major divisions, called *questions.* These are divided into chapters (*capitula*), which are the same size and scope as the "questions" of pts. 1 and 3.
25. Kramer, *Malleus,* fols. 20r–v, 53r (pp. 41, 109).
26. Ibid., fols. 55v–56r (p. 114).
27. Referring to the order laid out on ibid., fols. 20r–v (p. 41): Point 1 is discussed on fols. 53v–55v (pp. 109–12). There is an interpolation about women on fols. 54v–55r (pp. 111–12), moved from the original pt. 1, question 5 (discussed below). Point 2 is discussed on fols. 55r–v (pp. 112–13), point 3 on fol. 55v (pp. 113–14), and points 4–7 on fols. 55v–56r (p. 114).
28. Ibid., fol. 56r (p. 114).
29. Ibid., fol. 54v (p. 111).
30. Ibid., fol. 15v (p. 31), emphasis added (see also Kramer's table of contents, fol. 2r); fol. 54v (p. 111).
31. Ibid., fols. 53r–55v (pp. 109–13).
32. Ibid., fol. 54v (p. 111), emphasis added.
33. Here, as elsewhere, when discussing producers of *maleficia* before the current time, Kramer still uses the male-gendered *maleficos* instead of *maleficas.* Women are his ideal agents only for the combination of *maleficia* and demonic copulation. On incubi in medieval theology, see Lea, 1:145–62; and Cohn, *Europe's Inner Demons,* 234–37.
34. Kramer, *Malleus,* fol. 54v. Summers translates more readably, but he mistranslates "ante annos incarnationis dominice mille et quadringintos vel circiter" as "about 1400 years *before* the Incarnation of Our Lord" (p. 111, emphasis added).
35. Ibid., fol. 54v (p. 111), emphasis added.
36. Ibid., fol. 5v (p. 7).
37. Ibid., fol. 13r (p. 26).

38. Ibid., fol. 2r. The passage is not in Summers, who appears to have written his own table of contents (pp. i–iv).
39. The table of contents offers no more clarity: "Fourth question: whether it is catholic to assert that the function [*actus*] of incubus and succubus demons is appropriate only to spirits of the lowest rank [*infimis*]" (Kramer, *Malleus,* fol. 2r).
40. Ibid., fols. 15r–20r, 54v–55r (pp. 23–28, 111–12).
41. Ibid., fol. 10v; Summers (p. 21) translates very loosely.
42. This revised focus remains in the table of contents: "The sixth [question] concerns witches [*maleficos*] who cooperate with demons. Why women are found to be more infected with this heresy than men. And what sort of women above all others are involved is made clear by the five subsequent questions" (ibid., fol. 2r).
43. Ibid., fol. 26v (p. 54). There is the same focus in the table of contents: witches do this "virtute demonum," by the power of demons (fol. 2r).
44. "The eighteenth [question] against five arguments of laymen to the effect that God would never permit such power to the devil and witches; and in this matter the end rejoins [*coniungitur*] its beginning, since this last question is bound up in the first," i.e., that three things are necessary for witchcraft: the devil, the witch, and the divine permission (ibid., fol. 2r).
45. See n. 24 above.
46. Ibid., fols. 4r, 5r, 10v, 26v (pp. 2, 4, 20, 54). Each time, Kramer cites the canon law *Si per sortiarias,* which begins, "If sometimes by means of divinatory and malefic arts, by the permission of some just but mysterious judgment of God, and with the Devil's facilitation . . ." (1150). Summers omits Kramer's overt citations of this law.
47. Kramer, *Malleus,* fol. 15v (p. 31), emphasis added. The table of contents reads: "Whether in any way it can be catholic to believe that the origin and proliferation of the works of witches [*maleficorum*] proceeds from the influence of the celestial bodies, without any support from demons. Or [whether it comes] from separated substances, such as the movers of the celestial orbs [i.e., Aristotelian 'intelligences']. Or also from human malice, with some power of the stars being summoned by [human] utterances and words" (fol. 2r).
48. Ibid., fols. 15r–20r (pp. 31–41).
49. "Est ergo quaestio super influentias corporum celestium in qua tres alij errores reprobantur; et est quinta in ordine. Sed pro ampliori premissorum declaratione etiam obviandum quibuscumque pretensis obiectionibus. Queritur de maleficorum [*sic:* not maleficarum] operibus quo ad quintuplicem causam, quattuor ex illis reprobando ex quibus influere non possunt, quinta vero concludendo scilicet virtutem intellectivam ex qua fluere habent, que et licet bona secundum natura, est tamen mala secundum voluntatem. Quattuor autem cause reprobantur contra illos qui aut maleficas [*sic*] aut eorum [*sic*] opera esse negant: et sunt corporum celestium influentie, illorum corporum et orbium motores moventia, hominum excrescens malitia, et imaginum ac caracterum et verborum efficacia" (ibid., fol. 15r). The same text appears in the 1519 edition (see fol. 21v [sig. c5v]).
50. Even in Summers's translation, the ordering of the four refuted hypotheses is visible in the subheading titles that Summers used to introduce each of

them (see pp. 31, 36, 38, 39). In the first edition, these subheading titles do not appear in the body of the discussion (see Kramer/Jerouschek, *Malleus maleficarum 1487,* fols. 15v–20r).

51. In the first edition of the *Malleus,* and as late as the Nuremberg edition of 1519, the first sentence of the new pt. 1, question 5, is preceded by this title and summary paragraph. But, by 1580, editions of the *Malleus* had dropped them both. One could not blame an editor for suspecting that the summary and title had been corrupted and mixed up by previous printers. The deletion could also have occurred through a typesetter's oversight, although this seems less likely.
52. Kramer, *Malleus,* fol. 20v (p. 41).
53. This is implicit in the borrowings from Antoninus of Florence and influences some historians (e.g., Klaits, 65–74).
54. Cohn, *Europe's Inner Demons,* 164, 233–34.
55. Ibid., 164–205; Kieckhefer, *Magic in the Middle Ages,* and *Forbidden Rites.*
56. Kramer, *Malleus,* fol. 23r (p. 47).
57. However, succubi cannot be eliminated from Kramer's system, as we shall see in the next chapter. On demons and crimes against nature, see chap. 12 below. For other writers of the same opinion, see Lea, 1:161–62.
58. See the discussion of sodomy in chap. 12 below.
59. Kramer, *Malleus,* fol. 21r (p. 44), emphasis added.
60. Abbiati, "Appendice," 334.
61. Kramer, *Malleus,* fol. 4v (pp. 3–4); Guazzo/Ashwin, 39.
62. I quote from the bull as reproduced in Kramer/Jerouschek, *Malleus maleficarum 1487,* fol. Ir. As I state below, most early editions of the *Malleus* included the bull as a preface, but the first edition did not (ibid., xlv–xlvi). Summers (p. xliii) and George Lincoln Burr (Kors and Peters, eds., 108) translate differently.
63. Kramer, *Malleus,* fol. 10v (pp. 20–21).
64. See ibid., fol. Ir (p. xliii) (in the text of the *Summis*); Jerouschek, "500 Years of the *Malleus maleficarum,*" xli.

Chapter Three

1. *Oxford English Dictionary,* s.v. *reality,* citing Du Cange's *Glossarium* (5:606), gives 1120 as the earliest attestation. *Reality* is a complicated idea in the Christian tradition, as the dispute between nominalists and realists over the reality of abstract ideas illustrates. Battaglia, 15:615, credits Duns Scotus (d. 1308) with coining the term. See also Courtine, esp. 178–81; Latham, 392, 403. Salvatore Camporeale (personal communication) supports the latter three and cautions me that *quantity* and *quality* are *predicamenta* or *categories* deriving from Aristotle (*Categories,* 1b25), whereas, as a synonym (as well as a linguistic derivative) of *res* (thing), *realitas* is one of the *transcendentals* and thus a synonym of *truth* (*verum*) for late-Scholastic reasoning. Even Gianfresco Pico, writing in 1523, does not have a word for *reality* (see p. 290 and p. 408, n. 33, below).
2. I disagree, however, with Hopkin's absolutist defense of Aquinas, especially his conclusion that there are *no* innovations in Aquinas's demonology that "would lead us to look upon Thomas's version as richer in material for witchcraft than the Bible and Augustine for example" (177).

3. Keck, 89–91. Rabelais, who attended the Sorbonne in the early 1500s and loved his wine, still joked about drinking from the "Quart of Sentences."
4. Ibid., 91.
5. As Lansing, 96, observes, "The thirteenth century was an age not only of faith, but of skepticism."
6. Lombard, 1:327. The work is divided by book, distinction, and chapter.
7. Ibid., 1:348–51, 359–65, 379–83.
8. Lombard, *Sententiarum,* 2.8.1 (ibid., 1:365).
9. On the background to discussion of Augustine's views, see Keck, 71–92.
10. Augustine, 262, emphasis added. See Apuleius, *De deo Socratis.*
11. Augustine, 262.
12. Specifically, Augustine, *De civitate Dei,* 8.14–10.32. Suprahuman beings are also discussed at other points in the text.
13. Aquinas, *Summa theologiae,* 1.51.2 (9:37).
14. "[Aquinas] is the one who offered the church a method of conciliation of the tensions and a nonconflictual absorption of everything that could not be avoided. He is the one who taught how to distinguish contradictions in order to mediate them harmoniously. Once the trick was clear, [his followers] thought that Aquinas's lesson was this: Where yes and no are opposed, create a 'nes' " (Eco, *Travels in Hyperreality,* 267).
15. Aquinas, *Summa theologiae,* 1.51.2 (9:37).
16. Augustine, 262.
17. Aquinas, *Summa theologiae,* 1.51.2 (9:37).
18. Ibid., 1.51.3 (9:43). The reference is to Tob. 12:19. But Aquinas is glossing over a reference to *some* kind of body: else why would Raphael mention food and drink at all?
19. Aquinas, *Summa theologiae,* 1.51.3 (9:43).
20. On Bernard, see Jacobus de Voragine, 1:105–6; and Kramer, *Malleus,* fols. 80v–81r (p. 166). The fifth *distinctio,* or book, of Caesarius's *Dialogus* is composed entirely of stories of angels and demons, intended to prove that they can be seen and interacted with (see chap. 12 below).
21. See Tobit 6–8.
22. On Asmodeus, see Kramer, *Malleus,* fol. 15r (p. 30). The *Anchor Bible Dictionary* notes that the Book of Tobit "was a major step in the Biblical understanding of demons, and, especially, of angels" (C. A. Moore, 590). On the various versions of the text, see ibid., 591–92. The book is not canonical for Protestants and Jews, and Catholics reduced it to the compromise status of "deuterocanonical" at the Council of Trent.
23. Montaigne, "Of Cripples," 785; Ascoli; and, more schematically, Álvarez.
24. See Augustine, *De civitate Dei,* 15.23; and Stephens, *Giants in Those Days,* 75–92.
25. Aquinas, *Summa theologiae,* 1.51.3 (9:43). The first sentence reads: "Si tamen ex coitu daemonum aliqui interdum nascuntur . . . ," so a more literal translation might read: "Nevertheless, if occasionally some persons are born from the copulation of demons. . . ." However, the translation in the Gilby et al. edition fully renders the mood of Aquinas's bizarre passage because, in suggesting that devils might somehow sire children, Aquinas is not recording a mere afterthought. The sentence that I have left out (just before the final one of this passage) shows that Aquinas felt

that he needed to assure the reader that he was not simply making all this up: "Augustine, in *De Trinitate* (III, 23) speaks of devils using non-human seed in this way."

26. See the discussion of Silvestro Mazzolini (Prierias) below.
27. See Alexander of Hales, 2:75–76 (on Lombard, *Sententiarum,* 2.8). On the Augustinian theory behind this earlier theory, see Augustine, *De trinitate,* 3.7–10; Brady.
28. Hopkin, combating simplistic views that collapsed the differences between Aquinas and his fifteenth-century followers, maintained erroneously that "the incubus-succubus theory of Thomas Aquinas was [simply] designed to explain the stories of children being born as a result of a sexual union between demons and human beings. It was less adapted to the idea of the witches' sabbat than was the earlier incubus legend" (177; see also 1–27).
29. On Aquinas, see chap. 12 below. Keck overlooks this anxiety, in Bonaventure (his main author) and elsewhere. For Keck, Christian angelology (he discusses demonology only in passing) between the eleventh and the thirteenth centuries is a story of "deep changes and rich elaborations" (5), rarely one of worrisome problems. He repeatedly compares Scholastic angelologists to modern scientists, speaking of their "investigations" and their "discoveries," e.g.: "In the thirteenth century, angelologists were much like modern natural scientists, methodically exploring the biological aspects of the angel, one of the most marvelous creatures of the universe" (83; see also 16, 27, 34, 36, 53, 68–69, 103).
30. Aquinas, *Summa theologiae,* 1.51.3 (9:41).
31. Aquinas, *De malo,* 16.1 (Aquinas, *On Evil,* 445).
32. In addition to *Summa theologiae,* 1.50–64, and *De malo,* 16.1, there are Aquinas's *Commentum* on Lombard, *Sententiarum,* 2.8; the *Summa contra gentiles,* 2.91–93, 3.99; and three *quaestiones disputatae,* the *De potentia,* 4.2, the *De spiritualibus creaturis,* esp. arts. 5–8, and much of *De substantiis separatis.*
33. Aquinas, *Summa theologiae,* 1.51.2 (9:35–37). Vineti, sig. a8r, seems to attribute this opinion to Maimonides. For Boethius of Dacia's doubts (ca. 1270) about the reality of dreams of encounters with angels, see Keck, 190.
34. Kramer, *Malleus,* fol. 4r (p. 2) (see chap. 2 above). The quotation is from Aquinas's *Commentum* on Lombard, *Sententiarum,* 4.34.1.3, with a variant form in Aquinas's *Quaestiones quodlibetales* (see chap. 11 below).
35. Keck, 87–99.
36. Ibid., 99. See also Collins, 75–136; Colish, "Early Scholastic Angelology"; and Gilson, *Philosophy of Saint Bonaventure,* 222–26. Bonaventure's commentary on Lombard, *Sententiarum,* 2.8, is in his *Opera omnia,* 2:207–35.
37. Keck, 98. On the human soul in witchcraft theory, see chap. 13 below.
38. Lea, 1:157; Hopkin, 145–73.
39. Keck, 99 n. 22; Peters, *The Magician, the Witch,* 95–98; Lea, 1:289.
40. Keck, 94 n. 4; Wippel; *Index librorum prohibitorum,* 59–60.
41. Quoted from Tostado's epitaph in Abbiati, Agnoletto, and Lazzati, eds., 354 ("Note bio-bibliografiche").
42. Tostado, *Super genesim,* fol. 51r.
43. These words echo Aquinas's stipulation that "the child so begotten would not have the devil for its father, but the man whose semen had been used."
44. Tostado, *Matthei explanatio,* fol. 314v.

45. Kramer, *Malleus,* fol. 13v (p. 27). Compare Kramer's wording to Aquinas's *Commentum* on Lombard, *Sententiarum,* 2.8.1.4.
46. The references to Aristotle are from Aquinas's *Commentum* on Lombard, *Sententiarum,* 2.8.1.4, and are repeated by Bartolomeo Spina (see p. 83 below).
47. Kramer, *Malleus,* fol. 55r (p. 112); and see Aquinas's *Commentum* on Lombard, *Sententiarum,* 2.8.1.4 (wrongly cited by Kramer as 2.4.4).
48. Kramer, *Malleus,* fol. 55r (p. 112), emphasis added.
49. Ibid.
50. Ibid.
51. Ibid., fol. 55r (pp. 112–13).
52. Ibid., fol. 92r (p. 192). Kramer attributes his theory of changelings to William of Auvergne's *De universo* (ibid., fol. 51r [p. 105]).
53. On Mazzolini's career and works, esp. his writings on witchcraft, see Tavuzzi, esp. 122–27.
54. For the influence of the *Malleus,* see Lea, 1:354–65.
55. Mazzolini, *De strigimagarum,* 6.
56. Keck, 72–114.
57. Aquinas, *De malo,* 16.1 (Aquinas, *On Evil,* 447).
58. On Thomas Scoto's disbelief in spirits, see Hansen, ed., *Quellen,* 66n. For Pietro d'Abano, see Pico, *De rerum praenotione,* 4.9 (1:493). Pico says that Pietro defended himself by claiming that "it seemed logical that he would not have interrogated [*interrogasse*] demons unless he believed in them." In chap. 13 below, I argue that there is no illogic in attempts to contact demons while doubting their reality.
59. Kramer, *Malleus,* fol. 27v (pp. 56–57). See Aquinas, *De malo,* 16.1, and *De substantiis separatis,* 2. This idea derives from Augustine's discussion of Porphyry's epistle to Anebo, particularly the idea that Porphyry describes demons, "not as things of which he is himself convinced, but only with so much suspicion and doubt as to cause him to speak of them as commonly received opinions." Augustine claims that Porphyry "experienced difficulty" in "acquainting himself with and confidently assailing the whole fraternity of devils, which any Christian old woman would unhesitatingly describe and most unreservedly detest." Porphyry thought that, "by means of herbs, and stones, and animals, and certain incantations and noises, and drawings, sometimes fanciful, and sometimes copied from the motions of the heavenly bodies, men create upon earth powers capable of bringing about various results," but "all that is only the mystification which these demons practise upon those who are subject to them, for the sake of furnishing themselves with merriment at the expense of their dupes" (Augustine, 315–16, 317).
60. Keck, 84, quotes Alexander Murray that the term *supernatural* "arose only in the thirteenth century in order to 'accommodate an old idea of the divine in terms of a new idea of nature.'"
61. For Aristotle's view of heavenly matter, see Hetherington, ed., 95–103, esp. 101.
62. Kramer, *Malleus,* fol. 28r (p. 57). The book's first sentence asks "whether the belief that there are such beings as witches is so essential a part of the Catholic faith that obstinately to maintain the opposite opinion manifestly

savours of heresy" (fol. 4v [p. 1]). In pt. 1, question 8 (fol. 27v [p. 56]), Kramer says that, "although all the other doctors condemn as an unmitigated [*simplici*] falsehood" the notion that natural causes make witchcraft unnecessary and imaginary, "Saint Thomas impugns it more bitterly [*acrius*], and condemns it as an actual heresy, saying that this error proceeds from the root of infidelity [*ex radice infidelitatis*]," without specifying where (but see chap. 11 below). In part 3, question 24 (fol. 115v [p. 246]), Kramer explains how to sentence people "under strong suspicion" of witchcraft who will not confess and cannot be convicted. Inquisitors must make them declare "I abjure, renounce, and revoke that heresy, or rather, infidelity, which falsely and mendaciously maintains that there are no witches [*non aliquam maleficam*] in the world, and that no one ought to believe that those injuries can be caused with the help of devils."

63. Ibid., fol. 28r (p. 57), emphasis added.
64. Ibid.
65. French and Cunningham, 70–98; Haren, 194–211.
66. See Garin, 499; Schmitt, introduction, ix–xiii, "Perennial Philosophy," 527, and "*Prisca theologia,*" 223–24; and Walker, *Ancient Theology,* 40–41.
67. Steuco, 467. Compare Kramer on "the operation and cooperation of the angels" in forming comets, "which not even the philosophers can refute" (Kramer, *Malleus,* fol. 16v [p. 34]). Aquinas did admit, parenthetically and, apparently, only once, that "Aristotle did not posit any souls intermediate between the souls of the heavens [i.e., the 'intelligences' that move the spheres] and the souls of men, as Plato did; whence it cannot be found that *either he or his followers* ever mentioned demons [*unde de daemonibus nullam invenitur nec ipse nec eius sequaces fecisse mentionem*]" (*De substantiis separatis,* 4 [*Opera,* 3:516]).
68. Steuco, 460–61.
69. Ibid., 456.
70. For Steuco's references to angels in Tobit, see ibid., 420, 422, and 441 (all are allusions to angels' food), 452 (on Tob. 12:12–19), and 455. For his references to other biblical angels, see 426–27 (on Sodom and Gomorrah), 450 (on Jacob's ladder), and 478 (on Satan in the Book of Job).
71. Ibid., 473: "Nature will not permit and Philosophy will not accept that spirits denuded of a body can be taken with the love of women, or procreate with them. . . . Where there are no genitals, there is no love of sex [*coeundi*]; where no food and drink, no sperm; where no need of progeny and propagation, Nature gave no desire to generate. Just as pure [*nudi*] spirits cannot thirst or hunger, so they cannot be inflamed by Venus's cravings."
72. See the notes (9:9, 30–31)and app. 1 (9:301–5) to the Gilby et al. edition of Aquinas's *Summa theologiae;* this is also the implication of Bonaventure's hylomorphism.
73. Steuco, 463.
74. For more on Pomponazzi and immortality, see chap. 13 below.
75. Chapters 9–13 of Pomponazzi's *De naturalium effectuum causis* discuss Aristotle and demonology. Busson's introduction (Pomponazzi/Busson, 9–105) is useful, especially regarding Pomponazzi's effects on later discussions of demonology (39–62).

76. Pomponazzi, *De naturalium effectuum causis,* 181, quoting Aquinas, *Quaestiones quodlibetales,* 11.9.1. See chap. 11 below, pp. 318–20.
77. Pomponazzi, *De naturalium effectuum causis,* 191, emphasis added.
78. Ibid., 205–8.
79. Ibid., 204, quoting Plutarch, *Nicias,* 23.
80. Ibid., 207–8. Here, there is certainly a jab at Bartolomeo Spina, who called Pomponazzi's earlier book *De mortalitate animae,* or *On the Mortality of the Soul.* See chap. 13 below.
81. Pomponazzi, *De naturalium effectuum causis,* 205.
82. Cesalpino, sig. C1r.
83. De Ferrari.
84. See chap. 11 below.
85. For the attack on Pomponazzi, see chap. 13 below. On Spina's inquisitorial activities, see Ginzburg, *Clues,* 1–16; Bertolotti, 42–50; and Abbiati, "A proposito." Further bibliography on Spina can be found in Abbiati, Agnoletto, and Lazzati, eds., 366–68.
86. The colophon to the 1576 reprint of the first edition says, "These works were published in the year of Our Lord 1525," although the final words of *De strigibus* claim that it was published (*edita*) in 1523 (Spina, 90, 180). See also P. Castelli, *Bibliotheca lamiarum,* 121–22.
87. Spina, 16.
88. Ibid., 21.
89. Ibid., 47.
90. Ibid.
91. Augustine, 511–12.
92. In fact, it was not important to him because he had already explained the giants of Genesis 6 as the children of human fathers (the descendants of Seth) rather than incubi.
93. Spina, 46; references to Aristotle tie this passage to Aquinas and Kramer (see p. 71 and p. 383, n. 46, above).
94. Spina, 46–47.
95. Ibid., 46.
96. Ibid., 47, emphasis added.
97. This is not to downplay the influence of the Scholastic method of exposition itself, which, like the classroom methods on which it was based, began from the premise that "the method of teaching (*modus docendi*) ought to follow the pattern of discovery (*modus inveniendi*)" (Weisheipl, 1145).

Chapter Four

1. Spina, 91.
2. On Aristotle as empirical, see French and Cunningham, esp. 10–11. For Gianfrancesco, Aristotelianism was empirical since it depended more on observation and sensory data than on faith or Platonic idealism.
3. Schmitt, *Gianfrancesco Pico,* 49. See also Farmer, 133–79.
4. Biondi, introduction to Pico/Alberti, 32; Garin, 153; Schmitt, *Gianfrancesco Pico,* 53–54.
5. The classic study of Pico's *Strix* is Burke; see esp. 32–34.
6. P. Castelli, *Bibliotheca lamiarum,* 130–31 (although Passavanti's *Specchio della vera penitenza* was printed in 1495 [see chap. 5 below]).

7. Pico/Alberti, 50. On Alberti, see Almagià; Redigonda.
8. Pico/Alberti, 55–56.
9. Ibid., 10.
10. Given Alberti's imprecise usage, *biasimevoli ragionamenti* could mean "arguments *filled with blame,*" but he is asserting that such critiques are *worthy of blame* by right-thinking people like himself and Pico.
11. Pico/Alberti, 52–53.
12. Pico, *Strix,* sig. A4v.
13. See the account of Pico's character in Farmer, 133–79.
14. On relations between Pico, Spina, and Mazzolini, see Tavuzzi, 127.
15. Spina, 91.
16. Pico/Alberti, 53.
17. Ibid., 55. In modern terms, this would be "unbeliever" or "disbeliever." Alberti says that, when "convinced by the truth," Apistius changes his name to Pisticus, "that is, 'faithful' [*fedele*]" (ibid.).
18. Ibid.
19. Ibid., 55–56; cf. 50.
20. Pico, *Strix,* sig. E4v; Pico/Alberti, 132.
21. Pico, *Strix,* sigs. G3r–v.
22. This is both an Italian proverb and an inquisitorial byword: "And they most likely fear being accused, so they excuse themselves implicitly, before they can be accused. Whence it is clear that by thus excusing themselves they accuse themselves [*se sic excusando accusant*]" (*Recollectio casus,* 168).
23. Pico, *Strix,* sigs. G2v-3r; Pico/Alberti, 161–62.
24. Witches' demon familiars often have strangely banal names since accused witches were unfamiliar with clerical demonology. Pico compromised: Ludovicus, or Luigi, is a plausibly common name, but it hints at *ludo* and *ludificatio* (illude, illusion), recalling his title, *Strix, sive de* ludificationibus *daemonum.*
25. Pico, *Strix,* sig. D4v; Pico/Alberti, 109.
26. Turini translates *crassiores* as "bigger [*più grosse*] than those of men" (Pico/Turini, 103). Alberti left no doubt the "members" were genitals: "It seems to me that, as far as the pudenda [*parti vergognose*] are concerned, they are similar to flesh" (Pico/Alberti, 124).
27. Pico, *Strix,* sig. E3r. Alberti adds: "That's how they feel to the touch, but nonetheless they are always cold" (Pico/Alberti, 124). Alberti knew that coldness supposedly came from demonic bodies' airy composition and evidently wished that Pico had clarified it. In the original, Pico omits coldness in favor of this technical conversation:

> APISTIUS: I understand what flax is, Phronimus, but not cottonwool [*bombasium*].
> PHRONIMUS: I should think she meant tree wool [*xylinam lanuginem*].
> STRIX: By that I wanted you to understand the material that is used for stuffing bed quilts [*in lodicibus infarciri solet*].

28. The original (Pico, *Strix,* sig. D4v) attributes this speech to Phronimus, but Phronimus has just finished a long, erudite explanation. Alberti (Pico/Alberti, 112) attributes the question to Apistius, as Pico clearly intended.

29. Pico/Alberti, 113, emphasis added. The original (Pico, *Strix,* sig. D4v) is extremely laconic:

> DICASTES: He has now taken the form of a most salacious bird, not inconsistently [*non abhorrens*] with what this woman has said, whose lasciviousness surpasses all the monsters of lust.
> APISTIUS: I marvel that no one but her can perceive the form of that sparrow.
> DICASTES: In fact, no one can perceive it.
> APISTIUS: Perfectly marvelous!

30. Pico, *Strix,* sigs. E3r–v; Pico/Alberti, 125–26.
31. See Albano Biondi's introduction to Pico/Alberti, 22–24.
32. Pico, *Strix,* sig. E3v; expurgated by Pico/Alberti, 126.
33. Pico, *Strix,* sig. E3v; Pico/Alberti, 126–27.
34. Pico, *Strix,* sig. E3v. Sentence in italic added by Alberti (Pico/Alberti, 127).
35. Pico/Alberti, 126. Neither Pico's characters nor the editor (Biondi) appears to notice this.
36. The nickname means "greenhorn" (modern Italian *pivello*).
37. On Pivetto, see Pico/Alberti, 14–15 and the appendix, 217–22. In the real-life trials, Andrea Merlotti was nicknamed Il Piva, but there was also a Marco Piva. This Marco accused a certain "Piveta" of witchcraft (ibid., p. 221, no. 55).
38. Pico, *Strix,* sig. E3v; Pico/Alberti, 128, omits mentioning atheism.
39. Clark, *Thinking with Demons,* ix.
40. Levack, 56. See also Behringer, 6.
41. Levack, 102.
42. Kors and Peters, eds., 249–52.
43. Bodin, *Démonomanie,* 2.7 (Bodin, fol. 107v); De Lancre, 179.
44. Larner, *Enemies of God,* and *Witchcraft and Religion.*
45. Sharpe, 128–47.
46. Rosen, ed., 30.
47. Ibid., 32.
48. Levack, 200–202, 73–74.
49. Rosen, ed., 32.
50. Levack, 74ff.
51. Scot, *Discoverie,* 58–70, and *Discourse,* 433–35.
52. Willis explores maternal representations in English witchcraft.
53. Rosen, ed., 26.
54. Ibid., 81. Rosen notes that this was "a very equivocal offer."
55. Mather, 170.
56. Sharpe, 143.
57. Kramer, *Malleus,* fol. 55v (p. 114), emphasis added.
58. Ibid., fols. 55v–56r (p. 114).
59. This is the formal definition of witchcraft as *crimen exceptum* (see Levack, 79–80).
60. Kramer, *Malleus,* fol. 56r (p. 114).
61. Ibid.

62. Pictures of demons obviously copulating with humans tend to be details of larger tableaux: e.g., Robbins, 515; Hansen, ed., *Quellen,* 298 (also in Behringer, 75).
63. See the variant illustration, less crude, from another early edition of Müller in Grillot de Givry, fig. 49, p. 80. According to Giovanna Bosco (in P. Castelli, *Bibliotheca lamiarum,* 111), the illustrations to Müller are the only witchcraft images published in fifteenth-century demonological treatises. For a fourteenth-century manuscript illustration of an incubus inseminating Merlin's mother, the nun, see Kors and Peters, eds., fig. 14, p. 97. Following the prewitchcraft notion of predatory incubi and unwilling women, Merlin's mother is asleep.
64. Davidson, 24, is blunt: the drawing depicts "a young woman and a dragon-like demon which is engaged in cunnilingus." Unlike the "playful amoretti" (Lehner and Lehner, comps., fig. 92, p. 65) of an apparent witch engraving by Dürer, Baldung's infants have no wings or drapery. On putti in these pictures, see Davidson, 24. On Dürer and Baldung's witch illustrations, see Sullivan.
65. Reproduced, e.g., in Levack, pl. 10. Young and elderly nude witches are also represented in Baldung's engraving from 1514 (Lehner and Lehner, comps., fig. 89, p. 63). See further Davidson, esp. figs. 4–10.
66. Of Russell's five books on the Devil, the most useful for our purpose is *Lucifer,* esp. 208–301. Russell has some discussion of demonic corporeality and sexuality (mostly on 209–12, 295–301).
67. Baltrušaitis, 182–85; Lorenzi, 49–57; Link, 67.
68. For Wolfgang's pact with the Devil, see E. Castelli, 90.
69. Cuttler, 54, 37.
70. Ibid., 76–77.
71. Grillot de Givry, fig. 16, p. 41. The mirror reversal would be natural if van Meckenem copied his plate directly from a print of Schongauer: woodcuts and engravings are incised facing upward but printed facing downward.
72. Cuttler, 77. For Anthony's legend, see also Athanasius; and Jacobus de Voragine, 1:93–96.
73. Between the fifteen century and the seventeenth, demonic corporeality underwent still further permutations, including vegetable and inanimate forms, in representations of the temptation of Saint Anthony and related demonic subjects, the most famous examples being works by Hieronymus Bosch (d. 1516) and Pieter Brueghel the Elder (d. 1563). Abundant pictorial documentation of these and other works is in E. Castelli; and Tristan, esp. 103–79.
74. See E. Castelli; and Tristan.
75. E. Castelli, 129, reproduces an even more dramatic representation of a devil and a soldier by Graf, from 1516.
76. Russell, *Lucifer,* 231–32 (correctly, on Dante's Satan).
77. Janson, 391.
78. On this miracle, see chap. 8 below.
79. Stephens, "La demonologia nella poetica del Tasso." On the virtual bodies of Dante's dead, see *Purgatorio,* 25.76–108. Gragnolati gives the definitive reading of these bodies in Dante's system of corporeality.

80. Davidson, 101, declares that "most witchcraft art is an excuse for a wide variety of pornography."
81. Milton, *Paradise Lost,* 4.166–71, 5.219–23, 9.420–93.
82. Kramer, *Malleus,* fols. 13v–15r (pp. 28–31); and most early witchcraft theorists. Around 1700, Ludovico Sinistrari tried to attribute proper bodies and sex drives to incubi and succubi. In the *De demonialitate,* he "theorized" that incubi are a mere sexual nuisance, whereas true devils, lacking bodies and sex drives, want to cause human damnation. His attempt failed, and he had to equate "demoniality" (voluntary sex with incubi) with witchcraft (voluntary sex with demons).
83. 1 Cor. 11:10. See also Lea, 1:152–53 (William of Auvergne), 156–57.

Chapter Five

1. Levack, 38–44. See descriptions of the "witches' conclave" in Kramer, *Malleus,* fols. 48v–49r (pp. 99–100).
2. For the text of the Canon *Episcopi,* see either "Canon *Episcopi*" or Hansen, ed., *Quellen,* 38–39; the text is translated in Kors and Peters, eds., 29; cf. Abbiati, Agnoletto, and Lazzati, eds., 22–26; Lea, 1:178–80; and Levack, 46–49.
3. Kors and Peters, eds., 31.
4. Ibid. The references are to Ezekiel 1–3; Rev. 4:2; and 2 Cor. 12:1–6.
5. Kors and Peters, eds., 31.
6. See also Col. 1:16.
7. For the early history of Christian dream theory, see Le Goff, 193–231.
8. See Aquinas, *Commentum* on Lombard, *Sententiarum,* 2.7.2.2, and *Summa theologiae,* 2-2.95.6; Gregory, ed.; Fattori and Bianchi, eds.; P. Castelli, " 'Donnaiole, amiche de li sogni.' "
9. Kors and Peters, eds., 29–31.
10. On the relative newness of the concepts *nature* and *supernatural,* see Keck, 84.
11. French and Cunningham, 78 (William of St. Thierry to Bernard of Clairvaux about William of Conches's interpretation of the creation of Eve); see 70–98 for the "hostility of the orthodox to the use of 'nature' as a separate principle" in the twelfth century.
12. Aquinas, *Summa theologiae,* 1.2.3 (2:12–13).
13. All quotations are from Passavanti, 40–41. See also Abbiati, Agnoletto, and Lazzati, eds., 353.
14. The classic story of necromancy in the Middle Ages (1 Samuel 28).
15. On the wild host, see William of Auvergne, *De universo,* 3.2.24; Petzoldt, 22–23; Ginzburg, *Clues,* 163, and *Ecstasies,* 101–3. Ginzburg's main source is the sermons of the Dominican Johannes Herolt, from ca. 1418. Alonso de Espina refers to the "ancient host," demons "who appear to wakeful people on the road, as if they were a great army, and are seen to march along in great tumult, and are called *huesta antigua* in the vernacular. Sometimes they are even seen to perform great battles. . . . By these means they [the demons] have won a not insignificant multitude of souls" (sig. Z3r). On Saint Germanus (Germain), see Jacobus de Voragine, 2:28.
16. See Hopkin, 36; Keck, 109–12.

17. Bonomo (15–17, 59–60), Cohn (*Europe's Inner Demons,* 217–18), and Ginzburg (*Ecstasies,* 91–93) mention trials of women in Milan between 1384 and 1390, "not for imagining that they followed Diana, but for following her" (Cohn, *Europe's Inner Demons,* 217).
18. Jacquier, 136–40.
19. The term *synagoga* appears to be the earlier of the two. Ostorero, 143–44, relates usage of *synagoga* in trials from 1448 to early treatises like those in Ostorero, Bagliani, and Utz Tremp, eds. *Secta* designated groups of alleged heretics, *synagoga* their meeting place (Ostorero, 143n).
20. Jacquier, 140; cf. Lea, 1:278.
21. Vineti, sig. b1r.
22. Ibid., sig. b8r.
23. Ibid., sigs. b8r–v. See also Tostado, *Matthei explanatio,* fol. 162v.
24. Vineti, sigs. b8v–c1r.
25. Lazzati, preface to Giordano da Bergamo (Abbiati, Agnoletto, and Lazzati, eds.), 79, based on Ghigliazza, esp. 77–79, a simplistic local-historical defense of Giordano.
26. See Giordano da Bergamo (Hansen, ed.), 197–99.
27. Ibid., 200: "Cum obiectum fidei nostre sit veritas, nullo modo ipsi fidei falsum subesse potest."
28. Ibid., 200.
29. Clark, *Thinking with Demons,* 198–213. The Italian jurist Andrea Alciato (310–11) claimed that witches should be purged with hellebore (reputed to restore sanity to melancholics), not with fire.
30. Weyer, *De praestigiis,* 3.5-3.9 (Weyer, *Witches, Devils, and Doctors,* esp. 180–88); Scot, *Discoverie,* 1.8. Schiesari explores how melancholia was read as a sign of genius in men but transgressiveness in women.
31. Visconti, *Opusculum,* fol. 1v.
32. Ibid., fol. 1r.
33. Ibid. The same Bible verses are quoted by Rategno, 150, to justify punishing witches.
34. Visconti, *Lamiarum,* sig. a5v.
35. Ibid., sig. a6r.
36. Ibid., sig. a3v. Kramer also states that "among their chief operations are being bodily transported from place to place and the practice of carnal copulation with incubus demons" (Kramer, *Malleus,* fol. 51r [p. 104]).
37. Müller, *De lanijs,* 103.
38. In Abbiati, Agnoletto, and Lazzati, eds., 101.
39. Müller weakens Sigismund's supposed skepticism, having him assume that witches are guilty of *something.* Gianfrancesco Pico used the same strategy in portraying Apistius. Assuming that the reader identifies with the skeptic, these authors hoped to insinuate a subliminal message that witches *could not not* be guilty of something.
40. Müller, *De lanijs,* 80.
41. Ibid., 83.
42. Kramer, *Malleus,* fol. 5v; Summers (p. 7) garbles much of this passage.
43. Ibid., fols. 52v–53r (p. 108). On illusory transformations, see chap. 10 below.
44. Ibid., fol. 53r (p. 108).

45. "In the simplest terms, allegory says one thing and means another. It destroys the normal expectation we have about language, that our words, 'mean what they say'" (Fletcher, 2). On the "nut topos," see Robertson, 671–78.
46. Kramer, *Malleus,* fol. 5v (p. 7).
47. Ibid., fol. 52v (pp. 107–8).
48. Ibid.
49. Ibid., fol. 53r (p. 108).
50. Ibid., fol. 53r (p. 108); see also fol. 40r (p. 81) and fol. 49r (p. 100). This "witch of Breisach" was Kramer's favorite—perhaps principal—informant (see fols. 48v–49r [p. 100]).
51. Spina, 15.

Chapter Six

1. Lea, 1:385, remarked that Spina's *Quaestio* (examined later in this chapter) "seems to be an extended commentary on the Can[on] Episcopi."
2. For discussions of experiments with unguents by Giambattista Della Porta and Girolamo Cardano, see Bodin, *Démonomanie,* 2.5 (Bodin, fols. 89r–94v); Weyer, *De praestigiis daemonum,* 3.17 (Weyer, *Witches, Devils, and Doctors,* 225–28); and Tartarotti, 308–10. A later and particularly cruel example is in Tartarotti, 316–17. Predictably, Bodin finds diabolical explanations for all possible outcomes.
3. Cervantes, 232, emphasis added. The story considers problems of reality, including those raised by witchcraft mythology: unguents, Sabbat, infanticide, metamorphoses (are the dogs transformed humans?), and the permission of God.
4. Merchant, 168–69; Peters, *Inquisition,* chaps. 1–2, esp. pp. 12–17.
5. For other early references to experiments with witches, see Hansen, ed., *Quellen,* 107, lines 15ff. (from Tostado, *Matthaei explanatio,* fol. 165v), and 132, lines 7ff. (an example from 1456).
6. Tostado, *Super genesim,* fol. 125r. Compare to the burlesque scene in Cervantes, 235–38.
7. Tostado, *Super genesim,* fol. 125r. Tartarotti, 316–17, refers to this and "many" (*moltissimi*) later experiments.
8. Ginzburg, *The Night Battles,* describes several variations of soul travel.
9. See chap. 9 below.
10. Lazzati, preface to Alfonso Tostado, 46.
11. Tostado, *Matthaei explanatio,* fol. 165r.
12. Ibid.
13. Ibid.
14. Tostado, *Super genesim,* fol. 125r.
15. Ibid., fol. 51r.
16. Tostado, *Matthaei explanatio,* fol. 165r.
17. Ibid.
18. See Kramer, *Malleus,* fols. 51r–53r (pp. 104–9).
19. Tostado, *Matthaei explanatio,* fols. 165v–166v.
20. Allen, *Legend of Noah,* 68 (quotation), 66–91 (on scientific estimations about the Ark), appendix (on Kircher).
21. Allen, *Legend of Noah,* 75, emphasis added; see the example on 76.

22. Spina, 160–61, arguing against the jurist Ponzinibio, who had maintained that witches should not be punished because their crimes were imaginary.
23. On the composition date of the *Formicarius,* see Nider/Chène, 107.
24. Nider/Biedermann, 71 (sig. e4r) (Nider/Chène, 134). On witches in Nider's *Preceptorium,* see Lea, 1:271.
25. "Me recedentem videbis" (Nider/Biedermann, 41 [sig. e4r] [Nider/Chène, 134]).
26. The analyses that follow are based on Nider/Biedermann, 71 (sig. e4r) (Nider/Chène, 134–36).
27. Quoted in Nider/Chène, 210–12. Chène does not analyze the differences.
28. Nider did not assert unequivocally that night flying is possible, although he affirmed the existence of *maleficium* and of something like a Sabbat (see chaps. 7–9 below).
29. Nider/Biedermann, 1 (sig. a1r).
30. Nider/Biedermann, 70–71 (sigs. e3v–e4r) (Nider/Chène, 130–34). For the citation of Aquinas, see Nider/Chène, 128. See also Chène's analysis of Nider's theory (Nider/Chène, 206–7).
31. Nider/Chène, 207.
32. On the Christian distrust of dreams, see Le Goff, 210–14; on source vs. structure and contents, see ibid., 193–231, 238; on the duration of the uncertainty and distrust regarding dreams, see ibid., 16, 201, 211, 228, 229, 234. The quotation is from ibid., 203.
33. Ibid., 211–12, 225.
34. Ostorero, 29–30. See also Ostorero, Bagliani, and Utz Tremp, eds., 102–3, 107 (on Nider), 202, 269, 273–74, 435–36; and Blauert, 24–36.
35. See Borst, 101–22; and Ostorero, 5–32, esp. 18. The five texts in Ostorero, Bagliani, and Utz Tremp, eds., came from this area between about 1430 and 1440.
36. Spina, 5.
37. Ibid.
38. Ibid., 82.
39. Ibid., 83.
40. Ibid.
41. Ibid.
42. For example, Rémy, 245.
43. This anecdote is examined in chap. 9 below.
44. Mazzolini, *De strigimagarum,* 136, emphasis added. On the walnut tree of Benevento, see Bonomo, 309–330.
45. Mazzolini, *De strigimagarum,* 136.
46. Ibid.
47. Spina, 85.
48. Rategno, 144.
49. Mazzolini, *De strigimagarum,* 136; cf. ibid., 131 (same story).
50. Ibid., 136–37.
51. Spina, 36.
52. Guazzo/Ashwin, 15; Clark, *Thinking with Demons,* 381–82, 424–25, 431.
53. Nicolas Rémy, 245, claimed to have evidence of successful experiments by judges: "There have been seen cases of witches who as soon as the Judge has given them permission to rub or anoint themselves with the ointment,

have at once been carried aloft and have disappeared." The only example that Rémy gives is Pamphile in Apuleius's *Golden Ass,* the grandmother of all such tales. This story involves no judges, only a curious imitator, the hero of the novel; instead of becoming an owl, as he saw Pamphile do, he turned into a donkey.

54. Spina, 85.
55. Ibid.
56. Ibid.
57. Ibid., 41.
58. Ibid., 36.
59. Giordano da Bergamo tells a compressed variant of the story with an equally obvious point: "We read that the most holy Ambrose was transported from Milan to Rome [*sic*] and taken back to Milan in three hours at his own command [*ipso precipiente et cogente*], so that thereby might be shown the power of the saints over the powers of the Devil; for, according to Saint Augustine, evil things can be used for good. At any rate, uneducated people [*vulgares*] commonly maintain—and, indeed, the witches [*striges*] themselves confess [*fatentur*] it, that certain days or nights they anoint a stick with a certain ointment and ride it and are quickly taken to places chosen by the demon" (Giordano da Bergamo [Hansen, ed.], 199). Lazzati (Abbiati, Agnoletto, and Lazzati, eds., 85 n. 17) could find no source for this story. Given Giordano's point—the good can command demons—the source was probably a treatise on necromancy, not on witchcraft or hagiography.
60. Spina, 32–33.
61. Ibid., 33.
62. Ibid.
63. Ibid., 28.
64. On Mazzolini and Luther, see Tavuzzi, 104–22.
65. Spina, 48. On experience as *rerum magistra,* see Kramer, *Malleus,* fol. 56r. Summers (p. 114) erroneously translates *experientia rerum magistra edocuit* as "this is well known by the constant experience of Magistrates" rather than as "experience, the teacher of all things taught [us]."
66. Spina, 36.
67. Ibid., 28.
68. Ibid., 44–45.
69. Ibid., 45.
70. Ibid., 36–37, emphasis added.
71. Ginzburg, *The Night Travels,* and *Ecstasies.*
72. Abundantly documented in Ostorero; Hansen, ed., *Quellen;* and Hansen, *Zauberwahn.*
73. All references are to Elmer, 754–56.
74. All references are to Griffin, 756–57.
75. On Aquinas on pacts with the Devil, see Hopkin, 106–7; and Robbins, 369–79.

Chapter Seven

1. See, e.g., Thomas, *Religion and the Decline of Magic,* 26–50; Duffy, 266–98; Swanson, 182–88.

2. *Catholicism* is something of a misnomer until after the Council of Trent had defined doctrines as *Catholic,* in response to the objections of Protestants. I will use the terms as shorthand to denote the prevailing doctrines of the Western church, particularly the consensus about sacraments, even before Trent.
3. Kennedy, 299–301.
4. The Fourth Lateran Council (1215) allowed midwives and other layfolk to baptize newborns. The Council of Trent further specified that, in a life-threatening emergency, anyone (even Jews and Muslims) could baptize an infant or a pagan adult validly by speaking the proper words, sprinkling water, and having the sincere intention of baptizing (*Catechismo,* 180).
5. Quinn, 812.
6. One reason is the Protestant accusation that Catholic sacraments are "magic" or "witchcraft." See Clark, *Thinking with Demons,* 475–76, 533; Thomas, *Religion and the Decline of Magic,* 74–77, and "An Anthropology of Religion and Magic"; Geertz; and Kieckhefer, "The Specific Rationality of Medieval Magic," esp. 823–24.
7. *Catechismo,* 152, emphasis added. Sacramental theory is based on the theory of signs developed by Augustine. See *Catechismo,* 149–53; and Michel, "Sacrements," esp. 519 (*signum efficax*), 521 (*virtus sacramenti*).
8. The Tridentine catechism says that, according to Augustine, a sacrament is "the sign of a holy thing, or better . . . the visible sign of an invisible grace, instituted for our justification" (*Catechismo,* 150).
9. However, modern anthropologists have discovered that "primitive" theories of magic do not invariably presume "automatic" success. This misperception may derive from Protestant misunderstandings of sacraments. See Evans-Pritchard; and Douglas, *Purity and Danger.*
10. On the concept *ex opere operato,* see Michel, "Sacrementaux," 476–78; and Kennedy, 297, 298, 301, 304.
11. Kennedy, 297. Kennedy specifies: " 'Ex opere operato,' i.e. by virtue of the action, means that the efficacy of the action of the sacraments does not depend on anything human, but solely on the will of God as expressed by Christ's institution [of the sacrament] and promise [made for its effects]. 'Ex opere operantis,' i.e. by reason of the agent, would mean that the action of the sacraments depended on the worthiness either of the minister or of the recipient" (ibid.).
12. See Denzinger and Schönmetzer, pars. 1310, 1606.
13. Protestant ideas of *ex opere operato* influenced nineteenth-century English theories of witchcraft and magic: see Douglas, *Purity and Danger,* 18 ("ritual which is expected to have automatic effect"), 26 ("the assumption that ritual which works *ex opere operato* is primitive"), 108.
14. Camporeale, "Renaissance Humanism," esp. 111–18. I do not think, however, that Aquinas argued by analogy 100 percent of the time. The passages of his works that most stimulated witchcraft theory show a tendency to literalism. The great example is demonic corporeality (see chap. 3 above), but there are others, as I shall argue throughout this book. What counts is Aquinas's *overall* tendency to analogy; without it, he would have argued as a witchcraft theorist. See above, pp. 65–66, for example.
15. Camporeale, "La morte, la proprietà," 398–99. Camporeale is discussing

the vast increase in propitiatory masses (celebrated for the dead to shorten their time in purgatory) after the Council of Trent, but the same principles apply to the invention of witchcraft theory.

16. In fact, the two sorts of power do not have different sources but must conform to the axiom that "all power is from God."
17. See Michel, "Sacrementaux."
18. In 1913, the *Catholic Encyclopedia* still affirmed: "One of the most remarkable effects of sacramentals is the virtue to drive away evil spirits whose mysterious and baleful operations affect sometimes the physical activity of man. To combat this occult power the Church has recourse to exorcism and the sacramentals" (Kennedy, 293).
19. This distinction is found in both Aquinas and Bonaventure (see chap. 11 below).
20. Kramer, *Malleus,* fol. 108r (p. 230).
21. Nider/Biedermann, 208 (sig. n8v) (Nider/Chène, 176). Compare Nider/Biedermann, 196 (sig. n2v) (not in Nider/Chène); and Lea, 1:310, 327.
22. Kramer, *Malleus,* fol. 90r (p. 189).
23. The extreme case was reached with baptism. The Council of Trent's catechism would declare that, if necessary, "all people, even laymen and common folk, both male and female, and of whatever sect or false religion," including "Jews, infidels, and heretics," could perform valid baptism, "so long as such persons purpose and intend to do what the Catholic church is wont to do in such a ceremony" (*Catechismo,* 180).
24. Similarly, "If a person . . . double-crosses [*praevaricet*] on a pact established with a demon, say by uttering a sacred name while in flight, she will immediately be put down or abandoned by the demon and find herself far from the home she was returning to, most often scourged by the demons themselves, but sometimes unharmed" (Spina, 52).
25. On the ambiguity between saints, witches, and necromancers, see Dinzelbacher; and Kieckhefer, "The Holy and the Unholy."
26. Nider/Biedermann, 207–8 (sigs. n8r–v) (Nider/Chène, 174–76).
27. Robbins, 290.
28. "Urteil . . . ," 104; Monter, ed., 76.
29. Hansen (Hansen, ed., *Quellen,* 91 n. 2)and later Borst identified this judge as Peter von Greyertz, who was active between 1392 and 1406. However, Chène shows that, between 1392 and 1437/1438 (when the *Formicarius* was completed), there were at least three judges of the upper Simmenthal region named Peter (commentary in Nider/Chène, 223–31).
30. Nider/Biedermann, 208 (sig. n8v) (Nider/Chène, 178–80). On the name *Scadelem,* see Nider/Chène, 153n, 234.
31. Nider/Biedermann, 207 (sig. n8r) (Nider/Chène, 174).
32. Nider/Biedermann, 219–20 (sigs. o6r–v) (Nider/Chène, 188–92). All subsequent quotations of the passage on Peter and the sign of the cross are from these pages.
33. On *crimen exceptum,* see von Spee, 41 (question 4); Levack, 79–80; and Clark, *Thinking with Demons,* 205, 519, 675.
34. Nider does not specify that Peter thought that he had neglected the sign of the cross, but both context and Nider's verb *munio* (to fortify or defend) make this plain: "se diligenter crucis signo munire solebat"; "ut putabat

noctem neglexerat, non se ut debuit muniendo more solito." Chène misses this correspondence, taking the latter phrase to mean "religious practices of some sort [*d'éventuelles pratiques religieuses*] that he was supposed to perform during the night" (Nider/Chène, 260).

35. "[A]c si diceret: 'In nomine dyaboli.'" Either Peter or Nider was "stretching" Peter's *actual* utterance into an involuntary invocation of the Devil.
36. Caesarius of Heisterbach/Scott and Bland, 1:331–32: a wife was told "Go to the Devil," a child "Devil take you"; both came true.
37. Chène observes that Nider and/or Peter initially claimed that an old woman witch pushed Peter down the stairs, but Nider later says that the witches as a group invoked demons, who pushed Peter (Nider/Chène, 262–63). Nider adds that, "to deceive the minds of these sorcerers, [the demons] acted on the imagination of these superstitious persons so that they would believe [*viderentur*] that they themselves had been present" to push Peter (Nider/Biedermann, 221 [sig. o7r] [Nider/Chène, 196–98]).
38. This and subsequent paragraphs are based on Nider/Biedermann, 220–21 (sigs. o6v–o7r) (Nider/Chène, 192–94).
39. The witches' intention to harm Peter *veneficijs* could mean "with poisons," but in context *veneficijs* is a synonym for *maleficijs,* "with witchcrafts."
40. Nider does not reveal how Peter discovered the wine-cup-gazing incident.
41. Nider/Biedermann, 208 (sig. o8v) (Nider/Chène, 178). See also Lea, 1: 310, 332, 363.
42. See Clark, *Thinking with Demons,* 572–81; and Nider/Chène, 258, 426–28. Spina, 52, says, "On account of the protection of good angels, it commonly happens that demons cannot harm officials of the faith, nor can they snatch a heretic from such officials' prison."
43. See esp. Kramer, *Malleus,* 3.8, 15 (fols. 102r-v, 107r–8v [pp. 214–16, 227–30]).
44. Ibid., fols. 107r–v (p. 228).
45. Ibid., fol. 102r (p. 215), emphasis added.
46. Ibid., fols. 50r, 105v (pp. 102, 223).
47. Nider/Biedermann, 202–3 (sigs. n5v–n6r) (Nider/Chène, 155).
48. Nider/Biedermann, 207–8 (sigs. n8r–v) (Nider/Chène, 174–76); Kramer, *Malleus,* fol. 10v (p. 20). Compare Kramer, *Malleus,* fol. 8r (p. 14), quoting Isidore, *Eymologiarum liber,* 8.9.
49. Bonaventure, *Opera omnia,* 4:772, commenting on Lombard, *Sententiarum,* 4.34.2.2. On matrimony as a sacrament, see chap. 11 below. The conceptual opposition is almost explicit in Nider's *Formicarius,* 2.9 (Nider/Biedermann, 89 [sig. f5r]): A man married to a saintly woman who refuses to have sexual relations with him finds himself struck with impotence but does not suspect her of *maleficium.* The wife's obstinate chastity comes from her regular attendance at mass and her meditation on the *summum beneficium* of Christ's Passion.
50. Kramer, *Malleus,* fols. 56v, 57r (pp. 115, 116). Compare fol. 19r (p. 39).
51. Analyzed in chap. 8 below.
52. Clark, "Inversion, Misrule," 104, comes closest to my view, although he discusses relations as symbolic rather than physically efficacious. Clark, *Thinking with Demons,* 80–93, is comprehensive.

53. Nider/Biedermann, 203 (sig. n6r) (Nider/Chêne, 154) Kramer quotes this passage verbatim in the *Malleus* (fol. 49r [pp. 100–101]) Saint Bernardino of Siena was preaching similar witchcraft slanders in 1427 and claimed to have had a witch captured for performing them (see Cohn, *Europe's Inner Demons,* 46–54, esp. 49–50; Ginzburg, *Ecstasies,* 297–300; and Ostorero, Bagliani, and Utz Tremp, eds., 240).
54. Hsia. On legends of children and the eucharist, see chap. 8 below (Alonso de Espina's story of the Jew and the eucharist); and Rubin, *Gentile Tales,* chap. 1.
55. On *gazarii* for heretics, see Ostorero, commentary on *Errores gazariorum,* 301–4.
56. *Errores gazariorum,* 280–81, 291.
57. *Supradictum:* although Nider is ostensibly quoting the young man verbatim, "the abovementioned wineskin" refers to the confession of the witch who spoke of the baby broth, showing how tightly the two confessions fit into Peter's "research" and Nider's theory.
58. Nider/Biedermann, 203 (sig. n6r) (Nider/Chêne, 156).
59. Chêne sees ordination rather than confirmation in the ritual (Nider/Chêne, 243). I also disagree with her description of the ritual as parody.
60. Nider/Biedermann, 203 (sig. n6r) (Nider/Chêne, 156).
61. For a pessimistic view of such preemptive absolutions, even when granted by a pope, see Dante, *Inferno,* canto 27.
62. Nider/Biedermann, 203–4 (sigs. n6r–v) (Nider/Chêne, 156–58).
63. See French and Cunningham, 100–172; Lambert, 55–61, 105–46; and Strayer.
64. On genetic alteration caused by crime, see the discussion of Cain in Stephens, *Giants in Those Days,* chap. 2.

Chapter Eight

1. The classic study is de Lubac. See also Rubin, *Corpus Christi.*
2. Denzinger and Schönmetzer, par. 700; see also par. 690.
3. Ibid., par. 802. The first recorded use of the term *transubstantiation* is in a letter of Innocent's written in 1202 (ibid., par. 782). On usage from 1079 to 1215, see Michel, "Transsubstantiation," esp. 1398–99.
4. Denzinger and Schönmetzer, par. 802; cf. pars. 794, 846, 849. See also Jansen; Colish, *Peter Lombard,* 2:551–83.
5. Spilling consecrated wine was a scandal (*Catechismo,* 255–56), as was an animal's eating a consecrated host (Rubin, *Corpus Christi,* 67–68, 113).
6. Denzinger and Schönmetzer, pars. 1321, 1352, 1636, 1640, 1651.
7. Especially significant is de Lubac, 183, on Peter Lombard's treatment (ca. 1150) of eucharistic literality: "Formerly, theologians had proscribed the word *corporeum* for being synonymous with 'corruptible': now they proscribed *incorporeum* as being the equivalent of *phantasticum.*"
8. Kramer, *Malleus,* 116–17 (fol. 57r). Previous reference to toads and other venomous animals for preparing unguents and powders was in *Errores gazariorum,* 280–83.
9. See Rubin, *Gentile Tales;* and Nasuti.
10. De Espina, sigs. E1r–v, emphasis added.
11. Ibid., sig. E1v; cf. sigs. B2v-3r.

12. See Rubin, *Gentile Tales,* 40–48 (on de Espina's version, 46); and Netanyahu, 832–33 (on the *Fortalitium fidei* overall, 814–47).
13. White, "Natural Science and Naturalistic Art," 429–30. Thanks to Peter Travis for this reference. On popular doubt and skepticism about the eucharist, see Lansing, 96–103, esp. 102.
14. Compare Langmuir, 249–51, 259–61, 266, 300–301; Zafran, 119–92.
15. Eire, 126, 121, 128, 145–46.
16. Netanyahu, 840–47, contains some shrewd cui bono assessments of de Espina's charges against Jews, especially *conversos.* Neither Netanyahu nor Rubin (*Gentile Tales*) attends to evidence of Christians' resistance to skepticism, although Rubin discusses Christian reactions to Jewish disbelief in transubstantiation (29–39) and sees a Christian "wish to make Jews act as guarantors and witnesses of Christian faith" (31).
17. Cohn, *Pursuit of the Millennium,* 68–70, 102–3, 138–39.
18. Rubin, *Corpus Christi,* 245, 336–37, 294–97.
19. Rubin, *Gentile Tales,* 36, 37. But, for a subtle analysis of eucharistic miracle tales as a way of countering skepticism among Christians, see Rubin, *Corpus Christi,* 108–29.
20. Bynum, 51 (quotation), 59–60, 63–64, 76–77, and passim.
21. Probably this silence is due to Bynum's focus on lay piety. See her pp. 48–69.
22. Lansing, 162–66; Nasuti, 89–101. This is not to deny the influence of women on the institution of the feast (see Bynum, esp. 55). But the priestly miracle of Bolsena provided the crucial myth.
23. Rubin, *Corpus Christi,* 108–29, 176–77; Zika, 37–48; Nasuti, 15–85. Some supposedly pre-1263 miracles in Nasuti depend on documentation from a much *later* period, in one case 810 years after the alleged occurrence. The earliest accounts of the Bolsena miracle were written at least sixty years after its alleged occurrence (Lansing, 164).
24. See Bynum, 44–46, 51–52; but also Rubin, *Corpus Christi,* 185–91; and Lansing, 165–66.
25. Aquinas, *Commentum* on Lombard, *Sententiarum,* 4.11.1.1 (Aquinas, *Opera,* 1:474–75), emphasis added.
26. Aquinas, *Commentum* on Lombard, *Sententiarum,* 4.11.1.1 (Aquinas, *Opera,* 1:475). The Tridentine cathechism tells the faithful to forget "excessively subtle questions" and admire "the supreme providence of God" because, "since it is common human nature greatly to abhor the eating of human flesh or the drinking of blood, with great wisdom God has disposed that his most holy body and blood should be administered to us under the *species* [external appearance] of those things, namely bread and wine, the daily and universal [*comune*] consumption of which delight us above all else [*massimamente*]" (*Catechismo,* 245).
27. Occurrences too numerous to count in Cohn, *Pursuit of the Millennium;* Wakefield and Evans, eds.; and other works on medieval heresy.
28. This paragraph based on Zika, 48–59; and Watanabe, 215–21.
29. Compare R. I. Moore, 89–90, on the creation of the "medieval Manichee" stereotype, "which blended reality and fantasy into a whole that was consistent, coherent and terrifying," permitting the investigator "to understand the phenomenon before him as the fulfillment of a prophecy, . . . at

the modest price of attributing to the 'heretics' doctrines much more radical and much more coherent than those which they had in fact avowed." Witchcraft theorists also "seize[d] upon scattered expressions of popular belief in magic and sorcery as confirmation of their own nightmare of a Satanic conspiracy to overthrow Christendom."

30. Ostorero, Bagliani, and Utz Tremp, eds., 308, 316 (a Jew uses hosts to make poison to be spread by lepers), 346, 371.
31. Ostorero, 71–73.
32. Visconti, *Lamiarum,* sig. a3r.
33. Ibid., sig. b7v.
34. See the contentions of fourteenth-century Cathars in Wakefield and Evans, eds., 384; and Lansing, 94, 100. See also Stephens, "Metaphor, Sacrament," 222–23.
35. On Aquinas on chewing the *corpus gloriosum,* see p. 219 above.
36. Visconti, *Lamiarum,* sig. b3r–b4r.
37. 1 Cor. 11:27, 29. Visconti, *Lamiarum,* sig. b4r: "And just as those who unworthily take the body of Christ do not *truly* take the body of Christ in terms of its power and efficacy in divine matters [*quo ad virtutem divinorum et efficatiam*], but only in terms of [those forces'] judgment and punishment of those who take them unworthily, so those who trample the host do not bring shame on the divine majesty but only provoke its indignation and move it to revenge itself on them."
38. Visconti, *Lamiarum,* sig. b4r.
39. Ibid.
40. Segl. Kramer had published another treatise on the eucharist (*Tractatus novus*) in 1493. My discussion of Kramer's career is based on Quétif and Echard, 896–97.
41. Ibid., 897.
42. Ibid., 897. Summers's translation of Quétif and Echard's biography of Kramer (Kramer/Summers, xxxiv–xxxviii) is rhetorically overblown, filled with saccharine interpolations, and annotated by "credulous" eucharistic miracle stories (ibid., xxxvi). Rather than revise it, I have retranslated Quétif and Echard.
43. Quétif and Echard, 897; cf. Kramer/Summers, xxxv–xxxvi.
44. Quétif and Echard, 897.
45. Ibid. On the basis of Kramer's *Tractatus varii,* Zika, 27–30, says that the incident happened at Passau, not Padua, but gives the same outline of events.
46. Quétif and Echard, 897.
47. The use of the term *species* implies that these hosts have only the appearance of bread. If we assumed that the "other container" (*altero vase*) referred to a third vessel and that, given its characteristics, it obviously contained unconsecrated hosts, we would be unable to explain the outbreak of popular fervor, which obviously depended on the idea that the hosts *were* consecrated.
48. See Thomas, *Religion and the Decline of Magic,* 34–35; and Rubin, *Corpus Christi,* 334–35, 340–41.
49. Quétif and Echard, 897.
50. "At that time some were teaching that the eucharist was to be worshiped only on the condition of an implicit and understood [*subintellecta*] reserva-

tion that it should have been properly [*rite*] consecrated. Kramer argued against them publicly" (ibid., 896).

51. See Cohn, *Pursuit of the Millennium,* 169, 211.
52. On Hussites, Taborites, and Húskites, see Lambert, 335–37; and Cohn, *Pursuit of the Millennium,* 205–22. Cohn, *Pursuit of the Millennium,* 223–80, esp. 223–34, suggests that these groups possibly had links to Germany in Kramer's time.
53. See Lambert, 230 and passim.
54. See Watanabe, 215–16.
55. See Lambert, 316–20 and passim.
56. Ibid., 329, 330, 332, 339.
57. Ibid., 335–36.
58. Ibid.
59. See Pelikan, 4:92–98, 100, 122–25; Denzinger and Schönmetzer, pars. 1201–30, 1247–79; and Lambert, 284–360.
60. Lambert, 297.
61. On priests' alleged unsuitability to perform the sacraments, see Cohn, *Pursuit of the Millennium,* 39, 47–48, and passim.
62. Douglas, *Purity and Danger,* 175. Isaiah 59 is quoted by Nider, *Formicarius,* 2.1 (Nider/Biedermann, 58 [sig. d5v]).
63. See Lambert, 298, 300, 305, 307.
64. Kramer, *Malleus,* fol. 96v (p. 203), attributes the etymology to Saint Jerome ("heresis ab electione est dicta").
65. See the map in Ostorero, Bagliani, and Utz Tremp, eds., fig. 14, p. 525.
66. Lambert, 350–51, 359.
67. Ibid., 348–60, 381. A significant number of Hus's works were printed from the 1520s to the 1550s.
68. Ibid., 357. In session 22 (17 September 1562), the council formally left the decision to the wisdom of the pope, a decision that was confirmed four centuries later by the Second Vatican Council (4 December 1963). The relevant decrees can be found in Alberigo, ed., 727–28, 741, 831.
69. Pico, *Strix,* sig. F2r; Pico/Alberti, 140.
70. Pico, *Strix,* sigs. F1v–F2v; Pico/Alberti, 135–41.
71. Pico, *Strix,* sig. F2v; cf. Pico/Alberti, 141.
72. Pico, *Strix,* sigs. E4v–F1r; Pico/Alberti, 132–33.
73. Pico, *Strix,* sig. F2v; Pico/Alberti, 141–42.
74. Pico, *Strix,* sig. F2v; Pico/Alberti, 142.
75. Pico, *Strix,* sigs. F2v–3r; Pico/Alberti, 142–43.
76. Ibid. Although both Latin *sacramentum* and Italian *sagramento/sacramento* can mean a simple oath, Pico and Alberti interpret witches' confessions as sacramental. Pico distinguishes between *iureiurando* ("swearing on oath" by the serious witnesses) and *adacti sacramento* ("compelled by the sacrament," for the witches), Alberti's translation between *confermato con giuramento* and *con il sagramento costretti.* They imply that the host or some sacramental like holy water could be employed to compel confession, as Kramer suggests (*Malleus,* fol. 108r [p. 230]).
77. Pico, *Strix,* sigs. H3v; Pico/Alberti, 185.
78. Pico uses the technical term *pyx* (*pyxidem*); Alberti calls it a wooden box (*cassetta di legno*).

79. Pico, *Strix,* sig. H3v; Pico/Alberti, 185–86.
80. Pico, *Strix,* sig. H3v; Pico/Alberti, 186–87.
81. Pico, *Strix,* sigs. H3v–H4r; Pico/Alberti, 187–88.
82. Pico, like everyone until Hansen, believed that the *Malleus* was jointly authored. The passage in question was used as the epigraph to chap. 2 above.
83. Pico, *Strix,* sig. I1v.
84. Pico/Alberti, 197.
85. Lateran IV (1215) publicized the definition in its decrees (Michel, "Transsubstantiation," 1398–99). In 1562, the Council of Trent spelled out the implications of real sacrifice in response to Protestant objections (Denzinger and Schönmetzer, pars. 802, 1740–43). Trent defined the sacrifice as "visible" (ibid., 1742) even though the transubstantiation happens invisibly.
86. "Urteil . . . ," 105; Monter, ed., 77.
87. Robbins, 293, emphasis added.
88. Ibid., 292.
89. Color photographs of eucharistic relics are in Nasuti.

Chapter Nine

1. See Chène's commentary (Nider/Chène, 236–41).
2. Nider/Biedermann, 203 (sig. n6r) (Nider/Chène, 154).
3. Nider says that Peter acted because thirteen infants had recently died in Bern (ibid.).
4. Roper, 207.
5. Spina, 88. See Rom. 6:1–5; and Gal. 3:27.
6. Spina, 90.
7. "The New Testament contains no definite statement of a positive kind regarding the eternal lot of those who die in original sin without being burdened with grievous personal guilt" (Toner, 256, citing John 3:5, 9:4; Rom. 5:12ff.; Luke 12:40, 16:19ff.; and 2 Cor. 5:10).
8. *Catechismo,* 198, emphasis added. See Denzinger and Schönmetzer, pars. 1313 (Council of Florence, 1439), 1609 (Council of Trent, 1547). Innocent III was instrumental in gaining acceptance for the idea, beginning in 1201. William of Auvergne, *De sacramentis. De sacramentis in speciali, ac primum de sacramento baptismi,* chap. 3 (*Opera,* 1:421), described the action of baptism as a striking (*percussio*). Weyer claimed that the character of baptism keeps devils away (*De praestigiis daemonum,* 3.2, 6.24; *Witches, Devils, and Doctors,* 172, 551–52). In general, see Denzinger and Schönmetzer, p. 896 (Index systematicus J2cb); Moreau, esp. 1702–3 (in what way the character is real); and *Catechismo,* 166.
9. Defining the *age of reason* has a vague history; in the sixteenth century, the Council of Trent, with some waffling, implied that the age of reason was seven years. See Scannell, 216; and *Catechismo,* 166–67, 205–18, esp. 214–15.
10. Gurevitch paraphrases the *Elucidarium* of Honorius of Autun (ca. 1100), intended to help explain theology to the unlettered: "Children to the age of three who can still not speak will be saved, *if they are baptized,* for it is said 'Of such is the kingdom of heaven' (Matt. 19:14). Of those beyond the age of five a part will perish, a part will be saved" (155, emphasis added).
11. John 3:5; Innocent III, letter of 1201, Denzinger and Schönmetzer, par. 780.

12. Aquinas, *Summa theologiae,* 3.68.11; Eire, 140.
13. As we shall see, Visconti differs from Nider, claiming that witches prefer to kill *baptized* infants.
14. Toner, 257.
15. Aquinas, *De malo,* 5.3 (Aquinas, *On Evil,* 218–20).
16. Toner, 257.
17. Visconti, *Lamiarum,* sig. a3r, quoting Augustine, *De civitate Dei,* 21.13.
18. Exorcism—chasing devils away—was part of the baptismal ritual. See chap. 12 below.
19. Visconti, *Lamiarum,* sig. b3r.
20. Ibid., sig. a3r.
21. Compare Paul's attempt to justify God (Rom. 9:14–18) by explicitly refusing to attribute evil to him.
22. Visconti, *Lamiarum,* sig. b3r.
23. Toner, 258.
24. "Le turbe, ch'eran molte e grandi,/ *d'infanti* e di femmine e di viri" (Dante, *Inferno,* 4.29–30 [Dante/Durling and Martinez, 70–71, emphasis added]).
25. Like Dante, Montanari devotes barely a mention to the plight of the infants. Iannucci, 567–68, notes how the virtuous pagans are discussed in terms of the theology of infant limbo. See Padoan; Toner, 256; and Gaudel, esp. 770.
26. Dante, *Inferno,* canto 4; Montanari. Although Saladin was celebrated as a chivalrous opponent of the Crusaders, Averroës opposed the immortality of the individual soul (a doctrine that should have landed him among Dante's Epicureans in *Inferno,* canto 10).
27. In *Paradiso,* 19.70–81, Dante gives the traditional theological argument that God *cannot be* unjust, despite condemning those who have never heard of Christ to hell.
28. Dante, *Paradiso,* 32.40–84. Lines 75–84 assert that, before Moses, no ceremony was needed for salvation; from Moses to Christ, circumcision was necessary for males; "but, after the time of grace had come, without perfect baptism in Christ *such innocence was held there below*" (Dante/Singleton, *Paradiso,* 1:365) (*tale innocenza là giù si ritenne* [32.81–84]). Dante's language is less uneasy than Visconti's, but not serene: each of the last three tercets mentions the *innocenza* of little children, and the third tercet refers to limbo. Dante calls doubts about the justice of predestination a "hard knot"; he refers to predestination as happening "not without cause," but the cause is divine pleasure, and "the fact of it" has to suffice as an explanation.
29. Brieger, Meiss, and Singleton, 1:121–22; 2:67a, 70a, 74b.
30. In *Inferno,* 4.41–42, Dante presents the glass as half full: "*only so far* harmed [*offesi*] that without hope we live in desire" (Dante/Durling and Martinez, 72, emphasis added). So he could have agreed with Aquinas (*De malo,* 5.3 [*On Evil,* 220]) that the infants are *not unhappy*.
31. Spina, 90, emphasis added. This is the climax to chap. 33: "On the obligation through which witches promise the Devil that they will kill children, *and why God permits such an unjust (as it seems) slaughter of innocents.*"
32. Spina's earlier analysis (27–28)was an even less convincing attempt to prove that, as the Book of Exodus states, God justly punishes parents "to the third and fourth generation," by allowing witches and demons to harm children.

33. Similar vague connections between real or imagined unguents, transvection, and infanticide already appear in a trial from the Italian town of Todi in 1428. Saint Bernardino of Siena claimed, in a sermon preached in 1427, to have had a Roman woman arrested for thirty infanticides; the sermon contains references that lead some to suspect that it inspired the Todi trial (see Nider/Chène, 217–18n). On Bernardino and witches, see Mormando, 52–108.
34. Nider/Biedermann, 203 (sig. n6r) (Nider/Chène, 154). Kramer quotes this passage verbatim in the *Malleus* (fol. 49r [pp. 100–101]). Witch-cats will be examined in chap. 10 below. Nider implied on one occasion that transvection and the unguent were causally linked (see Nider/Chène, 212).
35. For examples of such preparations, see Guazzo/Ashwin, 90–91, 99–102; and refer to the discussion of the trial of Walpurga later in this chapter.
36. Kramer, *Malleus,* fol. 49r (p. 100).
37. Ibid., fol. 49r (p. 101). Kramer elsewhere uses *transmutatio* to describe how demons shift or transport images from one part of the brain to another (fol. 59v [pp. 121–22]). There is no support for any reading but *transmutaccionibus* in the manuscript tradition of the *Formicarius* (Nider/Chène, 154, variants).
38. Kramer, *Malleus,* fol. 52v (p. 107).
39. On fols. 48v (twice), 49r, and 52v (pp. 99, 100, and 107)of the *Malleus,* Kramer oscillates between the two options, sometimes on the same page.
40. Ibid., fol. 49r (p. 100), quoting Nider's witch who confessed that "we set our snares chiefly for unbaptized children" (Nider/Biedermann, 203 [sig. n6r] [Nider/Chène, 154]). Kramer interjects, "Reader, notice that at the Devil's command they attack the unbaptized for the most part, so that they will not be baptized."
41. Mazzolini, *De strigimagarum,* 5.
42. Kramer, *Malleus,* fol. 107v (p. 229): "It is clear that a hundred thousand [unbaptized] children" burned to ashes and carried as a talisman "could not cause the effect of such taciturnity with their natural properties [*ex naturali inclinatione*]." The Devil requires this only to ensure that their souls will be lost and to offend God (*in animarum perditionem et divinae maiestatis offensionem*).
43. Nider/Biedermann, 208 (sig. n8v) (Nider/Chène, 176). Compare Nider/Biederman, 196 (sig. n2v) (not in Nider/Chène); and Lea, 1:310, 327.
44. See chap. 12 below.
45. For example, Grillando, *De sortilegiis,* 7.2 (Grillando, 108–12); and Guazzo, *Compendium* (1608), 1.12 (Guazzo/Ashwin, 42–43; see also 37). In 1854, the Catholic encyclopedist Moroni (190–91) was still repeating the famous tale. Guazzo notes that, "with God's permission," devils can serve both salt and bread at the Sabbat despite the fact that they are the physical elements employed in baptism and the eucharist. Guazzo intimates that this exception was needed because witches often confessed (probably without or against their interrogators' prompting) that they had consumed bread and salt at the devil's banquets (Guazzo, *Compendium* [1608], 1.8 [Guazzo/Ashwin, 23]).
46. Pico, *Strix,* sigs. F2r, E2v; Pico/Alberti, 139, 121.

47. Pico, *Strix,* sig. E1v; Pico/Alberti, 117–18. Unbracketed phrases in italics added by Alberti.
48. Kramer, *Malleus,* fol. 56v (pp. 115–16).
49. Spina, 89. The *true* witches' ointment "is said to be made from filthy things by means of the abuse of the sacraments, which are things that, according to the judgment of medical doctors, are not able to induce sleep in any natural way" (ibid., 85).
50. Ibid., 81.
51. Ibid., 51.
52. Ibid.
53. Ibid. Contrary to Spina's argument, Augustine implicitly denies any sort of "Pavlovian" or mechanistic analogy between animals and spirits: "Devils are attracted to dwell in certain temples [in the guise of pagan gods] by means of . . . what suits their various tastes. *They are attracted, not by food like animals, but, like spirits, by such symbols as suit their taste,* various kinds of stones, woods, plants, animals, songs, rites" (Augustine, 772, emphasis added).
54. Spina, 81.
55. *Catechismo,* 157–59; Kennedy, esp. 298; see also chap. 3 above and chap. 11 below. Kennedy, 298, concedes that "the hylomorphistic theory . . . sheds much light on our conception of the external ceremony" but warns that "the comparison must not be carried too far" as "the attempt to verify the comparison (of sacraments to a body) in all details of the sacramental rite will lead to confusing subtilities [*sic*] or to singular opinions."
56. Aquinas, *Summa theologiae,* 1.2.3 (2:13), emphasis added; see van Steenbergen.
57. Nider/Biedermann, 208–9 (sigs. n8v–o1r) (Nider/Chène, 182).
58. Chène has greatly improved the situation; aside from the witchcraft passages in Nider/Chène, she plans a critical edition (including commentary) of the complete *Formicarius* (see ibid., 101).
59. Nider/Biedermann, 1 (sig. a1r).
60. Ibid. To my knowledge, only Chène mentions this overall organization (Nider/Chène, 105–6). However, she overlooks the importance of theodicy to Nider's organization, preferring to concentrate on his professed moral intentions.
61. Spina, 28.
62. Ibid.
63. Unbracketed words in italics are interpolations by Alberti.
64. Pico seems to refer to the Book of Revelation as if it were coming true in his time. Already in 1500 he had intimated that the end of time was near (*On Imagination,* 20 [end of dedicatory letter]).
65. Alberti omits the phrase "who was without faith" (*qui sine fide essent*); as usual, he is more adept at disguising Pico's doubt than Pico himself is.
66. Pico, *Strix,* sig. E4v; Pico/Alberti, 131–32.
67. Douglas, *Purity and Danger,* 174, emphasis added.
68. Spina, 50–51.
69. Ibid.
70. Moroni, 191.
71. "Urteil . . . ," 108, 105, 108–9; Monter, ed., 79–80, 77, 80.

72. "Urteil . . . ," 107–8; Monter, ed., 79.
73. See chap. 7 above.
74. Douglas, *Purity and Danger,* 175.
75. "Urteil . . . ," 107; Monter, ed., 79.
76. "Urteil . . . ," 109; Monter, ed., 81.
77. Ledrede, 63. See also Cohn, *Europe's Inner Demons,* 198–204.
78. For their accusations, see Ledrede, 28–29. See also ibid., 9; and Cohn, *Europe's Inner Demons,* 201–2. On Alice, see Williams.
79. Kors and Peters, eds., 82. And see the letter of Cardinal William of Santa Sabina (ibid., 80–81). See also Cohn, *Europe's Inner Demons,* 192–95.
80. Ledrede, 28, 27–28.
81. Ibid., 28, 63.
82. Ibid., 45.
83. Ibid., apps. 3–6, pp. 79–84.
84. Ibid., 1 and n. 1. Earlier, heretics were accused of interacting bodily with demons, but without accusations of *maleficium.* See the primary sources in Wakefield and Evans, eds.; and see Cohn, *Europe's Inner Demons,* 1–59 and passim.
85. Tuchman; Jordan. Whatever one thinks of Tuchman as a medieval historian, her subtitle—*The Calamitous Fourteenth Century*—was apt.
86. Boccaccio, 5–12. Herlihy, 17, maintains that some locales lost 70–80 percent of their population, that, about 1420, "Europe could have counted barely more than a third of the people it counted a hundred years before."
87. See Besserman. Job is cited abundantly by witchcraft theorists.
88. Camporeale, "Renaissance Humanism," 103–4.
89. Adémar de Chabannes, 75.
90. Paul of Chartres, 78–79.
91. Ibid., 79, emphasis added.
92. Guibert de Nogent, 103; Cohn, *Europe's Inner Demons,* 46–54, esp. 49.
93. *De operatione daemonum* was popular with Latin Christian demonologists from about 1580 on. Ficino had translated the most sensational parts in *Jamblicus de mysteriis,* 175–86.
94. Wakefield and Evans, eds., 82–85.
95. F. Patetta, quoted in Cuomo, 17. See also Bartlett.
96. Cuomo, 86–88. See Boccaccio, *Decameron,* 8.6.
97. "Itaque quicumque manducaverit panem hunc, vel biberit calicem Domini indigne, reus erit corporis et sanguinis Domini. . . . Qui enim manducat et bibit indigne, iudicium sibi manducat et bibit: non diiudicans corpus Domini" (1 Cor. 11:27, 29). Paul implies that taking communion unworthily caused some Corinthians to sicken and die: "Ideo inter vos multi infirmi et imbecilles, et dormiunt multi" (1 Cor. 11:30).
98. Cuomo, 90. Bartlett mentions trial by eucharist only in passing (17n, 72, 82, 95).
99. Guibert de Nogent, 104. See Cuomo, 76.
100. Sharpe, 3, 218–19, 282. Compare Bartlett, 146–51.
101. R. I. Moore. On Lateran IV and ordeals, see Bartlett, esp. 34–102; Baldwin.
102. Peters, *Inquisition,* 48; and see generally 48–53.
103. Of the biblical injunctions against tempting God, the most relevant is

Wisd. of Sol. 1:1–2, which declares that God is found by those who do not tempt [*tentant*] him and appears [*apparet*] to those who have faith.

104. Kramer, *Malleus,* fol. 110r (p. 235). On Kramer and this ordeal, cf. Bartlett, 145–46.
105. Kramer, *Malleus,* fol. 110r (p. 234). On this ordeal, see Cuomo, 62–64.
106. Kramer, *Malleus,* fol. 108r (p. 229). Summers mistranslates *fidem ipsorum ut iustam defendere* as "to say that their *heresy* must be true." Although Kramer seems to claim this as a personal experience, his story suspiciously resembles a tale told by Caesarius of Heisterbach in which a necromancer learns of the hidden charms (actually copies of a pact with the devil) by calling up the devil—*at the request* of the bishop of Besançon (Caesarius of Heisterbach/Scott and Bland, 1:339). Russell, *Witchcraft,* 120, thinks the borrowing "doubtful," but I fail to see why.
107. Alberigo, ed., 230.
108. "*Transsubstantiatis* pane in corpus et vino in sanguinem potestate divina" (ibid.).
109. Ibid., 230–31. On Catharism and sacraments, see Lambert, 44–61, 118–21.
110. Alberigo, ed., 233–34.
111. French and Cunningham, 112–16. See also Strayer, 22, 42. On real and imagined debates between Christians and Jews in the thirteenth and fourteenth centuries, cf. Zafran, 246–57.
112. Alberigo, ed., 244–45.
113. Ibid., 245.
114. The phrase "when the cause ceases, the effect ceases as well" recurs once in these statutes (ibid., 251)and is echoed yet again (ibid., 257).
115. French and Cunningham, 70–98.
116. Kramer, *Malleus,* fols. 107r–108r (pp. 227, 228, 230).
117. Ibid., fol. 107r (pp. 227–28).
118. Ibid., fol. 108v (pp. 230–31).
119. Ibid.

Chapter Ten

1. Evans-Pritchard; Douglas, *Purity and Danger,* and *Witchcraft Confessions;* and Kieckhefer, "Avenging the Blood of Children."
2. Pico, *Strix,* sig. E4v; Pico/Alberti, 132–33.
3. Pico, *Strix,* sigs. E4v–F1r; Pico/Alberti, 133.
4. Pico, *Strix,* sigs. G3r–G4v; Pico/Alberti, 164–65.
5. Mazzolini, *De strigimagarum,* 3.
6. Ibid. Abbiati (Abbiati, Agnoletto, and Lazzati, eds., 215 n. 1, 228 n. 3) shows that *masca* was common in Italian Piedmont dialects (Mazzolini was from Priero in the Piedmontese province of Cuneo). *Masca* was synonymous with *striga, strigia,* or *strega,* the term that subsequently became the normal word for "witch" in Italy. Mazzolini gave largely the same etymologies in his *Summa summarum,* fols. 302v–303r. See also Lea, 1:173; and Ostorero, Bagliani, and Utz Tremp, eds., 451n (for the French *masque,* ca. 1440).
7. Mazzolini, *De strigimagarum,* 3.
8. See Biondi's notes to Pico/Alberti, 202–3. Weyer, *De praestigiis,* 3.1 (*Witches, Devils, and Doctors,* 165–66), ridicules Jewish legends about the *lil-*

ith in Isaiah 34, which he identifies with the *strix*. This chapter is a compendium of lore about the *strix* and related infanticides.

9. Pico, *Strix,* sig. B1v; Pico/Alberti, 58–59. The joke is Lorenzo Da Ponte's (Mozart's librettist for *Così fan tutte*).
10. Pico, *Strix,* sig. B2r; Pico/Alberti, 59. The verb used (*vitiant, guastano*) carries the implication, not only of injury, but also of corrupting or ruining.
11. Lambert, 118–25. Lambert's somewhat condescending depiction of Cathar theology should be balanced with French and Cunningham, 127–45.
12. On Alanus de Insulis or Alain de Lille, see Cohn, *Europe's Inner Demons,* 22.
13. Rosen, ed., 73–74 (from 1566).
14. Pico, *Strix,* sig. F1r; Pico/Alberti, 135.
15. The early texts in Ostorero, Bagliani, and Utz Tremp, eds., have numersous references to werewolves: see, e.g., 87–88, 150–52, 239, 245–46, 451, 467. Only one implies erudite Latin tradition (the Roman writer Solinus); most involve infanticide and cannibalism. In the *Malleus,* Kramer discusses "wolves which sometimes seize and eat children out of their cradles and men, and whether this is also done by witches through illusion [*prestigiosa arte*]." He concludes that this is sometimes true; but at other times true wolves are possessed by devils without the intervention of witches. His one example of witch-wolves involves a man who believed that he was a wolf and devoured children, whereas a wolf possessed by a devil was actually the guilty party. Kramer explains neither how the man came to believe that the wolf's experiences were his own nor how witches were involved. His source is Scholastic, not popular, the *De universo* (3.2.13) of William of Auvergne (Kramer, *Malleus,* fols. 31v-32r [p. 65]). Summers's pseudocredulous note (Kramer/Summers, 65) cites a conviction for infanticidal lycanthropy from 1573. Summers published books on vampires and werewolves in 1929 and 1933 (*The Vampire in Europe, The Vampire, His Kith and Kin,* and *The Werewolf*) evincing close thematic and bibliographic connections to his interest in witches and demons.
16. Nider/Biedermann, 200 (sig. n4v) (Nider/Chène, 150–52).
17. Carl Sandburg, "Fog" (1916).
18. Thorndike, 4:229; other early-modern cat folklore can be found on 4:277. See also Darnton, 75–104, esp. 89–96.
19. Ostorero, Bagliani, and Utz Tremp, eds., 240. See also Ginzburg, *Ecstasies,* 297–300; and Cohn, *Europe's Inner Demons,* 49–50. For related infanticidal myths spread by Bernardino, see Mormando, 51–108, 178–79.
20. Spina, 27.
21. Ibid., 52–53.
22. Briggs, chaps. 1–5; Sharpe, chaps. 2, 6–7.
23. For instance, Kramer (*Malleus,* fols. 48r–v [p. 99]) reasons this way.
24. Spina is using his own terminology to describe the thought processes of Filippo and his wife. His technical legal terms indicate degrees of probable guilt and do not imply that Filippo or his wife personally took direct action against the old woman.
25. Spina, 52–53.
26. Further examples can be found in Lea, 1:174, 301; 3:1071.
27. Robbins, s.v. *werewolves;* Bodin, *Démonomanie,* 2.6 (Bodin, fols. 94v–104r);

Weyer, *De praestigiis,* 3.10, 4.23, 6.13, 6.14 (*Witches, Devils, and Doctors,* 192–94, 342–44, 511–14, 517–18).

28. Kramer, *Malleus,* fols. 62r–v (pp. 126–27).
29. Ibid., fols. 62r–v (p. 126).
30. Ibid., fol. 62v (p. 127).
31. Ibid., fols. 62r, 62v (pp. 126, 127).
32. Ibid., fols. 62v–63r (p. 128).
33. Pico, *Strix,* sigs. F1r–v; Pico/Alberti, 135. (Alberti adds some detail in his translation, which I quote here for its greater clarity.) On resuscitating animals that have been eaten, see Bertolotti.
34. Pico, *Strix,* sig. G3v; Pico/Alberti, 165.
35. For such speculation, see P. Castelli, " 'Donnaiole, amiche de li sogni.' "
36. Vineti, sig. d4r, quoting Aquinas, *Summa theologiae,* 1.84.6.
37. Spina, 25–26.
38. Ibid., 25.
39. Aquinas, *De malo,* 16.9–11 (Aquinas, *On Evil,* 514–30; parallel texts listed in nn. 362, 400, 415).
40. Aquinas, *De malo,* 16.9 (Aquinas, *On Evil,* 514). Aquinas quotes from Augustine's *De trinitate* to show that demons can gather the "seeds" of things and use them to produce natural changes, but more rapidly than nature does, so they seem supernatural.
41. Aquinas, *De malo,* 16.9 (Aquinas, *On Evil,* 515).
42. Aquinas, *De malo,* 16.9 (Aquinas, *On Evil,* 517, 518); Augustine, 624.
43. Augustine, 623–24. Compare Lea, 1:326. Later writers ignored or suppressed Augustine's frank recognition that skepticism about such sorcery was in order and that Apuleius's romance was a fiction. This was made easier by the fact that Augustine also cited Apuleius's philosophical treatise *De deo Socratis,* or *On the Daemon of Socrates,* to refute its representation of the daemons.
44. Augustine, 624.
45. Aquinas, *De malo,* 16.11 (Aquinas, *On Evil,* 529, 525).
46. Aquinas, *De malo,* 16.11 (Aquinas, *On Evil,* 525).
47. Aquinas, *De malo,* 16.11 (Aquinas, *On Evil,* 528).
48. Aquinas, *De malo,* 16.11 (Aquinas, *On Evil,* 525, 528, 529).
49. Aquinas, *De malo,* 16.11 (Aquinas, *On Evil,* 529).
50. The image in question, attributed to Jörg Breu the Elder, is reproduced in Troncarelli, ed., 182.
51. "The concept of lycanthropy was discussed by Geiler in one of the sermons as a kind of delusion caused by the Devil. Nonetheless, the illustrator showed a literal werewolf [*sic:* for wolf] attacking a man. He chose to illustrate the sensational rather than the theoretical" (Davidson, 22). See Geiler's discussion of werewolves (fols. 41v–42v; picture on fol. 41v). On Geiler, see Hansen, ed., *Quellen,* 286; Lea, 1:368–69; and Ostorero, Bagliani, and Utz Tremp, eds., 116n.
52. One wonders how the householders failed to notice the shambles in their yard, which, from the decomposition of the body in the foreground, must not be recent. Perhaps the dismembered bodies are symbolic, meant to forecast the fate of the stolen child.
53. Davidson, figs. 8, 9, 11. The drawing by Graf is my fig. 16 in chap. 11 below.

54. Ibid., 25: "vile-looking cat familiars."
55. See Grillot de Givry, fig. 28, facing p. 56.

Chapter Eleven

1. Davidson, 24: "using her . . . stick as a phallus." (The witch is not, however, penetrating herself with the pitchfork.) An identical picture is signed by Baldung; it cannot be determined which artist copied the other.
2. Ibid.
3. Cesalpino, sig. C1r. I have inserted *maleficia* in the last sentence, where Cesalpino uses *veneficium* as a synonym.
4. Ibid.
5. The final eleven of Cesalpino's fifteen chapters are heavily based on the *Malleus,* but Cesalpino makes only one devious reference to it: "In order to eradicate these people [witches] Pope Innocent VIII once appointed two inquisitors over Germany: in a short time one of them sentenced forty people to the stake and the other nearly fifty. And from the public confessions of these people at their trials I have borrowed much of what is written here" (sigs. D1r–v). The pope was a reputable source; Kramer was not.
6. To translate *praestigium* in Kramer's *Malleus,* Summers often uses the term *glamour* in its sense of something occult (from grammar; cf. *grimoire*). Since this can cause unnecessary confusion, I maintain the original term, as with *maleficium.*
7. Anania, *De substantiis separatis opusculum primum,* 3: "It has long been argued among Philosophers and those who are learned about the Ancients whether demons exist as something God made in the natural order or only as something that the intellect and genius of humanity represented to itself [*sibi effinxit*]; nor has there ever been any agreement among them." Anania says that he wrote the second part of this wrongly labeled "little work" to prove the existence of good angels: "Since I have already proved in the book that I wrote on the nature of demons that demons exist as something that God created in the order of reality [*in rerum ordine*], not as something that human ingenuity and art represented to itself so that by fearing them people would beware of committing evil" (*De substantiis separatis opusculum secundum,* 9).
8. Kramer, *Malleus,* fols. 59r–v (p. 121).
9. Boccaccio, 5.4; Battisti and Alessio, 5:3941. *Uccello* (bird) is still a common vulgar word for the penis in Italian, but German apparently has no such association. Winged phalluses are a feature in ancient art, particularly Etruscan. On winged phalluses in medieval pilgrim's badges and in manuscript illustrations of the *Roman de la rose,* see Koldeweij, esp. figs. 4 and 8, where women gather phalluses from a tree. Thanks to Craig Harbison for this reference.
10. For Bernardino's style, see Mormando.
11. On Kramer's Roman experience, see chap. 12 below.
12. Other jokes are at Kramer, *Malleus,* fols. 63r, 65r (pp. 128, 133).
13. Ibid., fols. 45v–46r (pp. 93–94). Also in Nider's *Formicarius,* 5.6 (Nider/Biedermann, 217–18 [sigs. o5r–v]).
14. Kramer, *Malleus,* fol. 59v (p. 121).
15. Jerouschek ("500 Years of the *Malleus maleficarum,*" xxxvii) asserts: "A . . .

central complex involves fantasies about castration, a syndrome that, considering its connection with the fear of sexuality, and especially women's sexuality, seems almost unavoidable." Barstow, 113, referring to Kramer/Summers, 114–22, solemnly takes the anecdote as evidence that "male fear runs through the *Malleus,* culminating in descriptions of how a witch can cause a man to become impotent or to lose his genitals; a particularly lewd story describes where the village priest lost his penis." See also Link, 153.

16. Kramer, *Malleus,* fols. 58r, 29v (pp. 118–19, 60).
17. Ibid., fol. 29r (p. 59); cf. fol. 58v (p. 119); and also Vineti, sigs. d2v–d3r.
18. Kramer, *Malleus,* fol. 29r (p. 59), citing Isidore, *Etymologiarum liber,* 8.9.33.
19. Kramer, *Malleus,* fol. 29v (p. 60). This corresponds to a human method of using "natural agents" to create illusion, mentioned on the previous page (fol. 29r [p. 59]).
20. Spina, 25–26.
21. Kramer, *Malleus,* fols. 30r–32r, 59v–61r (pp. 61–65, 122–24).
22. Ibid., fol. 29v (p. 60).
23. Ibid. There is some overlap between the fifth method and the second, in which the Devil is said to confuse percepts "in man's fancy." Kramer says that, "by the last three of these [five] methods, and even by the second, the Devil can cast a *praestigium* over the senses of a man" (ibid.), indicating awareness of overlap. The Devil's fourth and fifth methods reappear in the reprise of this discussion (ibid., fol. 58v [p. 120]).
24. Ibid., fol. 58v (p. 119). Kramer is uncertain whether fancy and imagination are the same. Having just listed them as two of five "interior senses," he adds: "But S. Thomas says they are only four . . . , reckoning fancy and imagination [*fantasiam et ymaginativam*] as one; and with some reason, for there is little difference between imagining and fancying [*imaginari et fantasiari*]."
25. Ibid., emphasis added. The nest of penises occurs only in the second discussion of illusory castration. The earlier discussion treated illusory castration only to exemplify hiding things from sensory detection. Perhaps, needing an equal and opposite illusion, Kramer "discovered" nesting penises after writing the first discussion. The pressing need for examples might explain why he used a joke as evidence.
26. Ibid., fol. 58v. Summers (119–20) deprives this passage of sense by suppressing all references to differences between sensory memory and intellective memory (the latter holds notions of things that cannot be perceived by the senses but understood only by intuition). He deletes the reference to the "common sense of the imagination." Summers seems unaware that Scholastic common sense is not "common" to all "sensible" people but the sense that combines the impressions of other senses to produce one's idea of an object, being, or action. Kramer is merely specifying that, in this case, the common sense is "of" the imagination because its function is to combine images (we would say *perceptions* or *percepts*) into a convincing illusion.
27. Ibid., fol. 59v. Summers (p. 121) has again confused matters by translating *specierum sensibilium* as "mental" images rather than sensory ones. Kramer has just explained how the Devil makes one see what is not there, but, before presenting witches who steal penises as an example, he apparently digresses for over a page and a half. The digression is not irrelevant, simply misplaced: Kramer wants to explain why God allows such nefarious illu-

sions. He would like to prove that anyone who suffers illusory castration is in a state of sin and that anyone "in a state of grace" is exempt. He cites the example of Saint Macharius (a favorite with witchcraft theorists), who, because he was holy, was able to see that a girl who seemed to have been turned into a filly was actually unchanged. As a corollary to the idea that the holy are unaffected by such *praestigia,* Kramer wants to demonstrate that the sacraments and sacramentals drive demons and witches away. The girl was bewitched because she neglected confession and the eucharist; Saint Macharius broke the *praestigium* by prayer. Likewise, Saint Anthony used the sign of the cross to drive away devils that two witches sent to tempt him. Despite these examples, Kramer has to conclude that, although a man in the state of grace cannot lose his own penis, he can still "see the loss of another, and to that extent the Devil can delude his senses." Finally, at two widely separated points, Kramer quotes the Book of Tobit to prove that the *praestigium* of castration afflicts only the lustful. Kramer's problem is, not logic, but organization: he tries to make all his proofs at once. All these "digressions" were in the earlier discussion of *praestigium* (ibid., fols. 30r–32r [pp. 61–65]). For instance, in the earlier discussion of Macharius and the filly-girl, he claims that "the devils seem to be unable to deceive the sight of holy men in the least" (fol. 30r [p. 61]).

28. Ibid., fol. 58r (p. 119).
29. Ibid.
30. Ibid.
31. Ibid., fol. 68v (p. 139).
32. Ibid., fol. 58r (p. 119).
33. An early reader of the copy that Jerouschek reproduces in his facsimile first edition felt the same way: he noted "Aliud mirum" (another wonder) in the margin (Kramer/Jerouschek, *Malleus maleficarum 1487,* fol. 58r).
34. Kramer, *Malleus,* fol. 28v (pp. 58–59).
35. Ibid., fol. 28v (p. 58).
36. Spina, 39, informs his readers that it is more difficult and marvelous for demons to create such *praestigia* in the mind than to perform the realities.
37. Kramer, *Malleus,* fol. 30v (pp. 62–63). Kramer's discussion is based on Aquinas, Augustine, and Saint Antoninus of Florence (Schnyder, 141).
38. Kramer, *Malleus,* fol. 61r (p. 125); Summers's translation erases the concrete physicality of this process.
39. Ibid., fol. 59v (p. 121).
40. Ibid.
41. Recalling Aquinas, *De malo,* 16.11, Kramer says: "But if it is asked how he can do this without causing pain in the head, the answer is easy. For in the first place he does not cause any actual physical change in the organs, but only moves the mental images." The Devil owes his exquisitely light touch to his complete lack of corporeality, for his nature is completely spiritual, says Kramer (ibid., fol. 61v [p. 125]; fols. 30r–v [p. 62] are also based on Aquinas, especially the *De malo,* 16.11).
42. Kramer, *Malleus,* fol. 59v (pp. 121–22).
43. See, e.g., ibid., fols. 10v, 20r, 23r, 48v, 54v, 55r, 55v, 59v.
44. Kramer, *Malleus,* fol. 13r (pp. 26–27), and fol. 11v (p. 22), emphasis added. The Latin reads: "Preterea, omnis actio est per contactum, ut dicitur primo

De generatione. Non videtur autem quod possit esse aliquis contactus demonis ad corpora cum nihil habeat cum eis commune." Summers's "point of contact" is not literally present but renders Kramer's idea succinctly.

45. Davis; Montaigne, "Of the Power of the Imagination," 70–71.
46. *Si per sortiarias;* Kramer, *Malleus,* fols. 4r, 26v–27r (pp. 2, 54–55, 56), etc.
47. Anonymous continuation of the *History of Spain* by Don Rodrigo Sanchez de Arévalo, quoted in Hansen, ed., *Quellen,* 262.
48. Ibid., emphasis added.
49. Kramer, *Malleus,* fol. 4r (p. 2), citing the *Si per sortiarias.*
50. See ibid., fols. 4r, 5r, 10v, 26v, 77r (pp. 2, 4, 20, 54–55, 157); *Si per sortiarias.*
51. Ibid., fol. 5r (p. 4). Kramer reveals seven ways whereby witches "infect with *maleficia* the venereal act and the conception of the womb." The third method is "removing [*auferendo*] the members accommodated to that act" (fol. 23r [p. 47]).
52. Kramer, *Malleus,* fols. 23v, 27v (pp. 48, 56). On the "debt of matrimony," see 1 Cor. 7:2–4.
53. Kramer, *Malleus,* fol. 41v (p. 84).
54. Ibid., fol. 5r (p. 5), emphasis added.
55. He gives no reason but several times quotes the Book of Job to prove that, if God did not restrain the demons, they would overthrow the entire creation (ibid., fol. 4r [p. 1] etc.).
56. Ibid., fols. 4v, 26v (pp. 4, 54). *Si per sortiarias* is crucial to Kramer's treatment, from the first page of the *Malleus* (fol. 4r [p. 2]).
57. *Catechismo,* 152, emphasis added.
58. See, specifically, Gen. 2:23–24; Matt. 19:1–6; Mark 10:2–9; and Eph. 5: 22–33. On matrimony as a sacrament, see Michel, "Sacrements," 546–53.
59. The Council of Florence declared: "The seventh sacrament is matrimony, which is the sign of the conjunction of Christ and his church according to the Apostle Paul when he said: 'This is a great sacrament; I say in Christ and in his Church' [Eph. 5:32]. The efficient cause of a normal matrimony is mutual consent expressed by words in the present tense. A threefold good is attributed to matrimony. The first is progeny, to be raised and educated in the worship of God. The second is faith, which each spouse must keep with the other. The third is the indivisibility of matrimony, which is due to the fact that it signifies the indivisible union of Christ and the church" (Denzinger and Schönmetzer, par. 1327; see also par. 761 [Council of Verona, 1184]; and see Colish, *Peter Lombard,* 2:628–98).
60. Denzinger and Schönmetzer, pars. 1601, 1797–1812, esp. pars. 1800–1801. The remaining Tridentine paragraphs on matrimony are also important, although not primary, to its sacramentality (ibid., 1813–16). See also Michel, "Sacrements," esp. 525–53. The issue of defining sacraments and sacramental signification had gained urgency in response to Hussitism and to the prospect of reunification with the Greek church and was further intensified after Luther's revolt. See Denzinger and Schönmetzer, p. 895 (Index systematicus J).
61. Kramer, *Malleus,* fol. 28r (p. 57). Kramer's view is old and even reactionary: between the late twelfth century and the early thirteenth, leading Catholic thinkers came to locate the sacramentality of marriage in the free con-

sent of both partners to the union, rather than in its sexual consummation (Lansing, 120–21). But Kramer insists, not only on consummation, but on conception and birth: "To return to the matter in hand. And first for the natural act of propagation instituted by God, that is, between male and female; that as though by the permission of God the sacrament of matrimony can be made void [*vitiari*] by the work of the Devil through *maleficia* . . ." (Kramer, *Malleus,* fol. 12v [pp. 25–26]). Kramer is even more explicit later: "The Canonists treat more fully than the Theologians of the impediment due to *maleficium;* and they say that it is *maleficium,* not only when anyone is unable to perform the carnal act. . . but also when a woman is prevented from conceiving, or is made to miscarry after she has conceived. A third and fourth method of witchcraft is when witches have failed to procure a miscarriage, and then either devour the child or offer it to a devil" (ibid., fol. 32r [p. 66]).

62. "It might be said that, the greater part of witches [*supersticiose*] being women, they lust more for men than for women. Also they act in the despite of married women, creating every opportunity for adultery when the husband is able to copulate with [*cognoscere*] other women but not with his own wife; and similarly the wife also has to seek other lovers" (ibid., fol. 27r [p. 55]). Kramer has prepared this moment by posing the question whether witches "can stir up such hatred between married couples that they can neither render nor exact the debt of matrimony for the procreation of children" (ibid., fol. 25r [p. 51]).
63. See Denzinger and Schönmetzer, par. 1327 (above, n. 59); Robinson.
64. Rupert of Deutz (d. 1135) uses the phrase "two in one flesh" to connect matrimony and the eucharist. See Bynum, 62–63, esp. 62.
65. Kramer, *Malleus,* fol. 41v (p. 84).
66. Aquinas, *Quaestiones quodlibetales,* 11.9.1, *Utrum maleficia impediant matrimonium* (Aquinas, *Opera,* 3:500). Peters translates more freely (see Kors and Peters, eds., 72–73).
67. Bonaventure, *Opera omnia,* 4:772, commenting on Lombard, *Sententiarum,* 4.34.2.2.
68. Aquinas, *Quaestiones quodlibetales,* 11.9, response (Aquinas, *Opera,* 3:501), emphasis added.
69. Ibid.
70. Aquinas, *Commentum* on Lombard, *Sententiarum,* 4.34.1.3 (Aquinas, *Opera,* 1:604).
71. Kramer, *Malleus,* fol. 4r. Summers's translation (p. 2) destroys any sense of Kramer's sources by a combination of mistranslation and typographical errors.

Chapter Twelve

1. Chène observes that there are two categories of malefactor in Nider's *Formicarius:* a sect of apostate infanticidal cannibals, both men and women, who have most of the characteristics of witches and isolated individual men like Scadelem who conform to the older stereotype of the necromancer or sorcerer (Nider/Chène, 243–44).
2. Aquinas, *De malo,* 16.1 (Aquinas, *On Evil,* 447). The same argument can be found in Aquinas, *De substantiis separatis,* 2 (Aquinas, *Opera,* 3:516).

3. Kramer, *Malleus,* fols. 27v–28r (pp. 56–57), revisits Aquinas's problems with Aristotle's neglect of demons. (See chap. 3 above.)
4. Vineti, sigs. e8r–e9v (or sig. f1v: single unquired leaf).
5. Vineti, sig. d5r, quoting Luke 10:19; and Aquinas, *Summa theologiae,* 2–2.95.2 (but erroneously: the quotation is from 2-2.90.2).
6. Vineti, sigs. d5r–v, quoting Aquinas's *Commentum* on Lombard, *Sententiarum,* 2.6.2.1 (but erroneously: the quotation is from 2.7.3.2). On pacts with demons, see also Aquinas, *Summa theologiae,* 1.118.3, 2-2.90.2–3, 2–2.92.2, 2-2.95.2–6, and 2-2.96.1–4.
7. Walker, *Unclean Spirits,* 5–7. See also Kieckhefer, *Forbidden Rites,* 127 (see also 14, 188).
8. Kieckhefer, *Forbidden Rites,* 14.
9. Vineti, sig. d2r. The female forms *malefica* and *malefice* (i.e., *maleficae*) do not occur at all. *Malefici* are mentioned through a quotation from Aquinas's *Commentum* on Lombard, *Sententiarum,* 4.34.1.3 (Aquinas, *Opera,* 1:604–5), the source of Vineti's and Kramer's worries about demons existing only in the imagination of the common people.
10. For Vineti's ideas on physical contact with demons, see chap. 1 above.
11. Vineti, sigs. a1v–a2r (table of contents).
12. Ibid., sigs. a2r–v (table of contents).
13. Ibid., sig. e3r.
14. Ibid.
15. Ibid., sigs. e3r–e4r, referring to Aquinas, *Summa theologiae,* 3.43.2–4, 3.44.1.
16. Vineti, sigs. e4r–v, referring to Mark 5.
17. Vineti, sigs. e4v–e5r, referring to Aquinas, *Summa theologiae,* 3.44.4 and 3.44.1 (both based on Chrysostom).
18. Vineti, sigs. e4v–e5r. For the definition of witchcraft as a witch, a demon, and divine permission, see Kramer, *Malleus,* fol. 4v (p. 2).
19. Vineti, sigs. e5r–e6r, referring to Aquinas's *Commentum* on Lombard, *Sententiarum,* 2.8 (the distinction on demonic corporeality), and *Summa theologiae,* 1.115.5.
20. Vineti, sigs. e6v, e7r.
21. Ibid., sigs. e6v–e7r, quoting Aquinas, *Summa theologiae,* 1.115.5, and *De substantiis separatis,* 2 (the same argument can be found in *De malo,* 16.1). Augustine, *De civitate Dei,* 10.11, discusses Porphyry's letter to Anebo ("Tremefons"), foreshadowing Aquinas's argument that "wonders . . . which quite surpass human power" demonstrate the reality of demons (317–18).
22. Vineti, sig. c3v, referring to Aquinas, *Summa theologiae,* 1.115.5, and *De substantiis separatis,* 2.
23. See particularly Vineti, sigs. c7v–d1v. Like Aquinas, Kramer, Spina, and a host of others, Vineti cites a passage where Augustine explained how demons seduced pagans into believing them gods by performing miracles, then directed them to make sacrifices: "They are attracted not by food like animals, but, like spirits, by such symbols as suit their taste: various kinds of stones, woods, plants, animals, songs, rites. And that men may provide these attractions, the devils first of all cunningly seduce them . . . by revealing themselves under a friendly guise. . . . For unless they first instructed men, it were impossible to know what each of them desires, what they

shrink from, by what name they should be invoked or constrained to be present" (Augustine, 772). On pacts in Aquinas, see n. 6 above.

24. Vineti, sig. e7v, based on Aquinas, *Summa theologiae,* 3.71.2.
25. Kelly, 274–75; for the relation to witchcraft, see 275–76n.
26. Vineti, sig. e8r, referring to Aquinas, *Summa theologiae,* 3.71.2–3. On the significance of these ritual actions, see Kelly, 274–76.
27. Vineti, sigs. e7v–e8r, quoting Aquinas, *Summa theologiae,* 3.71.3.
28. Kieckhefer, *Forbidden Rites,* 12.
29. Ibid., passim; Butler, *Ritual Magic,* passim.
30. Kramer, *Malleus,* fol. 64v (p. 132). "Hec verba ytalica que ex ore meo protulit" clearly implies that the demon spoke the Italian words.
31. Battaglia, 9:203, col. 1; Boccaccio, *Decameron,* 1.1; Dante, *Inferno,* cantos 14–16. In *Inferno* 11.91–111, Dante defines usury as a crime against nature and human industry; sodomy was a grievous sin against nature.
32. Kramer, *Malleus,* fol. 14v (pp. 29–30). On witchcraft and sodomy, see Monter, *Frontiers of Heresy,* 276–99.
33. Kramer, *Malleus,* fol. 64v (p. 131). In his note (ibid.), Summers lists the extensive collection of relics that was held in the Church of Santa Prassede, including "the Holy Pillar of the Scourging brought in 1223 from Jerusalem by Cardinal Giovanni Colonna." The column is still in this church (Cruciani and Corbella, 361). Saint Peter was supposed to have been crucified on the site of the Church of San Pietro in Montorio, on the Janiculum hill.
34. Kramer, *Malleus,* fol. 64v (p. 132). Stendhal, 120, mentioned this column as being in the chapel of Michelangelo's *Pietà,* but it appears to have been moved.
35. The third palindrome is from Doniger. Kieckhefer's *Forbidden Rites* and Marlowe's *Dr Faustus* suggest that palindromes were an important part of necromantic verbal techniques.
36. Kramer, *Malleus,* fol. 64v (p. 132). For slightly different versions of the Gospel incident, see Matt. 17:21; and Mark 9:29. The forty-day period recalls Christ's temptation in the desert, the archetypal scene of demonic molestation.
37. Kieckhefer, *Forbidden Rites,* 149, citing research by Lynn White, André Goddu, and Nancy Caciola.
38. Ibid.
39. Kramer, *Malleus,* fol. 65v (pp. 133–34), referring to Matthew 17 and Luke 13. Kramer says that, in the Gospels, the possessed are always continuously (*sine intermissione*) afflicted; thus, the Bohemian's novel form of possession must be caused by *maleficium,* the combination of demons, witches, and divine permission (ibid.).
40. Sister Jeanne des Anges was a famous example of this tendency, as were the other nuns of Loudun (see Jeanne des Anges; and Certeau). Menghi, *Compendio dell'arte essorcistica,* shows that the activation of possession by exorcism would become ever more commonplace, until theoretical explanations were needed.
41. Kramer, *Malleus,* fol. 64v (pp. 131–32).
42. Ibid., fol. 64v (p. 131).
43. On this "counterconversion," see James, *Varieties of Religious Experience,* 176–77. The experience that James quotes sounds plausible for the Bohemian.

44. Thomas, *Religion and the Decline of Magic,* 478, 521.
45. Godbeer, 106–8, 212.
46. Pico, *De imaginatione,* 10 (Pico, *On the Imagination,* 68–73).
47. Godbeer, 109, gives a similar explanation, although in moralizing terms: "Rather than accepting or rejecting responsibility for their condition, demoniacs did both: they displaced their sinful urges onto devils within them."
48. De Espina, sig. Z5r.
49. The consequences of this maxim are teased out by King James I/VI in his *Daemonologie:* "Doubtleslie who denyeth the power of the Deuill, woulde likewise denie the power of God, if they could for shame. For since the Deuill is the verie contrarie opposite to God, *there can be no better way to know God, then by the contrarie;* as by the ones power (though a creature) to admire the power of the great Creator: by the falshood of the one to considder the trueth of the other, by the injustice of the one, to considder the Iustice of the other: And by the cruelty of the one, to consider the mercifulnessse of the other: And so foorth in all the essence of God, and qualities of the Deuill. *But I feare indeed, there be over many Sadduces in this worlde, that denies all kinds of spirites: For convicting of whose errour, there is cause inough if there were no more, that God should permit at sometimes spirits visiblie to kyith*" (James I/VI, 34–35, emphasis added).
50. Guazzo, *Compendium* (1626), 1.1.
51. These are the *Flagellum daemonum,* or *A Scourge for Demons* (1577), and the *Fustis daemonum,* or *A Cudgel for Demons* (1584).
52. Menghi, *Compendio* (1584), fols. 8r–v, emphasis added.
53. "And because in the present little [*sic!*] work, beyond the use of reasoning, we shall adduce many examples taken from these two authors, Henry Institoris [Kramer] and Jacob Sprenger in the abovementioned book so as to confirm the truth, so that the gentle reader may be clear in future, he should notice that, whenever in the following chapters I will say 'the aforementioned authors,' or 'our authors,' etc., he must always understand that I refer to these two" (ibid., 184).
54. Ibid., 387–94 (on Aquinas's proofs), 399–403 (on Kramer's Bohemian).

Chapter Thirteen

1. Kramer, *Malleus,* fol. 64r (p. 131).
2. Ibid., fols. 64r–v (p. 131).
3. Ibid.
4. Ibid., fol. 64v (p. 131).
5. Certeau, Godbeer.
6. P. Castelli, *Bibliotheca lamiarum,* 151–52.
7. Ibid.
8. Cesalpino, sig. F3r.
9. Ibid.
10. Cesalpino, sigs. F2r–F3r.
11. On hysteria, see the apparatus provided by the physician-editors of Jeanne des Anges. For film, examples are Ken Russell's *Devils* (of Loudun, based on Aldous Huxley's book of that name) and the recent version of Arthur Miller's *Crucible.*

12. Kramer, *Malleus,* fol. 65r (p. 133); Cesalpino, sig. F3r.
13. Kramer, *Malleus,* fol. 64v (p. 131).
14. Kieckhefer, *Magic in the Middle Ages,* 55–94, 151–201; see also 201: "Those who prosecuted and condemned [people as witches] were, after all, men with some education, who would naturally tend to see popular magic in terms of what other educated people were doing. Recognizing the threat of demonic magic in the clerical underworld, they would spontaneously project that model onto humbler magicians."
15. Menghi, *Compendio* (1584), 430–35.
16. Kieckhefer, *Magic in the Middle Ages,* 17.
17. Ibid., 200.
18. Ibid., 116–50.
19. Caesarius of Heisterbach/Strange, 1:275–76 (Caesarius of Heisterbach/Scott and Bland, 1:314).
20. Caesarius of Heisterbach/Strange, 1:276–77 (Caesarius of Heisterbach/Scott and Bland, 1:314–15).
21. This gives rise to an exchange regarding sacramental efficacy:

    > NOVICE: Surely the knight can never have confessed these sins; for how could the devil know them if they had been confessed?
    > MONK: Because he had confessed with the intention of sinning again, he in no degree took away the devil's knowledge.
    > NOVICE: I am glad to hear what you say, because I remember you said the same thing in the sixth chapter of the third distinction. (Caesarius of Heisterbach/Strange, 1:278 [Caesarius of Heisterbach/Scott and Bland, 1:317])

    The evident intention is to demonstrate that sacramental confession destroys the memory of sin so thoroughly—unless it is ruined by insincerity—that demons cannot find out about it.
22. Caesarius of Heisterbach/Strange, 1:278, 277 (Caesarius of Heisterbach/Scott and Bland, 1:317, 316).
23. Caesarius of Heisterbach/Strange, 1:278–79 (Caesarius of Heisterbach/Scott and Bland, 1:317–18).
24. Caesarius of Heisterbach/Strange, 1:277 (Caesarius of Heisterbach/Scott and Bland, 1:316).
25. Caesarius of Heisterbach/Strange, 1:339 (Caesarius of Heisterbach/Scott and Bland, 1:390). Other examples, including poltergeists, are in Menghi, *Compendio* (1584), 507–16, to the same effect. Pages 523–96 of Menghi purport to prove the reality of demons and the efficacy of sacraments and sacramentals against them.
26. Based on discussions in Humanities 1 and 2, "The Classical Tradition," at Dartmouth College, academic years 1995–97.
27. Marlowe, 19.
28. Ibid., 29, 30.
29. Ibid., 39, 60, 62.
30. Faustus claims that he cannot really recall the dead but only "such spirits as can lively resemble" them (ibid., 51). On physically examining the demons that Faustus has conjured as Alexander the Great and his paramour, the em-

peror exclaims: "Sure, these are no spirits, but *the true substantial bodies* of those two deceased princes" (ibid., 52).

31. Ibid., 62.
32. Ibid., 50.
33. Ibid., 6–7.
34. Ibid., 67.
35. Ibid., 68.
36. Borges, 57.
37. "Sainthood and witchcraft were ascribed roles and could give occasion for competing ascription, with different observers thinking of a single person as a saint or as a witch, but the necromancer's role was essentially self-defined, and in the necromancer's own mind the holy and the unholy, the sacred and the explicitly demonic, entered into a rare and fascinating alliance" (Kieckhefer, "The Holy and the Unholy," 385).
38. "Satan has become the eternal absent. But his presence is demonstrated and assured precisely through his absence. . . . When one takes the image of Satan not for Satan but for an illusion, Satan demonstrates by this wrongful disbelief that he exists; and when one takes the image of Satan not for an illusion, but for Satan, then Satan shows by this vain belief that, once again, he exists" (Foucault, 23). I thank Stephen Greenblatt for this reference.
39. Pullman, 85–114.
40. Dante, *Inferno,* 10.13–16.
41. Boccaccio, *Decameron,* 6.9 (Boccaccio, 401).
42. Lucretius, *De rerum natura,* 3.830–31, 838–41 (Lucretius, 226–29).
43. "One must read Lucretius to understand *what* it was that Epicurus opposed: *not* paganism but 'Christianity,' which is to say the corruption of souls through the concept of guilt, punishment and immortality" (Nietzsche/ Hollingdale, 191).
44. Quoted in Jarrett, 42.
45. W. H. D. Rouse, in Lucretius, liv–lvi.
46. Kramer, *Malleus,* fol. 33v (pp. 68–69), emphasis added.
47. Ibid., fol. 35v (p. 73).
48. Vineti, sigs. a4r–v, referring to Aquinas, *Summa contra gentiles,* 3.99, *De potentia,* 6.6 (cf. 6.1), and *Summa theologiae,* 1.50.1. Aquinas is quoting Aristotle's discussion of the void in the *Physics,* 4.6.213a.
49. De Espina, sigs. i4r–v. De Espina quotes Acts 23:8 ("The Sadducees deny that there is any resurrection, or angel, or spirit, but the Pharisees accept them").
50. Randall, 274–75.
51. Benigni, 227.
52. Pomponazzi, *On the Immortality of the Soul,* 377, 379.
53. Abbiati, Agnoletto, and Lazzati, eds., 366–67; Garin, 569–70.
54. Randall, 275, quoting Pomponazzi, *Apologia,* 3.3.
55. Pomponazzi, *On the Immortality of the Soul,* 367, referring to Aristotle, *Metaphysics,* 12.8.1073a.28ff.: "Since we see that besides the simple spatial movement of the universe, which we say the first and unmovable substance produces, there are other spatial movements—those of the planets—which are eternal (for the body which moves in a circle is eternal and unresting: we have proved these points in the *Physics* [8.8–9]), each of *these* move-

ments also must be caused by a substance unmovable in itself and eternal. For the nature of the stars is eternal, being a kind of substance, and the mover is eternal and prior to the moved, and that which is prior to a substance must be a substance. Evidently, then, there must be substances which are of the same number as the movements of the stars, and in their nature eternal, and in themselves unmovable, and without magnitude" (Aristotle, 2:1696).

56. Pomponazzi, *On the Immortality of the Soul,* 318.
57. On attempts to identify Aristotle's celestial intelligences as angels, see Keck, 85–86.
58. Pomponazzi, *On the Immortality of the Soul,* 368–70.
59. Ibid., 372–73.
60. Ibid., 348–49.
61. Ibid., 365, quoting Aristotle, *De somno et vigilia,* 460b.3ff. (see Aristotle, 1: 732).
62. Ibid., 287.
63. Aristotle, *De anima,* 1.1.403a.3–12 (Aristotle, 1:642), emphasis added.
64. Aristotle, *De anima,* 3.7.431a.15–17 (Aristotle, 1:685), emphasis added.
65. Pomponazzi, *On the Immortality of the Soul,* 287, 291, 293, 295, 296, 305, etc.
66. Ibid., 282, 293.
67. Ibid., 296.
68. Ibid., 315, 317, 318.
69. Ibid., 324.
70. Randall, 277, quoting Pomponazzi, *De naturalium effectuum causis,* chap. 1.
71. Keats, in Adams, ed., 473. In *Paradise Lost,* the sleeping Adam dreams of Eve while she is being created from his rib: he awakes to find her every bit as delightful as his dream (8.452ff., esp. 482).

Conclusion

1. Beatrice Gottlieb, in Febvre, xxviii.
2. Febvre, 455.
3. Greenblatt, 22.
4. Thomas, *Religion and the Decline of Magic,* 171, 173. Thomas considers the problem of skepticism on 166–73 but does not distinguish voluntary from involuntary skeptics. On 469–77, he maintains that nearly everyone believed in the literal reality of devils, and, on 570–83, he traces the decline of ideas about Satan and witchcraft without considering the prehistory of skepticism in witchcraft theory.
5. Wesley, 5:265, emphasis added. Elsewhere, Wesley criticizes skeptics "whose manner of speaking concerning witchcraft must be extremely offensive to every sensible man who cannot give up his Bible" (5:375) and says, "I cannot give up to all the Deists in Great Britain the existence of witchcraft till I give up the credit of all history, sacred and profane" (6: 109).
6. See Kieckhefer, "Avenging the Blood of Children," esp. 91–93. "[The novelist Frank Peretti's] lavish and almost erotic attachment to the imagery of demons (and his simplistic and sentimental sense of evil) makes him the writer who best exemplifies American piety—which, to reverse the old

adage, loves the sin and hates the sinner. Peretti's books, and all these other Christian thrillers, roughly mirror the convictions of some significant portion of the 65 percent of Americans who say they believe in the Devil and the 86 percent who identify themselves as Christians" (Passaro, 69–70).

7. Mack, 406–7, emphasis added.
8. Ibid., 421.
9. Bob Seeger, "Against the Wind."
10. " 'Glaube' heißt Nicht-wissen-*vollen,* was wahr ist" (Nietzsche/Schlechta, 1218). The response to Saint Paul's definition of *faith* as "the substance of things hoped for, the evidence of things not seen" (Heb. 11:1), is evident.
11. Wills, *Papal Sin,* 9, quoting Aquinas, *Summa theologiae,* 1–2.6.8. Kramer uses this argument to argue against skepticism about witchcraft (Kramer, *Malleus,* fol. 6v [p. 10]).
12. Flew, 545–46.
13. Plato, *Symposium,* 202E-203A (Plato, 47).
14. I refer to Goya's illustration "El sueño de la razon produce monstros" (The sleep [or dreaming] of reason creates monsters).

WORKS CITED

Witchcraft Theorists

Alciato (Alciati), Andrea. Excerpt from *Parergon iuris libri X* [1543]. In *Quellen und Untersuchungen zur Geschichte des Hexenwahns und der Hexenverfolgung im Mittelalter,* ed. Joseph Hansen, 310–12. Bonn: Carl Georgi, 1901.

Anania, Giovanni Lorenzo. *De substantiis separatis opusculum primum de natura daemonum et occultis eorum operationibus.* Rome, 1654.

———. *De substantiis separatis opusculum secundum de natura angelorum et occultis eorum operationibus.* Rome, 1654.

Bodin, Jean. *De la démonomanie des sorciers.* Paris, 1582.

Canon *Episcopi.* First printed 1471. In *Corpus iuris canonici.* Vol. 1, *Decretum Magistri Gratiani.* Edited by Aemilius Ludwig Richter and Emil Friedburg, 1030–31. 1879. Photographic reprint, Graz: Akademische Druck, 1959.

Cesalpino, Andrea. *Daemonum investigatio peripatetica, in qua explicatur locus Hippocratis in Progn. "Si quid divinum in morbis habetur."* Florence, 1580.

de Espina, Alonso [Alphonsus a Spina]. *Fortalitium fidei contra Iudeos, Saracenos, aliosque christiane fidei inimicos.* Lyon, 1511.

De Lancre, Pierre. *Tableau de l'inconstance des mauvais anges et démons.* Paris, 1612.

Errores gazariorum, seu illorum qui scopam vel baculum equitare probant. [ca. 1430]. In *L'imaginaire du sabbat: Edition critique des textes les plus anciens (1430 c.–1440 c.),* ed. Martine Ostorero, Agostino Paravicini Bagliani, and Kathrin Utz Tremp, 267–300. Lausanne: Université de Lausanne, 1999.

Geiler von Kaisersberg, Johannes. *Die Emeis.* Strassburg, 1517.

Giordano (Jordanes) da Bergamo. Excerpt from *Quaestio de strigis* [ca. 1470]. In *Quellen und Untersuchungen zur Geschichte des Hexenwahns und der Hexenverfolgung im Mittelalter,* ed. Joseph Hansen, 195–200. Bonn: Carl Georgi, 1901. Also in *La stregoneria: Diavoli, streghe, inquisitori dal trecento al settecento,* ed. Sergio Abbiati, Attilio Agnoletto, and Maria Rosario Lazzati, 79–85. Milan: Mondadori, 1984. Reprint, Milan: Mondadori, 1991.

Glanvill, Joseph. *Saducismus triumphatus; or, Full and Plain Evidence concerning Witches and Apparitions . . . with a Letter of Dr. Henry More on the Same Subject. . . .* London, 1681.

———. *Saducismus triumphatus; or, Full and Plain Evidence concerning Witches and Apparitions.* 1689. Reprint, with an introduction by Coleman O. Parsons, Gainesville, Fla.: Scholars' Facsimiles and Reprints, 1966.

Grillando, Paolo. *De sortilegis.* [ca. 1525]. In *Tractatus duo: Unus de sortilegis D. Pauli Grillandi . . . alter de lamiis et excellentia iuris utriusque D. Ioannis Francisci Ponzinibij. . . .* Frankfurt, 1592.

Guazzo, Francesco Maria. *Compendium maleficarum.* 1st ed. Milan, 1608.

———. *Compendium maleficarum.* 2d ed. Milan, 1626.

———. *Compendium maleficarum.* Translated (from the 1st ed.) by E. A. Ashwin. Edited by Montague Summers. 1929. Reprint, New York: Dover, 1988.

———. *Compendium maleficarum.* Translated (from the 2d ed.) and edited by Luciano Tamburini. Turin: Einaudi, 1992.

Jacquier, Nicholas. Excerpt from *Flagellum haereticorum fascinariorum.* 1458. In *Quellen und Untersuchungen zur Geschichte des Hexenwahns und der Hexenverfolgung im Mittelalter,* ed. Joseph Hansen, 133–45. Bonn: Carl Georgi, 1901.

James I/VI. *King James the First, Daemonologie (1597), Newes from Scotland Declaring the Damnable Life and Death of Doctor Fian, a Notable Sorcerer Who was Burned at Edenbrough in Ianuary Last (1591).* 1597. Edited by G. B. Harrison. London: Bodley Head; New York: E. P. Dutton, n.d. Photographic reprint.

Jeanne des Anges, Soeur (d. 1665). *Soeur Jeanne des Anges Supérieure des Ursulines de Loudun (XVIIe siècle): Autobiographie d'une hystérique possédée.* Edited by Gabriel Lègue and Gilles de la Tourette. With a preface by Jean Martin Charcot. 1st ed. (hitherto unpublished). Paris, 1886.

Johann von Frankfurt. *Quaestio, utrum potestas cohercendi demones fieri possit per caracteres, figuras atque verborum prolationes.* 1412. In *Quellen und Untersuchungen zur Geschichte des Hexenwahns und der Hexenverfolgung im Mittelalter,* ed. Joseph Hansen, 71–82. Bonn: Carl Georgi, 1901.

"Judgment on the Witch Walpurga Hausmännin." 1587. In *News and Rumor in Renaissance Europe: The Fugger Newsletters,* trans. George T. Matthews, 137–43. New York: Capricorn, 1959.

Kramer, Heinrich. *Tractatus novus de miraculoso eukaristie sacramento, qui apparet in forma pueri, aut carnis vel sanguinis in hostia consacrata: Collectus a fratre h. i. . . .* Augsburg, 1493.

———. *Tractatus varii cum sermonibus contra errores adversus eucharistiam exortos.* Nuremberg, 1496.

———. *Sancte Romane Ecclesie fidei defensionis clippeum adversus Waldensium seu Pickardorum heresim.* Olmütz, 1502.

———. *Malleus maleficarum.* Speyer, 1487.

———. *Malleus maleficarum, opus egregium.* Nuremberg, 1519.

———. *Malleus maleficarum, in tres partes divisus. . . .* Frankfurt, 1580.

———. *Malleus maleficarum.* In *Malleus maleficarum: Ex plurimis auctoribus coacervatus.* Lyon, 1596.

———. *Malleus maleficarum.* In *Mallei maleficarum: Aliquot tam veterum quam recentiorum in unum corpus coacervati.* Lyon, 1620.

———. *The Malleus maleficarum of Heinrich Kramer and James Sprenger.* Translated by Montague Summers. 1928. Reprint, New York: Dover, 1971.

———. *Il martello delle streghe: La sessualità femminile nel transfert degli inquisitori.* Translated by Fabrizio Buia, Elena Caetani, Renato Castelli, Valeria La Via, Franco Mori, and Ettore Perella. With an introduction by Armando Verdiglione. Venice: Marsilio, 1977.

———. *Malleus maleficarum 1487 von Heinrich Kramer (Institoris): Nachdruck des Erstdruckes von 1487 mit Bulle und Approbatio.* 1487. Photographic reprint, with an introduction by Günter Jerouschek, Hildesheim: Georg Olms, 1992.

———. *Nürnberger Hexenhammer 1491 von Heinrich Kramer (Institoris): Faksimile der Handschrift von 1491 aus dem Staatsarchiv Nürnberg, Nr. D 251.* 1491. Photographic reprint, with apparatus by Günter Jerouschek, Hildesheim: Georg Olms, 1992.

Ledrede, Richard. *The Sorcery Trial of Alice Kyteler: A Contemporary Account (1324).* Translated by Gail Ward. Edited by L. S. Davidson and J. O. Ward. Binghamton, N.Y.: Medieval and Renaissance Texts and Studies, 1993.

Mather, Cotton. *The Wonders of the Invisible World: Being an Account of the Tryals of Several Witches Lately Executed in New-England: By Cotton Mather, D.D. to Which Is Added a Farther Account of the Tryals of the New-England Witches: By Increase Mather, D.D.* 1st ed., 1693. Reprint, Amherst, Wis.: Amherst Press, n.d.

Mazzolini, Silvestro [Prierias]. *Reverendi Patris F. Silvestri Prieriatis Or. Praed. Theologiae Profess. Sacrique Palatii Apostolici Magistri Dignissimi, De strigimagarum daemonumque mirandis, libri tres, una cum praxi exactissima, et ratione formandi processus contra ipsas, a mendis innumeris, quibus scatebant, in hac ultima impressione purgati, et indice locupletissimo illustrati.* 1521. Reprint, Rome, 1575. Excerpt in *La stregoneria: Diavoli, streghe, inquisitori dal trecento al settecento,* ed. Sergio Abbiati, Attilio Agnoletto, and Maria Rosario Lazzati, 224–29. Milan: Mondadori, 1984. Reprint, Milan: Mondadori, 1991.

———. *Summa summarum, que silvestrina dicitur.* 1st ed. Bologna, 1514. Excerpt in *La stregoneria: Diavoli, streghe, inquisitori dal trecento al settecento,* ed. Sergio Abbiati, Attilio Agnoletto, and Maria Rosario Lazzati, 220–24. Milan: Mondadori, 1984. Reprint, Milan: Mondadori, 1991.

Menghi, Girolamo. *Compendio dell'arte essorcistica, et possibilità delle mirabili, et stupende operationi delli demoni et de i malefici.* 1576. Photographic reprint, with an afterword by Ottavio Franceschini, Genoa: Nuova Stile Regina Editrice, 1987.

———. *Compendio dell'arte essorcistica, et possibilità delle mirabili, et stupende operationi delli demoni et de i malefici.* Bologna, 1584.

———. *Flagellum daemonum, exorcismos terribiles, potentissimos, et efficaces: Remediaque probatissima, ac doctrinam singularem in malignos spiritus expellendos, facturasque & maleficia fuganda de obsessis corporibus complectens, cum suis benedictionibus et omnibus requisitis ad eorum expulsionem* [1st ed., 1577]: *Accesit postremo pars secunda, quae Fustis daemonum inscribitur* [1st ed., 1584]: *Quibus novi exorcismi & alia nonnulla, quae prius desiderabantur, superaddita fuerunt.* Venice, 1644.

Müller [Molitoris], Ulrich. *De lanijs et phitonicis mulieribus.* [ca. 1489]. In *Ulrich Molitoris: Schriften,* ed. Jörg Mauz, 63–132. Konstanz: Hockgraben, 1997. Latin version of *Von den Unholden oder Hexen.*

———. *Von den Unholden oder Hexen.* [ca. 1489]. In *Ulrich Molitoris: Schriften,* ed. Jörg Mauz, 133–85. Konstanz: Hockgraben, 1997. German version of *De lanijs et phitonicis mulieribus.*

———. *Ulrich Molitoris: Schriften.* Edited by Jörg Mauz. Konstanz: Hockgraben, 1997.

Nider, Johannes. *Preceptorium divinae legis.* Augsburg, 1479.

———. *Formicarius (Vollständige Ausgabe der Inkunable Köln o[hne] J[ahre]).* [ca. 1480]. Photographic reprint, with an introduction by Hans Biedermann, Graz: Akademische Druck, 1971.

———. "Formicarius (livre II, chapitre 4 et livre V, chapitres 3, 4, et 7)." Edited by Catherine Chène. In *L'imaginaire du sabbat: Edition critique des textes les plus anciens (1430 c.–1440 c.),* ed. Martine Ostorero, Agostino Paravicini Bagliani, and Kathrin Utz Tremp, 122–99. Lausanne: Université de Lausanne, 1999.

Passavanti, Jacopo. *Lo specchio della vera penitenza.* Composed 1354. First printed 1495. In *Lo specchio della vera penitenza . . . Coi volgarizzamenti da Origene e da Tito Livio attribuiti al medesimo Passavanti,* ed. Filippo Luigi Polidori, 1–355. Florence, 1863. Excerpt in *La stregoneria: Diavoli, streghe, inquisitori dal trecento al settecento,* ed. Sergio Abbiati, Attilio Agnoletto, and Maria Rosario Lazzati, 32–45. Milan: Mondadori, 1984. Reprint, Milan: Mondadori, 1991.

Pico della Mirandola, Gianfrancesco. *De imaginatione.* 1st ed. Venice, 1501.

———. *De rerum praenotione.* 1507. In *Joannes Franciscus Picus Mirandulanus opera omnia* (1573), 1:366–709. Photographic reprint, with an introduction by Eugenio Garin, Turin: Bottega d'Erasmo, 1972.

———. *Examen vanitatis doctrinae gentium et veritatis Christianae disciplinae.* 1520. In *Joannes Franciscus Picus Mirandulanus opera omnia* (1573), 2:717–1264. Photographic reprint, with an introduction by Eugenio Garin, Turin: Bottega d'Erasmo, 1972.

———. *Dialogus in tres libros divisus: Titulus est Strix, sive de ludificatione daemonum.* Bologna: Jeronimo de Benedictis, 1523.

———. *Libro detto strega, o delle illusioni del demonio.* Translated by Leandro Alberti. 1524. Edited by Albano Biondi. Venice: Marsilio, 1989.

———. *On the Imagination: The Latin Text, with an Introduction, English Translation, and Notes.* Translated by Harry Caplan. Westport, Conn.: Greenwood, 1971.

———. *Über die Vorstellung/De imaginatione.* Translated by Eckhard Kessler. With an introduction by Charles B. Schmitt and Katharine Park. Munich: W. Fink, 1984.

———. *La strega, overo, de gli inganni de' demoni.* Translated by Turino Turini. 1555. Reprint, with an introduction by Ida Li Vigni, Genoa: Edizioni Culturali Internazionali Genova, 1988.

Plantsch, Martin. *Opusculum de sagis maleficis Martini Plantsch.* 1505. In *Quellen und Untersuchungen zur Geschichte des Hexenwahns und der Hexenverfolgung im Mittelalter,* ed. Joseph Hansen, 258–61. Bonn: Carl Georgi, 1901.

Ponzinibio, Francesco. *De lamiis et excellentia iuris utriusque.* 1520. In *Tractatus duo: Unus de sortilegis D. Pauli Grillandi . . . alter de lamiis et excellentia iuris utriusque D. Ioannis Francisci Ponzinibij. . . .* Frankfurt, 1592.

Psellus, Michael (d. 1078). *De operatione daemonum.* 1st Latin ed., 1615. Excerpted (as *De operibus daemonum*) in *Jamblichus de mysteriis Aegyptiorum: Sammelband neuplatonischer Schriften übersehen und herausgegeben von Marsilius Ficinus, Venedig 1503,* ed. Marsilio Ficino, 175–86 (sigs. N1r-N6v). Photographic reprint, Frankfurt: Minerva, 1972.

———. *Le opere dei demoni.* Translated by Pietro Pizzari. Palermo: Sellerio, 1989.

Rategno, Bernardo, of Como. *De strigiis.* [ca. 1510]. First printed 1566. In *Lucerna inquisitorum haereticae pravitatis R. P. F. Bernardi Comensis Ordinis Praedicatorum, et eiusdem Tractatus de strigibus,* 140–54. Venice, 1596. Excerpt in *La stregoneria: Diavoli, streghe, inquisitori dal trecento al settecento,* ed. Sergio Abbiati, Attilio Agnoletto, and Maria Rosario Lazzati, 200–214. Milan: Mondadori, 1984. Reprint, Milan: Mondadori, 1991.

Recollectio casus, status et condicionis Valdensium ydolatrarum, ex practica et tractatibus plurimum inquisitorum et aliorum expertorum atque etiam ex confessionibus et processibus eorundem Valdensium in Atrebato facta anno domini millesimo quadringentesimo sexagesimo. 1460. In *Quellen und Untersuchungen zur Geschichte des Hexenwahns und der Hexenverfolgung im Mittelalter,* ed. Joseph Hansen, 149–83. Bonn: Carl Georgi, 1901.

Rémy, Nicolas. *Demonolatreia.* 1595. Translated by E. A. Ashwin. London: Rodker, 1930. Excerpt in *Witchcraft in Europe, 1100–1700: A Documentary History,* ed. Alan C. Kors and Edward Peters, 236–46. Philadelphia: University of Pennsylvania Press, 1972.

Scot, Reginald. *A Discourse upon Divels and Spirits.* 1584. In *The Discoverie of Witchcraft,* ed. Brinsley Nicholson. London: Stock, 1886.

———. *The Discoverie of Witchcraft.* 1584. In *The Discoverie of Witchcraft,* ed. Brinsley Nicholson. London: Stock, 1886.

Sinistrari, Ludovico Maria. *De demonialitate.* [ca. 1700]. Edited and translated by Isidore Lisieux as *De la démonialité et des animaux incubes et succubes.* Paris: I. Lisieux, 1876.

———. *Demoniality.* Translated by Montague Summers. 1927. Reprint, New York: Dover, 1989.

———. *Demonialità, ossia possibilità, modo, e varietà dell'unione carnale dell'uomo col demonio.* Translated by Carlo Carena. Palermo: Sellerio, 1986.

Si per sortiarias. First printed 1471. In *Corpus iuris canonici.* Vol. 1, *Decretum Magistri Gratiani.* Edited by Aemilius Ludwig Richter and Emil Friedburg, 1150. 1879. Photographic reprint, Graz: Akademische Druck, 1959.

Spina, Bartolomeo. *Quaestio de strigibus, una cum tractatu de praeeminentia sacrae theologiae, et quadruplici apologia De lamiis contra Ponzinibium.* 1523. Reprint, Rome, 1576.

Tartarotti, Girolamo. Excerpt from *Il congresso notturno delle lammie.* 1749. In *La stregoneria: Diavoli, streghe, inquisitori dal trecento al settecento,* ed. Sergio Abbiati, Attilio Agnoletto, and Maria Rosario Lazzati, 298–331. Milan: Mondadori, 1984. Reprint, Milan: Mondadori, 1991.

Tasso, Torquato. *Il messaggiero.* [ca. 1580–87]. 1st ed. 1582. In *Dialoghi: Il messaggiero, Il padre di famiglia, Il Malpiglio, La Cavaletta, La Molza,* ed. Bruno Basile, 29–104. Milan: Mursia, 1991.

Tostado, Alonso (d. 1455). *Alphonsi Thostati in quinque prima capitula beati Matthei explanatio litteralis amplissima.* [ca. 1440]. First printed 1501–3. Venice, 1506. Excerpt in *Quellen und Untersuchungen zur Geschichte des Hexenwahns und der Hexenverfolgung im Mittelalter,* ed. Joseph Hansen, 105–9. Bonn: Carl Georgi, 1901.

———. *Alphonsi Thostati episcopi Abulensis hispani a se edita super genesim commentaria.* First printed 1501–3. Venice, 1507.

"Urteil gegen die Hexe Walpurga Hausmännin." 1587. In *Fugger-Zeitungen: Ungedruckte Briefe an das Haus Fugger aus den jahren 1568–1605,* ed. Victor Klarwill, 103–10. Vienna: Rikola, 1928.

Vieri, Francesco de'. *Intorno a' dimonij volgarmente chiamati spiriti.* Florence, 1576.

Vignate, Ambrosius de. *Tractatus de haereticis.* [ca. 1468]. Excerpt in *Quellen und Untersuchungen zur Geschichte des Hexenwahns und der Hexenverfolgung im Mittelalter,* ed. Joseph Hansen, 149–82. Bonn: Carl Georgi, 1901.

Vineti, Jean. *Tractatus contra demonum invocatores.* Composed ca. 1450–70. 1st printing, 1483. Cologne, 1487.

Visconti, Girolamo (d. ca. 1478). *Opusculum magistri Hieronimi Vicecomitis ordinis predicatorum in quo probatur lamias esse hereticas et non laborare humore melancholico.* [ca. 1460]. Cornell University Library, Special Collections, Witchcraft Collection, 4621 Bd MS 48.

———. *Lamiarum sive striarum opusculum.* Composed ca. 1460. In *Magistri Hieronymi Vicecomitis Lamiarum sive striarum opusculum ad illustrissimum Mediolani ducem Franciscum Sfortiam Vicecomitem,* sigs. a1r–c2r. Milan, 1490.

———. *Magistri Hieronymi Vicecomitis Lamiarum sive striarum opusculum ad illustrissimum Mediolani ducem Franciscum Sfortiam Vicecomitem.* Milan, 1490.

———. *Opusculum de striis, videlicet an strie sint velud heretice iudicande.* In *Magistri Hieronymi Vicecomitis Lamiarum sive striarum opusculum,* sigs. c2r–c8v. Milan, 1490.

Wagstaffe, John. *The Question of Witchcraft Debated; or, A Discourse against Their Opinion That Affirm Witches.* 2d ed. London, 1671.

Weyer, Johann. *De praestigiis daemonum, et incantationibus ac veneficiis libri sex . . . accessit liber apologeticus, et pseudomonarchia daemonum.* 6th ed. Basel, 1583.

———. *Witches, Devils, and Doctors in the Renaissance: Johann Weyer, De praestigiis daemonum.* Translated by Jon Shea. Edited by George Mora et al. Binghamton, N.Y.: Medieval and Renaissance Texts and Studies, 1991.

Anthologies of Witchcraft Materials

Abbiati, Sergio, Attilio Agnoletto, and Maria Rosario Lazzati, eds. *La stregoneria: Diavoli, streghe, inquisitori dal trecento al settecento.* Milan: Mondadori, 1984. Reprint, Milan: Mondadori, 1991.

Ficino, Marsilio, ed. *Jamblichus de mysteriis Aegyptiorum: Sammelband neuplatonischer Schriften übersehen und herausgegeben von Marsilius Ficinus, Venedig 1503.* Photographic reprint, Frankfurt: Minerva, 1972.

Hansen, Joseph, ed. *Quellen und Untersuchungen zur Geschichte des Hexenwahns und der Hexenverfolgung im Mittelalter.* Bonn: Carl Georgi, 1901.

Kors, Alan C., and Edward Peters, eds. *Witchcraft in Europe, 1100–1700: A Documentary History.* Philadelphia: University of Pennsylvania Press, 1972.

Lea, Henry Charles. *Materials toward a History of Witchcraft.* 3 vols. Edited by Arthur C. Howland. Philadelphia: University of Pennsylvania Press, 1939.

Lehner, Ernst, and Johanna Lehner, comps. *Picture Book of Devils, Demons, and Witchcraft.* New York: Dover, 1971.

Monter, E. William, ed. *European Witchcraft.* New York: Wiley, 1969.

Ostorero, Martine, Agostino Paravicini Bagliani, and Kathrin Utz Tremp, eds. *L'imaginaire du sabbat: Edition critique des textes les plus anciens (1430 c.–1440 c.).* Lausanne: Université de Lausanne, 1999.

Rosen, Barbara, ed. *Witchcraft in England, 1558–1618.* Amherst, Mass.: University of Massachusetts Press, 1991.

Troncarelli, Fabio, ed. *Le streghe: Tra superstitione e realtà storie segrete e documenti inediti di un fenomeno tra i più inquietanti della società europea.* 1983. Reprint, Rome: Newton Compton, 1992.

Other Primary Sources

Adémar de Chabannes (d. 1034). *Chronique.* Excerpt in *Heresies of the High Middle Ages,* ed. Walter L. Wakefield and Austin P. Evans, 74–76. New York: Columbia University Press, 1969.

Alberigo, Giuseppe, ed. *Conciliorum oecumenorum decreta.* Bologna: Istituto per le Scienze Religiose, 1972.

Alexander of Hales. *Magistri Alexandri de Hales glossa in quatuor libros sententiarum Petri Lombardi.* Edited by the Fathers of the College of Saint Bonaventure. 4 vols. Florence: Typographia Collegii S. Bonaventurae, 1952.

Antoninus, Saint, Archbishop of Florence. *Sancti Antonini Summa theologica.* 1740. 4 vols. Photographic reprint, Graz: Akademische Druck, 1959.

Apuleius (d. ca. 180). *De deo Socratis* (*De daemone Socratis*). In *Opuscules philosophiques (Du dieu de Socrate, Platon et sa doctrine, Du monde) et fragments [par] Apulée,* ed. Jean Beaujeu, 1–45. Paris: Les Belles Lettres, 1973.

Aquinas, Saint Thomas. *Angels (Ia. 50–64).* Edited by Kenelm Foster. In *Summa theologiae,* ed. Thomas Gilby et al., vol. 9. New York: McGraw-Hill, 1964.

———. *Commentum in quattuor libros sententiarum.* In *S. Thomae Aquinatis opera omnia,* ed. Roberto Busa et al., 1:1–708. Stuttgart/Bad Canstatt: Friedrich Frommann/Günther Holzboog, 1980.

———. *De malo.* In *S. Thomae Aquinatis opera omnia,* ed. Roberto Busa et al., 3:269–352. Stuttgart/Bad Canstatt: Friedrich Frommann/Günther Holzboog, 1980.

———. *De potentia* [*De potentia Dei*]. In *S. Thomae Aquinatis opera omnia,* ed. Roberto Busa et al., 3:186–269. Stuttgart/Bad Canstatt: Friedrich Frommann/Günther Holzboog, 1980.

———. *De spiritualibus creaturis.* In *S. Thomae Aquinatis opera omnia,* ed. Roberto Busa et al., 3:352–68. Stuttgart/Bad Canstatt: Friedrich Frommann/Günther Holzboog, 1980.

———. *De substantiis separatis.* In *S. Thomae Aquinatis opera omnia,* ed. Roberto Busa et al., 3:515–25. Stuttgart/Bad Canstatt: Friedrich Frommann/Günther Holzboog, 1980.

———. *Existence and Nature of God (Ia. 2–11).* Edited by Timothy McDermott. In *Summa theologiae,* ed. Thomas Gilby et al., vol. 2. New York: McGraw-Hill, 1964.

———. *On Evil.* Translated by John A. Oesterle. Edited by Jean T. Oesterle. Notre Dame, Ind.: University of Notre Dame Press, 1995.

———. *Quaestiones quodlibetales.* In *S. Thomae Aquinatis opera omnia,* ed. Roberto Busa et al., 3:438–501. Stuttgart/Bad Canstatt: Friedrich Frommann/Günther Holzboog, 1980.

———. *S. Thomae Aquinatis opera omnia.* Edited by Roberto Busa et al. 7 vols. Stuttgart/Bad Canstatt: Friedrich Frommann/Günther Holzboog, 1980.

———. *Summa contra gentiles.* In *S. Thomae Aquinatis opera omnia,* ed. Roberto Busa et al., 2:1–184. Stuttgart/Bad Canstatt: Friedrich Frommann/Günther Holzboog, 1980.

———. *Summa theologiae.* Edited by Thomas Gilby et al. 60 vols. New York: McGraw-Hill, 1964.

Aristotle. *The Complete Works of Aristotle: The Revised Oxford Translation.* 2 vols. Edited by Jonathan Barnes. Princeton, N.J.: Princeton University Press, 1984.

Athanasius (d. 373). *Vita di Antonio.* Translated by Pietro Citati, Salvatore Lilla, and Gabriella Apicella. Edited by G. J. M. Bartelink. 1974. Reprint, Milan: Fondazione Lorenzo Valla/Arnaldo Mondadori Editore, 1998.

Augustine. *The City of God* [*De civitate Dei*]. Translated by Marcus Dods, George Wilson, and J. J. Smith. New York: Modern Library, 1950.

Biblia latina cum glossa ordinaria: Facsimile Reprint of the Editio Princeps Adolph Rusch of Strassburg, 1480–81. 4 vols. Photographic reprint, with an introduction by Karlfried Froehlich and Margaret T. Gibson, Brepols: Turnhout, 1992.

Boccaccio, Giovanni. *The Decameron.* Translated by Mark Musa and Peter Bondanella. New York: Mentor, 1982.

Bonaventure. *Commentaria in quattuor libros sententiarum.* Vols. 1–4 of *Opera omnia.* 10 vols. Florence: Typographia Collegii S. Bonaventurae, 1882–1902.

Caesarius of Heisterbach. *Dialogus miraculorum.* [ca. 1225]. Edited by Joseph Strange. 2 vols. Cologne, 1851.

———. *The Dialogue on Miracles.* Translated by Henry von Essen Scott and Charles Cooke Swinton Bland. 2 vols. London: Routledge, 1929.

Cassirer, Ernst, Paul Oskar Kristeller, and John Herman Randall Jr., eds. *The Renaissance Philosophy of Man.* 1948. Reprint, Chicago: University of Chicago Press, 1975.

Catechismo, cioè istruttione, secondo il decreto del Concilio di Trento, a' Parochi, Publicato per comandamento del Santiss. S. N. Papa Pio V. Translated by Alessio Figliucci. Venice: Aldo Manuzio (Jr.), 1568.

Cervantes Saavedra, Miguel de. "The Dogs' Colloquy." In *Exemplary Stories,* trans. C. A. Jones, 195–252. Harmondsworth: Penguin, 1972.

Dante Alighieri. *The Divine Comedy: Paradiso.* Translated by Charles S. Singleton. 2 vols. Princeton, N.J.: Princeton University Press, 1975.

———. *The Divine Comedy: Purgatorio.* Translated by Charles S. Singleton. 2 vols. Princeton, N.J.: Princeton University Press, 1973.

———. *The Divine Comedy of Dante Alighieri.* Vol. 1, *Inferno.* Translated by Robert M. Durling and Ronald L. Martinez. New York: Oxford University Press, 1997.

Denzinger, Henricus, and Adolfus Schönmetzer, eds. *Enchiridion symbolorum definitionum et declarationum de rebus fidei et morum.* 1854. 36th ed. Barcelona: Herder, 1976.

Gui, Bernard. *Practica inquisitionis hereticae pravitatis.* [1323–24]. Excerpt in *Heresies of the High Middle Ages,* ed. Walter L. Wakefield and Austin P. Evans, 273–445. New York: Columbia University Press, 1969.

Guibert de Nogent (d. ca. 1121). *Da vita sua.* Excerpt in *Heresies of the High Middle Ages,* ed. Walter L. Wakefield and Austin P. Evans, 101–4. New York: Columbia University Press, 1969.

Hus, Jan. *De sanguine Christi.* [1406]. In *Spisy,* ed. Vaclav Flajšhaus, vol. 3. Prague: J. Bursika, 1903.

Index librorum prohibitorum Alexandri VII pontificis maximi iussu editus. Rome, 1667. Fictitious imprint.

Innocent VIII. *Summis desiderantes affectibus.* 1484. In *Malleus maleficarum 1487 von Heinrich Kramer (Institoris): Nachdruck des Erstdruckes von 1487 mit Bulle und Approbatio,* by Heinrich Kramer, fols. ir–v. Hildesheim: Georg Olms, 1992. Papal bull.

Isidore of Seville. *Etymologiarum sive originum libri XX.* Edited by W. M. Lindsay. 2 vols. 1911. Reprint, Oxford: Clarendon, 1971.

Jacobus de Voragine. *The Golden Legend: Readings on the Saints.* [ca. 1275–1300]. Translated by William Granger Ryan. 2 vols. Princeton, N.J.: Princeton University Press, 1993.

Lombard, Peter. *Sententiae in quattuor libris distinctae.* Edited by Ignatius C. Brady. 2 vols. 3d ed. Grottaferrata: Collegii S. Bonaventurae ad Claras Aquas, 1971–81.

Lucretius. *De rerum natura.* Translated by W. H. D. Rouse. 2d ed., rev. Martin Ferguson Smith. Cambridge, Mass.: Harvard University Press, 1982.

Marlowe, Christopher. *Dr Faustus.* Edited by Roma Gill. 2d ed. New York: W. W. Norton, 1989.

Montaigne, Michel de. "Of Cripples." [1585–88]. In *The Complete Works of Montaigne: Essays, Travel Journal, Letters,* trans. Donald M. Frame, 784–92. Stanford, Calif.: Stanford University Press, 1958.

———. "Of the Power of the Imagination." [1572–74]. In *The Complete Works of Montaigne: Essays, Travel Journal, Letters,* trans. Donald M. Frame, 68–76. Stanford, Calif.: Stanford University Press, 1958.

Paul of Chartres. Excerpt from *Vetus Aganon.* [ca. 1072]. In *Heresies of the High Middle Ages,* ed. Walter L. Wakefield and Austin P. Evans, 76–81. New York: Columbia University Press, 1969.

Petrarca (Petrarch), Francesco. *On His Own Ignorance and That of Many Others* (1371). Translated by Hans Nachod in *The Renaissance Philosophy of Man* (1948), ed. Ernst Cassirer, Paul Oskar Kristeller, and John Herman Randall Jr., 47–133. Reprint, Chicago: University of Chicago Press, 1975.

Plato. *Symposium.* Translated by Alexander Nehamas and Paul Woodruff. Indianapolis: Hackett, 1989.

Pomponazzi, Pietro. *De immortalitate animae.* 1st ed. 1516. Translated as *On the Immortality of the Soul* in *The Renaissance Philosophy of Man* (1948), ed. Ernst Cassirer, Paul Oskar Kristeller, and John Herman Randall Jr., 280–381. Reprint, Chicago: University of Chicago Press, 1975.

———. *Apologia Petri Pomponatii Mantuani.* Bologna, 1518.

———. *De naturalium effectuum causis, sive de incantationibus.* Composed 1520. 1st ed. 1567. Photographic reprint, Hildesheim: Georg Olms, 1970.

———. *Les Causes des merveilles de la nature; ou, Les Enchantements.* Translated by Henri Busson. Paris: Rieder, 1930.

Richter, Aemilius Ludwig, and Emil Friedburg, eds. *Corpus iuris canonici.* 2 vols. 1879. Photographic reprint, Graz: Akademische Druck, 1959.

Stendhal. *Promenades dans Rome.* Paris: Jean-Jacques Pauvert, 1955.

Steuco, Agostino. *De perenni philosophia.* 1540. Photographic reprint, with an introduction by Charles B. Schmitt, New York: Johnson Reprint, 1972.

von Spee, Friedrich. *Cautio criminalis, ovvero Dei processi alle streghe.* 1636. Translated by Mietta Timi. Edited by Anna Foa. Rome: Salerno, 1986.

Wakefield, Walter L., and Austin P. Evans, eds. *Heresies of the High Middle Ages.* New York: Columbia University Press, 1969.

Wesley, John. *The Journal of the Rev. John Wesley, Enlarged from Original Mss., with Notes from Unpublished Diaries, Annotations, Maps, and Illustrations.* Edited by Nehemiah Curnock. 8 vols. London: R. Culley, 1909–16.

William of Auvergne. *De sacramentis.* In *Opera omnia,* 1:407–555. Paris, 1674. Photographic reprint, Frankfurt a.M.: Minerva, 1963.

———. *De universo.* In *Opera omnia,* 1:593–1074. Paris, 1674. Photographic reprint, Frankfurt a.M.: Minerva, 1963.

———. *Opera omnia.* 2 vols. Paris, 1674. Photographic reprint, Frankfurt a.M.: Minerva, 1963.

Secondary Sources

Abbiati, Sergio. "Appendice." In *La stregoneria: Diavoli, streghe, inquisitori dal trecento al settecento,* ed. Sergio Abbiati, Attilio Agnoletto, and Maria Rosario Lazzati, 333–50. Milan: Mondadori, 1984. Reprint, Milan: Mondadori, 1991.

———. "A proposito di taluni processi inquisitori modenesi del primo cinquecento." *Bollettino della Società di Studi Valdesi* 146 (1979): 101–18.

———. Introduction and notes to Bernardo Rategno da Como, *De strigiis.* In *La stregoneria: Diavoli, streghe, inquisitori dal trecento al settecento,* ed. Sergio Abbiati, Attilio Agnoletto, and Maria Rosario Lazzati, 199–200, 214–17. Milan: Mondadori, 1984. Reprint, Milan: Mondadori, 1991.

———. Introduction and notes to Silvestro Prierias [Mazzolini]. In *La stregoneria: Diavoli, streghe, inquisitori dal trecento al settecento,* ed. Sergio Abbiati, Attilio Agnoletto, and Maria Rosario Lazzati, 218–220, 228–29. Milan: Mondadori, 1984. Reprint, Milan: Mondadori, 1991.

Adams, Hazard, ed. *Critical Theory since Plato.* New York: Harcourt Brace Jovanovich, 1971.

Allen, Don Cameron. *The Legend of Noah: Renaissance Rationalism in Art, Science, and Letters.* 1949. Reprint, Urbana: University of Illinois Press, 1963.

———. *Doubt's Boundless Sea: Skepticism and Faith in the Renaissance.* Baltimore: Johns Hopkins University Press, 1964.

Almagià, Roberto. "Leandro Alberti." In *Enciclopedia italiana,* ed. Giovanni Treccani, 2:180–81. Rome: Istituto Giovanni Treccani, 1929.

Álvarez, Jaime García. "Autorité." In *Dictionnaire encyclopédique du Moyen-Âge,* ed. André Vauchez et al., 1:152–53. Cambridge: James Clark; Paris: Editions du Cerf; Rome: Città Nuova, 1997.

Anglo, Sydney. *The Damned Art: Essays in the Literature of Witchcraft.* London: Routledge & Kegan Paul, 1977.

———. "Evident Authority and Authoritative Evidence: The *Malleus Maleficarum.*" In *The Damned Art: Essays in the Literature of Witchcraft,* ed. Sydney Anglo, 1–31. London: Routledge & Kegan Paul, 1977.

Ascoli, Albert Russell. "The Vowels of Authority (Dante's *Convivio* IV.vi.3–4)." In *Discourses of Authority in Medieval and Renaissance Literature,* ed.

Kevin Brownlee and Walter Stephens, 23–46. Hanover, N.H.: University Press of New England, 1989.

Baldwin, John W. "The Crisis of the Ordeal: Literature, Law, and Religion around 1200." *Journal of Medieval and Renaissance Studies* 24, no. 3 (1994): 327–53.

Baltrušaitis, Jurgis. *Le Moyen Age fantastique: Antiquités et exotismes dans l'art gothique.* Paris: Colin, 1955.

Baroja, Julio Caro. *The World of the Witches.* Translated by O. N. V. Glendinning. Chicago: University of Chicago Press, 1965.

Barstow, Anne Llewellyn. *Witchcraze: A New History of the European Witch Hunts.* San Francisco: Pandora, 1994.

Bartlett, Robert. *Trial by Fire and Water: The Medieval Judicial Ordeal.* New York: Oxford University Press, 1986.

Battaglia, Salvatore, ed. *Grande dizionario enciclopedico della lingua italiana.* 20 vols. to date. Turin: Unione Tipografico–Editrice Torinese, 1961–.

Battisti, Carlo, and Giovanni Alessio. *Dizionario etimologico italiano.* 5 vols. Florence: Barbèra, 1975.

Behringer, Wolfgang. *Witchcraft Persecutions in Bavaria: Popular Magic, Religious Zealotry, and Reason of State in Early Modern Europe.* Translated by J. C. Grayson and David Lederer. Past and Present Publications. Cambridge: Cambridge University Press, 1997.

Benigni, U. "Pomponazzi (Pomponatius)." In *The Catholic Encyclopedia,* ed. Charles G. Herbermann, 12:227. London: Universal Knowledge Foundation, 1913.

Bertolotti, Maurizio. "The Ox's Bones and the Ox's Hide: A Popular Myth, Part Hagiography and Part Witchcraft." In *Microhistory and the Lost Peoples of Europe,* ed. Edward Muir and Guido Ruggiero, 42–70. Baltimore: Johns Hopkins University Press, 1991.

Besserman, Lawrence L. *The Legend of Job in the Middle Ages.* Cambridge, Mass.: Harvard University Press, 1979.

Blauert, Andreas. *Frühe Hexenverfolgungen: Ketzer-, Zauberei-, und Hexenprocesse des 15. Jahrhunderts.* Hamburg: Junius, 1989.

Bonomo, Giuseppe. *Caccia alle streghe: La credenza nelle streghe dal secolo XIII al XIX con particolare riferimento all'Italia.* Palermo: Palumbo, 1959.

Borges, Jorge Luís. *Labyrinths: Selected Stories and Other Writings.* Edited by Donald A. Yates and James E. Irby. New York: New Directions, 1964.

Borst, Arno. *Medieval Worlds: Barbarians, Heretics, and Artists in the Middle Ages.* Translated by Eric Hansen. Chicago: University of Chicago Press, 1992.

Bosco, Giovanna, and Patrizia Castelli, eds. *Stregoneria e streghe nell'Europa moderna: Convegno internazionale di studi (Pisa, 24–26 marzo 1994).* Pisa: Ministero per i beni culturali e ambientali/Pacini Editore, 1996.

Brady, J. M. "Seminal Reasons." In *New Catholic Encyclopedia,* 13:68–69. New York: McGraw-Hill, 1967.

Brieger, Peter, Millard Meiss, and Charles S. Singleton. *Illuminated Manuscripts of the Divine Comedy.* Bollingen Series, vol. 81. 2 vols. Princeton, N.J.: Princeton University Press, 1969.

Briggs, Robin. *Witches and Neighbors: The Social and Cultural Context of European Witchcraft.* New York: Viking, 1996.

Burke, Peter. "Witchcraft and Magic in Renaissance Italy: Gianfrancesco Pico and His *Strix*." In *The Damned Art: Essays in the Literature of Witchcraft,* ed. Sydney Anglo, 32–52. London: Routledge & Kegan Paul, 1977.

Butler, Elizabeth. *Ritual Magic.* 1949. Reprint, University Park: Pennsylvania State University Press, 1998.

Bynum, Carolyn Walker. *Holy Feast and Holy Fast: The Religious Significance of Food to Medieval Women.* Berkeley and Los Angeles: University of California Press, 1987.

Camporeale, Salvatore I. "La morte, la proprietà, e il 'problema della salvezza': Testamenti e ultime volontà a Siena dal 1200 al 1800." *Memorie Domenicane,* n.s., 32 (1991): 381–404.

———. "Renaissance Humanism and the Origins of Humanist Theology." In *Humanity and Divinity in the Renaissance and Reformation: Essays in Honor of Charles Trinkaus,* ed. John W. O'Malley, Thomas M. Izbicki, and Gerald Christianson, 101–24. Leiden: Brill, 1993.

Castelli, Enrico. *Il demoniaco nell'arte: Il significato del demoniaco nell'arte.* Milan and Florence: Electa, 1952.

Castelli, Patrizia, ed. *Bibliotheca lamiarum: Documenti e immagini della stregoneria dal medioevo all'età moderna.* Pisa: Pacini, 1994.

———. " 'Donnaiole, amiche de li sogni' ovvero i sogni delle streghe." In *Bibliotheca lamiarum,* ed. Patrizia Castelli, 35–85. Pisa: Pacini, 1994.

Certeau, Michel de. *La Possession de Loudun.* 1970. Reprint, Paris: Gallimard/Julliard, 1990.

Clark, Stuart. "Inversion, Misrule, and the Meaning of Witchcraft." *Past and Present,* no. 87 (1980): 98–127.

———. "Protestant Demonology: Sin, Superstition, and Society (c. 1520–c. 1630)." In *Early Modern Witchcraft: Centres and Peripheries,* ed. Bengt Ankarloo and Gustav Henningsen, 45–81. Oxford: Clarendon, 1990.

———. "The 'Gendering' of Witchcraft in French Demonology: Misogyny or Polarity?" *French History* 5, no. 4 (1991): 426–37.

———. *Thinking with Demons: The Idea of Witchcraft in Early Modern Europe.* Oxford: Oxford University Press, 1997.

Cohn, Norman. *The Pursuit of the Millennium: Revolutionary Millenarians and Mystical Anarchists of the Middle Ages.* 3d ed. New York: Oxford University Press, 1970.

———. *Europe's Inner Demons: An Enquiry Inspired by the Great Witch-Hunt.* New York: Basic, 1975.

Colish, Marsha L. "Early Scholastic Angelology." *Recherches de théologie ancienne et médiévale* 62 (1995): 80–109.

———. *Peter Lombard.* 2 vols. Leiden: Brill, 1994.

Collins, J. D. *The Thomistic Philosophy of the Angels.* Washington, D.C.: Catholic University Press of America, 1947.

Courtine, J. F. "Realitas." In *Historisches Worterbuch der Philosophie,* ed. Joachim Ritter and Karlfried Gründer, 8:178–85. Basel: Schwabe, 1992.

Cruciani, Alessandro, and Giovanni Corbella. *Roma e dintorni.* 7th ed. Milan: Touring Club Italiano, 1977.

Cuomo, Franco. *Nel nome di Dio: Roghi, duelli rituali, e altre ordalie nell'Occidente medievale cristiano.* Rome: Newton Compton, 1994.

Cuttler, Charles David. "The Temptation of Saint Anthony in Art, from Earliest Times to the First Quarter of the XVI Century." Ph.D. diss., New York University, 1952.

Darnton, Robert. *The Great Cat Massacre and Other Episodes in French Cultural History.* New York: Vintage, 1984.

Davidson, Jane P. *The Witch in Northern European Art.* Freren: Luca, 1987.

Davis, Natalie Zemon. *The Return of Martin Guerre.* Cambridge, Mass.: Harvard University Press, 1983.

De Ferrari, A. "Andrea Cesalpino." In *Dizionario biografico degli italiani,* 24:122–25. Rome: Istituto della Enciclopedia Italiana, 1980.

de Lubac, Henri. *Corpus mysticum: L'Eucharistie et l'église au Moyen Age.* 2d ed. Paris: Aubier, 1949.

Dinzelbacher, Peter. *Heilige oder Hexen? Schicksale auffälliger Frauen in Mittelalter und Frühneuzeit.* Zurich: Artemis & Winkler, 1995.

Doniger, Wendy. "Site Specific." *Bookmark: Ephemera of Note from the University of Chicago Press* 1, no. 1 (2001): 4.

Douglas, Mary. *Purity and Danger: An Analysis of the Concepts of Pollution and Taboo.* 1966. Reprint, London: Ark, 1985.

———, ed. *Witchcraft Confessions and Accusations.* London: Tavistock, 1970.

Du Cange, Charles Dufresne, Sieur. *Glossarium mediae et infimae latinitatis.* 7 vols. Paris: Firmin Didot, 1840–50.

Duffy, Eamon. *The Stripping of the Altars: Traditional Religion in England, 1400–1580.* New Haven, Conn.: Yale University Press, 1992.

Duvergier, Arthur. *La Vauderie dans les états de Philippe Le Bon.* Arras, 1885.

Dworkin, Andrea. *Woman Hating: A Radical Look at Sexuality.* 1976. Reprint, New York: Dutton Plume, 1991.

Eagleton, Terry. *Literary Theory: An Introduction.* 2d ed. Minneapolis: University of Minnesota Press, 1996.

Eco, Umberto. *The Role of the Reader.* Bloomington: University of Indiana Press, 1979.

———. *The Name of the Rose.* Translated by William Weaver. 1983. Reprint, San Diego: Harcourt Brace, 1994.

———. *Travels in Hyperreality: Essays.* Translated by William Weaver. San Diego: Harcourt, Brace, Jovanovich, 1986.

———. *Interpretation and Overinterpretation.* Edited by Stefan Collini. Cambridge: Cambridge University Press, 1992.

Eire, Carlos M. N. *War against the Idols: The Reformation of Worship from Erasmus to Calvin.* New Haven, Conn.: Yale University Press, 1986.

Elliott, Dyan. *Fallen Bodies: Pollution, Sexuality, and Demonology in the Middle Ages.* Philadelphia: University of Pennsylvania Press, 1999.

Elmer, L. J. "Theology of Demon." In *New Catholic Encyclopedia,* 4:754–56. New York: McGraw-Hill, 1967.

Evans, G. R. *Philosophy and Theology in the Middle Ages.* London: Routledge, 1993.

Evans-Pritchard, E. E. *Witchcraft, Oracles, and Magic among the Azande.* Edited by Eva Gillies. Oxford: Clarendon, 1976.

Farmer, S. A. *Syncretism in the West: Pico's 900 Theses (1486): The Evolution of Religious and Philosophical Systems.* Tempe, Ariz.: Medieval and Renaissance Texts and Studies, 1998.

Fattori, M., and M. Bianchi, eds. *Phantasia e imaginatio: Atti del V. Convegno Internazionale del Lessico Intellettuale Europeo, 1986.* Rome: Edizioni dell'-Ateneo, 1988.

Febvre, Lucien. *The Problem of Unbelief in the Sixteenth Century: The Religion of Rabelais.* Translated by Beatrice Gottlieb. Cambridge, Mass.: Harvard University Press, 1982.

Fletcher, Angus. *Allegory: The Theory of a Symbolic Mode.* Ithaca, N.Y.: Cornell University Press, 1964.

Flew, Antony. "Theology and Falsification." In *A Modern Introduction to Philosophy: Readings from Classical and Contemporary Sources,* ed. Paul Edwards and Arthur Pap, 545–47. New York: Free Press, 1973.

Foucault, Michel. "Déviations religieuses et savoir médical." In *Hérésies et sociétés dans l'Europe préindustrielle, 11e–18e siècles,* ed. Jacques LeGoff, 19–25. Paris: Mouton, 1968.

Freedman, David Noel, et al., eds. *Anchor Bible Dictionary.* 6 vols. New York: Doubleday, 1992.

French, Roger, and Andrew Cunningham. *Before Science: The Invention of the Friars' Natural Philosophy.* Aldershot: Scolar Press, 1996.

Garin, Eugenio. *Storia della filosofia italiana.* 3 vols. Turin: Einaudi, 1966.

Gaudel, A. "Limbes." In *Dictionnaire de théologie catholique,* 9:760–72. Paris: Letouzey & Ané, 1926.

Geertz, Hildred. "An Anthropology of Religion and Magic, I." *Journal of Interdisciplinary History* 6, no. 1 (1975): 71–89.

Ghigliazza, T. "Fra Giordano e il problema delle streghe." *La Rivista di Bergamo* 33 (September 1982): 17–25.

Gilson, Etienne. *The Philosophy of Saint Bonaventure.* Translated by Dom Illtyd Trethowan and Frank J. Sheed. Paterson, N.J.: St. Anthony Guild Press, 1965.

Ginzburg, Carlo. *The Night Battles: Witchcraft and Agrarian Cults in the Sixteenth and Seventeenth Centuries.* Translated by John and Anne Tedeschi. New York: Penguin, 1985.

———. *Clues, Myths, and the Historical Method.* Translated by John Tedeschi and Anne C. Tedeschi. Baltimore: Johns Hopkins University Press, 1989.

———. *Ecstasies: Deciphering the Witch's Sabbath.* Translated by Raymond Rosenthal. New York: Penguin, 1992.

Godbeer, Ruchard. *The Devil's Dominion: Magic and Religion in Early New England.* Cambridge: Cambridge University Press, 1992.

Gragnolati, Manuele. "From Plurality to (Almost) Unicity of Forms: Statius's Embryology in *Purgatorio* 25." Paper presented at the conference "Dante 2000," Columbia University, 2 April 2000.

Greenblatt, Stephen. *Shakespearean Negotiations.* Berkeley and Los Angeles: University of California Press, 1988.

Gregory, Tullio, ed. *I sogni nel medioevo.* Rome: Edizioni dell'Ateneo, 1985.

Griffin, M. D. "Demonology." In *New Catholic Encyclopedia,* 4:756–57. New York: McGraw-Hill, 1967.

Grillot de Givry, E. A. *Le musée des sorciers, mages, et alchimistes.* 1929. Translated by J. Courtenay Locke as *Witchcraft, Magic, and Alchemy.* London: George G. Harrap, 1931.

Gurevitch, Aron. *Medieval Popular Culture: Problems of Belief and Perception.* 1988. Translated by János M. Bak and Paul A. Hollingsworth. Cambridge: Cambridge University Press, 1992.

Hansen, Joseph. *Zauberwahn, Inquisition, und Hexenprozeß im Mittelalter, und die Entstehung der großen Hexenverfolgung.* Munich: R. Oldenbourg, 1900.

Haren, Michael. *Medieval Thought: The Western Intellectual Tradition from Antiquity to the Thirteenth Century.* 2d ed. Toronto: University of Toronto Press, 1992.

Herlihy, David. *The Black Death and the Transformation of the West.* Edited by Samuel K. Cohn. Cambridge, Mass.: Harvard University Press, 1997.

Hetherington, Norriss S., ed. *Cosmology: Historical, Literary, Philosophical, Religious, and Scientific Perspectives.* New York: Garland, 1993.

Hill, P. J. "Limbo." In *New Catholic Encyclopedia,* 8:762–65. New York: McGraw-Hill, 1967.

Hopkin, Charles Edward. *The Share of Thomas Aquinas in the Growth of the Witchcraft Delusion.* New York: AMS, 1940.

Hsia, R. Po-chia. *The Myth of Ritual Murder: Jews and Magic in Reformation Germany.* New Haven, Conn.: Yale University Press, 1988.

Iannucci, Amilcare A. "Limbo." In *The Dante Encyclopedia,* ed. Richard Lansing, 565–69. New York: Garland, 2000.

"I Recognize You, Witch" ("Ti riconosco, Strega"). *La Repubblica,* 18 December 2000, 23. Advertisement for Liquore Strega.

James, William. *The Will to Believe.* New York, 1897.

———. *The Varieties of Religious Experience: A Study in Human Nature.* 1902. Reprint, London: Longmans, Green, 1929.

Jansen, F. "Eucharistiques (Accidents)." In *Dictionnaire de théologie catholique,* 5: 1368–1452. Paris: Letouzey & Ané, 1939.

Janson, H. W. *History of Art: A Survey of the Major Visual Arts from the Dawn of History to the Present Day.* 2d ed. New York: Abrams, 1969.

Jarrett, Derek. "The Doctor's Prescription." *New York Review of Books,* 18 March 1999, 39–42. Review of W. J. Bate, *Samuel Johnson,* and Lawrence Lipkin, *Samuel Johnson: The Life of an Author.*

Jerouschek, Günter. "500 Years of the *Malleus maleficarum.*" In *Malleus maleficarum 1487 von Heinrich Kramer (Institoris): Nachdruck des Erstdruckes von 1487 mit Bulle und Approbatio,* by Heinrich Kramer, xxxi–lv. Hildesheim: Georg Olms, 1992.

Jordan, William Chester. *The Great Famine: Northern Europe in the Early Fourteenth Century.* Princeton, N.J.: Princeton University Press, 1996.

Keck, David. *Angels and Angelology in the Middle Ages.* New York: Oxford University Press, 1998.

Kelly, Henry Ansgar. *The Devil at Baptism: Ritual, Theology, and Drama.* Ithaca, N.Y.: Cornell University Press, 1985.

Kennedy, D. J. "Sacraments." In *The Catholic Encyclopedia,* ed. Charles G. Herbermann, 13:295–305. London: Universal Knowledge Foundation, 1913.

Kieckhefer, Richard. *European Witch Trials: Their Foundations in Popular and Learned Culture, 1300–1500.* Berkeley and Los Angeles: University of California Press, 1976.

———. *Magic in the Middle Ages.* Cambridge: Cambridge University Press, 1989.

———. "The Holy and the Unholy: Sainthood, Witchcraft, and Magic in Late Medieval Europe." *Journal of Medieval and Renaissance Studies* 24, no. 3 (1994): 355–85.

———. "The Specific Rationality of Medieval Magic." *American Historical Review* 99 (1994): 813–36.

———. *Forbidden Rites: A Necromancer's Manual of the Fifteenth Century*. University Park: Pennsylvania State University Press, 1997.

———. "Avenging the Blood of Children: Anxiety over Child Victims and the Origins of the European Witch Trials." In *The Devil, Heresy, and Witchcraft in the Middle Ages: Essays in Honor of Jeffrey B. Russell,* ed. Alberto Ferreiro, 91–109. Leiden: Brill, 1998.

Klaits, Joseph. *Servants of Satan: The Age of the Witch Hunts*. Bloomington: Indiana University Press, 1985.

Koldeweij, A. M. "A Barefaced *Roman de la rose* (Paris, B.N., ms. fr. 25526) and Some Late Medieval Mass-Produced Badges of a Sexual Nature." In *Flanders in a European Perspective: Manuscript Illumination around 1400 in Flanders and Abroad: Proceedings of the International Colloquium, Leuven, 7–10 September 1993,* ed. Maurits Smeyers and Bert Cardon, 499–516. Leuven: Uitgeverij Peeters, 1995.

Lambert, Malcolm. *Medieval Heresy: Popular Movements from the Gregorian Reform to the Reformation*. 2d ed. Oxford: Blackwell, 1992.

Langmuir, Gavin. *History, Religion and Anti-Semitism*. Berkeley and Los Angeles: University of California Press, 1990.

Lansing, Carol. *Power and Purity: Cathar Heresy in Medieval Italy*. New York: Oxford University Press, 1998.

Larner, Christina. "Two Late Scottish Witchcraft Tracts: *Witchcraft Proven* and *The Tryal of Witchcraft*." In *The Damned Art: Essays in the Literature of Witchcraft,* ed. Sydney Anglo, 227–45. London: Routledge & Kegan Paul, 1977.

———. *Enemies of God: The Witch-Hunt in Scotland*. Baltimore: Johns Hopkins University Press, 1981.

———. *Witchcraft and Religion: The Politics of Popular Belief*. Edited by Alan Macfarlane. Oxford: Basil Blackwell, 1984.

Latham, R. E. *Revised Medieval Latin Word-List from British and Irish Sources*. 1973. Reprint, London: British Academy, 1975.

Lazzati, Maria Rosario. Preface to Alfonso Tostado, *Matthaei explanatio*. In *La stregoneria: Diavoli, streghe, inquisitori dal trecento al settecento,* ed. Sergio Abbiati, Attilio Agnoletto, and Maria Rosario Lazzati, 46. Milan: Mondadori, 1984. Reprint, Milan: Mondadori, 1991.

———. Preface to Giordano da Bergamo, *Quaestio de strigis*. In *La stregoneria: Diavoli, streghe, inquisitori dal trecento al settecento,* ed. Sergio Abbiati, Attilio Agnoletto, and Maria Rosario Lazzati, 79–80. Milan: Mondadori, 1984. Reprint, Milan: Mondadori, 1991.

———. Preface to Ulrich Müller. In *La stregoneria: Diavoli, streghe, inquisitori dal trecento al settecento,* ed. Sergio Abbiati, Attilio Agnoletto, and Maria Rosario Lazzati, 100–101. Milan: Mondadori, 1984. Reprint, Milan: Mondadori, 1991.

Leclercq, H. "Sacramentals." In *The Catholic Encyclopedia,* ed. Charles G. Herbermann, 13:292–93. London: Universal Knowledge Foundation, 1913.

Lefranc, Martin. Excerpt from *Le Champion des dames*. 1441. In *L'imaginaire du sabbat: Edition critique des textes les plus anciens (1430 c.–1440 c.),* ed. Martine Ostorero, Agostino Paravicini Bagliani, and Kathrin Utz Tremp, 438–508. Lausanne: Université de Lausanne, 1999.

Le Goff, Jacques. *The Medieval Imagination.* Translated by Arthur Goldhammer. Chicago: University of Chicago Press, 1988.

Levack, Brian. *The Witch-Hunt in Early Modern Europe.* 2d ed. London: Longman, 1995.

Link, Luther. *The Devil: The Archfiend in Art from the Sixth to the Sixteenth Century.* New York: Abrams, 1996.

Lorenzi, Lorenzo. *Devils in Art: Florence, from the Middle Ages to the Renaissance.* Translated by Mark Roberts. Florence: Centro Di, 1997.

Macfarlane, Alan. *Witchcraft in Tudor and Stuart England: A Regional and Comparative Study.* New York: Harper Torchbooks, 1970.

Mack, John E. *Abduction: Human Encounters with Aliens.* New York: Scribner's, 1994.

Mandrou, Robert. *Magistrats et sorciers en France au XVIIe siècle: Une analyse de psychologie historique.* Paris: Plon, 1968.

Mangenot, E., F. Jansen, F. Vernet, J. de Ghellinck, and L. Godefroy. "Eucharistic." In *Dictionnaire de théologie catholique,* 5:989–1368. Paris: Letouzey & Ané, 1939.

Merchant, Carolyn. *The Death of Nature: Women, Ecology, and the Scientific Revolution.* 1980. Reprint, San Francisco: Harper San Francisco, 1989.

Michel, A. "Sacrementaux." In *Dictionnaire de théologie catholique,* 14:465–82. Paris: Letouzey & Ané, 1939.

———. "Sacrements." In *Dictionnaire de théologie catholique,* 14:485–644. Paris: Letouzey & Ané, 1939.

———. "Transsubstantiation." In *Dictionnaire de théologie catholique,* 15:1396–1406. Paris: Letouzey & Ané, 1943–46.

Midelfort, H. C. Erik. *Witch Hunting in Southwestern Germany, 1562–1684: The Social and Intellectual Foundations.* Stanford, Calif.: Stanford University Press, 1972.

Montanari, Fausto. "Limbo." In *Enciclopedia dantesca,* ed. Umberto Bosco, 3: 651–54. Rome: Istituto della Enciclopedia Italiana, 1970.

Monter, William. *Frontiers of Heresy: The Spanish Inquisition from the Basque Lands to Sicily.* Cambridge: Cambridge University Press, 1990.

Moore, Carey A. "Tobit, Book of." In *Anchor Bible Dictionary,* ed. David Noel Freedman et al., 6:585–94. New York: Doubleday, 1992.

Moore, R. I. *The Formation of a Persecuting Society: Power and Deviance in Western Europe, 950–1250.* Oxford: Basil Blackwell, 1987.

Mormando, Franco. *The Preacher's Demons: Bernardino of Siena and the Social Underworld of Early Renaissance Italy.* Chicago: University of Chicago Press, 1999.

Moroni, Gaetano. "Strega." In *Dizionario di erudizione storico-ecclesiastica,* 70:184–94. Venice: Tipografia Emiliana, 1854.

Moureau, H. "Caractère sacramentel." In *Dictionnaire de théologie catholique,* 2: 1698–1708. Paris: Letouzey & Ané, 1939.

Murray, Alexander. *Reason and Society in the Middle Ages.* Oxford: Oxford University Press, 1990.

Nasuti, Nicola. *L'Italia dei prodigi eucaristici.* Siena: Cantagalli, 1992.

Netanyahu, Benzion. *The Origins of the Inquisition in Fifteenth Century Spain.* New York: Random House, 1995.

Nietzsche, Friedrich. *Der Anti Christ.* In *Werke in Drei Bänden,* ed. K. Schlechta, 2:1161–1235. Munich: Hanser, 1981.

———. *Twilight of the Idols and the Anti Christ.* Translated by R. J. Hollingdale. London: Penguin, 1990.

O'Brian, Patrick. *The Thirteen Gun Salute.* 1989. Reprint, New York: Norton, 1992.

Ostorero, Martine. *Folâtrer avec les démons: Sabbat et chasse aux sorciers à Vevey (1448).* Cahiers lausannois d'histoire médiévale, vol. 15. Lausanne: Université de Lausanne, 1995.

———. Commentary on *Errores gazariorum.* In *L'imaginaire du sabbat: Edition critique des textes les plus anciens (1430 c.–1440 c.),* ed. Martine Ostorero, Agostino Paravicini Bagliani, and Kathrin Utz Tremp, 301–37. Lausanne: Université de Lausanne, 1999.

Padoan, Giorgio. "Il limbo dantesco." *Letture classensi* 3 (1970): 187–217.

Passaro, Vince. "Dragon Fiction: The (Very Lucrative) Advent of the Christian Thriller." *Harper's Magazine,* September 1996, 64–70.

Pelikan, Jaroslav. *The Christian Tradition: A History of the Development of Doctrine.* Vol. 3, *The Growth of Medieval Theology (600–1300).* Chicago: University of Chicago Press, 1978. Vol. 4, *Reformation of Church and Dogma (1300–1700).* Chicago: University of Chicago Press, 1984.

Peters, Edward. *The Magician, the Witch, and the Law.* Philadelphia: University of Pennsylvania Press, 1978.

———. *Inquisition.* 1988. Reprint, Berkeley and Los Angeles: University of California Press, 1989.

Petzolt, Leander. "The Universe of Demons and the World of the Late Middle Ages." In *Demons: Mediators between This World and the Other,* ed. Ruth Petzoldt and Paul Neubauer, 13–25. Frankfurt: Peter Lang, 1998.

Popkin, Richard H. *The History of Skepticism from Erasmus to Spinoza.* Berkeley and Los Angeles: University of California Press, 1979.

Pullman, Bernard. *The Atom in the History of Human Thought.* Translated by Axel Reisinger. New York: Oxford University Press, 1998.

Purkiss, Diane. *The Witch in History: Early Modern and Twentieth-Century Representations.* London: Routledge, 1996.

Quaife, G. R. *Godly Zeal and Furious Rage: The Witch in Early Modern Europe.* New York: St. Martin's, 1987.

Quétif, Jacques, and Jacques Echard. *Scriptores ordinis praedicatorum recensiti, notisque historicis et criticis illustrati.* 1719–23. 2 vols. Reprint, New York: Burt Franklin, 1959.

Quinn, J. R. "Theology of Sacraments." In *New Catholic Encyclopedia,* 12:806–13. New York: McGraw-Hill, 1967.

Randall, John Herman, Jr. Introduction to Pomponazzi, *On the Immortality of the Soul.* In *The Renaissance Philosophy of Man,* ed. Ernst Cassirer, Paul Oskar Kristeller, and John Herman Randall Jr., 257–79. 1948. Reprint, Chicago: University of Chicago Press, 1975.

Redigonda, A. L. "Leandro Alberti." In *Dizionario biografico degli Italiani,* ed. Aldo Ferrabino, 1:699–702. Rome: Istituto della Enciclopedia Italiana, 1960.

Robbins, Rossell Hope. *The Encyclopedia of Witchcraft and Demonology.* New York: Crown, 1959.

Robertson, D. W., Jr. "Some Medieval Literary Terminology, with Special Reference to Chrétien de Troyes." *Studies in Philology* 48 (1951): 669–92.

Robinson, John A. T. *The Body: A Study in Pauline Theology*. Naperville, Ill.: Alec R. Allenson, 1957.

Roper, Lyndal. *Oedipus and the Devil: Witchcraft, Sexuality, and Religion in Early Modern Europe*. London: Routledge, 1994.

Rubin, Miri. *Corpus Christi: The Eucharist in Late Medieval Culture*. Cambridge: Cambridge University Press, 1991.

———. *Gentile Tales: The Narrative Assault on Late Medieval Jews*. New Haven, Conn.: Yale University Press, 1999.

Russell, Jeffrey Burton. *Witchcraft in the Middle Ages*. Ithaca, N.Y.: Cornell University Press, 1972.

———. *Lucifer: The Devil in the Middle Ages*. Ithaca, N.Y.: Cornell University Press, 1984.

Scannell, T. B. "Confirmation." In *The Catholic Encyclopedia*, ed. Charles G. Herbermann, 4:215–22. London: Universal Knowledge Foundation, 1913.

Schiesari, Juliana. *The Gendering of Melancholia: Feminism, Psychoanalysis, and the Symbolics of Loss in Renaissance Literature*. Ithaca, N.Y.: Cornell University Press, 1992.

Schmitt, Charles B. "Perennial Philosophy: From Agostino Steuco to Leibniz." *Journal of the History of Ideas* 27 (1966): 505–32.

———. *Gianfrancesco Pico della Mirandola (1469–1533) and His Critique of Aristotle*. The Hague: Martinus Nijhoff, 1967.

———. "*Prisca theologia* e *philosophia perennis:* Due temi del Rinascimento italiano e la loro fortuna." In *Il pensiero italiano del Rinascimento e il tempo nostro: Atti del V Convegno Internazionale del Centro di Studi Umanistici, Montepulciano, Palazzo Tarugi, 8–13 agosto 1968*, 211–36. Florence: Olschki, 1970.

———. Introduction to *De perenni philosophia of Augustinus Steuchus*, v–xvii. New York: Johnson Reprint, 1972.

Schnyder, André. *Malleus maleficarum von Heinrich Institoris (alias Kramer) unter Mithilfe Jakob Sprengers Aufgrund der dämonologischen Tradition zusammengestellt: Kommentar zur Wiedergabe des Erstdrucks von 1487 (Hain 9238)*. Göppingen: Kümmerle, 1993.

Sebregondi, Ludovica. "The Devil in Fifteenth- and Sixteenth-Century Florentine Engravings." In *Demons: Mediators between This World and the Other*, ed. Ruth Petzoldt and Paul Neubauer, 111–31. Frankfurt: Peter Lang, 1998.

Segl, Peter. "Heinrich Institoris. Persönlichkeit und literarisches werk." In *Der Hexenhammer: Entstehung und Umfeld des Malleus maleficarum von 1487*, ed. Peter Segl, 103–26. Cologne and Vienna: Böhlau, 1988.

Sharpe, James. *Instruments of Darkness: Witchcraft in Early Modern England*. 1996. Reprint, Philadelphia: University of Pennsylvania Press, 1997.

Stendhal. *Promenades dans Rome*. Paris: Jean-Jacques Pauvert, 1955.

Stephens, Walter. "Mimesis, Mediation and Counterfeit." In *Mimesis in Contemporary Theory: An Interdisciplinary Approach*. Vol. 1, *The Literary and Philosophical Debate*, ed. Mihai Spariosu, 238–75. Amsterdam: John Benjamins, 1984.

———. *Giants in Those Days: Folklore, Ancient History, and Nationalism*. Lincoln: University of Nebraska Press, 1989.

———. "Metaphor, Sacrament, and the Problem of Allegory in *Gerusalemme liberata*." *I Tatti Studies* 4 (1991): 217–47.

———. "Tasso and the Witches." *Annali d'Italianistica* 12 (1994): 181–202.

———. "La demonologia nella poetica del Tasso." In *Torquato Tasso e l'università,* ed. Walter Moretti and Luigi Pepe, 411–32. Florence: Leo S. Olschki, 1997.
Strayer, Joseph R. *The Albigensian Crusades.* 1971. Reprint, with an epilogue by Carol Lansing, Ann Arbor: University of Michigan Press, 1992.
Sullivan, Margaret A. "The Witches of Dürer and Hans Baldung Grien." *Renaissance Quarterly* 53, no. 2 (2000): 332–401.
Summers, Montague. *The Vampire, His Kith and Kin.* New York: E. P. Dutton, 1929.
———. *The Vampire in Europe.* New York: E. P. Dutton, 1929.
———. *The Werewolf.* London: K. Paul, Trench, Trubner, 1933.
Swanson, R. N. *Religion and Devotion in Europe, c. 1215–c. 1515.* Cambridge Medieval Textbooks. Cambridge: Cambridge University Press, 1995.
Tavuzzi, Michael. *Prierias: The Life and Works of Silvestro Mazzolini da Prierio, 1456–1527.* Durham, N.C.: Duke University Press, 1997.
Thomas, Keith. *Religion and the Decline of Magic.* New York: Scribner's, 1971.
———. "An Anthropology of Religion and Magic, II." *Journal of Interdisciplinary History* 6, no. 1 (1975): 91–109.
Thorndike, Lynn. *A History of Magic and Experimental Science.* Vol. 4. New York: Columbia University Press, 1934.
Toner, P. J. "Limbo." In *The Catholic Encyclopedia,* ed. Charles G. Herbermann, 9:256–59. London: Universal Knowledge Foundation, 1922.
Tristan, Frédérick. *Les Tentations.* N.p.: Balland Massin, 1981.
Trueblood, Elton. *The Logic of Belief.* New York: Harper & Bros., 1942.
Tuchman, Barbara. *A Distant Mirror: The Calamitous Fourteenth Century.* 1978. Reprint, New York: Ballantine, 1979.
van Steenberghen, Fernand. *Le Problème de l'existence de Dieu dans les écrits de S. Thomas Aquin.* Louvain-La-Neuve: Éditions de l'Institut Supérieur de Philosophie, 1980.
Vauchez, André, et al., eds. *Dictionnaire encyclopédique du Moyen-Âge.* Cambridge: James Clark; Paris: Editions du Cerf; Rome: Città Nuova, 1997.
Walker, D. P. *The Ancient Theology: Studies in Christian Platonism from the Fifteenth to the Eighteenth Century.* London: Duckworth, 1972.
———. *Unclean Spirits: Possession and Exorcism in France and England in the Late Sixteenth and Early Seventeenth Centuries.* Philadelphia: University of Pennsylvania Press, 1981.
Watanabe, Morimichi. "The German Church Shortly before the Reformation: Nicolaus Cusanus and the Veneration of the Bleeding Hosts at Wilsnack." In *Reform and Renewal in the Middle Ages and Renaissance: Studies in Honor of Louis J. Pascoe, S.J.,* ed. Thomas M. Izbicki and Christopher M. Bellitto, 210–23. Leiden: Brill, 2000.
Watt, Ian P. *The Rise of the Novel: Studies in Defoe, Richardson, and Fielding.* Berkeley and Los Angeles: University of California Press, 1964.
Weisheipl, J. A. "Scholastic Method." In *New Catholic Encyclopedia,* 12:1145–46. New York: McGraw-Hill, 1967.
White, Andrew Dickson. *A History of the Warfare of Science with Theology in Christendom.* 2 vols. London, 1896.
White, Lynn, Jr. "Natural Science and Naturalistic Art." *American Historical Review* 52 (1947): 421–35.
Williams, Bernadette. "'She Was Usually Placed with the Great Men and Lead-

ers of the Land in Public Assemblies'—Alice Kyteler: A Woman of Considerable Power." In *Women in Renaissance and Early Modern Europe,* ed. Christine Meek, 67–83. Dublin: Four Courts, 2000.

Willis, Deborah. *Malevolent Nurture: Witch-Hunting and Maternal Power in Early Modern England.* Ithaca, N.Y.: Cornell University Press, 1995.

Wills, Garry. "The Rescuer." *New York Review of Books,* 25 June 1992, 28–34.

———. *Papal Sin: Structures of Deceit.* New York: Doubleday, 2000.

Wippel, John F. "The Condemnations of 1270 and 1277 at Paris." *Journal of Medieval and Renaissance Studies* 7 (1977): 169–201.

Zafran, Eric M. "The Iconography of Anti-Semitism: A Study of the Representation of the Jews in the Visual Arts of Europe, 1400–1600." Ph.D. diss., Institute of Fine Arts, New York University, 1973.

Zika, Charles. "Hosts, Processions, and Pilgrimages: Controlling the Sacred in Fifteenth-Century Germany." *Past and Present,* no. 118 (1988): 25–64.

INDEX